Toward a History of Jewish Thought

Toward a History of Jewish Thought

The Soul, Resurrection, and the Afterlife

Zachary Alan Starr

WIPF & STOCK · Eugene, Oregon

TOWARD A HISTORY OF JEWISH THOUGHT
The Soul, Resurrection, and the Afterlife

Copyright © 2020 Zachary Alan Starr. All rights reserved. Except for brief quotations in critical publications or reviews, no part of this book may be reproduced in any manner without prior written permission from the publisher. Write: Permissions, Wipf and Stock Publishers, 199 W. 8th Ave., Suite 3, Eugene, OR 97401.

Wipf & Stock
An Imprint of Wipf and Stock Publishers
199 W. 8th Ave., Suite 3
Eugene, OR 97401

www.wipfandstock.com

PAPERBACK ISBN: 978-1-5326-9305-2
HARDCOVER ISBN: 978-1-5326-9306-9
EBOOK ISBN: 978-1-5326-9307-6

Manufactured in the U.S.A.   FEBRUARY 26, 2020

Contents

Introduction | vii

1. The Ancient Israelites Had No Notion of a "Soul" and Envisioned Neither Reward Nor Punishment in a Postmortem Existence but Were Focused on the Here and Now | 1

2. Resurrection as a Means of Postmortem Reward and Punishment Did Not Come to Be a Widely Accepted Idea Until Late in the Second Temple Period, but Has Roots in Earlier Biblical Material | 33

3. During the Second Temple Period, Greek Ideas about the Soul and the Afterlife Penetrate Jewish Thought and are Used to Resolve the Problem of Moral Evil | 60

4. Views about the Soul, Resurrection, and the Afterlife Continue to Evolve During the Rabbinic Period | 91

5. During the Geonic Period, Saadia Systematizes Jewish Thinking about the Afterlife | 123

6. Jewish Neoplatonic Philosophers Associate an Afterlife Reward with the Soul's Ascension to the Divine Realm, Not Bodily Resurrection; and Belief in Intercessory Acts to Aide in the Purgation of Impure Souls Develops | 151

7. Maimonides Represents a Turning Point from Neoplatonism to Aristotelianism | 178

8. Nahmanides and Other Early Kabbalists Adopt the Concept of Transmigration of Souls | 206

9. Baruch Spinoza Challenges the Scriptural Basis for Belief in the Immortality of the Soul and a Postmortem Reward or Punishment, and Denies that there Is Any Personal Immortality | 234

10. In the Mid-Eighteenth Century, Moses Mendelssohn Publishes His *Phädon, or On the Immortality of the Soul* | 259

11. In the Nineteenth and Twentieth Centuries, Reform Judaism Presents a Hodgepodge of Conflicting and Confused Ideas about the Soul, Resurrection, and the Afterlife | 287

12. Conservative Judaism, Orthodoxy, and Hasidism Take Varying Approaches to the Soul, Resurrection, and the Afterlife | 317

13. The Principle of Immanence Comes to Dominate the Intellectual Landscape of the Nineteenth and Twentieth Centuries | 342

14. Increasing Numbers of Jews in the Nineteenth and Twentieth Centuries Reject Belief in a Soul, Resurrection, and an Afterlife as Unfounded, Unscientific, and Superstitious, and Emphasize that Virtue Is its Own Reward | 366

15. Mordecai Kaplan, the Founder of Reconstructionism, Advocates Naturalism and This-Worldliness, as Does Sherwin Wine, the Leading Voice in Humanistic Judaism | 393

16. Concluding Considerations Regarding the History of Jewish Thought with Respect to the Soul, Resurrection, and the Afterlife | 414

Bibliography | 431

Introduction

THE JEWISH INTELLECTUAL HISTORY set forth in this work demonstrates that there has been extensive cross-fertilization between Jewish thought and the thought of other people, and that this cross-fertilization contributed to substantial changes in Jewish thinking. More specifically, the work describes the ways in which, and the reasons why, Jewish beliefs pertaining to the soul, resurrection, and the afterlife have been repeatedly altered. Thus, for example, it is shown that the Hebrew Bible evidences no notion of a "soul" but that the idea of a soul entered into Jewish thought during the Second Temple period, under Greek influence, in order to resolve a problem that also gave rise to a belief in bodily resurrection. The problem was that of moral evil—that the righteous suffer and the wicked prosper. It is also shown that the manner in which a soul was conceived and the understanding of what happened to a soul after death, as well as notions pertaining to bodily resurrection, continued to evolve in subsequent periods.

So, for instance, Saadia, in the tenth century, conceived of the soul as a *material* substance similar to that of the heavenly spheres which is created by God *simultaneously* with the creation of the body. According to Saadia, after death the soul receives neither reward nor punishment but is simply "stored up" until such time as it is reunited with the body in a world to come. Yet, tenth- and eleventh-century Jewish Neoplatonic philosophers, influenced by pagan and Islamic Neoplatonists, conceived of the soul as an *immaterial* substance which is immediately rewarded after death by its return to God in the upper regions of the world from whence it came (and where it had existed *before* it was joined to a body), and they gave no consideration to a reunification of the soul with the body.

In the twelfth and thirteenth centuries, Jewish Aristotelians, influenced by pagan and Islamic Aristotelians, held somewhat different notions about the soul than the Neoplatonists. The Aristotelians, but not the Neoplatonists, held that only that part of the soul is immortal which they called the "acquired intellect," and they believed that after death the acquired intellect united with what they called the "active intellect." Further, the Aristotelians, but not the Neoplatonists, debated whether or not immortality is individual, and some concluded that immortality is *not* individual. In either case, the afterlife experience of a soul (or acquired intellect) was conceived very differently by the Jewish Aristotelians than by other Jews.

Much later, Jewish philosophers of the Enlightenment held still different notions about the soul. Moses Mendelssohn essentially adopted the view of the soul expounded by the German philosopher Gottfried Leibniz. The Leibnizian view was itself influenced by the ideas of René Descartes, the so-called founder of modern philosophy, and the Cartesian view of the soul markedly diverged from the Aristotelian conception which had held sway during the Middle Ages. For Aristotle, the soul is the form of matter, but Descartes associated the soul with the mind; and for Descartes, consciousness is the defining criterion of the mental, not intelligence or rationality as it was for Aristotle. Moreover, mental activity for Descartes included not only understanding and willing but seeing, hearing, and feeling.

Belief in the soul's transmigration after death to a new body, a view associated with the Greek philosophers Pythagoras and Plato, was not originally accepted by Jews. No influence of this belief can be found in rabbinic sources and the belief was vehemently attacked by Saadia. Yet, beginning in about the twelfth century, belief in the transmigration of souls was accepted by the proponents of Kabbalah, and later, in the eighteenth century, it was accepted by the founders of Hasidism. The early kabbalist Nahmanides accepted the notion of *metempsychosis* in order to satisfactorily resolve the problem of moral evil. Despite many principles that Nahmanides employed to justify the prosperity of the wicked and the afflictions of the righteous, he felt that these principles couldn't explain every situation. Particularly vexing to him were the suffering of Rabbi Akiba and Job. He thought, however, that these cases *could* be explained on the basis of *metempsychosis*.

This work gives a central place in the history of Jewish ideas about the soul, resurrection, and the afterlife to Baruch Spinoza. Spinoza merits a central place because of his insistence that philosophy should neither be made to conform to Scripture nor be made ancillary to Scripture, and because of his claim that this-worldly existence is all there is. The contemporary Israeli philosopher Yirmiyahu Yovel credits Spinoza with a "philosophical revolution" based on what Yovel calls the "principle of immanence."[1] According to Yovel, this principle "views this-worldly existence as the only actual being, and the unique source of ethical value and political authority. All being is this-worldly and there is nothing beyond it, neither a personal creator-God who imposes His divine will on man, nor supernatural powers or values of any kind. The laws of morality and politics, too, and even religion, stem from this world by the natural power of reason."[2]

The intellectual history presented in this work supports Yovel's claim by demonstrating the development in the nineteenth and twentieth centuries of a this-worldly, scientific point of view (held by Jews and non-Jews alike) which rejects

1. Yovel, *Adventures of Immanence*, ix.
2. Yovel, *Adventures of Immanence*, ix.

INTRODUCTION

supernaturalism and any notion of an afterlife, understands mankind from an empirical perspective that excludes any notion of a soul, and embraces a moral point of view that has no need for postmortem rewards and punishments. It is shown that during the nineteenth century, psychology came into its own as a natural science, biology moved away from vitalism, and a "psycho-physical" view of human nature came to dominate both fields of study. There was little, if any, talk among psychologists or biologists of a "soul" and its postmortem existence. The emphasis was on understanding the relationship between physical and mental occurrences. Ultimately, William James explicitly eliminated the idea of a soul from empirical psychology. Then too, in the mid-nineteenth century, the British philosopher John Stuart Mill argued that the belief in human immortality is not grounded on scientific arguments and that human conduct should be directed toward achieving happiness in *this* life, not in an afterlife. In the twenty-first century, the neuroscientist Antonio Damasio, in *Looking for Spinoza*, explained that mental phenomena are dependent on the operation of many specific systems of brain circuits, not on a soul.

Among the Jewish advocates of the principle of immanence are the psychologist Sigmund Freud and the biologist Jacques Loeb. Freud argued that religious doctrines (including doctrines about an immortal soul, resurrection, and an afterlife) are all illusions and do not admit of proof, so no one can be compelled to consider them as true or to believe them. According to Freud, by withdrawing our expectations from the other world and concentrating our liberated energies on this earthly life, humanity will be better off. For his part, Loeb supports the view that there is no need for the concept of a soul by demonstrating that life can be explained entirely in physico-chemical terms. Also important are the this-worldly viewpoints of the Jewish philosophers Hermann Cohen and Morris Raphael Cohen. The former was a nineteenth-century Neo-Kantian who argued that conduct which has moral worth has nothing to do with achieving happiness in an afterlife and that Jewish monotheism is, in fact, opposed to all eudaemonism. The latter was a twentieth-century rationalist, naturalist, and liberal who fiercely defended the scientific method and opposed "religious morality," which he understood to emphasize the fear of eternal punishment and the illusory hope of resurrection for the purpose of a material reward.

Probably the most important and influential Jewish advocate of the principle of immanence has been Mordechai Kaplan. Kaplan believed that Jewish survival in the twentieth century required a naturalistic and a this-worldly focus because one could not be a modern person without it, and Judaism would not survive, he thought, if it remained at odds with modernity. Kaplan claimed that he and his contemporaries are "habituated to the modern emphasis upon improvement of life in *this* world as the only aim worthy of our endeavors."[3] The conduct of people today, claimed Kaplan, is not motivated, as it was in the past, by a yearning for an ideal existence in a future world. It has "dawned upon man that he can transform his physical and social

3. Kaplan, *Judaism as a Civilization*, 8 (emphasis added).

environment and deliberately change the conditions under which he lives."⁴ Consequently, modern people are motivated "by the desire to win for themselves a share of life in this world, to win success, honor, love and everything that contributes to human well-being and self-fulfillment *on earth*."⁵

Notwithstanding that a this-worldly, scientific point of view is held by a large percentage of modern Jews, many contemporary rabbis and Jewish authors have advocated for the acceptance of resurrection, immortality of the soul, transmigration of souls, and/or communicating with dead people. Among such rabbis and authors are Neil Gillman, Simcha Paull Raphael, Jon Levenson, and Elie Kaplan Spitz. Spitz, for example, relies on accounts of near-death experience and past-life regression to contend that reincarnation is possible. He also describes stories about so-called mediums who purportedly can communicate with dead people as evidence that "another realm does exist, to which our souls pass upon death and from which they may return into a new physical life."⁶ The views of Spitz are described and critiqued, as are the views of Gillman, Raphael, and Levenson.

Although the relevant history of Jewish thought recounted in this work was originally written to be as complete as possible, ultimately, it was necessary to limit the work to a single volume. Discussion of many non-Jewish thinkers who influenced Jewish thought about the soul, resurrection, and the afterlife had to be left out. For instance, a discussion of the development of the concept of the soul (or *psyche*) in Greek thought from the time of Homer until the Hellenistic period, which would place Jewish thinking about a soul in a full context, could not be included. Nor was there room for a discussion of pagan and Islamic commentators on Aristotle, and the ways in which they interpreted Aristotle to arrive at the concepts of the acquired intellect and the active intellect utilized by Jewish Aristotelians. Similarly, a chapter on the English, French, and German Enlightenment thinkers had to be omitted even though they greatly influenced modern Jewish thinking about the soul, resurrection, and the afterlife.

More regrettably, discussion of many Jewish thinkers and relevant intellectual developments in the Jewish community had to be foregone. This omission included, among other matters, any description of (1) the relevant thought of many medieval Jewish philosophers such as Halevi, ibn Saddiq, ibn Daud, Gersonides, ibn Falaquera, ben Samuel, Crescas, and Albo, all of whom addressed topics related to the soul, resurrection, and the afterlife; (2) Isaac Luria's kabbalistic school of thought and the methods Luria devised to stimulate what was called "holy *'ibbur*," as well as any description of the superstitious practices related to dybbuk possession and exorcisms that arose in the wake of Lurianic kabbalah; and (3) the seventeenth-century controversies in Amsterdam between Uriel de Costa and Samuel da Silva concerning the immortality

---

4. Kaplan, *Meaning of God*, 50.
5. Kaplan, *Meaning of God*, 44 (emphasis added).
6. Spitz, *Does the Soul Survive?*, 125.

INTRODUCTION

of soul, and between Rabbis Saul Levi Morteira and Isaac Aboab de Fonseca concerning the eternality of punishment.

Furthermore, the discussion of those Jewish thinkers and intellectual developments that *are* included in this work could not be as full and complete as desired. Despite these deficiencies, the reader may, nevertheless, gain from this work a very good understanding of the history of the ideas of the soul, resurrection, and the afterlife in Jewish thought, and their relation to the history of Jewish thought in general. It should be kept in mind, however, that, due to the above-mentioned limitations, and because the work is restricted to the limited (albeit critically important) topics of the soul, resurrection, and the afterlife, the work is only as a *first step* toward a fulsome history of Jewish thought.

1.

The Ancient Israelites Had No Notion of a "Soul" and Envisioned Neither Reward Nor Punishment in a Postmortem Existence but Were Focused on the Here and Now

To the authors of the Hebrew Bible death

> is simply the end of life, determined by God, and to be as readily accepted at his decision as the gift of life itself . . . There are neither attempts to overcome the mystery of death by mythopoeic fantasies, by bold analogical reasoning from the life of Nature, or by rituals of power, nor palliations of death's final decree by efforts to maintain a link with the departed. Whatever of such is still present in traces of feeding the dead, or enquiring from them, is placed under strict interdict by unconditional attachment to Yahweh.'[1]

Consistent with this view, apart from Enoch and Elijah, "all biblical personalities die and the Bible repeatedly emphasizes that death is the ultimate fate of all human beings."[2] The biblical view is well-expressed in the book of Job:

> Man born of woman is short-lived and sated with trouble.
>
> He blossoms like a flower and withers;
>
> He vanishes like a shadow and does not endure . . .
>
> His days are determined;
>
> You know the number of his months;

---

1. Eichrodt, *Theology of the Old Testament*, 2:500–1 (citing 2 Sam. 12:23, Ps 89:49, and Job 7:9 as examples of absolute resignation to death). See generally Lewis, *Cults of the Dead*, 1–2 (identifying several other twentieth-century scholars who maintained that cults of the dead didn't exist in Israel, and arguing, in opposition to such scholars, that while "'normative Yahwism' may have been resolute in its condemnation of cults of the dead, a strong circumstantial case can be built for their existence in some forms of 'popular religion.'").

2. Gillman, *Death of Death*, 60.

> You have set limits that he cannot pass . . .
> There is hope for a tree;
> If it is cut down it will renew itself;
> Its shoots will not cease.
> If its roots are old in the earth,
> And its stump dies in the ground,
> At the scent of water it will bud
> And produce branches like a sapling.
> But mortals languish and die;
> Man expires, where is he?
> As the waters fail from the sea,
> And the river is drained dry;
> So man lies down and rises not . . .[3]

The concern of the Hebrew Bible, for the most part, is "this-worldly." The focus of attention is on achieving well-being in the here and now. Accordingly, in Deuteronomy 11:13–15 and 28:1–14, the rewards the Israelites are offered for obedience to God's commandments are material well-being—rainfall, crops, food, children, military victory, national security, health, and length of days—and, in Deuteronomy 11:16–17 and 28:15–68, the punishment the Israelites are threatened with for disobeying God's commandments are the opposite—famine, poverty, illness, military defeat, and early death. Indeed, there does not appear to have been any idea on the part of the authors of the Hebrew Bible that, in the normal course of events, a person can survive death. Much less is there any idea until postexilic times that God will reward or punish someone in an afterlife.[4] Accordingly, the Hebrew Bible evidences no notion of a place of customary postmortem reward or of customary postmortem punishment.

Nor does the Hebrew Bible express the notion that a certain *part* of a person—the "soul"—is rewarded or punished in an afterlife. In fact, the ancient Israelites had no notion of a soul at all. Human beings are not conceived dualistically, as composed of a body and a soul. Rather, human beings are conceived as psycho-physical wholes, composed of earthly stuff and having a life force given by God. Upon death, the earthly stuff returns to the earth, and the life force returns to God. While having no notion of a soul or of a postmortem reward and punishment, the ancient Israelites *did* believe that there is *something* that survives a person's death. This something is neither the

---

3. Job 14:1–12. See Gillman, *Death of Death*, 60–65.

4. But see Brichto, "Kin, Cult, Land and Afterlife," 49–50 (emphasizing that Deut 11:18–21 promises, in return for obedience to the divine will, "the continuation of [one's] posterity (on the land)," and suggesting that such continuation is for the purpose of benefitting the dead ancestors). Whatever rites, if any, were performed to benefit dead family members were at odds with the *essence* of the biblical concept. Brichto himself states that "reward and punishment after death [is] the one element [of the Israelite conception of the afterlife] whose existence is denied by all scholars" (49–50).

person himself or herself, nor the person's soul. Rather, it is a shadowy double of the person (a "shade"), lacking vitality, knowledge, and feelings. The shade is conceived as residing underground in a place called *Sheol*. *Sheol* is viewed neither as a place of reward nor punishment, although it is inhospitable and undesirable.

Notwithstanding that the practice of necromancy is central to an episode in the life of King Saul, necromancy is at odds with the generally accepted conception of postmortem existence found in the Hebrew Bible. It likely reflects a cult of the dead existing in Canaanite culture and also probably practiced by many ancient Israelites but condemned by the authors of the Hebrew Bible.[5] Finally, certain biblical passages express a concern for a positive postmortem existence, but these passages are relatively late and do not alter the dominant this-worldly focus of the Hebrew Bible.

A. *Nephesh* Does Not Mean "Soul"

The Hebrew word *nephesh* has, until relatively recently, been translated in English versions of the Bible as "soul." However, modern biblical scholarship has established that this translation is erroneous. Although the exact meaning of *nephesh* is elusive,[6] the word was originally associated with the throat or the neck, which is to say, with that part of the body through which life-giving air passes.[7] For example, Psalm 69:2–3 has traditionally been translated:

> Save me O God; for the waters are come in unto my soul (*nephesh*).
> I sink in deep mire where there is no standing:
> I am come into deep waters, where floods overflow me.[3]

A better, modern translation, however, is that "the waters are come unto my *throat.*" Similarly, the prophet Isaiah used *nephesh* in the sense of throat when he compared the captivity of the people to being swallowed up by the underworld, saying:

> *Sheol* hath widened its throat (*nephesh*),

---

5. See generally Hallote, *Death, Burial, and Afterlife*, 11–68. Hallote contends that, despite the efforts of the "official religion of Israel" to eradicate the cult of the dead (which was inconsistent with monotheism), most ancient Israelites worshipped their dead family members. Lewis similarly argues "that there was an ongoing battle by the Yahwism which emerges as normative against the practice of necromancy and other death cult rituals such as self-laceration and presenting offerings to the deceased . . . In other words, the legal material we find in the Deuteronomistic and Priestly literature is decidedly against cults of the dead and from this we infer that such laws were formulated in reaction to existing death cult practices" (Lewis, *Cults of the Dead*, 176). See also Lewis, *Cults of the Dead*, 174 (cults of the dead "seem to have held a lasting appeal in certain forms of 'popular religion'").

6. Johnson, *Vitality of the Individual*, 3 (it admits "a remarkably wide range of meaning"). But see Eichrodt, *Theology of the Old Testament*, 2:216–20.

7. See Gillman, *Death of Death*, 76; Eichrodt, *Theology of the Old Testament*, 2:134; Johnson, *Vitality of the Individual*, 3–5, 6n1.

8. Cf. Jonah 2:5 ("Waters encompassed me up to the neck (*nephesh*)"). See Johnson, *Vitality of the Individual*, 92–93.

And opened its mouth without limit.⁹

That *nephesh* is related to the throat, or the part of the body through which air passes, can also be seen in Job 41:13, in which the author speaks in parallel verse of a flame coming out of the mouth and a fire coming out of the *nephesh*, and in Proverbs 3:22, in which *nephesh* is used in parallel verse with "neck."

The part of the body that has life-giving air pass through it, at a later time, becomes associated with the seat of the life force itself, or, in other words, with the living part of a person. Eichrodt, in explaining this development, states that, in the case of *nephesh*, it is possible:

> to establish *the basic physical connotation*, namely first of all the 'neck,' 'throat' or 'gullet,' and then by extension that which comes out of the throat, the 'breath' or 'breath of life' . . . As the characteristic sign of the living, both in human beings and in animals, the breath may appear to be the 'extra thing which the living possess,' that which distinguishes them from the dead. Thus it becomes a substance which inheres in the living even apart from the breath; in short, it becomes *equated simply with 'life.'* Hence it is granted to animals as well, and one can speak equally of the [*nephesh behema*/animal *nephesh*] and of the [*nephesh adam*/human *nephesh*].¹⁰

Stated differently, *nephesh* may be used

> to denote that common vital principle in man or beast which reveals itself in the form of conscious life, as when Solomon is congratulated upon having asked Yahweh for wisdom rather than the life [*nephesh*] of his enemies, or when the infatuated youth is said to be lured on, "As a bird will hasten to the snare, Not knowing that its life [*nephesh*] is at stake."¹¹

Because blood is also seen as a life force, *nephesh* came to be associated with blood, in addition to breath.¹² Indeed, *nephesh* came to be used with reference to "what is a comprehensive and unified manifestation of sentient life, as when it is said of the right kind of master that he understands the [*nephesh*] (i.e. the feelings) of his beast, or when the Israelites are reminded that in view of their own experience in Egypt they are in a position to know the [*nephesh*] (i.e. the feelings) of a resident alien."¹³

---

9. Isa 5:14. See Johnson, *Vitality of the Individual*, 5.

10. Eichrodt, *Theology of the Old Testament*, 2:134–35 (emphasis original). See also Johnson, *Vitality of the Individual*, 6–8.

11. Johnson, *Vitality of the Individual*, 8 (citing 1 Kgs 3:11; Prov 7:23). See also Gen 37:21.

12. The Bible states that "the *nephesh* is in the blood" and "the blood is the *nephesh*" (Lev 17:11; Deut 12:23). See also Urbach, *Sages*, 1:215 ("Although the Bible states 'for the blood is the [*nephesh*]' . . . yet the verse does not mean to say that the essence or material of the [*nephesh*] is blood. It merely informs us that when blood is shed human life grows weak and comes to an end. Blood is here only a manifestation of life like breathing, which is a symptom of life.").

13. Johnson, *Vitality of the Individual*, 10 (citing Prov 12:10; Exod 23:9).

Further, the fact that feelings may be seen to wax or wane suggested to the ancient mind that the *nephesh* itself may wax or wane.

> Thus the sensations of hunger and thirst may be attributed (explicitly or implicitly) to the [*nephesh*]; and this may be done in such a manner as to emphasize a shrinking or weakening of its power, as when it [viz., the *nephesh*] is said, not merely to be shriveled up or empty, but even to faint and so to pour itself out or drain away . . . Contrariwise, when such lack of nourishment is met, the vitality of the [*nephesh*] is restored . . . Similarly various emotional states are attributed to the [*nephesh*] as when it is said to be distressed or troubled, and thus prey of bitter feelings. Under such conditions . . . the [*nephesh*] may be said to waste or pine away, to melt or to faint, and indeed to drain away.[14]

Corresponding to this increase and decrease in the power of the *nephesh*, which is to say, in the vitality of the life force, there is a recognized "oscillation in mood," so that the *nephesh* "may be said to grieve (or weep) but also to be glad (or rejoice), to have a sinking feeling of despair but also hope, to be impatient but also to be patient, and above all . . . to hate but also to love, and more often and far more emphatically, to loathe but also to desire."[15] Thus, it is no surprise that the term *nephesh* "is often used by itself with an obvious emphasis on desire in some form or another. This is especially true . . . of the desire for food; and we may compare the use of the corresponding Arabic term . . . to indicate what we should call one's appetite."[16]

Ultimately, by extension, *nephesh* is used to represent the whole living person. As Eichrodt explains:

> [*Nephesh*] undergoes a minor extension of meaning, but one implicit in the logic of the concept, when it comes to denote not just the life within the individual, but *the living individual himself* . . . In the taking of a census the persons counted were designated simply by [*nephesh*], rather as we today might speak of 'seventy souls.' This is especially the usage in Hebrew when referring to slaves; but the individual is also described in this way in legal contexts. Here the aspect of the concept which makes it the characteristic term for the individual has become so predominant that [*nephesh*] even comes to mean a single being without qualification, regardless of whether it is alive or not; one is simply speaking of the individual. The recollection of the original meaning has here been so completely eradicated that a special qualification is added to indicate whether the individual in question is alive or dead: [*nephesh hayya*], the living being, is opposed to [*nephesh met*], the dead one, the corpse."[17]

---

14. Johnson, *Vitality of the Individual*, 10–11. See also Eichrodt, *Theology of the Old Testament*, 2:138.

15. Johnson, *Vitality of the Individual*, 12.

16. Johnson, *Vitality of the Individual*, 13. See also Eichrodt, *Theology of the Old Testament*, 2:139.

17. See Eichrodt, *Theology of the Old Testament*, 2:137 (emphasis original; citing numerous biblical verses). See also Johnson, *Vitality of the Individual*, 15–22 (discussing use of the term *nephesh* "to

This use of *nephesh* to refer to the whole person can be seen in Genesis 2:7, where *nephesh* "denotes the totality which has come about through the combination of the body formed out of the earth and the divine breath breathed into it." [18] That the whole human being, or the totality of what constitutes a human being, is expressed by the term *nephesh* is suggested by frequent reference to the fact that man *is* a *nephesh*. In these passages, *nephesh* is appropriately translated as "person." Thus, Speiser translates Genesis 12:5:

> Abram took his wife Sarai, his brother's son Lot, all the possessions that they had acquired, and all the persons (*ha-nephesh*) they had obtained in Haran.[19]

The word *nephesh* is also used to signify one's own self, becoming the equivalent of a personal or reflexive pronoun, as when Job says:

> Did I not weep for the hapless, My self (my *nephesh*) grieve for the poor?[20]

In this instance *nephesh* parallels and balances the pronoun "I," so that the second part of the verse implies "Did not I, myself, grieve for the poor?" Similarly, Job answers Eliphaz, saying:

> I, too, could talk like you, If you (your *nephesh*) were in my (my *nephesh*'s) place."[21]

In sum,

> it is . . . clear that the Hebrew mind, when using the term [*nephesh*], was far from conceiving of a soul in the sense of a spiritual *alter ego* of the physical person. What the Hebrew sought to express was rather that the impulses and emotions . . . were manifestations of the vital energy within the person, being closely bound up with the life of the individual, and only existent in it . . . It may be taken as an assured conclusion that in no instance does there underlie the use of [*nephesh*] that conception of an immaterial *alter ego* [that is, a "soul"], the origins of which have perforce been assumed to lie in primitive observation of the breath . . . This theory is as little verifiable in the case of Israel as it has proved susceptible of confirmation for primitive peoples. Equally remote from the concept of [*nephesh*] . . . is the signification of a numinous substance in Man which survives death and forms the necessary presupposition of a cult of the dead such as flourished in Canaan among Israel's neighbors. The

---

denote one's 'person' or 'self' as a centre of consciousness and unit of vital power," and, ultimately, it's use with reference to a corpse, so that "at one extreme [*nephesh*] may denote that vital principle in man which animates the human body and reveals itself in the form of conscious life, and at the other extreme it may denote the corpse from which such conscious life has departed!").

18. Eichrodt, *Theology of the Old Testament*, 2:137. See Johnson, *Vitality of the Individual*, 18–19.
19. Speiser, *Anchor Bible*, 85.
20. Job 30:25. See Eichrodt, *Theology of the Old Testament*, 2:138.
21. Job 16:4.

vital force connoted by [*nephesh*] has no independent numinous character, but is the gift of the Creator to the creature. It remains susceptible to the grip of death, and can offer no protection against the ultimate limit set to life in fellowship with God.[22]

B. The Biblical Concept of Man Is That of a Psycho-Physical Whole

The biblical depiction of the creation of man is that God molded the earth into a human form and then made this creation come alive by infusing it with air. Specifically, Genesis 2:7 is traditionally, but erroneously, translated:

> And the Lord God formed man of the dust of the ground,[23] and breathed into his nostrils the breath of life (*nishmat hayyim*); and man became a *living soul* (*nephesh hayyah*).

Modern biblical scholars believe that a more accurate translation of Genesis 2:7 is that man became a "living being" or a "living person," *not* a "living soul."[24]

Clearly, the image in Genesis 2:7 is that the body, composed of the same stuff as the earth, is made to come alive (that is, given vitality) by air which comes from God, and which, when it is infused (or breathed) into a human body, becomes human breath [*neshamah*]. This air which God breathed into man's nostrils is elsewhere referred to as the *ruach Elohim* (the "wind/air/breath of God");[25] and it is the *ruach Elohim* that functions as the life force which, *once infused in a human body*, becomes human breath [*neshamah*], which, as the life force, is called the *nishmat hayyim*, the breath of life.[26]

That the *ruach Elohim*, the breath of God, is the world's animating and life-giving force derives from the fact (or, rather, is the reason for the fact) that the *ruach Elohim* is part of the original "stuff" existing prior to the act of creation.[27] The breath of God is, in other words, the divine vital force which pervades the whole of creation. In the narrative of the flood, *ruach* is used in a genitive form along with *neshamah* to refer to the entire animal creation as that which has breath in its nostrils, now characterized as

---

22. Eichrodt, *Theology of the Old Testament*, 2:139–40 (See also 2 135n4). But see, Steiner, *Disembodied Souls*, 1–127. Steiner contends that, contrary to the modern scholarly consensus, the Hebrew Bible evidences a belief in disembodied souls. Unfortunately, space prohibits a complete statement and critique of Steiner's argument.

23. Elsewhere the "dust" [*'aphar*] is referred to as mud or "clay" [*homer*], or as "earth" [*eretz*]. See Job 10:9, 33:6; Qoh 12:7.

24. See e.g., Speiser, *Anchor Bible*, 14; Friedman, *Bible with Sources Revealed*, 35; Johnson, *Vitality of the Individual*, 19; Eichrodt, *Theology of the Old Testament*, 2:137.

25. See Eichrodt, *Theology of the Old Testament*, 2:47n2.

26. See Kohler, *Jewish Theology*, 212. See generally Eichrodt, *Theology of the Old Testament*, 2:46–47, 131–34.

27. See Gen 1:2. See generally Johnson, *Vitality of the Individual*, 32–33, and 32n8.

"*ruach*-like," or "life-giving," breath (*nishmat-ruach hayyim*).[28] This life-giving breath may also be referred to, more simply, either as the *nishmat hayyim* or the *ruach hayyim*.[29] It is this "breath of life" which serves as a common characteristic which man shares with the whole of the animal world.[30]

Though associated with the life force, *ruach* retains its literal meaning of "wind," and as such simply denotes the movement of air, both outside of human beings and inside of human beings (where it is called "breath").[31] As Eichrodt says:

> [I]n the blowing of the wind and the rhythm of human respiration ancient Man detected a divine mystery, and saw in this element in Nature, at once near to him and yet so incomprehensible, a symbol of the mysterious nearness and activity of the divine. As the bearer of life, therefore, the wind tends to become in the theistic religions the breath of life, proceeding from God, and both animating Nature and bestowing life on Man. The living breath in each human being may, then, be regarded as an effect of the divine breath of life, as, for example, in Egypt, where exactly as in Israel the deity breathes the life-breath into Man, and thus calls him into living existence.[32]

At some point the term *ruach* could even be used as a substitute for *neshamah*.[33] The relationship between the *ruach* (or the *ruach Elohim*) and the *neshamah* is made clear in Israelite poetry found throughout the Hebrew Bible. For example, the following lines appear in the book of Job at 33:4:

> The wind of God (*ruach Elohim*) has made me,
> The breath of the Almighty (*nishmat Shaddai*) gives me life.

Again, Job 27:3 states:

> All the while my breath (*neshamah*) is in me
> And the wind of God (*ruach Elohim*) is in my nostrils.

The prophet Isaiah employs *ruach* and *neshamah* as being practically synonymous when he refers to God as the one:

> Who created the heavens and stretched them out,
> Who fashioned the earth and its products,
> Who giveth *neshamah* to the people thereon,

---

28. See Johnson, *Vitality of the Individual*, 28.
29. Gen 2:7, 6:17, 7:15.
30. See Kohler, *Jewish Theology*, 212.
31. See Eichrodt, *Theology of the Old Testament*, 2:46–47. See also Johnson, *Vitality of the Individual*, 23–24.
32. Eichrodt, *Theology of the Old Testament*, 2:46–47.
33. Johnson, *Vitality of the Individual*, 28–29. See Eichrodt, *Theology of the Old Testament*, 2:47n2.

CHAPTER 1.

And *ruach* to those who walk therein.[34]

There is also a close relationship between *ruach* and *nephesh* since both words are associated with air as a life force. However, *nephesh*, in contradistinction to *ruach*, denotes "*life bound up with a body.*"[35] Put differently, *ruach* is the life force present everywhere and existing independently of any particular individual, and *nephesh* is that life force when it has become individuated. But this distinction is not consistently made, and *ruach* is used, just as *nephesh* is used, to describe psychic characteristics of human beings, including thoughts, decisions and moods.[36] Indeed, since, as discussed above, the *nephesh* could increase and decrease in vitality or power, and since the *ruach*, qua "wind," is readily observed to wax and wane, it is logical that the ebb and flow in human vitality came to be described in terms of the absence or presence of *ruach*.

> Thus it is said of Jacob, for example, when he recovered from the shock of being told by his sons that Joseph was still alive and actually ruling over Egypt, that his [*ruach*] 'lived' or 'came to life' . . . Similarly it is said of Samson, when he was faint with thirst after a particularly strenuous conflict with the Philistines, that . . . 'his [*ruach*] returned . . . and he lived.[37]
>
> In short, amid all the changing circumstances of life man's ordinary physical powers were rightly felt to ebb and flow, just as one's variable moods obviously come and go; and for the Israelite all this might be expressed in terms of the presence or absence of [*ruach*].[38]

In fact, the vagaries of *ruach*, qua "wind," "made it the obvious term for denoting almost any mood, disposition, or frame of mind (as we say); and indeed it seems to have been possible to resort to it as a means of expressing the whole range of man's emotional, intellectual, and volitional life."[39] This was often achieved by simply referring to a particular type of *ruach*, "suitably defined by a following noun in the genitive and operating as an extraneous influence, the origin of which is sometimes ascribed to Yahweh and sometimes left unindicated."[40] So, Isaiah can think of God "as reducing the citizens of Jerusalem to a state of coma by 'pouring out' upon them "a [*ruach*] of

---

34. Isa 42:5. See Johnson, *Vitality of the Individual*, 29.
35. Eichrodt, *Theology of the Old Testament*, 2:135 (emphasis original). See also 2:136.
36. See generally Eichrodt, *Theology of the Old Testament*, 2:48n3 (distinguishing "life-giving spirit [*ruach*] of God . . . from the individual human spirit, also denoted occasionally by the word [*ruach*]," and stating: "The latter as an organ of psychic life forms the focal centre of thoughts, decisions and moods, and thus constitutes a psychological concept as opposed to the cosmological one of the breath of life.").
37. Johnson, *Vitality of the Individual*, 25 (citing Gen 45:27; Judg 15:19).
38. Johnson, *Vitality of the Individual*, 26.
39. Johnson, *Vitality of the Individual*, 31.
40. Johnson, *Vitality of the Individual*, 31.

deep sleep," while Hosea speaks of Israel's proneness to apostasy as being due to "'a [*ruach*] of whoredom.'" [41]

All this is to evidence that in the Hebrew Bible man is *not* seen as a composite of a body and a soul. There is no such dualism. There is no concept of an immaterial substance that is separate and apart from the body, and that is responsible for life, intellect, and feelings. Rather, the human organism is seen as a psycho-physical whole, a single entity, with air serving as a life force.[42] According to Johnson, "in Israelite thought man is conceived, not so much in dual fashion as 'body' and 'soul,' but synthetically as a unit of vital power or (in current terminology) a psycho-physical organism." [43] Eichrodt similarly states that "a strict dualism, which feels that flesh and spirit, body and soul, are irreconcilable opposites, is completely unknown [to the ancient Israelites]." [44] Urbach takes the same position as Johnson and Eichrodt, saying:

> *In the Bible a monistic view prevails. Man is not composed of two elements— body and soul, or flesh and spirit*. In Genesis [2:7] it is stated 'and man became a living soul [*nephesh*],' but the term [*nephesh*] is not to be understood in the sense of *psyche, anima. The whole of man is a living soul. The creation of man constitutes a single act*. The [*nephesh*] is in actuality the living man, and hence [*nephesh*] is also used in place of the word [*adam*] ['man']. When the Lord says to Moses 'For all the men who were seeking thy life [thy *nephesh*] are dead' (Exodus iv 19), the reference is not to his *psyche* [soul] but to his whole being, and the same applies to the words of Elijah, when he states ' . . . And they seek my life [my *nephesh*], to take it away' [1 Kgs 19:10]. But on the other hand [*nephesh*] also expresses all the feelings and sentiments of a person, In the verse 'for ye know the heart [*nephesh*] of a stranger' [Exod 23:9], and in similar verses, the word [*nephesh*] is used in the sense of 'existence,' 'feeling,' 'attitude'—in brief, what is called today the 'human condition.' . . .
>
> [T]here is no difference between [the *nephesh*] and the flesh. 'O God . . . my [*nephesh*] thirsts for Thee; my flesh faints for Thee . . .' [Ps 63:2], the poet sings. [*Nephesh*] is in parallelism here with 'flesh' . . . Similarly, [*ruach*] is only a

---

41. Johnson, *Vitality of the Individual*, 31. Other texts speak of "a *ruach* of jealousy," "a *ruach* of judgment," and "a *ruach* of justice." See Johnson, *Vitality of the Individual*, 31–32.

42. See generally Gillman, *Death of Death*, 69, 76–78, 106; Kohler, *Jewish Theology*, 213. There is a strong urge among some people to transpose the biblical portrayal of each human as *single* entity into a portrayal of each human as a *composite* entity made of a body and a soul. Thus, Hirsch writes: "Man is viewed in the Bible as a composite being, consisting of body and soul, or flesh and breath. The body, created of earth, is animated by a breath of life which God breathed into it at the time of creation. The soul is thus associated with the breath" (Hirsch, *Rabbinic Psychology*, 57). Clearly, Hirsch is reading into the Bible his own concept of a soul by associating the biblical notion of the "breath of life" with the nonbiblical notion of a "soul." Hirsch then associates the biblical words "nephesh," "neshamah," and "ruach," which he considers essentially interchangeable, with the English word "soul." Hirsch interposes his own dualistic conceptions on the biblical view even while acknowledging that the biblical view is *not* dualistic. See Hirsch, *Rabbinic Psychology*, 64, 66.

43. Johnson, *Vitality of the Individual*, 87.

44. Eichrodt, *Theology of the Old Testament*, 2:147.

manifestation of life. 'In whose hand is the soul [*nephesh*] of every living thing, and the breath [*ruach*] of all mankind' [Job 12:10]. The [*ruach*] is not part of the components of man, but the form in which he finds expression . . . Pedersen rightly perceived that the [*ruach*] is not the centre of the [*nephesh*] but the power that moves it, the force that acts on the centre and thrusts it forward in a given direction . . . [*Nephesh*], [*guf* ('body')], and [*ruach*] form an indivisible entity, and it may be said that man is a psycho-physical organism."[45]

A possible intimation of the concept of a "soul" in the Hebrew Bible is found in the book of Ecclesiastes (in Hebrew, Qoheleth), at 3:21. Significantly, Qoheleth was probably composed around 250 BCE, more than 100 years after the death of Plato, and well after the dissemination of Greek ideas and culture throughout the ancient world, including Judea.[46] In general, chapter 3 of Qoheleth questions the belief that there is any kind of afterlife. It contends that one should concern oneself with what happens in this life, for "who shall bring him to see what shall be after him" (v. 22)? In this context, the author further contends that men are no different than beasts. They both have the same life force, that is "they [both] have one breath [*ruach*]," and they both die when they lose that life force—"as the one dies, so does the other" (v. 19). Then follows the relevant verse:

> Who knows whether the spirit (*ruach*) of man rises upward and the spirit (*ruach*) of the beast goes down to the earth?"

The meaning of his verse seems to be that, in keeping with the view that we cannot know what happens after we die, no one can say that after death the *ruach* of human beings goes upward and the *ruach* of beasts goes downward. Therefore, this verse seems to indicate that at least some people had voiced the view that, at death, the *ruach* of different categories of beings goes to different locations, the *ruach* of superior beings ascending and the *ruach* of inferior beings descending. Accordingly, the verse may reflect a view that 200 years later would be explicitly stated by Philo of Alexandria, namely that the *ruach* (or life-giving air that God breaths into human beings) is to be equated with the Platonic *psyche* or soul.[47] Part of the Platonic concept of *psyche*

---

45. Urbach, *Sages*, 1:214–15 (emphasis added).

46. See Gordis, *Faith for Moderns*, 63–68; Gillman, *Death of Death*, 77–78; Madigan and Levenson, *Resurrection*, 182. See generally Eichrodt, *Theology of the Old Testament*, 2:150 ("It was left to Greek philosophy in the Hellenistic period to make a breach [in the Israelite conception of man as psycho-physical unity]. Thus for the writer of II Maccabees the [*ruach*] as the principle of life indwelling Man disappears in favour of a dichotomistic application of the concepts of [*nephesh*] and [*basar*] as the two components of human nature. In the Wisdom of Solomon [*nephesh-psyche*] becomes the imperishable substance which as an indestructible principle of life guarantees Man immortality . . . This alliance between the Old Testament ways of thought and the concepts of Alexandrian-Platonic philosophy led in Philo to a complete capitulation to the Greek view of Man."); ch. 3 of this book.

47. See ch. 3, sec. C, 2. See also Moore, *Judaism in the First Centuries*, 2:292 (Qoheleth 3:18–22 "suggests that the author had heard some such discrimination of human and animal souls as was current in Greek circles.").

is that after death some souls travel to an upper region of reward and other souls go to a lower region of punishment, and the author of Qoheleth seems to doubt that anyone can have certain knowledge of this supposed postmortem divergence.

C. The Conception of Man as a Psycho-Physical Whole Is Seen in the Use of the Terminology for the Various Parts of the Body to Describe Mental Phenomena

That the human organism is seen as a psycho-physical unity is further evidenced by the fact that "the various members and secretions of the body, such as the bones, the heart, the bowels, and the kidneys, as well as the flesh and the blood, can all be thought of as revealing psychical properties."[48] Thus, for instance, "the flesh [*basar*] is clearly associated with psychical functions, as when the psalmist says:

> How lovely the place where Thou dost dwell,
> Yahweh of Hosts!
> My whole being [*nephesh*] longeth, yea pineth,
> For Yahweh's courts;
> My heart and my flesh [*basar*] acclaim
> The Living God.[49]

By synecdoche (in which a part is put for the whole) *basar* is used to refer to the entire body itself,[50] and then, probably because *basar* and many other parts of the body are associated with psychic activity, *basar* comes to denote, as *nephesh*, the whole person.[51] So, "all flesh" means every living being, both human and animal, and *kol-basar* [all flesh] can be used in the same sense as *kol-nephesh*.[52] That the whole person can be referred to in terms of the flesh/body as well as in terms of the *nephesh* highlights the fact that the human organism is seen as a psycho-physical unity. "Indeed the parallelism with [*nephesh*] is occasionally so marked that the use of the term for 'flesh' almost approaches the common use of the former term as a periphrasis for the personal pronoun . . . [as, for example]:

> Yahweh, Thou art my God! Thee do I seek!
> My whole being [*nephesh*] thirsteth for Thee.

---

48. Johnson, *Vitality of the Individual*, 87. See Johnson, *Vitality of the Individual*, 37 ("The conception of man as a psycho-physical organism may be seen . . . clearly when one examines the use of the terminology for the various parts of the body."), 41–86; Eichrodt, *Theology of the Old Testament*, 2:142–47.

49. Johnson, *Vitality of the Individual*, 38 (quoting Ps 84:2–3).

50. Johnson, *Vitality of the Individual*, 37 (citing 1 Kgs 21:27; Lev 13:38, 17:15; Num 8:7; Job 4:15; Prov 4:22).

51. See Eichrodt, *Theology of the Old Testament*, 2:147 (citing Lev 13:18; Qoh 4:5, 5:5; Neh 5:5).

52. Eichrodt, *Theology of the Old Testament*, 2:147 (citing Gen 6:13, 17, 7:15, 21).

CHAPTER 1.

> My flesh [*basar*] fainteth for Thee, a very land in drought,
> Exhausted for lack of water.[53]

The conception of man as a psycho-physical whole can also be seen in the relationship between mental states and internal parts of the body.

> Despondency, for example, is felt to have a shriveling effect upon the bones . . . just as they are said to decay or become soft with fear or distress . . . Indeed they are seen to form so fundamental a part of man's being that they provide an obvious parallel to the term [*nephesh*], when this denotes the whole personality conceived as functioning psychically; so that a suppliant of Yahweh, having begun his prayer with a plea for the destruction of his enemies, can continue:
>
> > Then I myself shall rejoice in Yahweh;
> > I shall exult in His salvation.
> > (lit. Then my [*nephesh*] will rejoice in Yahweh;
> > It will exalt in His salvation.)
> > All my bones will say:
> > Yahweh, who is like unto Thee?[54]

The internal organ that is most often associated with mental states is the heart [*leb*].[55]

> That strong emotion was actually physically felt by the heart, either in the slowing-down or quickening of the heart-beat, in an intermittent pulse or in direct sensation of pain, must have turned attention to this organ, and accorded it an important place in the description of psychical conditions . . . It is made the organ equally of feelings, intellectual activities, and the working of the will. The fact that Accadian shows an exactly corresponding usage for the cognate word *libbu* suggests that the employment of the term forced itself on primitive Man as axiomatic. The result in Hebrew, when feelings are in question, is a marked area of contact between [*leb*] and [*nephesh*]. As regards joy and sorrow it is possible equally well to talk of 'strengthening the heart' or 'refreshing the [*nephesh*],' of 'pouring out the heart' or 'pouring out the [*nephesh*]. Similar overlapping with [*ruach*] was unavoidable. One can speak either of a 'broken heart' or of a 'broken [*ruach*],' and describe pride as a lifting up either of the heart or of the [*ruach*] . . . The great majority of instances of the

---

53. Johnson, *Vitality of the Individual*, 38 (quoting Ps 63:2).

54. Johnson, *Vitality of the Individual*, 67–69 (quoting Ps 35:9–10). See Eichrodt, *Theology of the Old Testament*, 2:146 (the bones "provide a particularly forcible illustration of the immediacy with which the Hebrew conceived the physical as an expression of the psychical.").

55. See Johnson, *Vitality of the Individual*, 75–87; Eichrodt, *Theology of the Old Testament*, 2:142–45.

word refer to intellectual and volitional processes, and it is this which gives it its distinctive stamp in Hebrew thought.[56]

The heart is thus used with a force which approximates what we would call the "mind" or "intellect," and

> is frequently employed by metonymy to denote one's thought and therefore, on occasion, one's wish, purpose, or resolve; for one's thought or wish is essentially 'that which is in the heart,' or, as we should say, 'what one has in mind.' Similarly, whereas we speak of a matter in English as 'entering one's mind,' the Israelite says that it 'mounts upon the heart'; and in much the same way 'to lay to heart' is 'to bear in mind,' 'to bring back to the heart' is 'to recall to mind,' and for a thing to 'turn aside' from the heart is for one to 'forget' it.[57]

Eichrodt sums the matter up in a manner which makes clear that for the ancient Israelite the human being is a psycho-physical whole, and the body is not something separate and apart from a human's emotional, intellectual, and volitional essence:

> Of the greatest consequence . . . is the realism in biblical psychology, which brings the body into organic connection with psychic life. Here we have an affirmation of human existence in the body, with all that follows from this. For the body is not an object which we possess, but which stands outside our real being; it is not simply the natural basis and instrument to which we are assigned, but which does not belong to our essential self. It is the living form of that self, the necessary expression of our individual existence, in which the meaning of our life must find its realization. Hence the body cannot be despised as the prison of the soul . . . Instead it is understood as in all its parts the medium of a spiritual and personal [that is, emotional, intellectual and volitional] life . . . The repercussions of this holistic view of human nature on the shaping both of the God-Man relationship and Man's relations with his world can be detected at every turn. Where Man knew nothing of an immortal soul-substance, he was bound to be conscious with peculiar immediacy of his constant dependence on God as the only source of life in every peril. Equally the high value set on earthly goods appears in a new light, when we consider their direct connection with psychic realities . . . But the lines extend even further, affecting Israel's views on sin and redemption. For it is a consequence of their outlook on the psychic life that sin cannot be explained one-sidedly as *concupiscentia*, the desire of the flesh, but must be understood as a reality of the psyche as a whole, drawing the body into sympathy with it.[58]

56. Eichrodt, *Theology of the Old Testament*, 2:142–43 (citing numerous biblical verses). See Johnson, *Vitality of the Individual*, 77 ("for all that the heart is . . . brought so often into relation with man's psychical life at the *emotional* level . . . it is as the seat or instrument of his *intellectual* and *volitional* activity that it figures most prominently in Israelite thinking.") (emphasis added).

57. Johnson, *Vitality of the Individual*, 77–78 (citing numerous biblical verses).

58. Eichrodt, *Theology of the Old Testament*, 2:149 (emphasis original).

CHAPTER 1.

D. The Biblical Concept of Death Did Not Include Any Reward or Punishment in an Afterlife

In keeping with the conception of a human being as a single entity with air as its life force, death is *not* seen as a separation of the soul from the body, with the soul continuing to exist while the body disintegrates. Rather, death is seen as the end of any vital personhood, without any real (or vital) *you* continuing in some other place. Indeed, since the physical and the psychic were merely different aspects of one and the same entity, it would make no sense to imagine the continuation of the psychic aspect without the continuation of the physical aspect—both aspects reflect the same entity.

At death, the earthly matter from which human beings are formed returns to that earthly matter, and the portion of the wind of God that constitutes human breath, and served as the animating or life force of the human being, returns to God.[59] The thought is made clear in the book of Job, which reads, at 34:14:

> If He (God) set his heart upon man,
> if He gather unto Himself his wind (*ruach*)
> And His breath (*neshamah*),
> All flesh shall perish together
> And man shall return to dust.

A similar idea appears in the book of Qoheleth, at 12:7:

> The dust returns to the earth as it was,
> And the wind (*ruach*) returns to God, who gave it.[60]

It is also the book of Qoheleth in which it can be seen most clearly that, for the Israelite, there is no entity that survives death that in any way constitutes who a person really is, which is to say that there is nothing surviving death which has consciousness, emotions, and intelligence. The author of Qoheleth laments:

> The living know . . . that they shall die, but the dead know nothing, nor have they any reward . . Their loves, their hates, their jealousies, all have perished— no longer have they a share in all that is done under the sun.[61]

Nor did the ancient Israelites, prior to about 164 BCE, have any widespread belief that people could be resurrected (brought back into vital existence) after death and burial for the purpose of reward and punishment. To the contrary, certain biblical passages make it quite clear that resurrection for any purpose was generally believed to be, if not wholly impossible, unexpected and abnormal. For example, Job states:

---

59. See Johnson, *Vitality of the Individual*, 88; Eichrodt, *Theology of the Old Testament*, 2:214.
60. See also Qoh 3:19–20; Pss 104:29, 146:4; Gen 35:18; 1 Kgs 19:4.
61. Qoh 9:5–7.

> A cloud evaporates and vanishes,
>
> So he that goes down to *Sheol* does not come up;
>
> He returns to his house no more,
>
> His home never sees him again.[62]
>
> If a man dies, may he live again?[63]

Similarly, in 2 Samuel 14:14, the wise woman of Tekoa observes that "we must all die; we are like water that is poured out on the ground and cannot be gathered up."[64] There is also the story of the death of King David's first child by Bathsheba in 2 Samuel 12. While the child was very sick, David fasted, lay all night upon the earth, and wouldn't hearken to the voice of the elders of his house. But when the child died, David arose from the earth, washed, anointed himself, came into the house, and ate. His servants asked David why he fasted and wept while the child was still alive but when the child died, he rose and ate bread. David answered:

> While the child was yet alive, I fasted and wept: for I said, Who can tell whether God will be gracious to me, that the child may live?
>
> But now he is dead, wherefore should I fast? Can I bring him back again? I shall go to him, but *he shall not return to me*.[65]

Although there is no *soul* which survives death, there is *something*, some entity that stands in relation to the whole person, which *does* survive death. It is called a *repha* (plural, *rephaim*).[66] The *rephaim* are what anthropologists call "free souls."

---

62. Job 7:9–10. Job sees *Sheol* as a place of "no return." See Job 10:22, 16:22.

63. Job 14:14.

64. See Madigan and Levenson, *Resurrection*, 163. See also Ps 88:11 ("Wilt Thou work wonders for the dead? Or shall the shades arise and give thee thanks?"); Qoh 3:22 (discussed above in sec. B). There are two passages, 1 Samuel 2:6 and Deuteronomy 32:39, which are interpreted by Madigan and Levenson as demonstrating a belief that "death, or at least unjust death, will be miraculously reversed" (Madigan and Levenson, *Resurrection*, 160–63). Other scholars interpret these verses differently (Johnston, *Shades of Sheol*, 218–20; Johnson, *Vitality of the Individual*, 108–9; Eichrodt, *Theology of the Old Testament*, 2:141. See also Eichrodt, *Theology of the Old Testament*, 2:213–14 ("If it is sometimes said that the [*nephesh*] goes down into Sheol, or is rescued from it, this does not refer to actual death, but is poetic diction for mortal danger."). Further, even if these verses did express belief in a future resurrection, they would constitute a "rare exception" to the normal belief that death is irreversible. See Madigan and Levenson, *Resurrection*, 165. Mention should also be made of three incidents in biblical narrative where the "newly dead return to life . . . through contact with the prophets Elijah and Elisha" (Johnston, *Shades of Sheol*, 220–21). None of these incidents constitute *resurrection* of one who is dead and buried, and none concern reward or punishment. Rather, they constitute only miraculous *resuscitation*. Scholars have noted that these incidents have "similarities with resuscitation and healing accounts from Shamanistic societies" (Johnston, *Shades of Sheol*, 221). See Eichrodt, *Theology of the Old Testament*, 2:135n7; Madigan and Levenson, *Resurrection*, 131.

65. 2 Sam 12:22–23 (emphasis added).

66. See Isa 14:9, 26:14; Ps 88:11; Prov 2:18, 9:18, 21:16; Job 26:5. See also Eichrodt, *Theology of the Old Testament*, 2:214 ("That . . . which lives on in the grave is not a soul which had once been present in the living person but the whole man. Hence the dead are called neither [*nephesh*] nor [*nephashot*]

Free souls are not "souls" in the sense of conscious, intelligent, and sentient beings but rather they are shadowy doubles of people, active when people are unconscious, which continue to exist after a person dies.[67] Nor is the biblical *repha* to be equated with the person who lived. The *repha* has neither consciousness, emotions, nor intelligence; it is simply the shadowy double of the person who lived. As Eichrodt puts it:

> Israel fully shared the primitive belief that a shadowy image of the dead person detached itself from him and continued to eke out a bare existence; and we only confuse this idea if we mix it up with our own concept of the soul . . . What survives . . . is not a *part* of the living man but a shadowy image of the *whole* man.[68]

The term *rephaim* connotes "a relative weakness on the part of the dead as compared with the state of the living."[69] Their weakness is a consequence of the "disintegrating power of death," occasioned by the loss of vitality that occurs when the life force, the breath of life, departs.[70]

> Moreover, just as death in the strict sense of the term is for the Israelite the weakest form of life, so any weakness in life is a form of death . . . Thus it is said of Joshua's followers, for example, that, after they had been circumcised [which occasioned a loss of vitality], they remained where they were in camp 'until they *lived*,' i.e. until they recovered . . . Indeed, this method indicating a clearly recognized ebb and flow in one's vitality may be reinforced . . . by a reference to the absence or presence of [*ruach*].[71]

According to Johnston, the Hebrew word *rephaim* is often translated "shades" because "this translation evokes well the shadowy, insubstantial existence which the texts describe . . . The dead Rephaim are lifeless and flaccid."[72] Similarly, Johnson comments that the "conception of death as a weak form of life may . . . be seen in the fact that man is . . . pictured as living on, a mere shadow of his former self . . ."[73]

---

nor [*ruach*] but [*metim*] or [*rephaim*], the 'dead' or the 'weak.'").

67. See Bremmer, *Early Greek Concept of the Soul*, 9; Rohde, *Psyche*, 1:6–7; ch. 4, n. 35.

68. Eichrodt, *Theology of the Old Testament*, 2:214 (emphasis original).

69. Johnson, *Vitality of the Individual*, 89–90. See Johnston, *Shades of Sheol*, 130 ("Whatever the term's etymology, the Rephaim were understood in Israel as 'weak,' as shown when they greet the newly arrived king: 'You too have become weak as we' (cf. Is. 14:10).").

70. See Johnson, *Vitality of the Individual*, 102.

71. Johnson, *Vitality of the Individual*, 95–97 ((citing Josh 5:8; emphasis original).

72. Johnston, *Shades of Sheol*, 128.

73. Johnson, *Vitality of the Individual*, 88.

The place where *rephaim* go, after the person dies, is called *Sheol*.[74] Significantly, the term *Sheol* seldom appears in the Hebrew Bible.[75] And references in the Hebrew Bible to *rephaim* are even more sparse than references to *Sheol*.[76] This shows that neither the place of any afterlife nor the inhabitants of such a place are of great concern to the authors of the Hebrew Bible.[77] Their concern is this-worldly, not otherworldly. This is consistent with the fact that the promised reward for following God's commandments is material well-being in this life, and the threatened punishment for disobedience is the deprivation of material well-being in this life.[78] No mention is made in the context of the giving of God's commandments of any postmortem reward and punishment for obedience or disobedience.[79] In other words, *Sheol* is not a place of judgment or of reward or punishment. As stated by the author of Qoheleth, quoted above, "the dead know nothing, *nor have they any reward* . . ."[80]

The etymology of the term *Sheol* is uncertain, but it is generally accepted by scholars of the Hebrew Bible to be a kind of underworld.[81] Johnson says that:

> this underworld of Sheol, which swallows up mankind like some insatiable monster, is thought of as a great pit which lies, not only deep beneath the surface of the earth, but also beneath the waters of the great cosmic sea on which the whole world rests, and in which are sunk the bases of earth's mountains as the very pillars of heaven. To die, therefore, is to find oneself [or one's *repha*] sinking beneath these waters into a veritable cistern or well; and to be with the [*rephaim*] in Sheol is to be 'beneath the waters and their inhabitants' . . . Once

---

74. See Johnson, *Vitality of the Individual*, 88. See also Hirsch, *Rabbinic Psychology*, 81 ("The relation of the grave to Sheol remained obscure. No difficulty was felt in associating the dead with the grave and Sheol at the same time. The two terms, indeed, are often interchangeable.") (citing Isa 38:18, Ps 30:4); Moore, *Judaism in the First Centuries*, 2:289–90 ("Sometimes . . . Sheol seems to be only a metaphorical equivalent for the grave. Between the presence of the dead in their several tombs and the assembly of the dead in Sheol no contradiction was felt, and no attempt was made to reconcile the two notions.").

75. See Johnston, *Shades of Sheol*, 70–73.

76. Johnston, *Shades of Sheol*, 128.

77. See Johnston, *Shades of Sheol*, 72 ("the underworld is not a central feature of the Old Testament"), 124 ("The underworld truly was a place of little interest to the Hebrew writers."), 128 ("the underworld and its inhabitants are not a major Old Testament concern"). See also Madigan and Levenson, *Resurrection*, 66 (the focus of the Hebrew Bible "is not on the world of the dead, but on that of the living").

78. See e.g., Deut 11:13–28, 28:1–26; Lev 26:3–46.

79. See Kohler, *Jewish Theology*, 279–80.

80. Qoh 9:5–7. See Moore, *Judaism in the First Centuries*, 2:289–91; Bernstein, *Formation of Hell*, 140–46; Raphael, *Jewish Views of the Afterlife*, 55. See generally Johnston, *Shades of Sheol*, 70–85, 128–42; Eichrodt, *Theology of the Old Testament*, 2:210–15.

81. See Johnston, *Shades of Sheol*, 77–79; Eichrodt, *Theology of the Old Testament*, 2:210; Sarna, *JPS Torah Commentary*, 262–63 (*Sheol* "was imagined to be [a region] situated deep beneath the earth and to be enclosed with gates."). Many scholars have attempted, unsuccessfully, to derive the Hebrew word from seemingly related words in cognate languages. It now seems to be widely accepted that *Sheol* is an original Hebrew word.

inside this foul region of virtual annihilation, the gates of the Underworld are locked fast upon one; and there can be no return to former conditions in 'the land of the living,' nor indeed any fellowship with Yahweh—the Giver of Life. In fact, for the most part it is a still and silent 'land of forgetfulness,' which even at its best is but a pale and gloomy reflection of the world of light and life which is Yahweh's special sphere."[82]

Eichrodt offers a similar depiction of *Sheol*:

Like most nations, Israel knows of a place of the dead, which from the fact that one has to go down to reach it . . . appears to have been a kind of underworld. This is the [*Sheol*]. The word seems to be of immemorial antiquity; it is one of those concepts which no longer require the article, and thus have virtually become proper names. The etymology is in dispute . . . Generally speaking, existence in Sheol is a faithful, if shadowy, copy of existence on earth. There, too, kings sit on their thrones [Isa 14:9–11] and the prophet wears his mantle [1 Sam 28:14], and therefore rank and calling continue. But it is a place of silence and stillness where the impotence of the shadow beings makes the boisterous vigour of real life quite impossible. Indeed, the shades themselves bear the name [*rephaim*], the 'weak' or 'powerless' ones . . . Going down into the underworld is characterized as becoming weak, [*hullah*], [Isa 14:10], and the state of the dead is compared to men who sleep [Nah 3:18] . . . As a rule the dead know nothing of events in the world above.[83]

According to Johnston, "Sheol is a place of no return [Job 16:22], a place of captivity with gates [Isa 38:10] and bars [Jonah 2:6] . . . It is a place of darkness . . . of inactivity and silence . . ."[84] In the book of Job there are several passages, in addition to 16:22, describing *Sheol*. There is 7:9–10, quoted above, describing *Sheol* as a place that one goes down to, but does not come up from. There is 10:21–22, in which Job says that *Sheol* is "a land of utter darkness, Of gloom without order, Which shines like darkness," and from which there is no return. Finally, there is Job 14:10–12 about which Pope states: "Job expresses the standard OT view, shared by his friends . . . [that

---

82. Johnson, *Vitality of the Individual*, 90–94 (citing numerous biblical verses). See generally Johnston, *Shades of Sheol*, 114–24 (discussing relationship of water to the underworld and stating that water "is associated with the underworld, but is not confused with it."); Madigan and Levenson, *Resurrection*, 48–51 (discussing image of *Sheol* as "lethal waters").

83. Eichrodt, *Theology of the Old Testament*, 2:210–11. See Johnston, *Shades of Sheol*, 76.

84. Johnston, *Shades of Sheol*, 76. See Sarna, *JPS Torah Commentary*, 262–63 (*Sheol* "was a place of unrelieved darkness and gloom and of complete silence. None who entered it could return."); Moore, *Judaism in the First Centuries*, 2:291 ("Of a revivification of the dead there is no hope . . . The expectation of a resurrection of the flesh . . . is read *into* the text, not *in* it"; emphasis original). See also Madigan and Levenson, *Resurrection*, 45–54 (discussing images of *Sheol*, including images of grave, pit, underworld, engulfing waters, subterranean city, and prison).

there] is no afterlife worthy of the name. The torpor of the shades in the netherworld cannot be regarded as life."[85]

The description of *Sheol* as a place of no return brings to mind the Akkadian description of a place that was specifically called the "Land of No Return."[86] A poem about the Akkadian goddess Ishtar's descent to this place describes it as one "'which none leave who have entered it,'" a world "'from which there is no way back,'" one in which there is no light, only darkness, and where the inhabitants eat dust and clay.[87] The descriptions of *Sheol* are also reminiscent of the place called Hades in the epic Greek poems attributed to Homer in that it is simply a place in the earth where the shades, or shadowy doubles, go; it is not a place of judgment, or a place where anything happens.[88]

Scholars of the Hebrew Bible have generally portrayed *Sheol* "as the destiny of all without qualification."[89] Indeed, several biblical texts explicitly say that this is the case. For example, according to Job 3:19, "The small and the great are there alike." Especially unambiguous is Psalm 89:49:

> What man can live and not see death,
>
> can save himself from the clutches of Sheol?

One should note here the equivalence of death and Sheol, "with the clear implication that individuals, no matter how they have died, cannot escape the dreary netherworld."[90]

Madigan and Levenson have recently argued that whenever death is due to unnatural causes *Sheol* is mentioned but when death occurs "in the course of nature,

---

85. Pope, *Anchor Bible*, 102.

86. Pope, *Anchor Bible*, 59 ("The netherworld was called in Akkadian 'the land-of-no-return.'"). See Hirsch, *Rabbinic Psychology*, 25.

87. See Madigan and Levenson, *Resurrection*, 44 (quoting translation of Speiser). See also Eichrodt, *Theology of the Old Testament*, 2:211–12 (discussing depiction of the underworld in myth of Ishtar's Descent, as well as in Gilgamesh epic.).

88. See Kohler, *Heaven and Hell*, 8 ("*Sheol*, the Hebrew nether world, remained . . . like the Greek Hades, the dreary realm of the shades, the gathering of the departed, devoid of light and life, *without moral relation to earthly life*, 'the Land of Silence (Dumah),' from which there is no coming back"; emphasis added); Kohler, *Jewish Theology*, 279 ("Until long after the Exile the Jewish people shared the view of the entire ancient world . . . that the dead continue to exist in the shadowy realm of the nether world (*Sheol*), the land of no return [Beliyaal] of eternal silence [Dumah], and oblivion [Neshiyah], a dull, ghostly existence without clear consciousness and without any awakening to a better life . . . [and] throughout the Biblical period no ethical idea yet permeated this conception, and no attempt was made to transform the nether world into a place of divine judgment, of recompense for the good and evil deeds accomplished on earth, as did the Babylonians and Egyptians"; citing biblical verses).

89. Johnston, *Shades of Sheol*, 81; Sarna, *JPS Torah Commentary*, 262; Moore, *Judaism in the First Centuries*, 2:290; Hirsch, *Rabbinic Psychology*, 80–81. See Madigan and Levenson, *Resurrection*, 42–43.

90. Madigan and Levenson, *Resurrection*, 73. See Johnston, *Shades of Sheol*, 82–83 (discussing Ps 89:48–49 and Qoh 9:7–10).

Sheol does not appear."[91] Stated differently, if "the deceased has died prematurely, violently, bereft of children, rejected by God, or broken hearted, he or she faces Sheol"; otherwise not.[92] According to Madigan and Levenson, the distinction between death due to natural causes and death due to unnatural causes reflects a more important distinction between those who die in God's favor and those who do not. They contend that there is an "inconsistency" or "tension" in the Hebrew Bible "between two competing theologies."[93] One theology, which "comports well with ancient Mesopotamian and Canaanite notions," sees *Sheol* as the "universal destination," the "ultimate destination of all humankind."[94] This is the older theology. In addition, according to Madigan and Levenson, there is a newer theology based upon "a bold and younger affirmation of the Lord as savior."[95] This newer theology is related to the "ubiquitous distinction between God's anger and his favor. If the circumstances of death do not suggest divine anger, then death (whether we judge it to be natural or unnatural) need not be feared."[96] Those who die "in God's good graces . . . have no reason to think that they will be dispatched to that 'wholly undesirable' existence in the dark, dank netherworld."[97]

But if some of the dead do not go to *Sheol*, where do they (or their *rephaim*) go? No answer is given by any of those who assert that only the ungodly, unfortunate, or disfavored wind up in *Sheol*. For their part, Madigan and Levenson state:

> What exactly was the fate of those fortunate enough to avoid the netherworld? Where, if not Sheol, did the ancient Israelites who wrote of their lives and heard their tales believe *them* to have gone? On this, the Hebrew Bible is strikingly silent and forces us into conjecture."[98]

The conjecture offered by Madigan and Levenson is that those who die blessed survive "in their lineage (including, in some cases, the larger lineage that is the whole people of Israel). Thus Abraham dies after arranging the marriage of his favored son Isaac and begetting, in addition to the firstborn Ishmael, six other sons, some of them (like Isaac and Ishmael) destined to beget great nations in fulfillment of God's explicit promise to the founding patriarch."[99] Madigan and Levenson go on to point out:

91. Madigan and Levenson, *Resurrection*, 71 (quoting dissertation of R. Rosenberg).
92. Madigan and Levenson, *Resurrection*, 76.
93. Madigan and Levenson, *Resurrection*, 73.
94. Madigan and Levenson, *Resurrection*, 73.
95. Madigan and Levenson, *Resurrection*, 73.
96. Madigan and Levenson, *Resurrection*, 71.
97. Madigan and Levenson, *Resurrection*, 71.
98. Madigan and Levenson, *Resurrection*, 73 (emphasis original) See Johnston, *Shades of Sheol*, 199 ("there is no clearly articulated alternative to Sheol, no other destiny whose location is named, no other fate whose situation is described, however briefly. So the majority of Israelites may well have envisaged no alternative.").
99. Madigan and Levenson, *Resurrection*, 74.

In other words, Sheol can be thought of as the prolongation of the unfulfilled life. There is no equivalent prolongation of the fulfilled life precisely because it is fulfilled. The prolongation of those who die fulfilled comes, rather, not in the form of residence in a particular place, a joyful antipode to the miserable Sheol, but in the form of descendants, such as those three or four generations that Jacob, Joseph, and Job are privileged to behold just before they die. It also comes in the form of the survival of the decedent's 'name' (*shem*), which is itself closely associated with his lineage . . . [However], some vestiges of the older view, the view that all who die end up in Sheol, linger. [Qoheleth] (to cite an extreme example) appeals to the universality of the unfortunate death and thus the unfulfilled life to bolster his overall skepticism about the redeeming God).[100]

Whatever the merit of Madigan and Levenson's conjecture, and whatever the merit of the claim that only some, but not all, are destined for *Sheol*,[101] the central point at issue is unaltered. There is no postmortem reward or punishment.[102] In particular, there is no heaven where the "souls" of the righteous go to receive a postmortem reward.[103] And, as Madigan and Levenson themselves admit, it is wrong to equate *Sheol* with "hell"—*Sheol* is neither a place of judgment nor a place of punishment.[104]

100. Madigan and Levenson, *Resurrection*, 77–79 (citing Qoh 9:2).

101. On this matter, it must be mentioned that, upon their death, righteous people are said to be reunited with their fathers or kinsmen. See sec. F. This evidences that the righteous have a postmortem existence *somewhere*. It is true that *Sheol* is never mentioned in this context. See Madigan and Levenson, *Resurrection*, 71–73. But, as Johnston acknowledges, "most scholars assume this reunion takes place in Sheol," and Johnston points to Psalm 49 in which the ungodly who descend to *Sheol* are said to go to "the generation of their fathers," just like those who are favored by God are said to be reunited with *their* fathers (Johnston, *Shades of Sheol*, 34). So, being reunited with one's fathers suggests descent to *Sheol*. On Eichrodt's analysis, (1) the concern to be reunited with one's fathers and the other members of the family "derives from a belief that the dead still survive in some way or other in the grave," (2) this belief became replaced by the idea of a "general gathering-place of the dead," *Sheol*, and (3) descriptions of the righteous being reunited with their kinsmen, without mention of *Sheol*, merely indicates that the idea of *Sheol* "was manifestly never able to efface entirely belief in the presence of the dead in the grave, and this for the quite simple reason that the latter had appearances on its side" (Eichrodt, *Theology of the Old Testament*, 2:213). See generally Eichrodt, *Theology of the Old Testament*, 2:222 ("By shifting survival from the grave to a distant shadow kingdom it made it easier to establish the gulf between this world and the one beyond.").

102. At one place Madigan and Levenson *do* state that *Sheol* "very often has to do with punishment" (Madigan and Levenson, *Resurrection*, 71). But I do not understand this to mean that those disfavored by God and, thus, destined for *Sheol*, undergo, once there, some torture over and above just being in "the dark, dank netherworld." See Madigan and Levenson, *Resurrection*, 71. Indeed, Madigan and Levenson elsewhere make a point of emphasizing that *Sheol* is not "hell" and does not have anything to do with punishment. See *infra*, n. 104.

103. See Sarna, *JPS Torah Commentary*, 262 ("There is no concept of 'heaven' and 'hell' in the Hebrew Bible."); Madigan and Levenson, *Resurrection*, 80 (". . . in the Hebrew Bible there is no antipode to Sheol in the sense of a heavenly locale to which the blessed go after death—no postmortem Heaven or Garden of Eden to which those loyal to God can look forward.").

104. Madigan and Levenson, *Resurrection*, 75–76 ("Sheol is not a punishment from God or any other agent. It does not come in response to sin; it is the continuation of the depressing circumstances

CHAPTER 1.

E. The Bible Prohibits Necromancy, but at One Time There Was an Israelite Cult of the Dead

The practice of necromancy, or the consultation of the dead, stands in sharp contrast to the view that the dead know nothing. Necromancy was widespread among ancient Near Eastern peoples, but is prohibited in two of the biblical legal codes.[105] For example, Deuteronomy 18 admonishes: "Let no one be found among you who . . . consults *ghosts* or *familiar spirits*, or one who inquires of the dead." The italicized expressions "ghosts" and "familiar spirits" are translations commonly used for the Hebrew terms, respectively, *obot* and *yiddonim*. The term *yiddoni* is said to derive from the verb "to know" and, accordingly, has the literal meaning of "knowing one;" the exact meaning of the Hebrew word *ob* is a matter of some dispute, but most scholars interpret *ob* as "spirit of the dead" or, in other words, as "ghost."[106]

Although necromancy is prohibited under Israelite legal codes, there is reason to believe that the practice of necromancy existed to some degree in ancient Israel. Indeed, the prohibition is itself evidence that the practice existed.[107] Acceptance of necromancy is probably rooted in the practice of burying the body in a tomb and attributing consciousness to the dead person's shadowy double believed to inhabit the tomb.[108] Indeed, it has been argued by Friedman and Overton that ancestor worship or the cult of the dead "thrived for centuries" in ancient Israel and was not diminished until "an increasingly radical monotheistic urban elite gained ascendancy in Judah under Kings Hezekiah and Josiah."[109] The Hebrew Bible, in fact, preserves some of the earlier beliefs of the cult of the dead and the consultation of the "spirits of the dead" in the well-known account of Saul's conjuring the ghost of Samuel at *En-Dor*.[110]

---

that existed at the time of the individual's death.").

105. Deut 18:10–12; Lev 19:31, 20:6, 27. See generally Johnston, *Shades of Sheol*, 150–66; Lewis, *Cults of the Dead*, 102–17, 161–65.

106. See Johnston, *Shades of Sheol*, 151, 161–66; Eichrodt, *Theology of the Old Testament*, 2:215; Lewis, *Cults of the Dead*, 113–14. See also Friedman and Overton, "Death and Afterlife," 44.

107. See Madigan and Levenson, *Resurrection*, 59; Hirsch, *Rabbinic Psychology*, 73.

108. See Moore, *Judaism in the First Centuries*, 2:187 ("The tomb was the abode of the dead. There the body reposed, and it was doubtless believed that the ghost also inhabited the tomb, an attenuated material double of the body, ordinarily invisible, but sometimes seen in dreams or as an apparition in waking states; the conscious wraith of the man that had been."). See also *supra*, n. 74.

109. Friedman and Overton, "Death and Afterlife," 40. See Hallotte, *Death, Burial, and Afterlife*, 23 ("The Cult of the Dead was so deeply entrenched in everyday practice . . . that in spite of prophetic whining it survived beyond the destruction of Judah itself."); Bernstein, *Formation of Hell*, 136–40. See generally Hirsch, *Rabbinic Psychology*, 73–79. See also Setzer, *Resurrection of the Body*, 9–10 ("Several scholars suggest a deliberate and only partially successful suppression of a cult of the dead in Israel, though they offer different reasons for it. Mendenhall proposes that the emerging Yahwism sought to unify the people and discourage tribal and clan loyalties . . . Friedman and Overton suggest that landless priests wanted to suppress local forms of worship . . . that would compete with a centralized priesthood.").

110. See Madigan and Levenson, *Resurrection*, 57–59 ("1 Samuel 28 reminds us . . . that the patterns of religion generally regarded as normative in the Hebrew Bible reflect only a segment of the

It is impossible to say precisely how, if at all, the recognition that there are entities with knowledge which survive a person's death was reconciled with the belief that the only entity that survives death is the *repha* which knows nothing; but there exists a parallel situation in ancient Greek literature which is instructive. In epic poems attributed to Homer the *psyche* is conceived much as the Hebraic *repha*, a shadowy double of a person that lacks vitality and knowledge existing in an underground world.[111] Yet, in the *Odyssey*, Odysseus found it necessary to consult the *psyche* of the dead seer Teiresias. In order, however, to speak with Teiresias, Odysseus had to bring with him to the Land of the Dead sheep which he slaughtered and whose blood he gave to Teiresias to drink.[112] It was only upon being revivified by the blood that Teiresias could speak with Odysseus. In other words, although a *psyche* had no vitality, it could be revitalized by a life-giving substance. While no mention is made in 1 Samuel 28 of Samuel being similarly revived, perhaps some such means of being reenergized was understood to have occurred.[113]

Most importantly, however, the story of Saul at *En-Dor*, and the biblical recognition of necromancy, does not undermine the fact that the Hebrew Bible contains no word which is accurately translated as "soul," no concept of a postmortem reward or punishment, and (except as discussed herein)[114] no reference to resurrection.

F. The Biblical Expression "Gathered to His Kin" Does Not Suggest the Existence of a "Soul"

Two distinctive phrases found in biblical texts seem to present death as joining one's ancestors: (1) "gathered to his kin," and (2) "to sleep with one's fathers." The first phrase—"gathered to his kin" [*ve'asef el ammav*]—is used only in the Torah, and only on ten occasions.[115] Thus, it is said of Abraham, in Genesis 25:8–9:

> And Abraham breathed his last, dying at a good ripe age, old and contented; *and he was gathered to his kin.* His sons Isaac and Ishmael buried him in the cave of Machpelah, in the field of Ephron son of Zohar the Hittite, facing Mamre . . .

---

ancient Israelite population, many of whom doubtless once engaged without scruple in the very rites therein designated as deviant."); Johnston, *Shades of Sheol*, 156–57. See generally Friedman and Overton, "Death and Afterlife," 46–50.

111. See Bremmer, *Early Greek Concept of the Soul*, 70–124.

112. Homer, *Od.*, ch. 11.

113. See Friedman and Overton, "Death and Afterlife," 46 ("Samuel in the En-Dor episode . . . may simply be understood to be disturbed from eternal unconscious rest rather than from a place where persons are conscious after death.").

114. See ch. 2, sec. C, 1.

115. See Sarna, *JPS Torah Commentary*, 174; Johnston, *Shades of Sheol*, 33; Milgrom, *JPS Torah Commentary*, 169–70.

Although "gathered to his kin" is literally translated "gathered to his peoples," it is understood by scholars to refer to "the immediate kinship group."[116] Contemporary scholars often refer to a detailed study of the phrase published by Bern Alfrink in 1948.[117] According to Johnston, Alfrink "plausibly argued" that the expression is "an ancient stereotyped formula,"[118] and Johnston infers that the texts in which the expression occurs "reflect genuinely ancient usage."[119] Johnston then provides the following analysis and conclusion:

> 'Gathered to his people' clearly does not indicate death or burial, since it is mentioned alongside them, and is used of Jacob several months before his actual burial [Gen 49:33; 50:13]. Nor can it mean burial with ancestors in the family grave, since this did not occur for the burial of Abraham, Aaron and Moses. It may be derived from this practice, but if so its use became divorced from its origin . . . More likely, *'gathered to his peoples' indicates joining one's ancestors in the afterlife. Most scholars assume this reunion takes place in Sheol* (as Ps 49), even if Sheol is never mentioned.[120]

The second phrase, "to sleep with one's fathers," does not indicate rejoining one's ancestors in *Sheol* but "simply takes the place of the verb 'he died.'"[121] The phrase is "reserved for national leaders," and "with few exceptions it occurs of kings who died peacefully . . . Conversely, the stark description 'he died' is used of those who died violently."[122]

Sarna is in substantial agreement with Johnston's overall analysis of these phrases, except that Sarna sees them as *both* indicating rejoining one's ancestors in *Sheol*. Commenting on the phrase "gathered to his kin" in Genesis 25:8, Sarna states that the phrase "is not the same as burial in an ancestral grave" and "is also not identical with internment in general." He then concludes:

> It would seem, therefore, that the existence of the idiom, as of the corresponding figure 'to lie down with one's fathers,' testifies to a belief that, despite his mortality and perishability, man possesses an immortal element that survives the loss of life. Death is looked upon as a transition to an afterlife where one is united with one's ancestors. This interpretation contradicts the widespread, but apparently erroneous, view that such a notion is unknown in Israel until later times.[123]

116. See Johnston, *Shades of Sheol*, 33.
117. See e.g., Johnston, *Shades of Sheol*, 33; Milgrom, *JPS Torah Commentary*, 170n54.
118. Johnston, *Shades of Sheol*, 33–34 (quoting Alfrink).
119. Johnston, *Shades of Sheol*, 34.
120. Johnston, *Shades of Sheol*, 34. (emphasis added). See Eichrodt, *Theology of the Old Testament*, 2:213.
121. Johnston, *Shades of Sheol*, 34.
122. Johnston, *Shades of Sheol*, 34.
123. Sarna, *JPS Torah Commentary*, 174. In a footnote to this statement Sarna adds: "Outside the

Milgrom, commenting on Numbers 20:17 ("Let Aaron be gathered to his kin"), agrees that the phrase "gathered to his kin" "can neither mean to die nor to be buried in the family tomb."[124] Instead, "it means 'be reunited with one's ancestors' and refers to the afterlife in Sheol."[125] In a related "Excursus," Milgrom states that, as concerns the patriarchs, "the language of the Bible presumes three stages concerning death: They die, they are gathered to their kin, and they are buried."[126] He then quotes Alfrink: "'It (the term "gathered") designates something which succeeds death and precedes burial, the kind of thing which may hardly be considered as other than reunion with ancestors in Sheol.'"[127]

Tigay takes the same view as Sarna and Milgrom regarding the phrase "gathered to his kin"—that it refers to being reunited with one's ancestors. Unfortunately, Tigay uses an easily misinterpreted expression (viz., "the spirit") to designate the entity being reunited. With regard to Deuteronomy 32:50 ("You shall die . . . and be gathered to your kin"), Tigay claims: "This refers to the reunion of *the spirit* with one's kin in Sheol after death."[128]

Perhaps because Tigay claims that "the spirit" is the thing being reunited with one's ancestors, and because "the spirit" is associated by many with the disembodied soul, some, relying on JPS commentators Sarna, Milgrom, and Tigay, have argued that the biblical references to being gathered with one's kin are evidence of a biblical belief in the existence of a soul, as well as in the soul's immortality. So, for example, Spitz, quoting Sarna, Milgrom, and Tigay, writes:

> I believe that "gathered to his people" signifies a duality of body and soul and suggests an afterlife . . . My reading is that "gathered to his people" presents a reward experienced by the disembodied spirit for a life well lived. I am reassured in my judgment by recent writings of some of America's most prominent biblical scholars in their JPS Torah commentary.[129]

Spitz's reliance on Sarna, Milgrom, and Tigay is misplaced.[130] The scholarship of these commentators provides *no* evidence of a biblical belief in the existence of a

---

Pentateuch, the standard idiom is 'to lie down with one's fathers' . . . No perceptible difference in meaning between the two [phrases] can be determined" (Sarna, *JPS Torah Commentary*, 174n16). See also Sarna, *JPS Torah Commentary*, 324 (commenting on Gen 47:30), 346 (commenting on Gen 49:29).

124. Milgrom, *JPS Torah Commentary*, 170.

125. Milgrom, *JPS Torah Commentary*, 170 (citing Alfrink).

126. Milgrom, *JPS Torah Commentary*, 407.

127. Milgrom, *JPS Torah Commentary*, 407.

128. Tigay, *JPS Torah Commentary*, 317 (emphasis added). See also Tigay, *JPS Torah Commentary*, 293 (commenting with respect to "lie with your fathers" in Deuteronomy 31:16: "That is, die; the idiom stands for 'die and lie with one's fathers.' It refers specifically to the reunion of one's spirit after death with those of one's ancestors in Sheol, as in the phrase 'be gathered to one's kin' in 32:50.").

129. Spitz, *Does the Soul Survive?*, 189. See also Hirsch, *Rabbinic Psychology*, 74–75.

130. Equally misplaced is Spitz's reliance on "premodern rabbinic commentators" mentioned on

"soul," let alone evidence of a duality of body and soul, or of the postmortem reward for one's "soul." This is because the entity that is reunited with one's ancestors is *not* one's "soul," but one's *repha*. This is made abundantly clear by Eichrodt:

> This concern to be reunited with one's fathers and other members of the family clearly derives from a belief that the dead still survive in some way in the grave. This is, in fact, the oldest form of belief in survival, being found even among primitive peoples. Strictly understood it is incompatible with the idea of Sheol, the general gathering-place of the dead; but it is perverse to seek to iron out this contradiction by assuming a line of development: one grave—many graves—great burial cave—underworld. For the same contradiction is found among primitives. The idea of Sheol, deriving as it does from the exercise of the imagination, was manifestly never able to efface entirely belief in the presence of the dead in the grave, and this for the quite simple reason that the latter had appearances on its side. The custom of giving food to the dead, which even though taboo continued in Israel down to the latest period (cf. Deut. 26.14; Ecclus 30.18; Tobit 4.17), indicates the toughness of this belief ... *That, however, which lives on in the grave is not a soul which had once been present in the living person but the whole man.* [Emphasis added] Hence the dead are called neither [*nephesh*] nor [*nephashot*] nor [*ruach*] but [*metim*] or [*repahaim*], the 'dead' or the 'weak.' Israel fully shared the primitive belief that a shadowy image of the dead person detached itself from him and continued to eke out a bare existence; and we only confuse this idea if we mix it up with our own concept of the soul. For death results from God's withdrawing the breath of life, the [*ruach*], whereupon Man expires and once more becomes dust, that is, inanimate matter ... Equally the [*nephesh*], the life or individual existence, comes to an end ... What survives, therefore, is not a *part* of the living man but a shadowy image of the *whole* man.[131]

G. A Few Biblical Texts Suggest an Increasing Concern for a Positive Afterlife for the Righteous, but They Do Not Alter the Very Dominant This-Worldly Outlook of the Hebrew Bible

In addition to those biblical passages rightly seen by Madigan and Levenson as suggesting the importance in Israelite thought of survival, of sorts, in one's "name" and in

---

Does the Soul Survive?, 190. The mode of exegesis of these commentators allowed them to read their own beliefs into the Bible, so they provide no evidence of the actual biblical point of view. Other points made by Spitz are similarly lacking in merit. See ch. 12, sec. C, 6.

131. Eichrodt, *Theology of the Old Testament*, 2:213–14 (emphasis original). But see Steiner, *Disembodied Souls*, 93–100. Steiner fails to adequately distinguish a free soul from "our own concept of the soul."

one's descendants,[132] there are two texts that hint at immortality in the sense of earthly life ending without death. These are passages concerning Elijah and Enoch.

In 2 Kings 2 there is an account of the prophet Elijah commissioning a successor, Elisha. The two men went to Bethel and then to Jericho. At both places, disciples of the prophets came to Elisha and asked him, "Do you know that the Lord will take [*loqeach*] your master away from you today?" Elisha replied "I know it, too; be silent." Then the two prophets stopped at the Jordan River, and the account continues:

> Thereupon Elijah took his mantle and, rolling it up, he struck the water; it divided to the right and left, so the two of them crossed over to dry land. As they were crossing, Elijah said to Elisha, 'Tell me, what can I do for you before I am taken ['*ellaqach*] from you?' Elisha answered, 'Let a double portion of your spirit pass on to me.' 'You have asked a difficult thing,' he said. 'If you see me as I am being taken [*luqqach*] from you, this will be granted to you; if not, it will not.' As they kept walking and talking, a fiery chariot with fiery horses suddenly appeared and separated one from the other; *and Elijah went up to heaven* [*shamayim*] *in a whirlwind* . . .[133]

Madigan and Levenson comment on this passage as follows:

> Where was Elijah after 'he went up to heaven in a whirlwind' (v 11)? The Hebrew word *shamayim* is better rendered 'sky' than 'heaven,' because the latter term suggests a paradisiacal abode unknown in the Hebrew Bible. There is, in fact, no reason to think that Elijah is here assumed into heavenly glory, rewarded for his service, or brought into the company of other righteous servants of God. Rather, the God of Israel, whose throne several texts locate in the sky, whisks his servant Elijah away from the earth and toward his own mysterious and unapproachable abode . . .
>
> The mysterious closeness to God, manifest in the awesome display of divine power at the end of Elijah's earthly life, accounts for his eerie transport into the sky. To speculate about his destination is as fruitless as speculating about his origin or the way in which he acquired those miraculous powers. Indeed, so little is known about his destination that we cannot safely say even that he never died. Perhaps 2 Kings wants us to think that death followed his miraculous disappearance.[134]

Nevertheless, Jewish tradition soon came to conceive of Elijah as "a prophet who never died and thus continually stands ready to serve as the messenger or human agent of heavenly reconciliation."[135] But even if one accepts that Elijah attained im-

---

132. See Madigan and Levenson, *Resurrection*, 74–80, 109–19.
133. 2 Kgs 2:7–11(emphasis added). See Madigan and Levenson, *Resurrection*, 99.
134. Madigan and Levenson, *Resurrection*, 100.
135. Madigan and Levenson, *Resurrection*, 100.

mortality in that he never died, Madigan and Levenson insist that the biblical story "says nothing about the *nature of* immortality."[136]

The sole biblical reference to Enoch is just as mystifying as the account of Elijah's being "taken," but is even more cryptic.[137] In the antediluvian genealogy that appears in the early chapters of the book of Genesis, the following reference to Enoch appears:

> When Enoch had lived 65 years, he begot Methuselah. After the birth of Methuselah, Enoch walked with God 300 years; and he begot sons and daughters. All the days of Enoch came to 365 years. Enoch walked with God; then he was no more, for God took [*laqach*] him.[138]

This language diverges from the regular genealogical pattern, where every other person mentioned is said to have died, the paragraph ending with the phrase "and he died." Enoch's fate is clearly acknowledged to be different than the other persons mentioned in the antediluvian genealogy, though no further detail about Enoch is added. Some connection to the prophet Elijah seems to exist in that both men are said to have been "taken" by God, but it is less clear whether the "taking" in the case of Enoch signified something other than death.[139]

With regard to both Elijah and Enoch, Johnston comments:

> It is hard to know what ancient Israelites thought to be the fate of these two men, if indeed they knew these traditions and reflected on them. The silence on Enoch implies ignorance or unconcern with his nondeath, and the sole reference to Elijah suggests that it was only much later, well into the postexilic period, that he was seen as a potential messenger . . . Nowhere is the fate of Enoch and Elijah presented as a paradigm for the righteous: not in narrative of impending death, not in prophetic aspiration, nor in wisdom musing, nor—most strikingly—in the numerous psalms which grapple with the inequity and reality of death. Thus the experience of Enoch and Elijah remained entirely marginal for Israel's writers.[140]

Although the experience of Enoch and Elijah remained marginal for writers in the biblical period, this is not the case for writers in the period of the Second Temple, and later. Especially in the case of Enoch, a significant body of literature developed in his name speculating about what happens after death.[141] The book of Jubilees, dated in

---

136. Madigan and Levenson, *Resurrection*, 101 (emphasis added).
137. Madigan and Levenson, *Resurrection*, 101.
138. Gen 5:21–24.
139. See Madigan and Levenson, *Resurrection*, 101.
140. Johnston, *Shades of Sheol*, 200.
141. See Madigan and Levenson, *Resurrection*, 101 (referring to "massive amount of Enoch literature that Jews authored between (roughly) the third century B.C.E. and the sixth century C.E."); ch. 2, sec. E; ch. 3, secs. A, 3 and B, 2.

the second century BCE, describes the fate and activity of Enoch in terms of a belief in a heavenly paradise called the Garden of Eden:

> And Enoch bore witness against all of them. And he was taken from among the children of men, and we led him to the garden of Eden for greatness and honor. And behold, he is there writing condemnation and judgment of the world, and all of the evils of the children of men. And because of him none of the water of the Flood came upon the whole land of Eden, for he was put there for a sign and so that he might bear witness against all of the children of men so that he might relate all of the deeds of the generations until the day of judgment. And he offered the incense which is acceptable before the Lord in the evening (at) the holy place on Mount Qater.[142]

In addition to Elijah and Enoch, there are several psalms that may be interpreted as saying that the righteous will have a better postmortem fate than existence in *Sheol*. These psalms say that the righteous will be "taken" by God but, yet again, no details about what this means are provided. First is Psalm 49. Most of the psalm seems clearly to be an admonishment to the wealthy (but foolish and ungodly) that their wealth is powerless to prolong their life or to ransom them from the underworld. To the contrary,

> Sheeplike they head for *Sheol*,
> With Death as their shepherd.[143]

These people are said to rejoin their ancestors and never again see the light (v. 20). But there is a single line of the psalm in which the psalmist expresses the belief that his own fate will be different. He says:

> But God will redeem my life [my *nephesh*] from the clutches of *Sheol*, For He will take me [*yiqqacheni*].[144]

According to Madigan and Levenson, this verse may be interpreted to mean either that God will not allow the psalmist to remain in *Sheol* when he has died, or that God will prevent him from descending to *Sheol* in the first place.[145] But in either case, they say, it is ambiguous as to where the psalmist is "taken," just as it is ambiguous as to where Enoch and Elijah are "taken." They write: "Where does God 'take' the faithful servant who relies on him, rather than on wealth and status, for his felicity? We again find no answer."[146] Johnston comments as follows:

---

142. Jub. 4:22–25. See Madigan and Levenson, *Resurrection*, 102.
143. Ps 49:15. See Madigan and Levenson, *Resurrection*, 102.
144. Ps 49:16. See Madigan and Levenson, *Resurrection*, 103.
145. See Madigan and Levenson, *Resurrection*, 103.
146. Madigan and Levenson, *Resurrection*, 103.

God will ransom [the psalmist] from Sheol and will 'take' or 'receive' him. What humans are powerless to do, God will do for his faithful follower: God will provide an alternative destiny to the underworld. Here, more explicitly than anywhere else in the Hebrew Bible, the consignment of the ungodly *to* Sheol is contrasted with the ransom of the godly *from* Sheol.[147]

Psalm 73 is of a similar nature to Psalm 49. Like Psalm 49, it expresses concern that the wicked prosper and gain in wealth, while the psalmist, who is righteous, is chastised every morning.[148] The psalmist begins by confessing his envy of the prosperity of the wicked (vv. 1–14), "but he then enters 'the sanctuary,' where he perceives the ruinous end of these wicked people (vv. 15–20). Castigating himself for bestial stupidity, he asserts that continued communion with God forms the essence of his existence."[149] The significant line is in verse 24 where the psalmist affirms:

> You guide me with your counsel, and afterward you will receive me [*tiqqacheni*] with honour.[150]

According to Johnston:

> Scholars are divided over whether the psalmist envisages "honour" in the present life or in some unspecified future existence. Both views can be argued from the immediate context.[151]

Even assuming that Psalms 73 and 49 envisage an afterlife for the righteous that is better than existence in *Sheol* (and includes communion with the living God), while they still recognize that a lifeless existence in *Sheol* is a fitting end for the ungodly, it is important to note that both psalms are described as being "postexilic or late."[152] As such, neither psalm alters the fact that the texts of the Hebrew Bible in the *pre*exilic period have a definite this-worldly focus,[153] and that the *pre*exilic biblical world view includes (1) no rewards or punishments in the afterlife, and (2) a postmortem existence

---

147. Johnston, *Shades of Sheol*, 203 (emphasis added). See also Eichrodt, *Theology of the Old Testament*, 2:523.

148. See generally Johnston, *Shades of Sheol*, 204–6; Madigan and Levenson, *Resurrection*, 103–4. See also Eichrodt, *Theology of the Old Testament*, 2:520–23. Psalm 16 is also mentioned as seeming "to glimpse a different perspective" than the normative view that "this life is the only forum for relationship with Yahweh" (Johnston, *Shades of Sheol*, 200–1). Accord, Eichrodt, *Theology of the Old Testament*, 2:524–25.

149. Johnston, *Shades of Sheol*, 204.

150. See Johnston, *Shades of Sheol*, 204. Cf. Madigan and Levenson, *Resurrection*, 103 (translating, "You guided me by your counsel and will receive me [*tiqqacheni*] with glory.").

151. Johnston, *Shades of Sheol*, 205, but see 205n21. See also Madigan and Levenson, *Resurrection*, 104.

152. Johnston, *Shades of Sheol*, 206.

153. Even in the postexilic period. "[f]or most Israelites, hope remained firmly anchored in the present life" even if "a few seem to glimpse some form of continued communion with God beyond it" (Johnston, *Shades of Sheol*, 217).

only in the grave or in *Sheol*. In other words, these psalms suggest that, perhaps, beginning no earlier than about 500 BCE, the concern arises among *some* individuals that in the world of the living, wicked people prosper while righteous people suffer, and these individuals begin to seek a rectification for this injustice in differing postmortem existences.[154] Indeed, this *is* what happens, and it is just this emerging desire for differing postmortem existences that is discussed in the next chapter.

---

154. Evidence that this concern is arising may also be found in Proverbs. Proverbs 15:24, 23:14, 12:28, and 14:32 suggest that *Sheol* "is not for the wise and disciplined" (Johnston, *Shades of Sheol*, 207–9). After analyzing these proverbs, Johnston asserts: "To conclude, there are very few proverbs which suggest a positive life after death. These few suggestions are conceptually and textually uncertain, and they may reflect the later emendation or re-reading of misunderstood texts. So at best they testify to an afterlife belief which was becoming more widespread during the period of the text's transmission and translation" (Johnston, *Shades of Sheol*, 209).

2.

Resurrection as a Means of Postmortem Reward and Punishment Did Not Come to Be a Widely Accepted Idea Until Late in the Second Temple Period, but Has Roots in Earlier Biblical Material

WHILE THE DOMINANT FOCUS of the Hebrew Bible is this-worldly, sometime after the building of the Second Temple an otherworldly focus begins to emerge. The otherworldly focus is primarily a result of an emphasis on individual justice that was largely absent in preexilic times. The concern for individual justice caused people to ponder the problem of moral evil, that is, the problem that righteous individuals are often in a distressed state while wicked individuals are often in a state of well-being. Since God is just, the circumstances of the righteous and the wicked should be the reverse. The absence of justice *in this life* led to an imagined rectification *in another life*. However, for there to be a rectification in another life, persons who died in a state of injustice needed to be brought back to a state of renewed vitality. Hence, some people were attracted to the idea that the *rephaim* of those who had died, and were now in *Sheol*, could be revitalized and brought back to life, or reborn.

The seed for this idea of resurrection is present in the biblical belief that God is all-powerful, and that such power included the ability to bring about the revival or rebirth of that which has died.[1] Indeed, death and rebirth were believed to happen regularly in the natural order. There are also preexilic biblical texts evidencing belief in the possibility that human beings who had "died" (that is, lost all signs of vitality) could be brought back to life (really, revitalized or resuscitated) by the miracle-working

---

1. See generally Madigan and Levenson, *Resurrection*, 132–70. The Hebrew idiom for "resurrection" is *mehaye hametim,* which more literally means "revives or revitalizes the dead." For the ancient Israelites death was seen as merely an extreme form of the loss of vitality that happens regularly to living human beings, including when they sleep, so that "resurrection" could be seen as simply a more extreme form of the revitalization that happens regularly to living human beings, including awakening from sleep. See Johnson, *Vitality of the Individual*, 88, 95–97; Levenson, *Resurrection and the Restoration*, 168–72, 186–87.

prophets Elijah and Elisha. Certain texts might even be understood to affirm that human beings already in the netherworld could be brought back up from *Sheol*.[2] But even those who might have believed in such "resurrections" would have understood them to be extremely rare exceptions to the ordinary situation; in preexilic times, death for human beings was accepted as normally irreversible.[3] In the Second Temple period, however, *as a means of resolving the problem of moral evil,* what had been a rare exception became accepted as likely to occur normally.[4] Moreover, an additional feature was added to all past examples of revitalization; now the revitalization would be for eternity.

Although the idea of resurrection as a means of rewarding the righteous and punishing the wicked appears in a few texts that are dated to early postexilic times, the idea does not become widely accepted until around 167–164 BCE. This was when Judea was controlled by the Hellenistic King Antiochus IV, when there was a division in the Jewish community between those Jews who favored hellenization and those Jews who opposed hellenization, and when Antiochus persecuted those who opposed hellenization.[5] Jews who adopted the idea of resurrection at this time conceived of it as limited to Jews who had recently died without being properly rewarded or punished. This is discussed below in section C. Discussed in section D is the extension and universalization of the idea of resurrection associated with the events of the Jewish-Roman War of 66–70 CE. Sections E and F concern, respectively, (1) the conversion of *Sheol* to a place of punishment for the wicked who, at a time of judgment, were expected to be resurrected, and (2) texts and persons evidencing that, though the expectation of resurrection became widespread, in the period of the Second Temple it was not universally accepted. But first, sections A and B deal with emergence of the problem of moral evil during the period of the Second Temple.

A. The Problem of Moral Evil Is of Relatively Little Concern in the Preexilic Period Due to the Doctrines of Intergenerational and Collective Reward and Punishment

Preexilic Israel believed that God is omnipotent, good, and just, and administers justice in *this* world in the form of material well-being. The reward and punishment meted out by God, according to the Torah, is all in this life. In Deuteronomy 11:13–28, for example, God cautions that, if you obey his commandments, he will give you rain, you will have bountiful crops and grass for your cattle, and you will live well; but, if

---

2. See generally Johnston, *Shades of Sheol*, 218–28; Hirsch, *Rabbinic Psychology*, 85–87.

3. See generally Eichrodt, *Theology of the Old Testament*, 2:496–504; Hirsch, *Rabbinic Psychology*, 71–72.

4. See also Madigan and Levenson, *Resurrection*, 165.

5. See Scheindlin, *Short History of the Jewish People*, 33–49.

you disobey his commandments, he will *not* give you rain, you will have *no* harvest or grass for your cattle, and you will perish.[6]

These beliefs about God pose a problem that is referred to as the problem of evil. If God is all powerful and good, why is there evil in the world, why are there natural disasters such as floods and earthquakes? Furthermore, if God is all-powerful and *just* (rewarding those who obey his commandments and punishing those who disobey), then why are there people who obey God's commandments but suffer, and people who disobey but have an abundance of material well-being? It would seem that God is either not just or not omnipotent. This is the problem of *moral* evil.

In preexilic Israel the problem of moral evil was not apparent for two related reasons. First, it was accepted that God's reward and punishment is intergenerational, which is to say that you could be rewarded or punished for the conduct of your distant ancestors. It is stated in Exodus 20:5–6, for example:

> I, YHWH, your God am a jealous God, counting parents' crimes on children, on the third generation, and on the fourth generation for those that hate me, but practicing kindness to thousands for those who love me and for those who observe my commandments.[7]

This idea is also reflected in a popular proverb that "The fathers have eaten sour grapes, and the children's teeth are blunted."[8]

Second, it was accepted that God's reward and punishment is collective, that reward and punishment is not meted out for *individual* behavior but for the behavior of the people of Israel as a group. If the people obeyed God's commandments, the people would be rewarded, but if the people disobeyed, the people would be punished. This is because the ancient Israelites, as other ancient peoples, saw themselves not primarily as individuals but as members of a tribe or group. They accepted that one's own fate was linked to the fate of the group, including its ancestors.[9]

It was in light of intergenerational and collective reward and punishment that the Israelites understood the national calamity that befell them at the time of the Babylonian exile. The Babylonian exile was especially traumatic because it violated God's promise made to Abraham to give the Israelites the promised land forever.[10] The trauma of the exile was understood by many as God's punishment for earlier generations of Israelites having failed to live up to their side of the bargain, having failed to fully obey God's commandments. Lamentations 5:7–8 states:

---

6. See Nickelsburg, "Judgment, Life-After-Death, and Resurrection," 141; Prov 11:31 ("the righteous shall be requited *in the earth*", meaning, according to Johnston, "the inhabited world").

7. See also Exod 34:6–7; Deut 5:9–10.

8. Ezek 18:2; Jer 31:29.

9. See Cohen, *From the Maccabees to the Mishnah*, 84; Madigan and Levenson, *Resurrection*, 107. See also Adkins, *Moral Values*, 43–44. See generally Eichrodt, *Theology of the Old Testament*, 2:175, 231–42.

10. See Gen 17:8.

Our fathers have sinned, and are not;

And we have borne their iniquities.

Servants rule over us;

There is none to deliver us out of their hand.

B. The Traditional Conceptual Scheme of Intergenerational and Collective Reward and Punishment Began to be Challenged in the Postexilic Period, Giving Rise to Questions of Theodicy

The understanding of reward and punishment as intergenerational and collective began to be seriously challenged after the Babylonian exile.[11] People began more and more to see themselves as individuals rather than as merely members of the family, clan, tribe, or nation, and consequently began to have concern for individual justice.[12] When this happened the problem of moral evil became a *real* problem. The authors of the books of Job and Qoheleth are among the first to address this matter, seeking a justification of God's ways. The door to such theodicies was opened by people like Ezekiel, Jeremiah, and the author of Deuteronomy 24:16.

1. Ezekiel, Jeremiah, and Deuteronomy insist on individual justice

The questioning of intergenerational and collective reward and punishment is reflected in the teaching of the prophets Ezekiel and Jeremiah, who were active at the beginning of the period of the exile. Ezekiel rejected the belief that we are punished for the sins of others. He prophesies in chapter 18 of Ezekiel:

> And the word of the Lord came unto me: What do you mean by quoting this proverb upon the soil of Israel, 'Fathers eat sour grapes and their children's teeth are blunted'? As I live—declares the Lord God—this proverb shall no longer be current among you in Israel (vs. 1–3) . . . The person who sins, he alone shall die. A son shall not share the burden of a father's guilt; the righteousness of the righteous shall be accounted to him alone, and the wickedness of the wicked shall be accounted to him alone (v. 20) . . . Be assured, O house of Israel, I shall judge each one of you according to his ways—declares the Lord God (v. 30)[13]

Similarly, Jeremiah says:

---

11. See Cohen, *From the Maccabees to the Mishnah*, 10, 84–88.

12. The break-up of the clan had, in fact, begun with the settlement of Canaan. See Eichrodt, *Theology of the Old Testament*, 2:240–41. Cf. Bremmer, *Early Greek Concept of the Soul*, 124.

13. See generally Madigan and Levenson, *Resurrection*, 165–68.

In those days, they shall no longer say, 'Fathers have eaten sour grapes and children's teeth are blunted.' But everyone shall die for his own sins; whosoever eats sour grapes, his teeth shall be blunted.[14]

The preaching of Ezekiel and Jeremiah found expression in the Deuteronomic Law Code, generally dated to a time shortly preceding the Babylonian exile. According to Deuteronomy 24:16: "Parents shall not be put to death for children, nor children be put to death for parents; a person shall be put to death only for his own crime."

2. The book of Job raises the problem of moral evil[15]

The book of Job begins by describing Job as "blameless and upright"[16] and by recounting the material rewards that he merited and possessed. Then God asks Satan, or "the Adversary," if he has noticed Job and seen how righteous he is, how he obeys God. Satan says that, of course, Job obeys God because God has given him great material well-being. But, if God took away Job's material well-being, Job would not obey God but would curse him. So, God decides to test this hypothesis. God takes away all the blessings that had been bestowed on Job. He takes away all Job's animals, the source of his wealth; he takes away his children; and he inflicts Job with disease. Job's wife tells him to curse God but Job responds: "Shall we accept good from God, and not accept evil?"[17]

When friends of Job hear about the calamities that have befallen him, they go to console and comfort him, but they really don't offer consolation and comfort. The friends take the position that Job must have committed some grave offense because otherwise God would not be inflicting such horrendous punishment on Job. None of the friends mention that Job may be being punished for the wrongdoing of his ancestors or for the wrongdoing of others in the community. Individual reward and punishment is assumed. They claim that it is Job himself who must be responsible. Thus, the friends are in accord with the views voiced by Ezekiel and Jeremiah. Neither does Job himself refer to being punished for the sins of others. Rather, Job insists that he is innocent, and he complains that he is being wrongfully punished by God.

The book ends with God addressing Job out of a whirlwind, and with God saying that Job's friends had not spoken the truth about God. But in exactly what way had the friends not spoken the truth? No explanation is given. The message given by God to Job is that God's ways are unknowable. Presumably this implies that God cannot be confined to neat explanations of rewarding the righteous and punishing the wicked.

---

14. Jer 31:29–30.

15. See Madigan and Levenson, *Resurrection*, 182 ("The book of Job . . . deals with an innocent sufferer whose experience dramatically refutes the mechanistic theology that holds that one always and only gets what one deserves.").

16. Job 1:1, 8.

17. Job 2:10.

What is most relevant for present purposes is that the book of Job suggests that serious thought is being given at this time to the problem of moral evil, and that, once the concepts of intergenerational and collective reward and punishment are abandoned, satisfactory answers are hard to come by. One possible answer advanced in the book of Job is that evil may befall the righteous because God is testing them. But this answer becomes inadequate when the righteous are being killed, for then there can be no possibility of being restored, as was Job, to a state of well-being after the test is passed.[18]

3. The author of book of Qoheleth is troubled by the fact that the righteous and the wicked share the same fate

The book of Qoheleth also raises the problem of moral evil. Qoheleth explicitly rejects the idea that there is any reward or punishment in an afterlife.[19] But Qoheleth also observes that, in this life, the righteous often receive no reward and the wicked often receive no punishment. Specifically, it is stated:

> Here is a vanity that takes place on the earth—there are righteous men who receive the recompense due to the wicked, and wicked men who receive the recompense due to the righteous. I say, this is indeed vanity . . . All this I grasped and clearly understood, that the just and the wise, together with all their works, are in God's hands; men can be certain of neither God's love nor His hate—anything may happen to them. One fate awaits all men, one lot comes to the just and the unjust, to the good and pure and the impure, to him who brings his offerings and him who does not; as with the good man, so with the sinner . . .[20]

Qoheleth notes that many of those who disobey God's commandments are eulogized as benefactors of the city, and, since God does not appear to immediately punish wrongdoers, they are encouraged to continue their evil conduct. Further, to say that *ultimately* it will be better for you to obey God is not, to Qoheleth, a satisfactory answer. This leads Qoheleth to ponder that the righteous all too often are treated by God the way the wicked should be treated, and *vice versa*. Qoheleth seems to conclude that we cannot be assured that any particular conduct will result in either reward or punishment, but that God will do what he wants to do. This seems to be a rejection of the idea that God is just. So Qoheleth decides that the only thing to do in this life is to

---

18. See Madigan and Levenson, *Resurrection*, 112–13 (arguing that Job "foreshadows" the doctrine of resurrection). See also Johnston, *Shades of Sheol*, 209–13 (raising the possibility that Job "envisages some form of vindication after death, though without any indication of physical change or continued communion with God.").

19. See ch. 1, sec. D.

20. Qoh 8:10—9:3.

enjoy it as far as it lies in man's power to do so—to eat, drink, and be merry. Madigan and Levenson state that Qoheleth:

> casts into grave doubt the belief in a personal and just God who providentially directs the destinies of nations and individuals and who restores innocent sufferers like Job. For Qoheleth rather, 'God' refers to an inexorable and ultimate fate unresponsive to human action and thus human merit. This is indeed a frontal assault on the previous thinking.[21]

C. The Messianic Idea and the Idea of Resurrection of the Dead Became Prominent in Response to the Intensified Problem of Moral Evil Occasioned by the Persecution of Antiochus IV Epiphanes

During the time of Antiochus IV Epiphanes, the Seleucid king of Hellenistic Syria who ruled from 175–164 BCE, the problem of moral evil became acute, and it led to widespread belief in the resurrection of the dead. The problem became acute because, beginning in 167 BCE, Antiochus, who controlled the land that was once ruled by the Israelites, began a campaign of persecution. The worship of Yahweh and all Jewish rites were forbidden on pain of death. In the temple, an altar to Zeus Olympios was erected, and sacrifices were ordered to be made at the feet of an idol in the image of the king.

The *Hasidim* (the "pious ones"), the very people who were punctilious in observance of God's commandments, were abused and killed by Antiochus. Conversely, the Jewish Hellenists (those Jews who were willing to abandon observance of God's commandments) were rewarded for their wickedness—they were given high positions of authority by Antiochus. This problem of righteous Jews being punished and wicked Jews being rewarded was related to a broader problem, that the Jews were under the dominion of the non-Jews. The question had arisen as early as the Babylonian exile, "Why has God given dominion to the gentile nations?" Even if it be conceded that the Jews as a whole are sinful and that God is using the nations of the world to punish them, aren't the gentile nations also sinful? Why doesn't God punish them?[22] Yet, in the time of Antiochus, the contrast between the dominion of the gentile and the subjugation of the Jew was less pressing than the contrast between the *Hasidim* and the Jewish Hellenists.[23]

Since the *Hasidim* firmly believed in God's justice, they firmly believed that the conditions as then existed under Antiochus would not endure. God would restore the nation of Israel to its former prominence. This restoration, they believed, would

---

21. Madigan and Levenson, *Resurrection*, 183. See generally Lev. Rab. 28:1 ("the Sages wanted to store away the Book of Ecclesiastes, for they found in it ideas that leaned towards heresy" such as the denial of a postmortem reward).

22. Cohen, *From the Maccabees to the Mishnah*, 92–93.

23. Cohen, *From the Maccabees to the Mishnah*, 93–94. See also Kohler, *Jewish Theology*, 282–83.

be ushered in by an anointed one, a messiah, from the House of David—a military leader who would bring the righteous Jews military victory over both gentiles and wicked Jews (who would perish). They envisioned the reestablishment of the Davidic kingship and the ingathering of the Jewish diaspora.[24]

However, a problem still remained. Even if the righteous were ultimately vindicated in a new reestablished Davidic kingdom in which justice prevailed, this would be of little consolation to the hundreds of *Hasidim* who, during the reign of Antiochus, had been killed precisely because they were pious and refused to disobey God's commandments. Justice demanded that they be vindicated.[25] Moreover, many of the impious Jewish Hellenists had died of natural causes without having been dishonored. Justice demanded that they be dishonored. Clearly, the deaths of the pious precisely because they had willfully chosen to obey the Torah, and, conversely, the well-being of the hellenizing Jews despite gross disobedience of the Torah, presented a theological problem.[26] "Resurrection to life, on the one hand, and to punishment, on the other, was an answer to this problem."[27]

So, the idea arose that recently deceased persons would be brought back to life—resurrected—to receive their just desserts: the pious, who had suffered, to participate in the reestablished Davidic kingdom; the impious, who had imposed suffering on others, to be dishonored and perish. Thus, in its origin, the idea of an individual's resurrection was, in large part, a response to the problem of moral evil, and, for many, was also indissolubly linked to the idea of the national redemption.[28]

The extent to which the Israelite concept of bodily resurrection may have been influenced by the Persian religion of Zoroastrianism has been debated by scholars with the consensus opinion seeing only minimal influence.[29] In addition to having a possible foreign influence, the concept of human bodily resurrection may also have arisen, internally, merely by an awareness of death and rebirth in the natural world. Death is seen every winter, and a rebirth in the spring is universally celebrated, including by the ancient Israelites.[30] No great leap of the imagination is required to apply to

---

24. See Nickelsburg, *Jewish Literature*, 14.

25. See Moore, *Judaism in the First Centuries*, 2:312–13.

26. See Nickelsburg, *Resurrection, Immortality, and Eternal Life*, 32.

27. Nickelsburg, *Resurrection, Immortality, and Eternal Life*, 32. But see Madigan and Levenson, *Resurrection*, 180–85.

28. See Moore, *Judaism in the First Centuries*, 2:312–14, 319. But see Nickelsburg, *Resurrection, Immortality, and Eternal Life*, 5–6; Collins, "Afterlife in Apocalyptic Literature," 21, 127–28. See also Eichrodt, *Theology of the Old Testament*, 2:510.

29. See generally Moore, *Judaism in the First Centuries*, 2:394–95; Gillman, *Death of Death*, 96; Segal, *Life After Death*, 271; Eichrodt, *Theology of the Old Testament*, 2:516; Collins, "Afterlife in Apocalyptic Literature," 128; Madigan and Levenson, *Resurrection*, 147, 199–200; Setzer, *Resurrection of the Body*, 10. For a general discussion of Zoroastrianism and its influence on Jewish thought, see Segal, *Life After Death*, 173–203; Hirsch, *Rabbinic Psychology*, 47–56. See also Kohler, *Heaven and Hell*, 8, 32–39; Johnston, *Shades of Sheol*, 230–39.

30. See Frazer, *Golden Bough*, 361–78; Eichrodt, *Theology of the Old Testament*, 2:505–6; Cohon,

human beings the idea of death and rebirth seen every year in nature, especially since human death was understood as simply a loss of vitality, requiring only a revitalization to be reversed.³¹ Recently, Madigan and Levenson have contended that the Israelites always thought God had the power to rescue from death, and they always thought resurrection of the dead to be possible,³² so that, Madigan and Levenson argue, the origin of the belief in resurrection of the dead "does not lie *simply* in the embarrassment caused by the deaths of the Jews martyred by the Seleucid king Antiochus IV at the time the book of Daniel was composed."³³

Notwithstanding debate concerning the weight that should be assigned to the varying factors responsible for the origin of the idea of bodily human resurrection among the Israelites, all scholars agree that the "first transparent and indisputable prediction of the resurrection of the dead in the Hebrew Bible" is in the book of Daniel, generally agreed to have been written at "the time of the Seleucid persecution of 167–164 B.C.E."³⁴ Further, "resurrection in Daniel (as in 2 Maccabees) is seen as a theological response to the crises of the Antiochene persecution and of the martyrdom of faithful Jews."³⁵

Jewish Theology, 364; Gastor, *Festivals of the Jewish Year*, 31–32.

31. Job, at 14:7–12, compares the hopelessness of human death with the regenerative properties of death in the natural order, and then, in verses 13–15, imagines something different for human beings. Commenting on verses 13–15, Pope states: "Job here gropes toward the idea of an afterlife" (Pope, *Anchor Bible*, 102). Also, both Isaiah and Hosea compare God's awakening of the dead, or the healing of the nation, to the "fresh growth" that dew brings forth in the fields. See Isa 26:19; Hos 14:5–6; and Levenson, *Resurrection and the Restoration*, 198, 203. But see Eichrodt, *Theology of the Old Testament*, 2:505–6.

32. See Madigan and Levenson, *Resurrection*, 121–31. See also Johnston, *Shades of Sheol*, 218–20 (discussing Deut 32:39 and 1 Sam 2:6, and finding that they suggest "that Yahweh's power to 'raise up from Sheol' is a *potentiality* which is affirmed rather than an actuality which has been witnessed"; emphasis added).

33. Madigan and Levenson, *Resurrection*, 199 (emphasis added).

34. Madigan and Levenson, *Resurrection*, 171, 180. See Collins, "Afterlife in Apocalyptic Literature," 126 (Daniel 12:1–3 "is the only passage in the Hebrew Bible that clearly predicts the resurrection of individuals."); Nickelsburg, *Resurrection, Immortality, and Eternal Life*, 23 (Daniel 12:1–3 "is our earliest datable intertestamental reference to a resurrection of the dead"); Johnston, *Shades of Sheol*, 225 (Daniel 12:2 is the "one text [that] speaks unmistakably and unambiguously of personal resurrection."). There is considerable debate as to whether or not Isaiah 26:19, which has clear parallels to Daniel 12:2, refers to a literal resurrection or to a metaphorical national restoration. See Levenson, *Resurrection and the Restoration*, 199; Madigan and Levenson, *Resurrection*, 186–88; Nickelsburg, *Resurrection, Immortality, and Eternal Life*, 30–31; Johnston, *Shades of Sheol*, 224–25. See generally Gillman, *Death of Death*, 90–95. See also Eichrodt, *Theology of the Old Testament*, 2:504–5 (discussing Hos 6:1–2); Johnston, *Shades of Sheol*, 221–22, 227–28 (discussing Hos 6:1–2; Ps 1:5; and Isa 53:10–12).

35. Johnston, *Shades of Sheol*, 226–27.

1. The book of Daniel

The second half of the biblical book of Daniel contains a series of visions that Daniel allegedly saw during the reigns of several Persian kings, but in reality date from the time of Antiochus's persecution of the Jews, and they reflect various events in that persecution.[36] Through the use of mythic symbolism, they depict the persecution as a rebellion against heaven and they announce an act of divine judgment that will quash the rebellion and usher in an era of salvation.

In chapter 11, the author describes a vision concerning what will happen at the end of days, saying "'a contemptible man,' a violent king [in reality, Antiochus] . . . will be determined to do harm to 'the holy covenant,' 'desecrate the temple,' and 'set up the appalling abomination'—an idol in the most sacred place on earth."[37] Reflecting the tension in the reign of Antiochus between the *Hasidim* and the Jewish Hellenists, Daniel states that the foreign king would "have regard unto them that forsake the holy covenant" but that "the people devoted to their God will stand firm."[38] The passage continues:

> The wise among the people will make the many understand; and they shall fall by sword and flame, suffer captivity and spoliation. In defeat, they will receive a little help, and many will join them insincerely. Some of the wise will fall, that they may be refined and purged and whitened until the time of the end, for an interval still remains until the appointed time.[39]

The author soon moves to describing the "time of the end" itself. It is at this time that the patron angel of Israel, Michael, will confront the wrongdoers. Michael is both the warrior chieftain of the heavenly armies and God's appointed agent in rendering judgment. Michael will strike down the demonic power behind the foreign king [Antiochus] and his kingdom, and render judgment separating the righteous and wicked of Israel.[40] The text specifically states:

> And at that time, the great prince, Michael, who stands beside the sons of your people, will appear. It will be a time of trouble, the like of which has never been since the nation came into being. At that time, your people will be delivered, all who are found inscribed in the book. Many of those that sleep in the dust of the earth [or "dusty earth"], will awake, some to eternal life, others to reproaches, to everlasting abhorrence. And the wise shall be radiant like the

---

36. See generally Nickelsburg, *Jewish Literature*, 67–89; Nickelsburg, *Resurrection, Immortality, and Eternal Life*, 23–59; Moore, *Judaism in the First Centuries*, 2:296–99.

37. Madigan and Levenson, *Resurrection*, 171.

38. Dan 11:30–32, but see Nickelsburg, *Resurrection, Immortality, and Eternal Life*, 6.

39. Dan 11:33–35. See Madigan and Levenson, *Resurrection*, 172.

40. See generally Nickelsburg, *Resurrection, Immortality, and Eternal Life*, 23–42; Nickelsburg, *Jewish Literature*, 80–88; Moore, *Judaism in the First Centuries*, 2:296–98.

bright expanse of the sky, and those who lead the many to righteousness will be like the stars for ever and ever.[41]

"Many of them that sleep in the dust of the earth" refers to many of the dead. And to say that they will "awake" refers to their revitalization or resurrection. The resurrection envisioned "is not a general resurrection calculated to mete out justice to all humanity."[42] Rather, it is a resurrection of recently departed Israelites to participate in divine judgment.[43] Those Israelites found to have suffered for their righteousness will "enter eternal life"; those Israelites found to have been wicked in inflicting suffering on others, according to Nickelsburg, will be "pitched into Gehenna, where they will be a contemptible sight to all who pass by."[44]

Although no scholar doubts that the book of Daniel envisions a resurrection of the dead, there is an issue as to how to describe the nature of such resurrection.[45] Generally speaking, the resurrection implied in Daniel has been understood to be a physical resurrection, entailing the reconstitution of the human body. However, John Collins has asserted that Daniel 12:1–3 "does not necessarily imply that the resurrection must be physical; it may be a resurrection of the spirit from Sheol."[46] Unfortunately, Collins is unclear as to what precisely constitutes a "resurrection of the spirit." He may mean that what is resurrected is something entirely nonphysical (something immaterial or incorporeal). However, since Collins goes on to refer to Paul's discussion of resurrection in 1 Corinthians 15 where Paul envisions a *bodily* resurrection, albeit a body that is transformed so as to be incorruptible, Collins may mean a resurrection of a *transformed* human body. Indeed, if the resurrection implied in Daniel is a reconstitution of the human body, it *must* envision a body that is in some way transformed, for the righteous are to attain *eternal* life and the wicked are to receive *everlasting* abhorrence. There could be no possibility of an *eternal* or *everlasting* aspect of reward and punishment unless the human body was transformed in some manner that would prevent future death.[47]

Regardless of the manner in which the resurrection of the "ordinary" righteous and the wicked was conceived by the author of Daniel, the resurrection of "the wise" (*maskilim*) who turn the many to righteousness may have been conceived somewhat

41. Dan 12:1–3. See Madigan and Levenson, *Resurrection*, 171.

42. Nickelsburg, *Resurrection, Immortality, and Eternal Life*, 42. See generally Eichrodt, *Theology of the Old Testament*, 2:512–13.

43. See Johnston, *Shades of Sheol*, 226.

44. Nickelsburg, *Resurrection, Immortality, and Eternal Life*, 42.

45. See generally Madigan and Levenson, *Resurrection*, 178.

46. Collins, "Afterlife in Apocalyptic Literature," 126. See also ch. 3, sec. A, 3 (quoting Collins with regard to 1 Enoch).

47. See Madigan and Levenson, *Resurrection*, 176 (discussing that in comparison with other biblical references to resurrection, Daniel is "truly novel" in using the expression "eternal life," that is, in envisioning no second death), 178 ("resurrection was thought to yield a transformed and perfected form of bodily existence and thus a state of being both like and unlike any we can know.").

differently. The text states that the *maskilim* "shall shine like the bright expanse of the sky . . . like the stars." In other words, the bodies of the *maskilim* will be even more radically transformed than the bodies of the others, for the *maskilim* shall become like the stars in the sky. This type of transformation is referred to by scholars as "astral immortality."[48]

2. Second Maccabees[49]

Second Maccabees, one of the works included in the Apocrypha,[50] is a condensation of a five-volume history of Israel during the years from 180 to 161 BCE. In his account of hellenization in Jerusalem, the author stresses that Israel or its leaders have forsaken the covenant and violated the laws. This explains the disaster that subsequently befalls the nation. Antiochus is viewed as the agent of God's judgment. Next, the deaths of certain martyrs, including seven brothers and their mother, are recounted, and it is noted that these martyrs (or most of them) are put to death precisely because they refuse to capitulate to sin. This obedience to the Torah, and these innocent deaths, are seen as instrumental in reversing Israel's dire circumstance, and in facilitating the Maccabean victories that are recounted through the rest of the book.[51]

The book emphasizes that God will undo the violent and unjust deaths of the martyrs by raising the dead to life. The seven brothers make individual statements before they are martyred. One says, "You accursed wretch, you dismiss us from this present life, but the King of the universe will raise us up to an everlasting renewal of life, because we have died for his laws."[52] A second says, "One cannot but choose to die at the hands of mortals and to cherish the hope God gives of being raised again by him. But for you there will be no resurrection to Life."[53] As Nickelsburg says, "Resurrection, then, vindicates the conduct of the righteous . . . Vindication is *quid pro quo*. Because they lost their physical limbs, theirs must be a bodily resurrection; what has been destroyed must be restored . . ."[54]

Notice that on this view there is only resurrection of the martyrs, the recently deceased righteous. The punishment of the wicked is to miss out on resurrection to everlasting life. This is in contrast to Daniel in which, as generally interpreted, resurrection is of both the righteous and the wicked. In either case, the theological problem

---

48. See Grabbe, *Judaic Religion*, 260. See also *infra*, nn. 77 and 82.

49. See Nickelsburg, *Jewish Literature*, 91–117 (discussing 2 Macc and related texts in their historical context); Raphael, *Jewish Views of the Afterlife*, 110–11.

50. The Apocrypha is the name used to describe fifteen books or parts of books that were written by Jews during the Second Temple period but which were not included in the Hebrew Bible. See Raphael, *Jewish Views of the Afterlife*, 77–81; Winston, *Wisdom of Solomon*, ix.

51. See generally Nickelsburg, "Judgment, Life-After-Death, and Resurrection," 148–49.

52. 2 Macc 6:9.

53. 2 Macc 6:14.

54. Nickelsburg, "Judgment, Life-After-Death, and Resurrection," 149.

of moral evil is resolved by the idea that, if God's justice is not imposed on the living, it will be imposed on the dead in the time of the Messiah when the nation Israel as a whole would receive its promised reward. God could impose justice on those who had recently died by means of their resurrection.

All who envisioned such vindication, envisioned the resurrection of the righteous Israelites who had suffered on account of their righteousness, for the purpose of receiving their just reward. "Most naturally it was felt that, of all men, the martyrs who had laid down their lives for their religion in the persecution, and the heroes who had fallen in the final conflict with heathenism, had earned a part in the salvation that was at hand; and it was easy to believe that God, who must recognize their desert, would bring them to life to enjoy it."[55] But some also envisioned the resurrection of those hellenized Jews who had inflicted suffering on the righteous but died before having been dishonored or punished; the wicked needed to be resurrected in order to receive the dishonor or punishment they merited but hadn't gotten while alive. In either case, the idea of resurrection fully emerged in the persecution of the religion by Antiochus. As stated by Moore, "the assurance that the hour of deliverance was at hand and the new era about to begin, gave both the motive and the limitation of the first conception of resurrection."[56]

D. The Resurrection Idea Is Extended from the Messianic Time to an End Time, and from Those Recently Departed to Remote Generations (and to Gentiles), in Part Due to the Jewish-Roman War and Its Aftermath

Besides the idea of the political restoration of the nation of Israel achieved by the Messiah, there were some people who further envisioned a time when the current world order would end, God's kingdom (the *Malkut Shamayim*) would be established, and evil would be eliminated—a time when all men would worship the one true God. Such ideas had their roots in sayings of the biblical prophets.[57] It was part of the belief in this end time that when it came every person would be judged individually, and saved or damned by their own deeds.[58]

Gradually, the idea also crystallized that at this end time there would be a general resurrection, including the righteous and wicked of all past generations, not just the recently deceased who had suffered or had inflicted suffering. That the idea of a resurrection of all the pious of Israel should arise in the context of thoughts about the resurrection of the recently departed pious is not surprising. The promises of salvation made by the biblical prophets were made to Israel as a whole, and generations had

---

55. Moore, *Judaism in the First Centuries*, 2:312–14.
56. Moore, *Judaism in the First Centuries*, 2:314.
57. See Moore, *Judaism in the First Centuries*, 2:371.
58. Moore, *Judaism in the First Centuries*, 2:377.

lived in the hope of seeing it, but yet had died without doing so. They too should be vindicated. As explained by Moore:

> In the original apprehension this resurrection was to occur at the inauguration of the Messianic Age, and was for the righteous dead of Israel only, who were brought back to life to enjoy in their own land the blessings of that time. This belief was not displaced by the eschatological conception of a resurrection of righteous and wicked to judgment, but persisted beside it.[59]

In some apocalypses the gentile, as well as the Jew, would be resurrected to appear in a last judgment.[60] The idea of a universal resurrection appears in texts that are dated to a time immediately following the destruction of the Second Temple in 70 CE, and may have been brought into prominence by such an event. In the earlier period of development, the age of political restoration, called *Yemot Ha-Maschiach* (the Days of the Messiah), was the final period of history, and the names *Olam Ha-Bah* (the "World-to-Come") or *Atid La-Bo* (the "Future") were applied to it. But with the advent of the idea of a final order of things, *Olam Ha-Bah* came to refer to the end time as well, with the result that "the periodization of the hereafter is not always consistent either in conception or in designation."[61]

Among the texts which express the idea of an end time and a universal resurrection are several which were written in the aftermath of the destruction of Jerusalem in 70 CE.[62] The destruction of Jerusalem and the Second Temple caused the authors of the apocalyptic books 4 Ezra and 2 Baruch, as well as the author of the Sibylline Oracle 4, to focus on the problem of theodicy in a more general way than had the authors of Daniel and 2 Maccabees. The latter texts are primarily concerned with the question of how the recently departed *Hasidim* would be able to participate in the political restoration of Israel which was anticipated, and which they merited on account of their martyrdom. The former texts are more concerned with the question of why God had allowed the sinful gentiles to defeat God's chosen people, devastate the holy land promised to Israel, and destroy God's temple. The answer was related to an end time and a last judgment when there would be appropriate rewards and punishments for all mankind.

Other texts referring to either the resurrection of earlier generations of the righteous of Israel or to a universal resurrection include material forming part of the collection of texts referred to as the Testaments of the Twelve Patriarchs, especially the Testament of Judah and the Testament of Benjamin.[63]

---

59. Moore, *Judaism in the First Centuries*, 2:379.

60. Moore, *Judaism in the First Centuries*, 2:385.

61. Moore, *Judaism in the First Centuries*, 2:378.

62. For discussion of the historical background of these texts see Cohen, *From the Maccabees to the Mishnah*, 1–5; Nickelsburg, *Jewish Literature*, 231–36, 263–70.

63. Moore, *Judaism in the First Centuries*, 2:307 ("In the Testaments of the Twelve Patriarchs the resurrection is extended to the dead of remote generations, back to the beginnings of the people.").

CHAPTER 2.

1. Testament of Judah

Chapter 25 of the Testament of Judah is concerned with the restoration of Israel following a period of persecution, as well as with a postmortem judgment. Postmortem vindication is promised to those who had been persecuted because of their refusal to abandon God's commandments. As in Daniel 12:1–3, the Testament of Judah states:

> They who die for the Lord's sake will awake.[64]

In this same context, it speaks of the resurrection of the patriarchs:

> And after these things, Abraham, Isaac, and Jacob will rise to life.[65]

It next states that the children of Jacob will rise to be the heads of their tribes in the new Israel that is to be restored.[66]

2. Testament of Benjamin

The Testament of Benjamin (which is dated later than the Testament of Judah) postulates a universal resurrection and judgment, including gentiles.[67] It also mentions the resurrection of biblical figures prior to Abraham. Specifically, chapter 10 includes the following vision:

> Then you will see Enoch, Noah, and Shem, and Abraham, Isaac, and Jacob rising on the right hand in gladness. Then we also shall rise [the twelve patriarchs], each over our tribe, worshipping the king of heaven . . .
>
> Then all will rise, some to glory and some to dishonor. And the Lord will first judge Israel for their iniquity . . . And then he will judge all the nations.[68]

The function of resurrection in this text, and in 4 Ezra discussed below, is broader than in Daniel and 2 Maccabees. In this text: "The righteous are rewarded because of their obedience to the Torah, even if they have been rewarded during their lives, and although they may not have suffered or died because of their righteousness. The sinners are condemned for their wickedness in general and not specifically because they

---

For a general discussion of the Testaments of the Twelve Patriarchs, see Nickelsburg, *Jewish Literature*, 301–13.

64. T. Jud. 25:4. See Nickelsburg, *Resurrection, Immortality, and Eternal Life*, 49.

65. T. Jud. 25:1. See Nickelsburg, *Resurrection, Immortality, and Eternal Life*, 50.

66. Nickelsburg, *Resurrection, Immortality, and Eternal Life*, 50 (also citing, T. Zeb. 10:2). Accord, Moore, *Judaism in the First Centuries*, 2:307.

67. See Moore, *Judaism in the First Centuries*, 2:307–8 and 307n1; Nickelsburg, *Resurrection, Immortality, and Eternal Life*, 176–77.

68. T. Benj. 10:6–10. See Nickelsburg, *Resurrection, Immortality, and Eternal Life*, 176.

have mistreated the righteous. They are punished eternally, even though they may have suffered punishment during their life time."[69]

3. Fourth Ezra 7[70]

Fourth Ezra (or Esdras in Greek) contains revelations purporting to be made to Ezra in Babylon after the fall of Jerusalem to Nebuchadnezzar, but which are dated to the first century CE, after the destruction of the Second Temple (and perhaps to the reign of the Roman Emperor Domitian), or early second century CE.[71] The author is trying to make sense of the events of 70 CE and to come to grips with the problem of moral evil that those events accentuate.

Ezra challenges God to compare Israel's deeds to those of the gentiles, and questions why God punishes the Jews at the hands of the gentiles when the latter's deeds are worse than the former's deeds. Attention is turned to the idea of an end time as a solution to the problem, and the text describes the last days which entail "a four-hundred-year reign of the Messiah, the expunging of all life and a week when the earth returns to its primordial silence, the resurrection, and the great judgment over which God will preside . . . Judgment will be on the basis of deeds, and even the gentiles will be punished for not having served the Most High and obeyed the commandments."[72] The new age to be ushered in will be without the troubles of the present age, and a general resurrection and judgment are eagerly anticipated.

The judgment anticipated at the end time in 4 Ezra is *not* related to the persecution of the righteous or to the suffering of the Jewish people in general. "The wicked and the righteous are not judged on the way they have treated other people, or the way they themselves have been treated. They receive reward and punishment for their obedience or disobedience to God's law."[73]

Significantly, the idea of resurrection in 4 Ezra is combined with the idea of a soul. Given a belief that human beings possess a soul which can exist after the body decomposes, and given a belief that there will be a resurrection of the body and judgment at the end-of-days, the question is raised as to whether there is a process of judgment that takes place *with respect to the soul alone* immediately after death.[74] In answer to this question, it is explained that when souls leave their bodies immediately

---

69. Nickelsburg, *Resurrection, Immortality, and Eternal Life*, 177. See also Nickelsburg, *Resurrection, Immortality, and Eternal Life*, 214.

70. For a general discussion of this text, see Nickelsburg, *Jewish Literature*, 270–77; Segal, *Life After Death*, 491–94; Raphael, *Jewish Views of the Afterlife*, 99–102.

71. Moore, *Judaism in the First Centuries*, 2:283; Nickelsburg, *Resurrection, Immortality, and Eternal Life*, 171.

72. Nickelsburg, *Jewish Literature*, 271–73. See Segal, *Life After Death*, 492 ("the central issue of the book is theodicy, justifying God's ways to humanity.").

73. Nickelsburg, *Resurrection, Immortality, and Eternal Life*, 173.

74. See Raphael, *Jewish Views of the Afterlife*, 100.

after physical death they are stored in chambers in the earth, with separate chambers being designated for the wicked and the righteous.[75] The "souls of the unrighteous do not immediately enter into habitations but wander grieving in torments, because they realize the error of their ways."[76]

At the time that bodies are resurrected, the souls and bodies will be rejoined. After the judgment, those found to be righteous will be transformed and will shine like the light,[77] while the wicked face "the furnace of Gehenna."[78] The text reads:

> the earth shall give up those who are asleep in it, and the dust those who dwell silently in it; and the chambers shall give up the souls that have been committed to them . . .
>
> And recompense shall follow, and the reward shall be manifested; righteous deeds shall awake, and unrighteous deeds shall not sleep. Then the pit of torment shall appear, and opposite it shall be the place of rest; and the furnace of Gehenna shall be disclosed, and opposite it the paradise of delight. Then the Most High will say to the nations that have been raised from the dead, 'Look now, and understand whom you have denied, whom you have not served, whose commandments you have despised!'[79]

4. Second Baruch[80]

As in 4 Ezra, 2 Baruch uses the fall of Jerusalem in 586 BCE as its setting. Its alleged author is the Baruch who was Jeremiah's scribe, secretary, and disciple.[81] The text contains a set of disputations between Baruch and God that corresponds to those between Ezra and God in 4 Ezra. Baruch laments the paradox that Babylonia prospers while

---

75. See Raphael, *Jewish Views of the Afterlife*, 101-2. Cf. 1 En. 22, quoted in Nickelsburg, *Resurrection, Immortality, and Eternal Life*, 168-71 (souls or spirits stored in hollow places until the day of their judgment).

76. Collins, "Afterlife in Apocalyptic Literature," 130. See Setzer, *Resurrection of the Body*, 16.

77. Nickelsburg, *Resurrection, Immortality, and Eternal Life*, 174 (citing 4 Ezra 7:97, 125). See Collins, "Afterlife in Apocalyptic Literature," 130 (the righteous "are to be made like the light of the stars."). This seems to imply astral immortality See Setzer, *Resurrection of the Body*, 16 ("they pass into astral immortality"); *infra*, n. 82. Astral immortality is mentioned by Philo of Alexandria as an opinion that some affirm. Wolfson suggests that astral immortality reflects the view of the Stoic philosopher Chrysippus, "according to whom immortality, which to him is confined to the wise, means that the soul, which consists of an element similar to that of the stars, will upon the death of the body mount to heaven and there assume the spherical shape of stars" (Wolfson, *Philo*, 1:398-99). Those who affirmed this view, which according to Wolfson included the authors of 4 Ezra 7:97, 2 Baruch 51:10, and 1 Enoch 104:2, "must have found support in the scriptural verse, 'And they that are wise shall shine as the brightness of the stars for ever and ever.' [Daniel 12:3]" (Wolfson, *Philo*, 1:398-99).

78. 4 Ezra 7:36. See Nickelsburg, *Resurrection, Immortality, and Eternal Life*, 172.

79. 4 Ezra 7:32-37. See Nickelsburg, *Resurrection, Immortality, and Eternal Life*, 171-72.

80. For general discussion of this text, see Nickelsburg, *Jewish Literature*, 277-83; Segal, *Life After Death*, 495-97.

81. See Jer 36:4-10.

Israel suffers. He sees Israel's misfortune as divine chastisement for the evil deeds of Israel's wicked, notwithstanding the good deeds of Israel's righteous. He also notes that though they prosper, the gentiles fail to appreciate that such prosperity is God's doing. Baruch anticipates that the gentiles will ultimately fall victim to God's wrath and that God will eventually reverse Israel's misfortune.

The text turns to a discussion of the end time when Israel will be redeemed. The age and world of sorrow will give way to a new age and world in which even death itself will be overcome. There will be a Messiah and a period of woe. When the reign of the Messiah is completed, the dead will rise. Baruch asks whether in the resurrection "the righteous will be rid of those bodies that have partaken of the weakness and evil of this world," and "God states that after recognition has taken place . . . the righteous and the wicked will be separated . . . Those who have been faithful to the Torah and have trusted in its wisdom will ascend into the heights of heaven, be transformed into the likeness of the stars and the angels [astral immortality] . . . and enjoy the blessings of paradise and the world—now invisible—that does not die . . ."[82] The wicked will go into torment and will be punished in fire.[83]

According to Nickelsburg:

> Although the author contrasts this present corrupt world with the incorruptible realm of heaven . . . and although he describes the resurrected righteous soaring in the heights of heaven, he also envisions the renewal of creation . . . and the restoration of Zion . . . Most probably we are dealing with different traditions that stand in tension with one another.[84]

It is worth noting that 2 Baruch, as 4 Ezra, makes reference to storehouses in which the souls of the dead are kept awaiting the resurrection and judgment. The text reads:

> And it shall come to pass at that time that the treasuries will be opened in which is preserved the number of the souls of the righteous, and they will come out, and the multitude of souls will appear together in a single assembly;

---

82. Nickelsburg, *Jewish Literature*, 280–81. See *supra*, n. 77; Segal, *Life After Death*, 496 ("The dead must be raised in their exact form so that God's justice will be evident to all. But the righteous will be changed into a much more glorious form . . . The evil ones are transformed into the terrible beasts of the Daniel vision while the righteous are explicitly transformed into stars."); Collins, "Afterlife in Apocalyptic Literature," 131; Setzer, *Resurrection of the Body*, 16–17 ("combination of resurrection and transformation to a luminous, deathless state may be similar to Paul's image of a raised spiritual body in 1 Corinthians 15."). Transformation into the stars or heavenly bodies is referred to as "astral immortality." See Grabbe, *Judaic Religion*, 260; Segal, *Life After Death*, 265, 307, 491 (to be transformed into shining stars "can only mean to the Jews that they shall become angels."). Cf. Mark 12:24–27 (the only statement of Jesus concerning resurrection is that "when they arise from the dead, they neither marry nor are given in marriage, but are as angels in the heavens."). See Chilton, "Resurrection in the Gospels," 215–17. See also Wolfson, *Philo*, 1:366–85 (discussing unbodied souls or angels in the writing of Philo of Alexandria).

83. 2 Bar. 44:15, 51:2, 59:3, 64:7, 10.

84. Nickelsburg, *Jewish Literature*, 283. See Collins, "Afterlife in Apocalyptic Literature," 130–31.

and those who are first will rejoice, and those who are last will not be cast down. For each one of them will know that the predetermined end of the times has come. But the souls of the wicked, when they see all this, will be the more discomforted. For they will know that their torment is upon them and that their perdition has arrived.[85]

5. Sibylline Oracles 4

The term "sibyl" is used "to designate a woman who in a state of ecstasy uttered generally gloomy oracles about the future."[86] A collection of such oracles comprising fourteen books written in Greek are referred to as the Sibylline Oracles.[87] The fourth oracle in the collection is dated around 80 CE. The last lines in the oracle describe an end time and the universal destruction of all life brought about by God to vent his wrath on a wicked world. It then speaks of a resurrection for the purpose of judgment and reward or punishment. Specifically, it states:

> God himself will again form the bones and ashes of men, and he will raise up mortals again, as they were before. And then judgment will take place, in which God himself will pass judgment . . .[88]

Like 4 Ezra 7, Sibylline Oracles 4 describes the fate of those judged to be wicked as being cast into Gehenna, which is likened to the Greek Tartarus and River Styx (the river in Greek mythology that the souls of the dead were ferried across into Hades). In contrast, those judged to be righteous will be allowed to again live on the earth:

> And as many as sinned in impiety a heap of earth will cover again—dark Tartarus, and the Stygian recesses of Gehenna. But as many as are godly will live again on earth, When God gives breath and life and grace to them, the pious.[89]

Also like 4 Ezra 7, and unlike earlier texts, Sibylline Oracles 4 envisions a resurrection of all humans for the purpose of being judged for their deeds.[90] "The wicked are not specifically charged with the maltreatment of the righteous, nor are the latter given a new life because they have suffered in this life."[91] Rather, all are simply judged on the basis of how faithful they were to God's commandments, regardless of whether

---

85. 2 Bar. 30:2.
86. Nickelsburg, *Jewish Literature*, 193.
87. See generally Nickelsburg, *Jewish Literature*, 193–96; Collins, "Afterlife in Apocalyptic Literature," 135–36.
88. Sib. Or. 4:181–83. See Nickelsburg, *Resurrection, Immortality, and Eternal Life*, 174; Setzer, *Resurrection of the Body*, 15–16.
89. Sib. Or. 4:184–90. See Nickelsburg, *Resurrection, Immortality, and Eternal Life*, 174.
90. Nickelsburg, *Resurrection, Immortality, and Eternal Life*, 175.
91. Nickelsburg, *Resurrection, Immortality, and Eternal Life*, 175–76.

or not they had been rewarded previously. However, in contrast to 4 Ezra 7, no mention is made of storing souls and of restoring souls to the resurrected bodies. Commenting on this aspect of the Sibylline Oracles 4, John Collins notes: "The physical, earthly character of the resurrection here is remarkable in a text from the diaspora written in Greek but goes to show that Hellenistic culture did not always give rise to a belief in immortality of the soul, any more than Semitic culture necessarily gave rise to belief in resurrection of the body."[92]

E. *Sheol* Is Converted into *Gehenna*, a Place of Punishment for the Wicked, While the Heavens Are Seen as a Place of Reward for the Righteous

Special locations in the afterlife were created during the Second Temple period for the punishment and reward, respectively, of the wicked and the righteous. Such punishment and reward could be visited upon the resurrected body or upon the soul when it separated from the body, or, in some cases, initially upon a separated soul and subsequently upon a resurrected body.[93]

More specifically, *Sheol* is converted from its biblical concept, generally understood as a neutral place for all *rephaim* where there is neither reward nor punishment,[94] to *Gehenna*, a place of punishment for the wicked. As explained by Charles, this conversion occurred in two stages.[95] Before discussing these stages, however, the use of the word *Gehenna* as the name of the place where the wicked would be punished after death needs to be explained.

In preexilic times *Ge Hinnom*, the valley of Hinnom, or *Ge ben-Hinnom*, the valley of the son of Hinnom, was a large ravine on the southwestern corner of Jerusalem that was apparently both a city garbage dump and, more importantly, a place where altars to Canaanite gods had been built and where children had been passed through fire as a sacrifice to the Canaanite god Molech.[96] Thus, the valley came to be associated with burning, shame, and wickedness. In Isaiah 66:24, there is a clear reference to the valley of Hinnom as the place where the slain enemies of the messianic kingdom should suffer by fire in the presence of the righteous.[97]

The Greek translation of the Bible, the Septuagint,[98] transliterated the Hebrew name *Ge Hinnom* as *Gehenna*. Since *Gehenna* (or *Gehinnom*) was associated as a place

---

92. Collins, "Afterlife in Apocalyptic Literature," 136.
93. See ch. 3 (discussing the emergence of the concept of the soul in Jewish thought).
94. See ch. 1, sec. D.
95. Charles, *Book of Enoch*, 168n10.
96. See 2 Kgs 16:3, 23:10; 2 Chr 28:3, 33:6; Jer 7:31, 32:35; Neh 11:30; Segal, *Life After Death*, 135; Bernstein, *Formation of Hell*, 167–68.
97. See Charles, *Book of Enoch*, 100n1.
98. See ch. 3, sec. A, 1.

of wickedness, and as a place where the wicked should perish by fire, and since, in general, the punishment imagined for the wicked included being destroyed by fire as in the case of the residents of Sodom and Gomorrah,[99] *Gehenna* came to be seen as the place where the wicked will be punished by fire in the afterlife. In numerous places *Gehenna* is described as an "abyss . . . full of fire" (1 En. 90:26) or a place where there is "a burning worse than fire" (1 En. 100:9).[100]

In 1 Enoch 26:2-3, Uriel, one of the angels guiding Enoch on a cosmic tour, shows Enoch a deep and narrow ravine between two mountains.[101] Enoch inquires as to the purpose of the valley between the mountains, and Uriel replies:

> "This accursed valley is for those who are accursed forever: here will all those be gathered who utter unseemly words with their lips against God, and speak hard things of His Glory; here will they be gathered, and here is the place of their punishment. And in the last days there will be the spectacle of a righteous judgment upon them, in the presence of the righteous continually forever."[102]

Returning now to the conversion of *Sheol*, the first stage of its conversion from the biblical concept of *Sheol* to *Gehenna* occurred in the second century BCE and "was the product of the same religious thought that gave birth to the doctrine of Resurrection—the thought that found the answer to its difficulties by carrying the idea of retribution into life beyond the grave."[103] In this stage, *Sheol* "became essentially a place where [the souls of] men [as distinguished from the biblical *rephaim*] were treated [during an intermediate period] according to their desserts with a division for the righteous, and a division for the wicked."[104]

The first stage in the conversion of *Sheol* is illustrated by 1 Enoch 22, discussed below.[105] Enoch is shown the place (presumably in *Sheol*) where the spirits or souls of the dead are kept until the day of final judgment. Thus, rather than being the unending abode of the departed, *Sheol* becomes an intermediate place where souls are stored until the day of final judgment.[106]

In the second stage of its conversion, *Sheol*

> no longer signified the intermediate state of the righteous and of the wicked, but came to be used of the abode of the wicked only, either as their preliminary

---

99. Gen 19:24. See also Ps 21:8-9; Mal 4:1; Isa 66:15-16.
100. Raphael, *Jewish Views of the Afterlife*, 90.
101. See ch. 3, sec. B, 2.
102. 1 En. 27:2-3. See Collins, "Afterlife in Apocalyptic Literature," 122 (In Enoch we have "the beginnings of the idea of Hell."); Bernstein, *Formation of Hell*, 179-99.
103. Charles, *Book of Enoch*, 168n10.
104. Charles, *Book of Enoch*, 168-69n10.
105. See ch. 3, sec. B, 2.
106. See also 1 En. 51:1 (in the day of final judgment "the earth [will] give back those who are treasured up with it, and *Sheol* also will give back that which it has received . . ."); 4 Ezra 7.

abode … or as their final one … This was probably due to the fact that the Resurrection was limited to the righteous, and thus the souls of the wicked simply remained in *Sheol*, which thus practically became hell or Gehenna …[107]

Alongside the conversion of *Sheol* to *Gehenna* as the place of punishment for the resurrected wicked, the notion of heaven was created as the place of reward for the resurrected righteous in those cases in which resurrection was not intended for participation in a restored nation of Israel here on earth.[108] The notion of heaven as the abode of the righteous has biblical roots in passages concerning Enoch and Elijah. As discussed above,[109] in the genealogy contained in chapter 5 of Genesis, the description of Enoch (vv. 21–24) is unique. All other persons mentioned in the genealogy are said only to have lived a certain number of years and then to have died. However, regarding Enoch it is said, not that he died, but that he "walked with God" and that "he was not, for God took him." This description suggested that Enoch did not die, but was "taken" by God, and God's abode is, of course, in the sky, or in "the heavens."[110] Similarly, it is said of Elijah that he will be "taken," and then, later, Elijah ascends by a fiery chariot into the sky.[111] Thus, there existed in biblical material some limited association of the sky, or the heavens, with a place where certain select righteous are taken, perhaps to live eternally, just as in Homer, Menelaus does not die but is taken to the Elysian Fields to live forever.[112]

By the second century BCE the place to which Enoch is taken by God had come to be associated with the Garden of Eden.[113] This might be because Enoch is said to have "walked with God," and "Adam is described as having walked with God in Eden at the cool of the day (Gen 3:8)."[114] Raphael states: "Prior to the first century B.C.E. Heaven, or paradise (the Hebrew term is *Pardes*, meaning 'orchard'), had been the abode of only two individuals: Enoch and Elijah, both of whom had never died, but ascended to the heavenly realms. However, in the apocryphal era, Heaven becomes

---

107. Charles, *Book of Enoch*, 169n10. See 4 Ezra 7 and Sib. Or. 4. Here it is worth recalling that already in preexilic times there may have been an effort to restrict the inhabitants of *Sheol* to only the wicked. See ch. 1, sec. D (discussing the view of Madigan and Levenson).

108. See Davies, "Death, Resurrection, and Life After Death," 191 ("once 'Sheol' ceases to be seen as a neutral place, accommodating good and wicked alike, and becomes a place of punishment … then the heavens correspondingly invite the righteous, as the place of eternal bliss for the righteous.").

109. See ch. 1, sec. G.

110. Segal, *Life After Death*, 154–55.

111. 2 Kgs 2:10–11. See ch. 1, sec. G.

112. Homer, *Od.* 4:631–36. See Rohde, *Psyche*, 1:55–61; Guthrie, *Orpheus and Greek Religion*, 151; Burkert, *Greek Religion*, 198. It is also possible that the idea of heaven among hellenized Jews was influenced, to at least some extent, by Plato's conception of the earth's upper region as a place of reward. See Plato, *Phaed.* 109a–114d.

113. See ch. 1, sec. G (quoting *Jub.* 4:22–25). See also Raphael, *Jewish Views of the Afterlife*, 97–99.

114. Segal, *Life After Death*, 154.

somewhat democratized and is conceived of as the final resting pace of the righteous and the elect"; it is "conceived as a 'garden of righteousness' (1 Enoch 77:3) and the 'garden of the righteous' (1 Enoch 90:23)."[115]

During the Second Temple period, the association between Enoch and an ascension to heaven is elaborated upon. In 1 Enoch, there is an account of Enoch's journey up to heaven and then out to the ends of the cosmos. In 2 Enoch (a work preserved only in Slavonic manuscripts which translate an original Greek text dated to the first century CE) the account of Enoch's journey is expanded to include a tour of seven heavens.[116] Enoch tells how he was taken up in his sleep by two angels to each of the seven heavens in succession. In the first and fourth heavens he sees the celestial phenomena—the sun, moon, stars, etc.[117]—which is comparable to what he sees in 1 Enoch 17:1—18:6; 33–36; and 72–77. In the second heaven the fallen angels are imprisoned, but most significant for present purposes is the third heaven. It is here that he beholds the celestial paradise with its tree of life from whose roots four streams flow, one of honey, one of milk, one of wine, and one of oil.[118] This, he is told, is the place prepared for the righteous as an eternal inheritance. Also in the third heaven, however, is a place of torture with a fiery river as well as ice and cold, to burn and to freeze various classes of sinners.[119] Clearly, this tradition stands somewhat in opposition to the tradition that comes to be more generally accepted, which makes the place of punishment—*Gehenna*—underground.

F. The Belief in Resurrection Was Not Accepted by All Jews

It is important to keep in mind that the belief in resurrection of the dead that emerged in Jewish thought during the Second Temple period was not a belief embraced by all Jews. Some Jews opted to accept the belief that there is a reward and punishment after death, but to reject the belief that the body can be reconstituted after death so as to receive such reward or punishment. These people choose to accept the Greek idea that

---

115. Raphael, *Jewish Views of the Afterlife*, 92.

116. For a general discussion of 2 Enoch, see Nickelsburg, *Jewish Literature*, 221–25. See also Raphael, *Jewish Views of the Afterlife*, 94–96; Bernstein, *Formation of Hell*, 178–202 (discussing 1 Enoch). The seven heavens first recur in the vision of Levi in the Testaments of the Twelve Patriarchs. See T. Levi, ii, 3. For a brief discussion of apocalyptic writings that take the form of an ascent of a visionary through the heavens, see Collins, "Afterlife in Apocalyptic Literature," 131–35.

117. 2 En. 3–6, 11–17.

118. Cf. Gen 2:10–14 (referring to four streams that branch off the river that issues from Garden of Eden). See Levenson, *Resurrection and the Restoration*, 87.

119. The fact that paradise is not located in the highest heaven, but in the third heaven, is explained as a result of the third heaven being, at one time, the highest heaven (Collins, "Afterlife in Apocalyptic Literature," 133). Also, though in "earlier Jewish, and general Near Eastern tradition, the abode of the dead was always in the Netherworld . . . Hellenistic cosmology . . . had no place for a Netherworld, and so philosophical authors increasingly located Hades in the heavens" (Collins, "Afterlife in Apocalyptic Literature," 133).

humans have a *psyche* or soul which is separate from the body and which can survive the destruction of the body to receive a postmortem reward or punishment. The introduction into Jewish thought of this concept of a soul is discussed in chapter 3.

Moreover, many people accepted neither the belief in resurrection of the dead nor the belief in an immortal soul. Rather, they maintained the dominant biblical view that death is the common lot of all human beings, that from death there is no return, and that after death we can receive neither reward nor punishment. Such a viewpoint can be seen clearly in the book variously called Sirach, Ecclesiasticus, or the Wisdom of Ben Sira, and can also be inferred from documents found in the caves of Qumran, the so-called Dead Sea Scrolls. Further, such a view is ascribed by the Jewish historian Josephus to the group called the Sadducees, and is ascribed to unidentified people in other texts.

1. The Wisdom of Ben Sira[120]

This work was written a few years prior to the persecutions of Antiochus IV.[121] It employs the traditional form of the proverb in order to teach the author's views of right and wrong and their consequences. However, these consequences all come *in this life*.[122] Ben Sira mentions neither resurrection of the dead nor reward or punishment for an immortal soul. Death is followed by a gloomy existence in *Sheol*, from which there is no reprieve.[123] The reader is admonished to: "Give, take, and treat yourself well, for in the netherworld [*Sheol*] there are no joys to seek."[124]

2. The Dead Sea Scrolls

In the winter of 1946/1947 a treasure trove of ancient scrolls was found in the limestone cliffs near the northwest shore of the Dead Sea in the vicinity of Qumran. These materials have been dated between 250 BCE and 60 CE.[125] Archeological excavations at Qumran have revealed two phases of Jewish occupation there between 100 (or 130) BCE and 68 CE, when the Roman army overran the site during the Jewish War.[126] The Qumranites are believed to have been part of a substantial reform movement, perhaps a splinter group among the people called Essenes by Josephus.

Examination of the Dead Sea Scrolls reveals that the Qumranite sect held a worldview that was to some degree dualistic. Although God created everything,

---

120. For a general discussion of this work, see Nickelsburg, *Jewish Literature*, 53–63.
121. Moore, *Judaism in the First Centuries*, 2:316; Nickelsburg, *Jewish Literature*, 62.
122. Nickelsburg, *Jewish Literature*, 61.
123. Nickelsburg, *Jewish Literature*, 61 (citing Sir 40:1—41:13).
124. Sir 14:16–17. See Segal, *Life After Death*, 254–55.
125. Nickelsburg, *Jewish Literature*, 119.
126. Nickelsburg, *Jewish Literature*, 120.

among God's creation are two cosmic beings that exercise supervision over human beings: the Prince of Lights and the Angel of Darkness.[127] Some human beings, called the sons of light, follow the Prince of Lights, and some human beings, called the sons of darkness, follow the Angel of Darkness. However, the cosmic battle is fought not only between the two groups but "within the human heart, and people act according to their particular proportions of light and darkness . . ."[128] Corresponding to the two groups are two ways of acting—the ways of the righteous and the ways of the wicked.

Notwithstanding concern with conflict between good and evil, "[t]he published Scrolls of Qumran . . . contain not a single passage that can be interpreted with absolute certainty as a reference to resurrection or immortality."[129] Nickelsburg suggests that the absence of such a reference may be due to the fact that these materials "make no reference to a persecution unto death which requires a post-mortem vindication," and they do not "speak of injustices and oppression in this life that need to be adjudicated after death."[130] But whatever the reason, the lack of any explicit mention of a postmortem reward or punishment evidences that the primary concern of the Qumranites was with this life and not another one after death.[131]

3. Texts referring to the Sadducees' denial of an afterlife

The Sadducees were a Jewish group, active in the Second Temple period, described by the Jewish historian Josephus[132] and referred to in the New Testament. The name "Sadducee" derives from the Hebrew *zeduqi* and means "a descendant or adherent of Zadok the priest."[133] The Sadducees were an aristocratic and priestly segment of society that saw themselves as descendants of Zadok the priest.[134] As described by

---

127. Nickelsburg, *Jewish Literature*, 139.

128. Nickelsburg, *Jewish Literature*, 140.

129. Nickelsburg, *Resurrection, Immortality, and Eternal Life*, 179. But see Gillman, *Death of Death*, 104 (stating that the Dead Sea Scrolls contain "few references" to the doctrine of resurrection, but citing the Messiah Apocalypse as having such reference); Segal, *Life After Death*, 299 (relies on the Messiah Apocalypse in saying that "the Qumranites believed in resurrection of the dead"); Johnston, *Shades of Sheol*, 229–30. Reliance on the Messiah Apocalypse may be misplaced. According to Nickelsburg, the Messiah Apocalypse is not "demonstrably a Qumran sectarian text" (Nickelsburg, *Resurrection, Immortality, and Eternal Life*, 12).

130. Nickelsburg, *Resurrection, Immortality, and Eternal Life*, 205.

131. But see Nickelsburg, *Resurrection, Immortality, and Eternal Life*, 206–9 ("In spite of [its] general lack of concern about death, the Scrolls do refer to eternal life and use other eschatological vocabulary."). See generally Davies, "Death, Resurrection, and Life After Death," 195–210 (although "there is no statement of a doctrine of resurrection" it is likely that the Qumranites "embraced a variety of beliefs about personal survival beyond death"); Collins, *Jewish Wisdom*, 185 ("the dominant expectation of afterlife in the Dead Sea Scrolls, as found especially in the Hodayot, also avoids resurrection language but speaks instead of exaltation and fellowship with the angels.").

132. See ch. 3, sec. D.

133. Cohen, *From the Maccabees to the Mishnah*, 152.

134. Cohen, *From the Maccabees to the Mishnah*, 153; Segal, *Life After Death*, 376. Zadok was

Josephus, the Saducees denied any type of life after death.[135] Similarly, the Gospels and Acts of the New Testament relate that the Sadducees deny the resurrection of the dead,[136] and Avot of Rabbi Nathan asserts the Sadducees "erroneously concluded that there is no reward and punishment in the next world and no resurrection of the dead."[137]

4. Other texts evidencing the rejection of a meaningful afterlife

Several texts which express a belief in a postmortem reward and punishment juxtapose this belief with the opposite belief held by others, evidencing that these unnamed others rejected the view that there can be any reward or punishment after death. Instead, these others embraced the biblical view that all meaningful existence ends at death. Thus, for example, the Wisdom of Solomon[138] expresses the point of view of certain "godless men" as follows:

> . . . they said to themselves, reasoning in their faulted way:
>
> our life is short and full of trouble;
>
> there is no remedy at man's end,
>
> and no one has been known to have returned from the grave.
>
> By mere chance did we come to be,
>
> and thereafter we shall be as though we had never been,
>
> for the breath in our nostrils is but a puff of smoke;
>
> our reason is a mere spark within our throbbing heart,
>
> and when that is extinguished, our body will turn to ashes,
>
> and our life breath will be scattered like thin air.
>
> Our name will be forgotten with the passage of time,
>
> And none will recall our deeds . . .
>
> Come then, let us enjoy the good things at hand,
>
> And make use of creation with youthful zest.
>
> Let us take our fill of costly wine and perfumes,

---

installed by King Solomon as chief priest in place of Abiathar after the latter participated in Adonijah's attempt to seize the throne (1 Kgs 2:35). However, it is not certain that the name "Sadducees" was derived from a connection with this particular Zadok (Moore, *Judaism in the First Centuries*, 1:69–70). See generally Glatzer, *Hillel the Elder*, 17–18.

135. Josephus, *Ant.* 18:16. See Cohen, *From the Maccabees to the Mishnah*, 138–39; Segal, *Life After Death*, 376; Setzer, *Resurrection of the Body*, 24–26.

136. Matt 22:23–33; Mark 12:18–27; Luke 20:27–38; Acts 23:6–9. See Chilton, "Resurrection in the Gospels," 21. See generally Setzer, *Resurrection of the Body*, 26–32.

137. Cohen, *From the Maccabees to the Mishnah*, 149. See generally Setzer, *Resurrection of the Body*, 33–36.

138. See ch. 3, sec. A, 2.

and let no spring blossom pass us by.

Let us crown ourselves with rosebuds before they wither . . .

Let us tyrannize the poor honest man,

let us not spare the widow,

nor reverence the elder's hair long grey . . .

they were ignorant of God's mysteries;

they entertained no hope that holiness would have its reward . . .[139]

Although it may likely be that the "godless men" being referenced are gentiles,[140] there is no reason why some Jews may not also be included among the godless, as the view attributed to the godless is similar to the view attributed to Jews by Qoheleth and Ben Sira. Further, similar views are ascribed in 1 Enoch 94–104 to "the sinners" who seem clearly to be Jews, as they are those who "disregard the foundation and the eternal inheritance from their fathers."[141]

---

139. Wis 2:1–22.

140. See generally Winston, *Wisdom of Solomon*, 63–64 ("author is primarily addressing his fellow Jews"); Clarke, *Wisdom of Solomon*, 4 (book was addressed, in part, to "fellow Jews who had abandoned the faith of their fathers").

141. 1 En. 99:1. See Nickelsburg, *Resurrection, Immortality, and Eternal Life*, 142; ch. 3, sec. A, 3.

3.

During the Second Temple Period, Greek Ideas about the Soul and the Afterlife Penetrate Jewish Thought and are Used to Resolve the Problem of Moral Evil

AFTER ALEXANDER THE GREAT conquered the Persian empire in the late fourth century BCE, Greek language and ideas spread throughout the Middle East and beyond. In particular, Alexandria, a city which Alexander the Great built in Egypt, became home to a large population of diaspora Jews who quickly adopted the Greek language and culture. This Alexandrian Jewish population produced out of its midst a school of philosophers who consciously, deliberately, and systematically set about remaking Greek philosophy according to a Jewish pattern of belief and tradition.[1] The most important and prolific of these Alexandrian Jewish philosophers is one named Philo.

Recognizing the merit of the Greek philosophers, the Scripture-trained Jews came to see Judaism as a philosophy that not only had much in common with Greek philosophy but, having a divine origin, was superior to it. According to Wolfson, the pre-Philonic Alexandrian Jewish philosophers desired to present Judaism as a philosophy like that of the Greek philosophers; yet,

> they constantly stress certain fundamental differences. The Jewish God indeed is incorporeal and free of emotions as is the God of the philosophers, but still He is not without personal relation to man. He can be prayed to. God has established a fixed order of nature, but still He can miraculously change that order. God is providence, as philosophers say, but His providence is individual: He rewards and punishes . . . The soul is immortal as philosophers say, but it is also destructible as a punishment.[2]

As is suggested by the last sentence just quoted, in gaining a knowledge of Greek philosophy, the Jewish Hellenistic philosophers came to embrace the Platonic idea of

---

1. See Wolfson, *Philo*, 1:4.
2. Wolfson, *Philo*, 1:26.

an immortal soul—a soul that may survive the death of the body—or, at least, something akin to the Platonic idea of an immortal soul. This idea was attractive to the Jews in part because it provided a satisfactory answer to the problem of moral evil that had arisen following the abandonment of intergenerational and collective reward and punishment.[3] On the basis of the Platonic doctrine of a *psyche* or soul,[4] the problem of moral evil is resolved in a manner fundamentally similar to the solution offered by the doctrine of the resurrection of the body—if God's judgment is not imposed on someone while they are living, it can be imposed on that person, or on that person's soul, after they die. Indeed, part of what attracted Plato himself to the notion of an immortal soul was precisely that it provided a means for the punishment of those wicked persons who escaped punishment in this life.[5]

Unlike Plato, however, the Hellenistic Jewish philosophers of Alexandria, being "Scripture-trained," could not accept a doctrine, however attractive, that was not based in the teaching of the Torah. Therefore, the Jewish philosophers looked for and found scriptural evidence for their belief in the immortality of the soul and for their belief that immortality permitted God to reward righteous conduct performed in the here and now.[6] The attempt of the Jewish philosophers to find the origin of beliefs about the soul in scriptural texts was essentially the same as the attempts of Palestinian rabbis to find the origin of beliefs about bodily resurrection in scriptural texts.[7] There was a difference, however, in the method each used to interpret the scriptural texts. The Jewish Alexandrian philosophers, but not the Palestinian rabbis, primarily used the allegorical method.[8] Despite its novelty,

> [t]he readiness with which Philo, and . . . his predecessors among Hellenistic Jews, adopted the allegorical interpretation was facilitated by the fact that in Jewish tradition the Jew was not bound to take his Scripture literally. What is known in Judaism as the Oral Law meant freedom of interpretation of the scriptural text, whether dealing with some legal precept or some historical or some theological doctrine. Every verse in Scripture, whether narrative or law, was subject to such free interpretation.[9]

---

3. See ch. 2, sec. B.

4. By a "Platonic" soul is meant an entity that gives a person life, constitutes all the psychological and emotional aspects of a person, exists separate from the body, and survives the destruction of the body to receive a reward or punishment. It thus implies a dualistic point of view (soul vs. body) that is foreign to the biblical concept of a person. For a complete discussion of Plato's concept of a soul, see Robinson, *Plato's Psychology*, 3–157.

5. See Plato, *Phaed.* 107c ("If death were a release from everything, it would be a boon for the wicked.").

6. See Wolfson, *Philo*, 2:302–3.

7. See Wolfson, *Philo*, 1:397 ("Hellenistic Jews undoubtedly must have been engaged in a similar search for proof-texts [as the Palestinian rabbis]."). See also ch. 4, sec. E.

8. See generally Wolfson, *Philo*, 1:115–38.

9. Wolfson, *Philo*, 1:133.

For one who accepts the concept of a Platonic soul, resurrection of the body is not only unnecessary but makes little sense since death under the Platonic doctrine is understood as the separation of an immortal soul from a mortal body. The body, being mortal, disintegrates; the soul, being immortal, perdures and may receive a postmortem reward or punishment. In short, while Jews living in Palestine, and mostly of the lower socioeconomic class, were developing the idea of bodily resurrection of the dead to explain the martyrdom of the righteous for their religious views, hellenized Jews, mostly living in the diaspora and mostly from the higher socioeconomic class, were developing a different idea, taken from Greek philosophy, to resolve the same theological problem.[10] The different idea developed by the hellenized Jews was the idea of an immortal soul which receives a reward or punishment in an afterlife for conduct exhibited in this life.[11] Both ideas—the bodily resurrection of the dead and the immortality of the soul—were attractive to Jews of the Second Temple period for the same reason, namely, they each offered a solution to the problem of moral evil. There were even Jews who affirmed *both* the concept of a Platonic soul *and* the concept of a future bodily resurrection.

Texts of the Second Temple period incorporating into Jewish thought the idea of a soul and/or the idea of the soul's reward or punishment in an afterlife are discussed below in section A. Texts which combine the concept of a soul with the concept of bodily resurrection are discussed in section B. The ideas of Philo concerning the soul and its immortality are presented in section C. Philo offers by far the most extensive body of work—all written in Greek—of any Alexandrian Jew. Section D considers the relevant portions of the writings of the famous Jewish historian Flavius Josephus, and section E summarizes the evolution of Jewish thought during the Second Temple period with regard to these matters.

A. The Idea of a Platonic Soul, and Its Reward and Punishment in an Afterlife, Is Introduced into Jewish Thought by Hellenized Jews

1. The Septuagint brings the idea of a *psyche* into Jewish thought

The Septuagint is the Greek version of the Hebrew Bible.[12] Sometime in the third century BCE the Jews living in Alexandria had become so hellenized that many of them could no longer speak Hebrew and thus required that the Torah be translated into Greek.[13] After this was done, the other books of the Hebrew Bible were also translated into Greek. The completed work, with the inclusion of some books whose Hebrew

---

10. Even those who opted for resurrection as opposed to the immortality of the soul as the means to resolve the theological problem of moral evil may nonetheless have accepted the idea that man is composed of both body and soul. See Eichrodt, *Theology of the Old Testament*, 2:150.

11. See Wolfson, *Philo*, 1:396. See also Eichrodt, *Theology of the Old Testament*, 2:526–27.

12. See generally Nickelsburg, *Jewish Literature*, 192–93 (discussing the Septuagint).

13. Cohen, *From the Maccabees to the Mishnah*, 200.

originals have not been preserved or which were written originally in Greek, is known as the Septuagint.[14]

Several passages in which the Hebrew text refers to God's power to preserve life, such as Deuteronomy 32:39 and 1 Samuel 2:6, are translated in the Septuagint so as to refer to resurrection.[15] The Septuagint more blatantly alters other biblical passages to make them also endorse resurrection.[16] Though the Septuagint thus evidences the emergence of the doctrine of resurrection of the dead, according to Segal there are no passages which "unambiguously insert the immortality of the soul."[17] Similarly, Freudenthal argues that an analysis of how certain key Greek psychological terms (including *psyche* and *nous*) are used in the Septuagint "unequivocally" demonstrates that the translators were not familiar with how these terms were used in Greek philosophy.[18] Freudenthal concludes that Greek philosophy was not even known to the translators of the Septuagint, and that the "Septuagint bears no traces of the inroad of Greek philosophy into Jewish Hellenism."[19]

Even if the analyses of Segal and Freudenthal are meritorious and the Greek translators of the Torah did not intentionally insert a belief in the immortality of the soul into their translations, it also is true that the Septuagint's Genesis translates the Hebrew word *nephesh* in virtually all instances by the Greek word *psyche*.[20] Such instances include Genesis 2:7.[21] Thus, those later-day Jews who read the Septuagint, and who *were* familiar with the philosophical use of the Greek term *psyche* to designate the soul in contrast to the body, would find it very natural to interpret passages such as Genesis 2:7 as referring to an immortal soul. Furthermore, since later-day Jews interpreted the Bible allegorically, modifications made to the Hebrew text to make the Septuagint endorse a belief in resurrection could also easily be, and were, understood by them to endorse a belief in the immortality of the soul. Thus, it may fairly be argued that the Septuagint helped to incorporate the Greek idea of an immortal soul or *psyche* into Jewish thought.

---

14. Cohen, *From the Maccabees to the Mishnah*, 200.
15. Segal, *Life After Death*, 363–67.
16. Segal, *Life After Death*, 366.
17. Segal, *Life After Death*, 366.
18. See Freudenthal, "Are There Traces of Greek Philosophy?," 209–13.
19. Freudenthal, "Are There Traces of Greek Philosophy?," 222.
20. Pietersma and Wright, *New English Translation of the Septuagint*, 2 ("In the 41 of the 43 contexts in which [the word *nephesh*] is found (95%), the [Septuagint] translator's equivalent is [*psyche*].").
21. See Brenton, *Septuagint with Apocrypha*, 3. But see Winston, *Wisdom of Solomon*, 287.

2. The Wisdom of Solomon postulates immortality of the soul as a reward God grants to the righteous but denies to the wicked

"The *Wisdom of Solomon* is an exhortatory discourse written in Greek by a learned and thoroughly hellenized Jew of Alexandria some time after that city's conquest by Rome, in 30 BCE."[22] However, chapters 2 and 4–5 may have been composed in the second century BCE.[23] The author of this text is concerned with the problem of moral evil, and he uses the idea of an immortal soul to resolve the problem.[24]

The author begins by exhorting those "who rule the earth" to love justice because no one who acts unjustly will escape God's notice.[25] He next sets forth the point of view of the wicked. The wicked claim that this life is "short and full of trouble" and that there is no afterlife ("no one has been known to have returned from the grave").[26] Accordingly, the wicked say that one should "enjoy the good things at hand" by any possible means, including tyrannizing the poor and defenseless members of society and taking advantage of, and persecuting, those who are righteous.[27] But, says the author of the Wisdom of Solomon, by entertaining no hope that righteousness will be rewarded, the wicked pass up "the prize of unblemished souls," that prize being the soul's reward of a peaceful eternal afterlife.[28] The physical death of the just is in reality only the beginning of a better existence, inasmuch as their souls will enjoy a blissful immortality, a reward reserved only for the righteous.[29] The author writes:

> But the souls of the just are in God's hand,
>
> And torment shall in no way touch them.
>
> In the eyes of the foolish they seemed to be dead;
>
> Their end was reckoned as suffering
>
> and their journey hence utter ruin.
>
> But they are at peace.
>
> For even if in the sight of men they shall have been punished,
>
> Their hope is full of immortality . . .[30]

---

22. Winston, *Wisdom of Solomon*, 3. But see Clarke, *Wisdom of Solomon*, 2–3.
23. Nickelsburg, *Resurrection, Immortality, and Eternal Life*, 102.
24. See Nickelsburg, *Resurrection, Immortality, and Eternal Life*, 67, 113.
25. Wis 1:1. Translations of this text are from Winston.
26. Wis 2:1.
27. Wis 2:6–17 (quoted in ch. 2, sec. F, 4). Cf. Qoh 8:10—9:3.
28. 2:22–23.
29. See Winston, *Wisdom of Solomon*, 125; Wolfson, *Philo*, 1:409.
30. Wis 3:1–4. See Winston, *Wisdom of Solomon*, 125 ("The author assures his readers that the physical death of the just is in reality only the beginning of a better existence, inasmuch as their souls would enjoy a blissful immortality . . ."). But see Porter, "Pre-Existence of the Soul," 88 (arguing that the phrases "souls of the just" (or "souls of righteous men") and "unblemished souls" (or "blameless souls') "are not conclusive proof that immortality belongs to the soul apart from the body.").

Although the Jewish writer of these lines is universally believed to have acquired a belief in the existence of an immortal soul from Platonic and Stoic sources, he clearly has modified the acquired concept, for the idea that the soul's immortality is a reward granted by God to the righteous, but denied to the wicked, is not part of any Platonic or Greek notion of *psyche*.[31] Moreover, Porter has persuasively argued that despite using the Greek word *psyche* (soul) and distinguishing the *psyche* from the *soma* (body), the author's world outlook is more Hebraic than Greek—he sees human beings more holistically than is allowed by Platonic dualism. In Porter's words: "The writer is a Jew writing Greek; and when he uses [*soma*] and [*psyche*] for the two parts of human nature he inevitably thinks of man somewhat more dualistically than he would have done had he been writing in Hebrew. But he is still a Jew, and man still consists, in his thought, in the union of these two parts, and not in either one alone . . ."[32] Yet, a distinction between *psyche* and *soma* is made in Greek, and, being a Jew, it is natural for the author to associate the Greek concept of *psyche* with the life-giving energy that man receives from God—the breath of God—and to state, in verse 15:11, that God "infused him with an active soul [*psyche*] and breathed into him a vital spirit."[33] But because of his Hebraic outlook he does not, as required by Platonic doctrine, view the physical part of human nature as a hindrance to the *psyche* or identify the body as the source of sin; nor does he see a need, as required by Platonic doctrine, to disassociate himself from his body by living an ascetic life. To the contrary, according to Porter: "The contrast between [*psyche*] and [*soma*] is like that of Prov. 11:17 rather than that of Greek dualism. The words are Greek but the thought is Hebraic. Man is a unity, and his character, good or bad, belongs to both of the two parts of which he is composed."[34]

Seeing man as a unity, the author of the Wisdom of Solomon cannot fully follow Platonic doctrine and associate his essential being with his soul alone. He does, however, seem to associate his essential being with his *psyche* more than with his body. Porter explains the move from an Hebraic view of man—which understands man as a psycho-physical unity—to a Greek or Platonic view of man—which understands man dualistically, as a *psyche* imprisoned in a *soma*—as follows: "When Jews began to speak Greek and called the two parts of man [*soma*] and [*psyche*] they would naturally use [*psyche*] of that which God breathed into man, the neshamah or ruah, and then

31. See generally Wolfson, *Philo*, 1:407–10.

32. Porter, "Pre-Existence of the Soul," 68. See also Porter, "Pre-Existence of the Soul," 59 (The "breath or spirit of God seemed to the Hebrews to belong to God to such a degree that for a long time they did not even individualize each man's share in it, still less connect with it the man's personal consciousness. It remained more natural for them to apply the personal pronoun to the pre-existing body than the pre-existing neshamah . . . But we should expect the idea to arise in the course of time that the breath of God also was for each man in some sense a distinct entity.").

33. See Porter, "Pre-Existence of the Soul," 63, 71 ("The [soul or spirit] of man is what God breathes into him, and is first of all vitality, life itself."). See also Winston, *Wisdom of Solomon*, 287 (the author of the Wisdom of Solomon is following the distinction made by the Greek physician Erasistratus of Alexandria between a "*pneuma psychikon*" (an "active soul') and a "*pneuma zotikon*" (a "vital spirit").

34. Porter, "Pre-Existence of the Soul," 65.

the thought would be in easy reach that the personality, the 'I,' might associate itself as well with that part of the future man which comes from above as that part which come from below."³⁵ Then, after Jews had been immersed in Hellenistic culture for centuries, the author of the Wisdom of Solomon decides to associate his personality *more* with his soul than with his body. The critical passage is 8:19–20:

> I was, indeed, a child well-endowed,
> having had a noble soul fall to my lot;
> or rather being noble I entered an undefiled body.³⁶

The original thought, expressed in the first two lines, is that the author's personhood is to be associated with his embryonic body into which a soul is breathed by God.³⁷ But then it "occurs to him that it would be better to connect the personality with the soul, and to say [in the third line] that the body was happily matched to the soul, rather than that the soul was matched to the body."³⁸

This passage, 8:19–20, also seems to evidence that its author believed that the soul preexists the coming into being of the body, an idea which is clearly Platonic.³⁹ But, again, according to Porter, the outlook of the author is still more Hebraic than Platonic—he does not associate the preexisting *psyche* with the self, as does Plato. In Porter's opinion:

> His [*psyche*] may have been a somewhat more independent and personal being than the neshamah of the rabbis, but I think not much more; and so far as preexistence is concerned he seems to me to have had nothing but the Jewish conception, namely this: The neshamah, which God has created, remains his and in his keeping before and during and after the life of man. It is not the man's self, the person, but is an individualization and personification of that breath or spirit of God which is the life of man, and, uniting with the earthly body, make him a living being. The preexistence of this neshamah was no doubt thought of as real; but since it was not the man himself, its preexistence was of more significance for the conception of God than for that of man. It

---

35. Porter, "Pre-Existence of the Soul," 70.
36. Wis 8:19–20.
37. See Porter, "Pre-Existence of the Soul," 68.
38. Porter, "Pre-Existence of the Soul," 68. See also Winston, *Wisdom of Solomon*, 199 ("The expression *mallon de* [or rather] is often used, as here, to correct and state with greater precision what was first stated more loosely.").
39. See Winston, *Wisdom of Solomon*, 198 (verse 8:19 "is as clear a statement of the concept of preexistent souls as one could wish"). See also Winston, *Wisdom of Solomon*, 25–32; Collins, *Jewish Wisdom*, 185; Hirsch, *Rabbinic Psychology*, 175. But see Porter, "Pre-Existence of the Soul," 63–95; Clarke, *Wisdom of Solomon*, 9–10, 61 (although these verses "develop the idea that the personality resides in the soul," the author "did not fully develop the Greek idea of the pre-existence of the soul" and did not consider the soul and the body "as two independent substances"); Urbach, *Sages*, 1:235–36.

expressed the idea that God foreknows and has predetermined the number and lot of all men.[40]

Also Platonic is a possible reference to rational and irrational parts of a soul in 4:12.[41] Yet, the Platonic idea of *metempsychosis* or transmigration of souls "does not appear to be part of our author's thinking."[42] Nor is there any reference to the Platonic doctrine of *anamnesis*, that the soul had knowledge prior to being implanted into a body, forgets such knowledge when implanted, and must recollect such knowledge thereafter.[43] Further, in contrast to the Platonic position that the soul is inherently immortal, in the Wisdom of Solomon the soul acquires immortality as a result of a person's actions, which is why only the souls of the righteous are immortal.[44]

Although the text gives no indication as to whether the soul is viewed as an immaterial entity, as Plato views the soul in *Phaedo*,[45] that the author of the Wisdom of Solomon was acquainted with *Phaedo* may be gleaned from the statement of the godless that "our life breath will be scattered like thin air,"[46] for in *Phaedo* the doubters of the Platonic view contended that when the *psyche* is released from the body "it may be dissipated like breath or smoke, and vanish away."[47] In any event, the Wisdom of Solomon does *not* agree with Plato that the soul's reward is attained by shunning the body, despite acknowledging that "the perishable body weighs down the soul."[48]

The reward of the just and the punishment of the wicked occur immediately after physical "death," although "the righteous man does not really die."[49] The reward of the

40. Porter, "Pre-Existence of the Soul," 113.

41. Winston, *Wisdom of Solomon*, 29 (also noting that there is no reference to the tripartite soul of Plato's *Republic*).

42. Winston, *Wisdom of Solomon*, 198. Accord, Winston, *Wisdom of Solomon*, 28.

43. Winston, *Wisdom of Solomon*, 29.

44. Nickelsburg, *Resurrection, Immortality, and Eternal Life*, 222; Nickelsburg, "Judgment, Life-After-Death, and Resurrection," 154 ("Different from Platonic thought . . . the soul is not inherently immortal"); Winston, *Wisdom of Solomon*, 30, 63 (whereas for Plato souls "have a natural claim to immortality . . . the author of Wisdom places the emphasis not on this natural claim but on whether or not one has lived a life of righteousness."); Porter, "Pre-Existence of the Soul," 85–87.

45. In the *Phaedo* Plato does not specifically state that the *psyche* is immaterial. He says only that *psyche* "is more like" immaterial things and the body "is more like" material things, and that *psyche* is "*very nearly* indissoluble" (Phaed. 79c–80b; emphasis added).

46. Wis 2:3.

47. Phaed. 70a. See Porter, "Pre-Existence of the Soul," 55 (some scholars find "conclusive proof" that the writer of the Wisdom of Solomon had read the *Phaedo* in the parallel between 9:15 in the former and 81c in the latter). See also Porter, "Pre-Existence of the Soul," 85–87.

48. Wis 9:15. See Winston, *Wisdom of Solomon*, 207–8 (discussing Platonic motif concerning bodies weighing down the soul); Porter, "Pre-Existence of the Soul," 62, 72–75 (discussing the relation between 9:15 to *Phaedo*, 81c, and commenting that, in contrast to Platonic thought, the Wisdom of Solomon "contains no ascetic doctrine").

49. Nickelsburg, *Resurrection, Immortality, and Eternal Life*, 113–14. See Nickelsburg, "Judgment, Life-After-Death, and Resurrection," 154 ("Rewards and punishments are received at the time of one's physical demise.").

just person is, again, to attain "immortality."⁵⁰ After separation from their bodies, the souls of the just are "portrayed as being in the hand of God and perfectly at peace."⁵¹ For the just, according to the text, "their reward is in the Lord…"⁵² And as Winston notes, "Conversely, the wicked who had oppressed their weaker brothers with apparent impunity, become ignominious carcasses, eternal objects of outrage among the dead."⁵³ Regarding any further reward and punishment at a possible end time, the text is unclear,⁵⁴ but, according to some, "the author does not know the resurrection of the body."⁵⁵

Isaiah 56:1–5 is suggested as scriptural support for the belief in immortality. The passage in Isaiah promises a reward (specifically, "an everlasting name which shall not cease") to those that are righteous and keep the sabbath, even if they are eunuchs; and the promised reward is proclaimed to be "better than sons and daughters."⁵⁶ With the passage from Isaiah in mind, the author of the Wisdom of Solomon proclaims that those who are virtuous will ultimately be rewarded, even if they are eunuchs or are otherwise sterile in life; and, conversely, "the swarming multitude of the wicked [sc., their illicitly conceived progeny] will be of no profit."⁵⁷ In short, it is better to be childless and virtuous than fruitful and promiscuous, for in virtue there is immortality but in vice there is death. The full passage reads:

> Blessed indeed is the barren woman who is unstained,
>
> who has not gone to bed in sin,
>
> she shall be fruitful at the great assize of souls.
>
> And the eunuch who has not acted unlawfully
>
> or meditated wickedness against the Lord
>
> will receive the exquisite gift of grace in return for his steadfastness…
>
> It is better to be childless, provided one is virtuous,
>
> for in virtue's remembrance there is immortality,
>
> since it wins recognition both from God and from men…

---

50. Wis 3:4. See also Wis 5:15 ("the just live forever").

51. Winston, *Wisdom of Solomon*, 32. See Wis 3:1.

52. Wis 5:14.

53. Winston, *Wisdom of Solomon*, 32. See Nickelsburg, *Resurrection, Immortality, and Eternal Life*, 67 ("The thesis of Wisdom of Solomon 1–6 is that unrighteousness leads to death and destruction (1:12; 5:9–14), while righteousness leads to life and immortality (1:15, 5:15).").

54. See Nickelsburg, *Resurrection, Immortality, and Eternal Life*, 113–14; Winston, *Wisdom of Solomon*, 32–33.

55. Porter, "Pre-Existence of the Soul," 56. But see generally, Porter, "Pre-Existence of the Soul," 87–95, 112–13 (we cannot assume that the author shared the rabbinical idea that "the reunion of soul and body, the resurrection, is necessary to a true life of man after death," but, given his conception of the soul, we also cannot assume that resurrection is unnecessary).

56. Isa 56:5.

57. Wis 4:3.

CHAPTER 3.

> But the swarming multitude of the wicked will be of no profit;
>
> sprung from bastard shoots they will not strike deep root
>
> nor secure a firm footing . . .
>
> For children who are the product of illicit sex
>
> are witnesses against their parents' vice on their day of scrutiny.[58]

Referring to the line stating that it is "better to be childless, provided one is virtuous," Wolfson comments:

> What the author is really trying to do in this verse is to quote as proof-text for the belief in the immortality of the soul a verse from Isaiah with regard to childless persons who keep justice and do righteousness. Concerning such childless persons God says: 'I will give them, in my house and within my walls, a memorable place, better than sons and daughters; I will give them an everlasting name which shall not cease.' [Isa 56:1–5] We can almost hear the voice of the author asking himself, after the manner of Palestinian rabbis: 'What does the expression "an everlasting name which shall not cease" mean?' And his answer is, again after the manner of Palestinian rabbis: 'You must admit, it cannot mean anything else but immortality.'[59]

3. First Enoch 102–104[60]

First Enoch is a fragmentary survival of an entire apocalyptic literary work that once circulated under that name. These various materials were attributed to Enoch on the basis of Genesis 5:24, which states that "Enoch walked with God; then he was no more; for God took him." First Enoch contains several originally independent texts that were combined by a later redactor. There are extant texts of 1 Enoch in Ethiopic and Greek.[61]

First Enoch 102–104 belongs to that portion of 1 Enoch (specifically, chapters 92–105) which is referred to as the "Epistle of Enoch." These chapters of 1 Enoch are said by Charles to have been written between 134 and 94 BCE.[62] The author of the document, writing in the name of the biblical Enoch, composed an epistle ostensibly

---

58. Wis 3:13—4:6.

59. Wolfson, *Philo*, 1:397. See also Winston, *Wisdom of Solomon*, 132 (commenting on the phrase "the eunuch," Winston states: "The reference is clearly to Isa 56:3–5, where the prophet refers to those Jewish youth who were castrated at the hands of the Babylonian tyranny, and consequently despaired of any share in Israel's future redemption (Deut 23:1–2).").

60. See generally Nickelsburg, *Resurrection, Immortality, and Eternal Life*, 141–55; Nickelsburg, *Jewish Literature*, 110–14.

61. For a discussion of 1 Enoch and, especially, the Epistle of Enoch, see Nickelsburg, *Jewish Literature*, 43–53, 110–14; Charles, *Book of Enoch*, 25–33; Nickelsburg, *1 Enoch 1*, 430–55; Collins, "Afterlife in Apocalyptic Literature," 121–25; Raphael, *Jewish Views of the Afterlife*, 84–85.

62. Charles, *Book of Enoch*, 28. Accord, Nickelsburg, *Resurrection, Immortality, and Eternal Life*, 143.

for Enoch's children, on the basis of knowledge Enoch received during his tour of the heavenly realm. As is true of all apocalyptic literature, the aim of the work is to address the issue of the suffering of the righteous on earth; that is, to address the problem of moral evil. As discussed above, difficulties arise from the disparity between the reward that the righteous (either the nation Israel or, more typically, the righteous individuals of the nation) have been promised and the reality of what the righteous have actually received.

The main section of the epistle (94:6—104:8) describes the wicked ways of "the sinners" and assures "the righteous" that, if they remain steadfast, they shall ultimately receive the reward they have been promised, for God's "day of judgment" is near. The announcement of the coming judgment reaches its climax in 102:4—104:8. The righteous who have died, and whose "souls" are in *Sheol* (along with the souls of the wicked), are addressed as follows:

> Fear not, souls of the righteous, and be hopeful, you who have died in righteousness, and do not grieve because your souls have descended in grief into Sheol, and the body of your flesh has not fared in your life according to your piety.[63]

The writer continues by setting forth the obituary that the living sinners speak over the dead righteous—"As we die, so die the righteous; and what have they gained from their deeds?"[64] The sinners also (1) state that fellow sinners "have died in splendor and wealth," and that "judgment has not been executed on them in their life," and (2) indicate that they consider this life to be the only place of reward and punishment.[65] The writer next addresses the righteous dead in response to the claims of the sinners. He does not presume a resurrection of the body but says instead:

> Good things and joy and honor have been prepared and written down for the spirits of those who die in righteousness, and much good will be given to you in place of your toils ... And the spirits of you who have died in righteousness will live and rejoice and your spirits will not perish.[66]

Addressing the righteous who are still alive, the author states that they "will not have to hide on the great day of judgment," but that they will shine "as the light(s) of heaven," that "the portals of heaven will be opened for [them]," and that they "will be companions with the hosts of heaven."[67] Grabbe describes these occurrences as an instance of "astral immortality."[68] In contrast, the sinners are told that their sins are

---

63. 1 En. 102:4–5; See Nickelsburg, *Resurrection, Immortality, and Eternal Life*, 145.
64. 1 En. 102:6b–c. See Nickelsburg, *Resurrection, Immortality, and Eternal Life*, 146.
65. 1 En. 103:5d–6d. See Nickelsburg, *Resurrection, Immortality, and Eternal Life*, 147.
66. 1 En. 103:3a–4b. See Nickelsburg, *Resurrection, Immortality, and Eternal Life*, 148.
67. 1 En. 104:2c–6d. See Nickelsburg, *Resurrection, Immortality, and Eternal Life*, 150–51.
68. Grabbe, *Judaic Religion*, 259. Presumably, astral immortality in this case entails a transformation of the spirit, rather than a bodily transformation, but Grabbe does not so state. See also Wolfson,

"searched out and written down,"[69] and that their souls (or spirits) will be made to descend to *Sheol* where they will experience great anguish, darkness, burning flame, and will have no peace.[70]

In sum, the epistle does not resolve the problem of moral evil by resorting to the doctrine of a resurrection of the body at the time of judgment (the end time) but instead relies on the reward or punishment of the soul or spirit. As explained by Nickelsburg:

> [Although the writer] mentions the fact that the bodies of the righteous have been mistreated in life (102:5), he does not say that these bodies will be given new life. It is their spirits that will live and not perish, and for which good things are prepared. Similarly it is the spirits of the sinners that will descend into Sheol to face judgment and torment. At death, the spirits of the righteous descend to Sheol (102:5). At the judgment they will leave Sheol and ascend to heaven along with the righteous who are still alive.[71]

Thus, if Grabbe is correct in stating that at the time of judgment the living righteous will experience astral immortality, presumably the spirits of the dead righteous, which at the judgment will ascend to heaven, will similarly experience astral immortality at that time, while the spirits of the wicked will remain in *Sheol*.[72]

Collins considers the Epistle of Enoch to be an example of what he terms "the resurrection of the spirit" as distinguished from both bodily resurrection and the Platonic concept of rewarding and punishing an immortal soul. With regard to the Epistle of Enoch, Collins writes:

Philo, 1:398–99, 402 (linking 1 Enoch 104:2 ("Now ye shall shine as the lights of the heaven") to the view Wolfson associates with the Stoic philosopher Chryssipus, that the soul "will upon the death of the body mount to heaven and there assume the spherical shape of the stars," and linking 1 Enoch 104:6 ("Ye shall become companions to the hosts of heaven") to the view Wolfson associates with Plato in the *Phaedrus* and with Philo, "that the immortal souls find their final abode in the heavens by the side of the angels [Philo] or demons [Plato]").

69. 1 En. 104:7b.

70. 1 En. 103:7a–8c. See Nickelsburg, *Resurrection, Immortality, and Eternal Life*, 149 ("spirits"); Charles, *Book of Enoch*, 294 ("souls").

71. Nickelsburg, *Resurrection, Immortality, and Eternal Life*, 155. See also Grabbe, *Judaic Religion*, 259 ("The *Epistle of Enoch* assumes that the spirits of the righteous will be rewarded at death and the spirits of the wicked punished in Sheol."); Raphael, *Jewish Views of the Afterlife*, 93 ("in 1 Enoch we encounter a clear dualism of body and soul. At the end of the second century B.C.E., the notion of a dualistic separation between eternal spirit and mortal body emerges as a fully integrated philosophical concept, at least within the Hellenistic Jewish world. As a result, sacred writings of the apocryphal period speak about a postmortem soul, or spirit, existing totally independent of the physical body. Long after mortal destruction of the body, this spirit persists, experiencing due compensation in the postmortem realm.").

72. See Nickelsburg, *Resurrection, Immortality, and Eternal Life*, 155 (the text might imply that "the sinners will be brought up out of Sheol for judgment and then led down there again to be tormented," a sort of resurrection, but this isn't clear).

The reward of the righteous is to share the eternal, spiritual life of the angels in heaven. This is not the Greek idea of immortality of the soul, but neither is it the resurrection of the body. Rather it is the resurrection, or exaltation, of the spirit from Sheol to heaven. The bodies of the righteous will presumably continue to rest in the earth. A similar understanding of the resurrection is found explicitly in the book of Jubilees, another writing from the second century B.C.E. that may be some decades later than the Epistle of Enoch. There we are told that at a future time when people return to the path of righteousness their lives will grow longer until the number of their years becomes greater than once was the number of their days. After that 'their bones shall rest in the earth, and their spirits shall have much joy' [*Jub.* 23:26–31].[73]

It is important to mention that in the Greek text of chapter 103 of the Epistle of Enoch the words used to designate the immortal soul or spirit fluctuate between *psyche* and *pneuma*, and in the Ethiopic text of chapter 103 of the Epistle of Enoch the words used to designate the immortal soul or spirit fluctuate between *nafs* and *manfas*. Nickelsburg explains that the Greek word *psyche* (usually translated "soul") generally corresponds to the Ethiopic *nafs* and to the Hebrew *nephesh*, while the Greek word *pneuma* (usually translated "spirit") generally corresponds to the Ethiopic *manfas* and the Hebrew *ruach*.[74] He speculates that the fluctuation in both the Greek and Ethiopic texts "may witness to an overlapping in the meanings of the two words . . ."[75] The exact nature of the entity referenced by either *psyche/nafs* or *pneuma/manfas* (for instance, whether it conceived as something material or immaterial) is nowhere discussed.

4. The Testament of Abraham[76]

The Testament of Abraham was composed in Egypt in the late first century or early second century CE.[77] The text tells the story of events immediately preceding the death of Abraham. The archangel Michael is told by God to inform Abraham that the time of his death has arrived and that he should make his testament, or will. "The expectation is that the patriarch will voluntarily surrender his soul . . . [but Abraham] tells Michael that he wants to see all the wonders of the earth before he moves on to the next stage of existence."[78]

---

73. Collins, "Afterlife in Apocalyptic Literature," 124. See also Grabbe, *Judaic Religion*, 260 ("in Jubilees we appear to have resurrection of the spirit only (*Jub.* 23:22–31)").

74. Nickelsburg, *Resurrection, Immortality, and Eternal Life*, 154n45.

75. Nickelsburg, *Resurrection, Immortality, and Eternal Life*, 154n45.

76. For a discussion of the *Testament of Abraham*, see Nickelsburg, *Jewish Literature*, 322–27.

77. Collins, "Afterlife in Apocalyptic Literature," 136; Grabbe, *Judaic Religion*, 263; Nickelsburg, *Jewish Literature*, 327.

78. Segal, *Life After Death*, 503.

Michael takes Abraham in a chariot and shows him the inhabited world. Then Abraham is given a tour of heaven. He is shown many souls (of sinners) passing through a broad gate for destruction, and only a few souls (of the righteous) passing through a narrow gate to life or paradise. He is also shown Abel, the son of Adam, passing judgment on the souls. "Both scenes imply that the soul goes to its eternal destiny shortly after death. A bodily resurrection is not envisioned."[79]

As explained by Grabbe, "judgment of each individual seems to take place immediately after death, and the emphasis is on immediate judgment of the soul while the body rests in the grave."[80] Although the Testament of Abraham thus evidences the belief that reward or punishment is received by an immortal soul immediately after death, Collins asserts that such belief is a "re-conception" of the belief in "the resurrection of the spirit."[81] To the extent that Collins is correct, the author of the Testament of Abraham (as well as similar texts) simply eliminated the intermediate period found in the early apocalypses, during which period the "righteous souls" remained in *Sheol*, waiting for the day of judgment and their "resurrection" or heavenly ascent.[82] Moreover, Collins's assertion seems to suggest that the inchoate concept of a soul or spirit (*nephesh*) among Jews was that of a biblical *repha* or free soul to which other psychological aspects, associated with *ruach* or the life force, were added, mirroring to some degree the development of the Greek concept of a *psyche*.[83]

5. Fourth Maccabees[84]

Fourth Maccabees relates the same general account of the death of seven brothers and their mother during the persecutions of Antiochus IV as is related in 2 Maccabees

---

79. Nickelsburg, *Jewish Literature*, 326.

80. Grabbe, *Judaic Religion*, 263.

81. Collins, "Afterlife in Apocalyptic Literature," 129 ("In Alexandrian Judaism, the resurrection of the spirit is reconceived as the immortality of the soul.").

82. See also sec. B, 3.

83. The Greek concept of the *psyche*, which in the Homeric period was a shade, similar to the Hebrew *rephaim*, thereafter was used to describe various psychological functions of a human being, and also was adopted by the Orphic and Pythagorean cults and the mystery religions to refer to an immortal part of a human being considered to be divine or god-like. See generally Claus, *Toward the Soul*, 1–183; Adkins, *From the Many to the One*, 13–126; Rohde, *Psyche*, 3–462; Bremmer, *Early Greek Concept of the Soul*, 3–124; Guthrie, *Orpheus and Greek Religion*, 148–93; Bernstein, *Formation of Hell*, 21–129. See also Winston, *Wisdom of Solomon*, 126 ("In the extra biblical apocalyptic literature, the dead are no longer described as 'shades' but as 'souls' or 'spirits' and survive as individual conscious beings who may either enjoy a blissful existence as a reward for their righteousness or receive punishment for their wickedness. We find a similar distinction in Homer's view of the soul of the dead as a mere shadow or 'idol' (*eidōlon*) without conscious life, and the Orphic-Pythagorean view of the soul as something separable from the body, which must be kept pure and immaculate to enable it to return to its divine home after death.").

84. For a general discussion of this text, see Nickelsburg, *Jewish Literature*, 256–59; Nickelsburg, *Resurrection, Immortality, and Eternal Life*, 138–40, 199n105; Segal, *Life After Death*, 386–87.

7.[85] The story is told how Antiochus IV told the martyrs that they would be given positions of authority in government if they abandoned the laws of the Torah and adopted Greek ways, but that they would be tortured and killed if they refused to do so.[86] They, of course, refuse to violate the laws of the Torah, and they suffer the consequence. However, in 4 Maccabees (dated between 20 and 54 CE, and composed in the diaspora, possibly in Syrian Antioch)[87] the brothers never mention resurrection of the body; they never say, as in 2 Maccabees 7, that God will "raise [them] up" and that for Antiochus "there will be no resurrection." Instead, the author of 4 Maccabees repeatedly states that the brothers will not really die, but will be given "eternal life" and "immortality." It is also made clear that Abraham, Isaac, and Jacob "and all the patriarchs" have similarly been granted eternal life, "live to God," and will receive the brothers, presumably in heaven.

Although no specific mention is made of a soul that exists after the body is destroyed, since the bodies of the brothers are completely mutilated, it is reasonable to assume that what continues on eternally to live in God is the soul, which is seen as constituting the personhood of the brothers. Nickelsburg writes:

> Future resurrection of the body (2 Macc 7) is here replaced by immortality and an eternal life that begins at the moment of death.[88]

Relying on the language of 9:21–22 that one of the martyrs, in enduring the torture inflicted upon him, seemed "transformed by fire into immortality," Segal contends that the immortality envisioned is astral immortality.[89]

It should be noted that the punishment received by Antiochus IV is also different in 4 Maccabees than in 2 Maccabees. In the latter, the punishment is the failure to be resurrected. In the former it includes "eternal torture by fire."[90]

B. The Idea of a Soul Receiving Postmortem Reward and Punishment and the Idea of a Future Bodily Resurrection Are Combined in Certain Texts

1. Fourth Ezra 7 and 2 Baruch

As discussed above,[91] the authors of 4 Ezra 7 and 2 Baruch believed that (1) human beings possess souls—conceived as entities separate from their bodies, (2) souls leave

---

85. See ch. 2, sec. C, 2.
86. 4 Macc 8:6–8.
87. See Nickelsburg, *Jewish Literature*, 258.
88. Nickelsburg, *Jewish Literature*, 258. See Grabbe, *Judaic Religion*, 262.
89. Segal, *Life After Death*, 387.
90. 4 Macc 9:9. See also 4 Macc 13:15, 18:5, and Grabbe, *Judaic Religion*, 262 ("the wicked will be punished in fire"). But see Nickelsburg, *Jewish Literature*, 258n79; 4 Macc 18:17–18.
91. See ch. 2, secs. D, 3 and 4.

the body at death, and (3) the souls of the righteous are stored in chambers in the earth, and are protected by angels. At the time that people's bodies are resurrected, according to these same authors, the souls are taken from the chambers where they are being stored (or, if a soul of the wicked, taken from wandering the earth) and are rejoined to their bodies to receive judgment and recompense.

With reference to the immediate postmortem period, 4 Ezra 7, 79–101, states that "all souls appear before God soon after death to adore him. The souls of the wicked, being denied admission to the guarded chambers, wander about, grieving and sad. But the souls of the righteous are given seven days' freedom that they may understand better the divine plan, and at the end of this interval are gathered into the treasuries."[92]

2. First Enoch 22

Chapter 22 of 1 Enoch is found in a section of the work (chapters 20–36) which contains a tradition about a cosmic journey of Enoch in which Enoch is guided by a number of angels.[93] In this chapter Enoch is shown a deep and dark place inside a mountain (presumably associated with *Sheol*) where the spirits or souls of the dead are kept until the day of final judgment. "Here the righteous receive a foretaste of their coming bliss while the wicked are already suffering."[94]

On one interpretation of this chapter, Enoch is shown four compartments of the dead. One compartment is for "the spirits of the righteous, where there is a bright fountain of water."[95] A second compartment is for "sinners, when they die and are buried in the earth, and judgment has not been executed upon them in their life."[96] A third compartment is for those spirits of the righteous who have suffered a violent death.[97] The fourth compartment contains sinners who have been judged and punished prior to their death.[98] The spirits of the sinners in the second compartment are explicitly said to receive "great torment until the great day of judgment" at which time they will be "raised" from *Sheol*.[99] On the day of judgment the sinners in the second compartment will be "transferred to another place of torment, presumably Gehenna."[100] Nickelsburg explains:

---

92. Hirsch, *Rabbinic Psychology*, 269. See 4 Ezra 7, 79–101; Urbach, *Sages*, 1:240–41.

93. See Nickelsburg, *Jewish Literature*, 51–52; Moore, *Judaism in the First Centuries*, 2:301–3; Raphael, *Jewish Views of the Afterlife*, 86–94.

94. Nickelsburg, *Jewish Literature*, 52.

95. 1 En. 22:9. See Nickelsburg, *Resurrection, Immortality, and Eternal Life*, 168.

96. 1 En. 22:10. See Nickelsburg, *Resurrection, Immortality, and Eternal Life*, 168.

97. 1 En. 22:12. See Nickelsburg, *Resurrection, Immortality, and Eternal Life*, 169–70.

98. Nickelsburg, *Resurrection, Immortality, and Eternal Life*, 171.

99. 1 En. 22:11, 13.

100. Nickelsburg, *Resurrection, Immortality, and Eternal Life*, 169.

> The author appears to view this transferral as a kind of 'resurrection,' for he says that the spirits of the sinners in the other compartment 'will *not* be raised ... from there' ... He envisions a resurrection of *the spirits* of the sinners; their spirits, not their bodies, will be punished ... Although chapter 22 does not explicitly mention a resurrection of the righteous, it would be a unique passage if it envisioned only a resurrection of the sinners.[101]

Nickelsburg does not comment on the nature of the presumed resurrection of the righteous.

Regardless of how the nature of resurrection may have been envisioned, 1 Enoch 22, as 4 Ezra 7, is clearly different both from texts which simply mention the postmortem reward or punishment of the soul and from texts which simply mention a resurrection of the dead at the end time. Here we clearly have a two-step framework. A certain treatment of spirits or souls immediately after death followed by a resurrection of some sort for at least some of these spirits or souls at the end time, to be accompanied by a further reward and punishment.

It is also significant that in making *Sheol* the place where the spirits or souls of the dead reside from death until the end time, the nature of *Sheol* is transformed from a place where nothing of consequence happens to a place where rewards or punishments may be received.[102] The change in nature of *Sheol* parallels the change in the nature of Hades in Greek thought.

3. A reason for combining bodily resurrection with a postmortem reward and punishment for the soul may have been the failure of the expected end time to arrive

It has been suggested that the idea of a postmortem reward and punishment for the soul was combined with the idea of resurrection at an end time by apocalyptic writers who had been assuming that the end time was relatively close at hand. When the final judgment day didn't arrive as expected a need was felt that there be a more immediate dispensation of divine justice, a need "to understand why God had not yet intervened to save the righteous and punish the sinners."[103] According to Segal, "the delay of the

---

101. Nickelsburg, *Resurrection, Immortality, and Eternal Life*, 169–70 (emphasis original). See 1 En. 103:3–4 ("The spirits of those who died in righteousness shall live and rejoice"); Davies, "Death, Resurrection, and Life After Death," 193–95 (the "difference between Enoch and Daniel over whether the dead are raised bodily (Daniel) or in spirit (Enoch) is less important ... than what they share: a belief that the righteous will live forever in some (quasi?) angelic form"); Collins, "Afterlife in Apocalyptic Literature," 124 ("This is not the Greek idea of immortality of the soul, but neither is it the resurrection of the body. Rather it is the resurrection, or exaltation, of the spirit from Sheol to heaven."). See also Jub. 23:26–31.

102. See Raphael, *Jewish Views of the Afterlife*, 88–89 ("With the First Book of Enoch another new conception enters Jewish postmortem philosophy—the notion of Gehenna as a place of eternal damnation.").

103. Segal, *Life After Death*, 487.

apocalypse meant a turn to immortality of the soul and an interim 'waiting period' in which the souls were punished and rewarded in heaven before the end."[104]

A related development was the expanded use of the literary device of the cosmic tour, including tours of the seven heavens, like those in 1 Enoch, to include a tour of the punishments in hell.[105] The purpose of these angelically guided tours of hell was

> to confirm the moral nature of the universe, in contrast to the obvious and undeserved rewards that too many sinners and oppressors receive on earth. If the end is not just around the corner, if the end has not arrived in centuries, then it is no longer enough to think that God will punish the sinners at the end and reward the righteous there. Reward and punishment needs to be closer to the events of earthly existence. In short, there needs to be heaven and hell . . . The more that time passed without the good being rewarded by the end of the world, the more vindictive the faithful became against sinners . . . Hell was a convenient stick with which to whip the sinner and a great cautionary tale to encourage the faithful."[106]

C. Philo of Alexandria Adopts and Reads into the Torah an Essentially Platonic Concept of the Soul and its Immortality, but Modifies it to Better Harmonize with Other Jewish Beliefs

1. Philo used the allegorical method to reveal what he believed to be the hidden meaning of the Torah

"Philo lived in two worlds and imbibed the culture of both . . . [H]e believed that one could stand with one foot in each culture, that one could be, so to speak, a Jew and a Greek at the same time, and that the quest for truth could progress fruitfully through an appropriate synthesis of the two cultures."[107] Put differently, Philo saw the Torah as the true philosophy, and he also saw many of Plato's viewpoints as true. He attempted a reconciliation by effectively reading Plato's viewpoints into the Torah.[108] Of course, Philo didn't believe that he was reading Plato into the Torah any more than the Palestinian rabbis believed that they were reading the doctrine of bodily resurrection into

---

104. Segal, *Life After Death*, 487.

105. Segal, *Life After Death*, 487–88.

106. Segal, *Life After Death*, 488–89.

107. Nickelsburg, *Jewish Literature*, 217. Accord, Segal, *Life After Death*, 368; Hirsch, *Rabbinic Psychology*, 126; Guttmann, *Philosophies of Judaism*, 32. For an account of the life and works of Philo, as well as a listing of scholarly works on Philo, see Scholer, "Introduction to Philo Judaeus," ix–xvii; Schwartz, "Philo, His Family, and His Times," 9–31; Royse, "Works of Philo," 32–64.

108. See Hirsch, *Rabbinic Psychology*, 126 (Philo's objective was "to harmonize Jewish religious doctrine with Greek thought and to prove thereby that in Mosaic Law one could find instruction and perfect wisdom.").

the Torah. Both believed that they were only revealing the true meaning of the text. Philo writes:

> I venture not only to study the sacred commands of Moses, but also . . . to investigate each separate one of them, and to endeavor to reveal and to explain . . . things concerning them which are not known to the multitude.[109]

More specifically, Philo believed that there were philosophical truths in the Torah which were not known to the multitude because the multitude read the Torah literally. To get at the truths, he believed, the Torah had to be read allegorically. Allegory was a common hermeneutical method in the Greco-Roman period. The allegorical method entails reading the text as standing for or meaning something different than what the words literally say. A significant portion of Philo's works are commentaries on the Torah in which he provides an allegorical interpretation of each line.[110]

2. The Torah's hidden truth included for Philo an essentially Platonic concept of man as twofold (body and soul/mortal and divine), and an essentially Platonic concept of the soul

Philo reads both Genesis 1:26 and 2:7 (as well as many other biblical passages) allegorically in a way which incorporates Plato's view that man is composed of a corruptible body and an incorruptible soul which has both an irrational part and a rational part.[111] Philo maintains that it is absurd to read passages such as Genesis 2:7, which treat God anthropomorphically, in a literal manner. It is absurd to believe that God "breathes," as Genesis 2:7 states. Thus, the passage can only be properly read allegorically.

According to Wolfson, the difference between creatures which have souls and those which don't is explained by Philo in several passages.

> In one passage he says that the difference between them is that besouled creatures have sensation; in another passage he says . . . that besouled creatures have imagination . . . and impulse . . . adding that imagination is dependent

---

109. Philo, *Spec. Laws* 3, I (6). Translations of Philo are from Yonge. See Guttmann, *Philosophies of Judaism*, 26 (Philo "was sincerely convinced that he was not misrepresenting Judaism but revealing its deepest meaning.").

110. See generally Kamesar, "Biblical Interpretation in Philo," 77–85. See also Wolfson, *Philo*, 1:115–16.

111. Philo, *Alleg. Interp.* 1, XII (31)–XIII (41); *Alleg. Interp.* 3, XXXVIII (114–15). See Wolfson, *Philo*, 1:385–95; Zeller, "Life and Death of the Soul," 24. See also *QG* 1(4) (man "was formed out of dust and clay as far as his body was concerned; but he received his soul by God breathing the breath of life into his face, so that the temperament of his nature was combined of what was corruptible and of what was incorruptible."); Segal, *Life After Death*, 371 ("Man is made of flesh and spirit: the body is dust, though it is animated by divine spirit, which is not created but originates directly from the Lord . . . The body is created mutable and impermanent. The soul is immutable, immortal and permanent . . . So Philo called humanity the border between mortality and immortality."). See generally Grabbe, "Eschatology in Philo and Josephus," 165–69.

upon sensation; and in the third passage he says . . . that besouled creatures have sensation, imagination, and impulse. All this reflects Aristotle's statements that sensation is that which differentiates animal from plant, that imagination is never found by itself apart from sensation, and that animal cannot be appetitive . . . that is, cannot have what Philo calls impulse . . . without imagination.[112]

At any rate, Philo calls this kind of soul—which has sensation, imagination, and impulse—irrational [*alogos*], and he says that a part of the soul possessed by man is irrational. Although Philo refers to the irrational part of the soul of man as "earthlike,"[113] he does not mean that it is made of the element earth. What he means is that the irrational part of man's soul is mortal. Following Plato, Philo divides the irrational part of the soul into two component parts,

> the irascible [or spirited part, *thumikon*] and the concupiscent [or appetitive part, *epithymetikon*], locating the former in the chest and the latter in the abdomen. But, drawing also upon other classifications of the faculties of the soul which were common in his time, like Aristotle, he divides this irrational soul into the [nutritive, or vital, faculty and the sensitive faculty], or like the Stoics, he divides it into seven faculties, namely the five senses, speech, and generation.[114]

Again following Plato, Philo maintains that, in addition to the irrational soul that all animals have, man also has a rational soul or mind (*logos*).[115] And just as in Plato's *Timaeus*, where the rational soul is created by the Demiurge himself (and not the lesser gods who create the irrational soul),[116] so for Philo, the rational soul is created by God. Further, Philo, as Plato, generally assigns to the rational soul a place in the

112. Wolfson *Philo*, 1:386 (citing several works by Philo and Aristotle's *De Anima*).

113. Philo, *Alleg. Interp.* I, XII (31). See Wolfson, *Philo*, 1:387.

114. Wolfson, *Philo*, 1:389 (citing several works by Philo, Plato's *Timaeus,* and Aristotle's *De Anima*). Philo also refers to the Stoic division of the soul, consisting of a commanding faculty at the center with seven parts. See e.g., *Creation* XL (117); *Alleg. Interp.* 1, IV (11). More frequently Philo simply distinguishes between the rational and irrational parts of the soul. See e.g., *Heir* XXXV (167); Grabbe, "Eschatology in Philo and Josephus," 166 ("the really essential division is into rational and irrational soul"). See also Winston, *Wisdom of Solomon*, 29n41 (Philo "usually employs the bipartite division of the soul . . . sometimes the tripartite division of Plato's *Republic* . . . and at other times, the Stoic division"); Hirsch, *Rabbinic Psychology*, 127–28.

115. Wolfson, *Philo*, 1:389, 393. See also Urbach, *Sages*, 1:221 (Philo, following Plato, distinguishes in man three parts: "the body that is fashioned from clay, the animal vitality that is linked to the body, and the mind that is instilled in the soul, this being the Divine mind. Man is a synthesis of earthly substance and the spirit of God [*geodous ousias kai pneumatos theion*]. Man has been created both mortal and immortal—mortal in respect of his body, immortal in regard to his mind.") (citing *Creation* XLVI [134–35]).

116. Plato, *Tim.* 69c–70e ("Now of the divine, [the Demiurge] himself was the creator, but the creation of the mortal he committed to his offspring."). See Robinson, *Plato's Psychology*, 104–6. In other texts, such as *Phaedrus* 246a, Plato maintains that the soul is eternal, not created. See Wolfson, *Philo*, 1:389, 396.

body that is separate from the irrational soul, that place being, as in Plato's *Timaeus*, the head; but sometimes Philo places it in the heart, the heart being where the Stoics locate the entire soul and all its faculties, "for to them the rational faculties of the soul do not differ in their origin from the irrational faculties."[117] Unlike the irrational part of the soul whose faculties operate through, and are located in, various organs of the body, the rational soul, or mind, according to Philo, is "indivisible," and its separate faculties, such as intelligence, sagacity, apprehension, and prudence, "are not located in different parts of the body and do not operate through different organs of the body."[118] In other words, the rational soul is immaterial. It is also important to note that for Philo the rational soul "is graced by God with the power of free will by which it can control the desires and emotions of the irrational soul."[119]

Sometimes Philo uses the word "breath" [*pneuma*] to refer to the irrational soul, and in this usage, breath is something corporeal. But sometimes, based on his understanding of Genesis 2:7, Philo uses the word "breath" to refer to the rational soul, and in this usage, breath is something incorporeal.[120] Philo understands the passage that man is created in the image of God (Gen 1:26) as referring to the rational soul.[121] In interpreting another passage of Genesis, Philo writes:

> There are two ... parts of which we consist, the soul and the body; now the body is made of earth, but the soul consists of air, being a fragment of the Divinity, for 'God breathed into man's face the breath of life, and man became a living soul.' It is therefore quite consistent with reason to say that the body ... has nourishment which the earth gives forth ... but the soul ... is supported by nourishment which is ethereal and divine, for it is nourished on knowledge, and not on meat or drink, which the body requires.[122]

---

117. Wolfson, *Philo*, 1:392.

118. Wolfson, *Philo*, 1: 392.

119. Wolfson, *Philo*, 1:393. See also Hirsch, *Rabbinic Psychology*, 128 ("Endowed with reason, and able to choose and make decisions, the mind may be said to be the seat of virtue and vice.").

120. Wolfson, *Philo*, 1:394. See Philo, *Alleg. Interp.* 1, XII (31)–XIII (39); *Creation* XLVI (134–35). See also Hirsch, *Rabbinic Psychology*, 126 (Genesis 2:7 "suggested to [Philo] the Platonic conception of man as a combination of a material body and a divine, incorporeal soul").

121. Philo, *Creation* XXIII (69–70). See Hirsch, *Rabbinic Psychology*, 126 ("the statement that man was made in the image of God was taken [by Philo] to be a reference to the Platonic theory of Ideas, the image of God being an archetypical, immaterial form which served the creator as a model."). See also Philo, *Worse* XXIII ("Therefore, the faculty which is common to us with irrational animals, has blood for its essence. And it ... is ... a certain representation and character of the divine faculty which Moses calls by its proper name an image, showing by his language that God is the archetypal pattern of rational nature, and that man is the imitation of him, and the image formed after his model; not meaning by man that animal of a double nature, but the most excellent species of the soul which is called mind and reason.").

122. Philo, *Alleg. Interp.* 3, LV (161). See Termini, "Philo's Thought," 106 ("From the time of creation each man has in himself, in his mind, an image of the Logos, and on the basis of the spirit that was breathed into him, is able to know the creator and to remain in contact with Him.").

In sum, Philo conceives of humans, in a strictly Platonic way, as being *methorios*, that is, "on the border" between the material and immaterial, the mortal and the divine (or eternal), and the virtuous and evil.[123] Humans are mortal because, unlike purely incorporeal beings (such as angels and stars), human souls are entombed or imprisoned in a physical body which is associated with evil, is not part of the true self, and from which the rational soul must free itself to attain immortality.[124] Humans are divine or God-like because human beings possess a rational soul which is virtuous to the extent it avoids contamination by the body, constitutes the true self, and is potentially immortal. It is Philo's adherence to a strict Platonic dualism that distinguishes his outlook from that of both the author of the Wisdom of Solomon and the sages of the rabbinic period. In contrast to Plato, however, who (except in the *Timaeus*) speaks of the soul as ungenerated, Philo considers the soul to be generated, directly or indirectly, by God.

3. The rational soul, or mind, is immortal

The irrational part of the soul, for Philo, is, as the body with which it is closely associated, corruptible and mortal, but the rational part of the soul, or mind, is potentially incorruptible and immortal.[125] The proof text which Philo offers in support of the immortality of the mind is Genesis 15:15, which in the Septuagint reads: "But thou shalt go to thy fathers nourished with peace, in a goodly old age."[126] Commenting on this verse, Philo says:

> He [sc., Moses] here clearly indicates the incorruptibility of the soul, when it transfers itself out of the abode of the mortal body and returns as it were to the

---

123. See e.g., Philo, *Worse* XXII (82) ("every one of us . . . is two persons, the animal and the man. And each of these two has a cognate power in the faculties, the seat of which is the soul assigned to it. To the one portion is assigned the vivifying faculty according to which we live; and to the other, the reasoning faculty in accordance with which we are capable of reasoning."); *Creation* XLVI (135) ("man is on the boundaries of a better and an immortal nature . . . and that he was born at the same time, both mortal and immortal. Mortal as to his body, but immortal as to his intellect."). See also Philo, *Heir*, IX (45–46). The conception of human beings as *methoris*, with the divine part (the soul) being immortal for the righteous, finds expression in rabbinic texts. *Genesis Rabbah*, 8.11, states:

"Said the Holy One, blessed be He: 'Behold, I will create him [man] in [My] image and likeness, [so that he will partake] of the [character of the] celestial beings, while he will procreate, [after the nature] of the terrestrial beings.' R. Tifdai said in R. Aha's name: The Holy One, blessed be He, said: 'If I create him of the celestial elements, he will live [forever] and not die, and if I create him of the terrestrial elements he will die and not live [in a future life]. Therefore, I will create him of the upper and the lower elements: if he sins, he will die; while if he does not sin, he will live.'"

124. See Grabbe, "Eschatology in Philo and Josephus," 167 ("Human souls are of the same general substance as those who make up the ranks of angels and the stars. The difference is that in humans the souls are entangled with the body and the lower or irrational soul . . . The ultimate goal . . . [is] to escape the encumbrance of the body."); Wolfson, *Philo*, 1:366–85 (discussing unbodied souls or angels).

125. See Wolfson, *Philo*, 1:395–96. See also Winston, *Wisdom of Solomon*, 60–61; Hirsch, *Rabbinic Psychology*, 131; Grabbe, "Eschatology in Philo and Josephus," 167.

126. Wolfson, *Philo*, 1:398.

metropolis of its fatherland, from which it originally migrated into the body. Since to say to a dead man, 'Thou shalt go to thy fathers,' what else is this but to propose and set before him a second existence apart from the body...?[127]

This understanding of Genesis 15:15 is all but compelled by Philo's interpretation of Genesis 15:13 ("thy seed shall be a stranger in a land that is not theirs"). Regarding Genesis 15:13, Philo states: "[when] the [rational] soul . . . comes down from above . . . and enters a mortal and is sown in the field of the body, it is truly sojourning in a land which is not his own. Since the earthly nature of the body is wholly alien from pure Intellect . . ."[128]

The Jewish Alexandrian philosophers agreed that the soul is immortal but they disagreed as to the precise nature of that immortality, which is to say the nature of the fatherland to which the rational soul returns after its liberation from the body. This issue, in turn, related to differing views on the nature of the soul; whether, for example, it is material or immaterial. Wolfson expounds on the matter as follows:

> But what is that 'fatherland' intimated by the term 'thy fathers' in Scripture to which the soul returns? Besides his own view on the subject, Philo discusses elsewhere three other views, which . . . would seem to have been current among Hellenistic Jews who had adopted them from Greek philosophy . . .
>
> 'Some affirm,' he says, that the term 'thy fathers' refers to 'the sun, moon and other stars.' This evidently reflects the view of Chryssippus, according to whom immortality, which to him is confined to the wise, means that the soul, which consists of an element similar to that of the stars, will upon the death of the body mount to heaven and there assume the spherical shape of stars . . . For this view of immortality, these anonymous interpreters of the words 'thy fathers' must have found support in the scriptural verse, 'And they that are wise shall shine as the brightness of the firmament; and they that turn the many to righteousness as the stars for ever and ever.' [Dan 12:3] . . .
>
> 'Others think,' he continues, that the term 'thy fathers' refers to 'the ideas in which, as they say, the mind of the sage finds its new home.' This view is evidently based upon two statements in Plato . . . [and] they must have come to attribute to Plato the view that the immortal souls abide among the [Platonic Ideas or Forms], and hence to interpret 'thy fathers' to mean the [immaterial World of the Forms] . . .
>
> 'Others again have surmised that by "fathers" are meant the four first principles and potentialities of which the world is composed, earth, water, air and fire . . . [T]his interpretation of the term "thy fathers" reflects the view that

---

127. Philo, *QG* 3, 11. See Wolfson, *Philo*, 1:398. See also Philo, *Abraham* XLIV (258) (wisdom taught Abraham "that he was not to look upon death as the extinction of the soul, but rather as a separation and disjunction of it from the body, returning back to the region from whence it came; and it came, as is fully shown in the history of the creation of the world, from God.").

128. Philo, *QG* 3, 10.

the soul of each individual upon the death of the body is reabsorbed into the universal soul, that is, the primary fire or ether, of which it is only a part.

None of these three views could be acceptable to Philo. He could not accept the view that the souls become stars, for to him the stars are made of the element of fire, whereas the immortal souls are immaterial. For the same reason he could not accept the view that the souls are resolved into the primary fire or ether. Nor could he accept the view that the immortal souls go up to what Plato calls the supercelestial place to abide there among the ideas, for, to him, there is no supercelestial place such as conceived by Plato. His own view is that the souls, on departing from the bodies, do indeed go back to heaven, but there to rejoin that company of souls which have never descended into bodies, namely, angels."[129]

Philo expresses his view regarding the nature of the fatherland to which the rational soul returns in interpreting the biblical phrase used in the Septuagint with reference to Abraham (Gen 25:8), that he was "added to his people." Philo states: ". . . for Abraham also, leaving mortal things, 'is added to the people of God,' having received immortality, and having become equal to the angels; for the angels are the host of God, being incorporeal and happy souls . . ."[130]

4. Philo relies on the immortality of the soul to resolve the problem of moral evil

While reading the Platonic idea of an immortal soul into the Hebrew Bible, for Philo the rational part of the soul does not possess immortality as an inherent property (as it does for Plato), but immortality is granted by God.[131] God grants immortality, according to Philo, as a reward to the righteous, and

> since it is only by the providence of God that the soul of the righteous ceases to be mortal, it is quite reasonable [for Philo] to assume that the soul of the wicked never ceases to be mortal and never acquires immortality . . . The new element which [Philo] has introduced into the Platonic doctrine of the immortality of the soul is that by nature the soul is mortal, its immortality being due only to an act of divine grace.[132]

---

129. Wolfson, *Philo*, 1:358–401. But see Winston, *Logos and Mystical Theology*, 38 nn44 and 45.

130. Philo, *Sacrifices* II (5). See Wolfson, *Philo*, 1:401–3, and 401n44 ("In IV Macc. 13:17, the statement that 'when we shall have suffered thus, Abraham, Isaac and Jacob will receive us, and the fathers will praise us' would similarly seem to imply that the fathers, including Abraham, who are immortal souls and whose place is evidently in the heaven . . . have become equal to angels.").

131. Termini, "Philo's Thought," 109; Zeller, "Life and Death of the Soul," 24.

132. Wolfson, *Philo*, 1:410. See Wolfson, *Philo*, 1:416; Hirsch, *Rabbinic Psychology*, 130–31. According to Grabbe, however, one passage "suggests that just as the righteous go to heaven . . . the wicked are sent down to Tartarus," and Philo "also refers to punishment in Hades" (Grabbe, "Eschatology in Philo and Josephus," 168). This would imply the immortality of *both* the righteous and the

Philo puts it this way: Those "who die in the company of the pious" will receive "everlasting life . . . but everlasting death will be the portion of those who live in the other way."[133] Although Philo believes that the practice of virtue will be rewarded, he also urges "that man should practice virtue for its own sake."[134]

For Philo, to achieve immortality one must forsake bodily pleasure and the bonds which keep one tied to the material world, and must live virtuously, that is, according to the law. Conversely, to pursue bodily pleasure leads to transgression of the law, and prevents the soul (or it's rational part) from achieving immortality.[135] In other words, the immortality of the soul is in the end used by Philo to resolve the problem of moral evil.[136] Even if the virtuous person does not appear to be rewarded, he, in fact, is rewarded in that his soul will continue to live after the body in which it is imprisoned decomposes, and will go to heaven or a region above heaven; and even if the wicked person does not appear to be punished, he, in fact, is punished in that his wickedness (rule by passion rather than reason) results in the "death" of the soul, even while it is still embodied, and his soul will not go upward. As explained by Philo:

> The death of worthy men is the beginning of another life. For life is twofold; one is with the corruptible body; the other is without body incorruptible. So that the evil man dies 'by death'; even when he breathes, he is buried beforehand, as though he preserved for himself no spark at all of the true life, and this is excellence in character. The decent and worthy man, however, does not die 'by death,' but after living long, passes away to eternity . . .[137]

---

wicked, the one for reward in heaven, the other for punishment in Hades.

133. Philo, *Posterity* XI (39).

134. Wolfson, *Philo*, 2:297. See Wolfson, *Philo*, 2:294–97. Furthermore, "while in his discussion of divine providence Philo does not mention the fact that the wicked are sometimes dealt with kindly by God for the sake of the merit of their ancestors, we know that in several places of his writings he discusses this characteristically Jewish doctrine" (Wolfson, *Philo*, 2:292).

135. See e.g., Philo, *Creation* LIX (165); *Drunkenness* XXXV (140). Cf. Plato, *Crito* 47d–e (soul is made healthy by just actions, but damaged by unjust actions). See also Hirsch, *Rabbinic Psychology*, 129–30.

136. See generally Wolfson, *Philo*, 2:279–303. In these pages, Wolfson explains that the "problem of virtue and its reward presents itself in Greek philosophy and in Judaism after the same pattern. In both of them, it is assumed that in man there is a continuous struggle between two motive forces. In philosophy these forces are called emotion and reason; in Judaism they are called the evil imagination (*yeṣer ra', yeṣer ha-ra'*) and the good imagination (*yeṣer tob*) . . . These two traditions, the philosophic and the Jewish, are combined in Philo in his treatment of the same problem. The continuous conflict that goes on within man between good and evil is usually described by him in philosophic language as a conflict between the irrational soul and the rational soul or between emotion and reason. But it is also described by him in the traditional language of Judaism as a conflict between the evil *yeṣer* and the good *yeṣer* . . . Men are therefore urged by Philo, in the language of philosophy, to follow reason and virtue and, in the language of Scripture, to obey the commandments of the Lord their God, and as a reward for such a life of reason and virtue and obedience of the commandments he promises, in the language of philosophy, happiness and, in the language of Scripture, blessings" (Wolfson, *Philo*, 2:279, 288, 290).

137. Philo, *QG* 1 (16). See also Philo, *QG* 1 (51); *Flight* X (55). See Zeller, "Life and Death of the

Since Philo adopts the Platonic notion that we are composed of a corruptible, mortal body and a potentially immortal soul, and uses this belief to resolve the problem of moral evil, Philo had no need for the concept of resurrection of the body, and, as other Judeo-Hellenistic texts from Alexandria, makes no reference to such an idea. Nor does he place any emphasis on punishment of the wicked in Gehenna. However, though Philo only speaks of immortality of the soul, he describes this immortality in terms of resurrection. All references to bodily resurrection which Philo found in the traditional literature of his time, including references in the Septuagint (such as Isaiah 26:19 and Daniel 12:2) and in 2 Maccabees,

> were understood by him as being only a figurative way of referring to immortality. It is on this account . . . that he constantly draws upon the traditional vocabulary of resurrection to express his view of immortality . . . Such a restatement of the immortality of the soul in scriptural terms of the resurrection of the body is common in all the writings which consciously turned corporeal resurrection into something incorporeal. Thus the Ethiopic Enoch expresses itself in the language of bodily resurrection when it says that 'the righteous shall arise from their sleep,' for what it really means is a new incorporeal life, since it is only 'the spirits of you who have died in righteousness' that 'shall live and rejoice.'[138]

In accepting the Platonic idea of the immortality of the soul, Philo makes central to his notion of the Bible's message that the soul ascends through philosophical contemplation to achieve, ultimately, escape from the encumbrance of the body and communion with God. Indeed, for Philo salvation consists precisely in the achievement of this communion which is "based on knowledge and contemplation, is accompanied by peace and stability, and lasts for all eternity."[139] Accordingly, with Philo, salvation becomes primarily an individual matter; any concern with national or collective salvation is secondary for Philo.[140] Not surprisingly, therefore, both eschatology and messianism (the expectation of an earthly or celestial figure who will annihilate the enemies of Israel) have been said to be "absent from Philo's writings."[141]

Soul," 26–39; Termini, "Philo's Thought," 108. This idea that the righteous soul is eternal and that the wicked soul may be called dead even in life appears in rabbinic material. See Segal, *Life After Death*, 627 (quoting Tanh. b. Ber. 28b end); b. Ber. 18a–b ("The wicked, even in their lifetime, are called dead, but the righteous, even after death, are called alive.").

138. Wolfson, *Philo*, 1:404–6.

139. Termini, "Philo's Thought," 106. See Segal, *Life After Death*, 370 ("Philo . . . made central to his notion of the Bible's message an ascent to see God . . . Philo outlined a clear mystic allegory that culminates in the intellectual and spiritual ascent to heaven to the presence of God . . .").

140. Termini, "Philo's Thought," 106 ("The restoration of Israel . . in a historical and eschatological sense, is for Philo secondary."). See Grabbe, "Eschatology in Philo and Josephus," 169–72.

141. Termini, "Philo's Thought," 110. See Grabbe, "Eschatology in Philo and Josephus," 172–73 (Philo "says nothing about a cosmic cataclysm, the intervention of God at the end of history, a universal resurrection, or an end time judgment of all human beings."). But see Wolfson, *Philo*, 2:407–26 (discussing Philo's views on the Messiah and the messianic age).

D. Flavius Josephus Evidences a Belief in the Immortality of the Soul

Flavius Josephus is a Jewish historian born in Jerusalem in 37/38 CE. He is the author of the largest corpus of extant Jewish writings from the Second Temple period, and these works are a major source of information about this period.[142] Among his writings are the *Jewish War*, the *Jewish Antiquities*, and *Against Apion*. These works were written in Greek for a Greek and Roman readership.

At several places in his writings Josephus describes the views of "three schools of thought among the Jews," namely the views of the Pharisees, the Sadducees, and the Essenes.[143] He does not consistently provide specific information about the numbers of each group but he does say that the Sadducees are supported by "but a few" though they are "the people of highest standing," while the Pharisees "are extremely influential among the masses."[144] The Essenes "numbered only four thousand."[145] The only other Jewish group referred to by Josephus was not a philosophical school but a band of political activists, the Zealots. Thus, it seems that, as Josephus understood things, the three schools of thought include substantially all the major "philosophical" positions advanced by the Jews at the time.

Josephus depicts the beliefs of these three schools of thought in terms of their varying positions with regard to the soul and the afterlife. According to Josephus, the Essenes believed in the immortality of the soul. He writes:

> For this opinion is strongly held among them, that bodies are corruptible, and their material impermanent, but that souls will endure immortal forever; and that they come out of the most subtle air, and are united to their bodies as to prisons, into which they are drawn by a certain natural enticement; but that when they are set free from the bonds of the flesh, they then, as released from a long bondage, rejoice and mount upward.[146]

This description makes the opinion of the Essenes concerning the soul and the afterlife sound very much like the opinion of Philo. First, as Philo, the Essenes are described as dualists who distinguish between the corruptible, impermanent things (associated with the physical body) and the incorruptible, eternal things (associated with the soul). Second, the Essenes, as here described, see the soul as coming from a very rarified air, which sounds very much like Philo's understanding that the soul is immortal due to its being infused with the rarified air of God, that is, the *ruach elohim*, also called by Philo the breath of life. Third, both Philo and the Essenes, as described

---

142. For discussion of the life and writings of Josephus, see Nickelsburg, *Jewish Literature*, 288–96.

143. See e.g., Josephus, *Ant.* 13.5.9. See Cohen, *From the Maccabees to the Mishnah*, 119.

144. Josephus, *Ant.* 18.1.3–4. See Cohen, *From the Maccabees to the Mishnah*, 140.

145. Cohen, *From the Maccabees to the Mishnah*, 140.

146. Josephus, *J.W.* 2.8.11. See Nickelsburg, *Resurrection, Immortality, and Eternal Life*, 207. Accord, *Ant.* 18.1.5 ("the Essenes . . . regard the soul as immortal"). See Nickelsburg, *Resurrection, Immortality, and Eternal Life*, 208.

by Josephus, follow the Orphics and Pythagoreans in seeing the soul as "imprisoned" in the body. Finally, for both Philo and the Essenes of Josephus, once the soul (or, at least, the rational part of the soul of a righteous person) is released from its imprisonment in the body, it ascends upward to God. Josephus explicitly states that the opinion of the Essenes is "like the opinion of the Greeks" in that they envision a pleasant afterlife for virtuous souls and a very unpleasant afterlife for wicked souls. Josephus himself seems to have adhered to a

> radically dualistic anthropology very similar to that of Philo: 'All of us, it is true, have mortal bodies, composed of perishable matter, but the soul lives forever immortal: it is a portion of the Deity housed in our bodies.' (J.W. 3.8.5); cf. the words placed by Josephus in the mouth of the Zealot leader Eleazar at Masada: 'Life, not death, is man's misfortune. For death which gives liberty to the soul and permits it to depart to its own pure abode, there to be free from all calamity, but so long as it is imprisoned in a mortal body and tainted with all its miseries, it is, in sober truth, dead, for association with what is mortal ill befits that which is divine' (J.W. 7.8.7).[147]

Segal contends that Josephus's description of the Essenes is tendentious, that the Hellenistic audience for whom Josephus was writing would not understand the concept of resurrection, so Josephus translated the concept of bodily resurrection (which, says Segal, was the Essenes' actual belief) "into immortality of the soul, which his Hellenistic audience could understand more readily [than that of resurrection]."[148] Segal believes that evidence supporting the view that Josephus mischaracterized the position of the Essenes comes from the Dead Sea Scrolls since the Dead Sea Scrolls demonstrate, according to Segal, that the Qumran community, which is identified with the Essenes, believed in resurrection.[149]

Nickelsburg takes the opposite view. He argues that Josephus is correct in his description of the Essenes, and that the Essenes did, in fact, believe in the immortality of the soul but not resurrection.[150] As might be expected, Nickelsburg contends that the Qumran community believed in the immortality of the soul, not resurrection.[151]

---

147. Winston, *Wisdom of Solomon* 125–26. Accord, Porter, "Pre-Existence of the Soul," 54; Urbach, *Sages*, 1:222 (Josephus presents a "dualistic anthropology similar to Philo's in its extremism, but enunciated in rhetorical, homiletical fashion rather than in philosophical style... This concept lies at the heart of the oration that Josephus puts into the mouth of the leader of the Zealots at Masada...").

148. Segal, *Life After Death*, 298. See also Cohen, *From the Maccabees to the Mishnah*, 139.

149. Segal, *Life After Death*, 298–301 ("newly published passage puts the Dead Sea Scrolls clearly in line with those in the first century who accepted resurrection"). For relationship between Essenes and Qumran community, see Segal, *Life After Death*, 296 ("The Dead Sea Scrolls are now normally identified as Essene writings."); Cohen, *From the Maccabees to the Mishnah*, 146 ("likely that the Qumran community was a community of Essenes."); Nickelsburg, *Resurrection, Immortality, and Eternal Life*, 180n5, 206 ("I accept the identification of the Qumranites with the Essenes").

150. Nickelsburg, *Resurrection, Immortality, and Eternal Life*, 206–9.

151. See Nickelsburg, *Resurrection, Immortality, and Eternal Life*, 179–209.

In partial support of his position that Josephus's description of the Essenes is correct, Nickelsburg points to Josephus's description of the views of the Pharisees. Of the Pharisees, Josephus says in *Jewish Antiquities*:

> It is their belief that souls have an immortal power . . . Eternal imprisonment is allotted to some (those of the wicked) but to others (those of the virtuous), an easy passage to a new life [*anabioyn*].[152]

In the *Jewish War*, he says of the Pharisees:

> Every soul, they maintain, is imperishable but the soul of the good alone passes into another body, while the souls of the wicked suffer eternal punishment.[153]

According to Nickelsburg, the reference to "an easy passage to a new life" is a reference to the resurrection of the body, since elsewhere, says Nickelsburg, the noun *anabiosis* "is used in a clear reference to the resurrection of the body."[154] In Josephus, Nickelsburg contends, the Pharisaic idea of resurrection is hellenized, "but what emerges is not immortality of the soul, but transmigration, i.e., the soul enters a new body."[155] So, Nickelsburg concludes, "although Josephus describes the eschatology of both the Essenes and Pharisees in Hellenistic vocabulary, he does not attribute to the Essenes what he does attribute to the Pharisees, viz., a belief in a new *bodily* existence," and, therefore, the Essenes did not believe in bodily resurrection but believed only in immortality of the soul.[156]

Segal states that Josephus's description of Pharisaic belief in the *Jewish War*

> does not mean that Josephus attributed to Pharisees the Platonic notion of *metempsychosis* though he certainly used exactly that language to describe Pharasaic beliefs. Rather, Josephus described the Pharisees as envisioning another, different kind of body for imperishable souls . . . Josephus probably meant that the Pharisees believed that righteous persons will receive a new, incorruptible body. This is exactly what Paul says in I Corinthians 15.[157]

As discussed above,[158] the Sadducees are identified in sources other than Josephus as being those persons who denied any belief in an afterlife, and specifically denied resurrection. Josephus's description of the opinions of the Sadducees is consistent with

---

152. Josephus, *Ant.* 18.1.3. See Nickelsburg, *Resurrection, Immortality, and Eternal Life*, 208. See also Moore, *Judaism in the First Centuries*, 2:317.

153. Josephus, *J.W.* 2.8.14. See Moore, *Judaism in the First Centuries*, 2:317–18 (Josephus' description of pharisaic belief agrees with other sources "in the return to bodily life of the souls of the good only, and the eternal punishment of the bad.").

154. Nickelsburg, *Resurrection, Immortality, and Eternal Life*, 209n135.

155. Nickelsburg, *Resurrection, Immortality, and Eternal Life*, 208.

156. Nickelsburg, *Resurrection, Immortality, and Eternal Life*, 208–9.

157. Segal, *Life After Death*, 381. For a discussion of Paul's view of resurrection, see ch. 4, sec. F, 1.

158. See ch. 2, sec. F, 3.

the description found in these other sources. What is interesting about Josephus's account of those opinions, however, is that Josephus attributes to the Sadducees a belief in the idea that human beings have a soul. The Sadducees, according to Josephus, merely rejected the idea that the soul is immortal. According to *Jewish Antiquities*, the Sadducees believe "that the souls die with the bodies."[159] In the *Jewish War*, Josephus says that the Sadducees "take away the belief of the immortal duration of the soul, and the punishments and rewards in Hades."[160]

That Josephus's description of the opinions of the Essenes, Pharisees, and Sadducees was likely skewed, at least in part, to be more comprehensible to a non-Jewish readership does not mean that these descriptions were simply made-up. In other words, it is possible that Josephus accurately reflects a growing belief among Jews, due to Greek influence, that human beings have a *psyche* or "soul." That such a concept was infiltrating Jewish thought as Greek civilization spread following the conquests of Alexander the Great is undeniable. Specifically, the idea of a soul appears, as discussed above, in the Wisdom of Solomon, 4 Maccabees, 4 Ezra, 1 Enoch, and in other Jewish texts of the Second Temple period. More significantly, Philo shows how easily Greek ideas about a soul may be accommodated to the biblical texts, and how readily one may contend that such ideas were actually always in the Hebrew Bible, properly understood.

As will be seen in the next chapter, the idea that people have a soul was commonplace during the rabbinic period, so Josephus could not have been too far afield from Jewish views existing in the first century CE. Many, as the Essenes (on Nickelsburg's account), may have adopted a Platonic belief in an immortal soul, appropriately modified a la Philo. Others, perhaps including all or some of the Sadducees, may have rejected any belief in the afterlife, but nevertheless may have accepted the idea that human beings have a soul, such as did the Epicureans to whom the Sadducees were compared.[161] Still others, including some Pharisees, may have accepted the idea of resurrection at an end time, but may have combined it with the belief in a soul, such as in 4 Ezra 7 and 1 Enoch 22. Finally, some may have accepted the Pythagorean doctrine of *metempsychosis*. Josephus himself clearly believed in the immortality of the soul which, after surviving the death of the body, is rewarded or punished for deeds done when associated with the body, and seems also to have accepted *metempsychosis*, but gives no evidence of a belief in resurrection.[162]

It is important to make three other points. First, to whatever extent Jews were accepting the concept of a *psyche*, it is unlikely that anyone was particularly clear about what a *psyche* is. This is because the Greeks themselves (including, and especially, Plato) were not particularly clear about what a *psyche* is, and because the concept was still

---

159. Josephus, *Ant.* 18.1.4.

160. Josephus, *J.W.* 2.8.14.

161. See Segal, *Life After Death*, 378 (Sadducees "were seen as closely related intellectually to the Epicureans of the early Hellenistic period.").

162. See Grabbe, "Eschatology in Philo and Josephus," 175–77, 181.

being developed in varying directions. If people of a philosophical bent, such as Philo, could hold varying views about the soul, there is little prospect of the average person using the concept in a clear, well-defined manner. This leads to the second point. At the very least, Josephus underscores that at the beginning of the Common Era there was no single belief about the soul and the afterlife that was uniformly accepted by all Jews. To the contrary, Josephus evidences that there was a broad spectrum of belief among several groups. Even among the most dominant sect, the Pharisees, there was unlikely to have been uniformity of belief about these matters. Thirdly, Josephus also evidences that beliefs about the soul and the afterlife were linked to the problem of moral evil. He himself believed that after death the soul is rewarded or punished for one's deeds on earth, and he ascribes similar views to the Pharisees.[163]

E. Summary of Second Temple Period Views

In sum, the Second Temple period—from about 500 BCE to 70 CE—sees the emergence in Jewish thought of two similar, yet very distinct, approaches used to deal with the problem of moral evil. Both approaches resolve the problem by postulating an after-death reward and punishment. The one approach relies on the more or less homegrown concept of the physical resurrection of the dead; the other approach relies on the adopted Platonic view that humans have an immortal, or potentially immortal, soul—an entity separate from the body that is freed from the bodily prison at death.[164] Some, no doubt, maintained the biblical point of view that there is no reward and punishment except what is received in this life.

Even in the rabbinic period, despite the fact that the Pharisaic sect emerged victorious, a great variety of differing and even conflicting points of view are still found to exist. In general, however, a widely accepted point of view conflated the idea of an immortal soul with that of a bodily resurrection to occur at some time in the future.[165] This will be discussed in more detail in the next chapter.

---

163. Josephus, *J.W.* 3.8.1–7; 2.8.14; Grabbe, "Eschatology in Philo and Josephus," 177.

164. See Segal, *Life After Death*, 394–95 (resurrection of the dead "evolved out of religious martyrdom" giving worth to the death of the martyrs "by stating that God would make good his covenantal promises to reward the righteous and punish the iniquitous"; "immortality of the soul came from different circles and reflected different social concerns," being "adopted by a very well educated, very acculturated Jewish elite, completely at home or nearly at home in Greco-Roman culture."); Gillman, *Death of Death*, 112.

165. See Gillman, *Death of Death*, 134–40.

4.

Views about the Soul, Resurrection, and the Afterlife Continue to Evolve During the Rabbinic Period

FOLLOWING THE ROMANS' DESTRUCTION of the Second Temple in 70 CE and the defeat of Simon Bar Kokhba in 135 CE, the main centers of Jewish settlement in Palestine shifted to Galilee. Toward the end of the second century, Rabbi Judah the Patriarch composed and promulgated the Mishnah. A commentary on the Mishnah compiled in Palestine—the Palestinian Talmud—was completed in around 380 CE. Thereafter, conditions for Jews under Roman rule deteriorated.[1] Meanwhile, those Jews living in Babylonia fared much better and Babylonia came into its own as a center of religious studies. Rav introduced the Babylonian Jews to the Mishnah and established an academy in Sura; Samuel established an academy at Nehardea, later relocated to Pumbeditha. These schools would survive until the eleventh century as major centers of Jewish intellectual and religious activity.[2] The rabbis at Sura and Pumbeditha were responsible for compiling their own commentary on the Mishnah called the Babylonian Talmud, completed in around 499 CE. A type of literature called Midrash developed contemporaneously with the compilations of the Mishnah and the Talmuds.[3] The time during which all this material was created—from 70 CE to 500 CE—is referred to as the rabbinic period.

The rabbinic period offers no universally accepted or clearly articulated beliefs about the soul, resurrection, and the afterlife. Nevertheless, a widespread concern with an end time in which divine judgment would be rendered is evidenced by ubiquitous use of the expression *Olam Ha-Bah* [World to Come]. Furthermore, general acceptance of the concept of a soul, as distinct from the body, emerges,[4] and various

---

1. See Scheindlin, *Short History of the Jewish People*, 59–67.
2. Scheindlin, *Short History of the Jewish People*, 57–59.
3. See generally Hirsch, *Rabbinic Psychology*, 9–10.
4. See Porter, "Pre-Existence of the Soul," 57, 96 ("The older Hebrews had no word for body [*soma*], and what we call body was not to them the opposite of nephesh, but was inseparable from it. When the Jews wished to speak of that which preceded and survived the earthly life of man the word

depictions of the soul and its immortality are found in rabbinic texts; yet, these texts reveal no meaningful effort to clarify the exact nature and functions of the soul.[5]

Nor did the rabbis elucidate the precise relationship between the soul and the body. In fact, the Platonic antithesis between material (or bodily) things, which are inferior, and immaterial (or spiritual) things, which are superior, "is not to be found in Rabbinic teaching."[6] Despite the recognition of a dualism between the soul and the body, the *Tannaim* (the rabbinic sages whose views are recorded in the Mishnah) saw human beings as a unity.[7] The *Amoraim* (the rabbis who succeeded the Tannaim and who were responsible for the post-Mishnaic texts of the period) viewed humanity in a less holistic fashion than the Tannaim, but still never embraced a full Platonic dualism.[8]

Of far greater concern to the rabbis than specifics of the nature and functions of the soul, and its relation to the body, was their teaching that obedience to the Torah and rabbinic law brought reward, and disobedience brought punishment. In order to reinforce this notion in the community, the rabbis embraced belief in a postmortem reward and punishment. Some saw such postmortem treatment being meted out exclusively to the soul but most believed that such postmortem treatment would be given to a resurrected body-soul unity, and the Hebrew Bible was creatively interpreted to find that it contained the doctrine of bodily resurrection. Much less attention was paid to explaining the specifics of such bodily resurrection.

A. There Evolved No Universally Accepted or Clearly Articulated Beliefs about the Soul, Resurrection, and the Afterlife; Rather, There Were a Multitude of Varying and Sometimes Conflicting Points of View

The multitude of Jewish textual material that originated during the period from the destruction of the Second Temple until the time of the completion of the Babylonian

---

they naturally used was not nephesh but neshamah (less often ruaḥ), not the word which expressed the personal self of man, but the word that suggested the divine in contrast to the earthly element that entered into his making." The rabbis "provided themselves in the word [*guph*] with an equivalent for [the Greek *soma*]; and . . . adopted [*neshamah*] as its usual antithesis. They were able, therefore, to distinguish more clearly than Old Testament speech allows between the two parts of human nature [viz. body and soul].").

5. See Kohler, *Jewish Theology*, 288–89 ("no clear, consistent view of the soul prevailed as yet in the rabbinic age").

6. Urbach, *Sages*, 1:234. See also Hirsch, *Rabbinic Psychology*, 154, 162, 174; Porter, "Pre-Existence of the Soul," 96 ("the rabbis did not accept the Greek dualistic idea that the body is by nature, because made of matter, evil and the seat of the evil impulse, and that the soul is by nature pure and good, the seat of the good impulse . . . The ideas of the rabbis as to the relations of soul and body rested on the old Hebrew conception of the nature of man, not on the new Greek dualistic psychology.").

7. See Hirsch, *Rabbinic Psychology*, 160–61; Moore, *Judaism in the First Centuries*, 2:295.

8. Urbach, *Sages*, 1:248–50.

Talmud, and for centuries thereafter, does not present any fully developed or universally accepted viewpoint with regard to the concept of the soul, the concept of resurrection, or the concept of the afterlife.[9] This is not surprising. First, much of this material was intended to be dialectical—intended to present and analyze differing and competing points of view. Second, these materials sought neither to articulate nor to systematically set forth viewpoints about *any* "philosophical" issue.[10] We cannot, for instance, obtain from these materials "anything like a comprehensive statement or discussion which might give us a more or less complete view of what was believed [at the] time concerning the soul. The available material is fragmentary, consisting of stray statements and casual remarks, of anecdotes and aphorisms, which do not always indicate any doctrine or belief."[11]

"B. Terminology Concerning the Afterlife: *Olam Ha-Bah* and *Olam Ha-Zeh*

Perhaps the most pervasive and significant notion used during the rabbinic period relevant to the afterlife is used without any explanation as to its origin or precise meaning. This is the concept of the *Olam Ha-Bah*, usually translated "world to come" or "age to come."[12] This concept is contrasted with that of the *Olam Ha-Zeh*, usually translated "this world" or "this age."

While *Olam Ha-Zeh* refers to the time when and/or place where we presently live, it is impossible to say with precision to what *Olam Ha-Bah* refers. Clearly, it refers to a different time or place than *Olam Ha-Zeh*, but the question arises as to when this different time will occur and/or where this different place is located. There are three possibilities as to the temporal question:

1. The time immediately after any person dies.[13]

2. The time in history when there will be an ingathering of the diaspora to the land of Israel and the nation of Israel will be redeemed, a time of an earthly utopia characterized by social justice and material prosperity, referred to as *Yemot Ha-Mashiach*, usually translated as "Messianic Age."[14]

---

9. See Moore, *Judaism in the First Centuries*, 2:389; Raphael, *Jewish Views of the Afterlife*, 120, 160–61; Avery-Peck, "Death and the Afterlife," 244, 247, 248.

10. Neusner, *Jerusalem and Athens*, x. See Segal, *Life After Death*, 598 ("the Rabbis do not write systematic philosophical discourse."); Guttmann, *Philosophies of Judaism*, 47–48; Hirsch, *Rabbinic Psychology*, 12.

11. Hirsch, *Rabbinic Psychology*, 12.

12. See Moore, *Judaism in the First Centuries*, 2:378n6 ("The earliest known occurrence of the phrase . . . is in Enoch 71,15.").

13. Raphael, *Jewish Views of the Afterlife*, 127–28. See Segal, *Life After Death*, 626–27.

14. See Moore, *Judaism in the First Centuries*, 2:378 ("In an earlier stage of development, the national golden age, here called the Days of the Messiah, was the final period of history, and the names

3. The post-historical time when the present world will cease to exist and divine judgment will be meted out, perhaps to all the people of Israel, or all the people of the world who have ever lived, referred to as the end of days or time of final judgment.[15]

The only thing that can be stated with certainty is that *Olam Ha-Bah* is associated with a time and place of divine judgment, so that differing views as to when and where divine judgment will be meted out correlate with differing understandings of *Olam Ha-Bah*.

C. The Concept of the Soul Was Accepted, but the Character and Functions of the Soul Were Never Clearly Defined

Three Hebrew words—*nephesh*, *neshamah*, and *ruach*—were used more or less interchangeably in rabbinic texts to refer to the entity the Greeks called the *psyche*, although each Hebrew word was sometimes used to refer to a different characteristic or quality of this entity.[16] Regardless of which Hebrew word is used, the characteristics discussed in this section apply equally.

1. The soul is a life force

A prayer taken from the text of b. Berakhot 60b implies that the soul, referred to as *neshamah*, is something separate from the body, can survive apart from the body, and functions as a life force.[17] The soul in this text is not associated with who a person is but only with a part of who a person is since it refers to the soul "within me." The person appears to be equated with the body, but the body needs the soul for life. In discussing the concept of the soul in this prayer, Porter states:

> The neshamah is not the person, but is here, as uniformly in the rabbinical sayings, spoken as something distinct from the 'I,' and as objective to it. It is God's gift to the person, formed, or breathed, and kept in man by God . . . When, at death, God takes this 'soul' back, it is not the man's self that returns to the heavenly regions from which he came, but only the divine breath that

---

the World to Come or the Future were applied to it, and this usage continued in later times.").

15. See Moore, *Judaism in the First Centuries*, 2:391.

16. See Hirsch, *Rabbinic Psychology*, 151. Two additional words are also occasionally used to refer to the soul—*hayya* and *yehida*. See Gen. Rab. 14:9; Deut. Rab. 2:37; Eylon, *Reincarnation in Jewish Mysticism*, 51–52. Each of the five words refers to a specific quality of the soul. Eylon, *Reincarnation in Jewish Mysticism*, 51–52. See generally Nadler, *Spinoza's Heresy*, 57.

17. The prayer states: "The soul (*neshamah*) which you, my God, have given me is pure. You formed it in me, and you breathed it in me, and you keep it within me. Hereafter you will take my soul from me, to restore it to me again in the future [*atid la-bo*] . . . Praised are You, Lord who restores souls to dead bodies." b. Ber. 60b. See Porter, "Pre-Existence of the Soul," 97.

animated and preserved his body during his earthly life. Yet this divine breath is so far individualized and connected with this man that when the time comes for him to be raised from the dead, God will give back the same neshamah to the same body, and the man himself, the same man, will live again . . . Not only is it implied that the man's personality did not belong to the 'soul' in its preexistent state, but it is equally clear that the person does not go with the 'soul' when God takes it back at death . . . The neshamah is still primarily the 'breath of life.'"[18]

Another text that reflects the soul as a life force is Pesiqta Rabbati 1:6. In this text, as in Berakhot 60b, the life force is associated with "breath." Similarly, we read in Pirqe de Rabbi Eliezer:

> When God had formed man there was in him neither breath nor soul. What did God do? He breathed with the breath of His mouth, and a soul was cast into him.[19]

In his analysis of rabbinic psychology, Hirsch states: "The soul is the principle of life. Its presence animates the body; its departure results in death. The insensibility of swoon and sleep is caused by a partial withdrawal from the body of this life-giving agent, and the vitality of an organ depends on how closely the soul is attached to it . . . The soul is, therefore, called [*hayya*], the living one, for life is the essential part of its nature."[20]

2. The soul is endowed with reason and knowledge

Other texts refer to a soul that is more than a mere life force. In particular, they refer to a soul that possesses knowledge. For instance, there is rabbinic teaching that before birth the ensouled fetus knows the entire Torah but forgets it at the moment of birth.[21] The idea that the human soul is endowed with reason and knowledge is Platonic. The notion that this knowledge is possessed before birth but is forgotten at the moment of birth is also Platonic. In the *Phaedo*, *Meno*, and *Republic*, Plato claims

---

18. Porter, "Pre-Existence of the Soul," 97–98.

19. Pirqe R. El. 34. This passage evidences that Philo's allegorical interpretation of Genesis 2:7 was in essence adopted by the rabbis. The breath of life that God breathed into the human being is equated with the soul, understood as a life force. This life force is placed into the human being the moment he or she is formed (b. Sanh. 91b).

20. Hirsch, *Rabbinic Psychology*, 157. See Gen. Rab.14:9; Eylon, *Reincarnation in Jewish Mysticism*, 52. See also Hirsch, *Rabbinic Psychology*, 159.

21. See Guttmann, *Philosophies of Judaism*, 45; Hirsch, *Rabbinic Psychology*, 189–90; Urbach, *Sages*, 1:245–46 (quoting b. Nid. 30b). See also Midrash Tanhuma, Pekudei, 3 (Before the soul is placed in the womb of a women, it looks and peers about "from one end of the world to the other" and is shown the fate of the righteous souls in *Gan Eden* and the wicked souls in *Gehenna*. Then, upon going out of the mother's womb, the infant is struck on the head and forgets "everything he had witnessed and everything he knew.").

that the soul has knowledge before its union with a body but, immediately prior to its union, must drink from the waters of the Lake of Forgetfulness. This act causes the soul to forget but not to lose its knowledge. Thus, after its union with a body, a soul's preexisting knowledge can be recollected.[22] That the rabbis give expression to this notion evidences their exposure to the Platonic concept of *psyche*. Hirsch writes that in rabbinic material "the soul is endowed with reason. It is the thinking and knowing element in man, the power that discerns between right and wrong, and understands the consequences of evil."[23]

Notwithstanding the view which associates the soul with reason and intelligence, the rabbis also expressed the view that all mental functions, including thought and memory, as well as sensation, involve the body.[24] This view is in keeping with their overarching concept of man as a psycho-physical unity—body-soul—despite their acceptance of the idea that this unity has two distinguishable components.[25]

3. The soul is invisible, from heaven, pure, and indivisible

Texts from the rabbinic period are not concerned with metaphysical questions such as whether the soul is material or immaterial. At least one passage, however, suggests that there were some who may have viewed the soul as immaterial. This passage, attributed to Rabbi Simeon ben Pazzi, compares the soul to God. Included in this comparison is the statement that: "The soul sees and is not seen, so God sees and is not seen."[26] That the soul is "not seen" or invisible may imply that it is immaterial, as Plato associates the immaterial with the invisible. The soul's immateriality may also be gleaned from pervasive statements that man's soul comes from heaven which for Plato is the realm of the immaterial.[27] Hirsch contends, however, that the rabbinic contrast between heavenly and earthly should be seen, *not* as a contrast between "spiritual" and "material," but as a contrast between "holy, pure, sinless and immortal" and "unholy,

---

22. See Urbach, *Sages*, 1:246 ("In the motif of the unborn child's knowledge of the Torah and his forgetting it upon being born, scholars . . . have discerned the [*anamnesis*] of the Platonic myth.") (citing Plato, *Republic*, X, 621b). But see Hirsch, *Rabbinic Psychology*, 191.

23. Hirsch, *Rabbinic Psychology*, 157.

24. Hirsch, *Rabbinic Psychology*, 205.

25. See generally Hirsch, *Rabbinic Psychology*, 160–62, 203–7. See also Porter, "Pre-Existence of the Soul," 99 (In b. Šabb. 152b the man is more closely associated with the body than with the soul).

26. Hirsch, *Rabbinic Psychology*, 174 (quoting b. Ber. 10a). See also Hirsch, *Rabbinic Psychology*, 179–80 (quoting R. Isaac that prior to infusion into a body the souls "have no material substance").

27. See Hirsch, *Rabbinic Psychology*, 153–56.

impure, sinful and mortal."[28] According to Hirsch, the contrast between spiritual (or immaterial) and material is "altogether foreign to Rabbinic thought."[29]

However, Hirsch also acknowledges that the rabbis' conception of the soul is Platonic in origin, and that for Plato the soul originates from heaven because heaven is a place which is "pure and invisible," that is, immaterial.[30] Since for Plato the soul is immaterial because it is from heaven and because it is "pure and invisible," the rabbis' description of the soul, admittedly Platonic in origin, as from heaven, pure, and invisible suggests that they, similarly, conceived the soul as immaterial. But Hirsch insists that the purity of the soul for the rabbis related only to its "sinless origin and moral tendency" and not to the "unmixed nature of a spiritual essence."[31]

In any event, in addition to seeing the soul as invisible, from heaven, and pure, the rabbis also saw the soul as undivided.[32] They speak of one indivisible soul operating in unison with the body to achieve all human functions, including motion, nutrition and growth, sensation, and rationality. This is in keeping with ben Pazzi's comparison of the soul to God, for he stated: "The soul is one in the body, as God is one in the world."[33] Hirsch elaborates:

> The unity of God brought into harmony the various forces of creation and made the world really one. So the conception of one indivisible soul unified the diversity of psychic manifestations and gave them a common origin. Motion, sensation, intellection, all spring from the same source, the combination of a spirit and a body into a single unit . . . It is further explained that the soul

---

28. Hirsch, *Rabbinic Psychology*, 154. Cf. Porter, "Pre-Existence of the Soul," 96 (the rabbis' conception of body and soul "was not *so much* that of contrasted substances as of opposite origins; the guph was made of matter and the neshamah of spirit, but that the guph was from below, from the earth, and the neshamah from above, from God"; emphasis added), 103 ("the contrast between body and soul was not so much a contrast between material and spiritual being as between earthly and heavenly origin.").

29. Hirsch, *Rabbinic Psychology*, 154. See also Urbach, *Sages*, 1:234. Despite asserting that the purity and holiness of the soul has nothing to do with its being "spirit," Hirsch repeatedly indicates that the rabbis associated the soul with "the spiritual" and "the nonphysical" part of man in contrast to the "material" and physical part, the body. See e.g., Hirsch, *Rabbinic Psychology*, 194–95.

30. Hirsch, *Rabbinic Psychology*, 163, 170–72. See Eylon, *Reincarnation in Jewish Mysticism*, 49–51 ("The idea that the soul is pure and divine appears to be a direct influence of Plato . . ."). See generally Porter, "Pre-Existence of the Soul," 98, 101–3.

31. Hirsch, *Rabbinic Psychology*, 163, 172. See Porter, "Pre-Existence of the Soul," 104 ("It is [the] heavenly origin of the soul which the word pure [*tehor*] expresses.").

32. This is also a Platonic idea that may hint at a belief in the immateriality of the soul, for in the *Phaedo*, Plato claims that the *psyche* is immaterial and immortal because it is without parts or "incomposite" (Plato, *Phaed.*, 79b–80b).

33. b. Ber. 10a. Accord, Lev. Rab. 4 ("As God is one in the world so is the soul one in the body."). See Hirsch, *Rabbinic Psychology*, 174, 194 (quoting b. Ber. 10a, and Lev. Rab. 4). See generally Nadler, *Spinoza's Heresy*, 57 ("On some accounts, the soul is tripartite, constituted by *nefesh*, *ruach*, and *neshamah* . . . A more prevalent view, however, is that all three parts of the soul, while functionally distinct, form an indissoluble whole: the soul is one."); Hirsch, *Rabbinic Psychology*, 192–93.

is called Yeḥidah, the only one, because, while so many organs of the body are double, the soul is only one.[34]

4. The soul could be a free soul

In some passages it is clear that what is being referenced by a soul is what anthropologists call a "free soul," a shadowy double of a person that is active when the person is asleep and can leave the body to travel to other locations.[35] Thus, it is stated that the *ruach* goes up to heaven during sleep and descends when man is awake.[36] During its nocturnal travels the soul can see what is happening in the farthest parts of the world, and can also catch glimpses of what might happen in the future.[37] These visions appear to the sleeping person as dreams.[38]

Dreams were understood to be visions seen by the soul, including those experienced when, "detached from the sleeping body, it floats unhindered in limitless space. This explains why a person sleeping in one place may dream things in other places . . . Disentangled from the flesh, the soul of the sleeping body may come into contact with the spirits of the dead and receive information from them. This was a usual form of dream which was treated with much consideration."[39] In fact, according to Hirsch, it was believed that sleep was *caused* by the withdrawal of the soul from the body, "leaving the body with only the breath of life to keep it from death . . . During sleep the soul is not in the body, but remains somehow connected with it to maintain the circulation of the blood. The following statement is attributed to R. Meir: 'The soul fills the body. When man is asleep, it goes up and draws a new life from above.' Hence the invigoration of sleep."[40] Hirsch goes on to add:

34. Hirsch, *Rabbinic Psychology*, 192–93. See Eylon, *Reincarnation in Jewish Mysticism*, 51–52 ("*Yehidah* (= only one, single) denotes the uniqueness of the soul."). See also Hirsch, *Rabbinic Psychology*, 196 ("The Rabbis followed the view of the Neo-Platonists that the soul was diffused throughout the body and not localized in a particular organ."). According to Winston: "There appears to be no reference to bipartition of the soul in rabbinic literature" (Winston, *Wisdom of Solomon*, 29n40). Accord, Urbach, *Sages*, 1:234 ("The distinction between the rational and irrational soul is unknown to the Sages."). But see Wolfson, *Philo*, 2:279–303, discussed in ch. 3, n. 136 (relating the evil *yetser* and the good *yetser* to, respectively, the irrational and rational souls).

35. See generally Bremmer, *Early Greek Concept of the Soul*, 9, 14–53 (discussing free soul in the Greek concept of *psyche*); Rohde, *Psyche*, 1:6–7 ("It was the experience of an apparent double of the self in dreaming . . . that gave rise to the inference of a two-fold principle in the life of man, and of the existence of an independent, separable 'second self' dwelling within the visible self of daily life . . . [which] is *sleeping* when the limbs are active, but when the body is asleep it often reveals the future in a dream . . . [I]t survives death, though, indeed, only as a breath-like image . . .").

36. See Hirsch, *Rabbinic Psychology*, 152 (citing Gen. Rab. 14); Deut. Rab. 5:15. See also Eylon, *Reincarnation in Jewish Mysticism*, 48–49 (comparing Deut. Rab. 5:15 to Pythagorean beliefs).

37. Hirsch, *Rabbinic Psychology*, 200.

38. Hirsch, *Rabbinic Psychology*, 200 (citing b. Nid. 30b).

39. Hirsch, *Rabbinic Psychology*, 201–203 (citing b. Yoma 22b; b. Sanh. 102b; etc.).

40. Hirsch, *Rabbinic Psychology*, 199–200 (quoting Gen. Rab. 14). See Madigan and Levenson,

CHAPTER 4.

In keeping with this view of sleep, which is based on the primitive notion of the soul as a duplicate, is the belief that swoon, brought on by fright or illness, is due to a sudden flight of the soul from the body. The souls of Joseph's brothers flew out of their bodies, when Joseph revealed himself to them. The same thing happened to the Israelites at Sinai, when God spoke to them, and to Ezekiel, when he heard God's voice.[41]

5. The soul preexists the body

The notion that the soul preexists the creation of the body first appears in Jewish sources in the Wisdom of Solomon. It also appears in 2 Enoch, Josephus, and Philo.[42] In rabbinic literature the preexistence of the soul is first mentioned by Rabbi Meir, a Tanna of the second century CE. He says:

> In the seventh heaven, Araboth, are the souls of the righteous, the souls yet to be created (in the body), the treasuries of righteousness and justice, of life and blessing.[43]

More specifically, there are rabbinic teachings about a storehouse or treasure-house where souls abide prior to physical embodiment, often referred to as a *guph*.[44] For example, according to a teaching ascribed to the Tanna Rabbi Yossi: "The Messiah will not come before the souls which are in the *guf* have [all] entered physical life."[45] This storehouse, or *guph*, of preexisting souls is conceived as being in an upper region, in the seventh heaven or Arabot.[46] Upon creation of a new person, a soul from the storehouse is combined with a body, thought to come from a lower region.[47]

Resurrection, 205 (stating with reference to b. Ber. 60b that it "views the separation and reunification of [body and soul] as a daily occurrence" and sees sleep "as an anticipation of death"). Accord, Kohler, *Jewish Theology*, 287–88 ("Death to the pious is only a prolonged sleep . . . As at every awakening from sleep in the morning, so at the great awakening in the future, the souls which have departed in death shall return again to their bodies. These bodies could then hardly be conceived of as subject to decomposition").

41. Hirsch, *Rabbinic Psychology*, 200–1 (citations omitted).

42. Hirsch, *Rabbinic Psychology*, 175–76.

43. Hirsch, *Rabbinic Psychology*, 176 (quoting b. Hag. 12b). See also Guttmann, *Philosophies of Judaism*, 39 (citing b. Hag. 12b; b. Nid. 30b); Porter, "Pre-Existence of the Soul," 99–100. Midrash Tanhuma, Pekudei, 3, refers to all souls being "created on the sixth day of creation," being "fashioned with the first man," and being in the Garden of Eden.

44. Raphael, *Jewish Views of the Afterlife*, 155; Hirsch, *Rabbinic Psychology*, 176–77. See also Urbach, *Sages*, 1:237.

45. Raphael, *Jewish Views of the Afterlife*, 155 (citing b. 'Abod. Zar. 5a). See Hirsch, *Rabbinic Psychology*, 176; Urbach, *Sages*, 1:237 and 237nn79 and 80. See also b. Nid. 13b; b. Yebam. 62a—63b; Gen. Rab. 24:4; Lev. Rab. 15:1. See generally Porter, "Pre-Existence of the Soul," 105–6.

46. Raphael, *Jewish Views of the Afterlife*, 155 (citing b. Hag. 12b); Hirsch, *Rabbinic Psychology*, 269 ("Arabot, the highest heaven in which God dwells . . . [is the venue of] the unborn souls waiting to be sent on earth to animate new bodies.").

47. Raphael, *Jewish Views of the Afterlife*, 130 (citing Lev. Rab. 4:5). See Porter, "Pre-Existence of

Urbach asserts that the sayings attributed to the Tannaim Rabbis Meir and Yossi are wrongfully attributed and, in reality, are sayings of Ammoraim.[48] Urbach further asserts that,

> although the 'Treasure-house of souls' is indeed already mentioned in the period of the Tannaim, [it is] only in the sense of a place where the souls of the righteous are kept *after death*. The Tannaim were not exercised by the question of the soul's source and the way it came to be attached to the body, but by the fate of the souls of the righteous and the wicked ... Both the souls of the righteous and the souls of the wicked ascend on high, [but] only the souls of the righteous are placed in the Treasure-house, whereas the souls of the wicked are cast to the ground.[49]

On Urbach's account, the idea of preexistence doesn't arise until the period of the Amoraim.[50]

According to Hirsch, however, belief in the preexistence of souls appears *before* the belief that souls go to heaven after leaving the body[51] but use of the term *guph* as the location of the unborn souls does not. He says that the original belief concerning postmortem souls, found in apocalyptic literature such as 4 Ezra and 1 Enoch 22, was that until the day of judgment the souls of the dead are kept in chambers or treasuries that were well-guarded by angels "to protect the frail spirit from injury by the demons and evil spirits which haunt the limitless space of the universe."[52] Hirsch explains that the location of these chambers or treasuries, often referred to by the rabbis as the *otzar* (the "treasure-house"), "must originally have been on earth, not in heaven, where there are no evil spirits and demons ... and where such shelters would be unnecessary."[53] Subsequently, says Hirsch, the location of the righteous souls [after death] was transferred to heaven and

> the [*otzar*] went with them, though not with the purpose for which it was originally conceived. In [Qohelet Rab. 3] the following Baraita is quoted: 'The souls of the righteous and the souls of the wicked all go up to heaven. The souls of the righteous are put into the [*otzar*], but the souls of the wicked are thrust back to earth.' The scenes which once took place at the doors of the treasuries, all souls crowding to get in, the deserving being admitted, the

---

the Soul," 108.

48. See Urbach, *Sages*, 1:237, 238; 2:792.

49. Urbach, *Sages*, 1:238–39 (emphasis added).

50. See Urbach, *Sages*, 1:241.

51. Hirsch, *Rabbinic Psychology*, 268–69 ("The Rabbinic belief that souls go to heaven after leaving the body is ... based on their doctrine of pre-existence and cannot be older than it.").

52. Hirsch, *Rabbinic Psychology*, 263–64. See ch. 2, secs. D, 3 and 4; ch. 3, secs. B, 1 and 2.

53. Hirsch, *Rabbinic Psychology*, 264–65 (the *ozar* is the place "wherein the souls of the righteous were gathered after their separation from the flesh" while "the souls of the ungodly ... [were] obliged to wander about in torment, ever grieving and sad.").

undeserving driven away by the angels, were now taking place at the gates of heaven, scenes strongly reminiscent of what Er, son of Armenius, saw in the region of the spirits, large numbers of souls floating upwards, the good ascending through an opening in heaven, the bad forced back and dragged away to the underworld by fierce men of fire [Plato, *Republic*, X, 14, 615e] . . . The belief in the [*otzar*], wherein the disembodied souls assemble, gave rise in time to a belief in a similar receptacle, the [*guph*], containing the unborn spirits destined for the body.[54]

Although the soul preexists the creation of the body, souls are created beings, not, as Plato believed, eternal beings.[55] The view that souls are created, not eternal, is required by the belief that God's creation of the world is *ex nihilo*. According to the rabbis' erroneous reading of the opening verses of Genesis, in the beginning there was only God. All other things are created by God from nothing. Consequently, souls must have come into being at some point in time. Of course, the Bible does not specifically mention the creation of the soul, so "forced interpretations were resorted to find a hint or suggestion of its creation."[56]

A question arises as to why the rabbis, or some of them,[57] came to accept the idea of the preexistence of the soul. Based on the reading of Genesis 2:7 which understands the breath with which God gave life to the body as referring to the soul,[58] one might have thought it more natural to postulate that the soul is created simultaneously with the body. This is, indeed, the view accepted by Saadia Gaon.[59] Some have postulated a Greek origin to the rabbis' contrary view, but others dispute such an origin.[60] There is merit in Hirsch's suggestion that the purpose underlying the belief in the preexistence of the soul is "to express in concrete form the omniscience of God, and His determination of all things."[61] Because all prophesy, and indeed all wisdom, was understood as having been revealed at Sinai, it is reasonable to believe that all souls, as the repositories of visions and wisdom, were created at, or before, the Sinai event.[62]

54. Hirsch, *Rabbinic Psychology*, 267–68.
55. Hirsch, *Rabbinic Psychology*, 177.
56. Hirsch, *Rabbinic Psychology*, 178.
57. See Porter, "Pre-Existence of the Soul," 105–6 (distinguishing Babylonian conception from Palestinian conception).
58. See sec. C, 1 (quoting *Pirqe Rabbi Eliezer*).
59. See ch. 5, sec. B, 4.
60. See generally Hirsch, *Rabbinic Psychology*, 182–86.
61. Hirsch, *Rabbinic Psychology*, 183. See Porter, "Pre-Existence of the Soul," 99–100 ("pre-existence of the soul is more significant for the conception of God than for the conception of man; not the nature of the soul but the power of God is heightened by it."), 113 (pre-existence "expressed the idea that God foreknows and has predetermined the number and lot of all men").
62. See Hirsch, *Rabbinic Psychology*, 179–80. See also Eylon, *Reincarnation in Jewish Mysticism*, 47–48 (quoting Exod. Rab. 28:6 and concluding: "The fact that the souls, including those of the unborn, were all present at Mount Sinai presupposes their pre-existence."); Urbach, *Sages*, 1:236–37; Porter, "Pre-Existence of the Soul," 105–7; Midrash Tanhuma, Pekudei, 3 ("You should know that

Regardless of the reason for accepting belief in the preexistence of souls, generally speaking, the rabbis' understanding of the nature of the preexisting soul accords with the understanding of the author of the Wisdom of Solomon but not with the understanding of Plato and Philo. This is to say that for the rabbis the preexistence of the soul is not the preexistence of the person; rather, it is the preexistence of an individualization and personification of the *neshamah*, the life-giving breath of God, which, when infused into a human body, makes a living person.[63]

6. The soul is generally considered to be immortal, not subject to death

For the most part, the rabbis conceived the soul, essentially the individuated life-giving breath of God, to be immortal—not subject to death. While the conception of the soul as immortal is in keeping with the Platonic notion of *psyche*, the rabbis could not accept the related Platonic idea that the soul's immortality is part of its inherent nature.[64] Rather, for the rabbis the soul's immortality is granted to it by God.[65] However, the rabbis had no problem accepting the Platonic notion that death is caused by the departure of the soul from the body,[66] and they assigned the task of removing the soul from the body to a particular angel, Samael, called the angel of death.[67]

The Platonic notion of death as the separation of the soul from the body is superficially similar to the biblical notion that at death the body returns to dust and the life-giving breath of God returns to God. Of course, it is significant that for Plato, but not for the rabbis, the postmortem soul constituted not merely a life force but the true self, freed from the contamination of the body. For the rabbis the postmortem soul did not constitute the true self, although it was believed to retain a high degree of individuality and personhood, just as did the preexisting soul.[68] It is the divine breath's retention of individuality and personhood after separation from the body that distinguishes the

---

every soul, from Adam to the end of the world, was formed during the six days of creation, and that all of them were present ... at the time of the giving of the Torah, as it is said: *With him that standeth here with us this day, and also with him that is not here with us this day* [Deut 29:14].").

63. See Porter, "Pre-Existence of the Soul," 57, 63, 106–13; Hirsch, *Rabbinic Psychology*, 182 (prior to embodiment souls were seen to exist as "distinct individualities").

64. See generally Porter, "Pre-Existence of the Soul," 108 ("To a belief in the pre-existence of the soul, such as Plato and Philo represent, belongs inevitably the belief that the soul is immortal, that its original incorporeal state of existence is more native to it, and higher, than its earthly life, and that the recovery of this is its final destiny. But all this is foreign to rabbinical teaching ... The rabbis did not hope for a union of their self-conscious personalities with God after death at all. Their hope was a new life in the age to come.").

65. See Hirsch, *Rabbinic Psychology*, 156; Gillman, *Death of Death*, 136. See also Wolfson, "Immortality and Resurrection," 57.

66. Hirsch, *Rabbinic Psychology*, 238. Cf., Plato, *Phaed.*, 64c.

67. Hirsch, *Rabbinic Psychology*, 239. See also Raphael, *Jewish Views of the Afterlife*, 133–35.

68. See Porter, "Pre-Existence of the Soul," 97–98 (quoted above in text accompanying note 18).

rabbinic concept of the soul from the original biblical idea that the life-giving breath of God (not a "soul") separates from the body after death.

7. After death the immortal soul could be a ghost or familiar spirit remaining near the corpse

It was popularly believed during the rabbinic period that after death one's immortal soul continued to remain near the location of one's dead body and that the former entity not only retained individuality and personhood but consciousness and mental functions as well, and could be seen by, and could communicate with, living persons.[69] As visible and conscious beings existing near graves, such souls functioned somewhat as the biblical *ob* (ghost) or *yiddoni* (familiar spirit).[70] Indeed, the belief that the immortal soul remained near the dead body is but a modification of the ancient practice of ancestor worship or the cult of the dead.[71]

Numerous texts recount tales of the activity of such souls,[72] and the rabbis did not discredit "the prevalent practice of necromantic incantation."[73] An example of such stories is the following:

> 'Ze'iri deposited some money with his landlady, and while he was away visiting Rab she died. So he went after her to the cemetery and said to her, Where is my money? She replied to him: Go and take it from under the ground, in the hole in the doorpost in such and such a place, and tell my mother to send me my comb and my tube of eye-paint by the hand of So-and-so who is coming today.'[74]

It is possible that the association of the soul with a ghost or familiar spirit was reinforced by Platonic ideas. In Plato's *Phaedo* the idea is expressed that, if at the time of death the soul is pure and "does not drag along with it any trace of the body, because it has never willingly associated with it in life . . . then it departs to the place where things are like itself—invisible, divine, immortal and wise [the heavenly realm of immaterial things]."[75] However, "if at the time of its release the soul is tainted and impure; because it has always associated with the body and cared for it and loved it . . . [then the soul] is weighed down and dragged back into the visible world . . . and hovers about tombs and graveyards. The shadowy apparitions which have actually been

---

69. See generally Hirsch, *Rabbinic Psychology*, 257–63; Raphael, *Jewish Views of the Afterlife*, 136–40.

70. See ch. 1, sec. E; Johnston, *Shades of Sheol*, 150–66.

71. See ch. 1, sec. E.

72. See Hirsch, *Rabbinic Psychology*, 258–63.

73. Hirsch, *Rabbinic Psychology*, 261. See also Raphael, *Jewish Views of the Afterlife*, 139.

74. Raphael, *Jewish Views of the Afterlife*, 137–39 (quoting b. Ber. 18b). See Hirsch, *Rabbinic Psychology*, 261–62.

75. Plato, *Phaed.*, 80e—81a.

seen there are the ghosts of those souls which have not got clear away, but still retain some portion of the visible . . ."[76]

8. After death the immortal soul could remain at rest until it was reunited with the resurrected body or, alternatively, it could receive an immediate reward or punishment, but it could not transmigrate into a new body

In contrast to the ancient belief that after death the "soul" remained near the grave and could communicate with the living,[77] there arose a newer belief that after death the soul "maintained a separate existence in an intermediate place till the day of resurrection, when it would rejoin its former body."[78] A version of this newer belief first appeared in apocalyptic texts where the intermediate place was identified with the biblical *Sheol* and placed in subterranean chambers.[79] In 1 Enoch, for example, where the final judgment does not occur in the proximate future, the question naturally arose as to the whereabouts of souls between death and the great judgment.[80] In a tour of the world beyond the bounds of human exploration, "Enoch is shown a great mountain in the West in which are deep hollows with very smooth walls . . . The angel Raphael . . . tells [Enoch] that these hollow places were created that in them should be collected all the souls of men until the time appointed for the great judgment. The one that is light and has the fountain in it is for the spirits of the righteous; the others for different classes of the wicked."[81] The intermediate place for the righteous came to be identified as being the *otzar*, "treasuries, or chambers, where, guarded by angels, [the souls of the righteous enjoy] perfect quiet and peace."[82]

In the rabbinic period, under Platonic influence,[83] the *otzar* was moved to the heavenly or divine realm, under God's throne of glory, from which the soul came.[84] For the wicked, the intermediate place was earth where the impure soul was forced to wander about since it was unfit to be in the presence of God.[85] According to Hirsch:

76. Plato, *Phaed.*, 81b–d; Cf. b. Šabb. 152b ("The souls . . . of the wicked wander about the world.").
77. See ch. 1, sec. E.
78. Hirsch, *Rabbinic Psychology*, 257.
79. See ch. 2, secs. D, 3 and 4, and E; ch. 3, secs. B, 1 and 2.
80. Moore, *Judaism in the First Centuries*, 2:301–2. See ch. 3, sec. B, 2.
81. Moore, *Judaism in the First Centuries*, 2:302.
82. Hirsch, *Rabbinic Psychology*, 264 (citing 1 En., 4 Ezra, and 2 Bar.).
83. See *Rabbinic Psychology*, 264 (the newer doctrine "developed most probably under Greek influence").
84. See Hirsch, *Rabbinic Psychology*, 279–80 ("The doctrine that the righteous souls reside in heaven after death appears in Rabbinic literature in the second century, about the same time as that of pre-existence. The relationship of the two beliefs need hardly be pointed out."). See generally sec. C, 5 (discussing Hirsch's view that the chambers or *otzars* of the righteous souls described in apocalyptic texts of the Second Temple period were transferred to heaven during the rabbinic period.).
85. See b. Šabb.152b; Hirsch, *Rabbinic Psychology*, 257; Moore, *Judaism in the First Centuries*, 2:389–90; Gillman, *Death of Death*, 138. See also Hirsch, *Rabbinic Psychology*, 167, 263–71.

The Rabbis spoke often of the [otzar], the treasure-house, wherein the souls of the righteous were gathered after their separation from the flesh. They found Biblical authority for the conceit in [1 Sam 25:29], "The soul of my lord shall be bound in the bundle of life with the Lord thy God, and the souls of thine enemies shall He sling out, as from the hollow of a sling." The bundle of life, in which God will hold David's soul in safety as something precious, was identified with the closely guarded treasuries in which the souls of the righteous found protection, an interpretation to which the alliteration of the two Hebrew words [tzror, bundle] and [otzar] lent support. The curse flung at David's enemy seemed to allude to the torments which the souls of the unrighteous, being denied entry into the habitations of safety, were obliged to suffer.[86]

Hirsch also refers to the parable of the king who distributed garments among his servants. This parable interprets Qoheleth 12:7:

> This may be likened to a human king who distributed royal garments among his servants. The wise folded them up and laid them in a chest, the foolish went and did their work in them. After a time the king asked for his garments. The wise gave them back clean, the foolish gave them back soiled. The king was pleased with the wise, but was angry with the foolish. Concerning the wise he ordered that their garments be placed in the treasure-house, and that they go in peace to their homes. But concerning the fools he said that their garments should be cleaned, and that they should be imprisoned. So with regard to the bodies of the righteous, God says: "He enters in peace, they rest in their beds," [Isa 57:2] and of their souls He says: "They shall be bound in the bundle of life." [1 Sam 25:29] But to the bodies of the wicked He says: "There is no peace to the wicked," [Isa 57:21] and of their souls He says: "And the souls of thine enemies He will sling out" [1 Sam 25:29].[87]

The allegory suggests that the soul can be stained by sin and that unless it is kept clean and returned in its original state of purity it will be subjected to a harsh process of cleansing.[88] The allegory also suggests

> that after the dissolution of life the heavenly element of man, if it is pure and unsoiled by sin, returns to heaven and is put into the treasury. It can then be said, in the language of the parable, that the garment, given on loan, was returned to the owner. But if the soul was contaminated by sin, it is debarred from returning to its place of origin. This belief presupposes that the soul

---

86. Hirsch, *Rabbinic Psychology*, 265. See b. Šabb. 152b; ch. 6, sec. C, 2; *infra*, n.104.

87. Hirsch, *Rabbinic Psychology*, 167–68 (citing b. Šabb. 152b; Qoh. Rab. 9). See Urbach, *Sages*, 1:239–40; Eylon, *Reincarnation in Jewish Mysticism*, 50. Porter comments that in this passage man is more closely associated with his body than with his soul—it is not the body that is likened to a garment worn by the soul but the soul which is likened to a garment lent by God to man and which at death, if it has not been defiled, goes back into God's treasury (Porter, "Pre-Existence of the Soul," 99).

88. See Hirsch, *Rabbinic Psychology*, 195.

comes originally from heaven, and its return to heaven at the end of its earthly career is not a reward for special merit but the normal process of a soul that retained its true nature. It is its inability to return to its home, owing to deterioration, that constitutes a departure or a fall, the soiling of a clean garment, according to the wording of the parable.[89]

It is significant that the return of the soul to heaven is not a reward. Despite the notion that souls, by themselves, can become impure, an important rabbinic teaching is that sin involves both the body and the soul working together as one, and that, consequently, any reward must be administered to the body/soul unity, not just to the soul.[90] Thus, true postmortem reward and punishment required bodily resurrection. This teaching is expressed in a well-known account of a supposed exchange between Antoninus and Judah the Patriarch:

> Antoninus said to Rabbi: The body and the soul can free themselves from judgment [on the Day of Judgment]. How? The body can say: It is the soul that sinned, for since the day that it left me, I lie still as a stone in the grave. And the soul can say: The body has sinned, for since the day that I left it, I fly in the air as a bird. Said (Rabbi) to him: I shall give you an analogy. To what can the case be compared? To that of a human king who had a beautiful orchard that contained fine early fruit, and he posted two watchmen there, the one lame and the other blind . . . so the lame man was carried [piggyback] by the blind man, and they took them and ate them. After a time the owner of the orchard came. Said he to them: Where are the fine early fruits? Said the lame man to him: Have I then feet to walk with? Said the blind man to him: Have I then eyes to see? What did (the owner) do? He put the lame man astride the blind man and judged them as one. Even so the Holy One, blessed be He, takes the soul and casts it into the body and judges them as one, as it is written: *He summoned the heavens above, and the earth, for the trial of his people* [Ps 50:4]. '*He summoned the heavens above*' this refers to the soul; '*and the earth,*' [this refers] to the body.[91]

Yet, despite rabbinic teaching that sin involves both body and soul, there were many sages who taught that the *Olam Ha-Bah* commenced immediately following a person's physical death. For these sages, the reward and punishment meted out in the *Olam Ha-Bah* is meted out to the immortal soul alone.[92] This is evidenced by the following passage employing an analogy relating to ritual purity:

---

89. Hirsch, *Rabbinic Psychology*, 268.

90. See Hirsch, *Rabbinic Psychology*, 208 ("'The body cannot exist without the soul, the soul cannot operate without the body, therefore, they both sin.'") (quoting Tanḥ. Vayeekra 11).

91. b. Sanh. 91a–b. See Urbach, *Sages*, 1:223; Hirsch, *Rabbinic Psychology*, 208–9. See also Moore, *Judaism in the First Centuries*, 2:384; Avery-Peck, "Death and the Afterlife," 257–58; Eylon, *Reincarnation in Jewish Mysticism*, 55–56.

92. See generally Raphael, *Jewish Views of the Afterlife*, 127–30; Guttmann, *Philosophies of Judaism*,

It is like the case of a priest [Kohen] who had two wives, one was a priest's daughter and one was the daughter of an Israelite, and he handed them dough of heave-offering and they defiled it; he thereupon blamed the priest's daughter, but left the Israelite's daughter alone. Said she [the priest's daughter] to him: "Our lord, priest, you gave (the dough) to both of us together; why then do you blame me and leave her alone?" He answered her: "You are a priest's daughter, and have been trained in your father's home; but she is an Israelite's daughter and was not trained in her father's home. Hence I blame you." In the same way the Holy One, blessed be He, will in the hereafter say to the soul: "Why did you sin before me?" She will answer him: "Sovereign of the universe, the body and I have sinned together, why then dost Thou blame me and leave it alone?" He will reply to her: "You hail from the celestial beings on high, from a place where no sin is committed; whereas the body comes from among the earthly creatures below, from a place where sin is committed. Hence I blame you." The main responsibility rests on the soul, for it transcends all parts of the body.[93]

The rewards received by the souls of the righteous immediately after death were thought to be given in an upper region (heaven or *Gan Eden*), and the punishments to be received by the souls of the wicked immediately after death were thought to be given in a lower region (*Gehenna*).[94] The two separate regions are acknowledged in a legend about Rabbi Yohanan ben Zakkai who, in contemplation of his own death, stated: "[T]here are two roads before me, one leading to Gan Eden and the other to Gehenna, and I do not know by which I will be taken."[95]

The inconsistency between the older belief (that all souls remain near the grave) and the newer belief (that the souls of the righteous ascend to heaven) was "pointed out by a heretic to R. Abbahu. 'You say,' he argued, 'that the souls of the righteous are kept under God's throne of glory, how then did the witch of En-dor bring up Samuel from the grave?' The Rabbi replied: 'During the first twelve months after death, while the body still exists, the soul ascends to heaven, and also descends to visit the body. After twelve months, when the body has disappeared, it descends no more.'"[96]

37.

93. Urbach, *Sages*, 1:241–42 (quoting Lev. Rab. 4:5). See Raphael, *Jewish Views of the Afterlife*, 130; Eylon, *Reincarnation in Jewish Mysticism*, 58.

94. See generally Raphael, *Jewish Views of the Afterlife*, 140–56; Eylon, *Reincarnation in Jewish Mysticism*, 63; Moore, *Judaism in the First Centuries*, 2:390–91 (there is ambiguity in the terms *Gan Eden* and *Gehenna* with regard to whether an intermediate abode of disembodied souls is meant or the final state of the reembodied souls).

95. Raphael, *Jewish Views of the Afterlife*, 152 (quoting b. Ber. 28b). See Wolfson, "Immortality and Resurrection," 55. See also Avot R. Nat. 25; Midr. Pss. 31, 120a; b. Hag. 15a; Raphael, *Jewish Views of the Afterlife*, 129–30. That heaven is a place to reward the righteous is also made clear in Midrash Pesiqta Rabbati. Raphael, *Jewish Views of the Afterlife*, 133 (citing Pesiq. Rab. 44:8).

96. Hirsch, *Rabbinic Psychology*, 257–58. See b. Šabb. 152b—153a.

Clearly, the varying beliefs about that fate of the soul immediately following death were inconsistent and difficult to reconcile. Little thought was given to the many inconsistencies and confusions inherent in such notions. Notwithstanding these inconsistencies and confusions, it is beyond doubt that in the rabbinic period Platonic ideas about the soul, appropriately modified to conform with other Jewish ideas, had become generally accepted in Jewish thought.[97] One important Platonic idea not accepted by the rabbis was *metempsychosis*.[98]

D. The More Dominant Rabbinic View Accepted a Postmortem Reward or Punishment to a Recreated Body/Soul Unity

That *Olam Ha-Bah* refers not to the immediate postmortem existence of the soul but to either the messianic age or the end of days, and that divine judgment occurs only in the *Olam Ha-Bah,* not immediately after death, seems to have been the more dominant rabbinic view. On this view, reward or punishment is not received by the soul alone but only by the "entire person," only by a reconstituted body reunited with its soul. In other words, reward and punishment in an afterlife required resurrection and the soul's reinfusion into the resurrected body.[99]

In fact, when the rabbis speak of the resurrection of the body (*tehiyat hametim* in mishnaic materials or *mehaye hametim* in liturgical materials), they generally assume that this notion includes the restoration of an existing soul to the body.[100] This is to say that the rabbinic view, for the most part, adopted the Platonic idea that man is a composite of body and soul.[101] Yet, it must also be kept in mind that the terms *tehiyat hametim* and *mehaye hametim* are ambiguous, were perhaps used by the rabbis precisely because of their ambiguity, and could have implied, to some, a restoration to life that entailed something other than a resurrection of the physical body.[102]

Illustrative of the dualism that became dominant during the rabbinic period, as well as illustrative of the view that it is neither the reconstituted body alone nor the soul alone which is to be rewarded and punished, is the interchange between Antoninus and Judah the Patriarch quoted in section C, 8. This parable "asserts that the person can indeed be resolved into two components, body and soul, but with one

---

97. See Cohon, *Jewish Theology*, 377; Neusner, *From Politics to Piety*, 10.

98. Hirsch, *Rabbinic Psychology*, 272. See Urbach, *Sages*, 1:235; Eylon, *Reincarnation in Jewish Mysticism*, 45.

99. For example, a midrash comparing the binding of Isaac to his actual death and resurrection states that Isaac's soul was returned to his body. Pirqe. R. El. 31. See Levenson, *Resurrection and the Restoration*, 228.

100. See Gillman, *Death of Death*, 135, 138. See e.g., b. Ber. 60b.

101. See Gillman, *Death of Death*, 137; Hirsch, *Rabbinic Psychology*, 167.

102. Segal, *Life After Death*, 606–8. See Gillman, *Death of Death*, 135.

major qualification: separated, body and soul are each defective, handicapped, as it were, and if the person is be fully human, they must be reunited."[103]

Notwithstanding the idea that it is the reunited body and soul that are jointly to be judged, it has also been said that a prevalent rabbinic belief is that upon death the souls of the wicked enter *Gehenna* only temporarily; they are *purged* or *purified* for twelve months, after which time they enter *Gan Eden* where they remain until joined with the resurrected body.[104] Purging of the soul alone seems to be inconsistent with the view that it is only the reunited entity (that is, body and soul together) that is judged.[105] But, once again, that the views found in rabbinic literature are varied and inconsistent is not surprising. At least one rabbinic authority even insisted that Job 7:9 indicates a biblical denial of the doctrine of resurrection,[106] and we know from extraneous sources that there were Jews in the second century CE who also denied the resurrection of the dead.[107]

E. Rabbinic Efforts Were Directed Toward Establishing Resurrection as a Doctrine Derived from the Torah

1. The rabbis attempted to find a biblical basis for resurrection

The rabbis were little concerned with clarifying any issues relating to resurrection, such as explaining the nature of the resurrected body. Rather, their greatest concern was to establish that the doctrine of resurrection is biblically based.[108] Daniel 12:1-3

---

103. Madigan and Levenson, *Resurrection*, 205.

104. Raphael, *Jewish Views of the Afterlife*, 144-45, 160. See also Moore, *Judaism in the First Centuries*, 2:318 (discussing the disagreement between the Schools of Shammai and Hillel as to the fate of those who were neither totally righteous nor totally wicked, with the former contending that a period of purgation in the fires of Gehenna is required, and the latter maintaining that God "would incline the balance to the side of mercy, and not send them down to Gehenna at all . . ." citing Tosepheta Sanh. 13, 3; b. Roš.Haš. 16b—17a); Cohon, *Jewish Theology*, 394-95 ("The Shammaites distinguished between three classes with regard to the hereafter: The completely righteous will enjoy eternal life. The completely wicked will be consigned to everlasting reproach and abhorrence. The intermediary class [the *benonim*] will descend to Gehinnom and be purged. But the Hillelites hold that God's attribute of 'abundant mercy' means that He inclines toward mercy. He is compassionate even with the wicked."); Hirsch, *Rabbinic Psychology*, 266-67 ("Only the pure and perfect were fit to be under God's throne of glory. Another place had to be found for the souls which had not yet reached perfection, but which were yet too good for the fate of the wicked." Thus, "when the souls of the righteous were given a place in heaven, their former position was passed on to those of the middle state."); b. Šabb. 152b; ch. 6, sec. C, 2.

105. See Hirsch, *Rabbinic Psychology*, 168 (The "repeated exhortation to preserve the soul pure is difficult to harmonize with the Rabbinic conception of man as a unity.").

106. b. B. Bat. 16a. See Silver, *Maimonidean Criticism*, 115-17 ("The traditional treatment of resurrection was anything but consistent. Raba had insisted that Job 7:9 . . . indicated a Biblical denial of the entire doctrine.").

107. See Cohen, *From the Maccabees to the Mishnah*, 217.

108. See Gillman, *Death of Death*, 128-31; Segal, *Life After Death*, 614-19; Moore, *Judaism in the*

and Isaiah 26:19 provide an obvious biblical basis but were "not sufficient in and of themselves, probably because they are not from the Pentateuch which was considered supremely authoritative."[109] Accordingly, numerous attempts were made to ground resurrection in the Pentateuch but each attempt "is more fanciful than the other, simply because the doctrine is not really in the text."[110]

Consideration was given to Numbers 18:28 but the school of Rabbi Ishmael raised questions that had the effect of eliminating it as a proof text.[111] Deuteronomy 31:16 is, similarly, considered to be inadequate.[112] However, Deuteronomy 11:9, 21, and 4:4 were found to be acceptable.[113] A number of examples illustrating how the rabbis could use creative interpretations of biblical texts to support their conviction that the idea of resurrection is in the Torah are contained in *Sanhedrin* 90b–92a. Two such examples are:

1. Our Rabbis taught: *I kill and make alive* [Deut 32:39); I might interpret, I kill one person and give life to another, as the world goes on. Therefore, the Bible says: *I wound and I heal*. Just as the wounding and healing refer to the same person, so putting to death and bringing to life refer to the same person. This refutes those who maintain that resurrection is not intimated in the Torah.

2. R. Meir said, Whence do we know resurrection from the Torah? From the verse, *Then shall Moses and the children of Israel sing this song unto the Lord* (Exod 15:1): not *sang* but *shall sing* is written: thus resurrection is taught in the Torah.[114]

In short, the rabbis used their own hermeneutical techniques to read into the biblical text the idea of resurrection, much the same as Philo used allegory to read into the biblical text the Greek idea of an immortal soul. By this means the rabbis transformed an idea that developed "in a specific [post-biblical] setting to meet specific theological challenges [related to the problem of moral evil]" into one which could be claimed to represent "the eternal and unchanging word of God, part of God's original teaching to be accepted by all Jews."[115] Indeed, it was said that any Jew who denied that resurrection is a teaching that derives from the Torah would be separated from

---

First Centuries, 2:381–83; Raphael, *Jewish Views of the Afterlife*, 157; Madigan and Levenson, *Resurrection*, 208; Levenson, *Resurrection and the Restoration*, 219.

109. Gillman, *Death of Death*, 128.

110. Gillman, *Death of Death*, 128.

111. m. Sanh. 10:1. See Segal, *Life After Death*, 614; Madigan and Levenson, *Resurrection*, 210.

112. Segal, *Life After Death*, 615–16.

113. Segal, *Life After Death*, 616. See m. Sanh. 10:1. See also Moore, *Judaism in the First Centuries*, 2:382–83. Cf. Madigan and Levenson, *Resurrection*, 211.

114. See Madigan and Levenson, *Resurrection*, 208–9. See also Levenson, *Resurrection and the Restoration*, 23–34; Segal, *Life After Death*, 616–17; Gillman, *Death of Death*, 128–29; Raphael, *Jewish Views of the Afterlife*, 157.

115. Gillman, *Death of Death*, 131.

the people of Israel and punished by the forfeiture of their share in the *Olam Ha-Bah* belonging to all Israelites.[116]

2. The doctrine of resurrection was inserted into Aramaic translations of the Bible

During the rabbinic period, the Hebrew Bible was translated into Aramaic, the language spoken by the Jews of the Eastern diaspora and, to some extent, of the land of Israel as well.[117] These translations are known as *targumim*. Like the rest of rabbinic literature, the *targumim* are collective works, written over a long span of time.[118] As Flesher notes, "The Palestinian Targums to the Pentateuch are widely known for the material they insert into their translations of the Hebrew text . . . Nowhere is this more evident than with regard to the belief in resurrection of the dead. Although the Hebrew Pentateuch lacks any defined notion of the resurrection of the dead, the targums insert it."[119]

A prime example of the translators' insertion of the doctrine of resurrection into the Hebrew Bible is the *targumic* treatment of Genesis 3:19, in which God punishes Adam for eating the forbidden fruit. The Hebrew Bible states: "By the sweat of your brow shall you get bread to eat until you return to the earth, because from it you were created; because you are dust and to dust you are to return." Targum Neofiti inserts immediately after: "But from the dust you are to arise again to give an account and a reckoning of all you have done."[120] The same insertion also appears in other *targumim*, including Targum Pseudo-Jonathan.[121]

Similarly, several *targumim* expand the Hebrew of Deuteronomy 32:39, already used as a proof text for the doctrine of resurrection, to reinforce the rabbinic interpretation; specifically, the passage is translated to read: "I am he who causes the living to die in this world, and who brings the dead to life in the world to come."[122] Other passages that are expanded to make reference to the doctrine of resurrection include Genesis 4:8, 19:26, 25:34, and 30:22, Exodus 15:12, and Numbers 11:26.[123]

---

116. m. Sanh. 10:1.
117. Cohen, *From the Maccabees to the Mishnah*, 201.
118. Cohen, *From the Maccabees to the Mishnah*, 201.
119. Flesher, "Resurrection of the Dead," 311. See Segal, *Life After Death*, 629.
120. Flesher, "Resurrection of the Dead," 312.
121. Flesher, "Resurrection of the Dead," 312n4.
122. Flesher, "Resurrection of the Dead," 314.
123. See Flesher, "Resurrection of the Dead," 314–21; Segal, *Life After Death*, 629.

F. There Was Little Concern for, or Uniformity with Regard to, the Details of Resurrection and the Afterlife

1. The nature of the resurrected body is not adequately clarified

With regard to the type of body that is to be resurrected, rabbinic literature is mostly silent.[124] And once again such views about the nature of the resurrected body as can be found in rabbinic texts are inconsistent. There is even inconsistency with regard to the state of the body immediately following death, with Simeon ben Yohai suggesting the complete disintegration of the body, and certain texts suggesting the opposite.[125] As Kohler further notes, "Later still arose the legend of an indestructible bone of the spinal column, called *Luz*, which was to form the nucleus for the revival of the whole body."[126]

The most well-recognized text about the resurrected body is the gloss on the saying of Rav found in b. Berakhot 17a:

> It was a favorite saying of Rav: 'Not like this world is the World to Come.' In the World to Come there is neither eating nor drinking, no procreation of children or business transactions, no envy or hatred or rivalry. But the righteous sit enthroned, their crowns on their heads and enjoy the radiance of the *Shekhinah*.[127]

Yet, elsewhere rabbinic literature seems to envision that the resurrected body will engage in the very bodily functions that are specifically excluded in b. Berakhot 17a. For example, b. Ketubbot 111b emphasizes the ease with which grapes will be harvested in the *Olam Ha-Bah* and made into wine, in comparison to the difficulty required in the *Olam Ha-Zeh*, which would not be mentioned if there were to be no drinking of wine in the *Olam Ha-Bah*:

> Not like this world will be the World to Come. In this world one has the trouble to harvest grapes and press them; but in the World to Come a person will bring a single grape in a wagon or ship, store it in the corner of his house, and draw from it enough wine to fill it a large flagon . . . There will not be a grape which will not yield thirty measures of wine.[128]

---

124. See Gillman, *Death of Death*, 131–33.

125. See Kohler, *Jewish Theology*, 287–88.

126. Kohler, *Jewish Theology*, 288 (citing Qoh. Rab. 12:5). See also Gillman, *Death of Death*, 132–33 (citing Lev. Rab. 18:1). This notion of the *Luz* seems to presage the eighteenth-century doctrine of palingenesis advanced by Charles Bonnet and supported by Johann Herder. See Altmann, *Moses Mendelssohn*, 207–8; ch. 10, sec. D, 1.

127. Segal, *Life After Death*, 624. See also Raphael, *Jewish Views of the Afterlife*, 124.

128. See Raphael, *Jewish Views of the Afterlife*, 126 ("the Talmud states that in the World to Come 'grain will be produced after fifteen days and trees will grow fruit after one month' (*p. Taanit* 64a); 'the land of Israel will grow loaves of the finest flour and garments of the finest wool' (*Ketubbot* 111b); and 'women will bear children daily and the trees will produce fruit daily' (*Shabbat* 30b).").

The difference between a resurrected body which engages in the normal bodily functions of eating, drinking, procreation, etc. and one which doesn't may simply reflect the difference between resurrection in the *Olam Ha-Bah* as the end time and resurrection in the *Olam Ha-Bah* as the messianic age, but it may also reflect a fundamental problem in the concept of resurrection. The problem relates to whether, after the body is reconstituted, it will once again age, weaken, die, and decompose. Some might argue that if resurrection is to be lasting and eternal, the resurrected body must be something radically different than the body which exists in the *Olam Ha-Zeh*.

One is reminded of the contradictory concepts of resurrection found among those Jews who initiated the sect that was to become Christianity. The author of the Gospel of Luke describes the resurrection of Jesus as the resurrection of the very same flesh and blood body with which Jesus died, having the same appearance and possessing the same bodily functions.[129] However, in 1 Corinthians 15, Paul distinguishes the body that dies and is placed in the ground from the body that is raised or resurrected:

> It is sown in corruption; it is raised in incorruption: . . . It is sown a natural body; it is raised a spiritual body. There is a natural body, and there is a spiritual body . . . We shall not all sleep, but we shall all be changed. For this corruptible must put on incorruption, and this mortal must put on immortality.[130]

Further, Paul stresses that the resurrected, incorruptible, immortal body will not be of "flesh and blood,"[131] which directly contradicts the Gospel of Luke. The Pauline conception is that the body which is resurrected is a radically different body than the previously existing body.[132] Statements attributed to Jesus support Paul's understanding of resurrection in that they claim that those resurrected will be "as the angels of God in heaven" (Matt 22:30), or "equal unto angels" (Mark 12:25). Significantly, Paul's account may well reflect Pharisaic or rabbinic views.[133]

The radical transformation of the body envisioned by Paul raised difficult questions puzzled over by the church fathers.[134] Included among the questions they pondered are: (1) If a human body is eaten by cannibals, and if whatever is eaten becomes part of the body, then the same particles that were part of the first body will become a part of the second body, and how will God will be able to reassemble the first body? (2) Will aborted fetuses rise? (3) Will deformities and mutilations appear in heaven? (4) Will we all be the same sex in heaven? (5) Will we have to eat? (6) Will there

---

129. Luke 24:37.

130. Luke 15:42–53. See generally Segal, *Life After Death*, 428–34; Bynum, *Resurrection of the Body*, 3–6; Chilton, "Resurrection in the Gospels," 226–30.

131. 1 Cor 15:50.

132. Bynum, *Resurrection of the Body*, 6.

133. Segal, *Life After Death*, 401.

134. See Wolfson, "Immortality and Resurrection," 65–72.

be marriage? (7) Will we be resurrected with all our internal organs, as well as our external ones? (8) Will we be resurrected with the scars our bodies previously had?[135]

The degree to which the rabbis similarly concerned themselves with issues raised by the concept of resurrection is not clear. But the differing conceptions of the resurrected body as engaging in bodily functions of eating, drinking, and sex, and as not engaging in those functions, suggests that they did consider such questions. Further support for the rabbis' concern with such issues comes from the fact that such issues were considered in 2 Baruch (believed by some scholars to have been authored by the possible predecessors of the rabbis, and even attributed to Rabbi Akiba), and were later given attention by Saadia Gaon.[136]

In keeping with a thought that 2 Baruch had expressed,[137] it was assumed by some that in order for the resurrected body to be recognized it would have all the defects and deformities it had prior to death, but that after recognition God would heal all infirmities, for God says in Deuteronomy 32:39, "I wound, and I heal."[138] With regard to these "two stages of resurrection" Levenson comments:

> On the one hand, were the dead to come back already healed and transformed, they would no longer be the same persons—the same inextricable combination of body and soul—that they were in this life. On the other hand, were they to come back with their same defective moral bodies and morally ambiguous souls, they would be unfit for eternal life in the World-to-Come for which they are to be resurrected. The schema of two stages—first resurrection, then healing—navigates the paradox brilliantly. It preserves the continuity of personal identity and subjects the risen dead to a process of re-creation that renders them fit for life after death . . .[139]

It was also believed that the dead would not be resurrected naked, but "would rise clothed as they had been in life . . . or in the garments in which they had been buried."[140] With regard to the Pauline notion that the resurrected body would be spiritual and incorruptible, Segal observes: "The Rabbis do not seem to care much whether

---

135. See Bynum, *Resurrection of the Body*, 33, 37–38, 97–98. See generally Segal, *Life After Death*, 543–95. Cf. Matt 22:23–30 ("in the resurrection they neither marry, nor are given in marriage, but are as the angels of God in heaven.").

136. See Moore, *Judaism in the First Centuries*, 2:380 (The question raised in 1 Corinthians 15 concerning the sort of body in which one will be resurrected "confronted the Jews also," citing Syr. Bar.); ch. 5, sec. C, 3. See also Hirsch, *Rabbinic Psychology*, 149.

137. See ch. 2, sec. D, 4.

138. See Moore, *Judaism in the First Centuries*, 2:380; Gillman, *Death of Death*, 133. Sanhedrin 91b states: "R. Simeon b. Laquish contrasted [these two verses]: 'It is written, "I will gather them . . . with the blind and the lame . . ."' (Jer 31:8), and it is written, "Then shall the lame man leap as a hart and the tongue of the dumb sing . . ." (Is 35:6). How so [will the dead both retain their defects and also be healed]? 'They will rise [from the grave] bearing their defects and then be healed.'"

139. Levenson, *Resurrection and the Restoration*, 225.

140. Moore, *Judaism in the First Centuries*, 2:381.

resurrection is as literal, fleshy body, or as a perfected, spiritual body. Evidently, they believed that the nature of resurrection was for God to define."[141]

2. There is confusion as to precisely who will be resurrected for participation in the *Olam Ha-Bah*

As it was understood during the first century BCE, the *Olam Ha-Bah* concerned primarily the reestablishment of the nation of Israel to its rightful place, with only those righteous who had recently died being resurrected to participate. But in the rabbinic literature it was stated that those to participate in the *Olam Ha-Bah* would include all Jews who had died at any time. Specifically, in the Mishnah tractate Sanhedrin, chapter 10, mishnah 1, there is the following language:

> All Israelites have a share in the world/age to come, for it is written, 'Thy people also shall be all righteous, they shall inherit the land for ever; the branch of my planting, the work of my hands that I may be glorified [Isa 60:21].[142]

Despite the language in Mishnah Sanhedrin 10:1 that *all* Israelites would participate in the *Olam Ha-Bah*, the first mishnah of the tractate explicitly excludes certain persons. First to be excluded are those who claim "that there is no resurrection of the dead in the world/age to come."[143] These are followed by those who deny the divine origin of the Torah and by anyone who is "an *apikoros*."[144] The mishnah then adds that R. Akiba also excluded from participation anyone who "reads the heretical books" or attempts to heal a wound by means of incantation, and that Abba Saul excluded

---

141. Segal, *Life After Death*, 608. See also b. Nid. 70b; Saadia, *Book of Beliefs and Opinions*, 82 (referring to b. Nid. 70b).

142. See Madigan and Levenson, *Resurrection*, 206–7; Rosner, *Maimonides' Commentary on the Mishnah*, 164n1 (discussing whether quoted language is from chapter 10 or 11). The reliance on Isaiah 60:21 as a proof-text suggests to some that by the "world to come" the Tannaim had in mind the messianic age rather than the end time. See Avery-Peck, "Death and the Afterlife," 248. See generally Segal, *Life After Death*, 603–6 (questioning whether the "land" to which all Israel shall return is an "ideal land on this earth," a "reconstituted earth," or "a heavenly Israel"); Kellner, *Must a Jew Believe Anything?*, 33–34 (the land which the righteous will inherit for all eternity "must be in another dispensation altogether"). *Olam Ha-Bah* is sufficiently ambiguous to permit different understandings.

143. See Levenson, *Resurrection and the Restoration*, 24–26 (discussing differing versions of this language, with some versions excluding those who deny the resurrection of the dead and other versions excluding those who deny that the resurrection of the dead *is in the Torah*.).

144. See Madigan and Levenson, *Resurrection*, 207 (*apikoros* is "an umbrella term that seems to indicate one who denies the basic elements of rabbinic belief, most centrally the belief in divine providence and justice."); Kellner, *Must a Jew Believe Anything?*, 34 ("while it is highly probable that the term derives from the name of the Greek philosopher [Epicurus] . . . there is really no way of knowing what exactly the author of the mishnah meant. The Babylonian Talmud, however, in glossing this mishnah, is quite clear on its understanding of the term: the *epikoros* is that person who shows disrespect to the rabbis."); Setzer, *Resurrection of the Body*, 41–44; Jacobs, *Principles of the Jewish Faith*, 11–13; Kohler, *Jewish Theology*, 21n1 (citing Josephus, *Ant.* 10.11.7); Rosner, *Maimonides' Commentary on the Mishnah*, 65nn6–7.

anyone who uttered the Tetragrammaton.[145] The second mishnah of the tractate goes on to exclude from participation in the *Olam Ha-Bah* certain biblical figures—three kings (Jeroboam, Ahab, and Manasseh) and four "commoners" (Balaam, Doeg, Ahitophel, and Gehazi).[146] The third mishnah excludes the "generation of the Flood," the "generation of the dispersion," the "men of Sodom," the followers of Korah (who rebelled against Moses) and others.[147]

Later sages were to further add to the list of persons excluded from participation in the *Olam Ha-Bah*. As noted by Maimonides, those to be denied participation included: (1) "He who publicly shames his neighbor," (2) "he who calls his neighbor by his (evil) nickname," and (3) "he who takes honor in the disgrace of his neighbor."[148] In fact, according to Maimonides, despite the language that *all* Israelites shall share in the *Olam Ha-Bah*, the rabbis actually meant only the righteous. He writes that resurrection is:

> [only] for the righteous as stated in *Bereshit Rabbah*: 'The benefit of the rains is both for the righteous and the wicked, but the resurrection of the dead is only for the righteous.' How can the wicked live again, since they are (considered) dead even while alive? Thus have our Sages said: 'The wicked, even in their lifetime, are called dead, but the righteous, even after death, are called alive.'[149]

The rabbinic material is particularly unclear with respect to the participation of non-Jews in the *Olam Ha-Bah*, and with respect to their resurrection and ultimate fate. Contradictory rabbinic views about the participation of gentiles in the *Olam Ha-Bah* were set forth from a very early date. Two late-first-century CE masters, Rabbi Eliezer ben Hyrcanus and Rabbi Joshua ben Hananiah, interpreting the same biblical passage differently, took opposing positions. The former held that non-Jews do not have a portion in the *Olam Ha-Bah,* while the latter held that they did.[150] According to Raphael, in some instances "a universal belief is put forth that everyone ... [including gentiles] will be resurrected: 'They that are born are destined to die and the dead brought to life again' [m. Avot 4.29]. Other passages, however, claim that 'the resurrection is reserved for Israel' [Gen. Rab. 8:6]."[151]

---

145. See Segal, *Life After Death*, 603–4, 609; Rosner, *Maimonides' Commentary on the Mishnah*, 165n10.

146. See Segal, *Life After Death*, 609–10; Rosner, *Maimonides' Commentary on the Mishnah*, 158 and accompanying notes.

147. See Segal, *Life After Death*, 610–11; Rosner, *Maimonides' Commentary on the Mishnah*, 159–61 and accompanying notes. See generally Moore, *Judaism in the First Centuries*, 2:387; Raphael, *Jewish Views of the Afterlife*, 143–45.

148. Rosner, *Maimonides' Commentary on the Mishnah*, 150.

149. Rosner, *Maimonides' Commentary on the Mishnah*, 147. See also Raphael, *Jewish Views of the Afterlife*, 158.

150. Tosefta Sanh. 12:2. See Moore, *Judaism in the First Centuries*, 2:385–86; Gillman, *Death of Death*, 133–34; Kohler, *Heaven and Hell*, 116.

151. Raphael, *Jewish Views of the Afterlife*, 158. See also Raphael, *Jewish Views of the Afterlife*, 129.

Disagreement regarding the resurrection of gentiles may possibly also be gleaned from the *targumim*. Some *targumim* to Genesis 19:26 say that Lot's wife, who is not an Israelite, will remain a pillar of salt until the resurrection, when she will live again. However, Targum Pseudo-Jonathan deliberately omits mention of resurrection regarding Lot's wife.[152] There are also *targumim* that more clearly indicate that resurrection is only for Israel.[153] Moore asserts that the opinion of Rabbi Joshua ben Hananiah that non-Jews will participate in the *Olam Ha-Bah*, "prevailed" but Moore's earliest authority to support this assertion is Maimonides, citing Hilkot Teshubah 3:5.[154] Gillman, similarly relying on Hilkot Teshubah 3:5, states that "the consensus of rabbinic opinion, here codified by Maimonides, reflects the triumph of the universalist position."[155]

A universalist position is clearly expressed in the belief that the wicked among Jews and non-Jews will be punished in *Gehenna*, either for a twelve-month period or for eternity. According to Tosefta Sanhedrin 13:4–5:

> The wicked of Israel in their bodies, and the wicked of the nations of the world in their bodies go down to [*Gehenna*] and are punished in it for twelve months. After twelve months their souls become extinct, and their bodies are burned up, and [*Gehenna*] casts them out, and they turn to ashes, and the wind scatters them and strews them beneath the soles of the feet of the righteous . . . But the heretics and the apostates and the informers and the epicureans and those who deny the revelation (Torah), and those who separate themselves from the ways of the community, and those who deny the resurrection of the dead, and all those who sin and make the multitude sin, like Jeroboam and Ahab, and those who put the terror of them into the land of the living, and those who stretch out their hands against the temple—on these [*Gehenna*] will be locked, and they will be punished in it for generations.[156]

3. There is a split of opinion as to when the resurrection will occur

An issue existed as to whether there would be a resurrection of the dead at the time of the messianic age or at the end time. Since the tractate Sanhedrin, quoted above, states that all Israel will participate in the *Olam Ha-Bah*, and since the sense of *Olam Ha-Bah* in that passage seems to be the messianic age, the passage suggests that the resurrection of the dead would occur during the messianic age. However, the Talmud

---

152. Flesher, "Resurrection of the Dead," 323. See Segal, *Life After Death*, 629.

153. Flesher, "Resurrection of the Dead," 318, 321, 328.

154. Moore, *Judaism in the First Centuries*, 2:386. Accord, Kohler, *Heaven and Hell*, 116 (Joshua ben Hananiah's opinion "became the generally adopted one").

155. Gillman, *Death of Death*, 134. See also Cohen, *From the Maccabees to the Mishnah*, 209.

156. Moore, *Judaism in the First Centuries*, 2:387 (also citing, b. Roš.Haš.17a). See also m. Avot 5:20.

relates that a certain "Samuel" took an opposing position. Samuel, relying on Deuteronomy 15:11 as a proof text, is reported to have said, "This world differs from the Messianic era only in respect to servitude of the exiled, for it is said, *For the poor shall never cease out of the land*."[157] The proof text implies that poverty will continue in the messianic age. Therefore, according to Samuel, although the messianic age would bring about an ingathering of the exiles and an end to servitude, it would not initiate a new state of affairs such as was prophesied by Isaiah. It would not result in an end to hunger and want or the resurrection of the dead; rather, everything in the messianic age would be as it had been in the premessianic period.

In opposition to Samuel, "R. Hiyya b. Abba also said in the name of R. Johanan: All the prophets prophesied only for the days of the Messiah, but as for the world to come, 'Eye hath not seen, oh God, beside Thee.'"[158] In other words, according to Abba, the messianic age *would* initiate a new state of affairs, including the resurrection of the dead. During the Middle Ages, Saadia would reject the view of Samuel; Maimonides would accept it.[159] The same disagreement as the one between Samuel and Abba about the time of the resurrection emerges in the *targumim*.[160]

4. Relatively little attention is paid to the nature of the reward or punishment in the afterlife

Rabbinic descriptions of the kind of existence to be experienced in the afterlife are relatively sparse.[161] Moreover, such descriptions as do appear are neither consistent nor fully delineated. The rabbis were most concerned to establish that obedience to Torah leads to reward, and disobedience leads to punishment; delineating precise details concerning the nature of such reward or punishment was far less important. Furthermore, inconsistency regarding such details was a function of inconsistency about other related matters, such as (1) whether it is the soul or resurrected body that is to be judged, and, if the body, the nature of the resurrected body, and (2) whether the resurrection would occur in the messianic age or at the end time. Consequently, Rav could say: "In the World to Come there is neither eating nor drinking, no procreation of children or business transactions,"[162] while others could speak of the great abundance of wine to drink and food to eat.

---

157. b. Šabb. 63a (emphasis original). Accord, b. Ber. 34b; b. Sanh. 91b, 99a.

158. b. Šabb. 63a; b. Ber. 34b.

159. Saadia, *Book of Beliefs and Opinions*, 265–66; Maimonides, *Maimonides' Commentary on the Mishnah*, 147.

160. See Flesher, "Resurrection of the Dead," 312, 319–20.

161. See generally Kellner, *Must a Jew Believe Anything?*, 30 ("While classical Judaism clearly teaches that right behaviour in this world is rewarded in the next, and wrong behaviour in this world is punished in the next, it typically never seeks to establish precisely what happens.").

162. b. Ber 17a.

CHAPTER 4.

Gehenna is somewhat more fully described than *Gan Eden*. In keeping with the biblical location from which the word *Gehenna* is derived as well as with prerabbinic uses of the word, *Gehenna* is depicted as a place where there is fire of abnormal intensity.[163] Tosefta Sanhedrin 13:4 states that the wicked of Israel are sentenced "to twelve months of torture in hell where their souls are terminated and their bodies burnt." Yet, the rabbis also mention other conditions that were to be found in *Gehenna*, such as hail, snow, brimstone, smoke, and darkness.[164]

As *Gehenna* is variously depicted, so too is *Gan Eden*. It is sometimes referred to as being a "celestial" place "where the souls of the righteous dwell" but is also depicted as a "terrestrial . . . garden of lush vegetation and abundant fertility [presumably enjoyed, not by a disembodied soul, but by the resurrected body/soul unity]."[165] According to rabbinic thought, "just as Gehenna serves as a reminder and a warning . . . of the dangers of straying from God's ways, Gan Eden exists to provide inspiration . . . to lead a holy, God-fearing life. It is this ethical theme that underlies the rabbinic doctrine of Gan Eden."[156]

G. The Purpose of Resurrection and of Reward or Punishment in an Afterlife—to Foster Obedience to Torah—Was of Paramount Concern to the Rabbis

While details of the rabbis' views about the nature of the soul, resurrection, and the afterlife are unclear and inconsistent, there is little doubt as to their purpose in advocating a belief in a postmortem judgment and recompense. They sought to ensure absolute fidelity and obedience to rabbinic interpretations of the Torah. Adherence to the rabbis' Torah interpretations was of vital importance to them since they desired to use the law as interpreted by them as a replacement for the temple cult which had been destroyed.[167] They realized that the fulfillment of the laws of the Torah, as they interpreted it, would be enhanced if an eternal reward or punishment in an afterlife depended on it. Therefore, rabbinic material is replete with references to obedience to Torah as the means of achieving a reward after death. The details of an afterlife were less important to the rabbis than the means-end relationship: obedience leads to reward and disobedience to punishment.

163. See Raphael, *Jewish Views of the Afterlife*, 147–48.
164. See Raphael, *Jewish Views of the Afterlife*, 148.
165. Raphael, *Jewish Views of the Afterlife*, 149.
166. Raphael, *Jewish Views of the Afterlife*, 150–51.
167. Neusner, *From Politics to Piety*, 146. See generally Cohen, *From the Maccabees to the Mishnah*, 213–20 (discussing the emergence of rabbinic Judaism); Setzer, *Resurrection of the Body*, 36–39, 49–52 (arguing that the rabbis linked resurrection of the dead to "an assertion of their own legitimacy and authority . . . [I]t connects to a certain ethos that informs doctrine by supporting the claims of the Pharisees/rabbis of their own legitimacy. They are the ones who correctly understand God's power in this world (and the next).").

Before there is reward or punishment, however, there must be judgment, so the rabbis warn that there will be both a resurrection and a judgment that takes into account everything that one has done:

> [R. Eliezar Ha-Kappar] would say: 'Those who are born are [destined] to die, and those who die are [destined] for resurrection. And the [resurrected] are [destined] to be judged . . . And know that everything is subject to reckoning. And do not let your evil impulse persuade you that *Sheol* is a place of refuge for you. For . . . despite your wishes you are going to give a full accounting before the king of kings, the Holy One, blessed be he.'[168]

A positive outcome of such "full accounting" required adherence to Torah. So, the "idea of a world-to-come accentuates the value of Torah study and proper behavior in this world."[169] Neusner writes:

> Those who do not pass judgment then are condemned and do not pass on to eternal life . . . How to stand in judgment, meaning, go through the process of divine review of one's life and actions and emerge in the world-to-come, restored to the land that is Eden? Proper conduct and study of Torah lead to standing in judgment and consequent life of the world-to-come, and not keeping the one and studying the other deny entry into that life . . . The world-to-come, involving resurrection and judgment, will be attained through the Torah, which teaches proper conduct.[170]

Not surprisingly, the *targumim*'s expansions of the biblical text emphasize that what happens in the world-to-come is judgment, that resurrection of the dead is "for the purpose of judgment," and "that judgment would be on the basis of adherence to Torah."[171] For instance, one such expansion reads:

> 'Two thousand years before he created the world he had created the Torah; he had prepared the garden of Eden for the just and Gehenna for the wicked. He had prepared the garden of Eden for the just that they might eat and delight themselves from the fruits of the tree [of life], because they had kept precepts of the Torah in this world and fulfilled the commandments. For the wicked he prepared Gehenna, which is comparable *to a sharp sword* devouring with both edges. He prepared within it darts of fire and burning coals for the wicked, to be avenged of them in the world-to-come because they did not observe the precepts of the Torah in this world. For the Torah is a tree of life for everyone

---

168. m. Avot, 4:29. See Avery-Peck, "Death and the Afterlife," 248. See also Pesiq. Rab. 44:8 (quoted above); Raphael, *Jewish Views of the Afterlife*, 129–30, 132–33.

169. Avery-Peck, "Death and the Afterlife," 251.

170. Neusner, "Death and Afterlife," 273–74 (relying upon Lev. Rab.). See also Eylon, *Reincarnation in Jewish Mysticism*, 52 (quoting b. Menaḥ. 99b, which states that "whosoever keeps the Torah his soul is preserved, and whosoever does not preserve the Torah his soul is not preserved.").

171. Flesher, "Resurrection of the Dead," 315.

who toils in it and keeps the commandments: he lives and endures like the *tree of life* in the world-to-come. The Torah is good for all who labor in it in this world like the fruit of the tree of life."[172]

The *targumist* transforms the Torah into the tree of life.

> Not only is performing the Torah's precepts and commandments paralleled with eating the tree's fruit . . . but the fruit (and the Torah's precepts) gives the just person eternal life in the world-to-come, so 'he lives and endures like the tree of life in the world-to-come' . . . Those who followed the Torah in this world will receive the reward of the Garden of Eden and the Tree of Life in the world-to-come.[173]

It is true that the *highest* motive for proper conduct was said to be, not reward and punishment in this life or the afterlife, but simply reverence for the word of God. "That the law of God and every commandment in it should be kept 'for its own sake,' not for any advantage to be gained by it among men, is frequently emphasized [by the rabbis]."[174] A famous expression of this idea is found in Pirqe Avot where Antigonus of Socho is reported to have taught: "Be not like slaves who serve their master in the expectation of receiving a gratuity; but be like slaves who serve their master in no expectation of receiving a gratuity; and let the fear of Heaven be upon you."[175] Nevertheless, reward and punishment "are the motives to which the mass of mankind is most amenable, and the Jewish teachers, though well aware that they are not the highest, do not scruple on that account to appeal to them."[176]

H. Summary of Rabbinic Views

With regard to the soul, it seems to have been generally accepted in the rabbinic period that something exists that can be so designated but no definitive view of this entity can be ascertained. Hirsch writes that the rabbis

> discussed the nature, origin, and destiny of the soul, its premundane existence, its manifestations in life, and its state after death . . . [but that these] speculations were not developed into a doctrine, or definite religious belief, but formed a special field for the vague, rambling, explorations of the Haggadist . . . The ease with which one theory was exchanged for another, and the indifference with which contradictory ideas were allowed to settle down one

---

172. See Flesher, "Resurrection of the Dead," 315–16 (quoting Tg. Neof. expanding upon Gen 3:24; emphasis original).

173. Flesher, "Resurrection of the Dead," 316.

174. Moore, *Judaism in the First Centuries*, 2:96. See generally Moore, *Judaism in the First Centuries*, 2:89–111 (discussing motives of moral conduct in Rabbinic Judaism).

175. m. Avot 1:3. See Moore, *Judaism in the First Centuries*, 2:95–96.

176. Moore, *Judaism in the First Centuries*, 2:89–90.

beside the other, without adjustment or reconciliation, indicate that we have to do here not with a gradual, inner development, but with the acquisitions and adaptations resulting from external influence. The interaction between Greek and Jewish thought is perhaps nowhere more marked than in the Rabbinic speculations about man.[177]

Definitive statements regarding the rabbinic view of resurrection are no less difficult to find. The concept of the resurrection of the dead was generally accepted, though not without at least some dissenters.[178] But no definitive, unchallenged view can be ascertained as to precisely who will be resurrected, when the resurrection will occur, the nature of the resurrected body, whether it is the resurrected body (together with its reinfused soul) or just the soul that will be rewarded or punished in an afterlife, etc. No less difficult to pin down are rabbinic ideas about the nature of the afterlife. As Moore has succinctly stated with regard to rabbinic Judaism: "Any attempt to systemize the Jewish notions of the hereafter imposes on them an order and consistency which does not exist in them."[179] It would take the genius of Saadia to mold the multitude of rabbinic statements concerning the soul, resurrection, and the afterlife into a more or less consistent and unified point of view. It is to the work of Saadia that we next turn.

177. Hirsch, *Rabbinic Psychology*, 273.

178. The idea of resurrection was incorporated into the daily liturgy formulated by the rabbis, specifically, the second of the "Eighteen Benedictions" or *Amidah*, referred to as the *Gevurot* benediction. Gillman, *Death of Death*, 122–23. See Madigan and Levenson, *Resurrection*, 201–4; Cohen, *From the Maccabees to the Mishnah*, 62–63; Millgram, *Jewish Worship*, 101–2; Kohler, *Jewish Theology*, 284–85; Raphael, *Jewish Views of the Afterlife*, 158. See generally Millgram, *Jewish Worship*, 104–6 (discussing the origin of the *Amidah*).

179. Moore, *Judaism in the First Centuries*, 2:389.

5.

During the Geonic Period, Saadia Systematizes Jewish Thinking about the Afterlife

SAADIA BEN JOSEPH AL-FAYYUMI served as the *gaon* of the Sura rabbinic academy from 928 until his death in 942.[1] He wrote the first systematic presentation of Judaism, entitled in Hebrew translation from the original Arabic *Sefer ha-Emunot ve-ha-De'ot*.[2] This work for the first time attempted to present the various conflicting and sometimes contradictory views that had developed in Jewish civilization from the beginning of the Second Temple period until the end of the rabbinic period as a unified, consistent, and rational body of thought. Included in this work are (1) a systematic and sophisticated account of several views as to the nature of the soul, (2) an analysis of such views, and (3) Saadia's pronouncement as to the correct view. Also included are Saadia's arguments refuting those who deny the resurrection of the dead, his consideration of issues related to bodily resurrection, and his reasoning in support of a postmortem reward or punishment.

Saadia was prompted to compose *Sefer ha-Emunot ve-ha-De'ot* by his own doubts about traditionally accepted doctrines, including the "dogma of resurrection," as well as by the questioning, lack of clarity, and confusion about, *inter alia*, the nature of the soul, the revival of the dead, and life after death that he witnessed among many of the "people Israel."[3] As Heschel comments, "Convinced that certainty can be attained, Saadia's main effort was to establish . . . the truth about the principal controversial

---

1. For background on the life and thought of Saadia, see Malter, *Saadia Gaon*, 25–271; Saadia, *Book of Beliefs and Opinions*, xxiii–xxxii; Saadia, *Book of Doctrines and Beliefs*, 11–22; Guttmann, *Philosophies of Judaism*, 69–83.

2. The Hebrew title is that used by Judah Ibn Tibbon, who first translated Saadia's book into Hebrew in 1186. Saadia, *Book of Doctrines and Beliefs*, 5. The title is variously translated into English as the *Book of Doctrines and Beliefs* or the *Book of Beliefs and Opinions*.

3. Heschel, "Quest for Certainty in Saadia's Philosophy," 265–68. See Saadia, *Book of Beliefs and Opinions*, 414. See also Heschel, "Reason and Revelation in Saadia's Philosophy," 391–92.

issues of Judaism."⁴ Significantly, Saadia sought to arrive at such truth on the basis of rational arguments, and is generally considered the first Jewish thinker to do so. This chapter will offer an account of Saadia's epistemology, followed by a discussion of Saadia's understanding of the nature of soul, understanding of the doctrine of bodily resurrection, and proofs of a postmortem reward or punishment. A brief analysis of Saadia's arguments is also provided.

A. Saadia's Epistemology Recognizes Both Reason and Revelation as Sources of Truth

According to Saadia there are four sources of knowledge recognized by Jews: (1) knowledge gained by sense perception, (2) knowledge gained by rational intuitions, (3) knowledge inferred by logical necessity, and (4) the truth known by a reliable tradition.⁵ The first three of these sources of knowledge are based on the faculties possessed by each human being. They are grouped together by Saadia and referred to collectively as knowledge gained by "inquiry and speculation," or knowledge gained by reason. Knowledge gained by reason is distinguished from the fourth source of knowledge which consists of the written and oral traditions of Judaism (which Saadia refers to as "tradition").⁶ The fourth source of knowledge is distinguished from knowledge gained by reason in that tradition is understood by Saadia as knowledge revealed by God.⁷ In short, for Saadia there are two distinct types of knowledge: (1) knowledge acquired by human intellectual capacities, the knowledge of reason, and (2) knowledge that has been revealed by God, the knowledge of revelation.

Further, Saadia contends that the knowledge of reason and the knowledge of revelation both inform humans of the same truth. This is to say that truths that all humans know based on reason can never be in conflict with truths that Jews know based on revelation. They are simply alternative roads that lead to the same place.⁸

---

4. Heschel, "Quest for Certainty in Saadia's Philosophy," 290.

5. Saadia, *Book of Beliefs and Opinions*, 16–17.

6. "Saadia is not consistent in his use of the term tradition. It sometimes denotes both Scripture and oral tradition and sometimes oral tradition only." Heschel, "Quest for Certainty in Saadia's Philosophy," 311. See Saadia, *Book of Beliefs and Opinions*, 174 ("... the Bible is not the sole basis of our religion, for in addition to it we have two other bases. One of these is anterior to it; namely, the fountain of reason. The second is posterior to it; namely, the source of tradition.").

7. See Heschel, "Quest for Certainty in Saadia's Philosophy," 309 ("teaching that was communicated by God in His revelations to the prophets cannot be derived from the general three sources of knowledge . . . Tradition is to us, what revelation was to the prophets, namely a unique source of knowledge."), 311 ("tradition transmits what was received through revelation").

8. Malter, *Saadia Gaon*, 194–95; Guttmann, *Philosophies of Judaism*, 71; Heschel, "Reason and Revelation in Saadia's Philosophy," 394.

CHAPTER 5.

B. Saadia's Understanding of the Soul Diverges from the Platonic Soul in Significant Ways

Saadia rejects a strict Platonic dualism in which the soul is conceived as an immaterial entity that is distinct from the body and that must strive to free itself from the body. Rather, for Saadia the soul is something material that can only operate in conjunction with the body. Saadia is also opposed to the view that matter and the body are evil.

1. Knowledge that the soul exists and is endowed with reason may be inferred by logical necessity

Saadia takes it as an accepted truth that there is such an entity as the soul. His main concern is to establish the soul's nature. Yet, he offhandedly provides a proof of the soul's existence in explaining knowledge inferred by logical necessity. He writes that "knowledge inferred by logical necessity" consists of "conclusions, which, unless they are accepted by the individual as true, would compel his denial of the validity of his rational intuitions or the perception of his senses."[9] So, if one sees smoke, he says, one should conclude that there is a fire, since, unless it was accepted as true that there is a fire, one would be compelled to deny the knowledge gained by sense perception, namely that there is smoke. As an additional example, Saadia writes:

> Thus we are forced to affirm, although we have never seen it, that man possesses a soul, in order not to deny its manifest activity. [We must] also [agree], although we have never seen it, that every soul is endowed with reason, [merely] in order not to deny the latter's manifest activity.[10]

2. Saddia reviews and rejects various notions of the soul's essence

Saadia notes that there are a "bewildering variety of opinions" regarding the essence of the soul.[11] He refers to four theories concerning the nature of the soul which, he says, "have been listed previously" and which have "been refuted."[12] The reference is to his discussion of the creation of the world *ex nihilo*.[13] Most significant of these four previously refuted theories is Saadia's purported refutation of 'the theory of the spiritual [immaterial] elements" according to which "the creator of material bodies had at his

---

9. Saadia, *Book of Beliefs and Opinions*, 16–17.
10. Saadia, *Book of Beliefs and Opinions*, 17.
11. Saadia, *Book of Beliefs and Opinions*, 235.
12. Saadia, *Book of Beliefs and Opinions*, 235–36.
13. See Saadia, *Book of Beliefs and Opinions*, 236nn2–5. See also Saadia, *Book of Beliefs and Opinions*, 40 ("I say that our Lord, exalted be He, made it known to us that all things were created and that He had created them out of nothing. Thus Scripture says: *In the beginning God created the heaven and the earth* (Gen 1:1).").

disposal incorporeal and eternal [uncreated] substances, from which he created composite bodies."[14] In his refutation of this theory, Saadia states that its proponents "believe something the like of which cannot be found in our experience, viz. the existence of incorporeal things . . . This is something which Reason cannot accept."[15] Saadia has in mind the Platonic concept of the soul as an incorporeal substance which is uncreated and eternal [imperishable]. The other three theories which Saadia claims to have refuted all also assume this type of Platonic soul. Saadia rejects such a theory of the essence of the soul for at least three reasons.[16] First, he believes that he has proven that the only uncreated being is God; everything else is created.[17] Second, human beings cannot have knowledge of what is "of an extracorporeal character and not contained within a bodily frame."[18] Third, the soul has many accidents, "and every substance endowed with accidents must be material, according to Saadia."[19]

Passing over these four previously refuted theories, Saadia focuses on seven other theories. He rejects six of them. It has been shown by Davidson that the source of Saadia's list of theories is, for the most part, a work attributed to Plutarch entitled *De placitis philosophum*.[20] The first theory considered is the theory that the soul is not itself a substance or separate entity but an accident or attribute of things that themselves are substances. Within this first theory Saadia mentions five subtheories, including Aristotle's view that the soul is the "completion [perfection, entelechy or actualization] of a natural body" and the view considered in Plato's *Phaedo* that the soul is the harmony of the four primary elements—air, water, earth, and fire. Saadia rejects all theories which consider the soul to be an accident, rather than a material substance, on the ground that the soul is itself said to possess attributes such as wisdom (or ignorance) and purity (or wickedness), and "one accident could not be the bearer of another."[21]

Next Saadia considers several theories that identify the soul with one or another of the four primary substances. Specifically, he considers the views that the soul is "air," that the soul is "fire," and that the soul "consists of two kinds of air, one of which

---

14. Saadia, *Book of Doctrines and Beliefs*, 63. See Saadia, *Book of Beliefs and Opinions*, 50 (translating "eternal spiritual beings").

15. Saadia, *Book of Doctrines and Beliefs*, 64. See Saadia, *Book of Beliefs and Opinions*, 51 (translating "spiritual beings").

16. See Efros, *Studies in Medieval Jewish Philosophy* 104 (Saadia "rejected the view of Plato and Plotinus that the soul is an immaterial substance.").

17. Saadia, *Book of Beliefs and Opinions*, 50, 241 ("it would be wrong to ascribe eternity to aught except the Creator.").

18. Saadia, *Book of Beliefs and Opinions*, 93.

19. Efros, *Studies in Medieval Jewish Philosophy*, 104.

20. Davisdon, "Saadia's List of Theories of the Soul," 75–94.

21. Saadia, *Book of Beliefs and Opinions*, 237. In attributing such accidents to the soul, Saadia is in accord with rabbinic views. See ch. 4, secs. C, 2 and 3.

is internal while the other is external to the body."²² Davidson has shown that these views correspond in whole or in part with views expressed by Anaxagoras, Epicurus, Democritus, and the Stoics.²³ According to Saadia, these theories are unsound "for if the soul had been made of air, it would have been of a hot and humid nature, and if it had consisted of fire, it would have been of a hot and dry nature, whereas we do not find it to be of such a character."²⁴

Saadia also considers a theory "to the effect that the soul consists of two parts, one of which is intellectual, rational, intransient, with its seat in the heart, while the other is the source of vitality that is spread over the rest of the body and of a transient nature."²⁵ Davidson has shown that this view is a conflation of views expressed by Plato and Pythagoras with those expressed by Democritus and Epicurus.²⁶ Saadia rejects this view because it implies the existence of "two distinct souls."²⁷

Finally, Saadia mentions and rejects the view that "the soul is pure blood," a view which he ascribes to Anan ben David, the founder of the Karaite schism.²⁸ Saadia states that Anan was led to his view by the scriptural statement that "the blood is the soul [*nephesh*]" (Deut 12:23), but, says Saadia, Anan failed to consider the previous statement that "the soul of the flesh is in the blood" (Lev 17:11).²⁹ According to Saadia, the statement of Deuteronomy 12:23 "is only in keeping with the common usage of language which designates an object by the name of place in which it is located."³⁰

3. The theory of the essence of the soul deemed correct by Saadia is that the soul is a pure material substance, similar to the substance of the heavenly spheres, whose essential nature is reasoning

The correct theory of the soul, in Saadia's view, is that the soul is a pure substance "comparable in purity to that of the heavenly spheres."³¹ Both the soul and the heav-

---

22. Saadia, *Book of Beliefs and Opinions*, 237–38.

23. Davidson, "Saadia's List of Theories of the Soul," 81.

24. Saadia, *Book of Beliefs and Opinions*, 237.

25. Saadia, *Book of Beliefs and Opinions*, 237.

26. Davidson, "Saadia's List of Theories of the Soul," 82. See Saadia, *Book of Doctrines and Beliefs*, 143n5.

27. Saadia, *Book of Beliefs and Opinions*, 238.

28. Saadia, *Book of Beliefs and Opinions*, 238.

29. Saadia, *Book of Beliefs and Opinions*, 238.

30. Saadia, *Book of Beliefs and Opinions*, 239.

31. Saadia, *Book of Beliefs and Opinions*, 242. See Saadia, *Book of Beliefs and Opinions*, 206. The heavenly spheres are the layers of concentric spheres surrounding the earth at the center, containing the stars, the planets, the sun, and the moon, of which, in Greek philosophy, heaven was believed to be composed. Aristotle taught that the earth is a world filled with change, death, and decay; in contrast the planets, stars, moon, and sun are perfect, eternal, and unchanging. In addition to the four elements (fire, water, earth, and air) of which, according to traditional Greek thought, terrestrial things are composed, Aristotle postulated a fifth element—known as "aether"—as the matter of the heavenly

enly spheres are luminous and attain their luminosity as a result of light received from God, but the substance of the soul is even "finer," "more refined," "clearer," "purer," "simpler," and "more brilliantly illuminated" than the heavenly spheres.[32] In considering why we never see the soul when it departs from the body at death, Saadia explains that this "is due to its transparency and its resemblance to the air in its fineness, just as we are unable to see the heavenly spheres on account of the purity of their substances and their transparency."[33] It is because the soul is so highly refined that it is "endowed with intellect" or the power of cognition.[34] Indeed, intellect, or the power of cognition, describes the essential nature of the soul.[35]

Based on the view that the material stuff comprising the soul is for Saadia the "celestial fire," and taking into account that "the Stoics often failed to distinguish between *pneuma* and its two constituents (fire and air)," Freudenthal suggests that "Saadia's theory may well be a variant of the Stoic view of soul."[36] Altmann notes that in calling the soul a pure substance similar to the substance of the heavenly or celestial spheres, Saadia "follows . . . the view of [Heraclitus], who defines the soul, according to Stobaeus, as 'something shining,' and, according to Philoponos, as 'an ethereal, i.e. heavenly body.'"[37] Since "the Stoics derived many ideas from Heraclitus,"[38] and Heraclitus asserted that fire is the primary of the four elements, Altmann and Freudenthal may be basically in agreement. Whatever philosophical viewpoints may have informed Saadia's thinking, Saadia's position strongly resembles the rabbinic view that the soul is pure, from heaven, and endowed with reason.[39] Significantly, for Saadia, as for the rabbis, the purity of the soul is specifically related to its moral blamelessness.[40]

Saadia himself says that his view is based on the two sources of knowledge previously mentioned: reason and revelation.[41] Reason dictates the seventh view, says Saadia, based on the observation that the body is deprived of wisdom and intellectual

---

bodies, and which accounted for the difference between terrestrial things and celestial or heavenly things. Aether was believed to be a pure, perfect substance, devoid of the qualities of ordinary physical bodies. See generally Saadia, *Book of Beliefs and Opinions*, 42–43 (heaven consists "of many layers of spheres, one within the other, in which [are] set individual luminaries called 'stars,' . . . all of them fitted into these spheres.").

32. Saadia, *Book of Beliefs and Opinions*, 242; Saadia, *Book of Doctrines and Beliefs*, 145.

33. Saadia, *Book of Beliefs and Opinions*, 256.

34. Saadia, *Book of Doctrines and Beliefs*, 145.

35. Saadia, *Book of Beliefs and Opinions*, 243.

36. Freudenthal, "Stoic Physics in the Writings of R. Saadia," 130. See generally Davidson, *Alfarabi, Avicenna and Averroes*, 85n44.

37. Saadia, *Book of Doctrines and Beliefs*, 145n3.

38. Long, *Hellenistic Philosophy*, 145, 155–56.

39. See ch. 4, secs. C, 2 and 3.

40. Saadia, *Book of Beliefs and Opinions*, 246 (obedience to God's commandments "increases the luminosity of the soul's substance, whereas sin renders its substance turbid and black"). See also Saadia, *Book of Beliefs and Opinions*, 207; Malter, *Saadia Gaon*, 245. Cf. ch. 4, secs. C, 3 and 8.

41. Saadia, *Book of Beliefs and Opinions*, 242. See sec. A.

capacities when the soul is separated from the body, and on the belief that the soul could not perform these functions if it were made of earthy or terrestrial matter. Indeed, the soul must be of an even finer substance than the heavenly bodies since "if it were of the [exact same] consistency of the heavenly spheres, it would no more be endowed with reason than any of the latter."[42]

Although all souls are composed of a similar substance, the souls of the righteous are noble and shine with varying degrees of luminosity (depending on their degree of righteousness) while those of the wicked are base and do not shine (but are "turbid and black").[43] This idea has scriptural bases; Saadia says:

> proof is derived from the statement of Scripture to the effect that the virtuous souls shine like the heavenly spheres which are illuminated by the stars. This is expressed in the words: *And they that are wise shall shine as the brightness of the firmament* (Dan 12:3). The wicked souls, on the other hand, do not shine, but are on a lower level than the unspecified spheres, as Scripture says: *Behold, He putteth no trust in His holy ones; yea, the heavens are not clean in His sight. How much less one that is abominable and impure, man who drinketh iniquity like water* (Job 15:15, 16).[44]

4. Saadia rejects the rabbinic concept that souls preexist the creation of the body; for Saadia, the soul is created in the heart simultaneously with the creation of the body

Saadia accepts that the soul is neither an eternal (uncreated) being, nor a spiritual (incorporeal) being, but rather is created and material.[45] But he rejects the rabbinic concept of a *guph*, or storehouse of souls, existing prior to the creation of human bodies.[46] Rather, relying on an interpretation of Zechariah 12:1, Saadia asserts that one's soul is created simultaneously with one's body. He writes:

> I say, then, that the truth, so far as the nature of the soul is concerned, is that it is created. This view accords with my previous demonstration that all things existing in the world have been created and that it would be wrong to ascribe eternity to aught except the Creator. It is prompted furthermore by the declaration of God [that He was the one] *Who formed the spirit of man within him* (Zech 12:1). Now this creation of the soul by our Lord first takes place

---

42. Saadia, *Book of Beliefs and Opinions*, 242.
43. Saadia, *Book of Beliefs and Opinions*, 246.
44. Saadia, *Book of Beliefs and Opinions*, 242–43.
45. See Saadia, *Book of Beliefs and Opinions*, 50–54, 241; Saadia, *Book of Doctrines and Beliefs*, 63–66; sec. B, 2.
46. See ch. 4, sec. C, 5. Efros is puzzled by Saadia's rejection of this rabbinic idea. Efros, *Studies in Medieval Jewish Philosophy*, 101. But see Husik, *History of Mediaeval Jewish Philosophy*, 38 ("Saadia's opposition to the belief in the pre-existence of the soul at once does away with the Neo-Platonic view that the soul was placed in the body as punishment for wrongdoing.").

simultaneously with the completion of the bodily form of the human being, for it is stated in the above-quoted remark that it is created *within him*.[47]

Because Saadia rejects the idea that the soul preexists the creation of the body, he perforce rejects the Platonic idea of *anamnesis*,[48] again disagreeing with rabbinic texts.[49]

Saadia further asserts that the soul is located in the heart.[50] This is in contrast to certain rabbinic texts which assert that the soul is not localized in a particular organ but is diffused throughout the body.[51] Saadia selects the heart as the soul's location because "it is definitely known that the nerves, which endow the body with the powers of sensation and motion, all have their roots in the heart."[52] While this explanation may be biologically inaccurate, it does indicate that Saadia associates the soul with the powers of sensation and motion.

5. Saadia accepts Plato's tripartite division of the soul but denies that the soul can act other than through the instrumentality of the body

Saadia believes that the soul is virtually powerless except when it is united with the body; such functions as the soul performs, including strictly intellectual functions, it performs "by means of the body."[53] Put differently, despite being separate substances, the soul and the body constitute "one agent."[54] The reason for this is simply that it is part of the "essential character" of a human soul to act only in conjunction with a human body, and if it could function without the human body, it wouldn't be a human soul but "a star or a celestial sphere or an angel."[55] To demand the soul to act independently of the body is like "demanding that fire tend downward and water rise upward."[56]

As scriptural support for his belief that the body and the soul constitute one agent, Saadia relies on Genesis 2:7, though it is hard to see why this passage couldn't support the contrary belief.[57] For support from tradition, Saadia relies on the story

---

47. Saadia, *Book of Beliefs and Opinions*, 241–42. See also Saadia, *Book of Beliefs and Opinions*, 235, 346.
48. See Efros, "Saadia's Theory of Knowledge," 147.
49. See ch. 4, sec. C, 2.
50. Saadia, *Book of Beliefs and Opinions*, 235.
51. Hirsch, *Rabbinic Psychology*, 196. But Hirsch also notes that some rabbinic texts *did* hold that the soul is "localized in a particular organ" (Hirsch, *Rabbinic Psychology*, 196).
52. Saadia, *Book of Beliefs and Opinions*, 244.
53. Saadia, *Book of Beliefs and Opinions*, 243. See Saadia, *Book of Beliefs and Opinions*, 247–48.
54. Saadia, *Book of Beliefs and Opinions*, 250.
55. Saadia, *Book of Beliefs and Opinions*, 248.
56. Saadia, *Book of Beliefs and Opinions*, 248
57. Saadia, *Book of Beliefs and Opinions*, 250.

from b. Sanhedrin 91a, of a king who had an orchard in which he stationed two watchmen, one blind and one lame.[58]

Efros contends that Saadia rejects "the Platonic dualism of soul and body with their mutual hostility ... for two reasons. First, for systematic consistency ... [since he had elsewhere argued] that two agents cannot be the authors of one act ... And [second,] if we suppose that only the soul is the subject of all action, there would arise the difficulty, why should the body receive reward and punishment. Thus anthropological dualism endangers the belief in resurrection."[59]

Saadia also rejects the Platonic notion that the body is "the source of pain and filth and sin" from which the soul must separate itself.[60] The human body for Saadia, in and of itself, "contains no impurity" whatsoever. Indeed, the body is so far from being an impure thing to be shunned that, according to Saadia, the body is actually needed in order for the soul to get rid of any impurity and to be immortal. For to be alive and pure the soul must serve God, "and the soul has no means, by virtue of its nature, of rendering this service except through the instrumentality of the body."[61]

While rejecting a strict Platonic dualism, Saadia embraces the Platonic conception of the soul's basic powers. Specifically, Saadia believes that when united with the body a soul has three distinct powers: the power of reasoning, the power of appetite, and the power to exhibit passion or to be "angry."[62] He relates the three powers of the soul to three biblical words used interchangeably by the rabbis to denote the soul:

> When, now, the soul is united with the body, three faculties belonging to it make their appearance; namely, the power of reasoning, the power of appetition, and that of anger. That is why our language applied to them three distinct appellations, to wit: *nephesh, ruach,* and *neshamah.* By the appellative *nephesh* it alludes to the soul's possession of an appetitive faculty ... By the appellative *ruach,* again, it alludes to the soul's possession of the power to become bold and angry ... By means of the appellative *neshamah,* finally, it refers to the soul's possession of the faculty of cognition.[63]

---

58. Saadia, *Book of Beliefs and Opinions,* 253. See ch. 4, sec. C, 8.

59. Efros, *Studies in Medieval Jewish Philosophy,* 106.

60. Efros, *Studies in Medieval Jewish Philosophy,* 105 (citing Plato, *Phaed.* 66, 81). See also Plato, *Phaed.* 67c (purification is achieved by "separating the soul as much as possible from the body").

61. Saadia, *Book of Beliefs and Opinions,* 247.

62. Saadia, *Book of Beliefs and Opinions,* 243–44. Accord, Saadia, *Book of Beliefs and Opinions,* 360–61. See Saadia, *Book of Doctrines and Beliefs,* 147, 147n3 ("This is the well-known Platonic division of the soul into three parts"); Efros, *Studies in Medieval Jewish Philosophy,* 108n35 ("These are the three Platonic faculties of the soul: the rational, the spirited, and the appetitive."); Malter, *Saadia Gaon,* 245n205.

63. Saadia, *Book of Beliefs and Opinions,* 243–44.

Although Saadia reads the Platonic tripartite soul into the Bible, in keeping with rabbinic psychology which viewed the soul as a single entity that worked in unison with the body to achieve the variety of human functions,[64] Saadia says:

> *All three powers belong . . . to one soul*, to emphasize which fact the language of Scripture has coined two additional designations, besides those previously listed; namely, *chayyah* (living) and *yechidhah* (unique). It is called *chayyah* (e.g., Job 33:20) because of its capacity to survive when its Creator grants it survival. It is also *yechidhah* (e.g., Ps 22:21) because there exists nothing comparable to it among all creatures, either celestial or terrestrial.[65]

Consistent with the view that, despite having three distinct powers denominated by three particular Hebrew words, the soul is a single entity, when relying on biblical passages to support any of his beliefs about the soul, Saadia indiscriminately chooses passages that contain *nephesh*, *ruach*, or *neshamah*. Each word, though related to a particular power of the soul, can thus be used interchangeably to refer to the single entity.

6. What Saadia says about the fate of the soul after the death of the body is not entirely coherent

Saadia sets forth several possible positions regarding the fate of the soul after the death of the body. He relates these positions to what he believes are corresponding positions regarding the essence of the soul. Since he believes that he has previously refuted the relevant positions regarding the essence of the soul, he contends that he has thereby effectively refuted the corresponding positions on the postmortem fate of the soul. Thus, for instance, those who contend that the soul is a material thing of airy or fiery substance, and those who contend that it is an accident, also contend, says Saadia, that after the death of the body the soul "decomposes and disintegrates and disappears."[66] Because Saadia believes that he has previously refuted the views that the soul is an airy or fiery substance, or an accident, he believes he has effectively refuted the related view on the fate of the soul after the death of the body.[67]

The correct view of the fate of the soul after it exits the body, contends Saadia, is that it is "stored up" until the time when judgment is rendered and reward and

---

64. See ch. 4, sec. C, 3.

65. Saadia, *Book of Beliefs and Opinions*, 244 (emphasis added). See also Efros, *Studies in Medieval Jewish Philosophy*, 107. Cf. ch. 4, sec. C, 3 and nn. 16 and 34 (discussing rabbinic belief in the soul's indivisibility and rabbinic understanding of *hayyah* and *yehida*).

66. Saadia, *Book of Beliefs and Opinions*, 259. See generally Plato, *Phaed.* 70a (the average person believes that when the soul is released from the body "it may no longer exist anywhere but be dispersed and destroyed on the very day that man himself dies . . . that as it emerges it may be dissipated like breath or smoke.").

67. Saadia, *Book of Beliefs and Opinions*, 259.

punishment are meted out.[68] Pure souls are stored "on high" while impure souls are stored "below."[69] The purity of the soul is a function of how a person acted prior to death; as in talmudic thought, righteousness makes the soul pure and wickedness makes the soul impure. Since the body and soul constitute one agent, Saadia further insists that no reward or punishment may be given to the soul alone, but rather all reward and punishment must be meted out only when the soul is reunited with the resurrected body.[70] He asserts that this view is supported not only by reason but by Scripture and rabbinic tradition. In particular, Saadia refers to b. Sanhedrin 91a, and the parable comparing the soul and body to a blind watchman and a lame watchman charged with guarding the king's orchard.[71] This rabbinic tradition, he believes, conforms both the unity of body and soul and their joint reward or punishment in the world-to-come.[72]

Saadia admits that there are "many persons" who believe that reward or punishment is received only by the soul and there are "many persons" who believe that reward or punishment is received only by the body.[73] Saadia argues that these people are mistaken; specifically, "they [are] led astray by lack of acquaintance with the language of Scripture," and thereby misunderstand the biblical passages on which they rely.[74] Saadia makes a particular effort to dispute the position of the Karaite scholar Benjamin Nahawendi that only the body (specifically, the bones) receives reward or punishment.[75] After briefly discussing the relevant scriptural passages relied upon by his opponents, Saadia states:

> In general, . . . it may be remarked that whoever attributes actions to the soul only, or to the body alone or to the bones exclusively, does so out of ignorance of the rules of the language of Scripture and its usage. It is, namely, one of the peculiarities of the style of Holy Writ that an act performed by three or four or five different things is sometimes related by it to the first alone, and sometimes to the second alone, and sometimes to the third alone . . . Similarly, therefore, [in Scripture] it is sometimes the soul alone that is mentioned, or the body alone, or the bones, or the skin, when in reality all of them are meant. It even

---

68. Saadia, *Book of Beliefs and Opinions*, 257.

69. Saadia, *Book of Beliefs and Opinions*, 257 (citing b. Šabb. 152b). See Malter, *Saadia Gaon*, 230. Cf. ch. 4, sec. C, 8.

70. Saadia, *Book of Beliefs and Opinions*, 250, 336 ("the reward and punishment in the hereafter is meted out upon the body and soul unitedly, since they constitute together a single agent.").

71. See ch. 4, sec. C, 8.

72. Saadia, *Book of Beliefs and Opinions*, 253.

73. Saadia, *Book of Beliefs and Opinions*, 250.

74. Saadia, *Book of Beliefs and Opinions*, 250.

75. See Saadia, *Book of Beliefs and Opinions*, 250–52. Nahawendi had relied upon Ezekiel 32:27 (*And whose iniquities are upon their bones*) and Psalm 35:10 (*All my bones shall say 'Lord, who is like unto Thee?*) (Saadia, *Book of Beliefs and Opinions*, 251).

happens that a function pertaining only to the body or the soul is attributed to one member of the body alone.⁷⁶

Notwithstanding Saadia's belief that it is only the reunited soul and body that are to be judged, and rewarded or punished, he allows that after the soul exits the body, but before reunification, the soul alone receives a *sort of* reward or punishment. He says:

> During the first period after its separation from the body, however, the soul exists for a while without a fixed abode until the body has decomposed . . . It consequently experiences during this period much misery, occasioned by its knowledge of the worms and the vermin and the like that pass through the body, just as a person would be pained by the knowledge that a house in which he used to live is in ruins and that thorns and thistles grow in it . . . Now this painful experience comes to the soul in varying degrees according to its *desert* . . . The misery it experiences is, then, *in proportion to its deserts*.⁷⁷

Not only is this prereunification desert inconsistent with Saadia's belief that judgment is only rendered upon the reunited body/soul entity, but in attributing to the separated soul knowledge of the condition of the body Saadia is contradicting his position that the operation of all faculties of the soul, including intellectual ones, require the soul's union with the body. Saadia is driven to inconsistency due to a well-established tradition that he felt compelled to maintain, namely the judgment of the grave or the chastisement of the grave. Specifically, Saadia justifies the experience of an immediate postmortem misery by referring to the saying of "our early teachers . . . [to wit]: *Vermin are as painful to the dead as a needle to the flesh of a living person* [b. Šabb. 13b]. They base this remark on the statement of Scripture: *But his flesh grieveth for him, and his soul mourneth over him* (Job 14:22). That is what I understand is called *the judgment of the grave* or *the chastisement of the grave*."⁷⁸

For Saadia the idea of an immediate postmortem pain experienced by the soul alone is closely aligned with the rabbinic notion of an immediate postmortem review and accounting, since Saadia states that the degree of immediate postmortem pain experienced by the soul is a function of its desert. This rabbinic notion of an immediate postmortem judgment is mentioned in b. Ta'anit 11a, which articulates "that after death, each person must account directly for his or her actions."⁷⁹

---

76. Saadia, *Book of Beliefs and Opinions*, 252–53. Cf. ch. 1, sec. C.

77. Saadia, *Book of Beliefs and Opinions*, 257 (emphasis added).

78. Saadia, *Book of Beliefs and Opinions*, 257–58 (emphasis original). In a footnote added by Rosenblatt, the reader is directed to compare Saadia's statement to b. Ta'anit 11a. Saadia, *Book of Beliefs and Opinions*, 258n57. The judgment of the grave was actually understood by the rabbis as referring to postmortem pain experienced by the *body*, not the soul (Raphael, *Jewish Views of the Afterlife*, 136). Cf. Raphael, *Jewish Views of the Afterlife*, 166–73 (discussing the "pangs of the grave" (*hibbut ha-kever*) in later *midrashic* texts).

79. Raphael, *Jewish Views of the Afterlife*, 132–33.

CHAPTER 5.

7. Saadia's vigorous opposition to *metempsychosis* indicates that a significant number of Jews accepted this viewpoint

Saadia mentions, in an arrogant and dismissive tone, that he has

> found certain people, who call themselves Jews, professing the doctrine of metempsychosis, which is designated by them as the theory of the 'transmigration' of souls. What they mean by this is that the spirit of Reuben is transferred to Simon and afterward to Levi and after that to Judah Many of them would even go so far as to assert that the spirit of a human being might enter into a body of a beast or that of a beast into the body of a human being, and other such nonsense and stupidities.[80]

The "certain people" Saadia had in mind are Anan ben David, the founder of Karaism, and other Karaites.[81]

Saadia goes to great length to refute these views.[82] Efros asserts that Saadia discarded the theory of transmigration of souls "because that theory is based on the thought that the soul enters from the outside, that it is not created in the mother's womb," which undercuts the view that the soul and the body function as a "tight unit."[83] Efros continues: "Saadia saw clearly that transmigration is connected historically or ideologically with the idea of the independence of the soul, its separateness and preexistence originating in 'the viewpoint of the dualists and spiritualists.'"[84]

According to Saadia, the only "logical argument" given by the adherents of *metempsychosis* for their belief in the notion is based on theodicy. These adherents say: "'Inasmuch as the Creator is just, it is inconceivable that He should occasion suffering to little children, unless it be for sins committed by their souls during the time that they were lodged in their former bodies.'"[85] In rebutting this argument Saadia says that "they have forgotten what we have mentioned on the subject of compensation in the hereafter for misfortunes experienced in this world."[86] Saadia also says that reli-

---

80. Saadia, *Book of Beliefs and Opinions*, 259.

81. See Eylon, *Reincarnation in Jewish Mysticism*, 9, 17. See also Scholem, *Origins of the Kabbalah*, 192; Scholem, *On the Mystical Shape of the Godhead*, 198–99. For a general discussion of the Karaites, see Sirat, *Jewish Philosophy in the Middle Ages*, 37–56.

82. See Saadia, *Book of Beliefs and Opinions*, 259–63.

83. Efros, *Studies in Medieval Jewish Philosophy*, 106–7.

84. Efros, *Studies in Medieval Jewish Philosophy*, 107. See Saadia, *Book of Beliefs and Opinions*, 259 (Saadia says that those who accept the doctrine of *metempsychosis* "have derived it from the theory of the dualists and the spiritualists" which theories Saadia believes he has refuted). Saadia is referring to his refutation of (1) the spiritualist theory that the Creator "had at His disposal eternal spiritual beings out of whom He created . . . composite bodies" (Saadia, *Book of Beliefs and Opinions*, 50), and (2) the dualistic theory that the (immaterial) soul is good and the (material) body is bad (Saadia, *Book of Beliefs and Opinions*, 236)). See also Saadia, *Book of Doctrines and Beliefs*, 13, 63, 69.

85. Saadia, *Book of Beliefs and Opinions*, 260.

86. Saadia, *Book of Beliefs and Opinions*, 260.

ance on the Bible to support belief in *metempsychosis* is misplaced because the biblical interpretations by adherents to the doctrine are faulty.[87]

C. Saadia Endorses Belief in the Resurrection of the Dead

Saadia's central concern with respect to resurrection is to show that there will be a resurrection of the dead at the beginning of the messianic age *as well as* at the end time. This clearly is an attempt to harmonize the varying positions concerning the timing of the resurrection of the dead found in rabbinic tradition. Having distinguished two occasions at which there will be a resurrection of the dead, Saadia explains the difference of each in terms of the persons who will be resurrected and the nature of the resurrection.

1. Saadia believes that the resurrection of the dead will occur both at the time of redemption and in the world to come

Saadia begins his discussion of the doctrine of resurrection by asserting that the doctrine is "a matter upon which our nation is in complete agreement" and that he "does not know of any Jew who would disagree with this belief."[88] He acknowledges, however, that there is disagreement about the details of the doctrine. In particular, while all agree that there will be a resurrection of the dead "in the world to come" there is disagreement as to whether there will be a resurrection "at the time of the *redemption*."[89] While "the masses of our nation assert that [resurrection] will come about at "the time of the *redemption*" there are "some few of the Jewish nation" who disagree.[90]

Saadia's reference to "the world to come" is to an end time when the righteous will be rewarded;[91] and his reference to the time of redemption is to the messianic age. Saadia distinguishes three time periods—the present time, the time of the Messiah, and the end time.[92] He variously refers to the end time as "the world of compensation,"[93]

---

87. Saadia, *Book of Beliefs and Opinions*, 261–63.
88. Saadia, *Book of Beliefs and Opinions*, 264.
89. Saadia, *Book of Beliefs and Opinions*, 264–65 (emphasis original). See also Saadia, *Book of Beliefs and Opinions*, 409.
90. Saadia, *Book of Beliefs and Opinions*, 265 (emphasis original). See Malter, *Saadia Gaon*, 231.
91. Saadia, *Book of Beliefs and Opinions*, 323–24.
92. See Efros, *Studies in Medieval Jewish Philosophy*, 111n1.
93. Saadia, *Book of Beliefs and Opinions*, 208.

"the world of recompense,"[94] "the latter world,"[95] "the hereafter,"[96] the "future life,"[97] the "world to come,"[98] or "the time of retribution";[99] he variously refers to the messianic age as "the time of redemption,"[100] or "the time of the salvation"[101]; and he variously refers to the present time as "the workaday world"[102] or the "world of care."[103] The phrase "this world" refers to any time or place that precedes the world to come; therefore, "this world" could refer to either the time of redemption or the workaday world.[104]

Saadia says that there are four bases on which one might oppose the majority view that there will be a resurrection of the dead at the time of redemption: "nature, reason, Scripture, and tradition."[105] Regarding opposition based on nature, he considers the argument that resurrection defies the laws of nature.[106] He rejects this argument because, he contends, Jews "believe that the Creator is capable of changing the ordinary laws of nature and making them conform to His will at any time He pleases."[107] Indeed, he continues, to deny that the laws of nature may be violated would undermine the many "miracles" recounted in the Torah, such as the transformation of Moses' staff into a serpent and the transformation of water into blood.[108] Moreover, to deny that the laws of nature may be violated would compel the rejection of the doctrine of *creatio ex nihilo* since "the resurrection of the dead is easier to conceive of and more plausible than the doctrine of *creatio ex nihilo*."[109]

With regard to opposition based on both nature and reason, Saadia considers whether resurrection constitutes a "logical absurdity."[110] Specifically, it could be ar-

94. Saadia, *Book of Beliefs and Opinions*, 264.
95. Saadia, *Book of Beliefs and Opinions*, 208.
96. Saadia, *Book of Beliefs and Opinions*, 337.
97. Saadia, *Book of Beliefs and Opinions*, 185.
98. Saadia, *Book of Beliefs and Opinions*, 409.
99. Saadia, *Book of Beliefs and Opinions*, 229.
100. Saadia, *Book of Beliefs and Opinions*, 409.
101. Saadia, *Book of Beliefs and Opinions*, 430.
102. Saadia, *Book of Beliefs and Opinions*, 208.
103. Saadia, *Book of Beliefs and Opinions*, 183.
104. Saadia, *Book of Beliefs and Opinions*, 215 (referring to workaday world), 265 (referring to time of redemption), 333–34 (referring to any time and place preceding world to come).
105. Saadia, *Book of Beliefs and Opinions*, 410.
106. Saadia, *Book of Beliefs and Opinions*, 410. This is, presumably, an issue that concerns resurrection at the time of the redemption and not at the time of recompense because it is only at the former time that the laws of nature will still be operative.
107. Saadia, *Book of Beliefs and Opinions*, 411.
108. Saadia, *Book of Beliefs and Opinions*, 411.
109. Saadia, *Book of Beliefs and Opinions*, 411. Treatise I of *Sefer ha-Emunot ve-ha-De'ot* is devoted to establishing the doctrine of *creatio ex nihilo*. See Saadia, *Book of Beliefs and Opinions*, 38–50. The first literary record of the Jewish doctrine of creation out of nothing is 2 Maccabees 7:28. See Altmann, *Studies in Religious Philosophy*, 128–29.
110. Saadia, *Book of Beliefs and Opinions*, 412.

gued that there exist insufficient amounts of the four basic elements (air, earth, wind, and fire) to reconstitute all the bodies that will need to be resurrected.[111] Saadia rejects this argument on the basis of calculations which he believes prove that the "source materials" are more than sufficient to reconstitute the number of bodies that will be needed.[112] He also considers how someone who has been devoured by a lion or another animal could be resurrected since, arguably, the elements comprising the body of the devoured person will have been "metamorphosed" into the body of the devouring animal. This argument is rejected on the ground that it is wrong to suppose that the elements comprising the body of the devoured person are in fact assimilated into the body of the devouring animal.[113]

As to objection based on Scripture, Saadia considers whether there are any scriptural passages which contradict the belief in resurrection at the time of redemption. He admits that there are passages which do seem to cast doubt on the belief, but, by adroit use of the tools of scriptural interpretation, these are all explained away.[114] (One of the verses he cites is Job 7:9–10, cited in the Talmud as proof that the Bible denies the doctrine of resurrection.[115]) Saadia then goes on to consider scriptural passages which he considers to explicitly promise resurrection at the time of the redemption.[116] For example, he discusses Ezekiel 37:11–13.[117] Saadia states: "His statement: *And I will bring you into the land of Israel . . .* serves as an assurance that this promise is to be carried out in this world, lest it be mistakenly thought that it was meant for the world to come."[118] Saadia considers whether the biblical passages on which he relies in support of resurrection in this world should be discounted as being merely figurative, but concludes that a literal interpretation is warranted.[119] In particular, he asserts that Scripture confirms "the belief in resurrection [at the time of the redemption] . . . by

---

111. Saadia, *Book of Beliefs and Opinions*, 412. Accord, Saadia, *Book of Beliefs and Opinions*, 277.

112. Saadia, *Book of Beliefs and Opinions*, 412–13. Accord, Saadia, *Book of Beliefs and Opinions*, 277–78.

113. See Saadia, *Book of Beliefs and Opinions*, 413–14. Accord, Saadia, *Book of Beliefs and Opinions*, 278–80. Cf. Bynum, *Resurrection of the Body*, 127 (Anselm of Canterbury, facing the same issue, concluded: "just as fire is fed by the food of pieces of wood but wood is not however changed into the nature of fire, so the body is fed by the nourishment of food but this [food] is not converted into body.").

114. See Saadia, *Book of Beliefs and Opinions*, 417–20. Cf. Saadia, *Book of Beliefs and Opinions*, 273–75. The verses considered include Job 14:1, 14:12; Pss 78:39, 103:15–16; Qoh 9:3–6.

115. Ch. 4, sec. D (text accompanying note 106).

116. See Saadia, *Book of Beliefs and Opinions*, 267–71. Accord, Saadia, *Book of Beliefs and Opinions*, 420–23. The verses considered include Ezek 37:11–13; Isa 26:19; Dan 12:2.

117. See Saadia, *Book of Beliefs and Opinions*, 420. Accord, Saadia, *Book of Beliefs and Opinions*, 269.

118. Saadia, *Book of Beliefs and Opinions*, 420.

119. Saadia, *Book of Beliefs and Opinions*, 423–26. See Saadia, *Book of Beliefs and Opinions*, 265–67 ("every statement found in the Bible is to be understood in its literal sense except for those that cannot be so construed for one of . . . four reasons" which are discussed), 272–73.

expressly citing the resurrection in this world of the son of the *Zarephite* (1 Kgs 17:22) and that of the *Shunammite* (2 Kgs 4:35) woman."[120]

Finally, Saadia turns to objection based on tradition. Relying primarily on b. Sanhedrin 90a and b. Sukkah 52b, and ignoring the several talmudic passages which advance a contrary position, he concludes that tradition supports the doctrine of resurrection at the time of the redemption.[121]

2. At the time of the redemption all the righteous of Israel will be resurrected; and at the time of the next world, those Jews alive at, or born during, the time of the redemption, who subsequently died, will be resurrected, as will all those deserving of punishment

Saadia asserts that at the time of redemption every "righteous person and penitent of the Jewish nation" will be resurrected.[122] He also asserts that those resurrected at the time of redemption will include "the entire nation of Israel, the virtuous thereof as well as whoever died repentant."[123] The reason why the second assertion includes "the entire nation of Israel" is because those Jews who are neither righteous nor repentant are so "few in number" as to be insignificant.[124] Explicitly relying on b. Sanhedrin 92a, Saadia proclaims that all those resurrected at the time of the redemption will have eternal life—"they will not die but they will be transported from the era of the Messiah to the delights of the next world."[125]

Saadia recognizes a problem in excluding from the resurrection at the time of the redemption those who are deserving punishment in that Saadia understands Daniel 12:1–3 as referring to the time of redemption and Daniel states that some will awake to everlasting abhorrence. To make Daniel coincide with Saadia's schema, Saadia reasons:

> As for the statement: *Some to everlasting life, and some to reproaches*, he does not mean thereby a division of the resurrected, some being assigned to the Garden of Eden whilst others are destined for hellfire. He means, rather, that a division of those that lie in the graves will take place. Of them *many* will awake. These are the ones destined *for eternal life*. Others, on the other hand will not awake. It is these that are fated *for everlasting abhorrence*.[126]

---

120. Saadia, *Book of Beliefs and Opinions*, 267.

121. Saadia, *Book of Beliefs and Opinions*, 428–30. Accord, Saadia, *Book of Beliefs and Opinions*, 276.

122. Saadia, *Book of Beliefs and Opinions*, 430.

123. Saadia, *Book of Beliefs and Opinions*, 284.

124. Saadia, *Book of Beliefs and Opinions*, 431.

125. Saadia, *Book of Beliefs and Opinions*, 431. Accord, Saadia, *Book of Beliefs and Opinions*, 281.

126. Saadia, *Book of Beliefs and Opinions*, 423 (emphasis original). Accord, Saadia, *Book of Beliefs and Opinions*, 271.

There is also an issue in Saadia's mind as to what will happen to those Jews who are alive at the commencement of the time of redemption or who are born during it. He considers three possibilities and accepts as the correct position that "they will live a long life and die and then not come to life again until [the era of] the next world."[127] By a long life he means five hundred years.[128] After the messianic age: (1) those Jews who had been resurrected at the commencement of the period of redemption will not die but will be "transported" to the next world, (2) those righteous Jews alive at, or born during, the period of redemption, who are still alive, will die, but then will be resurrected together with those already deceased, and (3) all the dead among the gentiles, and the unrighteous Jews, will be resurrected for the occasion of their retribution[129]

Saadia rejects the idea that righteous gentiles will be resurrected at the end time for the purpose of receiving a reward. He states that those who deserve "perpetual torment" are "the nonbelievers and polytheists and then impenitent [Jewish] perpetrators of grave sins."[130] Concerning the nonbelievers and the polytheists Saadia believes that "their fate has been clearly described in the declaration of Scripture: *And they shall go forth, and look upon the carcasses of men that have rebelled against Me; for their worm shall not die* (Isa 66:24)."[131] Saadia's position ignores the rabbinic view attributed to Rabbi Joshua ben Hananiah that non-Jews have a portion in the *Olam Ha-Bah*.[132] While the impenitent Jews who have committed grave sins will receive perpetual torment along with non-Jews, those Jews who have committed lesser offenses will be pardoned. These latter Jews are pardoned because they have also committed good deeds which offset their offenses, and because they have been adequately punished in this world.[133]

3. The nature of the resurrected body depends on the time it is resurrected

Saadia is able to reconcile disparate statements in rabbinic tradition about the nature of the resurrected body by distinguishing between the two instances of resurrection. Those resurrected at the time of the redemption will have "normal" bodies, that is bodies similar to the ones that people have always had. They will be able to eat, drink,

---

127. Saadia, *Book of Beliefs and Opinions*, 434. Accord, Saadia, *Book of Beliefs and Opinions*, 288.

128. Saadia, *Book of Beliefs and Opinions*, 289.

129. Saadia, *Book of Beliefs and Opinions*, 281, 288, 431; *Book of Doctrines and Beliefs*, 155n2. See Efros, *Studies in Medieval Jewish Philosophy*, 114; Raphael, *Jewish Views of the Afterlife*, 244.

130. Saadia, *Book of Beliefs and Opinions*, 350–51. But see Malter, *Saadia Gaon*, 231 ("According to Saadia the world to come is not intended for Israel alone. The pious of all nations will have a share in it, a view expressed in the Talmud.").

131. Saadia, *Book of Beliefs and Opinions*, 351.

132. See ch. 4, sec. F, 2.

133. Saadia, *Book of Beliefs and Opinions*, 351. Cf. ch. 4, n. 104 (discussing disagreement between the Schools of Shammai and Hillel regarding punishment of the *benonim*).

and marry (have sexual relations).¹³⁴ "This is evident," says Saadia, "from the fact that the son of the *Zarephite* and the one of the *Shunammite* woman, who were brought back to life in this world, both ate and drank after their revival and were in the fit state for marriage."¹³⁵ Furthermore, the appearance of those resurrected at the time of the redemption will closely resemble the appearance they had in their former bodies since, Saadia says, they will be recognizable to family and friends; but although resurrected with all prior "blemishes," afterward they will be cured of all such blemishes.¹³⁶ This is, generally speaking, in keeping with rabbinic tradition, and Saadia cites b. Sanhedrin 91b. Finally, Saadia says that, despite having normal bodies, those resurrected at the time of the redemption will unfailingly choose to obey God and not rebel against him.¹³⁷

In contrast to those resurrected at the time of the redemption, those resurrected at the time of the next world will not have normal bodies; in keeping with b. Berakhot 17a, they will have a changed body, requiring neither food, drink, nor sexual release.¹³⁸ This raised the question as to what will happen in the next world to the people resurrected at the time of the redemption who have normal bodies still possessing the need for food, drink, and sex. The answer is that, although their physical constitution will be unchanged, they will simply forego eating and drinking, just as Moses neither ate nor drank for forty days.¹³⁹

4. Saadia considers questions raised by the notion of bodily resurrection

Saadia considers ten questions that occurred to him with respect to the concept of resurrection and with respect to inferences that could be drawn from the doctrine.¹⁴⁰ Most of these questions had already been addressed in discussing the time of resurrection and the nature of the resurrected body. One of the remaining questions is: Will there be enough room for all the resurrected people? Saadia's answer to this question suggests that he thought the time of redemption was near at hand. Specifically, he calculates that from the time of the first Israelite to the then-present time there had been thirty-two generations, each generation consisting of 1.2 million people, for a total of 38.4 million people that needed to be resurrected. Then, assuming that they will be granted 1/150th of the earth's surface, he concludes that there is ample room for everyone.¹⁴¹

---

134. Saadia, *Book of Beliefs and Opinions*, 280. Accord, Saadia, *Book of Beliefs and Opinions*, 432.
135. Saadia, *Book of Beliefs and Opinions*, 280. Cf. Saadia, *Book of Beliefs and Opinions*, 432.
136. Saadia, *Book of Beliefs and Opinions*, 286. Accord, Saadia, *Book of Beliefs and Opinions*, 432.
137. Saadia, *Book of Beliefs and Opinions*, 287.
138. Saadia, *Book of Beliefs and Opinions*, 432. Accord, Saadia, *Book of Beliefs and Opinions*, 281.
139. Saadia, *Book of Beliefs and Opinions*, 282, 339, 432–33.
140. Saadia, *Book of Beliefs and Opinions*, 430–34. Cf. Saadia, *Book of Beliefs and Opinions*, 277–89.
141. Saadia, *Book of Beliefs and Opinions*, 431–432. Cf., Saadia, *Book of Beliefs and Opinions*,

Saadia side-steps the need to provide answers to a myriad of further questions that might be posed, such as whether or not marriage bonds will be abrogated for those who are resurrected. He states that it is "not necessary to rack our brains" about such matters since "there will be available in the beyond prophets and prophetic inspiration and divine guidance."[142]

D. Saadia Offers Proofs of a Reward or Punishment in the World to Come, and Sets Forth His Views on the Nature, Duration, and Locations of Such Rewards or Punishments

Saadia takes it to be agreed by all Jews that there will be a resurrection of the dead in the world to come in order for the righteous of Israel to be rewarded with eternal life for their service to God, and for retribution to be executed on all others. He writes:

> The basis of this conclusion is . . . that man is the goal of creation. The reason why he has been distinguished above all creatures is that he might serve God, and the reward for this service is life eternal in the world of recompense. Prior to this event, whenever He sees fit to do so, God separates man's spirit from his body until the time when the number of souls meant to be created has been fulfilled, whereupon God brings about the union of all bodies and souls again [and requites the reunified person for their conduct in *this* world] . . . We consequently do not know of any Jew who would disagree with this belief. Nor is it hard for him to understand how his Master can bring the dead to life, since he has already accepted as a certainty the doctrine of creation ex nihilo.[143]

He begins Treatise IX of *Sefer ha-Emunot ve-ha-De'ot*, entitled "Concerning Reward and Punishment in the World to Come," as follows:

> Our Lord, blessed and exalted be He, has informed us that He has set aside a time for recompensing the righteous, in which, moreover, he will make a distinction between them and the godless. This is borne out by His statement:
>
> > *And they shall be Mine, saith the Lord of hosts, in the day I do make, even Mine own treasure; and I will spare them, etc. Then shall ye discern between the righteous and the wicked.* (Mal 3:17, 18).[144]

He then undertakes to prove that there will be a world to come with rewards for the righteous of Israel and a distinction made between them "and the godless." Consistent with his epistemology, he states that the sources of proof that he intends to rely

---

285–86.

142. Saadia, *Book of Beliefs and Opinions*, 282.

143. Saadia, *Book of Beliefs and Opinions*, 264 (emphasis added). Accord, Saadia, *Book of Beliefs and Opinions*, 235, 323–24.

144. Saadia, *Book of Beliefs and Opinions*, 323.

CHAPTER 5.

upon are "rational arguments, Scripture, and tradition."[145] After offering his proofs, Saadia addresses ten questions about the world to come: (1) the nature of the reward for the righteous of Israel, (2) the nature of the punishment for all others, (3) the locations for receipt of reward and punishment, (4) the nature of time, (5) the necessity for a perpetual reward, (6) the necessity for a perpetual punishment, (7) whether the extent of rewards and punishments will be equal for all, (8) whether there will be levels or classes among righteousness and the wicked, (9) who deserves perpetual torment, and (10) whether those to be requited in the hereafter will meet each other.

1. Rational proofs of a reward and punishment in the world to come are based on the need to resolve the problem of moral evil

Saadia begins his proof of reward and punishment in the world to come with rational arguments and offers three of them. First, he contends, since God is omnipotent, omniscient, and merciful:

> it is incompatible with His character, that the measure of happiness reserved for [the] human soul be restricted to the mundane well-being and pleasure it finds in this world For all well-being in this mundane world is bound up with misfortune, and all happiness with hardship, and all pleasure with pain, and all joy with sorrow. In fact, I find that these individual fortunes of which life is made up are either evenly balanced or that the things of a depressing nature outweigh those of a cheering nature.[146]

In other words, given what is accepted as true about the character of God, it follows that God wants happiness for human beings and is able to provide it. Yet, based on experience, Saadia takes it as certainly true that human beings do not, and cannot, attain happiness in this world. Thus, it logically follows that God "has set aside for it [the human soul] a place in which it can lead an untroubled existence and attain pure happiness."[147]

Saadia's second rational argument is that human beings have been created by God with both bodily appetites which make them desire to attain certain things, and reason which makes them repulsed by those very same things. For example, bodily desires might make a person want to have sex with someone who is married to another, while reason prohibits adultery.[148] If the dictates of reason are obeyed, the person

---

145. Saadia, *Book of Beliefs and Opinions*, 323.
146. Saadia, *Book of Beliefs and Opinions*, 324.
147. Saadia, *Book of Beliefs and Opinions*, 324. Saadia's reference here to the human soul is confusing since in the world to come the soul is reunited with the body. Presumably, his reference to the human soul is a poetic manner of expression in which the soul is meant to connote the whole person—the soul reunited with the body. See also Saadia, *Book of Beliefs and Opinions*, 208–9. See generally Saadia, *Book of Beliefs and Opinions*, 205–34.
148. Saadia, *Book of Beliefs and Opinions*, 325.

will be "overcome by feelings of regret and depression and sadness that pain him and cause him heartache."[149] Saadia comments: "Now it would not have been right that this should happen to [that person] were it not for the fact that [they are] to be compensated therefor by God [in the world to come]."[150] Similarly, Saadia claims that human beings have been created by God to approve of justice and truthfulness, but that acting on the basis of justice and truthfulness bring "enmity and hatred" from, and possibly bodily injury and death at the hands of, those persons negatively affected by acts of justice and truthfulness.[151] Again, Saadia claims that since, in this world, people are not rewarded, but punished, for acting in accordance with the nature God gave them to approve of justice and truthfulness, "fairness" demands that God intended to reward them in another world.[152]

Although some of these arguments touch on the problem of moral evil, that problem is most directly faced in the third rational argument. Here Saadia observes that a problem exists when men do violence against each other and it results in "the well-being of the one who committed the wrong and the misery [and death] of the [one] wronged..."[153] This is a problem, of course, because God is just and omnipotent, and these attributes mandate that He punish the one who committed the wrong and reward the one who was wronged. Therefore, argues Saadia, God "must perforce have reserved for them a second abode in which justice would be restored in their relationship to each other, reward being remitted to the one corresponding to the pain he has suffered at the hand of him that wronged, and punishment being brought down upon the other corresponding to the pleasure derived by his nature from his wrongdoing and violence."[154] Similarly, in this world the "godless" (gentiles) prosper while the "believers" (Jews) are in misery, which also requires rectification in a "second world."[155]

2. Saadia strains to come up with scriptural proof of a reward and punishment in the world to come

Turning to proof of reward and punishment in the world to come based on Scripture, Saadia acknowledges that "there is no explicit mention in the Torah of retribution anywhere else than in this world," and he offers two reasons why "the express statements of Holy Writ dwell [only] on this-worldly prosperity and hardship..."[156] First, "inasmuch as the reward of the world to come is demonstrable only rationally...

---

149. Saadia, *Book of Beliefs and Opinions*, 325.
150. Saadia, *Book of Beliefs and Opinions*, 325.
151. Saadia, *Book of Beliefs and Opinions*, 325.
152. Saadia, *Book of Beliefs and Opinions*, 325.
153. Saadia, *Book of Beliefs and Opinions*, 325.
154. Saadia, *Book of Beliefs and Opinions*, 325–26.
155. Saadia, *Book of Beliefs and Opinions*, 326.
156. Saadia, *Book of Beliefs and Opinions*, 327.

the Torah was terse in its explanation."[157] Second, "it is the character of prophecy to enlarge upon events of immediate urgency and be brief in regard to those of remote contingency."[158]

Not content to rely on these reasons to explain why Scripture omits any explicit reference to reward and punishment in a future world, Saadia attempts to find some type of scriptural basis. Saadia first mentions three biblical instances of the faithful who were willing to die in service of God: (1) Isaac, (2) Hananiah, Mishael, and Azariah, and (3) Daniel. He then contends that the persons involved in these instances would not have been willing to sacrifice themselves unless they believed in a future reward.[159] Saadia then argues that Moses, "the most pious and virtuous of men, did not attain ... any of the great mundane rewards" promised in scriptural passages, so that, if God's rewards were restricted to these mundane rewards, Moses would have received them.[160] Conversely, if there was no punishment outside of this world, all those who sin excessively would have received the same fate as the inhabitants of Sodom, but that doesn't happen.[161]

Lastly, Saadia interprets seven other groups of scriptural passages as supporting a reward or punishment in the hereafter,[162] contending that his interpretations are correct because they accord with reason, and any other interpretations of these passages are incorrect because other interpretations "would invalidate their use as proof of [the doctrine of] a world to come" and "reason demands retribution in another world."[163]

3. Support in rabbinic tradition of a reward and punishment in the world to come is easily found

Finally, with respect to proof based on tradition, Saadia states that the evidence is too extensive to be set forth in full, but provides numerous examples, including b. Avot, 4:16–17, b. Berakhot 17a, and b. Sanhedrin 10:1.[164] Also provided are examples from "the sages [who] translated the Torah [into Aramaic],"[165] that is the *targumim*. For example, Saadia notes that the Hebrew of Deuteronomy 33:6 (*Let Reuben live, and not die*) was rendered in Aramaic as "*Let Reuben live the life of eternity and not die a*

---

157. Saadia, *Book of Beliefs and Opinions*, 327. Cf., Saadia, *Book of Doctrines and Beliefs*, 184 (translating, "the Torah omitted a reference to it as superfluous"). Altmann notes that Saadia's reasoning here is "inconsistent with his general view that Revelation is necessary even in regard to matters which Reason can establish by its own effort" (Saadia, *Book of Doctrines and Beliefs*, 184n4).

158. Saadia, *Book of Beliefs and Opinions*, 328.

159. Saadia, *Book of Beliefs and Opinions*, 326–27.

160. Saadia, *Book of Beliefs and Opinions*, 327–28.

161. Saadia, *Book of Beliefs and Opinions*, 329.

162. Saadia, *Book of Beliefs and Opinions*, 330–33.

163. Saadia, *Book of Beliefs and Opinions*, 333.

164. Saadia, *Book of Beliefs and Opinions*, 333–35.

165. Saadia, *Book of Beliefs and Opinions*, 335.

second death."¹⁶⁶ He concludes by claiming that he has explained "how the doctrine of reward and punishment in the world to come is supported by the three sources of knowledge, namely: reason, Scripture, and tradition," that "our nation is fully agreed upon this matter," and that "the tradition concerning it is most firmly established and not subject to being explained away or changed."¹⁶⁷

4. The nature of the reward and punishment to be received in the world to come is related to an essence resembling fire which shines for the righteous and burns the sinful

Regarding the nature of the reward and punishment to be meted out in the world to come, Saadia proclaims:

> this reward and punishment will take the form of two very fine substances that our Master . . . will create at the time of the retribution, applying them to each of His servants in accordance with their dessert. They will both consist of the same essence, an essence resembling the property of burning, luminous fire, that will shine for the righteous [but] will burn for the sinful . . . Basically, . . . this substance that the Creator . . . will create will resemble the sun, except that . . . the heat and light of the sun are inseparable . . . whereas so far as this substance is concerned, the light can . . . be drawn off for the sake of the righteous and its heat collected for the sinful.¹⁶⁸

Saadia finds scriptural support for this in several passages in which righteousness is associated with light and wickedness with fire, including Proverbs 13:9, Psalm 140:11, and Psalm 11:6.¹⁶⁹

While the punishment of the wicked is clearly physical—they will perpetually burn and be in physical pain and torment, it does not appear to be the case that the righteous will experience any significant degree of physical pleasure. There will be no eating, drinking, or sex, so these physical pleasures are definitely excluded. Rather, "the righteous will subsist in the hereafter on light and not on ordinary nourishment."¹⁷⁰ Moses is suggested as an example of how such luminous nourishment is possible, for God kept Moses alive "three times for forty days and nights without food, as Scripture puts it: *And he was there with the Lord forty days and forty nights; he did neither eat bread, nor drink water* (Exod 34:28). He must, therefore, have been sustained solely by the light which God had [specially] created . . ."¹⁷¹ Thus, the reward of the righteous

---

166. Saadia, *Book of Beliefs and Opinions*, 335.
167. Saadia, *Book of Beliefs and Opinions*, 336.
168. Saadia, *Book of Beliefs and Opinions*, 337–38.
169. See Saadia, *Book of Beliefs and Opinions*, 338–39.
170. Saadia, *Book of Beliefs and Opinions*, 339.
171. Saadia, *Book of Beliefs and Opinions*, 339.

seems to consists solely in enjoying the light of the Creator, and the only physical pleasure is likened to the feeling of the warmth of the sun. According to Malter, the light will imbue the righteous "with the knowledge of divine things, bringing them nearer to the presence of God and the heavenly hosts, and making them participate in a life of continuous joy and happiness."[172]

5. The nature of space and time will be different in the world to come; the locations for reward and punishment will be a new heaven and a new earth, not Gan Eden and Gehenna

Saadia mentions *Gan Eden* and *Gehenna*, but not as referring to the *locations* in which reward and punishment, respectively, will be executed; rather, they refer to the *nature* of the reward and punishment. He says that the reward to be received "has been called *Garden of Eden*" and the future punishment "has been called *Gehinnom*" because the former had become a "byword" for magnificence and the latter had come to constitute "an example of baseness."[173]

Regarding the actual locations where reward and punishment will take place, Saadia argues that these must of necessity be physical places since the individuals receiving reward and punishment will be physical beings.[174] These newly created places are called in Scripture, according to Saadia, heaven and earth.[175] But the heaven and earth in the world to come will not be like the heaven and earth that currently exists; there will be a new heaven and earth that God will create simultaneously with the annihilation of the current heaven and earth.[176] A new earth is needed because in the world to come humans will need neither nourishment nor material possessions, so "there would be no purpose to the existence of fields or plants or rivers or valleys . . . or aught that resembles them."[177] While the righteous and the wicked will not meet, they will be able to see each other.[178]

In the world to come God will create a new time as well new spaces. Time in the hereafter will be "composed entirely of light uninterrupted by darkness," which is to say

> there will be no alternation of night and day following each other successively. For the reason that motivated [divine] Wisdom, when it caused men to dwell on earth, in making the distinction between night and day . . . was merely in order that they might employ the daytime in working for their livelihood

---

172. Malter, *Saadia Gaon*, 246.
173. Saadia, *Book of Beliefs and Opinions*, 340–41 (emphasis original).
174. Saadia, *Book of Beliefs and Opinions*, 341.
175. Saadia, *Book of Beliefs and Opinions*, 341.
176. Saadia, *Book of Beliefs and Opinions*, 341–43.
177. Saadia, *Book of Beliefs and Opinions*, 342.
178. Saadia, *Book of Beliefs and Opinions*, 351–52.

and other occupations and spend the night in relaxation, rest, cohabitation, the practice of solitude, and similar pastimes. Since, however, in the world to come none of these things have any place, the divisions of night and day can very well be dispensed with. The same applies to the divisions of time into months and years . . .[179]

6. The duration of reward and punishment in the world to come will be perpetual but the exact nature of such perpetual reward and punishment will be contingent upon the degree of righteousness or wickedness displayed in this world

The duration of the reward or punishment that will be received in the world to come is perpetual. Saadia supports this claim on the basis of reason, stating that perpetuity of reward and punishment are necessary to provide the strongest possible incentive and deterrent, respectively.[180] In addition, he relies on Daniel 12:2 ("*Some to everlasting life, and some to reproaches and everlasting abhorrence*") and other scriptural passages.[181]

Although the duration of the reward will be perpetual regardless of whether only one good deed was performed or a thousand were performed, and the duration of the punishment will be perpetual regardless of the extent of the wrongdoing, the exact nature of the reward or punishment will vary depending on the degree of righteousness or wickedness that one exhibited in this world.[182] Specifically, Saadia believes there will be seven gradations of righteousness and seven gradations of wickedness.[183]

7. The righteous and the wicked will see each other in the world to come, and the wicked will sigh regretfully over the reward which they forfeited

Regarding the tenth question about the world to come raised by Saadia, Saadia says:

> [S]o far as the righteous and the wicked are concerned, they will only look at one another with their eyes. Thus Scripture says concerning the righteous: *And they shall go forth, and look upon the carcasses of the men that have rebelled against me* [Isa 66:24] . . . and they will rejoice and be glad over their own condition.
>
> Likewise Scripture remarks concerning the wicked: *The sinners in Zion are afraid; trembling hath seized the ungodly: Who among us shall dwell with the devouring fire? Who among us shall dwell with everlasting burning* (Isa

---

179. Saadia, *Book of Beliefs and Opinions*, 343.
180. Saadia, *Book of Beliefs and Opinions*, 344–45.
181. Saadia, *Book of Beliefs and Opinions*, 345–46.
182. See Saadia, *Book of Beliefs and Opinions*, 347–48.
183. Saadia, *Book of Beliefs and Opinions*, 348–50.

33:14)? In amazement they will watch the righteous abide in the burning fire without being in the least hurt by it, and they will sigh regretfully over the reward which they forfeited . . .

So far as the righteous among themselves are concerned . . . those whose ranks are close to one another will meet, whereas those who are distant from each other in station will not. It would seem to me, however, that in the case of those destined for punishment there will be no meeting on the part of those who are of similar rank on account of the separation produced by their sufferings and their preoccupation with themselves.[184]

E. The Arguments Advanced by Saadia Are Subject to Serious Attack

Although Saadia explicitly seeks to adequately support the views he advances about the soul, resurrection, and the afterlife on the basis of both reason and revelation, he fails to do so. The rational arguments he advances are more often than not fallacious. An example of Saadia's fallacious reasoning is the suggestion that we must infer the existence of a soul "in order not to deny its manifest activities." The "manifest activities" include the powers of reasoning, appetition, anger, sensation, and motion.[185] In other words, Saadia explains certain human activities, such as reasoning, sense perception, and basic instincts and desires by attributing these activities to the soul, and then says that we must infer the existence of the soul in order not to deny the existence of these activities. This is circular reasoning, and thus fallacious. Nor does he consider whether these activities could be accounted for in some other way. Also seriously flawed, of course, are his arguments in support of a postmortem reward or punishment.

Saadia's reliance on Scripture is also subject to challenge. The biblical passages which he cites often support his position only because he creatively interprets those passages. For example, many biblical passages, such as Job 7:9–10, which clearly reject any afterlife, are said by Saadia not to preclude belief in an afterlife.[186] One of the most creative interpretations employed by Saadia is his use of the biblical words *ruach*, *nephesh*, and *neshamah* to read into the Hebrew Bible a belief in the Platonic concept of a tripartite soul.[187]

Finally, Saadia is able to say that rabbinic tradition supports his positions only by ignoring rabbinic texts that do not. Most fundamentally, Saadia ignores rabbinic texts which affirm that only the soul is rewarded in the world to come, not the body.

---

184. Saadia, *Book of Beliefs and Opinions*, 352.
185. See Saadia, *Book of Beliefs and Opinions*, 243–44; secs. B, 1 and 5.
186. Saadia, *Book of Beliefs and Opinions*, 417–18.
187. See Saadia, *Book of Beliefs and Opinions*, 243–44; sec. B, 5.

Further, it is clearly a perversion of rabbinic tradition for Saadia to assert that *Gan Eden* and *Gehenna* are not physical locations of reward and punishment.[188]

188. See sec. D, 5; ch. 4, sec. F, 4.

6.

Jewish Neoplatonic Philosophers Associate an Afterlife Reward with the Soul's Ascension to the Divine Realm, Not Bodily Resurrection; and Belief in Intercessory Acts to Aide in the Purgation of Impure Souls Develops

NEOPLATONISM IS A TERM coined in modern times to distinguish the form of the Platonic tradition inaugurated by Plotinus and lasting in its pagan form down to the sixth century from the teaching of Plato's immediate disciples and from the Platonism of the earlier Roman Empire.[1] Beginning with the first identifiable Jewish Neoplatonist, Isaac ben Joseph Israeli, who was born in Egypt in the ninth century, and continuing through the eleventh century in Andalusia,[2] Jewish thinkers were predominantly Neoplatonists, and as such held points of view at odds with those held by Saadia. In particular, whereas Saadia adamantly maintained that the world was created out of nothing, Neoplatonists maintained an emanation theory of creation, explicitly refuted by Saadia.[3] Also, whereas Saadia conceived the soul to be a material thing which acted only through the body, Neoplatonists conceived the soul to be an immaterial thing acting independently of the body. Finally, whereas the true self for Saadia is comprised of the soul-body unity, the true self for the Neoplatonists is comprised of the soul alone. These divergences from Saadia allowed Jewish Neoplatonists to accept the view that postmortem rewards and punishments belong exclusively to the soul.

Isaac ben Joseph Israeli ultimately settled in the influential city of Kairwān (part of present-day Tunisia) in the early tenth century and had many disciples. In the eleventh century, one of the most important Jewish Neoplatonists was Solomon Ibn

---

1. Wallis, *Neoplatonism*, 1. For a brief summary of the psychology of Plotinus, see Hirsch, *Rabbinic Psychology*, 138–49.

2. After Saadia, the Jewish community of Iraq gradually declined. Meanwhile, the Jewish community of Andalusia (the Muslim-controlled part of the Iberian Peninsula) flourished. See generally Scheindlin, *Short History of the Jewish People*, 82–84.

3. See Saadia, *Book of Beliefs and Opinions*, 50–55, 58–64.

Gabirol. Bahya Ibn Pakuda is also significant because his work, entitled *The Book of Direction to the Duties of the Heart* in the English translation, was intended for the general Jewish population and for centuries was widely read in Hebrew translation. Together with the devotional Hebrew poetry of Ibn Gabirol, *The Book of Direction to the Duties of the Heart* was instrumental in spreading Neoplatonic ideas into the mainstream of Jewish thought.

A. Pagan Neoplatonism Develops the Notion of an Immaterial Soul's Emanation from, and Return to, "the One"

Plotinus is reported to have been born in Upper Egypt and to have been taught by a Platonist named Ammonius Saccas.[4] In about 245 Plotinus went to Rome and established a school there. Among his pupils was Porphyry, whose stay with Plotinus lasted from 263 to 268. It was Porphyry who wrote a biography of Plotinus, and who collected and edited the writings of Plotinus in a work he called the *Enneads*. In keeping with the general tenor of Platonic thought, Plotinus believed that underlying the world of sense experience was a higher reality consisting basically of three incorporeal ontological levels or hypostases. These three hypostases he termed the One, the Intellect, and the Soul. The highest ontological level is the One. The One is that which is "utterly simple and undivided, all of a piece and utterly unique."[5] The One, sometimes called God, actually transcends all being which we can experience, and so is ineffable and beyond knowing.[6] Everything else that exists emanates directly or indirectly from the One. Regarding the concept of emanation, Copleston explains:

> God [the One,] . . . cannot create the world by a free act of His Will, since creation is an activity and we are not justified in ascribing activity to God and so impairing His unchangeability. Plotinus, therefore, had recourse to the metaphor of emanation . . . [He maintained] that the world issues from God or proceeds from God by necessity, there being a principle of necessity that the less perfect should issue from the more perfect.[7]

The first emanation, the Intellect, emanates directly from the One. In some places Plotinus says that "Intellect emanates from the One in the way that sweet odours are given off by perfume, or that light emanates from the sun . . . But elsewhere Plotinus

---

4. Wallis, *Neoplatonism*, 37. For further details of the life of Plotinus, see Copleston, *History of Philosophy*, I, part II, 207–8.

5. Kenny, *New History of Western Philosophy*, 1:311.

6. See Plotinus, *Enneades*, III. 8.8; Copleston, *History of Philosophy*, I, part II, 208 ("God is absolutely transcendent: He is the One, beyond all thought and all being, ineffable and incomprehensible."); Russell, *History of Western Philosophy*, 288 ("The one is somewhat shadowy. It is sometimes called God, sometimes the Good; it transcends Being.").

7. Copleston, *History of Philosophy*, I, part II, 210.

speaks of the Intellect as 'daring to apostatize from the One.'"[8] The Intellect performs the same function as Plato's Demiurge in the *Timaeus*. Ontologically speaking, the Intellect is pure thought, and can be associated with the realm of the Platonic Forms since thought and the objects of thought are, according to Aristotle, identical.

Emanating from the Intellect is the Soul. As Kenny states:

> Soul is the immanent, controlling element in the universe of nature, just as God was in the Stoic system, but unlike the Stoic God Soul is incorporeal. Intellect was the maker of the universe, like the Demiurge of the *Timaeus*, but Soul is intellect's agent in managing its development. Soul links the intelligible world with the world of the senses, having an inner element that looks upwards to Intellect and an external element that looks downward to Nature.[9]

Plato had viewed the World Soul as intermediate between the sensible and Intelligible worlds, describing the World Soul in the *Timaeus* as "blended of the indivisible substance and that which becomes (and is) divisible about bodies."[10] Plotinus interprets the Soul's "indivisibility" as nonspatiality and sees such nonspatiality as the Soul's essential nature. The fact that the Soul's activity entails the production and governance of bodies that are extended in space "makes her appear to undergo spatial division," but this "should not make us ascribe the body's spatial limitations to the soul itself."[11] It is the Soul's nonspatiality "that enables her to be present in her entirety throughout the whole body, as phenomena like sense-perception require."[12]

Plotinus's view of the individual human soul is that it is, as the Soul, nonspatial, with a division between the higher soul and the lower soul. The individual human soul is also immortal. Although Plato had referred to the human soul as having parts and had, in the *Timaeus*, associated each part with a certain organ or region of the body, Plotinus does not understand such language as implying that the soul, or any of its parts, is spatial; rather,

> the soul's various faculties are 'present' in their appropriate organs in the sense that their operation takes place there, and . . . this in turn results from the fact that not every part of the body is adopted to serve as an organ for every power of the soul . . . ; for instance, the blood around the heart is a suitable vehicle for anger . . . But reason, in his view, has no bodily organ . . . and is therefore situated in the head only in the sense that its function is to supervise perception and motion, which are 'present' in the brain insofar as their organs, the nerves, have their terminus there . . . Similar reasons explain why the individual soul,

---

8. Kenny, *New History of Western Philosophy*, 1:314.
9. Kenny, *New History of Western Philosophy*, 1:314. See Copleston, *History of Philosophy*, I, part II, 212.
10. Plato, *Timaeus*, 35a. See Wallis, *Neoplatonism*, 51.
11. Wallis, *Neoplatonism*, 51.
12. Wallis, *Neoplatonism*, 51.

while free from spatial limitations, is yet confined to the government of a particular body.[13]

The aspect of Plotinian thought most significant for Jewish intellectual history concerns the "law" that every being seeks to return to its cause.[14] Consistent with this principle, the individual human soul seeks to return to the One. Plotinus asserted that it is possible for the individual human soul to rise to the contemplation of, and to identify with, the Forms themselves. As Wallis states, "Simultaneously the soul overcomes attachment to her separate individuality and realises her inner identity with the whole Intelligible world."[15] Ultimately, the soul's goal is to return to, and unite with, the One. The Plotinian conception of the ascent of the soul to the One is described by Wallis as follows:

> The One, Plotinus emphasizes, ... is present whenever we turn within, away from our normal preoccupation with the sensible world, and so come to know ourselves and, ultimately, the One that is our source ... To see the latter we must 'divest ourselves of everything' ... or 'put away all otherness,' that is all multiplicity and everything that differentiates us from the One ... And just as ascent to the Intelligible world involved relinquishment of all sensible form, so now ascent to the formless One requires that the soul 'confound and annul the distinctions of Intelligence' ... and make herself formless.[16]

Later Neoplatonists placed greater stress on the practical and religious dimensions of Neoplatonism, that is, on theurgy.[17] For Porphyry, the end of philosophy is salvation, which is achieved by the soul purifying itself by turning away from that which is lower and focusing on that which is higher, thereby facilitating the soul's ascent to the Intelligible world and union with the One.[18]

B. Isaac ben Solomon Israeli

The Alexandrian School of Neoplatonism was moved to Baghdad in 900, and Neoplatonist works reached the Arabic-speaking world through many other routes as well. A major role was played by the so-called *Theology of Aristotle* which consists of extracts from *Enneads* IV–VI and supplementary or explanatory material perhaps derived from Porphyry's lost commentary. Although attributed to Aristotle, chapter III of the so-called *Theology of Aristotle* is based on *Enneads* IV.7.8 and actually refutes

---

13. Wallis, *Neoplatonism*, 76–77. See Hirsch, *Rabbinic Psychology*, 142. See also Wallis, *Neoplatonism*, 112. See generally Hirsch, *Rabbinic Psychology*, 139–40.
14. See Plotinus, *Enneades*, III. 8.7.17–18; Wallis, *Neoplatonism*, 65–66.
15. Wallis, *Neoplatonism*, 86 (citing Plotinus, *Enneades*, VI. 5.12.16).
16. Wallis, *Neoplatonism*, 88 (citing Plotinus, *Enneades*).
17. See Wallis, *Neoplatonism*, 93.
18. See Copleston, *History of Philosophy*, I, part II, 217.

Aristotle's own doctrine of the soul. As Copleston points out, "the result was that the Arabs' interpretation of Aristotle was at least as Neoplatonic as their interpretation of Plato—and perhaps more so."[19] Isaac Israeli was most directly influenced by the first great Islamic philosopher, al-Kindi, and by a lost pseudo-Aristotelian treatise originally written in Arabic and later translated into Hebrew by Abraham Ibn Hasday that has been dubbed by Altmann and Stern "Ibn Hasday's Neoplatonist."[20]

Israeli's own philosophical works, written in Arabic, include the *Book of Definitions*, the *Book of Substances*, the *Book on Spirit and Soul*, and the *Book on the Elements*.[21] The *Book on Spirit and Soul*, which is perhaps part of a larger work, "is the only one of Isaac Israeli's works that refers to the Bible and it seems that it was intended for the Jewish public."[22] In addition, Altmann and Stern have determined that a work called the *Chapter on Elements*, previously ascribed to Aristotle, is the Hebrew version of a work by Isaac Israeli, the Arabic original of which has been lost.[23] The *Chapter on Elements* is known from a single manuscript referred to as the Mantua Text.

1. Israeli accepts the Neoplatonic concept of emanation

Whereas for Plotinus emanation from the One comes about as a matter of necessity, Israeli emphasizes that emanation comes about as a result of the will of God. Further, whereas for Plotinus Intellect emanates directly from the One, Israeli interposes two simple substances—"first matter" and "substantial form"—between the Creator and Intellect. Substantial form "is perfect wisdom, pure radiance, and clear splendor."[24] By the conjunction of first matter and substantial form, Intellect came into being. After Intellect came into being,

> a radiance and splendour went forth from it like the radiance that goes forth from mirrors of glass set in the windows of baths and palaces when the radiance and splendour of the sun fall upon them. From this the nature of the rational soul came into being. Its radiance and splendour are less than the radiance and splendour of intellect . . . After the nature of the rational soul came into being, a radiance and splendour went forth from it . . ., and from this the nature of the animal soul came into being. Its radiance and splendour are less

---

19. Copleston, *History of Philosophy*, I, part II, 163. See also Husik, *History of Mediaeval Jewish Philosophy*, xxxvii ("The so-called 'Theology of Aristotle' is a Plotinian work . . . But the middle ages were not aware of the origin of this treatise, and so they attributed it to [Aristotle] and proceeded to harmonize it with the rest of his system as they knew it.").

20. Altmann and Stern, *Isaac Israeli*, xvii–xviii, xxix. See Stern, "Ibn Ḥasdāy's Neoplatonist," 59–78; Levin and Walker, "Isaac Israeli," §2.

21. See Altmann and Stern, *Isaac Israeli*, xvii; Sirat, *Jewish Philosophy in the Middle Ages*, 58–59; Levin and Walker, "Isaac Israeli," §5.

22. Sirat, *Jewish Philosophy in the Middle Ages*, 59.

23. Altmann and Stern, *Isaac Israeli*, 118.

24. Israeli, *Mantua Text*, §1.

than the radiance and splendour of the rational soul ... After the nature of the animal soul came into being, a radiance went forth from it ... and from this the nature of the vegetative soul came into being.[25]

The process continues with the "nature of the sphere" coming into being from the vegetative soul, and with the warmth of fire coming into being from "the motion of the sphere," followed by the creation of air, water, and earth, each having the property of wet or dry and the property of hot or cold.[26] As Israeli comments, "After the natures of the four elements ... had come into being as a result of the perfect, circular, and simple motion of the sphere, they mixed, combined, and penetrated one another. From this ... composite bodies and substances ... came into being, and the natures of animals, plants, and minerals arose."[27]

2. Israeli understands the human soul to be an "incorporeal spiritual substance" which is immortal, in contrast to the "vital spirit" which is corporeal and perishes with the body[28]

From what Israeli says about emanation, it seems that he adheres to the Aristotelian classification of a rational soul, an animal soul, and a vegetative soul.[29] This does not mean, however, that he accepts the Aristotelian view that the human soul, as the form of the body, cannot exist apart from the body. To the contrary, he accepts the Platonic position that the human soul is a separate entity and that it survives the destruction of the body. However, in the *Book of Definitions* Israeli explicitly states that Aristotle and Plato can be reconciled:

> The philosopher [Aristotle] said: The soul is a substance which perfects the physical body that possesses life potentially. Plato said: The soul is a substance which is united with the heavenly body and through this union it is joined to the bodies and acts in them. Isaac says: Someone may think that there is a difference between these two statements, but ... this would be an error. Plato ... had in mind the soul at the beginning of its movement and action. He says that the soul at the beginning of its movement is united with the body of the sphere, joins the bodies, and acts in them. This is so because the rank of the sphere is intermediate between the rank of the soul and that of the bodies; through this intermediate position the junction of the soul with the bodies is achieved, because through the movement of the sphere the four kinds of matter, which are the elements of the bodies, come into being. The philosopher,

25. Israeli, *Mantua Text*, §1. Cf. Israeli, *Book of Definitions*, §5:45–85; Israeli, *Book of Substances*, iv; Israeli, *Book on Spirit and Soul*, §9.
26. Israeli, *Mantua Text*, §2.
27. Israeli, *Mantua Text*, §1.
28. Israeli, *Book of Definitions*, §8:1–9.
29. See Kenny, *New History of Western Philosophy*, 1:243.

on the other hand, had in mind the soul at the completion of its movements and perfection of its acts. He said: 'The soul is a substance which perfects the physical body that possesses life potentially,' informing us that the bodies before the soul's junction with them possessed life potentially, while, when the soul was joined with them, it completed and perfected them and made them alive actually. Isaac says: When we say 'bodies were at the beginning alive potentially, and afterwards they passed into actuality,' we imply no temporal difference, separation, or distance . . . The junction of the soul with the bodies only means that the soul infuses into them some of its light and brilliance in order to make them alive, mobile, and sensible; in the same way as the sun infuses some of its light and brilliance into the world, in order to make it bright and brilliant, so that sight becomes possible. It is true that there is a difference between the brilliance and light of the sun and those of the soul, because the brilliance of the sun is corporeal and can be apprehended by sight in its substrate, which is the air; while the brilliance of the soul is spiritual and can only be apprehended by intellect through wisdom, not sense-perception.[30]

In addition to defining the soul, the *Book of Definitions* also defines the "vital spirit":

> The ancients agree that the spirit is a subtle body which pervades, from the heart and through the arteries, the whole body and gives it life, respiration in the lung and pulse in the arteries. It ascends to the brain and from there it pervades, through the nerves, the whole body and gives it sense-perception and movement. If someone asks about the difference between the soul and the spirit, we answer that the difference is twofold. (1) Firstly, the spirit is a corporeal substance contained, confined, and surrounded by the body, while the soul is an incorporeal spiritual substance which surrounds and contains the body from without. (2) Secondly, the spirit is dissolved and destroyed together with the body, while the soul persists and remains after its separation from the body, though its action does not penetrate the body after the absence of the spirit which has given it life, sense-perception, and movement; when the body is deprived of the spirit and is dead, the soul does not penetrate it.[31]

Israeli immediately reiterates in his definition of vital spirit that it "flows" through the arteries (as does the blood, albeit in a separate tube or channel) "to the whole body, giving it life and generating breath in the lung and pulse in the arteries in order to expel through them the warm vapours from the heart and draw in subtle air."[32]

In their comments on the definition of "vital spirit" Altmann and Stern state that the "physiological theories concerning the vital spirit, blood, arteries and veins

---

30. Israeli, *Book of Definitions*, §5:1–45.
31. Israeli, *Book of Definitions*, §8:1–15.
32. Israeli, *Book of Definitions*, §8:16–22. Cf. Israeli, *Book on Spirit and Soul*, §§1, 8.

are the conventional ones derived from Galen."³³ This may be true, and it associates the vital spirit with the blood mixed with air that Galen believed was in the arteries, but it doesn't explain Israeli's attribution of sensation and movement to both the vital spirit and the animal soul. The probable explanation is that (following the Plotinian doctrine that the soul's various faculties are "present" in their appropriate organs in the sense that their operation takes place there) Israeli believed the animal soul causes sensation and motion, but that the actual activity caused by the animal soul takes place by means of the vital spirit. Although Israeli never explicitly states that this is the case, he does say that the soul makes it possible for the body to move and to have sensation by infusing it with some of the soul's light and brilliance:

> The junction of the soul with the bodies only means that the soul infuses into them some of its light and brilliance in order to make them alive, mobile, and sensible; in the same way as the sun infuses some of its light and brilliance into the world, in order to make it bright and brilliant, so that sight becomes possible.³⁴

The likelihood that Israeli believed, consistent with Plotinian thought, that the animal soul causes sensation and motion but that the actual activity of sensation and motion takes place through the vital spirit, is supported by the fact that Israeli's notion that the soul "contains" the body, instead of being contained by it, also goes back to Plotinus.³⁵

Confusion concerning the vital spirit also arises due to Israeli's use of biblical proof texts. Galen associates the "vital spirit" with the Greek word *pneuma* (fiery air), and *pneuma* is often associated with the Hebrew word *ruach*. Indeed, the Septuagint "uses *pneuma* in 75 percent of the cases to translate the Hebrew word *ruach*."³⁶ So, one might expect Israeli to associate *ruach* with the vital spirit, and he does. He uses Psalm 78:39 as a proof text to establish that the vital spirit perishes, and so receives no reward or punishment in the afterlife: "we see that Scripture says: 'The spirit [*ruach*] passeth away and cometh not again' . . . it does not attribute reward and punishment to the [vital] spirit, but describes it as something which passes away and does not come again."³⁷ However, Israeli also associates *ruach* with the soul. The reason for this is that in at least one biblical passage, as interpreted by Israeli, *ruach* is seen to be that part of a human being which is immortal and returns to God, and Israeli understands that the part of a human being that is immortal and returns to God is the soul. The *Book on Spirit and Soul* states:

---

33. Altmann and Stern, *Isaac Israeli*, 49.
34. Israeli, *Book of Definitions*, §5:33–38.
35. See Altmann and Stern, *Isaac Israeli*, 50 (citing Plotinus, *Enneades*, IV.3.20).
36. MacDonald, *History of the Concept of Mind*, 2. In the Latin translation *ruach* is translated by *spiritus*. MacDonald, *History of the Concept of Mind*, 7.
37. Israeli, *Book on Spirit and Soul*, §8.

> The spirit is natural warmth which is in the heart; as the prophet says: 'Then shall the dust return to the earth as it was' [Qoh 12:7], i.e., the body will return to its component elements. But the soul returns upwards to the place of retribution; for this reason he says: 'and the spirit [*ruach*] shall return to God who gave it.' [Qoh 12:7][38]

Unlike Saadia, who differentiates the Hebrew words *neshamah*, *ruach*, and *nephesh*, associating each of these words with one of the three parts of the soul delineated by Plato—the rational, spirited, and appetitive parts, respectively—Israeli makes no such distinction. All three words simply refer to the same thing—the soul. Thus, in addition to interpreting *ruach* as referring to the soul, Israeli indicates that *neshamah* refers to the soul when he states: "The soul is splendour [a brilliant thing associated with light], as the prophet says: 'The spirit of man (*nishmat adam*) is a lamp of the Lord' [Prov 20:27]"[39]; and Israeli indicates that *nephesh* refers to the soul when he states that "if the soul inclines toward the intellect and towards wisdom [it will be rewarded by ascending to the intelligible realm]; if, however, it inclines towards the degree of the animal soul, it deserves punishment, according to the words of Scripture: 'The soul [*nephesh*] of my lord shall be bound in the bundle of life with the Lord God; and the souls of thine enemies, them shall he sling out, as from a hollow sling' [1 Sam 25:29]."[40]

3. For Israeli, the righteous soul that inclines toward wisdom is rewarded by returning to the supernal light of wisdom in the afterlife

Israeli explicitly states that it is wrong to say that a reward is given "in this world."[41] He argues that this world

> is the opposite of the next, as this world is the place for work, the next one the place for reward,[42] and it is fit that the righteous ones and the prophets should abide there [sc., the next world], but not the sinners; as it is written: 'Your fathers, where are they? And the prophets, do they live forever?' [Zech 1:5]—meaning that they have been raised to a nobler state. Similarly: 'But the wicked shall be cut off from the land' [Prov 2:22], meaning: from the enduring 'land,' i.e. the next world."[43]

---

38. Israeli, *Book on Spirit and Soul*, §8.
39. Israeli, *Book on Spirit and Soul*, §4.
40. Israeli, *Book on Spirit and Soul*, §8.
41. Israeli, *Book on Spirit and Soul*, §12. But see Altmann and Stern, *Isaac Israeli*, 193 (interpreting Israeli's mention in §13 of "two kinds of bliss: one which occurs without delay, the other remote" as including a reward in this world).
42. Cf. ch. 5, sec. C, 1 (Saadia distinguishes the "workaday world" from "the world of recompense").
43. Israeli, *Book on Spirit and Soul*, §12.

He also explicitly states that "reward and punishment belong to the soul."[44] Conversely, the vital spirit which, unlike the soul, is corporeal and part of the body, does not receive any reward or punishment.[45] The vital spirit, together with the entire human body "will return to its component elements."[46] More specifically, "the [vital] spirit returns to air, the phlegm and the humidities to water, the flesh and the bones, which are earthy, to dust."[47] But "the soul turns upwards to the place of retribution."[48] Elaborating on this understanding, Israeli writes:

> The soul . . . is the most noble of things, and is with the angels above the sphere, as he says: 'And I will give thee a place of access among those that stand by' [Zech 3:7], showing that its reward is to be with the angels, as these are granted bliss by God.[49]

The nature of the reward to be received by the soul in the next world is union with the supernal light of wisdom created by God as His first emanation. In the *Book of Definitions* Israeli states that the "reward of [the] Creator . . . is the union with the upper soul, and the illumination by the light of the intellect and by the beauty and splendor of wisdom," and that when a person attains this rank he "becomes spiritual, and will be joined in union to the light which is created, without mediator, by the power of God, and will become one that exalts and praises the Creator forever and in all eternity. This then will be his paradise and the goodness of his reward, and the bliss of his rest, his perfect rank and unsullied beauty."[50]

Those who merit this reward are identified as persons to whom the truths of science have "become clear" and who thus are able to "distinguish between good and evil, between what is laudable and what is not," so that they "do what corresponds to truth, in justice and rectitude," "sanctify, praise, and exalt the Creator, and recognize His dominion," and "avoid beastly and unclean actions."[51] In contrast to this is the person identified as deserving punishment, said to be one "who does not attach himself to the intellectual precepts which God has revealed . . . and [who thus] perseveres in his own injustice, sinfulness, coarseness, and in the evil ways."[52] Such a person "will be rendered unclean by his impurities, and they will weigh him down and prevent him

---

44. Israeli, *Book on Spirit and Soul*, §8.

45. Israeli, *Book on Spirit and Soul*, §8 ("Scripture . . . does not attribute reward and punishment to the spirit, but describes it as something which passes away and does not come again.").

46. Israeli, *Book on Spirit and Soul*, §8.

47. Israeli, *Book on Spirit and Soul*, §8.

48. Israeli, *Book on Spirit and Soul*, §8.

49. Israeli, *Book on Spirit and Soul*, §8.

50. Israeli, *Book of Definitions*, §2:56–65.

51. Israeli, *Book of Definitions*, §2:52–56. See also Israeli, *Book on Spirit and Soul*, §8 (the soul receives a reward if it "inclines towards the intellect and towards wisdom").

52. Israeli, *Book of Definitions*, §2:81–84.

from ascending to the world of truth."[53] Such a one "will not attain the light and the beauty of wisdom, but [will] remain contained under the sphere, sorrowful, in pain without measure, revolving with the revolution of the sphere in the great fire and the torturing flame. This will be his hell and the fire of his torture which God has prepared for the wicked and sinners who rebel against the precepts of the intellect."[54]

Elsewhere he speaks of the conduct of the soul itself, rather than the conduct of the person, as determining the soul's fate. He says that a reward will be received "if the soul inclines toward the intellect and toward wisdom; if, however, it inclines towards the degree of the animal soul, it deserves punishment, according to the words of Scripture: 'The soul of my lord shall be bound in the bundle of life with the Lord thy God; and the souls of thine enemies, them shall he sling out, as from a hollow sling' [1 Sam 25:29]."[55]

The way that Israeli describes the persons and the souls deserving of reward and punishment suggests that rewards or punishments for Israeli are primarily functions of intellectual achievement. This interpretation is supported by Israeli's explanation as to why humans receive a reward or punishment but other animals do not. According to the order of emanation, the rational soul, possessed only by humans, "came into being in the horizon and from the shadow of the intellect."[56] It is because the rational soul emanated directly from the intellect that "man became rational, discerning, susceptible of science and wisdom, distinguishing between good and evil, between praiseworthy and unpraiseworthy things, approaching virtues and shunning vices."[57] In short, man is rewarded or punished "because he knows the difference between the acts for which he is rewarded or punished."[58] In contrast, the animal soul does not come into being directly from the intellect but emanates "from the shadow of the rational soul, on account of which it is removed from the light of the intellect and acquires shadow; it becomes shadowy and inquiry and discernment leave it; it is, properly speaking, estimating . . . for it reveals things from outward appearance, not in reality."[59] Estimation is defined in the *Book of Definitions* as "a judgment concerning a thing with reference to what it appears to be and not with reference to what it is in truth."[60] Because the animal soul lacks inquiry, discernment, and knowledge, having only the ability to estimate, it is ruled by passions, not reason. The lion, for example, "seeks to overcome the other animals, without inquiry . . . or knowledge of what it is

---

53. Israeli, *Book of Definitions*, §2:84–86. Cf. Plato, Phaed. 81c.
54. Israeli, *Book of Definitions*, §2:86–91.
55. Israeli, *Book on Spirit and Soul*, §8.
56. Israeli, *Book of Definitions*, §5:49–50.
57. Israeli, *Book of Definitions*, §5:50–53.
58. Israeli, *Book of Definitions*, §5:54–55.
59. Israeli, *Book of Definitions*, §5:57–61.
60. Israeli, *Book of Definitions*, §33.

doing."[61] Consequently, says Israeli, "animals do not receive reward or punishment."[62] Reiterating, he says: "they [sc., animals] have no faculty of discernment and do not know for what action they should be rewarded, or, on the other hand, punished. The reason is that they are deprived of the faculty of inquiry and discernment and of perceiving the truth of things, and have a property of estimation and mediation."[63]

The reward and punishment of the soul are poetically depicted in a text believed to have been relied upon by Israeli that Altmann and Stern call "Ibn Hasday's Neoplatonist." The complete text, as we have it today, is incorporated into a book written by Abraham Ibn Hasday entitled *The Prince and the Ascetic*.[64] The relevant portion reads:

> If the rational soul is righteous, understands the truth of things, is purified from the defilement of this world, and not soiled by its evil and blameworthy desires, but acts according to truth, it is then worthy of receiving its reward and goes to the world of intellect and reaches the light which is created from the power, its pure brilliance and unmixed splendour and perfect wisdom, from whence it had been derived; it is then delighted by its understanding and knowledge. This delight is not one of eating, drinking, and other bodily delights, but the joy of the soul in what it sees and hears, a delight which has nothing in common with other delights except the name.
>
> If the sinful soul is not righteous and is not cleansed from the defilement of this world and its desires which destroy goodness, and its delights which carry with them all evil, and does not act in accordance with truth and does not understand it—it is worthy of remaining in exile from the world of the intellect and removed from the light and the splendour of its Creator and His great bounty which is treasured up for such as fear him. It remains sad and despondent and joins the fire which comes-to-be by the power of the movement of the sphere; that fire prevents it from passing to the great good—instead, it must revolve with the sphere's revolution, perplexed and full of desire, hungering and thirsting to find a way to go home to its country and return to its native place. It resembles a man who traveled away from his house, brothers, children and wife, relatives and family, and stayed abroad for a long time. When finally he was on his way back and approached his country and the goal of his desires, having passed through seas and rivers, forests and deserts, and was filled with the strongest desire to reach his home and rest in his house— obstacles were put in his way and the gates were shut and he was prevented

---

61. Israeli, *Book of Definitions*, §5:64–66.
62. Israeli, *Book of Definitions*, §5:72–73.
63. Israeli, *Book of Definitions*, §5:73–76. By "estimation and mediation" Israeli meant a faculty that grasps features of the world that are too abstract to be perceived merely by sensation, but not as abstract and universal as things grasped only by the intellect. Cf. Adamson, *Philosophy in the Islamic World*, 137, 149 (describing in this manner the use by Avicenna and al-Ghazali of the Arabic word *wahm*, translated as "estimation," and giving as an example of *wahm* a sheep's awareness of hostility when it sees a wolf).
64. See Altmann and Stern, *Isaac Israeli*, 95–96; Stern, "Ibn Ḥasdāy's Neoplatonist," 59–64.

from passing. He called, but it was to no avail, and he had to remain outside, hungry, thirsty, suffering from the heat of the day and the cold of the night, in continuous fear of wolves, lions, and other wild beasts. He wandered about, perplexed how to find a refuge, weeping bitterly and sorrowfully bewailing the great good which he had lost and the evil which had befallen him. The soul, if this is its fate, is sufficiently punished by the everlasting fire which is its lot.[65]

4. The upward way of the soul proceeds in three stages

The pagan Neoplatonist Proclus describes the soul's "ascent to the Divine" in three stages. In the first stage, called the stage of "self-purification," the soul is freed from sensible things in order to receive the light of Intellect; in the second stage Intellect "illumines" the soul; and in the third stage the soul, having reached the level of the Intellect, achieves "union" with God. The soul's three-stage ascent of self-purification, illumination, and union was adopted by Christian mystics, and may be found as well in Moslem sources, including al-Kindi.[66]

Israeli, too, adopts the Neoplatonic tradition of the three stages of the soul's upward ascent.[67] In *Chapter on the Elements* he describes the first stage of the ascent, the stage of "self-purification," as a turning away from the passions and appetites associated with the animal and vegetative souls, and an inclination toward the activity of the rational soul. Israeli takes it to be a basic truth that "[w]henever a man's soul inclines excessively towards some particular soul, he will incline towards the actions peculiar to the [particular] soul attracting him."[68] So, when a person's rational soul inclines toward the animal soul, rather than turning away from it, the person "will pursue the things that are vile, evil, and corrupt such as homicide, theft, falsehood and lust. [He] will abandon the good things, despise the pious and just, love the foolish and wicked, despise also those possessed of understanding, knowledge, and goodness."[69] Similarly, when both the rational and animal souls incline toward the vegetative soul "man will thereby be prone to pursue things such as excessive eating and drinking and the desire for the enjoyment of this world only."[70] It is only when the "vegetative soul inclines towards the animal soul, and the animal soul in turn inclines towards the rational soul, and the rational soul in turn inclines towards the intellect" that a person will become "balanced in his actions and pursue the good things such as the quest for wisdom and

---

65. Ibn Hasday, *Prince and the Ascetic*, ch. 35, in Altmann and Stern, *Isaac Israeli*, 115–16; Stern, "Ibn Ḥasdāy's Neoplatonist," 75–76.
66. See Altmann and Stern, *Isaac Israeli*, 185–86, 205.
67. See Altmann and Stern, *Isaac Israeli*, 186, 205.
68. Israeli, *Mantua Text*, §6.
69. Israeli, *Mantua Text*, §6.
70. Israeli, *Mantua Text*, §6.

knowledge," and that their physical desires and "desire for the pleasures of this world" will be "balanced and moderate."[71]

The second stage of the ascent—the "illumination" of the soul by the intellect—appears to require that the rational soul ("that soul of [a person] which is nearest to intellect") achieve "perfection."[72] When this occurs the person will become "perfect, clear minded, and truthful, and will pursue things which are good and true such as knowledge and understanding, purity and holiness, the worship and nearness to his Creator . . . and that which attaches to the Creator, like the souls of the prophets . . . which are joined to him."[73] The achievement of such perfection requires, in turn, the attainment of wisdom defined as the "true knowledge of the first, enduring, and everlasting things."[74]

The third and final stage of the ascent, that of union, is

> one at which the soul 'becomes spiritual' or 'becomes intellectual' . . . The union achieved at this stage is the union of the rational soul raised to the level of intellect with the supernal light of wisdom, thereby completing its ascent from bondage in the flesh and the two lower souls to the highest spiritual substance . . . There is no suggestion here of a final union with God Himself. All that the soul of man can hope to achieve is union with the supernal wisdom created by God . . . Mystical union with the supernal light of wisdom is regarded by Israeli as a stage which the rational soul can achieve even while still joined to the body, provided it 'withdraws' from the influence of the flesh and of the lower souls.[75]

As stated by Israeli in the *Book on the Elements*:

> One whose rational soul has withdrawn itself [i.e. from the lower souls] and upon whom intellect causes its light and splendour to emanate becomes spiritual, god-like, and longing exceedingly for the ways of the angels, as far as lies within human power.[76]

The ascent of the soul assumes its full significance in the context of the afterlife where the soul, separated completely from the body, is rewarded by its return to the region from which it first emanated and its complete and blissful union with the supernal light of wisdom. By asserting that such union constitutes paradise (or *Gan Eden*), "Israeli links the traditional Jewish eschatology with Neoplatonic mysticism."[77]

---

71. Israeli, *Mantua Text*, §6.
72. Israeli, *Mantua Text*, §6.
73. Israeli, *Mantua Text*, §6.
74. Israeli, *Book of Definitions*, §3:5–6. See Altmann and Stern, *Isaac Israeli*, 188.
75. Altmann and Stern, *Isaac Israeli*, 188–90.
76. Israeli, *Book on the Elements*, 139.
77. Altmann and Stern, *Isaac Israeli*, 192.

CHAPTER 6.

5. Bodily resurrection is of little importance to Israeli

The counterpart to the soul's afterlife reward of paradise—blissful union with the supernal light of wisdom—is the soul's afterlife punishment in hell. But hell is not the underworld *Gehenna* that was described in certain Second Temple and rabbinic texts. Hell, for Israeli, is primarily exile from the supernal light of wisdom. Those souls deserving of punishment are weighed down by their impurities and are unable rise past the sphere. In the process of the world's emanation from God, the sphere, it will be recalled, emanates out of the vegetative soul; and then out of the movement of the sphere the element of fire is created.

It thus becomes natural for Israeli to associate the wicked soul's punishment beneath the level of the sphere with a "great fire" and "torturing flame."[78] But for Israeli, who is philosophically sophisticated, the soul's real punishment is probably not physical torment, since in the afterlife the soul lacks a body needed to experience physical pain. Rather, the soul's real punishment is its "exile from the world of the intellect" and its inability to achieve a blissful union with the "light and the beauty of wisdom."[79] Significantly, Israeli takes no significant cognizance of the idea of an afterlife reward or punishment to a resurrected body.[80] This is not surprising since such idea is completely outside a Neoplatonic frame of reference.

C. Solomon ben Judah Ibn Gabirol

Ibn Gabirol was born in Málaga Spain between 1020 and 1022.[81] The most expansive of Ibn Gabirol's prose works was written in Arabic but is known only in its Latin translation done in the twelfth century entitled *Fons Vitae* [*Fountain of Life*]. *Fons Vitae* was attributed to one Avicebron. In addition, there is a thirteenth-century Hebrew translation/summary of the Arabic work called *Mekor Hayyim*. It was not until 1856 that a

---

78. Israeli, *Book of Definitions*, §2:86–89.

79. Altmann and Stern comment that Israeli's conception of hell as the consuming fire beneath the sphere and revolving with it, in which the souls of the wicked (weighed down by impurity) are caught, goes back to two sources: (1) "rabbinic tradition" in which "hell is described as the heat of the sun which burns the wicked or as a strange heat in their bodies which consumes them," and (2) "Plato [who] speaks [in *Phaedo*, 81c–d] of the corporeal element as 'burdensome and weighty and earthy,' hampering, depressing, and dragging down the soul into the visible world"; "Israeli combines these two traditions against the background of his own cosmology" (Altmann and Stern, *Isaac Israeli*, 193–94). See also Guttmann, *Philosophies of Judaism*, 126–27 (Israeli rejected the Greek Neoplatonists' idea of *metempsychosis* and, instead, "advanced the doctrine (which ultimately goes back to Greece) that the souls of the wicked, since they are weighed down by sensual pleasure, vainly try to rise to the supersensible world. In their vain longings they are driven hither and yon underneath the heavens; *in fact, this is their punishment*"; emphasis added).

80. The concept of resurrection is, however, mentioned at least once in relation to the existence of reward. See Israeli, *Book on Spirit and Soul*, §13.

81. For biographical information, see Loewe, *Ibn Gabirol*, 17–26; Ibn Gabirol, *Kingly Crown*, 3–5; Sirat, *Jewish Philosophy in the Middle Ages*, 68; Pessin, "Solomon Ibn Gabirol," §1.

scholar came upon the Hebrew summary and connected it with *Fons Vitae*, and thus discovered that Avicebron was Ibn Gabirol.[82] While the thought of Ibn Gabirol was, thus, known to later Jewish medieval thinkers from his strictly philosophical work, his ideas were more widely known in the Jewish community from his Hebrew poetry, especially from *Keter Malkhut* (variously translated as the *Kingly Crown*, *Kingdom's Crown*, or the *Royal Crown*).

1. For Ibn Gabirol the only afterlife reward is the soul's return to a place of repose in the higher world constituting the *Olam Ha-Bah*

Fons Vitae "is a purely metaphysical work, presenting an essentially Neoplatonic system, without as much as one word about its relationship to Judaism."[83] As Isaac Israeli had done before him, Ibn Gabirol adopts the Neoplatonic concepts of emanation and the return of the soul to the intelligible realm or the higher world. Indeed, it is the return of the soul that Ibn Gabirol contends is the purpose of life. Specifically, there is in *Fons Vitae* the following exchange between a master and his disciple:

> DISCIPLE: What then is the end and aim of the human race?
>
> MASTER: The union of its life-principle [soul] with the higher world, so that one may return to its counterpart.[84]

The goal of the return of the soul is accomplished by means of the pursuit of knowledge and the doing of good deeds.[85] Thus, Ibn Gabirol, as Israeli, accepts that the soul is immortal, survives the death of the body, and is rewarded in the afterlife by its return to the domain from whence it came, the higher world. There is no mention of resurrection.

These Neoplatonic themes are transposed into a more Jewish milieu in *Keter Malkhut*, with biblical proof texts being incorporated. In this regard, the poem serves the same purpose as the *Book of Soul and Spirit* for Israeli, namely, promulgating Neoplatonic views about creation, the soul, and the afterlife to the nonphilosophical, wider Jewish community. *Keter Malkhut* is "a long devotional poem exploring the ineffable splendor of the divine and tracing God's presence throughout the various

---

82. Ibn Gabirol, *Kingly Crown*, 31–32. See Loewe, *Ibn Gabirol*, 39–41; Pessin, "Solomon Ibn Gabirol," §1.

83. Guttmann, *Philosophies of Judaism*, 101. The conception of the soul in *Fons Vitae* is Aristotelian, delineating a vegetative principle, a sensing principle, and a rational principle. See Ibn Gabirol, *Fountain of Life*, 166–70 (*Fons Vitae*, 3.47, 3.48).

84. Ibn Gabirol, *Fountain of Life*, 5 (*Fons Vitae*, 1.2). See Hyman, *Eschatological Themes*, 70 (translating, "[The purpose of human life is] the attachment of the human soul to the upper world. By means of this everything returns to that which it resembles.").

85. See Ibn Gabirol, *Fountain of Life*, 5 (*Fons Vitae*, 1.2) ("knowledge and action free the life-principle from the bonds of materiality, cleanse it of darkness and obscurity, and enable it to return to its own higher realm."). Cf. Hyman, *Eschatological Themes*, 70–71. See also Ibn Gabirol, *Fountain of Life*, 4, 303 (*Fons Vitae*, 1.2; 5.43).

cosmological spheres which make up the universe."[86] It is included even today in many Jewish prayer books for recitation on Yom Kippur.[87]

The first part of the poem consists of a praise of God, it emphasizes "the unity of God, His existence, His preexistence, His greatness, His might, His light, His ineffable divinity, His wisdom, His will."[88] He is, in addition, said to be the source from which both the higher and lower worlds emanated, the latter "for works" and the former "for requital."[89] God is also identified as the "supreme light" which the pure of soul, but not sinners, can apprehend in the afterlife, or the "world of beauty."[90]

In the second part of the poem, the wonders of creation are described. Ibn Gabirol mentions ten levels or spheres that emanate from God constituting the heavens. Then he refers to the creation of the individual human soul which emanates, together with angelic spirits, from the radiance of the sphere of Intellect (referred to as the *Shechina*):

> Who can fathom Thy thoughts when from the splendor of the sphere of intelligence (*Shechina*) Thou madest the radiance of souls (*zohar ha-neshamot*) and lofty spirits (*ha-nephashot ha-ramot*)?
>
> They are the messengers of Thy Will, the ministers of Thy countenance.[91]

The most critical passages come in cantos 27–31:

> Who can do as Thy deeds, when under the throne of Thy glory Thou madest a place for the spirits of Thy saints [*lnaphshot hasidekha*] [cf. b. Šabb. 152b]. There is the abode of the pure souls [*neshamot*], that are bound in the bundle of life [1 Sam 25:29] . . .
>
> There shall the weary be at rest [cf. Job 3:17],[92] for they are deserving of repose.
>
> In it there is delight without end or limitation, for that is the world-to-come [*ha-olam ha-bah*].
>
> There are stations and visions for the souls [*nephashot*] that stand by the mirrors assembled [cf Exod 38:8], to see the face of the Lord and to be seen, . . .
>
> Delighting in the sweetness of the fruit of the Intelligence [*ha-sekhel*], which yields royal dainties [cf. Gen 49:20] . . .

---

86. Pessin, "Solomon Ibn Gabirol," §1.

87. See Pessin, "Solomon Ibn Gabirol," §1; Ibn Gabirol, *Kingly Crown*, 32; Hyman, *Eschatological Themes*, 66.

88. Ibn Gabirol, *Kingly Crown*, 40n3. See Hyman, *Eschatological Themes*, 66.

89. Ibn Gabirol, *Kingly Crown*, 42 (canto 1).

90. Ibn Gabirol, *Kingly Crown*, 48 (canto 7). Cf. Israeli, *Book of Definitions*, §2:63–64 (comparing paradise and reward with "unsullied beauty"). See Altmann and Stern, *Isaac Israeli*, 26.

91. Ibn Gabirol, *Kingly Crown*, 78 (canto 25).

92. "The poet is here following a midrashic interpretation of this verse" (Ibn Gabirol, *Kingly Crown*, 83n98).

Who can reveal Thy mysteries, when in the heights Thou madest chambers and treasure [*otzarot*], in which wonders are told, and the word of the mighty deeds?

Some of them treasures of life [*otzrot hayyim*] for the righteous and pure.

Some of them treasures of salvation, for penitent sinners,

Some of them treasures of fire and rivers of sulphur, for the transgressors of the covenant [cf. Joshua 7:15],

And treasures of deep pits of unquenchable fire, 'he that is abhorred of the Lord shall fall therein' [Prov 22:14].

And treasures of storms and tempests, of freezing and frost,

And treasures of hail and ice and snow, drought and also heat and bursting floods,

Steam and rime and mist and cloud and darkness and gloom.

All of them didst Thou prepare, in their time, either for mercy or for judgment Thou didst ordain them, 'O mighty God,

Thou hast established them for correction' [Hab 1:12].

Who can contain Thy might, when from the abundance of Thy glory [cf. Isa 66:11] Thou didst create a pure radiance, hewn from the quarry of the Rock, and dug from the mine of Purity?

And on it Thou didst set a spirit [*ruach*] of wisdom, and Thou didst call it Soul [*neshamah*].

Thou didst fashion it from the flames of fire of Intelligence [*sekhel*], and its spirit [*nishmatah*] is as a fire burning in it [cf. Isa 30:33].

Thou didst send it into the body to serve it and to guard it, and it is as a fire within, and yet it does not burn it.

From the fire of the spirit [*neshamah*] it was created, and went forth from nothingness to being, 'because the Lord descended upon it in fire' [Exod 19:18].

Who can reach Thy wisdom, when Thou gavest the soul [*nephesh*] the power of knowledge which inheres in her?

So that knowledge is her glory, and therefore decay has no rule over her, and she endures with the endurance of her foundation; this is her state and her secret.

The wise soul [*nephesh*] does not see death, but receives for her sin a punishment more bitter than death,

And if she be pure she shall obtain grace, and smile on the last day,

And if she be unclean, she shall stray amid a flood of anger and wrath,

All the days of her unseemliness she shall sit alone, captive and moving to and fro [cf. Isa 49:21]; 'she shall touch no hallowed thing, nor come into the sanctuary, until the days of her purifying be fulfilled' [Lev 12:4].

> Who can requite Thy bounties, when Thou gavest the soul [*neshamah*] to the body, to give it life, to teach and show it the path of life, to save it from evil [cf. Jonah 4:6]?
>
> Thou didst form man out of clay [cf. Job 33:6], and breathe into him a soul [*neshamah*] and set in him a spirit [*ruach*] of wisdom, by which he is distinguished from a beast, and rises to a great height.[93]

Though some details of the conceptual scheme depicted in these cantos are obscure, the basic ideas concerning the soul and the afterlife are clear. The soul is created in the upper world as an emanation of the Intellect—it is "fashioned from the flames of fire of Intelligence." It is associated with a body "as a fire within, and yet it does not burn it." Not only does the soul give the body "life" but, because the "power of knowledge" inheres in the rational soul ["a spirit of wisdom"], it is able to guide the body— "to teach and show it the path of life, to save it from evil." This power of knowledge, presumably mankind's rational soul, separates human beings from other creatures. The soul is, of course, immortal—"decay has no rule over her."[94]

Regarding the afterlife, if a person's soul is pure, after death such a pure soul will return to the upper world where, under the throne of God's glory, is its place of repose—"under the throne of Thy glory Thou madest a place for the spirits of Thy saints." In this place of repose "there is delight without end or limitation," and, most significantly, it is this place of repose for the pure souls that constitutes the world-to-come, the *Olam Ha-Bah*. Although it is not directly mentioned here, for Ibn Gabirol the soul purifies itself "by knowledge and the practice of pious exercises."[95] *Keter Malkhut*, as *Fons Vitae*, makes no reference to resurrection.

2. Keter Malkhut envisions a heavenly place of punishment and purgation

Among the details of the conceptual scheme contained in cantos 27 to 31 that are less than clear are the references to the several "treasures" [*otzarot*], including treasures of salvation for the penitent sinners and treasures prepared for mercy. In order to understand these references two preliminary matters must be addressed. The first is Lewis's translation of "treasures" for the Hebrew word "*otzarot*"; the second is the

---

93. See Ibn Gabirol, *Kingly Crown*, 82–88.

94. Ibn Gabirol, *Kingly Crown*, 82–88. Interestingly, in *Keter Malkhut*, Ibn Gabirol does not seem to equate the soul with his personhood. See e.g., Ibn Gabirol, *Kingly Crown*, 102 (canto 36) ("Thou hast put a holy soul in *me*—and with *my* evil deeds I soiled it"; emphasis added).

95. Sirat, *Jewish Philosophy in the Middle Ages*, 72 ("the 'practice' suggested . . . corresponds to a somewhat vague notion of moral conduct rather than to the precisely defined acts required by the rabbinical commandments."). The third and final part of *Keter Malkhut* provides a good idea of the type of conduct that will make the soul pure. See e.g., Ibn Gabirol, *Kingly Crown*, 94 (canto 33). See also Sirat, *Jewish Philosophy in the Middle Ages*, 72 ("In the conduct of one's body and one's senses . . . one should cleave to the happy mean."). See generally Loewe, *Ibn Gabirol*, 31–38 (discussing Ibn Gabirol's *The Improvement of Moral Qualities*).

categorization of souls during the rabbinic period to include an intermediate group (between the righteous and the wicked) which required purification before entering *Gan Eden*.

Lewis's translation of the Hebrew "*otzarot*" as "chambers" or "treasures" obscures what must surely be a reference to the rabbinic divine treasury [*otzar*],[96] and so a better translation of "*otzarot*" is "treasuries" or "treasurehouses." The connection with the rabbinic divine treasury is supported by the preceding canto which begins by stating that God has made a place under the throne of His glory for the pure souls "that are bound in the bundle of life." The

> divine treasury, or *otzar* [which the rabbis speak of] is often equated with the *tzror ha-hayyim*—translated as 'bond of life,' 'bundle of life,' or 'treasury of life'—a term that appears but once in the Bible, in the First Book of Samuel. There, Abigail, who was to become King David's wife, says: 'If any man sets out to pursue you, and take your life, your life [*nephesh*]shall be bound up in the bond of life [*tzror ha-hayyim*] with the Lord your God; but he will fling away the lives of your enemies, as from a hollow sling [*kaf ha-kela*]' . . . Through homiletical interpretation, the Rabbis . . . came to understand the term *tzror ha-hayyim* as referring to a transcendent realm of souls.[97]

This transcendent realm came to be understood as hidden under the throne of God's glory.[98]

The rabbinic idea that the souls of the righteous are stored in heaven in the divine treasury (*otzar*) awaiting the resurrection of the body has roots in Second Temple material which spoke of the souls of both the righteous and the wicked being stored in subterranean chambers.[99] So that, "[t]he place of the treasuries must originally have been on earth . . . In [4 Ezra 4:41], the chambers of the souls are closely connected with the underworld to which the dead are committed, and in [7:32], likewise the earth in which the dead sleep is associated with the habitations of souls."[100] The movement of the treasury from underground to heaven may have been facilitated by the rabbinic doctrine that all souls preexist in the seventh heaven, Arabot.[101] In any event, it came to be widely accepted "that after death the spirits returned to their former celestial

---

96. See ch. 4, sec. C, 8; Raphael, *Jewish Views of the Afterlife*, 154–55; Hirsch, *Rabbinic Psychology*, 265. Loewe's translation of the same canto refers to "treasure house" (Loewe, *Ibn Gabirol*, 141).

97. Raphael, *Jewish Views of the Afterlife*, 155. See Hirsch, *Rabbinic Psychology*, 265.

98. See Raphael, *Jewish Views of the Afterlife*, 155; Hirsch, *Rabbinic Psychology*, 265–66; ch. 4, secs. C, 5 and 8.

99. See ch. 4, sec. C, 5; ch. 2, secs. D, 3 and 4; ch. 3, secs. B, 1 and 2.

100. Hirsch, *Rabbinic Psychology*, 264.

101. See ch. 4, sec. C, 5; Hirsch, *Rabbinic Psychology*, 175–86. See also Hirsch, *Rabbinic Psychology*, 268–69 ("The venue of the returning souls, as we should expect, is in Arabot, the highest heaven in which God dwells.").

habitations, except those which were contaminated by sin on earth, and could not be admitted to the presence of God."[102]

With regard to the categorization of souls, during most of the Second Temple period there were, generally speaking, only two classes of souls in the afterlife—the pure souls of the righteous and the souls of the wicked.[103] During the rabbinic period this twofold division was augmented by a third category, namely the "moderately righteous."[104] Two rabbinic texts well evidence the development of this third category—b. Shabbat 152b and b. Rosh Hashanah, 16b. In Shabbat 152b, R. Eli'ezer is purported to say that the souls of the righteous are kept under God's throne of glory but angels cast aside the souls of the wicked. Then it is reported:

> Said Rabbah to R. Nahman: 'What of those who are intermediate between the completely righteous and the completely wicked?' R. Nahman answered: 'So said Samuel, 'Both (the souls of the moderately righteous and of the wicked) are handed over to the angel Duma, but the former have rest, the latter have no rest.'[105]

At issue in the Rosh Hashanah 16b is whether an intermediate category between the righteous and the wicked needs to undergo a process of purification or refining by fire in *Gehenna* (the position of Shammai) or whether God, in his mercy, will allow them to forego such purification process (the position of Hillel):

> It has been taught Beth Shammai says, there will be three groups at the Day of Judgment—one of thoroughly righteous, one of thoroughly wicked, and one of intermediate. The thoroughly righteous will forthwith be inscribed definitively as entitled to everlasting life; the thoroughly wicked will forthwith be inscribed definitively as doomed to *Gehenna*, as it says, 'And many of them

---

102. Hirsch, *Rabbinic Psychology*, 257. See also Hirsch, *Rabbinic Psychology*, 265 (citing Sifre Num. 139; "R. Eli'ezer . . . said: 'While a man is alive his soul is in the hand of the Creator [Job 12:10]; when he dies, it is kept in the treasure-house [1 Sam 25:29]. It might be understood that this applies equally to the souls of the wicked, therefore it is written, "And the souls of thine enemies He will sling out"' [1 Sam 25:29])." The fate of these unrighteous souls, unfit to be admitted into the heavenly realm, is not always clearly spelled out; but, according to some views, they were doomed to "to wander about in torment" and, according to other views, they would, at some point, receive punishment beneath the earth in *Gehenna* (Hirsch, *Rabbinic Psychology*, 264). See also Hirsch, *Rabbinic Psychology*, 267–68 (citing Qoh. Rab. 3 for the view that "the souls of the wicked are thrust back to earth."). See generally Raphael, *Jewish Views of the Afterlife*, 142–49; Shyovitz, "'You Have Saved Me,'" 63–64 ("The rabbis seemed split as to whether the wicked were (1) punished in hell for all of eternity; (2) punished for a discreet period of time, and then physically annihilated; or (3) punished for a discreet period of time and then allowed into heaven.").

103. See generally Hirsch, *Rabbinic Psychology*, 109, 267 ("The apocalyptic writers, apparently, had no idea of purgatory", and "know only two divisions, the righteous and unrighteous"); Le Goff, *Birth of Purgatory*, 26–33, 39–42.

104. See ch. 4, n. 104.

105. See Hirsch, *Rabbinic Psychology*, 266. The angel Duma, a "cohort of the Angel of Death," is "caretaker of the souls of the departed" (Raphael, *Jewish Views of the Afterlife*, 135). See Raphael, *Jewish Views of the Afterlife*, 299–301.

that sleep in the dust of the earth shall awake, some to everlasting life and some to reproaches and everlasting abhorrence' [Dan 12:2]. The intermediate will go down to *Gehenna* and squeal and rise again, as it says, 'And I will bring the third part through the fire, and will refine them as silver is refined, and will try them as gold is tried. They shall call on my name and I will answer them' [Zech 13:9]. Of them, too, Hannah said, 'The Lord killeth and maketh alive, he bringeth down to the grave and bringeth up' [1 Sam 2:6]. Beth Hillel, however, says: He that abounds in mercy inclines [the scales] towards mercy, [and does not send them to *Gehenna*], and of them David said, 'I love that the Lord should hear my voice and my supplication,' [Ps 116:1] and on their behalf David composed the whole of the passage, 'I was brought low and he saved me"[Ps 116:6].[106]

With the advent of this intermediate class, *Gehenna* became, not only a realm to eternally punish the wicked, but a realm to purge and purify the "moderately righteous."[107] Accordingly,

> as described in Midrash [*Pesiqta Rabbati*], 'after going down to *Gehenna* and receiving the punishment due him, the sinner is forgiven from all his iniquities, and like an arrow from the bow he is flung forth from *Gehenna*' [*Pesiq. Rab.* 53:2]. After this experience, the soul is sufficiently purified and able to enter the supernal postmortem realm of *Gan Eden*, the Garden of Eden [*Exod. Rab.* 7:4].[108]

With this background, one can more clearly understand what is happening in canto 28 of *Keter Malkhut*. Whereas the rabbis had transferred to the higher world only the chambers or treasuries of the wholly pure souls, leaving all other souls to the lower region, Ibn Gabirol has *all* souls returning, after separation from the body, to the higher world. The reason for this is clear. The soul, for Ibn Gabirol, emanates from the higher world, belongs to the higher world, and must return to the higher world. Therefore, in addition to the divine treasury (*otzar*) to which rabbinic texts refer, Ibn Gabirol adds to the upper world several additional treasuries (*otzrot*) for those souls that are insufficiently pure to rest under the throne of glory. Most of these additional treasuries serve the function previously attributed to *Gehenna*, namely, punishing the wicked. Indeed, paralleling the rabbinic *Gehenna*, where the wicked had to endure fire, hail, snow, brimstone, smoke, and darkness, Ibn Gabirol postulates these same hazards in different higher-world treasuries.

---

106. See also Kohler, *Heaven and Hell*, 115 ("Already in the first century we find the schools of Hillel and Shammai discussing the subject of punishment in the hereafter, and to Daniel's (xii, 2) two classes of men, the righteous to enter everlasting life and the wicked to go to everlasting doom, were added, as the third, those whose merits and demerits are found to be even, when weighed in the balance.").

107. See Le Goff, *Birth of Purgatory*, 39–41.

108. Raphael, *Jewish Views of the Afterlife*, 145.

More importantly, Ibn Gabirol is careful to build upon the rabbinic development of *Gehenna* as a place of purification or purgation. He does this by describing one of the heavenly treasuries as a place of "salvation for penitent sinners,"[109] and by stating that the treasuries in general were established "either for mercy or for judgment." The reason why Ibn Gabirol might be eager to provide for the purification of souls is found in the third part of *Keter Malkhut*. In this part, Ibn Gabirol acknowledges the "baseness and vileness," as well as the ignorance, of mankind:

> According to the potency of Thy power, so is the feebleness of my power; according to Thy perfection, so is the deficiency of my knowing ... And I am ... a vessel of shame, a dumb stone ... Twisted of heart, uncircumcised of heart, Fierce in wrath, reaper of vanity and deceit, Haughty of eye, swift to anger, foul of lip.[110]

Put differently, he recognizes the multitude and greatness of his sins, and the corresponding impurity of his soul:

> O my God! I know that my sins are too numerous to count, and that my guilt is too great to be told ... For Thou has put a holy soul in me—and with my evil deeds I soiled it, and with my evil imagining I profaned and defiled it.[111]

Given this recognition, few if any souls would be sufficiently pure to find rest below the throne of God, if not for a robust process of postmortem purification, and so Ibn Gabirol envisions treasuries for just such a process.[112]

It is instructive to compare Ibn Gabirol with Isaac Israeli with regard to these matters. Israeli makes no mention of any treasuries, and provides for no possibility of purgation in the afterlife. For Israeli, the pure souls return to the supernal light of wisdom, and the wicked souls "remain contained under the sphere, sorrowful, in pain without measure, revolving with the revolution of the sphere in the great fire and the torturing flame."[113] It is also instructive to compare Ibn Gabirol's emphasis on an intermediary class of souls that requires, after separation from the body, purgation of some sort with the development in Christianity of the concept of Purgatory.[114] Devel-

---

109. Ibn Gabirol, *Kingly Crown*, 84–86.

110. See Ibn Gabirol, *Kingly Crown*, 92–94 (canto 33).

111. Ibn Gabirol, *Kingly Crown*, 96, 102 (cantos 34 and 36).

112. Cf. Saadia, *Book of Beliefs and Opinions*, 247 (souls are capable of being purified only so long as they are within the body. Once the soul has separated from the body "it is incapable of being cleansed any longer of the corruption that has accumulated in it.").

113. Israeli, *Book of Definitions*, §2:86–91. See sec. B, 3.

114. The development of Christian views has been described in great detail by Jacques Le Goff. According to Le Goff, the concept of a separate place, distinct from hell and paradise, where some souls go after separation from the body to be purged, was not introduced until 1170–1180. See Le Goff, *Birth of Purgatory*, 154–76. See also Shyovitz, "'You Have Saved Me,'" 66; Ruderman, "On Divine Justice," 22.

opments in Christian thinking about the afterlife influenced similar developments in Jewish thinking, and *vice versa*.[115]

3. Increasing emphasis on purgation leads to intercessory prayers for the dead

The idea that souls too impure to be permitted into *Gan Eden* could, if purged, be granted such permission eventually gave rise to related liturgical developments. Specifically, beginning in the twelfth century, the Mourner's Kaddish was transformed into an intercessory prayer on behalf of the dead. As explained by Shyovitz, "in the late twelfth or early thirteenth century, the Jewish communities of northern Europe began to recite a weekly prayer for the dead," the Kaddish.[116] This prayer had been in existence well before the twelfth century but now it began to be used as an intercessory prayer for the dead, and it began to be used more often.[117] From the initial attestation of its intercessory use in several German liturgical guides, the recitation of the Mourner's Kaddish spread throughout the Rhineland, to northern and southern France, to Bavaria and Austria, and eventually to Spain and Italy, and from daily use it expanded to thrice-daily use.[118] The reason advanced by Shyovitz for these liturgical developments relates to the fact that the prayer was recited specifically in order to free one's family members from punishment in hell.[119] According to Shyovitz: "As the recitation of the Mourner's Kaddish spread, so too did the theology of divine recompense that undergirded it—namely a hell that was fundamentally temporary, from which anyone could be redeemed, and intended to ultimately purge the sinner of his deeds and elevate him, cleansed, to heaven."[120]

---

115. See generally Shyovitz, "'You Have Saved Me,'" 67–73 ("In high medieval northern Europe, both Jews and Christians were reimagining the nature of postmortem punishment, and were creating new means by which doctrinal beliefs could be manifested in practice. And they were doing so in dialogue with one another, telling themselves and one another tales that expressed these new beliefs, and that allowed them to spread rapidly throughout Europe and beyond.").

116. Shyovitz, "'You Have Saved Me,'" 49.

117. See generally Millgram, *Jewish Worship*, 153–56 (discussing development of the Kaddish).

118. Shyovitz, "'You Have Saved Me,'" 50–51.

119. Shyovitz, "'You Have Saved Me,'" 53–54 ("... the rise and spread of the Mourner's Kaddish was a manifestation of changing beliefs about the nature of the afterlife and the relationship between the living and the dead. Over the course of the High Middle Ages, both Jewish and Christian theologians developed new ideas about the nature and purpose of postmortem suffering. In particular, these thinkers stressed the fundamentally temporary duration of divine punishment in the afterlife, and the concomitant notion that the living could help cleanse the sins, and thus expedite the suffering, of their deceased relatives... The halakhists of medieval Ashkenaz thus added an intercessory prayer to their liturgy..."). See Millgram, *Jewish Worship*, 155 (discussing the change in the Kaddish from a prayer associated with the study of the Torah to a mourner's ritual and stating that the Kaddish began to be regarded "as a doxology of great merit for the redemption of the soul of the deceased. This doxology, if recited by the children of the deceased during the year after burial, [could] save the dead from the punishment visited upon sinners during the year after burial.").

120. Shyovitz, "'You Have Saved Me,'" 65.

That intercessory efforts on behalf of the dead were being made in Germanic areas by the late twelfth century is evidenced by *Sefer Hasidim*.[121] Several passages in *Sefer Hasidim* clearly refer to such practices.[122] One passage states that intercessory fasting or prayer could not be effective for a deceased person unless that person possessed virtues as well as sins. If it were otherwise, "how could there be any drawbacks for the wicked?"[123]

D. Bahya ben Joseph Ibn Pakuda

The Book of Direction to the Duties of the Heart "was not intended for philosophers, but for the religious congregation, to whom [Ibn Pakuda] wants to show the path towards the true worship of God."[124] Central to its teaching is the distinction between external duties of the body and duties of the heart, the former involving outward obedience and the later concerning intentions and thoughts. Ibn Pakuda asserts that "when our exterior opposes our interior, when our intention contradicts our words, when our conscience is not at one with the actions of our body, then is our worship of our Creator imperfect, for [God] does not accept an obedience that is false and counterfeit."[125] True obedience is necessary in order for the soul to return to its source in the world to come, the world of "pure spirituality."[126]

Ibn Pakuda accepts the Platonic dualism of soul (defined as a "spiritual substance") and body:

> You see that the body of man is composed of incompatible elements and various natures, all combined by the Creator's ability . . . Then the Creator joined it to a spiritual substance of [fire and] light, similar to the spirit of the superior

---

121. *Sefer Hasidim* (*Book of the Pious*) originated between the late twelfth and early thirteenth centuries in the Rhineland. Tradition attributes the authorship of *Sefer Hasidim* to Judah ben Samuel of Ratisbon, usually called Judah the Pious, one of the major figures associated with a circle or movement of German-Jewish pietists (*Haside Ashkenaz*) characterized by their distinctive combination of ethical and mystical concerns; scholars, however, have determined that *Sefer Hasidim* is a composite work of several authors. See generally Cronbach, "Social Thinking in Sefer Hasidim," 1–3.

122. See Cronbach, "Social Thinking in Sefer Hasidim," 48–50, 54 (translating para. 34, 35, and 357 of Parma manuscript of *Sefer Hasidim*).

123. Cronbach, "Social Thinking in Sefer Hasidim," 48–49. Cf. Cronbach, "Social Thinking in Sefer Hasidim," 50 ("if the deceased lacked merits, no amount of charity will do him any good. But if, along with his sins, he does have merits; if, because of some iniquities, he be excluded from paradise or be subject to penalties in Gehenna or to wearisome wanderings over thorn strewn paths or exposed to the jeers of hostile angels: or if he be a righteous person who, because of some shortcoming, is not admitted to the compartment of the righteous in heaven; in such case, there is advantage if prayer be offered and alms be rendered in behalf of the deceased"; translating para. 35 of Parma manuscript).

124. Guttmann, *Philosophies of Judaism*, 118.

125. Ibn Pakuda, *Book of Direction*, 99.

126. See Mansoor, "Introduction," 16 ("Bahya . . . speaks of the return of the soul to its source" in the world to come, which "he sometimes describes as the sphere of pure spirituality.").

bodies. By spiritual substance I mean his soul, which God bound to the human body.[127]

Death is similarly conceived Platonically as the separation of the soul from the body, and at such time the purified soul will be rewarded. In a supposed conversation, the mind says to the soul:

> When the days of your trial in this world are over . . . [the] connections and ties between you and your body are undone and disconnected, and you return to your primary state, while your body returns to its primary state, as it is said [Qoh 12:7]: "And the dust returneth to the earth as it was, and the spirit returneth unto God who gave it." Then you are shown the records of your deeds and thoughts, the choices you have made and the preferences you showed, everything you did in the world, and your reward is given you accordingly by the Creator.[128]

The goal or purpose of life is to reach the "highest stage and the supreme rank for those who obey God."[129] Ibn Pakuda explains:

> What does the love of God mean? It is the yearning of the soul, the desire of its very substance to be attached to God's supreme light. The soul is a simple spiritual substance which inclines by its nature to the spiritual beings that are like itself, and rejects by its nature the coarse bodies which are unlike it. The Creator has tied it to this coarse body of ours, a body full of darkness, in order to test it there by seeing how it manages and controls the body. Therefore, He charged it to protect the body and to benefit it . . .
>
> Since . . . the soul cannot escape its obligation of caring for the body . . . it has no peace from healing the ills of the body. It becomes too busy with the body's affairs to care for what is dear to itself, what is special to its own substance and conforms to it, what constitutes its happiness in the place of eternal rest. However, when the light of reason shines upon it and reveals to the soul the evil things toward which it has learned to love . . . when it reveals its negligence of deliverance both in this world and the next, then the soul turns away from all these and entrusts its affairs to the Creator . . . Thereupon it undertakes to practice asceticism in this world with all its pleasures, to scorn the body and its desires . . .
>
> Having understood His omnipotence and lofty greatness, it bows to him in submission and fear, in reverence and respect, in awe and veneration before His power and greatness. It preserves in this state until the Creator draws it near to him . . . Then it is filled with the love of God and devotes itself to him alone.[130]

127. Ibn Pakuda, *Book of Direction,* 161.
128. Ibn Pakuda, *Book of Direction,* 217.
129. Ibn Pakuda, *Book of Direction,* 426.
130. Ibn Pakuda, *Book of Direction,* 427–28. See also Guttmann, *Philosophies of Judaism,* 121–23

Those who reach this "highest stage" will be rewarded "both in this world and the next."[131] Since the reward envisioned is the soul's escape from concern for the body and return to the spiritual realm, bodily resurrection can hardly be seen as necessary or desirable. Indeed, it is precisely because Ibn Pakuda adheres to a strict Platonic dualism that associates an immaterial, independent, and immortal soul with the true self, and views the material body as an evil from which the soul must free itself, that he advocates the practice of asceticism. Yet, those who reach the highest stage do not act in order to reap a reward—they "consider neither reward nor punishment, but hasten rather to obey the Lord their God as an expression of the glory and honor He deserves."[132] Nevertheless, the nine lower stages of "the people of the Book" include those who "obey God only with the intention . . . of gaining His reward in this world and the next," and those who "do everything only for the sake of God's reward in this world . . . ignoring the truth of the reward in the hereafter."[133]

(Ethics for Bahya "is essentially the purification of the soul, its liberation from the fetters of sensuality, its elevation to the purity of spirit, and its final exaltation to communion with God.").

131. Ibn Pakuda, *Book of Direction*, 198.
132. Ibn Pakuda, *Book of Direction*, 198.
133. See Ibn Pakuda, *Book of Direction*, 195–98.

7.

Maimonides Represents a Turning Point from Neoplatonism to Aristotelianism

MOSES BEN MAIMON (MAIMONIDES or Rambam) represents a turning point in Jewish philosophy from a predominately Neoplatonist viewpoint to a primarily Aristotelian one.[1] Guttmann writes: "In the middle of the twelfth century Aristotelianism displaced Neoplatonism as the dominating influence in Jewish philosophy of religion."[2] This transition happened neither suddenly nor cleanly. Although the first work of Jewish Aristotelianism is considered to be Abraham Ibn Daud's *The Exalted Faith*, composed in 1161, evidence of Aristotelianism can be seen in works written much earlier.[3] Moreover, Neoplatonism had "absorbed many Aristotelian elements," and the subsequent Aristotelianism incorporated significant Neoplatonic elements.[4]

With specific regard to psychology, Aristotelianism meant that philosophers no longer conceived the soul to be a thing separate and apart from the body; instead, they defined the soul as the form of the body.[5] Nevertheless, since Aristotelian doctrine suggested that a part of the soul *might* exist independently of the body, Aristotelianism was shaped to be consistent with the idea that a part of the soul continued to exist after bodily death.[6] More specifically, the pagan Aristotelian commentators Alexander of

---

1. See Sirat, *Jewish Philosophy in the Middle Ages*, 157; Robinson, "Soul and Intellect," 534; Guttmann, *Philosophies of Judaism*, 152; Harvey, "Islamic Philosophy and Jewish Philosophy," 354–55.

2. Guttmann, *Philosophies of Judaism*, 152.

3. Guttmann, *Philosophies of Judaism*, 152 (mentioning Ibn Ezra and Judah Halevi). See Husik, *History of Mediaeval Jewish Philosophy*, 150–83, 187–96; Davidson, *Alfarabi, Avicenna and Averroes*, 180–94.

4. Guttmann, *Philosophies of Judaism*, 152. See also Robinson, "Soul and Intellect," 530, 533; Sirat, *Jewish Philosophy in the Middle Ages*, 141. See generally Husik, *History of Mediaeval Jewish Philosophy*, xxix–xxxix, 177–78.

5. Guttmann, *Philosophies of Judaism*, 153. See Sirat, *Jewish Philosophy in the Middle Ages*, 141.

6. See Guttmann, *Philosophies of Judaism*, 156. Accordingly, while rejecting certain Neoplatonic notions, Ibn Daud, nevertheless, agreed with the Neoplatonists that postmortem reward and punishment is meted out to the soul alone, or to the rational part of the soul called the "acquired intellect,"

CHAPTER 7.

Aphrodisias and Themistius, as well as many Islamic philosophers, including al-Farabi, Avicenna, Ibn Bajja, and Averroes, (1) interpreted Aristotle in a way that supported the immortality of what was called the "acquired intellect," (2) understood that aspect of intellect that Aristotle called "impassive" to be an eternal, transcendent, immaterial substance referred to as the "active intellect," and (3) understood that aspect of the intellect that Aristotle called "passive" to be the material part of a human being (called the "material intellect") having the *potential* for intelligence which when actualized by the active intellect results in human thought and intelligence—the acquired intellect.[7]

A major point of disagreement among Aristotelians concerned whether the immortality of the acquired intellect constituted a personal or individual immortality. Maimonides wrote about these topics in esoteric fashion and often disguised his true beliefs,[8] but most scholars accept that Maimonides agreed with al-Farabi, Ibn Bajja, and Averroes that the acquired intellect's immortality is neither personal nor individual;[9] rather, upon the destruction of the body the acquired intellect completely united with and merged into the active intellect. Some post-Maimonidean Jewish Aristotelians, such as Shem Tov ben Yosef Ibn Falaquera, agreed with Maimonides; others, such as Gersonides and Hillel ben Samuel, insisted that immortality is individual and personal.[10]

---

not to a resurrected body/soul unity.

7. See generally Davidson, *Alfarabi, Avicenna and Averroes*, 13–29. The active intellect, also referred to as the "agent intellect" or the "divine intellect," was associated by Alexander of Aphrodisias with God (or the First Cause of the universe). See Davidson, *Alfarabi, Avicenna and Averroes*, 3, 14.

8. See generally Sirat, *Jewish Philosophy in the Middle Ages*, 159–60, 162–64; Rudavsky, *Maimonides*, 3, 22–24; Husik, *History of Mediaeval Jewish Philosophy*, 241–43; Pines, "Introduction," lviii–lix.

9. See Pines, "Introduction," ciii–civ; Maimonides, *Guide of the Perplexed*, 1:221n11 (Ibn Bajja's doctrine of the Unity of the Intellect, which precludes any individual immortality, "seems to be accepted by Maimonides."); Davidson, *Alfarabi, Avicenna and Averroes*, 207 (Maimonides "refrains from defending the individual immortality of the human soul or intellect.'); Sirat, *Jewish Philosophy in the Middle Ages*, 170 ("if no Maimonidean text states his position without ambivalence, this was because he inclined towards the solution of nonindividual survival, a conclusion that he could not postulate openly in writing."); Husik, *History of Mediaeval Jewish Philosophy*, xlvii; Rudavsky, *Maimonides*, 102–3.

10. There is much concern among Western European Jewish Aristotelian philosophers (mostly in Provence and northern Spain) about whether the human soul, or rather that part of the human soul which they considered to be immortal (viz., the intellect or, more precisely, what they called the "acquired intellect") retains at least some of the individual characteristics of the deceased person, or whether those parts of the individual soul which survive the destruction of the body lose *all* the individual aspects of the deceased person. If the part of the soul which is immortal loses all its individuality after separation from the body, then there is no *personal* immortality. The immortality envisioned by Ibn Falaquera and Maimonides, in contrast to that of Gersonides and Hillel ben Samuel, is not a personal or individual immortality. See Sirat, *Jewish Philosophy in the Middle Ages*, 269; Husik, *History of Mediaeval Jewish Philosophy*, xlvii, 339; Robinson, "Soul and Intellect," 552.

A. Maimonides Expressed His Views on the Soul in Various Works Written Throughout the Course of His Lifetime

Maimonides expressed his views on the nature and functions of the soul, on its reward for obeying God's commandments, and on the afterlife, in the *Commentary on the Mishnah*, the *Guide of the Perplexed*, and parts of the *Mishneh Torah*.

1. *Shemonah Perakim*

Included in Maimonides's *Commentary on the Mishnah* is an introduction to Pirqe Avot that has become known as the Eight Chapters (*Shemonah Perakim*). The Eight Chapters includes a discussion of the human soul and its powers that adopts Aristotelian notions.[11] Maimonides states that although the soul of man is a "single soul" it has "several "parts."[12] He does not actually mean that the soul is divided into parts; rather, he means that the soul has certain discrete powers or faculties, some of which are shared with other living things—plants and animals. He enumerates five basic powers: "nutritive, sentient, imaginative, appetitive, and rational."[13] The nutritive power includes attracting, retaining, digesting, excreting, growing, procreating, and separating mixtures (isolating what is used for nourishment from what is excreted). The sentient power consists of the five external senses: sight, hearing, taste, smell, and touch. The imaginative power preserves the impressions of sensibly perceived objects. The appetitive power is that by which a being desires or is repulsed by things. The rational power, found only in humans, enables people to perceive *intelligibles*, deliberate, acquire the sciences, and distinguish between base and noble actions.[14]

In keeping with Aristotelian doctrine, the rational part of the soul is understood by Maimonides to engage in both practical and theoretical activities.[15] When engaged in practical activities it is concerned with the rationality of human emotions and conduct (and thus is tied to the body); when engaged in theoretical activities it is concerned with pure thought (and thus is not tied to the body). The part of the rational soul that engages in pure thought is referred to as the intellect. It is by means of the intellect that "man knows the essence of the unchanging beings."[16] Maimonides concludes this section by stating: "Know that this single soul, whose powers or parts are described above, is like matter, and the intellect is its form. If it does not attain its

---

11. Maimonides, *Eight Chapters*, 61–78. See also Rudavsky, *Maimonides*, 96; Robinson, "Soul and Intellect," 535.

12. Maimonides, *Eight Chapters*, 61.

13. Maimonides, *Eight Chapters*, 61. See Rudavsky, *Maimonides*, 96; Robinson, "Soul and Intellect," 535; Husik, *History of Mediaeval Jewish Philosophy*, 281–82.

14. Maimonides, *Eight Chapters*, 62–63. But see Maimonides, *Guide of the Perplexed*, 1:24.

15. Maimonides, *Eight Chapters*, 63. See Husik, *History of Mediaeval Jewish Philosophy*, 282. See also Aristotle, *Ethics*, 1102a27–1103a10.

16. Maimonides, *Eight Chapters*, 63.

form, the existence of its capacity to receive this form is for naught and is, as it were, futile ... This is not the place for a discourse about form, matter, or how many intellects there are and how they are attained."[17]

The importance of the rational part of the soul, especially the intellect, is emphasized again when Maimonides states: "Man needs to subordinate all his soul's powers to thought, ... and to set his sight on a single goal: the perception of God ..., I mean, knowledge of Him, in so far as that lies within man's power."[18] The ability to perceive God is achieved by the theoretical activity of the intellect, which is, as God is, a completely immaterial thing.

2. Perek Helek

The immateriality of the intellect, and its importance, is made clear in that part of the *Commentary on the Mishnah* addressing the tenth chapter of Tractate Sanhedrin.[19] The introduction to this portion of Maimonides's commentary is referred to as *Perek Helek*. Mishnah 1 of chapter 10, referring to all Israel's participation in the world to come, prompts Maimonides to discourse on the "good that man will reap" from the fulfillment of God's commandments, and "the evil which will befall [man]" from the transgression of those commandments.[20] He notes that there are many differences of opinion on this matter and that "opinions have become so confused that it is nearly impossible to find someone to whom this matter is clear."[21] He then considers five opinions regarding the ultimate good to be obtained through adherence to God's commandments (and the evil to be obtained by disobedience):

---

17. Maimonides, *Eight Chapters*, 64. See also Rudavsky, *Maimonides*, 95.

18. Maimonides, *Eight Chapters*, 75.

19. See Hyman, "Maimonides' 'Thirteen Principles,'" 121n16 ("Though in our editions of the Talmud this chapter appears as the eleventh chapter of the tractate *Sanhedrin*, [the tenth chapter] is its correct position.").

20. God's justice leaves it beyond doubt that obedience to the commandments is rewarded and disobedience is punished. See Maimonides, *Guide of the Perplexed*, 2 469; Maimonides, *Commentary on the Sanhedrin*, 156. Nevertheless, one should serve God out of love, not fear, which is to say that one should obey God's commandments without being compelled by the desire to receive a reward or avoid a punishment. See Maimonides, *Book of Knowledge*, 92a-93a (citing m. Avot 1:3) See generally Hyman, "Maimonides' 'Thirteen Principles,'" 143-44 ("To worship God without the expectation of reward is, for Maimonides, the highest form of worship, yet at the same time he is aware that such unselfish service can be expected only of the few. For that reason the majority of men to whom the Law is addressed require principles promising reward or threatening punishment, for it is only under these conditions that they will obey the Law."); Kellner, *Must a Jew Believe Anything?*, 151-55. Cf. Ibn Pakuda, *Book of Direction*, 195-98 (the highest stage in obedience to God consists in obeying God without consideration of reward or punishment).

21. Maimonides, *Commentary on the Sanhedrin*, 135.

1. The good and evil is the corporeal pleasure or pain to be obtained in, respectively, the Garden of Eden and *Gehenna*,[22] the first being conceived as "a place where one eats and drinks without physical effort . . . [where there are] rivers flowing with wine and fragrant oils, and many similar things," and the latter being conceived as "a place of blazing fire where bodies are burned and where human beings suffer various types of agonies . . ."

2. The good and evil is what is to be obtained in the messianic age [*Yemot Ha-Maschiach*], the good being that "all human beings [then alive] will be kings forever . . . and inhabit the entire world unto eternity . . . [and that] the earth will bring forth ready-woven garments, and ready-baked bread and many similar impossible things," and the evil being "that a person will not exist at that epoch and will not be worthy to see it."

3. The good "consists of the resurrection of the dead in which a person will live after his death, return to his family and his relatives, eat and drink, and never die . . . [a]nd the evil is that he will not live."

4. The good consists in "the attainment *in this world* of all worldly desires such as fertility of the land, and abundant possessions, and many children, and long life, and bodily health, and peace and security, and the presence of a Jewish king and dominion over our enemies," and the evil consists in "the opposite of these situations, such as we now experience in our own time, the time of the exile."

5. The good and evil consists of a combination of the goods and evils in 1 to 4, so that the good is "the coming of the Messiah, and that he will resurrect the dead and lead them to the Garden of Eden, and they will eat and drink there and live in good health, so long as the heaven and earth endure."[23]

Some important points about Maimonides's list of five opinions are:

1. Those who espouse these opinions adduce proofs in support of their point of view from "statements of the Sages" and/or from "scriptural passages."[24] It is not surprising that varying and inconsistent positions all rely on traditional texts, as the views found in these texts are multifaceted and inconsistent.

2. Maimonides states that, while there are persons who espouse all the various and conflicting opinions, those who espouse the fifth opinion "are the majority."[25]

---

22. It will turn out that the Garden of Eden and *Gehenna* "have virtually no role in Maimonides' eschatology"; and *Gehenna* for Maimonides "is not a place but the name for the pain and punishment that will befall the wicked" (Hyman, *Eschatological Themes*, 88; citing *Perek Helek*). See Maimonides, *Commentary on the Sanhedrin*, 146–47.

23. Maimonides, *Commentary on the Sanhedrin*, 135–36 (emphasis added). See Robinson, "Soul and Intellect," 535; Hyman, *Eschatological Themes*, 74–76.

24. Maimonides, *Commentary on the Sanhedrin*, 135–36.

25. Maimonides, *Commentary on the Sanhedrin*, 136.

3. There is no mention of any strictly spiritual reward meted out to an incorporeal soul. Why Maimonides omitted mention of the view of Jewish Neoplatonists is not known.[26]

4. Maimonides's list evidences that Jewish views as to the ultimate good to be obtained through adherence to God's commandments were hopelessly confused and conflicting.[27]

Since the adherents of the various opinions supported their position by adducing proofs based on statements found in traditional Jewish sources, Maimonides realized that a correct interpretation of traditional Jewish sources is required to arrive at a correct opinion regarding the ultimate good to be obtained by adherence to God's commandments, and he proceeds to discuss three groups of interpreters. A first group, because of their "ignorance of the sciences . . . [and] fields of knowledge" understands the words of the talmudic sages literally and doesn't interpret them at all. This is the majority group. The second group, also numerous, likewise understands the words of the sages literally, but, in contrast to the first group, they call these words foolish. This is presumably because the members of this second group, in contrast to the members of the first group, are not completely ignorant of the sciences and fields of knowledge. Then there is a third group, comprised of only a very few people, "who have a clear conception of the greatness of the Sages and the excellence of their intellect," but only because they recognize that the words of the sages must not be read literally; they know that the words of the sages "have both superficial and deeper meanings and that all of their statements which speak of impossibilities were said in the manner of riddle and parable, for this is the method of the great Sages."[28]

Turning now to his own view of the ultimate good to be obtained through adherence to God's commandments, Maimonides contends that it is crucial to distinguish between goods which are physical and goods which are spiritual. He says that most people only recognize "pleasures of the body and those (delights) achieved by our senses in regard to eating, drinking and sexual intercourse"; this is because we live in the physical world and, therefore, can only understand physical pleasures.[29] But Maimonides clearly believes that there is also a spiritual (nonphysical or incorporeal) world and that spiritual pleasures are far superior to bodily pleasures. Spiritual pleasures are "everlasting and without interruption."[30] Physical pleasures are base while spiritual pleasures are of "high worth."[31]

26. See generally Rudavsky, *Maimonides*, 8 ("Interestingly enough, medieval Jewish philosophers are not quoted in Maimonides' philosophical works."); Pines, "Introduction," lix–lx, cxxxii–cxxxiv; Sirat, *Jewish Philosophy in the Middle Ages*, 161.

27. See Raphael, *Jewish Views of the Afterlife*, 148.

28. Maimonides, *Commentary on the Sanhedrin*, 140–42.

29. Maimonides, *Commentary on the Sanhedrin*, 143.

30. Maimonides, *Commentary on the Sanhedrin*, 143.

31. Maimonides, *Commentary on the Sanhedrin*, 144.

Maimonides further believes that the statements of the sages, *when properly understood*, recognize that the ultimate good to be obtained by following God's commandments does not consist of the physical pleasures mentioned by the proponents of the five opinions he outlined but consists in spiritual pleasure that can only be experienced by the incorporeal intellect (which Maimonides here refers to as simply "the soul").[32] Further, the statements of the sages, again when properly understood, also recognize that this ultimate good will be received in the world to come, and that the world to come means the time immediately following the complete separation of the soul (really, the acquired intellect) from the body.[33] Specifically, Maimonides relies upon b. Berakhot 17a, which states that in the world to come there will be no eating, drinking, or sex, but that the righteous will sit with their crowns on their head, enjoying the brightness of the divine presence. As explained by Maimonides:

> 'Their crowns on their heads,' is the immortality of the soul in the intellectual sphere and the merging of the two into one, as described by the renowned philosophers... The Sages' statement, 'Enjoying the brightness of the divine presence [the *Shekhinah*],' means that those souls derive bliss from what they understand of the Creator, just like the holy spirits and the other ranks of angels in what they understand of His existence.
>
> For the happiness and the ultimate goal is to reach this lofty group and to become like one of them. The existence of the soul in the manner we have just stated, that is to say endless, is the existence of the Creator... And this is the great good to which no other good can compare and to which no pleasure can be likened...
>
> And the consummate evil... consists of the cutting off of the soul and its perishing so that it does not become perpetual. And this is the 'cutting off' mentioned in the Torah [Num 15:31], in that the punishment of *karet* means the cutting off of the soul.[34]

When Maimonides refers to "the merging" of the soul and the "intellectual sphere" into one "as described by the renowned philosophers," he has in mind the

---

32. See Hyman, "Maimonides' 'Thirteen Principles,'" 125–26, 141 ("In contrast to [the five] popular views, Maimonides holds that man's ultimate happiness—that is, the World to Come—consists in the immortal existence of the human intellect apart from any body—this intellect, being engaged in the contemplation of God," and "Maimonides... identifies the World to Come with the philosophical notion of the incorporeal existence of the human intellect, which takes place only when this intellect becomes actualized through the understanding of true opinions.").

33. See Maimonides, *Commentary on the Sanhedrin*, 149 ("the (ultimate) goal is the world to come and it is to it that (our) effort should be directed. And it is for this reason that the Sage who firmly grasped the truth looked toward the ultimate goal, omitted everything else, and declared: **All Israel have a portion in the world to come.**") (boldface original).

34. Maimonides, *Commentary on the Sanhedrin*, 144–45. Cf. ch. 5, sec. C, 3. See generally Hyman, *Eschatological Themes*, 89 ("whereas Saadiah uses [the relevant passage] to establish how in the World to Come human beings can have a body, even though these physical activities are lacking, Maimonides uses it to demonstrate that in the World to Come human beings exist as incorporeal intellects.").

conjoining of the acquired intellect with the active intellect, as taught by Aristotelian commentators such as Alexander of Aphrodisias, al-Farabi, Ibn Bajja, and Averroes.[35] In short, *Perek Helek* reinforces the statement made in the Eight Chapters that the highest goal of human activity is the perception or knowledge of God which may be achieved by the acquired intellect. This perception results in a spiritual pleasure that can only exist in the spiritual or incorporeal world. As Robinson puts it, in *Perek Helek* Maimonides "presents his own purely spiritualistic view [of the *summum bonum* and the divine reward]: Knowledge of God is the highest goal and contemplation of God the greatest reward; this alone is true delight, and it has no share whatsoever in anything material."[36]

Since the highest good is achieved by the incorporeal intellect after complete separation from the body, which is the time of the world to come, in the world to come there is no need for any postmortem corporeal rewards associated with resurrection of the body. Nevertheless, as one of the thirteen fundamental principles necessary for being considered an Israelite and for having a share in the world to come set forth in *Perek Helek*,[37] Maimonides states: "The *resurrection of the dead* is one of the fundamental principles of the Law of Moses, our teacher. He who does not believe in this has no tie to the Jewish people. But it is only for the righteous as stated in *Bereshit Rabbah* . . ."[38]

Maimonides also states in *Perek Helek* that belief in the days of the Messiah is a fundamental principle, and that during those days, which could last for thousands of years, there will be corporeal rewards ("plentiful harvests and . . . riches"), but that these do not constitute the ultimate goal—the ultimate goal is the spiritual rewards received in the world to come.[39] Maimonides marginally clarifies this entire eschatological scheme in the *Treatise on Resurrection*, but never adequately explains it.

---

35. See Davidson, *Alfarabi, Avicenna and Averroes*, 202. See also Hyman, "Maimonides' 'Thirteen Principles,'" 126–27.

36. Robinson, "Soul and Intellect," 536.

37. See Hyman, "Maimonides' 'Thirteen Principles,'" 119–29 (discussing Maimonides's "Thirteen Principles" as they appear in *Perek Helek*). As Maimonides interpreted this mishnah "the enumeration of those excluded from the World to Come can be used to derive from it a list of basic principles, the affirmation of which is required in order to be considered an Israelite and, hence, for having a share in the World to Come" (Hyman, "Maimonides' 'Thirteen Principles,'" 123). See Kellner, *Dogma in Medieval Jewish Thought*, 10 ("It is by way of defining the term 'Israelite' [in the tenth chapter of *b. Sanhedrin*] . . . that Maimonides lays down thirteen beliefs which must be upheld by every Jew in order to earn a place in the world to come.").

38. Maimonides, *Commentary on the Sanhedrin*, 147 (emphasis original). See also Maimonides, *Commentary on the Sanhedrin*, 157 (In setting forth the thirteen beliefs which must be held by every Jew in order to earn a place in the world to come, it is stated: "**The thirteenth fundamental principle is the Resurrection of the Dead, and we have already explained it.**") (boldface original). Accord, Kellner, *Dogma in Medieval Jewish Thought* 16 (setting forth the relevant text of *Perek Helek*).

39. See Maimonides, *Commentary on the Sanhedrin*, 147–49, 157 ("The *days of the Messiah* refers to the time when sovereignty will return to Israel who will return to the land of Israel . . . Anyone who rises against him will be destroyed . . . In regard to existing things, nothing will be different from what

3. The Guide of the Perplexed

Despite difficulty in deciphering Maimonides's *Guide of the Perplexed*,[40] it is clear that in it Maimonides retains a similar understanding of the soul as that found in the Eight Chapters. He suggests that there are various faculties of the soul and that one aspect of the rational faculty, the acquired intellect, is immortal. Maimonides's understanding of the human intellect as described in the *Guide of the Perplexed* is explained by Davidson, who writes:

> Maimonides does not formally list the stages through which the human intellect progresses, but [as other Islamic and Jewish Aristotelians] he does distinguish between 'potential' or 'material intellect,' which is the human rational faculty before it begins to think, 'actual intellect,' which is human intellect when thinking any intelligible thought [*Guide*, 1.68], and acquired intellect. Actual human intelligible thought comes, as in Avicenna, 'from the emanation of the active intellect.' Avicenna had explained the process whereby a man acquires actual intelligible thought as the man's entering into 'conjunction' (*ittiṣāl*) with the active intellect and receiving the active intellect's emanation. Maimonides similarly writes that man obtains intelligible thought through 'conjunction [*ittiṣāl*; Hebrew: *hiddabeq*] with the divine [active] intellect, which emanates upon him and from which the form [the intelligible thought] comes into existence.' [*Guide*, 3:8] He does not, however, employ another formula of Avicenna's, the characterization of all actual human thought as *acquired* intellect. A human intellect that has already passed to actuality, yet is not at the moment actually thinking, is described by Maimonides as neither 'actual intellect,' on the one hand, nor an unqualified potentiality, on the other. It is in a state of potentiality 'close' to actuality and resembles the 'skilled scribe when he is not writing.' [*Guide*, 3.51] . . .
>
> The human 'acquired intellect,' in contrast to the human potential intellect, is 'not a power in a body' but rather is 'completely separate from the body, and emanates upon it.' It is related to the individual 'man' as 'God is [related] to the world' [*Guide*, 1.72]; it thus apparently is something substantial . . . [While the statements Maimonides makes about the acquired intellect are] not very informative, [they] do tell us that acquired intellect is an advanced stage or state of human intellect, that it is something incorporeal, and that it exists independently of the human body. Maimonides further writes that man's 'final perfection consists in attaining "actual intellect" and he adds that such a condition comes about when one knows everything a man can know about all existent things.' [*Guide*, 3.2] Actual intellect in this sense, as man's final perfection, is different from actual intellect in the sense previously

---

it is now, except that the sovereignty will be Israel's . . . People will also live for a long time, because the removal of worries and sufferings results in prolongation of life.") (emphasis original).

40. See Robinson, "Soul and Intellect," 536.

> employed by Maimonides, in the sense of a human intellect actually thinking any thought whatsoever, and very plausibly is equivalent, in Maimonides' terminology, to *acquired* intellect. The term *acquired intellect* would, then, denote for Maimonides—as it did for Alfarabi and as one acceptation of acquired intellect did for Avicenna—human intellect at the culmination of its development. Maimonides does not mention the proposition that when human intellectual development is complete, man enters into permanent conjunction with the active intellect. But he does know of a closely related state, the human intellect's having incorporeal beings and the active intellect in particular as a direct object of thought . . .
>
> Possessing actual intellect at the level of 'final perfection' is, for Maimonides, the 'sole . . . cause' of human immortality. [*Guide*, 3.37; 2.27] . . . How far one may fall below absolute human intellectual perfection without losing immortality is left unclear. Despite his insistence on the enormous pleasure awaiting the human intellect in its afterlife, Maimonides cites without demurral the opinion of Ibn Bajja that individuality and all distinction between human intellects is inconceivable after the body's demise. [*Guide*, 1.74 (7), taken together with 2, introduction, proposition 16; 1.70].[41]

To further elaborate on Davidson's comments, in part 1, chapter 41 of the *Guide of the Perplexed,* Maimonides discusses the word *nephesh*. He states that *nephesh* is an equivocal term. It is used to denote (1) "the animal soul common to every sentient being," (2) "the rational soul, I mean the form of man," and (3) "the thing that remains of man after death."[42] Here it is most important to pay attention to the fact that Maimonides distinguishes the "form of man" from "the thing that remains of man after death." In strictly Aristotelian terms, the form of a material entity is not something separate and apart from the physical stuff from which the entity is composed, and cannot remain after the decomposition of that physical stuff. For many Islamic and Jewish Aristotelians, however, that which remains after death is not the soul in its entirety but only that aspect of the soul that is termed the "acquired intellect." The acquired intellect is a term coined by the Arabic translators of Alexander of Aphrodisius to describe the sum total of intellectual cognitions attained by an individual throughout his lifetime. Since the concept of the acquired intellect postdates the Hebrew Bible by hundreds of years, it is hardly surprising that there is no biblical equivalent, and that Maimonides must interpret the biblical word *nephesh* in a manner that includes its being the acquired intellect. So even though Maimonides does not here specifically use the term "acquired intellect" (or its Arabic equivalent), it is clear that he accepts the idea that it is only the acquired intellect, not the entire soul (that is, not the animal soul and not the form of man), which perdures.[43]

---

41. Davidson, *Alfarabi, Avicenna and Averroes*, 200–3 (emphasis original).
42. Maimonides, *Guide of the Perplexed*, 1:91.
43. See Maimonides, *Guide of the Perplexed*, 1:173–74 ("the *souls* that remain after death are not

Maimonides also interprets the word *ruach* as capable of meaning the "acquired intellect," without specifically using that term. He notes that the word *ruach*, as the word *nephesh*, is equivocal. Included among the several meanings of *ruach* that he delineates are "the animal spirit" and "the thing that remains of man after his death and that does not undergo passing-away."[44] In so doing, Maimonides acknowledges that these Hebrew words—*nephesh* and *ruach*—have no clearly defined meanings in Jewish tradition and can be used in some cases interchangeably. He does not recognize Saadia's tripartite division which restricts *nephesh*, *ruach*, and *neshamah* to certain specific faculties of the soul.[45]

When Maimonides defines *nephesh* and *ruach* as including that part of a human being that survives death, the part to which he is referring is the acquired intellect. This position is supported by other passages in the *Guide*. For example, in book 1, chapter 72, Maimonides compares a human individual to the "world as a whole."[46] As part of this comparison he compares the "rational faculty" to God, stating:

> The rational faculty is a faculty subsisting in a body and is not separable from it, whereas God . . . is not a faculty subsisting in the body of the world, but is separate from all parts of the world. For the governance and the providence of him . . . accompany the world as a whole in such a way that the manner and true reality of this accompaniment are hidden from us; the faculties of human beings are inadequate to understand this . . .
>
> Know that it behooved us to compare the relation obtaining between God . . . and the world to that obtaining between the acquired intellect and man; this intellect is not a faculty in the body but is truly separate from the organic body and overflows toward it. We should have compared, on the other hand, the rational faculty to the intellects of the heavens, which are in bodies. However, the case of the intellects of the heavens, that of the existence of separate intellects, and that of the representation of the acquired intellect which is also separate, are matters open to speculation and research. The proofs with regard to them are well hidden though correct.[47]

Although he is hesitant about providing details, it is clear that Maimonides thinks that the acquired intellect, in contrast to the "rational faculty," is something separate and apart from the body. The relationship between the acquired intellect and the body is akin to the relationship between God and the world. Just as God is separate from the

---

the *soul* that comes into being in man at the time he is generated. For that which comes into being at the time a man is generated is merely a faculty consisting in preparedness, whereas the thing that after death is separate from matter is the thing that has become actual and not the *soul* that also comes into being"; emphasis original).

44. Maimonides, *Guide of the Perplexed*, 1:90.
45. See ch. 5, sec. B, 5.
46. Maimonides, *Guide of the Perplexed*, 1:192.
47. Maimonides, *Guide of the Perplexed*, 1:192–93.

CHAPTER 7.

world but, yet, his governance and providence "accompany the world," so the acquired intellect is separate from the body but, yet, its governance and providence accompany the body.[48] Being separate from the body entails that the acquired intellect can subsist after the destruction of the body, and so the acquired intellect is clearly "the thing that remains of man after his death."[49] Consequently, the famous passage from 1 Samuel 25:29 (*Yet the soul [nephesh] of my lord shall be bound in the bundle of life*), which had been interpreted since rabbinic times as referring to the immortal soul, is now interpreted by Maimonides as referring to only a certain part of the soul—the acquired intellect.[50]

Next, Maimonides associates the acquired intellect with something like the sum total of intellectual cognitions attained by an individual throughout his lifetime. In book 1, chapter 30, he discusses the Hebrew word *'akhol* [eat]. In the course of this discussion he says:

> the *term eating* is applied figuratively to knowledge, learning, and, in general, the intellectual apprehensions through which the permanence of the human form endures in the most perfect of states, just as the body endures through food in the finest of states . . . This use is also frequent in the speech of the *Sages*, I mean the designation of knowledge as eating. Similarly they often designate knowledge as water . . . This use is frequent. *Jonathan ben Uziel* . . . translated the words: *With joy shall ye draw water out of the wells of salvation*, by the words: *With joy shall you receive a new teaching from the chosen of the righteous*. Consider accordingly that he interprets the word water as being the knowledge that will be received in those days.[51]

According to Kellner, this discussion establishes that "[p]erfection and permanent endurance (i.e., immortality) . . . are consequences of 'intellectual apprehensions.'"[52] Similarly, in last chapter of the *Guide*, Maimonides states that what gives the individual "permanent perdurance" is "the acquisition of the rational virtues" which he equates with the acquisition of the "intelligibles."[53] To the same effect is the discussion in book 3, chapter 27, where Maimonides equates the welfare of the soul with "the multitude's acquiring correct opinions corresponding to their respective capacity" and states that man's "ultimate perfection" which results in "perpetual [immaterial] preservation" is

---

48. The comparison between the relationship of the acquired intellect to the body and the relationship of God to the world is strengthened by the statement that the acquired intellect "overflows toward [the body]" for "the separate intellects" in the world, which are the intermediaries between God and the physical world, are all created as a result of an "overflow from God" (See Maimonides, *Guide of the Perplexed*, 2:259).

49. Maimonides, *Guide of the Perplexed*, 1:91.

50. See Maimonides, *Guide of the Perplexed*, 1:91.

51. Maimonides, *Guide of the Perplexed*, 1:63–64 (emphasis original).

52. Kellner, *Maimonides on Human Perfection*, 3.

53. Maimonides, *Guide of the Perplexed*, 2:635. See also Kellner, *Maimonides on Human Perfection*, 3–4 ("that which enables [man] to be permanently with God, is the conception of the intelligibles.").

"to become rational in actu" which means "to have an intellect in actu" which "would consist in his knowing everything concerning all the beings that it is within the capacity of man to know in accordance with his ultimate perfection."[54]

It is also clear that Maimonides accepts the existence of what is called the "active intellect." As Robinson notes:

> For example, in *Guide* I.72 and II.6-7 Maimonides presents a fairly standard Neoplatonized-Aristotelian emanationist cosmology, with the active intellect—the last of the celestial intelligences—construed as the cause of existence and final aim of knowledge... Many of the traditional theological doctrines in the *Guide* are understood with the help of the active intellect. Both prophecy and providence are explained as resulting from a divine overflow through the active intellect to individuals with properly prepared intellects.[55]

In book 2, chapter 4, Maimonides specifically states that the "tenth intellect is the Active Intellect, whose existence is indicated by the facts that our intellects pass from potentiality to actuality and that the forms of the existents that are subject to generation and corruption are actualized after they have been in their matter only in potentia."[56]

---

54. Maimonides, *Guide of the Perplexed*, 2:510-12 (emphasis original). An issue exists as to the exact nature of the knowledge required to actualize the intellect in a manner sufficient to achieve immortality. Hasdai Crescas, for instance, distinguishes two "versions" of the theory of the acquired intellect. According to one version, which Harvey says "represents the minority Avicennian view advanced by Gersonides [and which was also] held by Abraham Ibn Daud, . . . 'he who intellectually cognizes one *intelligible* of the *intelligibilia* of geometry . . . will live eternally!'" while according to the other version, which Harvey calls "the orthodox view among Muslim and Jewish philosophers," immortality is achieved only by intellectual apprehension of the "the essence of the incorporeal substances" (Harvey, "Hasdai Crescas's Critique," 44-47). In other words, according to the first version, "any true knowledge earns immortality," while according to the second version, "only true knowledge of incorporeal things—or, in theological language, God and His angels—earns immortality" (Harvey, "Hasdai Crescas's Critique," 34-35). The difference in versions may be reducible to the question of whether or not partial cognition of the active intellect suffices to secure immortality; according to the first version it does, while according to the second version only complete cognition of the active intellect suffices to secure immortality (Harvey, "Hasdai Crescas's Critique," 36-37). Harvey argues that the second version "is identifiable with the opinion of Maimonides" (Harvey, "Hasdai Crescas's Critique," 38). Although Harvey admits that Maimonides "does not reveal his position in detail" because the issue "as to what kind of knowledge is necessary for acquisition of immortality is one of the esoteric puzzles of the *Guide of the Perplexed*," he points to several passages in the *Book of Knowledge* and the *Guide of the Perplexed* in support of his position (See Harvey, "Hasdai Crescas's Critique," 40-44). See also Kellner, *Maimonides on Human Perfection*, 2 (for Maimonides "one achieves an acquired intellect only through cognition of God and the Separate Intellects."). But see Hyman, "Maimonides' 'Thirteen Principles,'" 141-42 (Maimonides makes "immortality possible for all"; discussed *infra*, n. 80).

55. Robinson, "Soul and Intellect," 536. See Maimonides, *Guide of the Perplexed*, 2:254-66; Davidson, *Alfarabi, Avicenna and Averroes*, 203-5 ("True prophesy takes place only when the rational and imaginative faculties together enjoy the emanation of the active intellect," citing *Guide of the Perplexed*, 2:37).

56. Maimonides, *Guide of the Perplexed*, 2:257. Maimonides goes on to explain, *inter alia*, that the "intellect in actu existing in us . . . derives from an overflow of the Active Intellect" (Maimonides, *Guide of the Perplexed*, 258). See also Rudavsky, *Maimonides*, 97 ("According to Neoplatonic ontology, in which the spheres form part of a cosmic chain of being, the last intellect in this emanated chain

Last, there can be little doubt that Maimonides, in accordance with the Aristotelian point of view of al-Farabi, Ibn Bajja, and Averroes accepted that the acquired intellect conjoins with the active intellect after the destruction of the body. This unification of the acquired intellect with the active intellect results in human immortality, but a human immortality that is nonindividual. This is because there are no individual differences with regard to pure intellect. In other words, the acquired intellect that survives the destruction of the body contains nothing that is tied to an individual person—no memories, emotions, feelings, thoughts that pertain solely to the individual, or personality. This is the import of Maimonides's interpretation of a rabbinic text (b. Hag. 12b) stating that in Arabot there exists "the soul of the righteous ones, and the souls and the spirits that shall be created in the future." Maimonides explains:

> How sublime is this notion to him who understood it! For the *souls* that remain after death are not the *soul* that comes into being in man at the time he is generated. For that which comes into being at the time a man is generated is merely a faculty consisting in preparedness, whereas the thing that after death is separate from matter is the thing that has become actual and not the *soul* that also comes into being . . . Because of this the Sages have numbered the *souls and spirits* among the things that come into being. *What is separate is, on the contrary, one thing only.*[57]

Similarly, in discussing the seventh method used by the Mutakallimun to prove the creation of the world in time, Maimonides specifically refers to Ibn Bajja's doctrine of the Unity of the Intellect:

> Now you know that regarding the things separate from matter—I mean those that are neither bodies nor forces in bodies, but intellects—there can be no thought of multiplicity of any mode whatever, except that some of them are the causes of the existence of others . . . However, what remains of Zayd is neither the cause nor the effect of what remains of Umar. Consequently *all are one in number as [Ibn Bajja] and others who were drawn into speaking of these obscure matters have made clear.*[58]

With regard to this reference to Ibn Bajja's doctrine, Pines writes:

> Maimonides . . . makes it pretty clear that he rejects Avicenna's views on the afterlife of the soul and that he has a certain preference for Ibn Bājja's

---

of spheres is what Islamic philosophers called the Active Intellect. Maimonides follows al-Farabi and Avicenna in positing the Active Intellect as the final link in the chain, serving as an intermediary between the superlunar and the sublunar spheres. The Active Intellect serves as the link between God and humans; it is a giver of forms, and as such plays a crucial role in the formation of existence. The Active Intellect plays a crucial role in the process of human knowledge and prophecy as well, and it serves as a foundation for immortality.").

57. Maimonides, *Guide of the Perplexed*, 1:173–74 (emphasis in last sentence added).
58. Maimonides, *Guide of the Perplexed*, 1:221 (emphasis added).

position. This is not fortuitous. As may be seen from the letter to Ibn Tibbon, Maimonides' attitude toward Ibn Bājja is not marked by the reticence that he shows toward Avicenna . . . In rejecting Avicenna's view concerning the disembodied soul, Maimonides makes one of his few explicit references to Ibn Bājja. He credits this philosopher quite correctly with having made clear that as far as only pure intellect is concerned there are no individual differences. In other words, Aristotle qua intellect is identical with the other 'happy ones'; they are not a multiplicity of beings, but 'one.' The intellect being regarded as the only portion of man that survives bodily death, this doctrine of Ibn Bājja means that, contrary to Avicenna, nothing individual remains after death. As has already been stated, Maimonides seems to incline to this opinion of Ibn Bājja, yet he does not wholly commit himself, these being, according to him, 'hidden matters' (I 74, seventh way).[59]

Rudavsky concurs in this understanding of Maimonides, stating:

> Maimonides suggests . . . that only part of the soul—the intellectual part—is properly immortal. When separated from the body, the immortal part of the individual, and not the entire soul per se, enjoys a special sort of existence akin to the Active Intellect. Like the Active Intellect, this intellectual part of the soul has no personal features.[60]

4. The *Mishneh Torah*

In the section of *Sefer Ha-Mada*, the first book of the *Mishneh Torah*, called *Hilkhot Yesodei ha-Torah* (Laws of the Foundations of the Torah), Maimonides describes the acquired intellect in the same manner as he did in the Eight Chapters, as the "form of the soul." He then reiterates that, as the form of the soul, the acquired intellect (1) is incorporeal, (2) knows and apprehends the *intelligibles*, (3) is separate and apart from the body, (4) survives death, and (5) constitutes the immortal part of a human being:

> This form of the soul is not compounded of elements into which it would again dissolve. Nor does it exist by the energy of the vital principle, so that the latter would be necessary to its existence, in the way that the vital principle requires

---

59. Pines, "Introduction," ciii–civ. See Husik, *History of Mediaeval Jewish Philosophy*, xlvii.

60. Rudavsky, *Maimonides*, 102. See also Rudavsky, *Maimonides*, 105, 107 ("it is not even clear whether anything more than the Active Intellect, which is totally bereft of personal characteristics, endures," and "[i]n accord with Averroes' 'monopsychism,' Maimonides appears to suggest that all immaterial souls form a united whole."). But see Hyman, *Eschatological Themes*, 84–86 ("One of the troublesome issues of Maimonides' description of the World to Come is whether he believes in individual or, as Ibn Bâjja and Averroes, in collective immortality. Some medieval commentators, such as Samuel Ibn Tibbon and Moses of Narbonne, and Shlomo Pines among the moderns, emphasizing the Ibn Bâjja passage in the *Guide*, concluded that Maimonides is a proponent of collective immortality, that is, that all immortal human intellects are one. Against this interpretation Alexander Altmann has argued (I believe convincingly) that Maimonides believed in individual immortality.").

a physical body for its existence. But it comes directly from God in Heaven. Hence, when the material portion of our being dissolves into its component elements, and physical life perishes—since that only exists in association with the body and needs the body for its functions—this form of the soul, is not destroyed, as it does not require physical life for its activities. It knows and apprehends the Intelligences that exist without material substance; it knows the Creator of All Things; and it endures forever.[61]

Matters pertaining to the soul and the afterlife are also set forth in chapters 8 and 9 of the section called *Hilkhot T'shuvah* (Laws of Repentance). It is here that Maimonides makes it clear that *Olam Ha-Bah* is the world inhabited by the acquired intellect after the destruction of the body. Rewards received *prior* to the destruction are only instrumentally good—they are the means whereby we are enabled to achieve that which is intrinsically good, life in the *Olam Ha-Bah*. Chapter 8 of *Hilkhot T'shuvah* begins by stating that the ultimate good that man will reap from the fulfillment of God's commandments is life in the world to come.[62] In the world to come the righteous attain bliss and abide in a state of happiness; conversely, the wicked will be cut off from this life and die.[63]

Next considered is the nature of the bliss or good to be obtained in the world to come. In keeping with the theme discussed in *Perek Helek*, that spiritual pleasures are of greater value than bodily pleasures, Maimonides contends that the pleasures to be obtained in the world to come are strictly spiritual pleasures, thereby again opposing all five of the opinions concerning the ultimate good he rejected in *Perek Helek*. He states bluntly:

> In the world to come, there is nothing corporeal, and no material substance; there are only souls of the righteous without bodies . . . None of the conditions occur there which are incident to physical bodies in this world such as sitting, standing, sleep, death, grief, merriment, etc.[64]

To support the view that spiritual pleasures are of greater value than bodily pleasures and that the spiritual pleasure to be sought is knowledge of God, he relies again

---

61. Maimonides, *Book of Knowledge*, 39a. See Kellner, *Maimonides on Human Perfection*, 1–2; Rudavsky, *Maimonides*, 95, 102.

62. Maimonides, *Book of Knowledge*, 90a (*Hilkhot T'shuvah*, 8:1).

63. Maimonides, *Book of Knowledge*, 90a (*Hilkhot T'shuvah*, 8:1).

64. Maimonides, *Book of Knowledge*, 90a (*Hilkhot T'shuvah*, 8:2) See Silver, *Maimonidean Criticism*, 28 (In the *Commentary on the Mishnah*, Maimonides avoided spelling out his preference for the immortality of the soul by insisting "that the delights of the next life are beyond the intellectual grasp of the human mind . . . However, in the *Mishneh Torah*, Maimonides' passion for orderliness and precision overcame his caution . . . The next life is entirely other and distinct from our mundane existence. All human attributes fall away. The soul participates in the pure spiritual existence of angelic spheres. In short, familiar bodily appetites and accidents no longer accrue. Talmudic statements seeming to promise familiar pleasures are figurative in force.").

on b. Berakhot 17a. After stating that the world to come is a nonmaterial world, he adds:

> So the ancient sages said, 'In the hereafter, there is no eating, no drinking, no connubial intercourse, but the righteous sit with their crowns on their heads and enjoy the radiance of the Shechinah.' This passage clearly indicates that as there is no eating or drinking there, *there is no physical body hereafter* . . . The phrase 'their crowns on their heads' refers to the knowledge they have acquired, and for the sake of which they have attained life in the world to come . . . So 'the Crown,' of which the sages here speak is not to be taken literally but refers to knowledge. And what is the meaning of the sages' statement: 'they enjoy the radiance of the Shechinah'? It means that the righteous attain to a knowledge and realization of the truth concerning God to which they had not attained while they were in the murky and lowly body.[65]

He then makes it crystal clear that this reward of the righteous, this ultimate good or bliss, can only be obtained by the acquired intellect. According to Maimonides:

> The soul, whenever mentioned in this connection [viz., in connection with the world to come], is not the vital element requisite for bodily existence, but that form of soul which is identical with the intelligence which apprehends the Creator, as far as it is able, and apprehends other abstract concepts and other things . . . And it is this which, in this connection, is called Soul. That life, as it is immortal,—death being only incidental to the body, which does not exist in the hereafter—is called 'the bond of life,' as it is said, 'but the soul of my lord shall be bound in the bond of life; and the souls of thine enemies, them he shall sling out . . .' [1 Sam 25:29]. And this is a recompense than which there is none higher; a bliss beyond which there is nothing more blissful.[66]

To again emphasize the inferiority of the physical pleasures sought by most people, and to make clear that such pleasures will not be available in the world to come, he goes on to add:

> Possibly you may esteem this boon (of life hereafter) lightly, and imagine that the only reward for fulfilling religious precepts and walking consistently in the ways of truth is to enjoy good food and drink; to have intercourse with 'beautiful forms'; to wear fine linen and brocade; to dwell in places of ivory; to be served on gold and silver plate and enjoy similar things . . . The wise and intelligent know, however, that all these pleasures are exaggerated and inane, and there is no profit in them. They are regarded by us as a great boon because we are beings with physical bodies . . .; and when the body ceases to exist, all these things become null and void.[67]

65. Maimonides, *Book of Knowledge*, 90a–90b (emphasis added) (*Hilkhot T'shuvah*, 8:2).
66. Maimonides, *Book of Knowledge*, 90b (*Hilkhot T'shuvah*, 8:3).
67. Maimonides, *Book of Knowledge*, 90b–91a (*Hilkhot T'shuvah*, 8:6).

Maimonides continues by stating that the world to come "now exists . . . It is called the World to Come . . . only because human beings will enter into it at a time subsequent to the life of the present world in which we now exist with body and soul,—and this existence comes first."[68] It is thus quite clear that for Maimonides the incorporeal part of the souls of the righteous Jews (that is, their acquired intellects) enter the world to come immediately upon separation from the body.[69] At this time, according to the views hinted at in the *Guide*, the acquired intellects unite with the active intellect and become one. In such condition, the bliss attained by the acquired intellects is something divorced from the individual person that existed when the acquired intellects accompanied a body.

In chapter 9 of *Hilkhot T'shuvah*, Maimonides considers the copious references in the Torah promising material rewards and punishments in this life. He asks: "What then is the meaning of the statement found everywhere in the Torah that 'if ye obey, it will happen to you thus; if ye do not obey, it will be otherwise'; and all these happenings will take place in this world, such as war and peace; sovereignty and subjection; residence in the Promised Land, and exile; prosperity in one's activities and failure, and all other things predicted in the words of the Covenant [Lev 26; Deut 28]"[70] Maimonides's answer to this question harkens back to the distinction made in *Perek Helek* between the ultimate goal and things that serve as the means to the ultimate goal. The material things promised as rewards in the Torah are intended as instrumental goods only, not as the ultimate or intrinsic good. In the words of Maimonides:

> When we fulfil all the commandments of the Torah, all the good things of this world will come to us. When however we transgress the precepts, the evils that are written in the Torah will befall us. But nevertheless, those good things are not the final reward for the fulfilment of the commandments. These matters are to be understood as follows: . . . Whoever fulfils what is written [in the Law] and knows it with a complete and correct knowledge will attain thereby life in the World to Come. According to the greatness of his deeds and abundance of his knowledge will be the measure in which he will attain that life. He has further promised us in the Torah, that, if we observe its behests joyously and cheerfully, and continually meditate on its wisdom, He will remove from us the obstacles that hinder us in its observance, such as sickness, war, famine, and other calamities; and will bestow upon us all the material benefits which will strengthen our ability to fulfil the Law, such as plenty, peace, abundance of silver and gold. Thus we will not be engaged, all our days, in providing for our bodily needs, but will have leisure to study wisdom and fulfil the commandment, and thus attain life in the World to Come . . . So too, He taught us in the Torah that if we deliberately forsake it . . . the true Judge will deprive

---

68. Maimonides, *Book of Knowledge*, 91a (citing Ps 31:19–20) (*Hilkhot T'shuvah*, 8:8).
69. See Gillman, *Death of Death*, 156.
70. Maimonides, *Book of Knowledge*, 91b (*Hilkhot T'shuvah*, 9:1).

the forsakers of all those material benefits . . ., and will send upon them all the calamities that will prevent their attaining the life hereafter, so that they will perish in their wickedness.[71]

At the end of chapter 9 Maimonides refers to the messianic era.[72] He says that the prophets and sages longed for it, not as the final goal, but, again, merely as an instrumental good. In the messianic era there will be "relief from the wicked tyranny that does not permit them properly to occupy themselves with the study of the Torah and the observance of the commandments; that they might have ease, devote themselves to getting wisdom, and thus attain to life in the World to Come."[73] Last, he reiterates what he had repeatedly said in many of his works—that the messianic era will be realized in this world which will continue as it had "except that independent sovereignty will be restored to Israel."[74]

Maimonides includes in *Hilkhot T'shuvah* virtually the identical list of those principles, first set forth in *Perek Helek*, that he deemed necessary for being considered an Israelite and, thus, for having a share in the world to come (that is, his "thirteen principles"), including resurrection of the dead.[75] Moreover, those principles of the thirteen concerning reward and punishment are discussed in *Hilkhot T'shuvah*, chapters 7 through 9, at some length, and a full discussion of the world to come is included in chapter 8. Yet, the principle of the resurrection of the dead (principle thirteen) is missing from this discussion.[76] As Hyman notes:

> Because of the omission some of Maimonides' contemporaries (as well as later scholars) questioned Maimonides' belief in this principle. Aware, however, of the furor caused by this omission, Maimonides, in his later years, wrote the *Treatise Concerning the Resurrection of the Dead* to fill the gap.[77] This *Treatise* . . . can be considered as a kind of appendix to the *Mishneh Torah*, designed to complete the full discussion of the 'thirteen principles.'[78]

---

71. Maimonides, *Book of Knowledge*, 91b (*Hilkhot T'shuvah*, 9:1). See generally Kellner, *Must a Jew Believe Anything?*, 156–61 (discussing that the commandments "are preparations which enable human beings to achieve their proper end, intellectual perfection.").

72. See generally Silver, *Maimonidean Criticism*, 29.

73. Maimonides, *Book of Knowledge*, 92a (*Hilkhot T'shuvah*, 9:2). Cf. Maimonides, *Commentary on the Sanhedrin*, 148.

74. Maimonides, *Book of Knowledge*, 92a (*Hilkhot T'shuvah*, 9:2). Maimonides made this point in Book II, chapter 29, of the *Guide of the Perplexed*, and in *Perek Helek* (see *supra*, n. 39), and will reiterate it yet again in the *Treatise on Resurrection* (see Maimonides, *Moses Maimonides' Treatise on Resurrection*, 38). As support for his position Maimonides relies on the rabbinic teaching that there is no difference between this world and the world to come except for servitude to foreign powers (in this world). See b. Ber. 34b; b. Šabb. 63a, 151b; b. Sanh., 91b, 99a.

75. See sec. A, 2; *supra*, n. 37.

76. Nor is the principle of the resurrection of the dead discussed in the *Guide of the Perplexed*. See Hyman, "Maimonides' 'Thirteen Principles,'" 134–36.

77. See sec. D.

78. Hyman, "Maimonides' 'Thirteen Principles,'" 133.

CHAPTER 7.

B. What Maimonides Says about Those Who Have a Portion in *Olam Ha-Bah* Is Not Entirely Consistent with the Belief That the Acquired Intellect Comes into Existence by Intellectual Apprehension

The only part of a person that survives death and enters the world to come is the acquired intellect, and the acquired intellect is associated with the actualization of a person's potential for intellectual apprehension; so, it might be thought that those who enter the world to come are only those who have actualized their potential for intellectual apprehension—who have achieved the requisite level of intellectual perfection—whether Jewish or gentile, or whether obedient to the commandments of the Torah or disobedient. In fact, Kellner interprets book 1, chapter 30 of the *Guide* as maintaining that "[p]erfection and permanent endurance (i.e., immortality) ... are consequences of 'intellectual apprehensions.'"[79] Yet, in several of the texts that have been discussed above, namely *Perek Helek* and the *Mishneh Torah*, Maimonides makes clear that entry into the world to come is not dependent on intellectual apprehensions alone, but on obedience to God's commandments.[80]

This apparent inconsistency concerning whether those who enter the world to come are those who achieve the requisite intellectual perfection or are those who adhere to God's commandments is highlighted in chapter 3 of *Hilkhot T'shuvah*. In this chapter Maimonides discusses at some length those persons who have a portion in the world to come and those persons who are cut off from the world to come. Interestingly, intellectual apprehension isn't specifically mentioned as a prerequisite for entry into the world to come.[81] The chapter is initiated with a discussion of the three classes of persons delineated in rabbinic material—the righteous, the wicked, and the intermediate class. Maimonides, recognizing that there are no wholly righteous or wholly wicked persons,[82] begins chapter 3 as follows:

79. Kellner, *Maimonides on Human Perfection*, 3. See text accompanying note 52.

80. Hyman suggests that belief in the first five of Maimonides's thirteen principles enables one to have sufficiently actualized the intellect to qualify for entry into the world to come (Hyman, "Maimonides' 'Thirteen Principles,'" 141). According to Hyman, "The Law, then, by commanding that all Israelites, the masses no less than the intellectual elite, must know certain true propositions about God, provides the possibility of immortality for all. The first five principles make it possible for Maimonides to embrace a philosophical understanding of human immortality without restricting immortality to a small philosophical elite" (Hyman, "Maimonides' 'Thirteen Principles,'" 141–42). If Hyman were correct, it would still leave unexplained why all commandments other than those concerning the first five of Maimonides's thirteen principles need be obeyed. It seems reasonable to suppose that obedience is necessary to achieve the material goods and the moral perfection required to sufficiently actualize one's intellect to qualify for entry into the world to come, but this is nowhere made explicit. See also Kellner, *Must a Jew Believe Anything?*, 162–63 ("the notion that the righteous are rewarded for the fulfilment of the commandments ... and that the wicked are punished ... for their transgressions, is ... a necessary belief without being a true one.").

81. Inconsistencies in Maimonides' writings can sometimes be explained as due to the different audiences he is addressing. See Maimonides, *Moses Maimonides' Treatise on Resurrection*, 51; Rudavsky, *Maimonides*, 127; Gillman, *Death of Death*, 164–65.

82. See also Shakespeare, *All's Well that Ends Well*, Act IV, scene 3 ("The web of our life is of a

> Every human being has merits and iniquities. One whose merits exceed his iniquities is righteous. He whose iniquities exceed his merits is wicked. If the two balance in an individual, he belongs to the intermediate class . . . This valuation takes into account not the number but the magnitude of merits and iniquities.[83]

Although a person's meritorious deeds and iniquities are weighed at the hour of death, they are also weighed annually on the New Year, and the threefold classification has more important ramifications with regard to the annual weighing than with regard to the one at the hour of death. This is because the Jewish intermediates and the Jewish wicked, and not just the Jewish righteous, "have a portion in the world to come; for all Israelites, notwithstanding that they have sinned, have a portion in the life hereafter, as it is said, 'Thy people shall be righteous, they shall inherit the land for ever' [Isa 60:21]. The expression *land* is a metaphor for the land of life, that is, the world to come. And so too, the saints among the gentile peoples have a portion in the world to come."[84]

There follows a discussion of those Jews who will be cut off from the world to come:

> The following have no portion in the world to come, but are cut off and perish, and for their great wickedness and sinfulness are condemned for ever and ever. Heretics and Epicureans; those who deny the Torah, the resurrection of the dead or the coming of the Redeemer; apostates; those who cause a multitude to sin, and those who secede from the ways of the community; anyone who commits transgressions like Jehoiakim, in high handed fashion and openly; informers; those who [terrorize] a community, not for a religious purpose; murderers and slanderers, and one who obliterates the physical mark of his Jewish origin.[85]

Each of the types mentioned as being cut off from the world to come even if they are Israelites are further discussed and, in some cases, subdivided.[86] Maimonides also adds that, even among those whose transgressions are less grave, if one's transgressions are "habitually" committed that person will have no portion in the world to come.[87] Finally, he goes on to discuss repentance, and states that, if a person repents and is accepted as a penitent, such person can, despite having transgressed, have a portion in the world to come.[88]

---

mingled yarn, good and ill together.").

83. Maimonides, *Book of Knowledge*, 83b (*Hilkhot T'shuvah*, 3:1–2).

84. Maimonides, *Book of Knowledge*, 84b (*Hilkhot T'shuvah*, 3:5). See ch. 4, n. 142. (discussing use of Isa 60:21 as a proof text).

85. Maimonides, *Book of Knowledge*, 84b (*Hilkhot T'shuvah*, 3:6).

86. See Maimonides, *Book of Knowledge*, 84b–85a (*Hilkhot T'shuvah*, 3:6–14).

87. Maimonides, *Book of Knowledge*, 85a (*Hilkhot T'shuvah*, 3:14).

88. See Maimonides, *Book of Knowledge*, 85b–86b (*Hilkhot T'shuvah*, 3:14).

Again, nowhere is intellectual apprehension specifically mentioned, and this seems at odds with the basic tenor of Maimonidean thought in that he has argued in the *Commentary on the Mishnah*, in *Hilkhot T'shuvah* chapter 8, and elsewhere "that one's portion in the world to come depends upon one's intellectual attainments."[89] This issue has been discussed by scholars with no decisive conclusion being reached.[90] Jewish Aristotelians coming after Maimonides, however, adhering to what came to be called the theory of the acquired intellect, seem less reluctant to make intellectual apprehension supreme; this led to Hasdai Crescas's attack on this theory in the late fourteenth century.[91]

C. Maimonides's Statements on the Resurrection of the Body Are Puzzling

In *Perek Helek* Maimonides unequivocally affirms the doctrine of the resurrection of the dead.[92] Indeed, according to him, the resurrection of dead is one of thirteen "fundamental principles" of the Torah, principles that must be truly believed to be part of the "collective unit of Israel."[93] Yet, *Perek Helek* provides almost no discussion of the details of this fundamental principle. Maimonides says only:

> The *resurrection of the dead* is one of the fundamental principles of the Law of Moses . . . He who does not believe in this has no religion and no tie with the Jewish people. But it is (only) for the righteous as stated in *Bereshit Rabbah*: 'The benefit of the rains is both for the righteous and the wicked, but the resurrection of the dead is only for the righteous' . . . Know also that man must of necessity die and decompose into the elements of which he is composed.[94]

An important unanswered question is: When is the resurrection of the righteous dead to occur? Furthermore, it is difficult to see what possible answer might be offered. It does not appear that the resurrection of the dead can occur in the *Olam Ha-Bah*, since, in *Perek Helek* (and elsewhere) Maimonides interprets b. Berakhot 17a to mean that in the *Olam Ha-Bah* the righteous will exist only as immortal souls in the intellectual (or immaterial) sphere.[95] Moreover, since the *Olam Ha-Bah* exists *now* in a different dimension, and one enters the *Olam Ha-Bah* immediately upon death, "a doctrine of bodily resurrection seems to be superfluous."[96]

---

89. Kellner, *Maimonides on Human Perfection*, 2.
90. See Kellner, *Maimonides on Human Perfection*, 1–45; Rudavsky, *Maimonides*, 184–96.
91. See generally Harvey, "Hasdai Crescas's Critique," 83–85, 114–24.
92. See sec. A, 2.
93. Maimonides, *Commentary on the Sanhedrin*, 157.
94. Maimonides, *Commentary on the Sanhedrin*, 147 (quoting Bereshit Rab. 13).
95. See Maimonides, *Commentary on the Sanhedrin*, 144.
96. Gillman, *Death of Death*, 156–57.

Neither is there any real place for a resurrection of the dead in *Yemot Ha-Maschiach*, since Maimonides repeatedly states that *Yemot Ha-Maschiach* refers to the time when sovereignty will return to Israel but that nothing extraordinary will otherwise occur. Specifically, he writes in *Perek Helek*:

> In regard to existing things, nothing will be different from what it is now, except that the sovereignty will be Israel's, and this is the meaning of the Sages' statement: 'There is no difference between this world and the days of the Messiah except the subjugation of foreign Powers alone.'[97]

Confusion about the fundamental principle of the resurrection of the dead is not lessened by other Maimonidean texts since resurrection of the dead is nowhere mentioned in them, except to say that denial of belief in resurrection of the dead precludes entry into the world to come.[98] This is especially puzzling in chapter 8 of *Hilkhot T'shuvah* for here he focuses on the good that man will reap from the fulfillment of God's commandments, and one might have thought that resurrection is such a good. Indeed, in *Perek Helek* he listed resurrection of the dead as one of the five possible opinions concerning the good that man will reap from the fulfillment of God's commandments. Yet, in *Hilkhot T'shuvah* Maimonides is silent about resurrection. Furthermore, the text of *Hilkhot T'shuvah* cannot be read so as to include bodily resurrection as an *intrinsic* or final good, since such a good is adamantly depicted as something immaterial. And even though Maimonides is careful in *Hilkhot T'shuvah* to mention that the material goods depicted in the Torah are *instrumental* goods, he says nothing about resurrection being an instrumental good.

Furthermore, in *Hilkhot T'shuvah* Maimonides repeats the understanding of *Yemot Ha-Maschiach* that precludes resurrection of the dead at that time.[99] Indeed, in the section of the *Mishneh Torah* called *Hilkhot Melachim* (The Laws of Kings) Maimonides states: "Let no one think that the custom of the world will any way cease to exist during the days of the Messiah or that something new will occur in the Work of Creation."[100] This is significant because Maimonides considered resurrection, which defies the laws of nature, to be like a miracle or act of creation, that is, as something new in the work of creation. Presumably this is why he makes the following further statement in *Hilkhot Melachim*:

---

97. Maimonides, *Commentary on the Sanhedrin*, 147. See *supra*, nn. 39 and 74. See generally Hyman, *Eschatological Themes*, 80.

98. Because Maimonides says nothing, perforce we can know nothing of his thoughts concerning such issues as the nature of the resurrected body or its relationship to the original body's acquired intellect (now conjoined with the active intellect).

99. Maimonides, *Book of Knowledge*, 92a (*Hilkhot T'shuvah*, 9:2).

100. Weiss and Butterworth, *Ethical Writings of Maimonides*, 174.

> Do not suppose that the messianic king needs to give signs, perform miracles, and make new things happen in the world, *or resurrect the dead* and do similar things. It is not so.[101]

It may be objected that Maimonides understood resurrection to be an example, not of the power of the messianic king to perform miracles, but of *God's* power to perform miracles, and that having a proper conception of God is the reason why belief in resurrection is a fundamental principle. Indeed, Maimonides says something along these lines in the *Treatise on Resurrection*, discussed in the next section.

D. The *Treatise on Resurrection* Was Intended to Respond to Critics

The description in *Hilkhot T'shuvah* of the world to come as completely immaterial, and its failure to include any details about resurrection, did not go unnoticed.[102] There were some who were merely confused as to what the Maimonidean view on resurrection really entailed. There were others who, independently rejecting the doctrine of bodily resurrection, cited Maimonides in support of their view.[103]

A particular incident involved a pupil in a Damascus Academy who openly declared that "there is no resurrection of the dead, and that the soul does not return to the body after it has left it."[104] In support of his position the pupil cited statements in the *Mishneh Torah* about the ultimate goal being the world to come, and about the world to come being an immaterial world.[105] Although others refuted the pupil's position by citing biblical verses and rabbinic statements to the contrary, the pupil defended his position by objecting to a literal interpretation of the verses and statements cited.[106] This incident was brought to the attention of Maimonides, but Maimonides paid no attention to it because, he said, "no one can be so foolish as to find it so difficult to understand what we wrote (clearly in our composition)."[107]

Then, in 1189, Maimonides received a letter from Yemen in which the writer

---

101. Weiss and Butterworth, *Ethical Writings of Maimonides*, 172 (emphasis added).

102. See Hyman, *Eschatological Themes*, 78 ("Maimonides' limited mention of the resurrection of the dead became the subject of controversy already in his own time."); Gillman, *Death of Death*, 156–57 (Rabbi Abraham ben David of Posquieres commented on Maimonides's *Mishneh Torah*: "'This man's words are in my eyes near to those who assert that there is no resurrection of the body but only of souls.'"); Silver, *Maimonidean Criticism*, 53–68, 90, 98–108, 116–29 (discussing attacks on Maimonides and the *Mishneh Torah*).

103. See Silver, *Maimonidean Criticism*, 114, 128–35.

104. Maimonides, *Moses Maimonides' Treatise on Resurrection*, 29.

105. See Rosner, "Brief Description of the Treatise," 15–16; Maimonides, *Moses Maimonides' Treatise on Resurrection*, 29. See also Silver, *Maimonidean Criticism*, 37n1. 64.

106. See Rosner, "Brief Description of the Treatise," 15–16; Maimonides, *Moses Maimonides' Treatise on Resurrection*, 29.

107. Maimonides, *Moses Maimonides' Treatise on Resurrection*, 29. See Rosner, "Brief Description of the Treatise," 16.

complained of the fact that the denial of resurrection was rife among many of his coreligionists, that in support of their heretical views they ascribed an allegorical purport to the biblical and Rabbinic statements regarding resurrection, and that they further fortified their denial by some passages in the works of Maimonides himself. In view of this, the writer requested a Responsum for the clarification of these mooted points. Maimonides complied with the request.[108]

He explained "that the resurrection of the dead is a cardinal principle in the Torah, to wit, the return of the soul to the body which should not be explained (allegorically but accepted literally); and that life in the world to come—after the resurrection of the dead—is as [he] stated it in the chapter [*Perek Helek*], and [he] thought that this would be sufficient."[109]

Several members of the Yemenite community showed this communication of Maimonides to a powerful Baghdad *gaon* named Samuel ben Ali and asked him to comment on the issue of resurrection.[110] Ben Ali then published an essay on resurrection in which he accused Maimonides of denying the truth of the resurrection of the dead and postulating a purely spiritual or incorporeal bliss in the *Olam Ha-Bah*.[111] A copy of the essay of Samuel ben Ali was sent to Maimonides and prompted Maimonides to write an exposition of his views on resurrection of the dead entitled, in Hebrew translation from the original Arabic, *Ma'amar Tehiyyat ha-Metim*, or, in English, *Treatise on Resurrection*.[112]

Maimonides begins the *Treatise on Resurrection* by questioning ben Ali's competence in philosophy:

> Rabbi Samuel declares that scholarly philosophers do not say that it is impossible for the soul to return to the body after it has separated from it but that it is theoretically possible. This treatise proves that . . . he has no knowledge

---

108. Rosner, "Brief Description of the Treatise," 16. See Maimonides, *Moses Maimonides' Treatise on Resurrection*, 29 (individuals in Yemen who denied resurrection cited as evidence in support of their position what Maimonides had said about the world to come). See also Silver, *Maimonidean Criticism*, 37, 64.

109. Maimonides, *Moses Maimonides' Treatise on Resurrection*, 29–30. See also Silver, *Maimonidean Criticism*, 64 ("Yemenite correspondents requested of Maimonides an elucidation of his position. He answered at some length, restating his understanding of the tenet but insisting that resurrection is a basic creed not to be rationalized away nor to be taken in a figurative sense.").

110. See Rosner, "Brief Description of the Treatise," 16; Maimonides, *Moses Maimonides' Treatise on Resurrection*, 30; Silver, *Maimonidean Criticism*, 64.

111. Silver, *Maimonidean Criticism*, 64. See Maimonides, *Moses Maimonides' Treatise on Resurrection*, 30 (Ben Ali "wrote a treatise for [the Yemenites] on the resurrection of the dead wherein he represented [Maimonides's] words in this matter partly erroneously and falsely and partly in a manner that can perhaps be justified."); Rosner, "Brief Description of the Treatise," 16.

112. See Silver, *Maimonidean Criticism*, 65; Maimonides, *Moses Maimonides' Treatise on Resurrection*, 30; Rosner, "Brief Description of the Treatise," 16.

at all of the ways by which philosophers distinguish between the certain, the impossible, and the possible . . .

[This] learned Rabbi decreed and affirmed that philosophers do not believe in the immortality of souls, and that they argue on this point. I wonder: who are those whom he calls philosophers?

And we observe another amazing thing, and that is, that the intellect is not at all mentioned by that learned Rabbi. I do not know whether the soul and the intellect are one and the same thing in this philosophy, or whether the soul remains and the intellect perishes, or whether the intellect remains and the soul perishes . . . Perhaps, he conceives that the intellect is a property of the body as stated by the advisors whom he considers to be scholarly philosophers. If that be the case, it will certainly perish. . . .

Our intent in this, our treatise, is not to argue with any of the points included in his treatise . . . Rather, our aim is to provide benefit to the reflecting student, and not . . . to humiliate or demean anyone.[113]

The substantive portion of the *Treatise on Resurrection* starts off by defining resurrection of the dead as the return of the soul to the body after its separation, and reiterating that the resurrection of the dead is a "fundamental principle" as to which "there is no disagreement among the nation."[114] Yet, it is also stated that life in the world to come is without death precisely because "there are no (physical) bodies there," and it is further asserted that "every intelligent person accepts . . . that in the world to come souls without bodies will exist like angels."[115]

Maimonides goes on to deny that he ever said that it is impossible for the soul to return to the body; to the contrary, he states that belief in the return of the soul to the body is important.[116] Its importance, however, apparently has nothing directly to do with reward and punishment. Rather, the problem with denying resurrection of the dead is that it "leads to the denial of all miracles (chronicled in the Bible) and the denial of miracles is equivalent to denying the existence of God and abandonment of our faith."[117]

Not until the end of the *Treatise on Resurrection* does Maimonides further discuss his understanding of miracles. Here he distinguishes between "miracles [that] occur in manners that are consistent with the laws of nature" and miracles that are "outside the realm of nature."[118] The resurrection of the dead is of the latter kind, and thus "one cannot prove it in a speculative manner" but must simply believe it on the

---

113. Maimonides, *Moses Maimonides' Treatise on Resurrection*, 30–31. See Hyman, *Eschatological Themes*, 78.

114. Maimonides, *Moses Maimonides' Treatise on Resurrection*, 32.

115. Maimonides, *Moses Maimonides' Treatise on Resurrection*, 33.

116. Maimonides, *Moses Maimonides' Treatise on Resurrection*, 35.

117. Maimonides, *Moses Maimonides' Treatise on Resurrection*, 35. See generally Guttmann, *Philosophies of Judaism*, 158–62.

118. Maimonides, *Moses Maimonides' Treatise on Resurrection*, 48.

basis of the words of a prophet.[119] Rudavsky has argued that Maimonides doesn't really believe in miracles that are outside the realm of nature but included this category in the *Treatise on Resurrection* because this work was intended for the general public and Maimonides believed "that the masses [were] not yet ready to subject the supernatural externals of miracles to natural explanation."[120]

While thus insisting to the general public that he accepts the doctrine of resurrection, Maimonides is still far from clear as to where and how resurrection fits into his general eschatological schema. He says only that it will happen "at the time of His choice," that this could be "during the era of the Messiah or before him or after his death," and that those to be resurrected will be "those He wishes to resurrect."[121] In this context he addresses those people who had "raised doubts about [his] words at the end of [his] [*Mishneh Torah*, in *Hilkhot Melachim*] where [he states] the following: 'Do not think that the King Messiah will have to perform signs and wonders, bring anything new into being, resurrect the dead or do similar things.'"[122] He says that "[s]ome people with weak intellects think that this assertion represents a denial in the resurrection of the dead," but in reality, all that he meant is that the Messiah "will not be required to perform a miracle"; it does not preclude God from performing a miracle.[123]

Maimonides also considers the complaint that in all his writings he had merely mentioned that resurrection is a cardinal principle without providing any further elaboration, while he had "described the world to come at great lengths."[124] His response to this complaint is that he only elaborates on that which "needs to be elucidated" such as "an obscure subject" that is difficult to understand, but that "a miraculous event is not obscure nor difficult (to comprehend) . . .; rather we perceive it with our senses or accept it (as fact) from one who personally witnessed it."[125] Nor should he be faulted, he writes, for failing to expound "on all the (rabbinic) homiletically expositions and Talmudic narratives related to [resurrection] . . . Such is more appropriate for people other than [him] according to the intent of what they write."[126]

Two matters of *biblical* interpretation, however, *are* addressed: (1) the numerous scriptural passages which seem to clearly prove that resurrection of the dead is impossible, and (2) the "fact that the Torah does not mention this fundamental principle at

---

119. Maimonides, *Moses Maimonides' Treatise on Resurrection*, 40–41, 46.
120. Rudavsky, *Maimonides*, 127. See also Rudavsky, *Maimonides*, 104–5
121. Maimonides, *Moses Maimonides' Treatise on Resurrection*, 37.
122. Maimonides, *Moses Maimonides' Treatise on Resurrection*, 36–37.
123. Maimonides, *Moses Maimonides' Treatise on Resurrection*, 37. Maimonides ignores his other statements to the effect that during the messianic period nothing extraordinary will occur.
124. Maimonides, *Moses Maimonides' Treatise on Resurrection*, 39.
125. Maimonides, *Moses Maimonides' Treatise on Resurrection*, 40.
126. Maimonides, *Moses Maimonides' Treatise on Resurrection*, 41.

all, either in the form of an allusion and certainly not explicitly."[127] Regarding the first matter, Maimonides cites many of the biblical passages which claim resurrection to be impossible such as "*If a man die, may he live again?* [Job 14:14]" and "*For we must needs die, and are as water spilt on the ground which cannot be gathered up again* [2 Sam 14:14]."[128] These passages, he says, are part of "narratives describing the existence of nature in its usual manner" and it is not part of nature that a living being "return and exist again after its death"; rather "they die and slowly dissolve until they disintegrate into the elements and the original substance from which they came" except that the human soul or intellect [in contrast to the human body] "does not perish nor become lost" but, as part of its nature, is immortal.[129]

Regarding the second matter—that the resurrection is not mentioned in the Torah—Maimonides, distinguishing between the Torah and the prophetic books, explains:

> The reason for this is that the resurrection of the dead will indeed occur as a miraculous event [unlike the world to come which is a natural event] . . . and the credibility of such an event can only be based on the words of the prophet. At that time [sc., the giving of the Torah at Sinai] (nearly) all mankind belonged to the sect of Sabeans who . . . deny the transmission of prophecy from God to mankind. . . . How then could the Torah describe a basic tenet which requires belief in (the words of) a prophet to someone to whom the whole concept of prophecy is unacceptable? . . . [After God] produced the great miracles recorded throughout the Torah to authenticate thereby the prophecy of the prophets . . . [and] there remained no doubt about the (truth of) the prophesies of the prophets nor about the occurrence of miracles . . . the prophets narrated to us that which they were told by the Almighty concerning the resurrection of the dead [e.g., Dan 12:2–3] and it became easy to accept it.[130]

In the final analysis, assuming that the laws of nature can be contravened (and that Maimonides does in fact believe that they can be contravened) so that resurrection is theoretically possible, Maimonides provides no compelling reason why resurrection is needed and should occur. It plays no significant role in his scheme of reward and punishment or eschatology. Even if one is resurrected, the real reward for obedience to God's commandments is the nonphysical life of the world to come. Thus, it isn't surprising that many have contended that, despite his assertions that resurrection is a fundamental principle and must be accepted, Maimonides, qua philosopher, didn't believe in resurrection, and certainly didn't consider it a truly important doctrine.[131]

---

127. Maimonides, *Moses Maimonides' Treatise on Resurrection*, 41–47.
128. Maimonides, *Moses Maimonides' Treatise on Resurrection*, 41–42.
129. Maimonides, *Moses Maimonides' Treatise on Resurrection*, 43.
130. Maimonides, *Moses Maimonides' Treatise on Resurrection*, 46–47.
131. Rudavsky has summed up the Maimonidean position on resurrection as follows: "Clearly, Maimonides' heart is not in proving that the doctrine of resurrection of the body is philosophically

8.

Nahmanides and Other Early Kabbalists Adopt the Concept of Transmigration of Souls

KABBALAH ORIGINATED IN THE twelfth century in Provence.[1] The kabbalistic movement soon spread from Provence to nearby Catalonia. According to Scholem, the "first recognizable group of kabbalists crystallizing in Spain had its center during the first half of the thirteenth century in Gerona, a small Catalan city situated between Barcelona and the Pyrenees."[2] The kabbalists in Gerona were composed of men whose ideas have been shown by Altmann to possess roots going back to the Neoplatonism of Isaac Israeli.[3] The best known among them is Rabbi Moses ben Nahman (Nahmanides or Ramban). Among the earliest kabbalistic texts is a pseudepigraphal book called *Sefer ha-Bahir*.[4] The *Bahir* represented the canonical text upon which the Spanish kabbalists based themselves and to which they made constant reference until it was replaced by the *Sefer ha-Zohar*.[5] The *Zohar*, as the *Bahir*, is written in pseudepigraphic form, but is now generally understood to have been authored, for the most part, by the Spanish kabbalist Moses de Leon.[6]

---

tenable. He presents it as a view outside the purview of rationality, as contrary to the national order, and does not even try to offer rational arguments on its behalf. Maimonides half-heartedly accedes to the masses, realizing how important the doctrine is to them theologically, but does not accept it himself" (Rudavsky, *Maimonides*, 106). See also Rudavsky, *Maimonides*, 107; Hyman, "Maimonides' 'Thirteen Principles,'" 144; Gillman, *Death of Death*, 163–64; Silver, *Maimonidean Criticism*, 38–40. But see Hyman, *Eschatological Themes*, 79.

1. See Scholem, *Origins of the Kabbalah*, 12. See generally Dweck, *Scandal of Kabbalah*, 2–4.

2. Scholem, *Origins of the Kabbalah*, 365.

3. See Altmann, *Studies in Religious Philosophy and Mysticism*, 128–39. See also Sirat, *Jewish Philosophy in the Middle Ages*, 247 ("the thought of Solomon Ibn Gabirol ... had a great influence on the Kabbalah.").

4. See Scholem, *Origins of the Kabbalah*, 39–43; Eylon, *Reincarnation in Jewish Mysticism*, 1–2. See also Scholem, *On the Mystical Shape of the Godhead*, 197; Verman, *Books of Contemplation*, 166–70.

5. See Scholem, *Origins of the Kabbalah*, 44.

6. See generally Scholem, *Major Trends in Jewish Mysticism*, 156–204.

CHAPTER 8.

What is most significant in the present context is the kabbalists' embrace of the notion they came to refer to as *gilgul neshamot*, the "transmigration of souls" or *metempsychosis*.[7] The early kabbalists taught this doctrine, as well as their basic theosophic doctrine, as a mystery to be strictly limited to initiates. Such esoteric views were in writings often merely alluded to. not clearly explained. This was certainly true in the case of Nahmanides—his kabbalistic writings "abound with half—and quarter—hints, or are couched wholly in the language of allusion."[8] Kabbalists were opposed to the rationalism of the Aristotelians;[9] and Aristotelians were opposed to *metempsychosis*.[10]

A. Nahmanides Challenges the Maimonidean Understanding of *Olam Ha-Bah* and Emphasizes Both Bodily Resurrection and Transmigration of Souls to Resolve the Problem of Moral Evil

Among Nahmanides's principal works is *Torat Ha-Adam*, the bulk of which deals with legal issues concerning illness, visiting the sick, death, burial and mourning, etc.[11] The last chapter of *Torat Ha-Adam* is called *Shaar Ha-Gemul* (The Gate of Reward). *Shaar Ha-Gemul* addresses matters involving reward and punishment resulting from performance or violation of the commandments, and from the doing of good or wicked deeds. Other relevant works of Nahmanides include his *Commentaries on the Torah* and a discourse that he delivered in the city of Acco dubbed the "Discourse on *Rosh Ha-Shanah*."

---

7. See generally Scholem, *Origins of the Kabbalah*, 457 ("The term *gilgul*, generally used at a later date for the transmigration of souls, seems to be as yet unknown among [the] early [kabbalistic] authors. Instead, they preferred to speak of *sod ha-'ibbur*."). The term *sod ha-'ibbur* was used by Nahmanides and his disciple, R. Sheshet des Mercadell (Eylon, *Reincarnation in Jewish Mysticism*, 7; Scholem, *On the Mystical Shape of the Godhead*, 208n21).

8. Scholem, *Origins of the Kabbalah*, 367. See also Verman, *Books of Contemplation*, 26; Chajes, *Between Two Worlds*, 15 ("Ramban, an active disputant with Christians over matters of messianic belief, may have thought it indiscreet to treat the subject of reincarnation openly, given the sensitivity of the issue. No less plausible a reason for the secrecy shrouding discussions of reincarnation in early kabbalistic literature is the simple fact that so much earlier Jewish literature implicitly or explicitly denied it as heretical, figuring nowhere in biblical or rabbinic literature, and complicating if not contradicting classical Jewish eschatological beliefs such as resurrection.").

9. See Guttmann, *Philosophies of Judaism*, 255; Scholem, *Major Trends in Jewish Mysticism*, 24. See generally Scholem, *Origins of the Kabbalah*, 6–12.

10. See Eylon, *Reincarnation in Jewish Mysticism*, 6; Fontaine, *In Defense of Judaism*, 80 (Ibn Daud's refutation of the notion of transmigration of souls is based on the Aristotelian principle that the body and soul "constitute a single whole."). See Sirat, *Jewish Philosophy in the Middle Ages*, 150; Davidson, *Alfarabi, Avicenna and Averroes*, 196 (Ibn Daud proves, as Avicenna did, "that transmigration is impossible because it would entail two souls in a single body, namely, the soul required by the 'blend' of matter and the transmigrating soul"; citing *Sefer ha-Emunah ha-Ramah*). Cf. Adamson, *Philosophy in the Islamic World*, 136. See also Scholem, *On the Mystical Shape of the Godhead*, 197 ("official Jewish theology, as represented by medieval Jewish philosophy, was emphatically opposed to this doctrine [of reincarnation].").

11. Hyman, *Eschatological Themes*, 8; Nahmanides, *Gate of Reward*, v; Raphael, *Jewish Views of the Afterlife*, 263.

One of the main interests of Nahmanides in *Shaar Ha-Gemul* is to correct the position of Maimonides and some "Spanish Sages," including especially Ibn Gabirol, that the *Olam Ha-Bah* is presently existing and that one's soul enters the world to come immediately after death.[12] For Nahmanides, the fate of the soul immediately after death is to be sharply distinguished from the *Olam Ha-Bah*. Another main concern of Nahmanides is theodicy; he wants to answer all questions concerning the problem of moral evil. It is in connection with this second concern that he mentions the doctrine of the transmigration of souls.

1. Nahmanides's view of the nature of man and the soul

Nahmanides is not interested in psychology; his concern is with eschatology and theodicy. He simply accepts as true what had become by then the generally accepted conception of the nature of man. This conception is essentially Platonic; man is composed of a body and a soul. He is, however, cognizant of the philosophical question whether there are three different souls—the "soul of growth," the "soul of movement," and the "rational soul"—or whether there is but one soul with "three forces."[13] He states that the "plain meaning" of Genesis 2:7 indicates that the soul is but one; yet he also cites Onkelos and rabbinic authorities that opine that there are various souls in man.[14] He doesn't seem interested in deciding the matter.

But Nahmanides *is* eager to object to the Neoplatonic view that the soul is something created through emanation. He states that Genesis 2:7 "affirms that [man's soul] is given through the breath of G-d, and is not something which evolved [from the Separate Intelligences]."[15] To say that it is given "through the breath of God" indicates to Nahmanides that the soul is part of the divine essence.[16] Commenting on Genesis 2:1, he says that "the souls of men are included in the host of heaven," the "host of the heaven" also including "the two luminaries and the stars" and "the Separate Intelligences."[17] Because the soul is part of the divine essence, and not a composite of the four elements, it is not subject to decomposition, and so, by its own nature, exists after the death of the body.[18]

---

12. Nahmanides, *Gate of Reward*, 127–28. See Hyman, *Eschatological Themes*, 8–9.
13. Nahmanides, *Commentary on the Torah*, 1:67.
14. Nahmanides, *Commentary on the Torah*, 1:67–68.
15. Nahmanides, *Gate of Reward*, 58. See Hyman, *Eschatological Themes*, 92. See also Nahmanides, *Commentary on the Torah*, 1:66 (the soul is not "an evolvement from the Separate Intelligences"). See generally Scholem, *Origins of the Kabbalah*, 455.
16. See Nahmanides, *Commentary on the Torah*, 1:66n286.
17. Nahmanides, *Commentary on the Torah*, 1:59.
18. See Nahmanides, *Commentary on the Torah*, 4:278–79 ("Scripture did not need to state that as a reward for [fulfillment of] the commandments the soul will exist [after the death of the body, for it is self-understood from a knowledge of the nature of the soul], but instead it states that as a punishment for sins, the soul will be desecrated and defiled, and become cut off from its proper existence.").

CHAPTER 8.

Regarding the exact nature of the soul, Nahmanides is not completely clear. He states that the soul is "not a [material] body"[19] and is not "confined by space,"[20] suggesting that the soul is something incorporeal. Yet, he also suggests the soul is made of light[21] and is something "ethereal,"[22] implying some degree of materiality, albeit a very refined materiality. He acknowledges that he is being intentionally cryptic, stating:

> This, though, is the position of our Rabbis of blessed memory: The Holy One, blessed be He, created the souls of the righteous, which are undoubtedly [composed] of the clearest and lightest spirits. They are neither some material body, nor are they limited or confined by space. They are unlike other spirits which can be caught in leather bottles but are rather of the class of angels and are most ethereal. *This is not the place to explain all the concepts thereof* . . . Our Rabbis of blessed memory said that [the souls] were formed on the first day [of Creation] as a part of the formation of light by the Will of G-d, Who established this lower world, the upper clear heavens, and all the material and intellectual hosts.[23]

Nahmanides recognizes that there is a problem in stating that the soul is incorporeal, and cannot be limited or confined by space, while at the same time stating that the soul is associated with a particular human body. He rejects the explanation of the Neoplatonists who claim that the soul is confined to the body only in the sense that it operates the functions of the body.[24] Instead, Nahmanides suggests that there may actually be two souls, the second one being "coarser" so that the two souls "become closely attached to each other, the thin one existing in the coarser one which is the power of movement covered in the natural heat of the blood. The coupling together of these two [souls] is analogous to [the relationship of] the knot of the flame to the wick, whose connection is maintained by means of the oil between them."[25] In the end Nahmanides says that we simply don't know how the soul is joined to the body, but he is certain that it is.[26]

---

19. Nahmanides, *Gate of Reward*, 62. Accord, Nahmanides, *Gate of Reward*, 58.
20. Nahmanides, *Gate of Reward*, 58.
21. Nahmanides, *Gate of Reward*, 58.
22. Nahmanides, *Gate of Reward*, 62. Accord, *Gate of Reward*, 58 (the souls of the righteous "are neither some material body, nor are they limited or confined to space . . . but are rather of the class of angels and are most ethereal."). See Hyman, *Eschatological Themes*, 92 ("Akin to angelic beings, the human soul consists of a 'pure and extremely subtle spirit' (*ruah zakah ve-dakah beyoter*)"; citing Hebrew version of previously quoted passage from *Gate of Reward*).
23. Nahmanides, *Gate of Reward*, 58 (emphasis added).
24. See ch. 6, sec. A.
25. Nahmanides, *Gate of Reward*, 62.
26. Nahmanides, *Gate of Reward*, 61–63. See Hyman, *Eschatological Themes*, 93 ("In the end, Nahmanides follows the rabbinic tradition").

2. There are three periods at which an individual is judged, the first of which is at the New Year

In *Shaar Ha-Gemul* Nahmanides contends that according to rabbinic tradition there are three periods when one is judged: (1) each year at the New Year, (2) immediately following death, and (3) at "the day of the great judgment," the time of resurrection.[27] The "thing" receiving reward or punishment is different at each of the three periods, as is the nature of the reward and punishment. What is most important to Nahmanides, however, is that the reward or punishment received by any being at any time be commensurate with the relevant conduct and be completely justifiable.[28] The thing receiving reward or punishment at the time of the New Year is the "body"[29]; the reward received is that it is "inscribed and sealed for life," which is to say that it is assigned "life, peace, riches, wealth and honor"; and the punishment received is that it is "sealed for death," which is to say that it is assigned "plagues, poverty, death of children, and similar mishaps."[30]

The "bodies" receiving reward or punishment are divided into three classes—the "thoroughly righteous," the "thoroughly wicked," and the "intermediates." This terminology is misleading, for one may have committed sins and yet be classified among the "thoroughly righteous," and one may have performed meritorious deeds and yet be classified among the "thoroughly wicked." This is because, if one who has committed sins is yet "acquitted" by God at "trial," he is considered "thoroughly righteous," and one "who is declared guilty in his trial is called 'thoroughly wicked' [although he may have performed many meritorious deeds]."[31] The third class of "intermediates" include those for whom the "scales are equal on each side."[32] Decision on the intermediates is postponed until the Day of Atonement. "If, through repentance, prayer, and charity, they acquire merit during that time, they are definitely inscribed for a judgment of life. If not, they are inscribed for a judgment of death."[33]

After providing this account of the judgment that takes place on the New Year, Nahmanides immediately raises the problem of moral evil, stating that "[It is quite plain that] any number of righteous people do indeed die forthwith and [that] any

27. Nahmanides, *Gate of Reward*, 4–5, 7, 76. See Nahmanides, "Discourse on *Rosh Ha-Shanah*," 47–48.

28. Nahmanides, *Gate of Reward*, 8 (each person is subject to reward or punishment "according to [their] deeds"). See Hyman, *Eschatological Themes*, 90.

29. See Nahmanides, "Discourse on *Rosh Ha-Shanah*," 41, 48.

30. Nahmanides, *Gate of Reward*, 3–4 ("The Sages refer to all punishments in this world . . . under the term 'death,' and they spoke of attaining meritorious reward as 'life.'"). See Nahmanides, "Discourse on *Rosh Ha-Shanah*," 41, 55.

31. Nahmanides, "Discourse on *Rosh Ha-Shanah*," 54. Cf. Maimonides, *Book of Knowledge*, 83b (*Hilkhot T'shuvah*, 3:1–2).

32. Nahmanides, "Discourse on *Rosh Ha-Shanah*," 54.

33. Nahmanides, "Discourse on *Rosh Ha-Shanah*," 54. Nahmanides, "Discourse on *Rosh Ha-Shanah*," 42n145. See Nahmanides, *Gate of Reward*, 2.

number of wicked people live prolonged lives in tranquility!"[34] Nahmanides raises the same concern more expansively in the "Discourse on *Rosh Ha-Shanah*."[35] Part of Nahmanides's explanation for this apparent injustice is to point to another period of judgment, specifically to the judgment that occurs at the time of the resurrection, which period he calls the "World to Come." He states that some iniquities and some good deeds must be punished or rewarded, respectively, in this world, while others must be punished or rewarded, respectively, in the World to Come. Accordingly, a wicked person who has performed some good deeds for which he is required to be rewarded in this world may at the New Year be included among the righteous and inscribed and sealed for life, though in the World to Come he will be "utterly destroyed"; correspondingly, one who is essentially a righteous person and whose good deeds will merit reward in the World to Come may have "stumbled by committing one sin and was [consequently] inscribed on the New Year for death."[36]

3. The second period of judgment occurs after death in the World of Souls

Regarding judgment that occurs at death, Nahmanides says:

> Each and every person . . . is subject to judgment at the time of his death, and his fate is decided in accordance with one of [the] three essential groups: the thoroughly righteous are immediately inscribed and sealed and enter *Gan Eden* . . .; the thoroughly wicked are immediately sealed and enter Gehenna and are punished there; the intermediates cry out [in prayer] to be removed therefrom to a place of tranquility, as we are prepared to explain.[37]

The "thing" that is the subject of reward and punishment at the time of death cannot be the body for "is not a person's body after death like a silent stone?"[38] Accordingly, the reward or punishment received must be "only for the soul."[39] Since the world to which the soul of a person goes immediately following the death of the body is a world comprised of the souls of the dead, Nahmanides refers to this world as the "World of Souls."[40]

The type of reward or punishment meted out in the World of Souls cannot be of a bodily or physical type for the soul is immaterial, not occupying any space. So, how can Scripture and rabbinic tradition speak of punishment by fire when "fire has

---

34. Nahmanides, *Gate of Reward*, 2.

35. Nahmanides, "Discourse on *Rosh Ha-Shanah*," 50–51. See Nahmanides, *Gate of Reward*, 27.

36. Nahmanides, *Gate of Reward*, 3–4. See Nahmanides, *Gate of Reward*, 9–10. See also Nahmanides, "Discourse on *Rosh Ha-Shanah*," 52–53. Cf. Nahmanides, *Gate of Reward*, 12–13 (discussing why most Israelites experience more trouble and pain in this world than the people of other nations).

37. Nahmanides, *Gate of Reward*, 7. Cf. b. Šabb. 152b, discussed in ch. 6, sec. C, 2.

38. Nahmanides, *Gate of Reward*, 51.

39. Nahmanides, *Gate of Reward*, 51.

40. Nahmanides, *Gate of Reward*, 5. See Nahmanides, "Discourse on *Rosh Ha-Shanah*," 47.

an effect only upon such things of physical properties?"[41] Similarly, if *Gehenna* is a physical place, how can *Gehenna* be the place where the soul is punished, as tradition states? Nahmanides begins his discussion of these questions by stating that "the entire Gemara and [all the] Midrashim of our Rabbis are explicit on the matter of Gehenna and [the nature of] that punishment."[42] Specifically, the rabbis say that after-death punishment is received in *Gehenna*, that *Gehenna* is an actual physical location hundreds of times larger than the "world," and that the nature of the punishment is by fire.[43] These teachings of the rabbis, says Nahmanides, must be taken literally—they "cannot be interpreted as a parable."[44]

Nahmanides states that in whatever way the soul can be confined to the individual body so too can the soul be confined to *Gehenna*. Moreover, the fire which punishes the soul in *Gehenna* is not the same as the fire in this world. The fire in *Gehenna* is of an ethereal or immaterial nature. This is established to the satisfaction of Nahmanides by the talmudic teaching that "'Our [earthly] fire was created on the night following the Sabbath, and the fire of Gehenna was created on the second day [of Creation]'" in that "things created on the first day are more refined . . . than those things created on the second day" and things created on the second day are more refined than those created on the third, etc.[45] The intensity of the punishment that each soul receives in *Gehenna* depends on the severity of its wickedness, for "in Gehenna, there can be more pain and suffering for one sinner than there is for another . . . Everything is done by true judgment and equitable law, as it is said, *for all His ways are justice* [Deut 32:4]."[46] For "the lesser [sins], there is no fixed time [for punishment]. Instead, each person is punished according to his deeds, and when he cries out [in prayer], he rises again. For the gravest sins, [however, the punishment extends] for all generations."[47] The time of punishment for those whose sins are no greater than their merits [sc., the "intermediates"] is twelve-months.[48]

In the World of Souls the place where reward is received is *Gan Eden*.[49] This is supported by numerous rabbinic passages in which *Gehenna* is contrasted with *Gan Eden* as the places, respectively, of punishment and reward.[50] Nahmanides then cites

---

41. Nahmanides, *Gate of Reward*, 51–52. See Hyman, *Eschatological Themes*, 91.
42. Nahmanides, *Gate of Reward*, 52.
43. See Nahmanides, *Gate of Reward*, 53–58.
44. Nahmanides, *Gate of Reward*, 58. See Hyman, *Eschatological Themes*, 91–92.
45. Nahmanides, *Gate of Reward*, 59 (quoting b. Pesaḥ. 54a). See Nahmanides, *Gate of Reward*, 58–64.
46. Nahmanides, *Gate of Reward*, 8.
47. Nahmanides, *Gate of Reward*, 8. See also Nahmanides, *Gate of Reward*, 70–73.
48. Nahmanides, *Gate of Reward*, 8.
49. Nahmanides, *Gate of Reward*, 82, 85.
50. See Nahmanides, *Gate of Reward*, 82–85.

numerous passages to demonstrate that *Gan Eden* is "an actual garden on the earth"[51]; but the "*Gan*" and "*Eden*" on earth are mere "illustrations of higher secrets," and "allude" to "higher matters" that "are also termed *Gan* and *Eden*."[52] He continues: "In the higher [spheres], there is a concept allusively designated *Gan* in the words of our Rabbis, and [there is] an even higher concept than that which is designated *Eden*. This is termed *the bundle of life*. The profound secrets of these [two concepts] is held by those who have received the faith."[53] The reference to "the bundle of life" indicates the divine treasury of souls that kabbalists well understood by this time to exist under the "Throne of Glory" and to which Nahmanides specifically refers to in the following paragraph.[54] He specifically states that when a person dies, God "places [the soul] in the [heavenly] treasury, as it is said, *and the soul of my lord* [David] *shall be bound in the bundle of life* [1 Sam 25:29]"[55]; the wicked soul, however, is cast out and sent to *Gehenna* for punishment.[56] The nature of the reward that Nahmanides envisions for the remaining righteous souls is the contemplation of the divine presence through either an "opaque speculum" or a "lucid speculum."[57] Nahmanides says the term "contemplating" [*histakluth*] is used by the rabbis "to indicate rational contemplation and [the achievement of] a superior degree of understanding."[58] Although not mentioned in *Shaar Ha-Gemul*, in the "Discourse on *Rosh Ha-Shanah*" Nahmanides suggests that there are gradations of merit in *Gan Eden*, and even seems to say that the higher and lower *Gan Eden* are related to such differing degrees of merit,[59] but he doesn't elaborate on this comment and his exact meaning is unclear.

One further point about reward and punishment in the World of Souls needs to be mentioned—the meaning of "the great punishment of excision."[60] Nahmanides explains excision as follows: Immediately after death each soul naturally ascends

51. Nahmanides, *Gate of Reward*, 88–90.

52. Nahmanides, *Gate of Reward*, 90.

53. Nahmanides, *Gate of Reward*, 90 (emphasis original). See also Nahmanides, "Discourse on *Rosh Ha-Shanah*," 47.

54. Nahmanides, *Gate of Reward*, 90 (quoting b. Šabb. 152b). The imagery of the bundle of life, or *tzror ha-hayyim*, was employed in the popular poetry of Ibn Gabirol, and came to be understood, especially by kabbalists, as referring to a transcendent realm of souls. Nahmanides also mentions b. Hagigah 12a, which refers to the "souls of the righteous . . . and souls destined to be born" existing in Arabot, the seventh heaven. (Nahmanides, *Gate of Reward*, 90).

55. Nahmanides, *Gate of Reward*, 92.

56. Nahmanides, *Gate of Reward*, 92.

57. See Nahmanides, *Gate of Reward*, 90–91.

58. Nahmanides, *Gate of Reward*, 91. The term *histakluth* is related to the religious, mystical experience for which the term *devekuth* comes to be used by later kabbalists. Scholem, *Major Trends in Jewish Mysticism*, 341–42.

59. Nahmanides, "Discourse on *Rosh Ha-Shanah*," 47 (When a person's soul is judged after death "all his deeds are individually accounted for before his Creator . . . [and it is determined] whether his soul deserves to be in the higher or lower Gan Eden and which gradation thereof he merits.").

60. See generally Nahmanides, *Gate of Reward*, 64–73.

upward and tries to cleave to the "higher existences" since the nature of the human soul, as that of the higher existences, is to return to the Creator.[61] However, the soul of a wicked person is inhibited by its "thick coarseness" from fully ascending, and it is instead "pulled into" and joins "the fire of Gehenna," a

> River of Fire, which emerges from under the Throne of Glory [and which is] comprised of the elements of the [fiery] sphere ... With [the souls of the wicked], it rolls and descends there [to Gehenna] ... *This is the essence of excision*, which is to say that the soul is cut off from its foundation as a branch is cut off from a tree which has given it life. Thus the Sages said [b. Šabb. 152b]: 'And [the souls of] the wicked are continually *zom'moth* (muzzled or tied up), as it is said, *and the souls of thine enemies, them shall he sling out, as from the hollow of a sling.*' [1 Sam 25:29].[62]

4. The third period of judgment occurs at the time of the resurrection preceding the World to Come

Nahmanides begins his discussion of the third period of judgment by declaring: "As far as the Rabbis are concerned, the principal reward for [the observance of] all the commandments lies in the World to Come."[63] According to Nahmanides, the rabbis have interpreted b. Sanhedrin 90a in a manner which leaves no doubt that the World to Come is to be understood as the time of the resurrection of the dead.[64] Nahmanides goes on to refer to rabbinic passages that "distinguished between the era of the Messiah and the future world, which is the world after the resurrection."[65] He concludes: "All these statements [of the rabbis] clearly indicate that the World to Come ... is not [synonymous with] the World of Souls and the reward which reaches the deceased immediately after death. Rather, it is the world which the Holy One, blessed be He, will create after the era of Messiah and the resurrection of the dead."[66]

The "being" that will be rewarded in the World to Come is the reunited body and soul, but the body and soul in the World to Come will be very different from the body and soul in the present world. In the present world, the soul has no ascendancy over the body because the soul must use the "physical powers" of the body. Further, in the present world the body is physical or material, and must be sustained by food

---

61. See Nahmanides, *Gate of Reward*, 66–67.

62. Nahmanides, *Gate of Reward*, 66–67 (emphasis added). Cf. ch. 6, sec. B, 3 (According to Isaac Israeli, the soul of the wicked will "remain contained under the sphere, sorrowful, in pain without measure, revolving with the revolution of the sphere in the great fire and the torturing flame.").

63. Nahmanides, *Gate of Reward*, 96.

64. Nahmanides, *Gate of Reward*, 97.

65. Nahmanides, *Gate of Reward*, 101.

66. Nahmanides, *Gate of Reward*, 105. Accord, Nahmanides, *Gate of Reward*, 109. See Hyman, *Eschatological Themes*, 100–1.

and drink. However, in the World to Come the soul "will be endowed with angelic qualities"[67] and will gain ascendancy over the body because the soul will not need the "physical powers" of the body but will "see" and "hear" by nonphysical means.[68] In addition, the body will not be sustained by food and drink. Instead, the bodies of those who are pure of soul will be composed of and sustained by subtle things (*devarim dakim*), and the bodies of the purest souls will be composed of and sustained by the subtlest things (*devarim dakim min ha-medakkim*).[69] More specifically, in the World to Come the body will be sustained by the "Higher Light" or the "Higher Glory."[70] Just as Moses was sustained on Mount Sinai for forty days without food by virtue of the glory of the divine presence, and just as "the *Chayoth* who bear the Throne are sustained by the Divine Glory," so the "ascendancy of the soul over the body annuls the physical powers . . . and causes the body to exist without food and drink."[71] Moreover, this body will not be subject to death.[72] For those who doubt that a body can exist without being subject to death, Nahmanides says that the cases of Elijah and Enoch prove otherwise.[73]

In the World to Come the intermediates join the righteous in *Gan Eden*, since "the Holy One . . . inclines the scale toward goodness [and does not condemn them]."[74] The fate of most of the wicked in the World to Come is the same as the intermediates, since "all Israel have a portion in the World to Come."[75] Only the most egregiously wicked are denied entry into the World to Come. Those having such great wickedness include worshippers of idols and heretics, the Sadducees, scoffers, deniers of the Torah, the people of the generation of the flood, those who says that the resurrection

67. Nahmanides, *Gate of Reward*, 113.

68. See Nahmanides, *Gate of Reward*, 95, 110.

69. See Nahmanides, *Gate of Reward*, 111; Hyman, *Eschatological Themes*, 101. This description suggests that the combined souls and resurrected bodies of the righteous will have gradations for merit to at least some degree, with the most righteous being given the most ethereal bodies and, consequently being closer to the Divine Presence.

70. See Nahmanides, *Gate of Reward*, 111–12 ("The people [of the generation of the wilderness], who ate the manna, were sustained by that food, which was absorbed into their limbs. The manna was the product of the Higher Light which became tangible through the Will of its Creator . . . [T]hose [inheriting eternal life in] the World to Come will exist by the substance of the manna which is the Higher Glory.").

71. Nahmanides, *Gate of Reward*, 110. See also Nahmanides, *Gate of Reward*, 95–96; Nahmanides, *Commentary on the Torah*, 2:226–28.

72. Nahmanides, *Gate of Reward*, 113 (all who merit existence in the future world "will live forever").

73. Nahmanides, *Gate of Reward*, 110–11. See Hyman, *Eschatological Themes*, 101.

74. Nahmanides, *Gate of Reward*, 5. See also Nahmanides, *Gate of Reward*, 66 ("the Rabbis said in Yerushalmi Tractate Peiah [I, 1]: 'One whose majority of deeds are meritorious inherits *Gan Eden*. One whose majority of deeds are sins inherits Gehenna. Rabbi Yosei bar Chanina said that if the scales on both sides are equal, the Holy One . . . seizes one count from the sins, and the merits [then] outweigh [the number of sins.]'").

75. Nahmanides, *Gate of Reward*, 74.

of the dead is not a doctrine of the Torah or that the Torah is not transmitted from heaven, those who abandon the ways of the community, those who sinned and caused the masses to sin, and those who spread their terror in the land of the living.[76] It is because only the most egregiously wicked are denied a share in the World to Come that all others (including the righteous, the nonegregiously wicked, and the intermediates) must receive the full measure of punishment for whatever iniquities they have committed in this world or in the World of Souls. Such punishment in this world might include, especially, "bodily excision," i.e., early death, and includes in the World of Souls being "cut off from life in *Gan Eden*."[77] Conversely, since even the egregiously wicked may have performed some good deeds, and since they receive no rewards in the World of Souls or in the World to Come, they must be rewarded in this world.[78]

It remains to describe the nature of the punishment of the egregiously wicked in the World to Come. They are, of course, "cut off" from the World to Come. But are their bodies resurrected and recombined with their souls? Nahmanides does not specifically say so, and it does not seem that he believed that they were. Rather, it appears that for Nahmanides resurrection was restricted to, and was part of the bliss of, the righteous.[79] This being so, it might be thought that the souls of the egregiously wicked would simply remain in *Gehenna* for perpetual torment from the refined, ethereal fire existing there. A problem with this thought is that it conflicts with the statement of a third-century Amora, Reish Lakish, who said that "there is no Gehenna in the future."[80] Accordingly, Nahmanides first asserts that the "sphere of the sun has a sheath" which weakens its strength so that it does "not go out and burn the world,"[81] and then asserts that in the World to Come, God "will strip [the protective sheath], and thereby burn the wicked with the sun."[82] By this means Nahmanides is able to

76. See Nahmanides, *Gate of Reward*, 6, 71, 75, 77, 97.

77. See Nahmanides, *Gate of Reward*, 69–70. This is why a person who "merits ascension to his deserved share of the portions of *Gan Eden*" may suffer bodily excision. See Nahmanides, *Gate of Reward*, 69–70. See also Nahmanides, *Gate of Reward*, 99 ("excision is the [untimely] loss of the soul from the body and its being prematurely cut off from this world.").

78. Nahmanides, *Gate of Reward*, 72–73.

79. See Nahmanides, *Gate of Reward*, 76 (Just as one is judged on the New Year and on the day of his death, "so will everyone be judged on the great day at the beginning of the resurrection concerning the subject of the future in the World to Come. [That is, it will be determined] whether he deserves to be resurrected and to enjoy the bliss of body and soul of that time."); Nahmanides, "Discourse on *Rosh Ha-Shanah*," 48 (On the day of great judgment it will be decided "whether this [particular individual] is worthy of the resurrection and the pleasant state of body and soul during the unending and continuous duration of all those times after the resurrection . . . , or if he should be condemned not to be resurrected and [to have his soul] remain in Gehinnom where it was or even double the measure of evil punishment upon it."). If the bodies of the egregiously wicked *were* to be resurrected, the question would arise as to the nature of such resurrected bodies. They certainly could not be the same type of ethereal body sustained by the Divine Light that the righteous receive.

80. See Nahmanides, *Gate of Reward*, 78–82.

81. Nahmanides, *Gate of Reward*, 79.

82. Nahmanides, *Gate of Reward*, 79–80.

reconcile the statement of Reish Lakish with statements about the wicked receiving punishment in *Gehenna*. Specifically, Nahmanides states:

> For those who are liable to excision, this judgment [cf terrible pain for the soul] is further increased twofold on the day of the great judgment. They are punished in Gehenna until they are destroyed there. According to Reish Lakish, [who says that there is no Gehenna in the future], they will be punished by the sun which will come out of its sheath. This [punishment] is still in the category of the suffering caused by the fire of Gehenna and originates from it.[83]

5. Nahmanides is unable to fully reconcile his disagreements with Maimonides concerning the World to Come

Nahmanides had great respect for Maimonides and strains to reconcile what Maimonides says about the afterlife with the views Nahmanides takes to be correct. In the end, however, full reconciliation proves to be impossible. The first problematic passages are in Maimonides's *Mishneh Torah* stating that the punishment of the wicked is that they will not merit bliss in the World to Come and that their souls will be "extirpated," or cease to exist.[84] The heart of one who sees these words, says Nahmanides, "may pound [for fear that] perhaps the opinion of the Rabbi . . . tends to state that there is no punishment and suffering for the sinning soul and that no trouble reaches it."[85] In other words, Maimonides could be understood to mean that the only afterlife punishment for the wicked is that their souls will be destroyed. For Nahmanides, such an afterlife "punishment" is not only "untrue by tradition"[86] but is unacceptable because the wicked soul would not really be punished and there would be no gradations of punishment for souls with varying degrees of wickedness.[87] Nahmanides deals with these Maimonidean passages by contending that they refer, not to punishment immediately after death, but to the "great punishment" *after* the soul was "first chastised with the punishments of Gehenna."[88] In support of this contention, Nahmanides quotes *Hilkhot T'shuvah* 3:5–6 which Nahmanides says shows that Maimonides "did

---

83. Nahmanides, *Gate of Reward*, 81–82.
84. Maimonides, *Book of Knowledge*, 90a, 90b (*Hilkhot T'shuvah*, 3:1, 5).
85. Nahmanides, *Gate of Reward*, 74.
86. Nahmanides, *Gate of Reward*, 65.
87. See Nahmanides, *Gate of Reward*, 65 ("Should [the sinner's soul] return to its elements . . . then it would be happy and [it would be] well with it."). Moreover, Nahmanides believes that, until the World to Come, nothing can be actually destroyed—things can only return to their constituent physical elements; and since human souls are not composed of physical elements, they have no physical components to which they can return (Nahmanides, *Gate of Reward*, 65).
88. Nahmanides, *Gate of Reward*, 74.

distinguish between those guilty of real excision and those guilty of [deserving only some] punishment."[89]

No such reinterpretation is available to reconcile the statement in Maimonides's *Commentary on the Mishnah* that *Gehenna* is not an actual place but only "a substitute designation for the punishment of the wicked."[90] Nahmanides is compelled to say that, in his opinion, "these are not satisfactory words" since "[i]n everyone's view, this [*Gehenna*] is a place which contains the wondrous ethereal fire that was created by G-d to punish and extirpate those that go far from him."[91] Interestingly, in his "Letter to the French Rabbis," written in 1232 in response to the ban on certain works of Maimonides imposed by the rabbinical authorities in northern France, Nahmanides defends Maimonides, while at the same time condemning anyone who denies the reality of punishment in *Gehenna*.[92]

By ignoring that for Maimonides the being existing in the *Olam Ha-Bah* is not the soul reunited with a body but only the soul, Nahmanides is able to say that the words "of the great Rabbi" are "precious," "pure," "excellent," "delightful," and "correct." The particular words so praised include (1) the statement that "[i]n the World to Come, our souls will attain the secrets of the Creator just as or [even] more than the stars and the spheres achieve those secrets," (2) the interpretation of b. Berakhot 17a (about there being no eating or drinking in the world to come but only delighting in the divine presence) as meaning that the souls of the righteous "will find delight in their attainment and knowledge of the Divine secret," and (3) the statement that no one knows the beauty and grandeur of the World to Come except God.[93] But then Nahmanides is compelled to again criticize Maimonides on two major points: Maimonides wrongly believes that (1) in the World to Come "there is no physical body or any material substance," and (2) "that the World to Come exists for the individual immediately after death."[94] In sharp contrast, Nahmanides holds that "the body exists in some fashion in the World to Come" and that "upon death those worthy of it enter *Gan Eden*, and the World to Come does not come to be until after the time of the

---

89. Nahmanides, *Gate of Reward*, 74–75. See Hyman, *Eschatological Themes*, 95.

90. Nahmanides, *Gate of Reward*, 75.

91. Nahmanides, *Gate of Reward*, 76. See Hyman, *Eschatological Themes*, 96 ("From Maimonides' explicit statement it follows that Maimonides believed that the judgment of sinners takes place immediately at the time of death and that this punishment consists of the excision of the soul, that is, its ceasing to exist. *Gehinnom*, for Maimonides, is simply another term for the nonexistence of the soul.").

92. Nahmanides, "Letter to the French Rabbis," 436–40 ("We have heard that you say that [Maimonides] is as one who denies the punishment in Gehinnom . . . But I . . . did not believe the report . . . G-d forbid [the entertaining] of a denial of the existence of Gehinnom . . . He who denies this [punishment in Gehinnom] rends the robe of the faith and the garment of the tradition in an unsewable, [irreparable] manner.").

93. Nahmanides, *Gate of Reward*, 119–21. See Hyman, *Eschatological Themes*, 104–5.

94. Nahmanides, *Gate of Reward*, 121–23. See Hyman, *Eschatological Themes*, 105.

Messiah and the time of the last judgment."[95] Yet, Nahmanides minimizes these differences by attributing them to "nomenclature."[96]

There may be merit in Nahmanides's assertion that the difference between him and Maimonides is one of nomenclature only. This is because Nahmanides's insistence on distinguishing the World to Come from the World of Souls has no significant practical consequence given that, according to Nahmanides, in the World to Come the body "will become like the soul" and the activity of the soul will be essentially identical with its activity in the World of Souls—it will cleave to the knowledge of the Most High. Later kabbalists followed Nahmanides in claiming that the "resurrected body will be totally spiritualized and transformed" so it is not surprising that these later kabbalists "deemphasized the doctrine of bodily resurrection."[97]

6. Resolving the problem of moral evil leads Nahmanides to accept the doctrine of the transmigration of souls

Much effort is expended by Nahmanides to explain the principles underlying God's reward and punishment so that it can be seen that such reward and punishment is just and proper. Except for things which "affect all people," such as eating certain bad foods which cause a stomachache or standing too long in the sun which causes a headache, all afflictions are caused by sin[98]; they are the result of either the commission of evil deeds, the failing to perform required deeds, or the failing to perform required deeds properly and with sufficient vigor.[99] No one suffers "for no sin whatsoever"; all suffering "comes only as an atonement [for sin]."[100]

Despite this bald assertion, Nahmanides does in fact recognize that other principles may also be at work. For example, there are "sufferings of trial," such as God's trial of Abraham.[101] These are not really "sufferings,"[102] and apply only to "His saints."[103] Additionally, there are "afflictions of love." When one "has neither committed any sins nor neglected the [positive] commandments, [then] his sufferings are but the visitations of [Divine] love. [He is being afflicted] . . . so that he will be given his complete

---

95. Hyman, *Eschatological Themes*, 105.

96. Nahmanides, *Gate of Reward*, 128. In footnote to the relevant sentence, Chavel writes, "While Maimonides uses the term *Olam Haba* (the World to Come) for both the World of Souls which one enters immediately after death and the World to Come after the resurrection, Ramban distinguishes between these two terms" (Nahmanides, *Gate of Reward*, 128).

97. Raphael, *Jewish Views of the Afterlife*, 324–25.

98. Nahmanides, *Gate of Reward*, 21–22.

99. Nahmanides, *Gate of Reward*, 16.

100. Nahmanides, *Gate of Reward*, 20–21.

101. Nahmanides, *Gate of Reward*, 22.

102. Nahmanides, *Gate of Reward*, 26 ("a trial cannot be classified among [forms of] suffering . . . It is instead an extension of the greater principle of [His] goodness.").

103. Nahmanides, *Gate of Reward*, 22.

reward in the World to Come."[104] Such afflictions are necessary because people may "sin through error"—for even though no true sin has been committed, the soul has been defiled. As Nahmanides states:

> The inadvertent [transgressor] . . . does not deserve to be punished for his error with Gehenna . . ., but he does require purification . . . For this reason, the Holy One . . . had compassion upon His people and His saints and gave them the offerings with which to atone for unintentional sins. [See Lev 4]. When the sanctuary is not in existence, He sends afflictions upon them in order to purify them from those unintentional sins and to [have them] atone for them with afflictions so that they will be cleansed [of transgression] in the World to Come.[105]

Paralleling these principles concerning afflictions visited upon the righteous are corresponding principles concerning "the suspension [of the punishment] of the wicked."[106] In this context Nahmanides mentions intergenerational reward.[107] He also mentions a sort of trial—God sometimes "ordains ease for the wicked in order to test men of wickedness . . . [But the wicked] will hold fast to their evil ways."[108] Most important, the wicked must be rewarded in this world for the few good deeds they have done in order that they may be utterly destroyed in the world to come.[109]

Although Nahmanides thus employs many principles to justify the prosperity of the wicked and the afflictions of the righteous, these principles don't explain every situation—"there are still thoroughly righteous men who . . . are chastised, and, thoroughly wicked people who live in ease and quietude in the world."[110] Nahmanides asks how such a thing is compatible with the way of God, and then asserts that this question "has no answer according to man's knowledge."[111] Most troubling of all to Nahmanides are the cases of Job and Rabbi Akiba. Regarding Rabbi Akiba, Nahmanides repeatedly refers to the following rabbinic teaching:

> Thus, the Rabbis related concerning Rabbi Akiba that the Holy One, blessed be He, showed [Rabbi Akiba] to Moses our teacher in the visions of prophesy.

---

104. Nahmanides, *Gate of Reward*, 17.

105. Nahmanides, *Gate of Reward*, 17–18.

106. Nahmanides, *Gate of Reward*, 26

107. Nahmanides, *Gate of Reward*, 26–27. Nahmanides also recognizes the possibility of intergenerational punishment. See Nahmanides, *Gate of Reward*, 29.

108. Nahmanides, *Gate of Reward*, 27.

109. See Nahmanides, *Gate of Reward*, 26.

110. Nahmanides, *Gate of Reward*, 31. See also Nahmanides, *Gate of Reward*, 50 ("we see any number of righteous people who perish [while studying] their books or while fasting and praying with the utmost intent of heart! There are people who are born deficiently, lacking certain organs of the body. There are those who die before reaching the age of twenty years, and yet from the moment they became knowledgeable, were righteous").

111. Nahmanides, *Gate of Reward*, 31.

[Moses] said before Him: 'Master of the universe! You have shown me erudition in Torah, [now] show me his reward.' Moses then saw how the Romans were cutting his flesh in a meat-market. Moses said before Him: 'Master of the universe! This is the Torah, and is this its reward?' He answered him: 'Be silent! The matter has entered in thought before Me.' The Sages intended to state therein that Rabbi Akiba did not deserve such a death of intolerable suffering in order to make allowance for his few evil deeds; he was thoroughly righteous all his life. [Their purport], rather, was that the matter is incomprehensible [to mortals].[112]

Despite the suggestion that the rabbis intended to convey the idea that human beings lack the ability to comprehend the afflictions of Rabbi Akiba, Nahmanides says that "this discussion contains a secret which is transmitted to Torah scholars and the tradition—intimated at in the words of our Rabbis and included in the subject of the secret of transmigration [of souls]—handed down by the Sages to their worthy pupils."[113] Similarly, in his discussion of the book of Job the doctrine of the transmigration of souls is again mentioned as resolving the challenge to God's justice that the book poses.[114] But as to how the doctrine of transmigration of souls resolves these challenges to God's justice Nahmanides remains silent.

B. The *Sefer ha-Bahir* Uses the Idea of Transmigration in the Context of Theodicy

The *Bahir* was published in Provence about twenty years prior to the birth of Nahmanides in Gerona, and the kabbalists of Gerona "were the first to embrace the teachings of the *Bahir*."[115] There is no doubt that the *Bahir* is a source for Nahmanides's acquaintance with the doctrine of the transmigration of souls.[116] The doctrine is presented in

---

112. Nahmanides, *Gate of Reward*, 31–32. See also Nahmanides, *Gate of Reward*, 50; Nahmanides, "Discourse on *Rosh Ha-Shanah*," 53; Nahmanides, *Commentary on the Torah*, 5:73.

113. Nahmanides, *Gate of Reward*, 32.

114. See Scholem, *Origins of the Kabbalah*, 458 ("Nahmanides discovered in the words of Elihu (Job 33) a clear indication and a great number of proof texts for [the doctrine of the transmigration of souls], in which all the problems of theodicy find their solution."); Scholem, *On the Mystical Shape of the Godhead*, 208 ("Nahmanides wrote an entire commentary to Job, finding the key to the book in [the doctrine of the transmigration of souls], which, according to him, is alluded to in Elihu's discourses to Job . . . [A]ll questions of theodicy, and especially the suffering of the righteous and the good fortune of the wicked, are answered by the doctrine of transmigration.").

115. See Eylon, *Reincarnation in Jewish Mysticism*, 7. See generally Scholem, *Origins of the Kabbalah*, 44. For a general discussion of the structure, sources, substance, and symbolism of the *Bahir*, see Scholem, *Origins of the Kabbalah*, 49–198.

116. See Eylon, *Reincarnation in Jewish Mysticism*, 7. See generally Scholem, *On the Mystical Shape of the Godhead*, 197–201 (In the *Bahir* the doctrine of *metempsychosis* "is taken for granted, and is elucidated without any apologetic tone . . . [which] is all the more remarkable, since during the period in which this book appeared, official Jewish theology, as represented by medieval Jewish philosophy, was emphatically opposed to this doctrine . . . [and] the classical Jewish tradition, as set down in the

the *Bahir* without yet using a special word for it (the term *gilgul* was used by later-day kabbalists).[117] In the *Bahir*, as in the writings of Nahmanides, transmigration of souls is used in the context of theodicy, as evidenced by section 135, which makes use of the parable in Isaiah 5 about one who planted the choicest grapes in his vineyard but saw it bring forth only wild or sour grapes:

> Why are there evildoers who are well off, and righteous who suffer evil? Because the righteous man was previously an evildoer in the past and is now being punished. But is a man to be punished for [the sins] of his youth? Has not Rabbi Simon said that one is only punished [by the heavenly court] from one's twentieth year on! Say to them: I am not speaking of the [same] life, but of that which was in the past. His colleagues said to him: How much longer will you speak unintelligibly? He said to them: Go and see. This is like a person who has planted a vineyard in his garden, and he hoped that it would bring forth grapes, and it brought forth wild grapes [after Isa 5:2]. He saw that he was not succeeding—so he replanted it, placed a fence around it, repaired the breaches, pruned [the vines of] the wild grapes, and planted it a second time. When he saw that he was not succeeding [for the second time]—he again fenced it off, and again replanted it after pruning. How often? He said to them: Until a thousand generations, as is written: 'He commanded a word to a thousand generations' [Ps 105:8]. This is what is meant by the [talmudic] saying [b. Hag. 13b]: 'Nine hundred seventy-four generations were lacking [for the figure of one thousand], when the Holy One, blessed be He, stood and planted them in every generation.'[118]

Transmigration of souls is thus compared to the replanting of a vineyard; as the owner of the vineyard seeks to improve the quality of his grapes by repeatedly replanting the vineyard, so God seeks to improve the purity of a human soul by "replanting" it into a new body.[119] Because a soul occupies more than one body, the righteous person who suffers evil may be being punished for the evil done when that same soul occupied a different body.[120] The references to Psalms and b. Hagigah concern the number of generations for which souls would be replanted. According to talmudic

---

Talmud and the midrash, knew nothing of transmigration.").

117. Scholem, *On the Mystical Shape of the Godhead*, 201.

118. Scholem, *On the Mystical Shape of the Godhead*, 201–2 (quoting *Bahir*). See Eylon, *Reincarnation in Jewish Mysticism*, 105. See also Scholem, *Origins of the Kabbalah*, 188 ("The doctrine of transmigration of souls appeared [in the *Bahir*] as an answer to the question of theodicy.").

119. See Eylon, *Reincarnation in Jewish Mysticism*, 105–7 (discussing varying sources which use the symbol of the vineyard; stating that in Isaiah 5:2 (1) "the acts of preparing the vineyard and the planting of the grapes refer to God's creation of this world," and (2) "the unsuccessful venture in which the grapes turned sour seems to refer to the sins of the wicked that ruin any good in the order of things"; and concluding that readers well-versed in talmudic and midrashic literature "would have associated the midrashic passage with the question of theodicy.").

120. See Eylon, *Reincarnation in Jewish Mysticism*, 110 ("the *Bahir* postulates that the righteous person in this world may suffer because in a previous life he was wicked and vice versa.").

chronology, the Torah was given twenty-six generations after the creation of the world, but according to rabbinic interpretation of Psalm 105, God gave the Torah ("a word") after 1,000 generations had passed. The contradiction is resolved in b. Hagigah 13b by saying that 974 generations of evildoers were foreseen by God before the world was created but were not then created. Instead, God "stood and sowed them in every generation, and these are the arrogant ones of every generation."[121] According to Scholem, in the *Bahir* "these evil ones are . . . the bad grapevines, which, however, are not denied the opportunity to submit to a new test and to emerge as righteous."[122]

Just as section 135 reads a parable from Isaiah as teaching the transmigration of souls, so section 86 reads a parable from b. Shabbat 152b as teaching this doctrine. Shabbat 152b interprets Qoheleth 12:7 to mean that God gives everyone a pure soul and one must keep their soul pure to be rewarded in the world to come. More specifically, it says that what is taught in the biblical passage "may be compared to a human king who distributed royal garments to his servants"; those who were wise took care of these garments, while those who were foolish did not. When the king asked that the garments be returned, the wise were able to return clean garments, but the foolish weren't. The king was happy with the wise; he took their clean garments to his storehouse and allowed them to go home in peace. However, the king was angry with the foolish; he sent the garments to be washed and sent the foolish to prison. The parable is reworked in the *Bahir* after first noticing that the biblical phrase "*from generation to generation*" evokes the idea that the human soul is reincarnated in one generation after another:

> R. Meir said: What is the meaning of the verse '*The Lord shall reign forever, your God, O Zion, from generation to generation*'? What is '*from generation to generation*'? R. Papias said: It is written '*A generation goes and a generation comes*' [Qoh 1:4]. And R. Akiba said: What is meant by: '*A generation goes and a generation comes*'? A generation that has already come once. To what is this similar?—To a fable about a king who owned slaves, and he dressed them with embroidered silk garments according to his best ability. They disarranged them. He expelled them and drove his presence from them, and stripped them of his garments, and they went away. The king then took the garments, washed them thoroughly until there was no soiled spot left on them and he placed them to be readily used. Then the king bought other slaves and dressed them with these garments. But he did not know whether or not these slaves were good. And here is a case where they [the new slaves] benefited from garments that had been worn previously by others and were not even new. However, the verse [Qoh 1:4] continues: '*But the earth stands forever.*' This is the same as

---

121. See Scholem, *On the Mystical Shape of the Godhead*, 202; Scholem, *Origins of the Kabbalah*, 189.

122. Scholem, *Origins of the Kabbalah*, 189. See also Scholem, *On the Mystical Shape of the Godhead*, 202–3 ("the wild grapes are the wicked, who must undergo rebirth and thereby receive the opportunity to emerge from their new test as righteous.").

the verse in [Qoh] 12:7: 'The dust returns to the earth as it was, but the spirit returns to God who gave it.'¹²³

In other words, just as the two parts of Qoheleth 12:7 refer, respectively, to the body and the soul, so do the two parts of Qoheleth 1:4 refer, respectively, to the transmigrating soul and the body. Scholem comments that the "Talmud speaks of the soul, which is to be returned to God in a state of purity, in terms of a royal garment loaned out to a man; in the *Bahir*, the same passage is used in relation to transmigration, rather than to reward and punishment in the future world—a significant turning."¹²⁴ Scholem also comments that this reworking of the talmudic parable in Shabbat 152b is "with utter disregard for its original meaning."¹²⁵

Although introducing the new doctrine of transmigration of souls, the *Bahir* maintains the traditional belief that it is important to keep one's soul pure, to be righteous. Indeed, righteousness is linked to eschatological concerns. To understand this connection, it must first be mentioned that the *Bahir* distinguishes between old souls and new souls. The old souls are continually circulating from generation to generation, that is, they are transmigrating. But, in addition, there are new souls that are stored in God's "treasurehouse of all souls."¹²⁶ When the Congregation of Israel "is bad" God only uses the old souls; but when the Congregation of Israel "is good" God will use the new souls. Among the new souls is the soul of the Messiah.

In sections 126–27, the *Bahir* "explains that the Messiah can come only when all the souls 'in the body of man' are exhausted and have ended their migration. 'Only then may the "new [souls]" come out, and only then is the son of David allowed to be born. How is that? Because his soul comes forth new among the others.' The soul of the Messiah is therefore not subject to migration."¹²⁷ In short, the use of the new souls is linked to redemption brought about through the goodness of Israel, which is further identified with the transmigrating souls becoming pure.¹²⁸ As Scholem writes: "The emergence of new souls is . . . viewed here as a special merit occurring when the community of Israel proves itself worthy."¹²⁹ According to Eylon:

---

123. See Eylon, *Reincarnation in Jewish Mysticism*, 89–90 (emphasis added); Scholem, *On the Mystical Shape of the Godhead*, 203; Scholem, *Origins of the Kabbalah*, 111–12.

124. Scholem, *On the Mystical Shape of the Godhead*, 203. See also Eylon, *Reincarnation in Jewish Mysticism*, 98–99 ("By changing a few details, the *Bahir* introduces a new concept: the 'used' garments are a symbol for reincarnated souls.").

125. Scholem, *Origins of the Kabbalah*, 90. See also Scholem, *Origins of the Kabbalah*, 111–13.

126. See Scholem, *On the Mystical Shape of the Godhead*, 204–5; Eylon, *Reincarnation in Jewish Mysticism*, 110–13.

127. Scholem, *Origins of the Kabbalah*, 190.

128. See Scholem, *On the Mystical Shape of the Godhead*, 204–6; Eylon, *Reincarnation in Jewish Mysticism*, 110–14.

129. Scholem, *On the Mystical Shape of the Godhead*, 205.

CHAPTER 8.

The fable in [section 127 of the *Bahir*][130] exemplifies the responsibility of the individual to take care of the soul, and the collective responsibility of the People of Israel for the continuity of the process of reincarnation and, ultimately, the coming of the Messiah. God deposits good and pure souls in his people, his soldiers in the fable. However, if His people allow their souls to become polluted with wrongdoing, they delay redemption and cause old souls to reincarnate despite their wish. As the king [in the fable] accuses his soldiers of 'killing' themselves and engaging in self-destruction, so does God accuse humans of neglecting to care for their souls and bodies, ruining them with their ignorance . .

[I]n section 104 the *Bahir* raises the issue of the renewal of human souls. There is a close relationship between morality and the renewal of souls. The renewal and descent of souls to this world is conditional upon certain ethical conduct on the part of the nation of Israel. If Israel behaves according to the laws of the Torah, God allows new souls to descend to earth. This in turn means that the process of reincarnation is shortened and redemption arrives sooner. However, if the nation of Israel misbehaves then it delays the process of reincarnation and new souls do not descend to the earth, arresting the souls' rate of renewal. The same old souls are to be recycled and reincarnated; thus postponing the coming of the Messiah . . .

Moreover, the coming of the Messiah is dependent solely on the ethical behavior of the nation of Israel. God has complete control over the divine source of souls . . . and He renews them conditionally. Once the inventory of new souls depletes entirely, the Messiah comes to redeem the nation of Israel . . .

The coming of the Messiah terminates the cycle of reincarnation and brings about perfection to the divine sphere.[131]

It is important to note that the idea of transmigration of souls is introduced in the *Bahir* by means of the traditional talmudic style of biblical exegesis. It is being tacitly suggested that these novel ideas are derived from the Bible.

---

130. In the fable the king sent plenty of food and bread to his army but because the soldiers were lazy they did not preserve the bread and it became moldy. The king became angry and ordered the soldiers to dry and restore the bread as much as possible, saying that he would not give them new bread until the moldy bread had been eaten. The industrious soldiers preserved the bread as best they could and ate all of their portion of it, but others did not, and starved to death. The latter were blamed for neglecting their body. They were also blamed because, had they not died, they might have given birth to good sons who might have prevented them from spoiling the bread. Finally, they are blamed for not studying Torah for "not by bread alone does a human being live, but from all that is uttered from God's mouth" (Deut 8:3). See Eylon, *Reincarnation in Jewish Mysticism*, 114.

131. Eylon, *Reincarnation in Jewish Mysticism*, 114–15.

C. The Concept of the Soul and Its Transmigration Is Developed in *Sefer ha-Zohar*

The *Zohar* is not a single book but "a whole library of mystical commentaries on the Bible and mystical treatises composed mostly during the last third of the thirteenth century."[132] Traditionally, the entire work was said to have been authored by Simeon bar Yohai, a second-century Palestinian rabbi, the material having been revealed to him by the prophet Elijah and accompanying angels. Twentieth-century scholarship has shown that the *Zohar* was mainly the product of Moses de Leon. It was de Leon who claimed that the author was bar Yohai; he made this claim for the same reason that he composed the work primarily in Aramaic, the language of the Talmud—he wanted the new ideas contained in the work, including ideas about transmigration of souls, to be backed by the authority of prophesy and the talmudic sages. The *Zohar* currently is printed in five volumes: "the first three volumes are a commentary on the Torah (*Sefer ha-Zohar al Ha-Torah*); the other two are *Tikkunei Ha-Zohar* ('Emendations of the *Zohar*') and *Zohar Hadash* ('New *Zohar*'). There is also a later work, dependent upon yet separate from the *Zohar* itself, entitled *Raaya Meheimma*, or 'The Faithful Shepherd,' composed by an anonymous author." [133]

The *Zohar* employs the three Hebrew words that had been used for centuries to refer to the soul—*nephesh*, *ruach*, and *neshamah*—but uses these words in new ways.[134] Saadia, for example, had said that each word refers to one of three faculties of the same soul which faculties appear when the soul is united with the body—basically, the Platonic appetitive, spirited, and rational faculties.[135] In contrast, Moses de Leon suggests that each word designates a distinct entity only contingently linked together and with the physical body. These three distinct entities represent three levels, grades, or forms of soul.[136] The lowest level of soul is *nephesh*, followed by *ruach*, and then *neshamah*. Only *nephesh* "stands in intimate relation to the body."[137] The *nephesh* is the "vital soul"; it is responsible for life as it "nourishes and upholds" the body.[138] Once the *nephesh* acquires "due worth, it becomes the throne for the 'spirit' [*ruach*] to rest upon, as it is written, 'until the spirit be poured upon us from on high' [Isa 32:15]."[139] The *neshamah*, the "holy soul" or "super-soul," is the highest level of soul. When the *nephesh* and *ruach* "have duly readied themselves, they are worthy to receive the

---

132. Scheindlin, *Short History of the Jewish People*, 116.

133. Raphael, *Jewish Views of the Afterlife*, 276–77 (citing Scholem, *Kabbalah*, 213–20).

134. See Scholem, *Major Trends in Jewish Mysticism*, 240; Scholem, *On the Mystical Shape of the Godhead*, 218.

135. See ch. 5, sec. B, 5.

136. See Scholem, *Zohar*, 19; Scholem, *Major Trends in Jewish Mysticism*, 240; Scholem, *On the Mystical Shape of the Godhead*, 218.

137. Scholem, *Zohar*, 19. See also Raphael, *Jewish Views of the Afterlife*, 278–79.

138. See Scholem, *Zohar*, 19.

139. Scholem, *Zohar*, 19.

'super-soul' [*neshamah*], resting in turn upon the throne of the spirit [*ruach*]. The super-soul stands preeminent, and not to be perceived."[140]

The relationship between the human body and each of the three souls is compared to the wick of a candle and different flames surrounding the wick:

> It is the [*nephesh*]. the lowest stirring, to which the body adheres; just as in a candle flame, the obscure light at the bottom adheres close to the wick, without which it cannot be. When fully kindled, it becomes a throne for the white light above it, and when these two come into their full glow, the white light becomes a throne for a light not wholly discernible, an unknowable essence reposing on the white light. and so in all there comes to be perfect light.[141]

Everyone has *nephesh* as it is "the natural soul given to every man," and through the study of Torah and meritorious action one may acquire *ruach*.[142] However, *neshamah* can only be acquired by

> the perfect devotee, who, for the author of the Zohar, is identical with the kabbalist, and it is only by penetrating into the mysteries of the Torah, that is to say, through mystical realization of his cognitive powers, that he acquires it. *Neshamah* is the deepest intuitive power which leads to the secrets of God and the universe. It is therefore natural that *neshamah* is also conceived as a spark of . . . the divine intellect itself. By acquiring it, the kabbalist thus realizes something of the divine in his own nature.[143]

Stated differently, only a person who has achieved perfection by penetrating the mysteries of the Torah can attain all three grades or forms of soul. As Scholem writes:

> The normal psychophysical constitution of a human being is already included in full in the lowest level, [*nephesh*] . . . The two higher levels of the soul, *ruach* and *neshamah*, are intuitive degrees or levels of the soul, achieved by mystics only after much practice and contemplation of the secrets of the Torah. Everyone is born with a [*nephesh*], but whether or not he will succeed in bringing down his own *ruach* and *neshamah* from the treasurehouse of souls, or some other heavenly source where these higher forms of his own soul abide, depends upon his own choice and spiritual development.[144]

Nephesh is capable of sin but not *neshamah* or *ruach*; *neshamah*, as a spark of the divine intellect, is beyond sin.[145] In another work of Moses de Leon, he asserts

---

140. Scholem, *Zohar*, 19.
141. Scholem, *Zohar*, 19.
142. Scholem, *Major Trends in Jewish Mysticism*, 241.
143. Scholem, *Major Trends in Jewish Mysticism*, 241.
144. Scholem, *On the Mystical Shape of the Godhead*, 218.
145. See Scholem, *Major Trends in Jewish Mysticism*, 241; Scholem, *On the Mystical Shape of the Godhead*, 219.

that in the act of sin *neshamah* actually abandons man. This is because *neshamah* "is substantially the same as God" and God cannot inflict punishment upon Himself.[146] Accordingly, it is *nephesh* that is punished after death, and in some passages *ruach*, but never *neshamah*.[147] At death, the three souls are destined to go to their separate ways to three different regions. The *neshamah* returns immediately after death to the higher Garden of Eden.[148] One passage of the *Zohar* explains the souls' after-death destinies thusly:

> While the body in the grave is decomposing and moldering to dust, [*nephesh*] tarries with it, and it hovers about in this world, going here and there among the living, wanting to know their sorrows, and interceding for them at their need.
>
> *Ruach* betakes itself into the earthly Garden of Eden. There, this spirit, desiring to enjoy the pleasures of the magnificent Garden, vests itself in a garment, as it were, of a likeness, a semblance of the body in which it had its abode in this world. On Sabbaths, New Moons, and festival days, it ascends to the supernal sphere, regaling itself with delights there, and then goes back to the Garden. As it is written: 'And the spirit [*ruach*] returneth unto God who gave it' [Qoh 12:7], that is, at the special holidays and times we have mentioned.
>
> But *neshamah* ascends forthwith to her place, in the domain from which she emanated... Never thereafter does she descend to earth... And until such time as *neshamah* has ascended to be joined with the Throne, *ruach* is unable to be crowned in the lower Garden and [*nephesh*] cannot rest easy in its place; but these find rest when she ascends...
>
> But if *neshamah* has for some reason been prevented from ascending to her proper place, then *ruach*, coming to the gate of the Garden of Eden, finds it closed against it, and, unable to enter, wanders about alone and dejected; while [*nephesh*], too, flits from place to place in the world, and seeing the body in which it once was tenant eaten by worms and undergoing the judgment of the grave, it mourns for it, as the Scripture says: 'But his flesh grieveth for him, and his soul mourned over him' [Job 14:22].
>
> So do they all undergo suffering, until the time when *neshamah* is enabled to reach to her proper place above. Then, however, each of the two others becomes attached to its rightful place; this is because all three are one, comprising a unity, embraced in a mystical bond.[149]

Elsewhere the *Zohar* discusses the after-death fate of the soul without clearly differentiating *nephesh*, *ruach*, and *neshamah*:

---

146. Scholem, *Major Trends in Jewish Mysticism*, 241.
147. Scholem, *Major Trends in Jewish Mysticism*, 241.
148. See Scholem, *Major Trends in Jewish Mysticism*, 241n126.
149. Scholem, *Zohar*, 69–71. See Raphael, *Jewish Views of the Afterlife*, 281–82.

[W]hen a man's soul leaves him, it is met by all his relatives and companions from the other world, who guide it to the realm of delight and the place of torture. If he is righteous, he beholds his place and ascends and is there installed and regaled with the delights of the other world. But if no, then his soul stays in this world until his body is buried in the earth, after which the executioners seize on him and drag him down to Dumah, the prince of Gehinnom, and to his allotted level in Gehinnom.

Rabbi Judah said: During seven days does the soul go from his house to his grave, And from his grave to his house, back and forth in mourning for the body, according to the verse: 'But his flesh shall suffer pain for him, and his soul shall mourn over him' [Job 14:22], and as it beholds the grief of the house, it also grieves.

Now we know that at the end of the seven days the decay of the body sets in, and the soul then goes to its place. It is first permitted into the cave of Machpelah up to a point, set in accordance with its merit. Then it comes to where the Garden of Eden stands, . . . and if it is deemed worthy to do so, it enters.

We know that there are four pillars waiting, and in their hands they hold the form of a body which the soul joyfully dons as its garment, and then it abides in its allotted circle of the Lower Garden for the stated time . . . [By] a pillar of three hues called 'the habitation of mount Zion' [Isa 4:5] . . . the soul ascends to the gate of righteousness, where are to be found Zion and Jerusalem. Happy is the lot of the soul deemed worthy to ascend higher, for then it is together with the Body of the King. If it does not merit to ascend higher, then 'he that is left in Zion, and he that remained in Jerusalem, shall be called holy' [Isa 4:3]. But when a soul is granted to ascend higher, then it sees before it the glory of the King, and is vouchsafed the supernal delight from the region which is called Heaven.[150]

As indicated by these passages, the suffering endured by the soul until it is able to reach "its rightful place" includes the "pangs of the grave" mentioned by Saadia.[151] It also includes purgation and purification in *Gehenna*.[152] Although the emphasis is placed on *Gehenna* as a place of purgation lasting twelve months, "eternal damnation

---

150. Scholem, *Zohar*, 32–33. See also Scholem, *Major Trends in Jewish Mysticism*, 242 (during its earthly stay the soul weaves a mystical garment from its good deeds which it wears in the lower paradise, but the souls of sinners are "naked," or the mystical garment they weave has "holes." "After death, the various parts of the soul . . . return to their original location, but those who have sinned are brought to court and purified in the 'fiery stream' of Gehenna, or, in the case of the most shameful sinners, burned."); Raphael, *Jewish Views of the Afterlife*, 279–80 (quoting the view expressed by Moses de Leon that even though the soul "is divided into three parts," they "really form one mystery . . . without any division.").

151. See ch. 5, sec. B, 6; Raphael, *Jewish Views of the Afterlife*, 251–293 (citing *Zohar*, III, 126b–127a; I, 245a).

152. See Raphael, *Jewish Views of the Afterlife*, 298–308.

is the due punishment for those who do not believe in the resurrection of the dead."[153] After completing the allotted time of punishment, the soul enters, first Lower, then Upper *Gan Eden*, to enjoy the delights of the higher worlds:

> The body is punished in the grave and the soul in the fire of Gehinnom for the appointed period. When this is completed she rides from Gehinnom purified of her guilt like iron purified in the fire, and she is carried up to the Lower Gan Eden...[154]

Although the early kabbalists, including Nahmanides, had used the doctrine of transmigration of souls to resolve issues related to theodicy, transmigration is drastically restricted by the author of the main part of the *Zohar*. Only a childless man and, under certain circumstances, his wife, are subject to *metempsychosis*. As Scholem points out, "One who has failed to fulfill this first and most fundamental law of the Torah, 'to be fruitful and multiply,' must return to the world a second time in order to do so."[155] Interestingly, the parable in section 135 of the *Bahir*, discussed above, "is applied by the *Zohar* to those who are childless, and to them alone."[156]

Because one who died childless had to return to fulfill the commandment "to be fruitful and multiply" the doctrine of transmigration of souls was used to explain the biblical institution of the levirate. According to Deuteronomy 25:5–10, if brothers live together and one of them dies childless, a surviving brother must take the dead brother's widow as his wife, and the first-born of this new marriage is regarded in law as the son of the deceased. One of two biblical examples of this institution is the story of Tamar in Genesis 38. Judah's first-born son, Er, died without having a child by his wife Tamar, and thus it was the duty of Er's brother, Onan, to marry Tamar, but Onan doesn't want to have a child who would not be, in law, his own. Nahmanides, in commenting on the specific passage *Onan knew that the seed would not be his* [Gen 38:9] states that this indicates "that Onan had some definite kind of knowledge in this matter which made him certain *that the seed would not be his*" and adds that the matter "is indeed one of the great secrets of the Torah."[157] Chavel comments: "Ramban here hints to the mystic doctrine of the transmigration of souls. Onan 'knew' that when he married his brother's wife his brother's soul would become incarnate in his son. Therefore Onan did not consider the child to be his own."[158] In the *Zohar*, transmigration of souls is used in the same manner: "If the dead man's brother marries his widow, he 'draws back' the soul of the deceased husband. He builds it up again and it becomes

---

153. Raphael, *Jewish Views of the Afterlife*, 303–5 (citing *Zohar*, I, 77a–77b; 107b–108a).

154. Raphael, *Jewish Views of the Afterlife*, 308 (quoting *Zohar*, III, 53a). See also Raphael, *Jewish Views of the Afterlife*, 308–14 (discussing Lower and Upper *Gan Eden*, and the soul's ultimate return to the holy celestial abode called *tzror ha-hayyim* ("bundle of the living")).

155. Scholem, *On the Mystical Shape of the Godhead*, 209.

156. Scholem, *On the Mystical Shape of the Godhead*, 209n24.

157. Nahmanides, *Commentary on the Torah*, 1:469.

158. Nahmanides, *Commentary on the Torah*, 1:469n155.

a new spirit in a new body."[159] However, the *Zohar* extends this usage. *Anyone* who has failed to fulfill the commandment to procreate "assumes a new existence in a new bodily abode, be it as a form of punishment or as a chance or restitution."[160]

D. Other Early Kabbalists Develop the Concept of Transmigration of Souls in Various Ways

1. Transmigration begins to be used more expansively

The move evidenced in the main part of the *Zohar* to limit transmigration was not uniformly accepted. Rather, during roughly the same time period, other kabbalists were employing transmigration in various, more expansive, ways. For instance, R. Sheshet des Mercadell, a disciple of Nahmanides, taught that all evildoers are subject to transmigration. According to him, though transmigration is "agonizing," and thus constitutes punishment, it also constitutes an act of divine love and mercy, saving the souls of the evildoers from obliteration in the fires of *Gehenna* and giving evildoers an opportunity to cleanse themselves.[161] In contrast, those in the intermediate class "are sentenced by the celestial court to Hell [*Gehenna*], which in the view of this Kabbalist is preferable to transmigration."[162]

Many others further expanded the scope of *gilgul neshamot*—to include the intermediate class, as well as the evildoers.[163] Still others believed that even the completely righteous could be subject to *gilgul*. This would occur, not primarily as punishment of course, but either for the benefit of the righteous persons themselves (such as to fulfill a commandment they may have been unable to fulfill in their prior life, or to atone for some minor sin) or, chiefly, for the benefit of the entire world.[164] In the writings of R. Solomon ben Abraham Adret, the most important disciple of Nahmanides, and in the later parts of the *zoharic* literature, *gilgul* increasingly becomes a universal law.[165] By the seventeenth century, it could be asserted:

> The belief of the doctrine of transmigration of souls is a firm and infallible dogma accepted by the whole assemblage of our [community] with one accord, so there is none to be found who would dare to deny it.[166]

---

159. Scholem, *Major Trends in Jewish Mysticism*, 243.

160. Scholem, *Major Trends in Jewish Mysticism*, 243.

161. Scholem, *On the Mystical Shape of the Godhead*, 210.

162. Scholem, *On the Mystical Shape of the Godhead*, 211. For a discussion of how *Gehenna* and *Gan Eden* are depicted in the Zohar, see Raphael, *Jewish Views of the Afterlife*, 298–314.

163. Scholem, *On the Mystical Shape of the Godhead*, 210.

164. Scholem, *On the Mystical Shape of the Godhead*, 210.

165. Scholem, *On the Mystical Shape of the Godhead*, 212. See Raphael, *Jewish Views of the Afterlife*, 316 ("Truly, all souls, must undergo transmigration"; quoting *Zohar*, III, 99b).

166. Raphael, *Jewish Views of the Afterlife*, 316 (attributing these words to Menasseh ben Israel).

2. The doctrine of soul sparks is developed

According to Scholem, the new doctrine of soul sparks developed in an effort to resolve the problem of what would happen at the time of the resurrection to the various bodies "inhabited" by the transmigrating soul.[167] Although some kabbalists assumed that only the last body would be resurrected, there were objections to this solution on grounds of divine justice: "as the previous bodies had also been instruments of certain good actions, how could they be ignored at the Last Judgement as though they had never existed?"[168]

The only way in which one soul could be reunited with multiple bodies was for the one soul to be divided, which is what the doctrine of soul sparks does. A single soul, it was reasoned, is actually composed of many sparks. Just as sparks from the light of one candle can light many other candles, so can sparks from a single soul (which is the light of God) be used to animate many bodies.[169] From this initial eschatological usage, the doctrine of soul sparks was expanded. Scholem quotes a thirteenth-century fragment:

> Know that the soul is never reincarnated alone, save in the case . . . of a totally wicked soul . . . But for the middling person (*beinoni*) . . . his situation is thus: sparks of his soul remain behind [i.e., in paradise] in accordance with the commandments he has performed; but the other parts enter into transmigration. This portion of his soul then comes mixed with the soul of a different reincarnate, who is in the same situation as he, or with [several] transmigrating souls . . . But then they do not enter [the new body] by themselves, but with a new soul. And this is what is meant by the verse "All these things doth God work, twice, yea thrice, with a man" [Job 33:29]—that is, two or three souls at once in one soul. But it must be "with a man"—that is, with a new soul that has not sinned.[170]

Thus, in general, it came to be accepted that a new soul implanted in a body can come with, or later acquire, sparks of various other souls. Under such circumstances, of course, the unity of the specific individual soul becomes "highly problematic."[171] In subsequent developments of this doctrine the sparks acquired by a soul "strengthen

---

167. Scholem, *On the Mystical Shape of the Godhead*, 215–16. See also Scholem, *Origins of the Kabbalah*, 460 (the doctrine of soul sparks was "used in the school of Solomon Ibn Adreth in order to eliminate the difficulty that would arise at the resurrection of the dead for the different bodies through which one single soul had passed. The different bodies of the resurrection would be inhabited by sparks from the same soul. According to Azriel there also exist souls of such exalted rank that they do not return to the world of bodies, but remain in the 'world of life' and thus do not participate at all, or only in a purely spiritual sense, in the resurrection.").

168. Scholem, *On the Mystical Shape of the Godhead*, 216.

169. Scholem, *On the Mystical Shape of the Godhead*, 216.

170. Scholem, *On the Mystical Shape of the Godhead*, 216–17.

171. Scholem, *On the Mystical Shape of the Godhead*, 217.

CHAPTER 8.

certain tendencies within the soul, because they attempt to attain, in the present life and through the medium of the new soul, that which they previously lacked."[172]

---

172. Scholem, *On the Mystical Shape of the Godhead*, 217.

9.

Baruch Spinoza Challenges the Scriptural Basis for Belief in the Immortality of the Soul and a Postmortem Reward or Punishment, and Denies that there Is Any Personal Immortality

As early as 1516, Pietro Pomponazzi denied that natural reason could determine whether the soul is immortal *vel non* but asserted that the immortality of the soul is revealed to be true in Scripture.[1] In 1624, Uriel da Costa effectively opposed Pomponazzi's assertion that the soul's immortality is a revealed truth. Da Costa asserted that the Hebrew Bible identifies the soul with blood, and thus that the Hebrew Bible proves that the soul is mortal.[2] Three decades after the death of da Costa, Baruch Spinoza effectively opposed both Pomponazzi and da Costa—Spinoza held that neither the immortality nor mortality of the soul is a question that could be, or should be, proven on the basis of Scripture. He further effectively opposed Pomponazzi's assertion that the soul's immortality *vel non* was indeterminable by natural reason. Spinoza argued that all matters concerning the nature of the world could only be ascertained

---

1. See generally Pomponazzi, *On the Immortality of the Soul*, 280–381; Randall, "Introduction," 257–79.

2. See generally Da Costa, *Examination of Pharisaic Traditions*, 267–425. In 1623, Uriel da Costa, a *converso* from Oporto, Portugal, who had arrived in Amsterdam with his extended family in 1615 and adopted Judaism, was excommunicated for professing heresies and persisting in "wrong opinions." The wrong opinions included da Costa's denial of the immortality of the soul, bodily resurrection, and any other afterlife. In that same year, 1623, da Costa's nemesis, Dr. Samuel da Silva, published a work entitled *Tratado da Immortalidade da Alma* (*Treatise on the Immortality of the Soul*) in which da Silva (1) reproduced three chapters from a then-unpublished work by da Costa attacking the doctrine of the soul's immortality, and (2) presented a refutation of what da Silva considered da Costa's "specious arguments." Da Silva's work was most likely commissioned by the Amsterdam Jewish authorities. Early in the following year, da Costa published the full version of the work from which da Silva had pilfered and reproduced three chapters. This full version had been revised by da Costa to respond to da Silva's attack. It was entitled *Exame das Tradicoes Phariseas Conferidas com a Lei Escrita* (*Examination of Pharisaic Traditions Compared with the Written Law*). See Salomon and Sassoon, "Introduction," 1–50.

through natural reason (not through revelation), and that true philosophy precluded the type of personal immortality of the soul envisioned by the multitude.

To elaborate upon Spinoza's contentions, after briefly describing Spinoza's life, this chapter will address Spinoza's views concerning (1) the nature of the soul and its relation to the body, including the issue of the soul's immortality, (2) whether there is any postmortem reward or punishment, and (3) the proper way of interpreting Scripture, and the impact of scriptural misinterpretation on beliefs about the immortality of the soul. Since Spinoza developed his ideas about the soul in response to the writings of René Descartes,[3] Descartes's views will be mentioned before discussing those of Spinoza.

A. The Life of Baruch Spinoza

While still in his early twenties Spinoza experienced a loss of faith and commitment.[4] In particular, he began to question in his own mind (1) the divine origin and Mosaic authorship of the Torah, (2) the traditional concept of God, and (3) the immortality of the soul as it was commonly understood.[5] The issue of the immortality of the soul had been a matter of intense focus by the Amsterdam rabbinate for the preceding quarter of a century, and was also a topic of widespread discussion in the Jewish community of Amsterdam at large.[6] One rabbi, Menasseh ben Israel, even argued that all fundamental Jewish beliefs rested on belief in the immortality of the soul.[7]

Spinoza's unorthodox beliefs soon came to the attention of the leaders of the Amsterdam Jewish community, and on July 27, 1656, he was excommunicated.[8] The writ of *herem* stated that the community leaders had long known of the "evil opinions and acts of [Spinoza]" and had recently received "more serious information about the abominable heresies which he practiced and taught and about his monstrous deeds," and, consequently, had decided that Spinoza should be "excommunicated and expelled from the people of Israel."[9] Nowhere does the writ of *herem* specify the "evil opinions" or "abominable heresies" which Spinoza held and taught, but Nadler has argued that

---

3. See Curley, *Behind the Geometrical Method*, x–xii, 3–4.

4. Nadler, *Spinoza's Heresy*, 29.

5. See Nadler, *Spinoza*, 134; Nadler, *Spinoza's Heresy*, 29–31; Kasher and Biderman, "Why was Spinoza Excommunicated?" 103–4.

6. See Kasher and Biderman, "Why Was Spinoza Excommunicated?," 106–8; Salomon and Sassoon, "Introduction," 15–50.

7. See Kasher and Biderman, "Why Was Spinoza Excommunicated?," 108. See also Kasher and Biderman, "Why Was Spinoza Excommunicated?," 110; Raphael, *Jewish Views of the Afterlife*, 316.

8. See Kasher and Biderman, "Why Was Spinoza Excommunicated?," 120–21, 134–35; Nadler, *Spinoza's Heresy*, 1–2, 29–30.

9. Nadler, *Spinoza*, 120; Nadler, *Spinoza's Heresy*, 2.

Spinoza's denial of the immortality of the soul was "an especially aggravating factor... in the decision to ban him."[10]

By early 1659, Spinoza was making periodic visits to study at Leiden University where Cartesian thought flourished.[11] Spinoza soon became "well known as someone who 'excelled in Cartesian philosophy.'"[12] Spinoza's interest in Descartes found expression in an intellectual circle in Amsterdam of which Spinoza became an integral and celebrated member.[13] In 1660 or early 1661, Spinoza moved to the small village of Rijnsburg, a few miles outside Leiden.[14] It was in Rijnsburg that Spinoza wrote (1) a geometrically ordered statement of Descartes's philosophy, (2) an unfinished work called *Treatise on the Emendation of the Intellect*, (3) a treatise entitled *Short Treatise on God, Man and his Well-being*, and, (4) a first draft of his most celebrated work, *Ethics*.[15]

In the spring of 1663, Spinoza moved to the village of Voorburg, just outside The Hague.[16] That same year Spinoza arranged for publication of his exposition of the philosophy of Descartes, calling it *Parts One and Two of Descartes' "Principles of Philosophy" Demonstrated in the Geometric Manner*.[17] To this work Spinoza attached an appendix entitled "Metaphysical Thoughts" which consisted of "a discussion of classical metaphysical problems that, he believed, Descartes did not adequately address."[18] The Cartesian exposition and "Metaphysical Thoughts," written in Latin, earned Spinoza a reputation for being a talented commentator on the Cartesian philosophy, and were soon translated into Dutch.[19]

Although Spinoza may have contemplated writing a work dealing with the Bible as early as 1659, it was not until the fall of 1665 that he put aside work on the *Ethics* to begin writing what would become the *Theological-Political Treatise*, published in 1670.[20] The impetus to complete and publish the *Treatise* was the imprisonment and death in prison of his friend Adriaan Koerbagh. In 1668, Koerbagh published a work in which he "denied the divine authorship of the Bible. It is, he insisted, a work of human literature, compiled from a variety of other writings by 'Esdras' (Ezra). And

---

10. Nadler, *Spinoza's Heresy*, 40. See Nadler, *Spinoza's Heresy*, 183–84.

11. See Nadler, *Spinoza*, 163–65; Kasher and Biderman, "Why Was Spinoza Excommunicated?," 131.

12. Nadler, *Spinoza*, 167.

13. See Nadler, *Spinoza*, 167–73.

14. See Nadler, *Spinoza*, 180–81; Hampshire, *Spinoza*, 230.

15. See Hampshire, *Spinoza*, 230, 234; Nadler, *Spinoza*, 175–76, 180–81; Nadler, *Book Forged in Hell*, 12.

16. Nadler, *Spinoza*, 203.

17. Nadler, *Spinoza*, 204–7; Nadler, *Book Forged in Hell*, 12. See generally Curley, *Collected Works of Spinoza*, 1:221–24.

18. Nadler, *Spinoza*, 210–11.

19. See Nadler, *Spinoza*, 211; Nadler, *Book Forged in Hell*, 13; Hampshire, *Spinoza*, 231.

20. See Nadler, *Spinoza*, 225–26, 243, 247–48, 269; Hampshire, *Spinoza*, 231.

the proper method for interpreting the meaning of Holy Scripture is, as for any book, a naturalistic one that relies mainly on its language and on the historical context of its authors and texts."[21] The publication of this book under his own name and in Dutch resulted in Koerbagh being interrogated and imprisoned.[22] He fell ill as a result of his incarceration, and died on October 5, 1669.[23]

The *Treatise* "reached the Dutch reading public in early 1670 . . . [and the] reaction, far and wide, was immediate, harsh, and unforgiving."[24] It was called "godless" and a book "forged in hell."[25] The religious authorities officially denounced it, asserting that it was "as vile and blasphemous a book as the world has ever seen."[26] In various places the book was banned and copies were confiscated, but, for the most part, it remained possible to buy it in the major towns.[27]

Around the time that the *Treatise* was published, Spinoza moved to The Hague.[28] In the following years, he returned to the *Ethics* and undertook to compose a Hebrew grammar.[29] Both of these works were published posthumously. Throughout 1676 his health deteriorated, and he died on February 21, 1677, at the age of 44. After his death Spinoza's friends prepared his various manuscripts for publication, under the title *Opera Posthuma* by B.D.S. As Hampshire notes: "His posthumous works, including the *Ethics*, were at first received with incomprehension and perfunctory abuse, and were generally neglected until the end of the eighteenth century."[30]

B. Descartes Postulates the Existence of Two Types of Substances—Immaterial Substances and Material Substances—and Asserts That the Soul or Mind, Being an Immaterial Substance, Is Immortal

René Descartes[31] conceived of the world as containing a great many substances which could be divided into two main kinds: material substances and immaterial substances.[32] Material substances have the attribute of extension, and immaterial substances

---

21. Nadler, *Book Forged in Hell*, 39. See Nadler, *Spinoza*, 265–66.
22. See Nadler, *Book Forged in Hell*, 42–43; Nadler, *Spinoza*, 267–69.
23. Nadler, *Spinoza's Heresy*, 43; Nadler, *Spinoza*, 269.
24. Nadler, *Spinoza*, 295.
25. Nadler, *Spinoza*, 295.
26. See Nadler, *Spinoza*, 296.
27. See Nadler, *Spinoza*, 296–97.
28. Nadler, *Spinoza*, 288.
29. See Nadler, *Spinoza*, 322–26.
30. Hampshire, *Spinoza*, 234.
31. For a brief summary of Descartes's life and writings, see Kenny, *New History of Western Philosophy*, 3:33–41. Descartes, considered to be the father of modern philosophy, was born in France, but lived most of his adult life in Holland. Kenny, *New History of Western Philosophy*, 3:33.
32. See Curley, *Behind the Geometrical Method*, 6.

have the attribute of thought.³³ The human body, being an extended thing (that is, having a certain figure, confined to a certain place, perceivable by one or more of the five senses, capable of being moved, but not capable of self-movement), is a type (or mode) of a material substance.³⁴ The human soul, in contrast to the human body, does not possess any of the properties of an extended thing; it does, however, have the attribute of thought.³⁵ Thus, the human soul, or the human mind, is a thinking thing, a mode of an immaterial substance.³⁶ Therefore, Descartes's view is dualistic. Humans are composed of two separate and distinct things, each being modes of two separate and distinct substances.³⁷

Descartes's concept of the human soul or mind is not the same as that of the medieval Aristotelians. For the latter, what essentially constituted the human soul were the faculties of intellect and will.³⁸ As Kenny notes:

> For Descartes and those who followed him . . . [it] was consciousness, not intelligence or rationality, that was the defining criterion of the mental: the mind is the realm of whatever is accessible to introspection. So, the mind included not only human understanding and willing, but also human seeing, hearing, feeling, pain, and pleasure. Every form of human experience, according to Descartes, included an element that was spiritual rather than material, a

---

33. See Curley, *Behind the Geometrical Method*, 6–8.

34. See Goetz and Taliaferro, *Brief History of the Soul*, 71 (quoting Descartes's *Meditations*).

35. See Goetz and Taliaferro, *Brief History of the Soul*, 72 ("according to Descartes, a soul is that which is nonextended and, thereby, without shape in a given place, is not divisible into parts and is not moveable in the sense that it cannot change spatial position. Therefore, Descartes believes that a soul is not located in space, period.").

36. See Goetz and Taliaferro, *Brief History of the Soul*, 71–72; Curley, *Behind the Geometrical Method*, 6–8; Curley, "Immortality of the Soul," 31 (Descartes stated: "when I achieve clarity and distinctness in my conception of the soul, I understand it as a thinking thing, and nothing more."). Following ordinary medieval usage, "Descartes uses the term 'human soul' in the sense of 'mind.' Among the philosophers of the Renaissance the [Latin] terms *animus* [soul] and *mens* [mind] were used as designations of the individual human soul, which was considered as being of divine origin and separable from the body, in contradistinction to the term *spiritus* [spirit], which was used as a designation of the vital force which was inseparable from the body, thus on the whole the term *spiritus* corresponding to the sensitive faculties in Aristotle and the terms *animus* and *mens* corresponding to the rational faculty in Aristotle . . . Descartes says that he prefers the term *mens* to *anima*, on the ground that the latter 'is equivocal and is frequently applied to what is corporeal'" (Wolfson, *Philosophy of Spinoza*, 2:43).

37. See generally Forstrom, *John Locke and Personal Identity*, 29–46 (discussing Descartes's analysis the of the distinction between the soul and the body, as well as his views on personal immortality, and how they are framed in relation to the papal bull issued in 1513 during the eighth session of the Lateran Council.) As Forstrom comments, "Descartes' discussion of immortality in the *Meditations* can and ought to be placed in relation to the council's decrees" directing philosophers to refute the arguments of those asserting that the soul is mortal (Forstrom, *John Locke and Personal Identity*, 37).

38. See Kenny, *New History of Western Philosophy*, 3:212.

phenomenal component that was no more than contingently connected with bodily causes, expressions, and mechanisms.[39]

So, when Descartes refers to the human mind as a "thing that thinks" (*res cogitans*), "thinking" must be understood broadly so as to include not only intellectual meditation but also volition, sensation, and emotion. These other activities possessed the feature which was the most important characteristic of a thinking thing, immediate consciousness.[40] As Descartes himself expressed it, "'I use this term [sc., thinking] to include everything that is within us in such a way that we are immediately conscious of it.'"[41]

Not only are the human body and the human mind distinct substances, conceived as each existing independently, but Descartes frequently speaks as if the real person is only the mind, not the composite of mind and body.[42] Nevertheless,

> Descartes' official position is . . . that human beings are composite substances, whose constituent substances are minds and bodies . . . Considered in themselves, [a person's] mind and [a person's] body are 'complete substances,' in the sense that each can be conceived to exist without the other, or without anything else except God. But [a person's] mind and [a person's] body need not be considered simply as isolated things. They can also be considered in relation to the whole human being they constitute.[43]

Considered in relation to the whole human being they constitute, the mind and the body coexist, not by a "mere presence or proximity of one to the other, but by a true substantial union."[44] In his *Meditations*, Descartes describes the substantial union of mind and body by distinguishing it from the relationship of a sailor to a ship, a metaphor first used by Aristotle. Descartes writes:

---

39. Kenny, *New History of Western Philosophy*, 3:213.

40. See Kenny, *New History of Western Philosophy*, 3:214.

41. Kenny, *New History of Western Philosophy*, 3:214 (quoting Descartes). See also Hatfield, "Psychology," 243 ("Aristotelian psychology regarded the *psyche*, or soul, as a vivifying principle having three main powers: vegetative, sensory, and intellectual or rational. The cognitive capacities associated with the sensory and intellectual powers were higher manifestations of a vital or living principle common to all living things, including plants. The Cartesian philosophy challenged the unity of the Aristotelian soul, by contending that animals are bare material machines devoid of feeling or sentience, thus separating merely vital phenomena, which were to be given a purely mechanistic account, from the phenomena of mind. The sensory, intellectual, and volitional phenomena of mind required an immaterial soul—but one that did not govern the vital processes of the body.").

42. See Curley, *Behind the Geometrical Method*, 7, 52–56. See Kenny, *New History of Western Philosophy*, 3:216–17 ("In human beings, Descartes argues for a sharp distinction between mind and body. In the sixth *Meditation*, he concludes that his nature or essence consists simply in being a thinking thing; he is really distinct from his body and can exist without it.").

43. Curley, *Behind the Geometrical Method*, 52–53.

44. Goetz and Taliaferro, *Brief History of the Soul*, 82 (quoting letter from Descartes to Roger Henricus).

> Nature teaches me, through those sensations of pain, hunger, thirst, etc., that I am not only present in my body as a sailor . . . is present in his ship, but that I am very closely conjoined to it, and as it were, mingled throughout it, so that together with it I compose one thing. For otherwise, when the body is injured, I who am [would be?] nothing other than a thinking thing, would not feel pain on its account, but would perceive that injury by pure intellect, as a sailor perceives by vision if something is broken on the ship; and when the body required food or drink, I would understand this explicitly, I would not have those confused sensations of hunger and thirst. For certainly, those sensations of thirst, hunger, pain, etc., are nothing but certain confused modes of thinking, which have arisen from the union, and as it were, thorough mingling of the mind with the body.[45]

This understanding of the substantial union of the mind and the body was immediately challenged by Descartes's contemporaries. How, it was asked, can two things whose natures are so completely different as the body and the mind interact with each other? How could the mind, being immaterial and nonextended, move the body, which is material and extended, and how could the body affect the mind?[46] The interaction between the mind and the body is made even more obscure when Descartes states that the mind is not directly affected by (and does not directly affect) any part of the body other than the pineal gland in the brain, which in turn is directly affected by (or directly affects) the animal spirits (corpuscular bodies that move very quickly).[47] So that when the mind wills something "'it brings about that the little gland to which it is closely joined moves in the manner required to produce the effect corresponding to this volition.'"[48] Conversely, when the mind perceives something through the exterior senses the process is reversed: "movements of the animal spirits in the bodily extremities ultimately produce movements of the pineal gland, which result in the soul's experiencing pain and pleasure, seeing, hearing, tasting, and the rest."[49] The inadequacy of Descartes's explanation as to how the mind and the body interact rendered his dualism "a fundamentally mistaken philosophy."[50]

---

45. Curley, *Behind the Geometrical Method*, 56–57 (quoting Descartes's *Meditations*).

46. See Curley, *Behind the Geometrical Method*, 57; Goetz and Taliaferro, *Brief History of the Soul*, 80–82.

47. See Kenny, *New History of Western Philosophy*, 3:217; Goetz and Taliaferro, *Brief History of the Soul*, 76–82.

48. Goetz and Taliaferro, *Brief History of the Soul*, 77 (quoting Descartes's *The Passions of the Soul*).

49. Goetz and Taliaferro, *Brief History of the Soul*, 78. See Kenny, *New History of Western Philosophy*, 3:217 ("the mind is not directly affected by any part of the body other than the pineal gland in the brain. All sensations and emotions consist of motions in the body which travel through the nerves to this gland and there give a signal to the mind which occasions a certain experience.").

50. Kenny, *New History of Western Philosophy*, 3:219. See also Goetz and Taliaferro, *Brief History of the Soul*, 83 ("Descartes conjectures that the locus of interaction [between the mind and the body] is at the pineal gland in the brain; but this answer has not withstood the test of time or that of science."). See generally Curley, *Behind the Geometrical Method*, 57–59.

Despite the fact that Descartes argues that the mind and the body are substantially united, he also wanted to allow for the possibility of philosophically proving that the mind continues to exist after the death of the body. The need to allow for this possibility was very much related, in his mind, to the need to contend that virtue brings a reward, if not in this life, then in an afterlife. He wrote:

> For though it suffices for those of us who are faithful to believe by faith that God exists and that the human soul does not die with the body, it certainly does not seem possible to persuade infidels of any religion, or even of any moral virtue, unless those two things have first been proven by natural reason. Often this life offers greater rewards to vice than to virtue; so few would prefer the right to the useful if they did not fear God and expect another life.[51]

That the soul is an immaterial substance, and thus is distinct from the body, allows for the possibility that the soul is immortal. According to Descartes's *Discourse on Method*:

> [O]ur soul is of a nature entirely independent of the body, and consequently . . . it is not bound to die with it. And since we cannot see any other causes which destroy the soul, we are naturally led to conclude that it is immortal.[52]

Curley has claimed that Descartes might have offered proof of the soul's immortality but doesn't.[53] Instead, in the synopsis of Descartes's *Meditations*, Descartes remarks on the difference between the mind and the body, and then states that he will not go on to state reasons in proof of the immortality of the soul because:

> . . . [the] arguments [concerning the difference between mind and body] are enough to show that the death of the mind does not follow from the corruption of the body, and hence are enough to give mortals the hope of an afterlife, and secondly, because the premises from which the immortality of the mind can be inferred [that is, proven] depend on an explanation of the whole of physics.[54]

51. Curley, "Immortality of the Soul," 27 (quoting Descartes's *Meditations*, the dedication). In the dedication of the *Meditations* Descartes also refers to the Lateran Council's condemnation of those who say that human reasoning leads to the conclusion that the soul dies with the body, and its call upon Christian philosophers to refute the arguments on which they are based, and to make known the truth.

52. Goetz and Taliaferro, *Brief History of the Soul*, 97 (quoting Descartes's *Discourse on Method*).

53. Curley, "Immortality of the Soul," 34.

54. Curley, "Immortality of the Soul," 35 (quoting Descartes's *Meditations*, Synopsis). Curley goes on to discuss Descartes's comment that proof of the immortality of the soul depends upon an explanation of the whole of physics. Curley, "Immortality of the Soul," 35–36. See also Kraye, "British Philosophy Before Locke," 290 (discussing position of Kenelm Digby that to prove the immortality of the soul "would require 'a totall Survey of the whole science of Bodyes,' which he duly went on to produce [in 1644]", and noting that when Descartes was asked what he thought of Digby's demonstration he said "that while reason enabled us to indulge in fine hopes, it did not provide any certainty of immortality, which could come only from faith.").

C. Spinoza Rejects Descartes's Views on the Nature of the Soul, Its Relation to the Body, and Its Personal Immortality; Instead, Spinoza Contends That the Human Mind and the Body Are Modes of a Single, Infinite Substance Which He Calls "God or Nature," and Denies That There Is a Personal Immortality

1. Spinoza's monism constitutes a rejection of the notion that human beings are a composite of two distinct substances, a material body and an immaterial mind

Spinoza denied Cartesian substance dualism; that is, he denied Descartes's view that the world is comprised of a great many substances divided into two main kinds, material substances, whose essence is extension, and immaterial substances, whose essence is thought.[55] As a corollary of his denial of Cartesian substance dualism, Spinoza denied the Cartesian notion that an immaterial mind and a material body could interact. In the *Ethics*, part 3, proposition 2, Spinoza states: "The body cannot determine the mind to thinking, and the mind cannot determine the body to motion, to rest, or to anything else." In the accompanying scholium, Spinoza replies to those who are "firmly . . . persuaded that, solely at the bidding of the mind, the body moves or rests, and does a number of things which depend upon the will of the mind alone, and upon the power of thought."[56] Spinoza argues that it is premature to be so persuaded because no one has yet come to understand what the body can do, *without being determined by the mind*, by the laws of nature alone, insofar as nature is considered merely as corporeal:

> For no one as yet has understood the structure of the body so accurately as to be able to explain all its functions, not to mention the fact that . . . sleepwalkers in their sleep do very many things which they dare not do while awake; all this showing that the body *itself* can do many things from the laws of its own nature alone at which the mind belonging to that body is amazed. Again, nobody knows by what means or by what method the mind moves the body . . . So that it follows that when men say that this or that action of the body springs from the mind which has command over the body, they do not know what they say, and they do nothing but confess with pretentious words that they know nothing about the cause of the action, and see nothing in it to wonder at. But they will say, that whether they know or do not know by what means the mind moves the body, it is nevertheless in their experience that if the mind were not fit for thinking the body would be inert. They say again, it is in their experience that the mind alone has power to speak and be silent, and to do many other things which they therefore think to be dependent on a

---

55. Cartesian thought was also dualistic in postulating both a material, multifarious, finite, changeable world and an immaterial, simple, infinite, immutable, and omnipotent God who created the world. See generally Wolfson, *Philosophy of Spinoza*, 1:79–80; Curley, *Behind the Geometrical Method*, 19–23.

56. Spinoza, *Ethics*, III, Prop. II, Scholium.

decree of the mind. But with regard to the first assertion, I ask them if experience does not also teach that if the body be sluggish the mind at the same time is not fit for thinking? When the body is asleep, the mind slumbers with it, and has not the power to think, as it has when the body is awake . . .

With regard to the second point, I should say that human affairs would be much more happily conducted if it were equally in the power of men to be silent and to speak; but experience shows over and over again that there is nothing which men have less power over than the tongue, and there is nothing which they are less able to do than to govern their appetites, so that many persons believe that we do freely only those things we have a weak inclination toward . . . but that we do not at all do freely those things we seek by a strong affect . . . So experience itself . . . clearly teaches that men believe themselves to be free simply because they are conscious of their own actions, knowing nothing of the causes by which it is determined: it teaches, too, that the decrees of the mind are nothing but the appetites themselves, which differ, therefore, according to the different temper of the body. For every man determines all things from his affect; those who are agitated by contrary affects do not know what they want, whilst those who are agitated by no affect are easily driven hither and thither *All this plainly shows that the decree of the mind, the appetite, and determination of the body are* coincident in nature, or rather that they are *one and the same thing,* which, when it is considered under the attribute of thought and manifested by that, is called a decree, and when it is considered under the attribute of extension and is deduced from the laws of motion and rest, is called a determination . . . Consequently, those who believe that they speak, or are silent, or do anything else from a free decree of the mind, dream with their eyes open.[57]

Instead of there being two kinds of substances which interact in human beings, as Descartes claimed, for Spinoza there is only *one* substance, which is infinite, and which he refers to as "God or Nature" ("*Deus sive Natura*").[58] All the particular things that Descartes regarded as finite substances, Spinoza says are merely "modes" of the one substance, the modes expressing the "attributes of God in a certain way."[59] The two main attributes of Spinoza's "God or Nature" are thought and extension, and so, for Spinoza, all the particular things that Descartes regarded as finite substances (either finite material substances, such as the human body, or finite immaterial substances,

---

57. Spinoza, *Ethics*, III, Prop. II, Scholium (emphasis added). See Curley, *Behind the Geometrical Method*, 81–82; Hampshire, *Spinoza*, 129–33. With regard to this scholium, the neuroscientist Antonio Damasio comments that Spinoza was not only undermining traditional notions concerning the supposed relationship between an immaterial mind and a material body but was also "preparing the stage" for future discoveries demonstrating that mental phenomena are essentially manifestations of bodily events. See Damasio, *Looking for Spinoza*, 216.

58. See Hampshire, *Spinoza*, 36; Curley, *Behind the Geometrical Method*, 8.

59. Curley, *Behind the Geometrical Method*, 8. See also Kenny, *New History of Western Philosophy*, 3:190; Wolfson, *Philosophy of Spinoza*, 1:64–72.

such as the human mind) are "modes" of the single, infinite substance, either a mode of God's attribute of extension or a mode of God's attribute of thought.[60] To say that something is a "mode" of a particular attribute of "God or Nature" is to say that it is a portion of that attribute,[61] or that it is "in" and "conceived through" that attribute, in a manner something like the way in which an individual thing is "in" and "conceived through" its species and genus (e.g., man is conceived through, and is in, his genus "animal" and his species "rational").[62] As explained by Hampshire:

> Spinoza . . . argued that the two pervasive features of the Universe as it presents itself to our minds, the Universe as a system of extended or spatial things and the Universe as a system of ideas or thought, must be interpreted as two aspects of a single inclusive reality; they are not to be conceived as two distinct substances, a conception which has been proved to be self-contradictory; they must be two attributes of the single substance . . .
>
> Everything which exists in the Universe is to be conceived as a 'modification' or particular differentiation of the unique, all-inclusive substance, whose nature is revealed to us solely under two infinite attributes, Thought and Extension.[63]

Kenny puts it this way:

> Thought and extension, the defining characteristics of mind and matter, are in fact attributes of God himself, so that God is both a thinking and an extended thing; he is mental and he is bodily . . . Individual minds and bodies are modes, or particular configurations, of the divine attributes of thought and extension.[64]

It follows from Spinoza's monism that human beings are not composite substances, having a material body and an immaterial mind which coexist by a true substantial union, as Descartes understood it. Rather, man,

> as a whole is not a substance, nor are his soul and body, taken individually, substances. Man is a combination of two modes. 'All that he has of thought are only modes of the attribute of thought,' and 'all that he has of form, motion, and other things, are likewise' modes of the attributes of extension. Or, as [Spinoza] expresses it in the *Ethics*, 'the essence of man consists of certain modifications of the attributes of God.' These modifications are mind and body, the human mind being 'a part of the infinite intellect of God,' and the human

---

60. For a detailed discussion of Spinoza's understanding of "God or Nature" and the modes of "God or Nature," see Wolfson, *Philosophy of Spinoza*, 1:214–331, 370–400; Hampshire, *Spinoza*, 30–81; Curley, *Behind the Geometrical Method*, 3–50.

61. See Curley, *Behind the Geometrical Method*, 31.

62. See Wolfson, *Philosophy of Spinoza*, 1:76.

63. Hampshire, *Spinoza*, 63, 69.

64. Kenny, *New History of Western Philosophy*, 3:191.

CHAPTER 9.

body being 'a mode which expresses in a certain and determinate manner the essence of God in so far as He is considered as a thing extended.'[65]

In the scholium to proposition 21 of the *Ethics*, part 2, Spinoza puts it this way:

> The mind and the body are one and the same individual, which is conceived now under the attribute of thought, now under the attribute of extension.

The attribute of thought ("Thought") and the attribute of extension ("Extension") "are not in Spinoza two partly parallel, or somehow coordinated, systems of things or events, as mental and physical events are ordinarily imagined to be. They are the same order of causes in the same substance, but conceived under two different attributes of this substance."[66] As Spinoza states it: "The order and connection of ideas is the same as the order and connection of things."[67] Each finite extended thing, conceived under the attribute of thought, is simply the idea of that finite extended thing. Accordingly, the human body, which is a thing as conceived under the attribute of extension, is the same thing which, when conceived under the attribute of thought, is the idea of the human body, or the human mind. There are not two things, the body and the mind; there is only one thing, conceived under the attribute of extension as the body, and conceived under the attribute of thought as the idea of the body.[68]

2. Spinoza is best understood as denying a personal immortality

Because the human mind is not a thing that is separate and distinct from the human body, but is the same thing as the human body, only conceived under the attribute of thought, and because the changes to that thing which, when conceived under the attribute of extension, are considered bodily changes, are the same changes which, when conceived under the attribute of thought, are considered mental changes, it follows that when the human body perishes, that same thing conceived under the attribute of thought as the human mind also perishes. As Spinoza states in the *Short Treatise*:

---

65. Wolfson, *Philosophy of Spinoza*, 2:41 (quoting Spinoza, *Short Treatise*, II, Preface, sect. 3; and *Ethics*, Part 2, Prop. 10, Corollary; Prop. 11, Corollary; Definition 1). See Curley, *Behind the Geometrical Method*, 60–62.

66. Hampshire, *Spinoza*, 64.

67. Spinoza, *Ethics*, Part 2, Prop. 7.

68. See Kenny, *New History of Western Philosophy*, 3:228 ("Peter's soul and Peter's body are one and the same thing, looked at from two different points of view . . . Peter's soul is a mode of the attribute of thinking, and Peter's body is a mode of the attribute of extension: they are both one and the same thing, expressed in two ways. This doctrine is meant to exclude the problem that bedeviled Descartes, namely, how to explain the manner in which soul and body interact. They do not interact at all, Spinoza answers: they are the very same thing.").

Now since the Idea proceeds from the existence of the object, then if the object changes *or is destroyed*, the Idea itself also changes *or is destroyed* in the same degree.[69]

Similarly, in the *Ethics*, Spinoza suggests that the mind or soul of a person, say Peter, exists only so long as that singular thing, Peter, exists. Specifically, Spinoza explains the difference between the idea of Peter which constitutes the essence of Peter's mind from the idea of the same Peter which is in the mind of another man, say Paul:

> The former directly expresses the essence of Peter's own body, *and involves existence only so long as Peter exists*; but the latter indicates the constitution of Paul's body rather than the nature of Peter, and therefore, as long as that disposition lasts, contemplates Peter as present even though Peter may not exist.[70]

Commenting on this quotation, Kenny states:

> The crucial passage here is the statement that the idea of Peter that is Peter's soul 'involves existence only so long as Peter exists.' Does this mean that Peter's soul goes out of existence when Peter does? This would seem to follow from Spinoza's statement that a human being consists of body and soul, and that body and soul are the same thing under two different aspects. Peter, Peter's soul, and Peter's body should, on this account, come into and go out of existence together.[71]

Yet, as Kenny recognizes, "if we ask whether the soul is immortal, Spinoza does not give a totally unequivocal answer."[72] This is primarily because proposition 23 of the fifth part of the *Ethics* states:

> The human mind cannot be absolutely destroyed with the Body, but something of it remains which is eternal.[73]

The exact meaning of this sentence is the subject of debate. Indeed, it has been well noted that "Spinoza's views on the immortality of the soul . . . are . . . notoriously

---

69. Spinoza, *Short Treatise*, Appendix II, sec. 7 (emphasis added).

70. Spinoza, *Ethics*, Part 2, Prop. 17, Scholium (emphasis added). See Kenny, *New History of Western Philosophy*, 3:229. See also Spinoza, *Ethics*, Part 5, Prop. 23, Scholium ("Our mind . . . can be said to endure, and its existence can be defined by a certain time, only insofar as it involves the actual existence of our body.").

71. Kenny, *New History of Western Philosophy*, 3:229–30.

72. Kenny, *New History of Western Philosophy*, 3:230.

73. See also Spinoza, *Short Treatise*, 116–17 ("*we have said nothing about the time of the human mind's creation*. Our reason is that it is not sufficiently established at what time God creates it, *since it can exist without the body*.") (emphasis added); 140–4 (if the soul is united with the body, and the body perishes, then the soul must perish also; but, "if it is united with another thing, which is, and remains, immutable, then . . . it will have to remain immutable also."); 152–56 (discussing the human soul and concluding that "from all this (as also because our soul is united with God, and is part of the infinite Idea arising immediately from God) we can see clearly . . . the immortality of the soul.").

difficult to fathom."[74] While it is clear that "something" of the mind or soul does not perish with the body,[75] the exact nature of this "something" is disputed. The dispute concerns, primarily, whether the "something" of the mind that survives the destruction of the body is of such a nature that it constitutes the personal immortality of the relevant person, or not.[76] Before discussing this dispute, however, it is best to say a word as to why the human mind cannot be absolutely destroyed with the body.

By way of demonstrating proposition 23, Spinoza points to proposition 22, which states that "in God there is necessarily an idea that expresses the essence of this or that human Body, under a species of eternity (*sub specie aeternitatis*)."[77] He then states that, because the object of the idea constituting the human mind is the body, the idea in God that expresses the essence of the body is "necessarily something that pertains to the essence of the human Mind."[78] He continues:

> But we do not attribute to the human Mind any duration that can be defined by time, except insofar as it expresses the actual existence of the Body, which is explained by duration, and can be defined by time, i.e. (by IIP8C), we do not attribute duration to it [sc., the human Mind] except while the Body endures. However, since what is conceived, with a certain eternal necessity, through God's essence itself (by P22) is nevertheless something, this something that pertains to the essence of the Mind will necessarily be eternal.[79]

In other words, the idea in God of the human body cannot be an idea of the human body as the body exists in time, but only an idea of the *essence* of the human body as it exists outside of time (*sub specie aeternitatis*), presumably as part of God's attribute of extension. Thus, the idea in God that has as its object only the nontemporal *essence* of the human body must itself pertain, not to the human mind as it exists in time, but only to the *essence* of the human mind as it exists outside of time (*sub specie aeternitatis*), presumably as part of God's attribute of thought. Therefore, it seems reasonable to say that the human mind cannot be absolutely destroyed because, although the human body as it exists as a finite thing in time is destroyed, the *essence* of the human body as it exists *sub specie aeternitatis* cannot be destroyed; and where

---

74. Nadler, *Spinoza's Heresy*, 105. See Curley, *Behind the Geometrical Method*, 84 (Curley comments that he doesn't feel that he himself adequately understands the relevant part of the *Ethics* and believes "that no one else understands it adequately either.").

75. See Curley, "Immortality of the Soul," 39–40.

76. See Nadler, *Spinoza's Heresy*, 105-8 ("there has been, since the posthumous publication of his writings, a great deal of debate over whether Spinoza believes in personal immortality or rejects it; even today no consensus has emerged.").

77. Spinoza, *Ethics*, Part 5, Prop. 22.

78. Spinoza, *Ethics*, Part 5, Prop. 23.

79. Spinoza, *Ethics*, Part 5, Prop. 23.

the *essence* of the body exists, so the *essence* of the mind (that is, the idea of the *essence* of the body) must exist, albeit *sub specie aeternitatis*.[80]

Nadler explains it this way:

> Given Spinoza's general parallelism between the attributes of Extension and Thought, and given the resulting and more particular parallelism in a human being between what is true of the body and what is true of the mind, there are then, likewise—and necessarily—two aspects of the human mind, which is nothing other than the idea *of* the body. First, there is the aspect of the mind that corresponds to the durational existence of the body . . .
>
> [T]his part of the mind comes to an end when the duration of the body comes to an end, that is, at a person's death . . . But there is another part of the mind—namely that aspect of it that corresponds to the eternal aspect of the body. This is the expression in the attribute of Thought of the body's extended essence. Like its correlate in extension, this aspect of the mind is eternal. It is a part of the mind that remains after a person's death.[81]

The part of the mind that remains after death is very different than the mind that is the idea of the body as it existed in time. For one thing, Spinoza very clearly says that the capacity for imagination and memory exists only so long as the finite human body endures.[82] So, the eternal part of the mind, after death, retains no memory of its prior existence, and is unable to even imagine such prior existence. Moreover, the eternal part of the mind is unable to have any notion of external objects because there can be no image formed of external objects without the imagination.[83] Nor can there be any determination that anything is pleasant or unpleasant because the imagination plays an important role in all such determinations.[84] So, the eternal part of the mind is only able to see things in their necessary and eternal aspect, or to have a certain type of knowledge that is called by Spinoza "adequate knowledge."[85]

It is because the eternal mind is limited in this way that some scholars contend that any immortality of the soul envisioned by Spinoza cannot be considered a personal immortality. Thus, for example, Curley states:

---

80. See generally Spinoza, *Ethics*, Part 5, Prop. 29; Hampshire, *Spinoza*, 66–67, 171–76.

81. Nadler, *Spinoza's Heresy*, 113. See also Curley, *Behind the Geometrical Method*, 83–85; Kenny, *New History of Western Philosophy*, 3:230 (that the human mind cannot be destroyed with the body "turns out only to mean that since our soul is an idea, and all ideas are ultimately in the mind of God, and God is eternal, there never was a time when our soul was totally nonexistent. Our life is but an episode in the eternal life of God, and when we die that life persists."); Yovel, *Marrano of Reason*, 169–70; Damasio, *Looking for Spinoza*, 216–17.

82. Spinoza, *Ethics*, Part 5, Prop. 21. See Curley, *Behind the Geometrical Method*, 85–86; Nadler, *Spinoza's Heresy*, 126; Wolfson, *Philosophy of Spinoza*, 2:291.

83. See generally Wolfson, *Philosophy of Spinoza*, 2:80–90.

84. See Wolfson, *Philosophy of Spinoza*, 2:165.

85. See Wolfson, *Philosophy of Spinoza*, 2:10–63. See also Nadler, *Spinoza's Heresy*, 116–18; Hampshire, *Spinoza*, 102–3.

If memory does not survive the destruction of the body, then *I* do not survive the destruction of the body. For some memory of my past actions is essential to my being the person who performed them. So, Spinoza's doctrine of the eternity of the mind cannot offer the kind of consolation provided by its analogue in Descartes. Whatever the doctrine of the eternity of the mind does mean, it does not mean that *I* can entertain any hope of immortality.[86]

In the same vein, Curley states that the portion of the mind that Spinoza proclaims to be eternal:

> cannot retain any sense of itself as an individual existing over time, with those memories of its past which are essential to its identity as the same person. Continuity of memory is destroyed when the traces in the brain which record past experience are destroyed. What survives must be something quite impersonal, with which we cannot really identify, and about whose fate we cannot deeply care.[87]

Nadler, similarly, refers to Spinoza's "blatant rejection of personal immortality,"[88] but offers a somewhat different analysis than Curley. Nadler argues that there can be no personal immortality for the reason that one human mind *sub specie aeternitatis* is not "quantitatively distinguishable" from any another human mind *sub specie aeternitatis* because the "adequate ideas that remain after one's death are not bound together in any way and thus separated from any other 'collection' of adequate ideas (say, those that belonged to someone else)."[89] Hampshire makes substantially the same point.[90]

At least one scholar, however, interprets Spinoza as supporting individual immortality. Wolfson asserts that Spinoza "*must have found* that there is nothing in his philosophy to preclude the assumption that, by the eternal order of nature, that portion of the infinite intellect of God which constitutes the human mind acquires, through its experience in life, a certain distinctness and individuality which remains with it even after death when it is reunited with that infinite intellect of God whence

---

86. Curley, *Behind the Geometrical Method*, 86 (emphasis original). See also Nadler, *Spinoza's Heresy*, 124 ("there can be no persistence of a *person* after his death"; emphasis original).

87. Curley, "Immortality of the Soul," 40. See also Kenny, *New History of Western Philosophy*, 3:230 (The immortality of the soul envisioned by Spinoza "is something very different from the personal survival in an afterlife which was the aspiration of popular piety.").

88. Nadler, *Spinoza's Heresy*, 130.

89. Nadler, *Spinoza's Heresy*, 129. Nadler also argues that "it is hard to see *how* one eternal mind—or, rather, the body of eternal adequate ideas that once belonged to a person's mind—could be qualitatively differentiated or individuated from another. Or, to put it more precisely, there is no reason why two eternal minds should *necessarily* be distinguishable from one another" (Nadler, *Spinoza's Heresy*, 124–25; emphasis original).

90. Hampshire, *Spinoza*, 174–75 ("The possible eternity of the human mind cannot . . . be intended by Spinoza to mean that I literally survive, as a distinguishable individual, in so far as I attain genuine knowledge; for in so far as I attain genuine knowledge, my individuality as a particular thing disappears and my mind becomes so far united with God or Nature conceived under the attribute of thought.").

it originally came."⁹¹ As to why Spinoza *must have found* this, Wolfson writes: "What sense is there in speaking of the immortality of the soul unless the soul, unlike the body, in its reabsorption in the universal soul [the attribute of thought] retains a certain kind of individuality which is not found in the body in its reabsorption in the universal body [the attribute of extension]?" Then Wolfson asserts that having "found this . . . view of immortality not inconsistent with his philosophy, Spinoza accepted it."⁹² Wolfson acknowledges that Spinoza maintains that imagination and memory are destroyed with the body, but asserts, without further explanation, that this is "quite in accordance with" not only individual immortality but personal immortality.⁹³

In any event, Spinoza is adamant in maintaining that whatever remains of the mind after death will not receive any reward or punishment for what the person did before death. By denying that there is any reward or punishment for the eternal part of the mind, the whole *raison d'etre* for a belief in the immortality of the soul, according to traditional Jewish thought, is undermined. So, any concept of a personal immortality that anyone sees in Spinoza is wholly at odds with the concept of a personal immortality held by all prior Jewish philosophers.

D. Spinoza Denies That There Is Any Postmortem Reward or Punishment

Spinoza, of course, could not possibly accept belief in bodily resurrection since bodily resurrection would contravene the laws of nature.⁹⁴ So, if Spinoza is interpreted as denying personal immortality of the soul, there can be no postmortem reward or punishment. Accordingly, Nadler contends that Spinoza attacked the well-established Jewish theodicy that was first expressed by the early sages, was reformulated and systematized by Saadia, and was followed by subsequent medieval Jewish philosophers.⁹⁵

---

91. Wolfson, *From Philo to Spinoza*, 60 (emphasis added). Under this view of immortality "distinctness and individuality, by the eternal order of nature, is retained by the soul even after it departs from the body" (Wolfson, *From Philo to Spinoza*, 59).

92. Wolfson, *From Philo to Spinoza*, 61.

93. Wolfson, *From Philo to Spinoza*, 61 (emphasis added). See also Wolfson, *Philosophy of Spinoza*, 2:294–95, 318–19 (Wolfson argues that "the immortality of the soul, according to Spinoza, is *personal* and individual."). Wolfson's argument is specious. In the first place, as Nadler has pointed out, nowhere in the *Ethics* does Spinoza actually use the phrase "immortality of the soul" (*immortalitas animae*); instead, Spinoza self-consciously uses the phrase "eternity of the mind" (*mentis aeternitas*). See Nadler, *Spinoza's Heresy*, 108, 110–11. Wolfson also errs in accepting that, if the eternal mind preserves *anything* that was peculiar to a human being during his life, this constitutes a *personal* immortality. See generally Forstrom, *John Locke and Personal Identity*, 6–28 (discussing John Locke's argument that personal identity requires more than numerical sameness of an immaterial substance; it requires memory of one's past self and actions continued under consciousness of being the same person).

94. See generally Yovel, *Marrano of Reason*, 76 (for Spinoza "the soul in the psychological sense is destroyed with the body and neither of them enjoys the prospect of resurrection").

95. See Nadler, *Spinoza's Heresy*, 142–53.

This Jewish theodicy is that "true reward and punishment occur in the world to come."[96] Nadler writes:

> Now when Spinoza denies the personal immortality of the soul, he is, in effect, confronting head-on this whole tradition of theodicy. And he does so for the sake of demonstrating that the true value of virtue is in this life. Human virtue—the striving for and acquisition of understanding and the third kind of knowledge—just *is* happiness . . . Spinoza is thus engaged . . . [in] forestalling a particular theodicy—namely, that practiced by the rabbis of the Talmud, by Saadya, Maimonides, and Gersonides, and by a host of other philosophers, Jewish and gentile—and persuading people not to look at virtue as a burden to be borne for the sake of some alleged otherworldly reward.[97]

But even if Spinoza is interpreted as accepting a personal immortality, it is, nevertheless, beyond doubt that Spinoza rejects the idea that there is any reward or punishment in the afterlife for what a person does before the body is destroyed. The sole reward for following God's law (as Spinoza understands God's law) is the achievement of the highest good or blessedness, which is the love of God (as Spinoza understands the love of God). In other words, virtue is its own reward; virtue is not an instrumental good but an intrinsic good. There is nothing else to be gained from the love of God, either in this life or in any afterlife. This point is made clear in the *Theological-Political Treatise* where Spinoza explains:

> Since the love of God is man's highest happiness and blessedness, and the final end and aim of all human action, it follows that only he observes Divine Law who makes it his object to love God not through fear of punishment nor through love of some other thing such as sensual pleasure, fame, and so forth, but from the mere fact that he knows God, or knows that the knowledge and love of God is the supreme good. So the sum of the Divine Law and its chief command is to love God as the supreme good; that is, as we have said, not from fear of some punishment or penalty nor from love of some other thing from which we desire to derive pleasure.[98]

The love of God is associated by Spinoza with intellectual perfection and achieving knowledge of nature. He, consequently, recognizes that the average person is not able to accept the love of God as the highest good, but instead seeks some physical, sensual pleasure as the highest good. So, the previously quoted passage from the *Theological-Political Treatise* continues:

---

96. Nadler, *Spinoza's Heresy*, 153 (quoting Gersonides's *The Wars of the Lord*).

97. Nadler, *Spinoza's Heresy*, 153 (emphasis original). See also Nadler, *Spinoza*, 131, 242–43; Yovel, *Marrano of Reason*, 170; Hampshire, *Spinoza*, 164–65.

98. Spinoza, *Theological-Political Treatise*, 51–52. See also Spinoza, *Short Treatise*, 142 ("God does not give man laws in order to reward him when he fulfills them.").

But carnal man cannot understand these things: He thinks them foolish because he has too stunted a knowledge of God, and in this supreme good, consisting as it does only in philosophic thinking and pure activity of the mind, he finds nothing to touch, to eat, or to feed the fleshly appetites which are his chief delight. But those who recognize that they have no more precious gift than intellect and a sound mind are sure to regard these as very substantial blessings.[99]

Substantially the same point is reiterated at the close of the *Ethics*. He begins in proposition 41 of the fifth part by stating that morality, religion, and virtue (which are all to be associated with following the divine law and achieving intellectual perfection and the highest good) would be of the first importance *even if we didn't know that our mind is eternal*. This suggests that any belief in an afterlife is irrelevant as a motive to following the divine law and achieving the highest good. He then states:

> The usual conviction of the multitude seems to be different. For most people apparently believe that they are free to the extent that they are permitted to yield to their lust, and that they give up their right [to yield to their lust] to the extent that they are bound to live according to the rule of the divine law. Morality, then, and Religion, and absolutely everything related to Strength of Character, they believe to be burdens, which they hope to put down after death, when they also hope to receive a reward for their bondage, that is, for their Morality and Religion. They are induced to live according to the rule of the divine law (as far as their weakness and lack of character allows) not only by this hope, but also, and especially, by the fear that they may be punished horribly after death. If men did not have this Hope and Fear, but believed instead that minds die with the body, and that the wretched, exhausted with the burden of Morality, cannot look forward to a life to come, they would return to their natural disposition, and would prefer to govern all their actions according to lust . . .
>
> These opinions seem no less absurd to me than if someone, because he does not believe he can nourish his body with good food to eternity, should prefer to fill himself with poisons and other deadly things, or because he sees that the Mind is not eternal, *or* immortal, should prefer to be mindless, and to live without reason. These [common beliefs] are so absurd they are hardly worth mentioning.[100]

The last proposition of the *Ethics* states: "Blessedness is not the reward of virtue, but virtue itself; nor do we enjoy it because we restrain our lusts; on the contrary, because we enjoy it, we are able to restrain them."[101] Curley comments that "Spino-

---

99. Spinoza, *Theological-Political Treatise*, 52.

100. Spinoza, *Ethics*, Part 5, Prop. 41, Scholium (emphasis original). See Nadler, *Spinoza*, 246–47; Hampshire, *Spinoza*, 202. See also Yovel, *Marrano of Reason*, 132–35, 197–98.

101. Spinoza, *Ethics*, Part 5, Prop. 42.

za is opposed to the Cartesian idea that we require the hope of reward and fear of punishment in the afterlife to motive a preference for the right over the useful. The reward of virtue is not blessedness in the world to come, but virtuous living itself."[102] Hampshire sums up Spinoza's point of view concerning reward and punishment as follows:

> The true philosopher will be uninfluenced by fear and hope, and unaffected by the superstitious fears and hopes of the anthropomorphic religions, with their futile imaginations of jealous Gods allotting rewards and punishments. He will know that 'virtue is its own reward,' in the strict sense that the best life is necessarily the happiest; the intrinsic satisfactions of the free mind are the most lasting and secure . . . Spinoza writes with disgust and contempt of the appeal of conventional religious morality to supernatural rewards and punishments, as being appeals which are essentially squalid and unworthy of adult intelligence.[103]

E. According to Spinoza, It Is Improper to Assert That the Immortality of the Soul, or a Postmortem Reward or Punishment, Are Revealed Truths, Since Revelation Has Nothing to Do with Knowledge of the Natural World

Spinoza's views concerning the Hebrew Bible are primarily to be found in the *Theological-Political Treatise*. Most relevant for present purposes are the following two points: (1) theologians have read ideas into the Hebrew Bible that are not actually contained in it, including ideas about the immortality of the soul and a postmortem reward and punishment, and (2) properly understood, there are no revealed truths in the Hebrew Bible having anything to do with the immortality of the soul or the nature of any afterlife because the aim of the Hebrew Bible is not to impart knowledge concerning philosophy or "scientific knowledge"; rather, reason and revelation, philosophy and theology, are separate and distinct endeavors, and the way to arrive at truths about the nature of the world is only through reason or philosophy, not revelation or theology.[104] Both of these points are mentioned by Spinoza in the *Treatise*'s Preface, as explained by Feldman:

---

102. Curley, "Immortality of the Soul," 40. Spinoza may be distinguished from Maimonides. Maimonides believed that one should be virtuous, not for the sake of a reward, but only out of love of God; yet, he also asserted that it is nevertheless true that external rewards and punishments are received for virtue and wickedness, respectively. See Maimonides, *Book of Knowledge*, 91a–93a (*Hilkhot T'shuvah*, 9–10).

103. Hampshire, *Spinoza*, 164–65.

104. Spinoza also claims that the traditional ascription of the authorship of the Torah to Moses is false, that the traditional ascriptions of authorship of the other books of the Hebrew Bible are also false, that the Hebrew Bible was "written by a number of men of . . . different generations over a period of time which . . . [extends] to about two thousand years," and that a significant portion of the text

> Already in the Preface ... Spinoza introduces two methodological principles that will govern his discussions throughout the treatise. *First, he makes it quite clear that one of the basic errors of previous exegetes of the Bible had been their tendency to read into the text ideas that they derived from some nonbiblical source, especially but not exclusively from philosophy.* These ideas then became authoritative, and the interpreters attained the status of an exegetical elite who believed that they alone had the right to interpret the Bible. Spinoza rejects this approach as arbitrary and arrogant: arbitrary, since it assumes that the Bible is a philosophical book from which all kinds of philosophical and scientific truths can be learned, at least by those competent to recognize these truths behind or beneath the literal text; arrogant, since it makes pretext to a level of intellectual insight that is unwarranted and self-serving. Spinoza proposes that we read the Bible as it is, literally, that we try our best to understand what it really says, not attempt to make it say what we want it to say. *Secondly*, in reading the Bible as it is written, we must rely upon our best tool, reason. This means that we must not, especially at the outset of our reading, subordinate reason to any theological dogmas or principles. The medieval doctrine that philosophy is the 'hand maiden' of theology Spinoza explicitly and scornfully rejects. But lest one think that Scripture will be made a hand maiden to philosophy, as some medieval philosophers attempted, *Spinoza will argue that philosophy and theology are separate and independent disciplines*, a theme that will be developed in detail in a later chapter of the [*Treatise*].[105]

With respect to the first of these points, Spinoza specifies the ancient Greeks—particularly Plato and Aristotle—as the original source of those ideas that he believes to have been improperly read into the Hebrew Bible. Regarding those responsible for this perversion of the true teaching of the Hebrew Bible, Spinoza writes:

> I grant that they have expressed boundless wonder at Scripture's profound mysteries, yet I do not see that they have taught anything more than the speculations of Aristotelians or Platonists, and they have made Scripture conform to these so as to avoid appearing to be the followers of heathens. It was not enough for them to share in the delusions of the Greeks: they have sought to represent the prophets as sharing in these same delusions.[106]

In chapter 7 of the *Treatise,* which concerns the proper method of interpreting Scripture, Spinoza again complains about the improper method of reading falsehoods into the Hebrew Bible:

---

of the Hebrew Bible is corrupt. See Spinoza, *Theological-Political Treatise*, 108–18, 163. See generally Nadler, *Spinoza*, 275–77.

105. Feldman, "Introduction," xix–xx (emphasis added).

106. Spinoza, *Theological-Political Treatise*, 5.

CHAPTER 9.

> We see that nearly all men parade their own ideas as God's Word, their chief aim being to compel others to think as they do, while using religion as a pretext. We see I say, that the chief concern of the theologians on the whole has been to extort from Holy Scripture their own arbitrarily invented ideas, for which they claim divine authority . . . [So] that religion takes the form not so much of obedience to the teachings of the Holy Spirit as of defending what men have invented.[107]

That these "arbitrarily invented ideas" are ones that come from the ancient Greek philosophers is reiterated in subsequent chapters. Specifically, in chapter 13, Spinoza states that Scripture does not contain "abstruse speculation or philosophic reasoning."[108] He then writes:

> I am therefore astonished at the ingenuity displayed by those, of whom I have already spoken, who find in Scripture mysteries so profound as not to be open to explanation in any human language, and who have then imported into religion so many matters of philosophic nature that the Church seems like an academy, and religion like a science . . . I should indeed be surprised if they taught any purely philosophic doctrine which was new and not already a commonplace in ages past among gentile philosophers (whom they nevertheless accuse of blindness); for *if you enquire as to the nature of the mysteries which they see lurking in Scripture you will certainly find nothing but the notions of an Aristotle or a Plato or the* like, which often seem to suggest the fantasies of any uneducated person rather than the findings of an accomplished biblical scholar.[109]

Although Spinoza leaves no doubt that the "arbitrarily invented ideas" that were being read into the Hebrew Bible were "the delusions of the Greeks," he never specifies which ideas of the ancient Greeks he thought were the "delusions" being read into the Hebrew Bible. But it seems reasonable to suppose that among these "delusions" are the beliefs that the soul is a thing distinct from the body, constitutes the real person, and will be rewarded or punished in an afterlife for conduct in this life. He clearly thought that these beliefs are false. And he also was well aware that Scripture had been "made to conform" to such beliefs. Even in his youth, Spinoza had declared that (1) whenever Scripture speaks of "soul" that word "is used simply to express life, or anything that is living [and it] would be useless to search for any passage in support of immortality," and (2) "nothing is to be found in the Bible about the nonmaterial or incorporeal."[110] In addition, he must have known both that several works had been written in Amsterdam in the first half of the seventeenth century opposing da Costa's assertion that

---

107. Spinoza, *Theological-Political Treatise*, 88.
108. Spinoza, *Theological-Political Treatise*, 157.
109. Spinoza, *Theological-Political Treatise*, 157–58 (emphasis added).
110. Nadler, *Spinoza's Heresy*, 29. See Wolfson, *Philosophy of Spinoza*, 2:324.

the Hebrew Bible does not assert the immortality of the soul, and that Menasseh ben Israel taught that belief in the immortality of the soul was the foundation for all the basic tenets of Judaism.

Turning to the second point, that philosophy and theology are separate and distinct disciplines, Spinoza says that Scripture "has nothing to do with philosophy, each standing on its own footing."[111] This point is pursued in detail in chapters 13 and 14. In chapter 13 Spinoza contends that "Scripture's aim was not to impart scientific knowledge" and that, except for the knowledge necessary to obey God's commandment to love one's neighbor, "philosophic questions . . . whether they be concerned with knowledge of God or with knowledge of Nature, have nothing to do with Scripture, and should therefore be dissociated from revealed religion."[112] The clear implication of this teaching is that one should not look to Scripture to ascertain answers to questions concerning the existence or nature of a soul or concerning the existence or nature of an afterlife. These are philosophic questions, the answers to which require knowledge of the nature of the world; and, says Spinoza, Scripture does not reveal any truths about the nature of the world.

Chapter 14 focuses specifically on the difference between faith and philosophy. Spinoza defines faith as "the holding of certain beliefs about God such that, without these beliefs, there cannot be obedience to God," and from this definition he deduces seven "tenets of faith," none of which concerns immortality of the soul or the afterlife.[113] Thus, faith requires no belief in the immortality of the soul or the afterlife. Chapter 14 of the *Treatise* concludes with the following thought:

> It now remains for me to show finally that between faith and theology on the one side and philosophy on the other there is no relation and no affinity . . . The aim of philosophy is, quite simply, truth, while the aim of faith . . . is nothing other than obedience and piety. Again, philosophy rests on the basis of universally valid axioms, and must be constructed by studying Nature alone, whereas faith . . . must be derived only from Scripture and revelation . . . So faith allows to every man the utmost freedom to philosophize, and he may hold whatever opinions he pleases on any subjects whatsoever.[114]

There is no doubt that the proposition that faith and revealed truth have no affinity with philosophy and the truths of reason has as a corollary that it is improper to assert that the immortality of the soul, or a postmortem reward or punishment, are matters of faith or are revealed truths. If they are truths at all, this must be established by philosophy and rational argument.

---

111. Spinoza, *Theological-Political Treatise*, 6.
112. Spinoza, *Theological-Political Treatise*, 158.
113. Spinoza, *Theological-Political Treatise*, 165–66.
114. Spinoza, *Theological-Political Treatise*, 169.

CHAPTER 9.

F. Spinoza Occupies a Pivotal Place in the History of Jewish Thought as a Result of Insisting That Philosophy Should Neither Be Made to Conform to Scripture Nor Be Made Ancillary to Scripture, and Emphasizing That There Is Only a This-Worldly Existence—There Is No Afterlife

Both Wolfson and Yovel see Spinoza as occupying a central position in the history of Jewish thought, and of intellectual history in general. Specifically, both see Spinoza as rejecting traditional religious points of view and advocating ideas leading to modern secularism. However, each sees the break with past religious traditions somewhat differently.

Wolfson sees Spinoza's break with past religious traditions as the rejection of a complex of principles that Wolfson dubs "Philonic philosophy."[115] Philonic philosophy is "that system of thought which flourished between pagan Greek philosophy, which knew not of Scripture, and that body of philosophic writings which ever since the seventeenth century has tried to free itself from the influence of Scripture."[116] It was the method of Philonic philosophy to harmonize Scripture and Platonic and Aristotelian ideas as they developed over time.[117] According to Wolfson, "[Spinoza's] daring consists in overthrowing the old Philonic principles which by his time had dominated European religious philosophy for some sixteen centuries."[118] Wolfson identifies several Philonic principles that Spinoza attacked, including principles regarding (1) God and God's relation to the universe, (2) Man and Man's soul (in particular, "that the human soul is of divine origin, and has been especially created by God apart from the body, so that even after it is placed in the body it continues to exist there as something apart from it"), and (3) a happiness for Man that is "twofold: happiness in the present life and happiness in what is called the hereafter."[119]

Yovel sees Spinoza's break with past religious traditions more narrowly, as the break with one principle—otherworldliness. Spinoza's rejection of otherworldliness

---

115. See generally Wolfson, *From Philo to Spinoza*, 17–38.

116. Twersky, "Introduction," 11. See Wolfson, *From Philo to Spinoza*, 17 (". . . between ancient Greek philosophy which knew not Scripture and the philosophy which ever since the seventeenth century has tried to free itself from the influence of Scripture there was a philosophy which placed itself at the service of Scripture and was willing to take orders from it.").

117. See Twersky, "Introduction," 11.

118. Twersky, "Introduction," 11. See Wolfson, *From Philo to Spinoza*, 35 ("Spinoza it was who for the first time launched a grand assault upon . . . the Philonic philosophy.").

119. See Wolfson, *From Philo to Spinoza*, 41–64. See Harvey, "Portrait of Spinoza as a Maimonidean," 151–52. See also Schwartz, *First Modern Jew*, 196–98 (recognizing that Spinoza played a significant role in the origins of Jewish secularism). Arguably, the most important aspect of Spinoza's break with Philonic philosophy is not his rejection of particular principles but his rejection of the *method* of "Philonic philosophy," that is, the attempt to harmonize Scripture and philosophy. See generally Spinoza, *Theological-Political Treatise*, 170. See Feldman, "Introduction," xxxvi; Nadler, *Book Forged in Hell*, 180–82.

and his embrace of this-worldliness is called by Yovel the "philosophy [or principle] of immanence."[120] As Yovel expresses it, "Spinoza's great innovation... was his 'philosophy of immanence,' with its emphasis on the fact that 'this-worldly existence [is] all there is... the only actual being and the sole source of ethical value.'"[121] In *Spinoza and Other Heretics*, Yovel claims that "Spinoza took the first step in the eventual secularization of Jewish life by examining it empirically as a natural phenomenon subject solely to the forces of secular history."[122] Yovel analyzes the relationship between Spinoza and a host of subsequent thinkers, both Jewish and Christian—Kant, Hegel, Heine, Hess, Feuerbach, Marx, Nietzsche, and Freud. Such consideration is aimed at establishing that "Spinoza's philosophy of immanence has tacitly or expressly penetrated the major currents of modern thought and has helped to shape the modern mind far beyond what is usually recognized... [and] that much of the history of modern thought can be retold—and illuminated—from the standpoint of Spinoza's immanent revolution."[123]

More broadly speaking, Spinoza helped to usher in the Age of Enlightenment. No longer were philosophers and intellectuals satisfied to rely upon revelation, or Scripture, as the main source of knowledge and truth; instead, they relied upon what they called "the natural light of reason."[124] Moreover, Enlightenment philosophers in England and France (1) shunned Aristotelianism, (2) embraced deism, atheism, empiricism, and materialism, (3) denied a rational basis to accept the immortality of the soul or resurrection, and (4) rejected reward and punishment in an afterlife as the motivation for proper conduct. The German Enlightenment, however, was not in the same empiricist, materialist mold as the English and French Enlightenments. The leading German philosopher, Gottfried Wilhelm von Leibniz, was a rationalist as well as an immaterialist. Leibniz maintained a belief in the immortality of the soul and of its reward or punishment in an afterlife, and it was Leibniz, not Spinoza, who would most influence the leading philosopher of the Jewish Enlightenment, Moses Mendelssohn. Although Mendelssohn acknowledged the importance of Spinoza, it was only "as a necessary, if erroneous precursor to the philosophy of Leibniz."[125] Therefore, before considering the influence of Spinoza and the principle of immanence in modern Jewish thought, we first turn to Mendelssohn and modern Jewish movements which have tenaciously clung to otherworldliness.

---

120. Yovel, *Marrano of Reason*, ix; Yovel, *Adventures of Immanence*, ix.
121. Schwartz, *First Modern Jew*, 193 (quoting Yovel, *Marrano of Reason*, ix).
122. Yovel, *Marrano of Reason*, 199.
123. Yovel, *Marrano of Reason*, x.
124. Spinoza, *Theological-Political Treatise*, 6.
125. Schwartz, *First Modern Jew*, 36.

10.

In the Mid-Eighteenth Century, Moses Mendelssohn Publishes His *Phädon, or On the Immortality of the Soul*

MOSES MENDELSSOHN, THE FOUNDING father of the *Haskalah*, wrote *Phädon, or On the Immortality of the Soul, in Three Dialogues* (1767) to prove that the soul is immaterial and immortal. It "was an international bestseller" and made Mendelssohn a "philosophical star."[1] Although *Phädon* was written in German, Mendelssohn published an essay in Hebrew that presented the essence of the *Phädon*.[2] This essay, together with a letter written by Mendelssohn dealing with the doctrine of preestablished harmony advanced by Leibniz,[3] and with various theories about the relationship between body and soul, was published in 1787 under the title *Sefer Ha-Nephesh*.[4] A Hebrew translation of *Phädon* appeared that same year.[5] Since Mendelssohn's arguments for the immateriality and immortality of the soul are based, not on revelation, but on reason—on philosophical arguments which give rise to the truths of what he calls "natural religion"—before discussing the *Phädon* and *Sefer Ha-Nephesh* mention will be made of Mendelssohn's general epistemology.

A. Mendelssohn Distinguishes the Eternal Truths of Reason Naturally Revealed to All Thinking People from the Legislation Supernaturally Revealed Only to the Jews

Mendelssohn believed that truths about fundamental principles such as the existence and providence of God, the immortality of the soul, and the vocation of man are

---

1. Gottlieb, *Moses Mendelssohn*, xiv.
2. Altmann, *Moses Mendelssohn*, 181.
3. The theory of preestablished harmony is that God has preestablished the corporeal realm and the incorporeal realm, the mind and the body, to act in a harmonious and finely coordinated way.
4. Altmann, *Moses Mendelssohn*, 181.
5. Altmann, *Moses Mendelssohn*, 192.

"open to the understanding of the natural, unspoiled intellect of every man," which is to say, open to "natural reason."[6] Because these truths are universal and accessible to all, they are "eternal truths"; collectively, they constitute a universally valid "natural religion."[7] In *Jerusalem* (1783), Mendelssohn proclaimed:

> I . . . do not believe that the powers of human reason are insufficient to persuade men of the eternal truths that are indispensable to human felicity, and that God had to reveal them in a supernatural manner.[8]

Mendelssohn states that the eternal truths of natural religion can be reduced to a few fundamental principles, and he compares the three basic principles of Judaism enunciated by Joseph Albo[9] to the principles of reason identified by Herbert of Cherbury, the founder of English deism.[10] But Mendelssohn is not a deist; he accepted supernatural revelation as an alternative source of knowledge, at least for Jews. The distinction between truth *naturally* revealed to all thinking people and truth *supernaturally* revealed only to the Jews is elucidated by Mendelssohn in *Jerusalem*. Mendelssohn contends that the substance of what God supernaturally revealed to the ancient Israelites at Sinai included "no doctrinal opinions, no saving truths, no universal propositions of reason. These the Eternal reveals to . . . all men, at all times, through nature and thing, but never through word and script."[11] What God supernaturally revealed to the ancient Israelites at Sinai was "a divine legislation—laws, commandments, ordinances, rules of life, instruction in the will of God as to how they should conduct themselves in order to attain temporal and eternal felicity."[12]

In a letter to Elkan Herz, Mendelssohn defends himself from an accusation that he is a deist by asserting that his reliance on reason rather than supernatural revelation to establish the principles he accepted as true is consistent with belief in the supernatural revelation that is part of Judaism because the latter includes no universal principles other than those that could be derived from reason, i.e., no principles that are not part of *natural* religion.[13] Although supernatural revelation is unnecessary to

---

6. Guttmann, *Philosophies of Judaism*, 337–38.

7. See Mendelssohn, *Jerusalem*, 81; Altmann, *Moses Mendelssohn*, 542.

8. Mendelssohn, *Jerusalem*, 84. See Altmann, *Moses Mendelssohn*, 535.

9. The existence of God, the existence of divine law, and reward or punishment for, respectively, obedience or disobedience to divine law.

10. Mendelssohn, *Jerusalem*, 90–91. See Mendelssohn, *Jerusalem*, 90n116 (Lord Herbert of Cherbury "identified five religious truths of reason: (1) The existence of a Supreme God; (2) the obligation to worship God; (3) morality as the main part of divine worship; (4) the opportunity and obligation to repent; and (5) the existence of rewards and punishments after this life.").

11. Mendelssohn, *Jerusalem*, 81.

12. Mendelssohn, *Jerusalem*, 81.

13. Altmann, *Moses Mendelssohn*, 249 (quoting Mendelssohn correspondence).

ascertain the truths of natural religion, such truths, Mendelssohn believed, may in fact be found in the Hebrew Bible and rabbinic sources.[14]

Because Mendelssohn believed that God's supernatural revelation was only for the Jews, he rejected the Maimonidean position that in order to have a share in the world to come non-Jews must follow Noahide laws "from obedience to God's command as expressed in the [Torah]."[15] Mendelssohn wrote to Rabbi Jacob Emden: "I . . . consider [the position of Maimonides] harder than flint. Shall all the inhabitants of the earth from east to west, except for us, be cast into a pit of annihilation and be abhorrent to all flesh if they do not believe in the Torah . . . I have found in the words of the sages . . . no obligation for descendants of Noah to occupy themselves with studying the Torah relating to their seven commandments, but only permission to do so."[16] For Mendelssohn, virtuous conduct alone enabled one to achieve eternal bliss, and he associated virtuous conduct with striving for moral and intellectual perfection as a human being. This idea is stressed by Mendelssohn in *Phädon* as is the idea that a postmortem reward for achieving the greatest moral perfection humanly possible is available *to the whole human race*. Left unstated in *Phädon* is Mendelssohn's view that "the Jews can expect a 'particular reward' since God would not have laid [the] extra burden on them [of following the revealed legislation] without some special compensation. What God's 'special reasons' were for giving the revelation, or in what the 'particular reward' consists, Mendelssohn does not say." [17]

B. In the *Phädon* Mendelssohn Offers Three Proofs of the Soul's Immortality

Mendelssohn's objective in *Phädon* was to present "a Socrates redivivus who spoke the language of the modern Enlightenment; who talked in the way in which Socrates would have talked if he had lived in Mendelssohn's time. *The author's overriding concern was to secure the notion of immortality against the sophists of the eighteenth century, that is, against the French materialists.*"[18] The importance to Mendelssohn of

---

14. See Mendelssohn, *Jerusalem*, 88–89. See also Guttmann, *Philosophies of Judaism*, 333–34.

15. Altmann, *Moses Mendelssohn*, 217 ("those who kept the seven Noachian laws merely on rational grounds . . . could be called 'wise' but not 'pious' and were, therefore, not entitled to the bliss of the hereafter."). See generally Rudavsky, *Maimonides*, 178–79.

16. Mendelssohn, "Letter to Rabbi Jacob Emden," 32–34. See Mendelssohn, "Open Letter to Lavatar," 9; Altmann, *Moses Mendelssohn*, 217–18, 294. See also Meyer, *Origins of the Modern Jew*, 20, 37.

17. Meyer, *Origins of the Modern Jew*, 37.

18. Altmann, *Moses Mendelssohn*, 150 (emphasis added). By "modern Enlightenment" Altmann means the *Aufklärung*, and specifically Leibnizian/Wolffian philosophy. The French materialists whose views Mendelssohn opposed included, Voltaire, d'Holbach, and de La Mettrie. Voltaire, for example, considered the theory of the soul as an immaterial substantial being to be an unnecessary hypothesis. "In the article on Soul in the Philosophical Dictionary [1764] he argues that terms such as 'spiritual soul' are simply words which cover our ignorance" (Copleston, *History of Philosophy*, VI, part 1, 34). In Britain, Thomas Hobbes, William Coward, and David Hume all enthusiastically argued

proving the immortality of the soul was related to his concerns about the "worthwhileness of virtue,"[19] as well as to his thoughts about the purpose or vocation of man. Mendelssohn came to accept that the vocation of man is to reach perfection as a rational and moral being, and that, since perfection is not attained in this life, it must be attained in a future life.[20] The "Leibnizian idea of a deathless world in which each monad strives toward perfection was turned [by Mendelssohn] into the notion of infinite perfectibility..."[21] Related to the objective of presenting Socrates as, essentially, an adherent of Leibnizian philosophy is the objective of presenting a *rational* proof of the immortality of the soul, foregoing any reliance on supernatural revelation.[22]

After a short preface, *Phädon* is divided into two parts. The first part is entitled "The Life and Character of Socrates." The second part is divided into three dialogues written in the manner of Plato's *Phaedo*, with the setting being the day of the death of Socrates. The main participants in the dialogues, as in Plato's *Phaedo*, are Socrates and two interlocutors, Simmias and Cebes. There is also an appendix to the third edition of *Phädon*, published in 1769, in which Mendelssohn responds to some objections which were made to him following the book's original 1767 publication.

1. The first dialogue

In Plato's dialogue, Socrates comments to his interlocutors that a philosopher should welcome death. The nub of this discussion includes a reference to Plato's Theory of Forms. All agree that the Forms exist and that they cannot be accessed through the bodily senses but only through "the unaided intellect."[23] In fact, it is agreed that so long as we "keep to the body[,] and our soul is contaminated with this imperfection, there is no chance of our ever attaining satisfactorily to our object, which we assert to be the Truth [that is, the apprehension of the Forms]."[24] Everyone also agrees that upon death the soul separates from the body.[25] Since a philosopher is one who seeks the truth, since the truth can only be apprehended when the soul is unhindered by the

---

for materialism. In 1777, Joseph Priestly published *Disquisitions Relating to Matter and Spirit* which advanced a materialist position and responded to objections to materialism.

19. Altmann, *Moses Mendelssohn*, 27 (quoting Mendelssohn correspondence).

20. See also Tomasoni, "Mendelssohn's Concept of the Human Soul," 146.

21. Tomasoni, "Mendelssohn's Concept of the Human Soul," 146.

22. See Meyer, *Origins of the Modern Jew*, 29 ("When [Mendelssohn] wrote on immortality he put his largely Leibnizian thoughts into the frame of a Socratic dialogue, choosing a pagan protagonist to escape the controversial question of revelation."). See also Altmann, *Moses Mendelssohn*, 156 (in the Age of Reason supernatural revelation "could no longer be invoked to secure the belief in immortality").

23. Plato, *Phaed.*, 65d–66a.

24. Plato, *Phaed.*, 66b.

25. Plato, *Phaed.*, 64c.

body, and since the soul becomes unhindered by the body after death, the philosopher can achieve his objective only after death. Thus, a philosopher should welcome death.

Up to this point Mendelssohn's first dialogue closely follows Plato, and this portion of the dialogue closes with the same conclusion reached in Plato's dialogue—that "death is never terrifying to true philosophers, but must always be welcome."[26] There is, however, one significant alteration. Mendelssohn does not include any reference to Plato's Theory of Forms. Instead, Mendelssohn includes a reference to a belief in God; and the interlocutors agree with Socrates that "God is our Proprietor, we His property, and His providence procures what is best."[27] Further, Socrates's interlocutors agree that God is "the All Perfect Being, without which nothing can exist" and that God has the attributes of "Maximum [or Highest] Perfection," "Maximum Good," and "Maximum Wisdom."[28] Then Socrates contends that "the man who loves wisdom must distance himself from the senses and their objects, if he wants to grasp, what is true felicity to grasp, the All Maximum and Most Perfect Being" and that "[i]n this quest for ideas he must close his eyes and ears, and pay no attention to pain and sensual pleasure, and, if possible, forget his body entirely, in order to focus himself all the more completely on the capacities of his soul and its inner activity."[29] The philosopher cannot apprehend God "as long as [his] soul resides in the body, so we must assume one or the other; either we shall never know the truth, or we shall know it after death, because then the soul leaves the body . . . [So] we can hope, freed from the follies of the body, to behold the source of truth, the Maximum and Supreme Being, *with pure and holy senses.*"[30]

In this first part of their dialogues neither Plato nor Mendelssohn presents proof of anything. Rather, they set forth the assumptions on which their subsequent proofs of immortality are based. Both accept that (1) there such a thing as a soul, (2) the soul is an immaterial thing which is separate and distinct from the body, (3) it is only the soul which can apprehend the truth, (4) the body hinders the soul from fully apprehending the truth, (5) at death the soul is separated (released) from the body, and (6) only after death can one fully apprehend the truth. Plato (but not Mendelssohn) also assumes the existence of the Forms and beliefs related to the Forms. Mendelssohn (but not Plato) also assumes the existence of God and beliefs related to God—specifically, that God is an immaterial being possessing maximum perfection, wisdom, and goodness. Mendelssohn also assumes that the soul is a Leibnizian/Wolffian monad—an immaterial being or spirit which (1) is part of the City of God, (2) "recognizes its kindred spirits, in so far as it observes itself" and thus "can generally grasp the possibility" of "a thing of superior nature than itself, or form an idea of a thing of higher

---

26. See Mendelssohn, *Phädon*, 69–85.
27. Mendelssohn, *Phädon*, 74–75.
28. Mendelssohn, *Phädon*, 80.
29. Mendelssohn, *Phädon*, 82.
30. Mendelssohn, *Phädon*, 83–84 (emphasis added). See Altmann, *Moses Mendelssohn*, 152.

ability than it possesses itself," and (3) has an internal driving force to perfection or perfect knowledge.[31]

These assumptions having been set forth, Cebes raises the question of the soul's immortality.[32] In response, the Socrates of Plato's *Phaedo* presents four arguments to prove that the soul is immortal: (1) the argument based on the principle that opposites come from their opposites, (2) the argument based on the theory that all learning is a matter of recollection, (3) the argument from affinity, and (4) the final argument.[33] Mendelssohn ignores the second of these arguments because it is based on Plato's Theory of Forms and Mendelssohn has eliminated reference to this doctrine, but he does use the first argument, albeit in an altered form.[34] The Socrates of Mendelssohn's *Phädon* relies not on the principle that opposites come from their opposite but on a principle of natural change. Socrates in the *Phädon* states that "we say a thing has changed, when among two opposite determinations, which can belong to it, the one ceases and the other actually begins to exist. For example, beautiful and ugly, just and unjust . . . are . . . opposite determinations, which are possible to one and the same thing."[35] It is possible for a beautiful thing to become ugly, and it possible for a just thing to become unjust. It is also claimed that all changes in nature have "an intermediate state, which serves as a transition . . . to go from one state to the opposite," so that, for example, night follows day by means of evening twilight.[36] Next, it is agreed that natural change must be produced by powers that exist in nature, and that these powers must have been operating "since time immemorial."[37] It is further deemed undeniable that "all changeable things cannot remain unchanged for even a moment . . . since the powers of nature are never at rest" and every changeable thing changes as a result of "a power to do something and an ability to be acted upon by something."[38] So that even though we, being limited to a specific zone of the earth, differentiate the morning, afternoon, evening, and midnight, one who considers the whole earth knows that "the revolutions of day and night follow continuously on each other, and every moment in time—morning and night, midday and midnight is joined together."[39] As Mendelssohn

31. See Mendelssohn, *Phädon*, 82.

32. Plato, *Phaed.*, 70a–b; Mendelssohn, *Phädon*, 87.

33. Plato, *Phaed.*, 69e–72d, 72e–77d, 77e–80b, 102b–106e. See Bostock, *Plato's Phaedo*, 42–121, 169–93.

34. See generally Altmann, *Moses Mendelssohn*, 152 ("In [Mendelssohn's] finished work the second proof is dropped altogether, [and with regard to the first, whereas Plato's proof is based on] . . . the Platonic concept of generation as a circular process . . . Mendelssohn's proof is built on a different presupposition, that there can be no absolute generation and corruption in nature. All changes proceed gradually, without a leap. Between being and nonbeing no transition is possible. Hence the soul cannot be annihilated through death.").

35. Mendelssohn, *Phädon*, 88.

36. Mendelssohn, *Phädon*, 88.

37. Mendelssohn, *Phädon*, 89.

38. Mendelssohn, *Phädon*, 90.

39. Mendelssohn, *Phädon*, 94.

makes clear in the appendix to the third edition, the principle of natural change relied upon by his Socrates is based upon Leibniz's law of continuity. Therefore, in the first dialogue Mendelssohn essentially substitutes Leibniz's law of continuity for Plato's principle that opposites come from their opposite.[40]

These general principles of natural change having been established, natural change is distinguished from change in being. In contrast to natural change, there is no transitional or intermediary state between "being" and "not-being."[41] This implies that "nature can produce neither being nor annihilation."[42] Therefore, since death and life are *natural* changes, having a transitional or intermediary state called "dying," death does not constitute annihilation.[43] This, all *Phädon* interlocutors agree, is clearly the case with regard to the body.[44] The question is whether this is also the case with regard to the soul, a noncompound thing.[45] While the annihilation of the soul is a possibility, annihilation could only occur as the result of a supernatural force (a miracle performed by God) because there can be no annihilation in nature. Leaving aside the objection that it would be sacrilege to suggest that God would annihilate the soul, it is presumed that the point in time when such annihilation might occur would be "when the body no longer needed [the soul], in the moment of death."[46] However, since it was already agreed that there is no moment when it can be said that the animal body dies (is annihilated), there can be no moment when the soul might be annihilated. As stated by *Phädon*'s Socrates: "Therefore, if the death of the body is also supposed to be the death of the soul: there must be no moment at which one can say, now the soul vanishes; but gradually, as the movements in the parts of the machine cease to harmonize towards one unified goal, the soul must diminish in power and internal activity also."[47] Therefore, the soul must be "eternally existent," and, so long as it exists,

40. Mendelssohn, *Phädon*, 150–51 (Mendelssohn says that he conveyed the propositions existing "in the argument of Plato of the opposite states [conditions] and the transition from one to the other . . . in the manner of Plato, but with the clarity appropriate to our times . . . [T]hey obtain a high degree of certainty only through the doctrine of continuity."). See Tomasoni, "Mendelssohn's Concept of the Human Soul," 147 ("Mendelssohn abandoned the cyclic and mythological vision . . . and brought Plato's argument closer to the principle of the continuity of nature, following the conception of Leibniz.").

41. Mendelssohn, *Phädon*, 93.

42. Mendelssohn, *Phädon*, 93.

43. Mendelssohn, *Phädon*, 92–94.

44. Mendelssohn, *Phädon*, 94.

45. In the appendix to the third edition Mendelssohn states that when he refers to the soul, he is referring to the ability or power to think and to will, which, in the first dialogue, he assumes to be the attributes of a "simple being" (Mendelssohn, *Phädon*, 150).

46. Mendelssohn, *Phädon*, 95–96.

47. Mendelssohn, *Phädon*, 96 (emphasis original). See Smith, *Commentary to Kant's "Critique of Pure Reason,"* 470 ("Mendelssohn's argument is that the soul, as it does not consist of parts, cannot disappear *gradually* by disintegration into its constituent elements. If, therefore, it perishes, it must pass out of existence *suddenly*; at one moment it will exist, at the next moment it will be nonexistent. But, Mendelssohn maintains, for three closely connected reasons this would seem to be impossible. In the first place, the immediate juxtaposition of directly opposed states is never met with in the

it must act and be acted upon—it must feel, think, and will.[48] But since it is no longer with the body, and no longer needs to care for the needs of the body, "nothing remains to it . . . but wisdom, love of virtue, and knowledge of the truth."[49]

2. The second dialogue

In Plato's *Phaedo*, after the first three arguments in support of the soul's immortality are presented, renewed objections to the immortality of the soul are raised by Socrates's interlocutors, Simmias and Cebes. Simmias refers to the "attunement theory" of the soul pursuant to which the *psyche* is not seen as a substance separate and apart from the body but as an expression of a certain condition or state of the body, namely, the state of attunement or harmony.[50] Cebes objects that, although he believes that Socrates has proven that the soul can exist after the death of the body, Socrates has not proven that the soul is immortal; after the soul transmigrates to another body and then, after that second body dies, to a third body, and so on, the soul may ultimately be annihilated.[51]

Mendelssohn's *Phädon* follows the design of *Phaedo* in presenting objections to the immortality of the soul raised by Simmias and Cebes. In the case of Simmias, the objection raised reflects the concern expressed by Simmias in *Phaedo*. The Simmias of *Phädon* says to Socrates:

> Where I have understood you correctly, your proof was approximately the following: the soul and the body exist in the most intimate connection; the latter is gradually dissolved into its parts, the former must either be annihilated, or still have ideas. Nothing can be annihilated by natural powers: therefore through natural means our soul can never cease to have concepts. But suppose . . . I were to prove through similar reasons, that musical harmony would have to continue when the lyre was smashed to pieces, or that the symmetry

---

material world. Complete opposites, such as day and night, waking and sleeping, never follow upon one another abruptly, but only through a series of intermediate steps. Secondly, among the opposites which material processes thus bridge over, the opposition of being and not-being is never found. Only by a miracle can a material existence be annihilated. If, therefore, empirical evidence is allowed to be relevant, we must not assert of the immaterial soul what is never known to befall the material existences of the visible world. Thirdly . . . the sudden cessation of the soul's existence would also violate the law of continuity of time. Between any two moments there is always an intermediate time in which the moment passes continuously into another.") (emphasis original).

48. Mendelssohn, *Phädon*, 98. See Mendelssohn, *Phädon*, 151.

49. Mendelssohn, *Phädon*, 100.

50. Plato, *Phaed.*, 85d-86e. See Altmann, *Moses Mendelssohn*, 153; Bostock, *Plato's Phaedo*, 120, 122-25. See generally Bostock, *Plato's Phaedo*, 125-34 (discussing the refutation of Simmias's objection).

51. Plato, *Phaedo*, 86e-88b; Altmann, *Moses Mendelssohn*, 153; Bostock, 120, 134. See generally Bostock, 135-93 (dealing with Socrates' response to Cebes's objection and analyzing Plato's "final argument" for the immortality of the soul).

> of a building still must exist, even if all the stones were ripped apart from each other and crushed to dust? ... If we compare the lyre or the building with the body, and harmony or symmetry with the soul: then we have proved that the playing of the stringed instrument must last longer than the strings, the elegant proportions would have to last longer than the building. But this is highly absurd in regard to harmony and symmetry; [since harmony exists only in conjunction with the composition of the lyre, and symmetry exists only in conjunction with the composition of the building]: they [viz., harmony and symmetry] cannot endure longer than the composition itself [viz., longer than, respectively, the lyre and the building].
>
> The same can be asserted about [the] health [of the body]: It is an attribute of the body ... [existing only in conjunction with the composition of the body], and disappears, when the composition is dissolved into its parts ... Perhaps [sensation in animals], and even man's reason [that is, man's ability to think], are nothing other than attributes of the composition, [that is, exist only in conjunction with the composition of the body, and, as is the case with life, health, harmony, and symmetry,] ... cannot last longer than the composition [viz., longer than the body].[52]

This objection of Simmias is basically the objection of the French and English materialists and reflects Locke's comment that it is not inconceivable that "God can superadd to matter a faculty of thinking" if he chooses to do so.[53]

The influence of Locke is also reflected in the objection of *Phädon*'s Cebes in that Cebes accepts the Lockean position that personal identity is tied to self-consciousness and memory. Thus, Cebes in *Phädon*, as in *Phaedo*, contends that it is insufficient for Socrates to prove that the soul survives the death of the body. However, the reason why survival is insufficient has now nothing to do with immortality as such; the concern is rather with theodicy. If God is to be justified, there must be appropriate reward and punishment in the afterlife, and this requires that the soul surviving the death of the body be identified with the person who performed the acts in this life meriting reward or deserving punishment, and survival of the same person requires that self-consciousness and memory persist. Cebes complains to Socrates:

> If your proofs are defended against objections, still nothing more follows from them, than that our soul continues after the death of our body and has ideas; but continues how? Perhaps in a swoon, in a faint or as in sleep ... Now if our soul should sink into a kind of sleep or state of lethargy with its separation from the body, and never wake again, what would we have gained by its continuation? ... If that which befalls the spirit after death concerns us, and

---

52. Mendelssohn, *Phädon*, 105–6.
53. See Altmann, *Moses Mendelssohn*, 153 ("Simmias becomes the advocate of the French school of materialism ... [and] suggests the possibility of attributing to matter more than extension and solidity."); Tomasoni, "Mendelssohn's Concept of the Human Soul," 148–49. Cf. ch. 9, sec. C, 1; ch. 13, n. 72.

> should already arouse fear or hope here below in us: so we who are conscious of ourselves here in this life, must still keep that awareness of self in this life after death and be able to remember the present . . . The lack of all consciousness is not an impossible state for our soul: daily experience convinces us of this. How [then can you expect a better life after death, a greater enlightenment of the understanding,] if such a state without consciousness should continue in eternity after death?[54]

This objection is clearly reflecting the point of view of those, such as Hobbes, who espoused the doctrine of mortalism.[55]

After raising the objections of Simmias and Cebes, the remainder of *Phädon*'s second dialogue is devoted to responding to the objection of Simmias, while the response to Cebes's objection is taken up in the third dialogue. In order to answer Simmias's objection that sensation and thinking may be attributes of, and derived from, a skillfully formed body, and thus cease to exist when the body ceases to exist, Mendelssohn has his Socrates prove that thinking is an activity of an *immaterial* substance, not an activity associated with the parts of the body being ordered in a certain way, in contrast to, for example, the symmetry of a building which *is* a matter of the building's component stones being ordered in some way.[56] He does this, generally speaking, by contending that thinking cannot be derived from anything composite. If thinking cannot be derived from anything composite, thinking must be derived from a simple substance, and, if it is a simple substance, it must be unextended (that is, *immaterial*) "for the extended thing is divisible, and the divisible is not simple."[57]

Moreover, this simple, immaterial substance must be capable of grasping and uniting all of our innumerous "collection of concepts, perceptions, inclinations, and passions" as we "would not even be the same person that we had been a moment before, if our conceptions would be divided among many and were not encountered together somewhere in their closest connection."[58] Consequently, since we think,

---

54. Mendelssohn, *Phädon*, 107–8. See Altmann, *Moses Mendelssohn*, 153–54 (The objection Cebes raised in *Phaedo* "is completely reformulated. It now concerns the problem of immortality as the continuity of the person conscious of its past and active in the exercise of its intellectual functions.").

55. See Forstrom, *John Locke and Personal Identity*, 66–67 (Hobbes "adopts a view known as mortalism, which is sometimes called soul-sleeping. Mortalism is the view that what happens at bodily death is nothing in terms of the soul. The soul 'sleeps,' that is it is basically unconscious (and thus cannot be affected by prayers or the intercession of saints) until the Day of Judgment when the body is resurrected. There is no natural immortality of the soul that preserves it in a conscious state between death and the resurrection. This understanding or critique of the soul and immortality is not unique or original to Hobbes.").

56. Altmann, *Moses Mendelssohn*, 154 (Mendelssohn had to show "why matter could not think.").

57. Mendelssohn, *Phädon*, 120. Mendelssohn indicates in the preface that this proof of the soul's immateriality is one which "the students of Plato gave, and some modern philosophers adopted from them" (Mendelssohn, *Phädon*, 42). The student of Plato to which Mendelssohn refers is Plotinus, and the modern philosopher who adopted it is Leibniz. See Mendelssohn, *Phädon*, 42n57; Altmann, *Moses Mendelssohn*, 154. See also Mendelssohn, *Phädon*, 154–57 (discussing Plotinus).

58. Mendelssohn, *Phädon*, 119–20.

there must be "in our body at least one single substance, which is not extended, not compound, but is simple, has a power of intellect, and unites all our concepts, desires, and inclinations in itself."[59] Having determined that there must be some such substance, nothing prevents us, says *Phädon*'s Socrates, from calling it "our soul."[60]

The merit of this argument depends on the claim that thinking cannot be derived from anything composite. So, what supports this claim? According to Mendelssohn, the alternative hypothesis—that thinking *is* derived from something composite "is impossible, self-contradictory, and [is] therefore to be rejected."[61] Why so? The explanation begins with the statement that in any composition "a certain order comes into being, which is more or less perfect" and "the powers and efficacies of the component parts are changed more or less by the composition."[62] More specifically, a harmony and symmetry can be found in the whole "even if every component part has neither harmony nor symmetry in itself."[63] So, for example, an individual note by itself is not harmonic but several notes together may be harmonic, and none of the individual stones of a building may be symmetrical or well-proportioned but the building itself may be symmetrical or well-proportioned. In other words, the harmony of the notes and the symmetry of the building are, in these cases, a result of "the manner of the composition."[64]

At this point it is stated that harmony and symmetry, as well as order, regularity, and, in general,

> all proportions which require gathering together and contrasting of the manifold parts, are effects of the power to think. Without the addition of the thinking being, without comparison and contrasting of the manifold parts, the most regular building is a mere heap of sand, and the voice of a nightingale, not more harmonic than the creak of a night owl... *The thinking capacity, and this alone in all of nature, is able, through an inner activity, to make comparisons, combinations, and contrasts a reality: therefore the source of everything compound,* of number, greatness, symmetry, harmony, etc. in so far as they require a comparison and contrast *must be sought solely in the ability to think. And since this is granted, thus this ability to think... cannot possibly exist in a*

---

59. Mendelssohn, *Phädon*, 120. Although the text states that the soul is *in* the body, there is some reason to think that Mendelssohn may have actually had a different view. In relating the substance of a conversation with Mendelssohn, August Hennings reports Mendelssohn saying: "'In the same way in which the moon is not in my eye... when I look at her, though she affects my eye, so *my soul is not included in my body*, though it exercises its effect primarily upon the body." (Altmann, *Moses Mendelssohn*, 341, quoting Hennings's correspondence; emphasis added). Cf. ch. 5, secs. A and B, 2.

60. Mendelssohn, *Phädon*, 120.

61. Mendelssohn, *Phädon*, 121.

62. Mendelssohn, *Phädon*, 113.

63. Mendelssohn, *Phädon*, 114.

64. Mendelssohn, *Phädon*, 114

whole, which is composed from parts existing separate from each other. For all these things assume the actions and functions of the thinking being."[65]

It follows that the view "that our power to feel and to think should be sought in the situation, structure, order, and harmony of the components of the body [must be] . . . rejected as impossible."[66]

Preceding the objections of Simmias and Cebes, the second dialogue focuses on concerns about the vocation of man. The relevant passages evidence that Mendelssohn's interest in proving the immortality of the soul is directly tied to his interest in confirming his understandings of the nature of God, the vocation of man, and the meaning of life, as well as directly tied to his interest in resolving the problem of moral evil. Absent the immortality of the soul, the goal of reaching moral and intellectual perfection becomes a chimera and, consequently, God becomes less than infinitely good and loving. Similarly, absent the immortality of the soul there can be no postmortem reward and punishment and, consequently, God becomes less than infinitely just and omnipotent. It is due to these concerns that the second dialogue begins with Simmias saying that he cannot deny the doctrine of the immortality of the soul and the related doctrine of a postmortem divine judgment without seeing everything which he regards as true and good "shaken to its foundation."[67] Continuing, Simmias makes clear that the everything which he regards as true and good concerns his "conceptions of divinity, of virtue, of the dignity of man, and of the relationship in which [man] stands to God," all of which relate to the vocation of man. So that to deny the immortality of the soul is to create "difficulties" for his entire conceptual scheme and to undermine all that, for him, makes life purposeful and meaningful.[68] More specifically, he says:

> [I]f our soul is mortal, then our reason is a dream . . . [and] virtue lacks all the brilliance, which makes it divine in our eyes. Then the beautiful and the sublime, moral as well as physical, is not an imprint of divine perfection; . . . and so we, like cattle, have been put here to seek food and die . . . And man, robbed of the hope of immortality . . . must fear death and despair. Not the most-kind God, who takes delight in the felicity of his creatures, but a sadistic being must have bestowed man with virtues, which only make him more pitiable. I can't express, what oppressive anguish overcomes my soul, when I put myself in the place of the wretched people, who fear annihilation. The bitter reminder of death must embitter all their joys . . . The hope of a future life resolves all these

---

65. Mendelssohn, *Phädon*, 116 (emphasis added).
66. Mendelssohn, *Phädon*, 117. Cf. Mendelssohn, *Phädon*, 154–56. See also Altmann, *Moses Mendelssohn*, 154–55 ("the soul cannot be regarded as the result of a composition of material elements because its activity has to be presupposed in order to explain that a composite 'appears' different from its parts.").
67. Mendelssohn, *Phädon*, 104.
68. Mendelssohn, *Phädon*, 105.

difficulties, and brings the truths, which we are convinced of in various ways, into harmony again. This hope sanctifies the Deity, establishes virtue in its nobility, . . . and even makes the plagues of this life worthy of worship in our eyes . . . A doctrine, which stands in harmony with so many known and established truths, and by means of which we so easily resolve an array of difficulties, finds us very much inclined to accept it; it needs almost no further proof.[69]

3. The third dialogue

In the preface to *Phädon* Mendelssohn discloses that in the third dialogue he "had to take [his] refuge completely in the moderns, and allow [his] Socrates almost to speak like a philosopher from the eighteenth century."[70] Accordingly, his Socrates espouses a Leibniz/Wolffian conception of the soul which entails that the soul retains self-consciousness and memory after its separation from the body. The argument advanced is that to deny that the soul retains self-consciousness and memory creates "difficulties" with respect to, or contradicts, other beliefs which are regarded as well-established and true, whereas to affirm that the soul retains self-consciousness and memory "stands in harmony with"[71] these other beliefs. The other beliefs upon which Mendelssohn relies may be placed into three general categories: (1) beliefs about God, His "great plan of creation,"[72] and the vocation of man, (2) beliefs about man's moral obligations, and (3) beliefs about God's providence—God's justness and goodness.

The dialogue begins with Cebes expressing his "firm conviction" that all human beings "are loved most tenderly" by the "All-Holiest Being" who created them, and that, consequently, he entertains no fear "that the Almighty would doom [him] to eternal torment, and guilty or innocent would allow [him] to be eternally miserable."[73] Cebes states as a general proposition that when considering "future events, which depend solely on the will of the Almighty" we can reject as impossible any future event that "would not be in accordance with divine perfections."[74] After Cebes affirms "that the soul is a simple being, which has its own existence independent of the body" and is "imperishable,"[75] he reasserts his doubts "about the future destiny of the human spirit . . . Will [the Almighty] let the human spirit continue in a waking state for eternity, conscious of the present and the past? Or has He decreed it to sink into a state similar

---

69. Mendelssohn, *Phädon*, 104–5. See Altmann, *Moses Mendelssohn*, 156 (the sentiment that, if our soul is mortal, reason is a mere dream and virtue lacks all splendor "represents the overriding concern of the book.").
70. Mendelssohn, *Phädon*, 42.
71. See Mendelssohn, *Phädon*, 105.
72. Mendelssohn, *Phädon*, 128.
73. Mendelssohn, *Phädon*, 125.
74. Mendelssohn, *Phädon*, 125.
75. Mendelssohn, *Phädon*, 126.

to sleep with the departure of the body, and never to wake?"[76] It is further acknowledged that experiences such as sleep, fainting, and dizziness "teach us that a total depravation of all consciousness . . . would not be totally impossible."[77] There follows an agreement that Cebes can be freed from his doubts about the future destiny of the soul by "the certainty that [these doubts] run contrary to the intentions of God, and could have been chosen just as little, as the eternal misery of his creatures."[78]

It is then stated that "the whole human race" must be treated alike since "in the wisest plan of creation, similar beings have similar determinations," and that, consequently, "a similar destiny must be in store for the whole human race. Either they all awake [after the death of the body] to a new consciousness—[in which] . . . the oppressed innocent person would expect a better fate than his persecutors—or they all end their determination [or, vocation] with this life."[79] In this context, Socrates asserts, Cebes's anxiety about a possible cessation of consciousness becomes "absurd."[80] To explain this absurdity, Socrates launches into a long discourse on the nature of thinking things and their place in the design and final purpose of creation which follows the teaching of Leibniz/Wolffian philosophy. He says that all thinking things (finite spirits or, in Leibnizian terminology, monads) are simple substances which "have innate capabilities, which they develop through exercise and make more perfect."[81] In this regard thinking things are very different than compound things. As discussed in the second dialogue, compound things can be neither orderly, harmonious, nor perfect without the prior existence of a thinking thing. So, compound things were not created

> in the great design of this universe for their own sake: since they are lifeless and unconscious of their existence, and as such are not capable of any perfection. The final goal of their existence is rather to be sought in the living and feeling part of creation: the lifeless serves the living as an instrument of sensations, and bestows on it not only the sensuous feeling of manifold things, but also concepts of beauty, order, symmetry, method, final purpose, perfection, or at least bestows the material for all these concepts, which the thinking being develops afterwards, by virtue of its inner activity.[82]

In addition, compound things are incapable of enduring but "are in constant transformation and flux of changes"; and "if the composition in itself is not capable of

---

76. Mendelssohn, *Phädon*, 126.
77. Mendelssohn, *Phädon*, 126.
78. Mendelssohn, *Phädon*, 126.
79. Mendelssohn, *Phädon*, 126–27.
80. Mendelssohn, *Phädon*, 126–27.
81. Mendelssohn, *Phädon*, 126–27.
82. Mendelssohn, *Phädon*, 129–30.

enduring: how much less will its perfection endure, which can never be attributed to it in itself, ... but only in relation to the feeling and thinking beings in creation?"[83]

Turning to the status of "the living part of creation," Socrates divides living things into two classes: (1) things of a "sensuously feeling" nature, and (2) things of a thinking nature. Both classes have in common "that they are of continuous being and always can possess and enjoy a self-subsisting perfection."[84] The first class, however, which includes "all animals which dwell on earth," does not exhibit "constant progress to a higher perfection."[85] In sharp contrast, the second class, which includes human beings, "cannot refrain from exercising [their] powers of cognition and desire, to develop, to change in capabilities, therefore to approach perfection more or less."[86] In short, living, *thinking* things (human beings), but not living, *feeling* things (animals), exhibit constant progress to a higher perfection. Indeed, the vocation or purpose of thinking beings is associated with "this striving toward perfection."[87] That "their life here on earth is not intended to be a steady progress toward perfection ... is an indication that [living, feeling things, i.e., animals] were not the final goal in the great design of creation."[88] Conversely, the constant striving toward perfection of rational beings indicates that their perfection is "the highest final goal of creation."[89] The perfection of rational beings includes, most importantly, the acquisition of virtue because virtue "alone leads to felicity, and we cannot please the Creator in another way than by striving towards our true felicity."[90]

The highest final goal of creation, that each human being achieve perfection, cannot be reached within one's lifespan on earth. This leads Mendelssohn's Socrates to state:

> The Supreme Being cannot possibly have chosen and brought into the plan of the universe ... that [rational beings] stop dead completely still in the middle of their course [of striving to achieve perfection], [and] not only to stand still, but [to be] pushed back into the abyss, and ... lose all the fruits of their efforts. Is it befitting wisdom to create a world, such that the spirits which are put there may contemplate its wonders, may be blissful, and on the other hand, a moment later, to withdraw even the capability of contemplation and felicity from these spirits forever? ... Oh no, my friends!, providence has not given

83. Mendelssohn, *Phädon*, 130.

84. Mendelssohn, *Phädon*, 130.

85. Mendelssohn, *Phädon*, 130–31. Mendelssohn states that the "spiritual essence" which animates animals "is of infinite duration," and that he "is inclined to believe" that the "animal, simply sensuous and feeling natures ... will lift themselves aloft into the spheres of spirits" (Mendelssohn, *Phädon*, 132). Cf. Leibniz, *Monadology*, §§74–77; Leibniz, *New System of the Nature of Substances*, 100–1.

86. Mendelssohn, *Phädon*, 134. Cf. Leibniz, *Principles of Nature and of Grace*, §18.

87. Mendelssohn, *Phädon*, 135. Cf. Leibniz, *New System of the Nature of Substances*, 101–2.

88. Mendelssohn, *Phädon*, 131.

89. Mendelssohn, *Phädon*, 135.

90. Mendelssohn, *Phädon*, 133–34.

us a desire for everlasting felicity in vain. It can and will be satisfied . . . As well we serve the Regent of the world here on earth, while we develop our capabilities: in like manner we will also continue in that life after death under His divine care, exercising ourselves in virtue and wisdom, constantly making ourselves more perfect and efficient, fulfilling the chain of divine purposes which extend us into infinity. To stop anywhere on this path, contends openly with divine wisdom, goodness, or omnipotence, and would be pleasing to the Most Perfect Being as little as the most intense misery of innocent creatures in His design of the plan of the world.[91]

In sum, to deny that the soul persists with self-consciousness and memory contradicts the great plan of creation which has as its final goal the perfection of man.

Mendelssohn's Socrates goes on to argue that the relevant denial also contradicts well-established beliefs about our moral obligations, when he says, "He who hopes for a future life and locates the purpose of his existence in the progress to perfection can say to himself: Behold! You have been sent here, to make yourself more perfect by the advancement of the good: you may therefore promote the good, even at the expense of your life, if it cannot be obtained otherwise."[92] However, for those who deny the prospect of a future life, "the present existence would have to be the highest good."[93] Consequently, says *Phädon*'s Socrates, no other goal could precede the goal of staying alive—"as soon as we think we lose all our existence with this life, . . . [living] ceases to be simply a means," and it "becomes the ultimate goal, the final aim of our desires, the highest possession we strive for, . . . and no possession in the world can come into comparison with it . . . Therefore, I cannot possibly believe that a man who thinks this life is all there is, could possibly sacrifice himself for the welfare of his fatherland, or for the welfare of the entire human race."[94] Indeed, according to his principles, he would be justified in causing the destruction of his fatherland (indeed, the destruction of the entire world), if his life would be prolonged thereby by the smallest degree. Yet, Socrates continues, it is universally accepted that any citizen is morally obligated to sacrifice themselves for the fatherland and for the general welfare. So, for those who think this life is all there is, there would be a moral conflict, a war "between the fatherland and this citizen."[95] Thus, the view that there is no future life must be false, for "a doctrine which can only exist if we accept self-contradiction, irresolvable doubts, or undecided uncertainties in the realm of truths, must necessarily be false."[96]

---

91. Mendelssohn, *Phädon*, 135–36.
92. Mendelssohn, *Phädon*, 137.
93. Mendelssohn, *Phädon*, 136.
94. Mendelssohn, *Phädon*, 137.
95. Mendelssohn, *Phädon*, 137.
96. Mendelssohn, *Phädon*, 138. See Altmann, *Moses Mendelssohn*, 155–56 (calling this the "argument from the collision of duties").

CHAPTER 10.

In addition to the moral conflict, the denial of an afterlife with self-consciousness and memory also calls into question God's "providence"—God's justness and goodness. The facts that in this world (1) there are physical evils such as "storms, tempests, earthquakes, floods, plagues, etc.," and (2) "good and evil . . . seem to be distributed among men entirely unintentionally with regard to virtue and merit"—the wicked prosper, the oppression of the innocent and virtuous succeeds, and the righteous suffer not less seldom than the evil-doer—contradict God's goodness and justice.[97] Absent a belief in a future life, "one could believe that the fate of men [was] designed by a cause, which [finds] pleasure in evil."[98] But, "we are all certain that we stand under Divine Care."[99] The conflict between the belief in divine care, or providence, and the physical and moral evil found in this world is resolved by the doctrine of the immortality of the soul. Linking the resolution of this conflict with the resolution of the other related conflicts, Socrates states:

> He who fulfills his duty here on earth with steadfastness in defiance of misfortune and endures adversity with surrender to the Divine Will, must finally enjoy the recompense of his virtues; and the wicked cannot pass away, without being brought in one way or the other to the recognition, that evil deeds are not the way to felicity. In a word, all attributes of God, His wisdom, His goodness, His justice would be contradicted if He had created rational beings, which strive for perfection only for a limited time.[100]

Before ending the third dialogue with the account of the death of Socrates that parallels the account in Plato,[101] Mendelssohn gives a nod to Plato's myths about the fate of the soul after death.[102] Alluding to Plato's myths of the afterlife, the Socrates of *Phädon* doubts their truth but accepts their utility:

> Whether the souls of the godless have to suffer frost or heat, hunger or thirst, whether they toss and turn in the morass of Acherusia, in gloomy Tartarus, or must spend their time in the flames of Phlegethon until they are purified; whether the blessed breathe in the purest air of heaven on a radiant earth of pure gold and precious stones, and sun themselves in the brilliance of the sunrise, or if they rest in the arms of everlasting youth and are fed with nectar and ambrosia: *all this . . . I know not. If our poets and fable teachers know it better: may they assure others of it. Perhaps it is not harmful, if some people's*

---

97. See Mendelssohn, *Phädon*, 139–42.
98. Mendelssohn, *Phädon*, 140.
99. Mendelssohn, *Phädon*, 141.
100. Mendelssohn, *Phädon*, 142. See Tomasoni, "Mendelssohn's Concept of the Human Soul," 150 ("in Mendelssohn's view, the absurdity of this consequence showed the falsity of the premises; the supreme good required some prospect after this life, an immortality in which the person continued to exist and was either rewarded or punished.").
101. See Mendelssohn, *Phädon*, 143–46; Plato, *Phaed.*, 115b–18a.
102. See Plato, *Phaedo*, 107b–15a.

imagination is occupied and exerted in such a way. As far as I am concerned, I content myself with the conviction that I will exist eternally under Divine Care, that His holy and just providence will reign over me in that life as in this, and that my true felicity exists in the beauties and perfections of my spirit: these are temperance, justice, freedom, love, benevolence, knowledge of God, promotion of His intentions, and surrender to His Holy Will.[103]

C. *Sefer Ha-Nephesh* Stresses That the Immortality of the Soul Is a Fundamental Tenet of the Torah

After the publication and success of *Phädon*,

> Mendelssohn seems to have felt a sense of obligation to present at least an outline of its arguments to the Jewish public . . . A translation of the *Phaedon* into Hebrew seemed to him an utter impossibility. He had therefore to find a literary form that was manageable . . . It was probably in the latter part of 1769 . . . that he produced an essay shorn of the setting and the trimmings of the *Phaedon* and yet presenting, in neat and precise terms, the essence of the work . . . It was only after his death, [however,] in 1787, that David Friedländer edited it, together with another piece, under the title *Sefer Ha-Nefesh* ("Book on the Soul").[104]

1. *Sefer Ha-Nephesh* includes a letter to Hartog Leo discussing the body/soul relationship

The other piece included in *Sefer Ha-Nephesh* is a letter of unknown date written in Hebrew to Mendelssohn's friend Hartog Leo in which Mendelssohn responds to an objection raised by Leo to Leibniz's doctrine of a preestablished harmony between the body (which in Leibnizian terminology belongs to the kingdom of nature) and the soul (which belongs to the kingdom of grace).[105] The thrust of Leo's objection is that, in his view, the Leibnizian doctrine made free will impossible and, consequently, left no room for reward and punishment, jeopardizing morality and religion.[106]

Mendelssohn's response "dealt at length with the various theories about the relationship between body and soul."[107] Specifically, Mendelssohn analyzes three theo-

---

103. Mendelssohn, *Phädon*, 143 (emphasis added).

104. Altmann, *Moses Mendelssohn*, 181.

105. Altmann, *Moses Mendelssohn*, 181. See Leibniz, *Monadology*, §87 (distinguishing between the physical kingdom of nature and the moral kingdom of grace, and asserting "a perfect harmony between [these] two natural kingdoms").

106. Altmann, *Moses Mendelssohn*, 187. Leibniz believed that in the kingdom of nature there is no free will, as whatever happens is determined by the laws of motion.

107. Altmann, *Moses Mendelssohn*, 181.

ries: (1) "influxionism," which Mendelssohn associates with Aristotle, but which is better associated with Descartes; (2) "occasionalism," which Mendelssohn identifies as Cartesian, but is more particularly the theory of Nicolas Malebranche; and (3) "harmonism," Leibniz's theory of preestablished harmony.[108] Since there were no Hebrew equivalents for philosophical terms that were not found in medieval Jewish philosophy, Mendelssohn had to coin Hebrew equivalents for modern philosophical terminology. He used the Hebrew *ba'aley ha-geram* to render "adherents of occasionalism" and *ba'aley ha-haskama* for "adherents of the doctrine of preestablished harmony."[109] Additionally, he offers a biblical illustration to explain the differences among these theories. Altmann summarizes Mendelssohn's illustration as follows:

> Jacob saw Rachel and fell in love with her. What happened was an impression of Rachel's figure being made on Jacob's heart as a result of seeing her: because of the power of his own idea of her a train of thought was set in motion that caused him to serve her father seven years, and they seemed to him but a few days. No philosopher would deny that it was the effect of the internal image of Rachel in Jacob's heart that produced his desire for her and all his subsequent actions. What was in dispute was the manner in which the image arose in the soul. There were three opinions concerning this matter: (1) the influxionists (Aristotle and his followers) held that the soul was affected by the power of an external object perceived through the senses; (2) the occasionalists (the Cartesians) believed that the external object was not the agent that affected the soul but merely the occasion for the activity of God upon the soul; and (3) the harmonists (Leibniz and his school) were of the opinion that even the first representation arose in the soul by its own limited power as a result of preceding representations and, at the same time, in harmony with the external object.[110]

Next Mendelssohn offered the well-established objection to the influxionist theory (or theory of body/soul interaction), which seemed to be favored by Leo. The influxionist theory is based on the idea that all finite substances act on each other causally, so that the body can act on the soul and *vice versa*. The standard objection to this theory is the inability to explain how something that is corporeal can act on something incorporeal, and *vice versa*.[111] Mendelssohn also suggested that this theory was "incompatible with a fundamental law of nature, namely, that governing motion," and, more specifically, Newton's third law of motion that for every action there must be an equal and opposite reaction.[112]

---

108. See Altmann, *Moses Mendelssohn*, 184–85.
109. Altmann, *Moses Mendelssohn*, 184–85.
110. Altmann, *Moses Mendelssohn*, 185.
111. Altmann, *Moses Mendelssohn*, 186. See ch., 9, sec. B.
112. Altmann, *Moses Mendelssohn*, 186.

With regard to the concerns raised by Leo about the harmonist theory, Mendelssohn both responded to the issue of free will and addressed the issue of divine punishment:

> Following Leibniz, he defined free will as the choice of the good, be it the true good or the apparent one. Once the will had made its decision, the event called 'exercise of free will' was over. The action by which the body implemented that decision was a free action only insofar as it resulted from free will... [So] predeterminism, which was inherent in the doctrine of preestablished harmony, [did not] invalidate free will. For the choice of the will was made through the consideration of the good. It was motivated by purpose. The preordained decree was not part of the motivation. It did not operate upon the will but was merely in harmony with it.[113]

As for the issue of divine punishment, Mendelssohn reiterated a view he had repeatedly expressed in several of his works, that the purpose of divine punishment is not to avenge misdeeds: "In Mendelssohn's view, there was no divine punishment except for the benefit of the sinner, that is, for the sake of his improvement."[114] He believed that this view was justified on the basis of reason and was found in the Torah.[115]

2. *Sefer Ha-Nephesh* includes a Hebrew treatise on the soul's immortality

The essay or treatise in *Sefer Ha-Nephesh* dealing with the immortality of the soul discusses the topic in three chapters corresponding in form, but not in substance, to the three dialogues of *Phädon*.[116] The treatise begins with an initial remark that the doctrine of the immortality of the soul is a "fundamental tenet" (*yesod*) of the Torah.[117] This is not surprising because, as previously noted, Mendelssohn believed that eternal truths ascertainable through reason alone are also to be found in the Hebrew Bible and rabbinic material. With specific reference to the immortality of the soul, as early as 1758 Mendelssohn had conceived of a plan to express his rationally based belief that the soul is immortal completely on the basis of rabbinic sources, instead of placing them in the mouth of Socrates.[118] As he explained in a letter to Hartwig Wessely:

> I wanted to depart completely from the way of Plato and write my own book on the nature and immortality of the soul. My idea was to base my teaching

---

113. Altmann, *Moses Mendelssohn*, 188.
114. Altmann, *Moses Mendelssohn*, 188.
115. Altmann, *Moses Mendelssohn*, 188.
116. See Altmann, *Moses Mendelssohn*, 181.
117. See Altmann, *Moses Mendelssohn*, 181. See also Altmann, *Moses Mendelssohn*, 190 (quoting Mendelssohn's correspondence stating that the immortality of the soul is "'a truth that is not doubted by anyone "called by the name of Israel," since it is an integral part of the principles of our holy faith.'").
118. See Altmann, *Moses Mendelssohn*, 179–80; Guttmann, *Philosophies of Judaism*, 333–34.

on the utterances of our rabbis of blessed memory as found in the haggadic portions of the Talmud and in the Midrashim, for most of them agree to a very large extent with what I have expounded philosophically [*be-derekh ha-emmet*] and in no way contradict [philosophical] truth.[119]

Having made clear in his opening remarks that traditional sources of authority accord with reason with regard to the immortality of the soul,[120] he begins the first chapter of the Hebrew treatise by describing the basic nature of the soul in accordance with Leibnizian notions. In contrast to the body which is said to be "a composite held together by the order and relation of its constituent parts," the soul is said to be "a simple substance and the single substratum of sensation, desire, and conceptual knowledge."[121] Then, following a contrivance initiated by Saadia Gaon, Mendelssohn uses the Hebrew words *nephesh*, *ruach*, and *neshamah* to refer, respectively, to three faculties of the soul he delineates—sensation (or perception), desire, and conceptual knowledge (or reason).[122] He writes:

> This simple substance qua substratum of perception is called *nefesh*, qua faculty of desire and abhorrence is called *ruach*, and in respect of its being the substratum of reason and conceptual knowledge *neshama*.[123]

The second chapter of the treatise demonstrates the incorruptibility of the soul, a topic Mendelssohn discussed in the first dialogue of *Phädon*. But the demonstration he now offers diverges from what he offered in *Phädon*. In *Phädon* the argument was based on Leibniz's law of continuity, that

> nature produces no change abruptly and is therefore incapable of annihilating a thing. This argument . . . is . . . replaced [in *Sefer Ha-Nephesh*] by an ontological line of reasoning. Composite things come into being through the composition of their parts, and they cease to be when the order of their parts is destroyed. The parts both precede and outlast the composite thing. A simple thing (the soul), on the other hand, can come into being only ex nihilo and ceases to be only by annihilation . . . Natural causes being limited and time-bound, can neither create a thing ex nihilo nor annihilate it. Only an infinite being (God) can do this by way of miracle. Man's body [being a composite thing] is generated in time through natural causes. The soul, [however, being] . . . a simple substance, comes into being through a miracle by the will of God, and it can perish only through a miracle. God, however, annihilates nothing:

---

119. Altmann, *Moses Mendelssohn*, 180 (quoting Mendelssohn's correspondence).

120. See Altmann, *Moses Mendelssohn*, 184 (Mendelssohn's arguments "are based on reason alone . . . The biblical and rabbinic quotations are not adduced as theological proof texts but as stylistic devices that help give the essay a decidedly Jewish flavor.").

121. Altmann, *Moses Mendelssohn*, 181.

122. See Altmann, *Moses Mendelssohn*, 182.

123. Altmann, *Moses Mendelssohn*, 181–82 (quoting Mendelssohn).

'For all actions of God (be his Name blessed) are good in themselves, and if they sometimes appear to us as being evil, this is due, as is well known, to the deficiency of our comprehension... Now, annihilation is a true evil, not an apparent one, as is obvious, and all consequences of true evil are truly evil... This being the case, God can never desire the annihilation of any creature. It is demonstrated, therefore, that the soul of man does not die a natural death when the body dies and does not suffer annihilation through the mere will of God, but lives eternally.'[124]

The third chapter of the treatise corresponds to the *Phädon*'s third dialogue in that Mendelssohn argues that the denial of the immortality of the soul contradicts other beliefs accepted as true, whereas belief in the soul's immortality stands in harmony with these other beliefs. Altmann summarizes the argument:

The question [Mendelssohn presents] is: Are we to believe that after its separation from the body the soul continues to be a substance endowed with reason and will and possessed of all its acquired perfections?... He suggests that there are... five possible ways of answering the question, and that the answer we accept depends on our concept of what best agrees with our notion of God. The five possibilities are: (1) The souls remain eternally in the same condition... (2) All souls rise eternally in rank through an increase in perfection and happiness. (3) All souls rise for a time and then descend to previous levels down to the low grade of merely sentient beings. (4) All souls repeat the process of rise and fall ad infinitum. (5) Some souls rise and increase in perfection, while others descend and decrease in happiness.

Mendelssohn seems to have considered a modified form of the fourth possibility as the most likely fate of the soul, since it best agreed with 'the rules of wisdom and the infinite and abundant love' of God: 'Even as rational beings have commenced to rise on the ladder of perfection and happiness, so they will continue eternally; yet at times they will descend for some period and thereafter rise again to enjoy their felicity.' It appears that the measure and duration of the soul's rise and fall are held to depend on the soul's merits and demerits, and that descents represent punishments it deserves... Only in this manner are the ways of God well-balanced, while otherwise there would be 'one event to the good and to the wicked, to him that serveth God and to him that serveth him not.'[125]

Thus, in the final analysis, the postmortem fate of the soul is directly tied to the problem of moral evil.

---

124. Altmann, *Moses Mendelssohn*, 182–83 (quoting Mendelssohn).
125. Altmann, *Moses Mendelssohn*, 183–84.

CHAPTER 10.

D. After the Initial Publication of *Phädon* Objections to Mendelssohn's Arguments for the Immortality of the Soul Were Raised by Critics

The third edition of *Phädon* includes an "Appendix, Concerning Some Objections, Which Have Been Made to the Author" in which Mendelssohn describes and responds to several criticisms.[126] He also engaged in a brief exchange of letters with Johann Gottfried Herder, a philosopher who maintained a naturalistic and anti-dualistic position, and who attacked traditional metaphysics on the bases that it sought to transcend experience and was, accordingly, useless and even harmful. Equally worthy of attention is Immanuel Kant who, in his *Critique of Pure Reason* (1787), included a small section refuting Mendelssohn's proof of the incorruptibility of the soul.

1. In response to objections from Herder and others Mendelssohn asserts that "the soul must have a *vehiculum*"[127] and that he "had nothing against palingenesis"[128]

In his initial letter, "Herder admitted that the arguments for the incorruptibility of the human soul were 'very strong' . . . [but disputed] that the surviving 'thinking substance' remained without a body."[129] On a related point, he acknowledged that Mendelssohn, along with "most philosophers and theologians," viewed "the liberation from sensual perceptions and the entirely spiritual perfection" as the state from which are derived "the rewards of the future condition" of the soul. He queried, however: "what is a soul liberated from all sensual perceptions, and what is a purely spiritual perfection in a human soul? I must confess: I do not know."[130]

Herder also criticized Mendelssohn's notion of a progressive rise toward perfection. While acknowledging that the purpose of life, or the vocation of man, is to perfect man's faculties, he saw a process that "flows back into itself . . . [while with Mendelssohn, he said,] the stream flows uphill."[131] In short, Herder doubted the truth of a disembodied soul striving in a postmortem world to achieve ever higher degrees of perfection: "We enter this world only to become perfect *here*, to increase and decrease, to learn and apply, to enjoy ourselves and the world."[132] Thus, the training of

---

126. See Mendelssohn, *Phädon*, 147–60. See also Altmann, *Moses Mendelssohn*, 160–79.
127. Altmann, *Moses Mendelssohn*, 161 (quoting Mendelssohn correspondence).
128. Altmann, *Moses Mendelssohn*, 174 (quoting Mendelssohn correspondence).
129. Altmann, *Moses Mendelssohn*, 170. See Beiser, "Mendelssohn Versus Herder," 237 ("Herder argued that he could not conceive the soul as an immaterial being, as a completely disembodied being, one existing without the sensibility and desires that come with the human body.").
130. Altmann, *Moses Mendelssohn*, 170 (quoting Herder's correspondence). See generally DeSouza, "Soul-Body Relationship," 154–59.
131. Altmann, *Moses Mendelssohn*, 170–71.
132. Altmann, *Moses Mendelssohn*, 173 (emphasis original).

our mental faculties had no bearing on our future condition; and all we could hope for after death, Herder believed, was palingenesis, the regeneration of our body, and another life.[133]

What is most significant about Mendelssohn's response is his assertion that "he agrees entirely with Herder about the impossibility of a disembodied soul, and he now regrets that he ever seemed to countenance the existence of such a soul in his *Phädon*."[134] Indeed, while rejecting Herder's belief in the transmigration of souls,[135] Mendelssohn "accepts Herder's doctrine of palingenesis, i.e., that in the afterlife body is regenerated."[136] Mendelssohn's agreement with Herder did not represent a new-found point of view. He had expressed basically the same position in a letter to Isaak Iselin, stating that "the soul must have a *vehiculum*."[137]

In reply to Mendelssohn's letter, Herder said that they were both in agreement that (1) "an incorporeal human soul is a mere chimera, and hence . . . reject all the nonsense that our Platonists conclude from a nonsensual human nature about our future bliss," and (2) "the purpose of our present existence is the training [*Ausbildung*] of the faculties of our soul, presuming that the soul is our self [*Ich*] and our body is, as it were, merely the phenomenon of its existence and the mediating organ of its representations."[138] Herder added that he was convinced of the indestructibility of the soul, "which implied its immortality and continued existence as a thinking thing."[139]

---

133. See Altmann, *Moses Mendelssohn*, 171.

134. Beiser, "Mendelssohn Versus Herder," 237. See also Beiser, "Mendelssohn Versus Herder," 238 (Mendelssohn "agreed wholeheartedly with Herder that the soul has to be embodied."). Mendelssohn may be seen as following Leibniz who had asserted that "every monad has a body belonging to it as the monad's sensorium" (Altmann, *Moses Mendelssohn*, 172, citing Leibniz, *Monadology*, §§ 61–63). See Beiser, "Mendelssohn Versus Herder," 243 (Leibniz "held both that monads must be embodied and that they are independent mental substances.").

135. See Altmann, *Moses Mendelssohn*, 172.

136. Beiser, "Mendelssohn Versus Herder," 238. Specifically, Mendelssohn states: "'Delete, in the first place, all passages in the Phaedon that distinctly state that in the hereafter our soul will be altogether bereft of body. So far as I remember, my intention was to leave the matter undecided so as not to complicate the knotty question of immortality by too many side issues. Yet in my heart I was, and still am, completely convinced that no limited spirit can be entirely without a body . . . I do consider the sensual element in human nature as the flower of its perfection . . . A soul liberated from all sensuality? . . . I agree with you that in the future life, as in the present, such a thing is a mere chimera'" (Altmann, *Moses Mendelssohn*, 172, quoting Mendelssohn's correspondence). See also Altmann, *Moses Mendelssohn*, 174.

137. Mendelssohn had sent Iselin a copy of the *Phädon* immediately after its publication. Iselin sent criticisms to Mendelssohn to which Mendelssohn responded. In his response Mendelssohn states: "'I myself believe—and here I entirely concur with you—that the soul must have a *vehiculum*. Nevertheless, I considered it advisable to leave this doctrine in abeyance, since it did not seem to be necessary for my purpose. Should the spirit of man always retain such a sensorium in which the changes of the world are reflected, the doctrine of immortality could only gain thereby.'" Altmann, *Moses Mendelssohn*, 160–61 (quoting Mendelssohn correspondence).

138. Altmann, *Moses Mendelssohn*, 175 (quoting Herder correspondence).

139. Altmann, *Moses Mendelssohn*, 175. See Beiser, "Mendelssohn Versus Herder," 238 (listing five basic points of agreement between Mendelssohn and Herder: (1) immortality of soul, (2) vocation

Yet, he insisted, there still remained a "knotty point" left untied, namely, whether, as Herder maintained, our seeking perfection was only for "our condition here below," or whether, as Mendelssohn believed, it impacted our future condition.[140] So, "Herder thinks that the vocation of man has to be limited to this world alone, and . . . the ideal of human perfection cannot be extended beyond this life to the next world to come . . . [whereas Mendelssohn] assumes that the faculties we have in this life are transferrable or extendable to another life."[141] Mendelssohn never responded to Herder but in a note included in his *Notes to Abbt's Friendly Correspondence* "he held firmly to his view of the matter."[142]

2. Kant's refutation of Mendelssohn's proof of the soul's immortality is part of Kant's critique of rational psychology and speculative metaphysics in general

The first edition, or "A-edition," of Kant's *Critique of Pure Reason* was published in 1781. A second edition, the "B-edition," was published in 1787. The chapter of the *Critique* entitled "The Paralogisms of Pure Reason" was entirely restated in the B-edition. The restatement includes a section called "Refutation of Mendelssohn's Proof of the Permanence of the Soul." In this section Kant addresses the argument in the first dialogue of *Phädon* that there is no definite moment in time when it can be said that the soul is annihilated. Referring to Mendelssohn, Kant writes:

> This acute philosopher soon noticed that the usual arguments by which it is sought to prove that the soul—if it be admitted to be a simple being—cannot cease to be through *dissolution*, is insufficient for its purpose, that of proving the necessary continuance of the soul, since it may be supposed to pass out of existence through simply *vanishing*. In his *Phaedo* he endeavored to prove that the soul cannot be subject to such a process of vanishing, which would be a true annihilation, by showing that a simple being cannot cease to exist. His argument is that since the soul cannot be diminished, and so gradually lose something of its existence, being by degrees changed into nothing (for since it has no parts, it has no multiplicity in itself), there would be no time between a moment in which it is and another in which it is not—which is impossible.[143]

---

of man to perfect faculties, (3) soul has to be embodied, (4) palingenesis, and (5) human perfection involves development of sensibility).

140. Altmann, *Moses Mendelssohn*, 175 (quoting Herder correspondence).

141. Beiser, "Mendelssohn Versus Herder," 240. Alternatively stated, "Herder insists that the purpose of this life is *entirely* immanent, that nothing we do here can count as a preparation for the next life. Mendelssohn, on the other hand, thinks that the purpose of life is not only immanent but also transcendent, that we can prepare ourselves for the next life by developing our powers here and now, because the next life will be nothing more than a continuation of the development of the powers we have had in this life" (Beiser, "Mendelssohn Versus Herder," 241). See also Altmann, *Moses Mendelssohn*, 174.

142. Altmann, *Moses Mendelssohn*, 176–77.

143. Kant, *Critique of Pure Reason*, B 413–14 (emphasis original).

Kant then proceeds to argue that Mendelssohn failed to consider that

> the supposed substance ... may be changed into nothing ... by gradual loss (*remissio*) of its powers, and so, if I may be permitted to use the term, by elanguescence. For consciousness itself has always a degree, which always allows of diminution, and the same must hold of the faculty of being conscious of the self, and likewise of all the other faculties. Thus, the permanence of the soul, regarded merely as object of inner sense, remains undemonstrated, and indeed indemonstrable. Its permanence during life is, of course, evident *per se*, ... But this is very far from satisfying the rational psychologist who undertakes to prove from mere concepts its absolute permanence beyond this life.[144]

The refutation of Mendelssohn's argument for the soul's immortality constitutes just a small part of Kant's critique of rational psychology in general; in turn, the criticism of rational psychology constitutes just a part of Kant's overall criticism of speculative metaphysics.[145] Kant considered his entire project one of "transcendental criticism," that is

> pure reason's systematic detection, correction, and explanation of its own excesses. These excesses occur, according to Kant, because reason constantly strives to transcend the bounds of sense in its pursuit of speculative knowledge. In Kant's view, all such attempts to 'rise above the world of sense through the mere might of speculation' (A 591 / B 619) are destined to fail. In particular, pure speculative reason can afford us no knowledge of the nature of the self as it is in itself, none of the world considered as the totality of appearances, and none of the existence (or nonexistence) of God.[146]

According to Kant, even sophisticated philosophers (including Leibniz, Wolff, and Mendelssohn) have believed that pure speculative reason *could* provide us with knowledge of the soul and of God because they succumbed to a powerful illusion "grounded in the very nature of human reason itself" which Kant called the "transcendental illusion."[147] When one is in the grip of transcendental illusion one can be persuaded of the soundness of certain unsound arguments. Unsound arguments which may persuade one, under the influence of transcendental illusion, that we can know the character of the self, or soul, to be a simple, incorruptible, immaterial, and

---

144. Kant, *Critique of Pure Reason*, B 414–15 (emphasis original). See Smith, *Commentary to Kant's "Critique of Pure Reason,"* 470–71 ("Kant's reply to ... Mendelssohn's argument is that though the soul must not be perceived as perishing suddenly, it may pass out of existence by a continuous diminution through an infinite number of smaller degrees of intensive reality."). See also Altmann, *Moses Mendelssohn*, 179 ("The 'law of continuity,' Mendelssohn could have objected ... also ruled out the possibility of a fading out through a remission of powers.").

145. See generally Russell, *History of Western Philosophy*, 706–10 (discussing Kant's *Critique of Pure Reason*).

146. Proops, "Kant's First Paralogism," 449–50 (quoting Kant's *Critique of Pure Reason*).

147. Proops, "Kant's First Paralogism," 450–51.

naturally immortal substance are called by Kant "paralogisms of pure reason."[148] In reality, Kant believes, "the thinking being that we refer to by means of the word 'I' is something about whose inner nature we must remain forever ignorant."[149] It is only a paralogism that makes one believe that the soul is a substance—something that can exist only as a subject, as a self-subsisting being.[150]

While Kant thus debunks the claims of rational psychology to prove the existence of God and the immortality of the soul, he accepts that there is a God and a future life on other grounds: "The argument is that the moral law demands justice, i.e., happiness proportional to virtue. Only Providence can insure this, and has evidently not insured it in *this* life. Therefore there is a God and a future life."[151] In other words, belief in the immortality of the soul is justified on the basis of what Kant calls practical reason, not pure reason. According to Kenny:

> Our natural drive to go beyond the limits of merely empirical psychology leads us into fallacies—Kant calls them 'paralogisms' or bogus syllogisms . . .
>
> The rational proof of the immortality of the soul is nothing but delusion. But that does not mean that we cannot believe in a future life as a postulate of *practical* reason. In the present life happiness is clearly not proportioned to virtue; so if we are to be motivated to behave well, we must believe that the balance will be addressed in another life elsewhere. The refutation of rational psychology, Kant claims, is a help, not a hindrance, to faith in an afterlife. 'For the merely speculative proof has never been able to exercise any influence on the common reason of men . . .' (B, 424).[152]

Kant, in the *Critique of Practical Reason*, argued that nothing we know about the physical world suggests that "virtue is the efficient cause of happiness."[153] Nevertheless, he held that to promote the *summum bonum* is an obligation imposed on all men; and, since, according to him, "ought implies can,"[154] this *summum bonum* must be realizable. Some other (and moral) force must, therefore, be operative in the universe that will at some future time bring about the distribution of happiness in accordance with virtue. It is on this bases that Kant says that the possibility of the *summum bonum*

---

148. See Kant, *Critique of Pure Reason*, A 341–51=B 399–413.

149. Proops, "Kant's First Paralogism," 460.

150. See Proops, "Kant's First Paralogism," 461, 465. See also Kenny, *New History of Western Philosophy*, 3:242 (summarizing the four paralogisms of pure reason mentioned by Kant, and stating that, on the basis of these paralogisms "rational psychology concludes that the self is an immaterial, incorruptible, personal, immortal entity.").

151. Russell, *History of Western Philosophy*, 710 (emphasis original).

152. Kenny, *New History of Western Philosophy*, 3:242–43 (quoting Kant's *Critique of Pure Reason*; emphasis added). See generally Copleston, *History of Philosophy*, VI, part 2, 126–31.

153. Kant, *Critique of Practical Reason*, Pt. 1, Bk. II, ch. 2, §1.

154. See, Kant, *Critique of Pure Reason*, A 548=B 576.

leads to, or postulates, the existence of God.[155] Moreover, the possibility of the *summum bonum* must also lead to, or postulate, the immortality of the soul:

> The *perfect accordance* of the [will] with the moral law [*i.e.*, complete virtue] is ... perfection of which no rational being ... is capable at any moment of his existence. Since, nevertheless, it is required as practically necessary [*i.e.*, it is a state that ought to exist], it can only be found in a *progress in infinitum* towards that perfect existence ...
>
> Now, this endless progress is only possible on the supposition of an *endless* duration of the *existence* and personality of the same rational being ... The *summum bonum*, then, practically is only possible on the supposition of the immortality of the soul; consequently this immortality, being inseparably connected with the moral law, is a postulate of pure practical reason (by which I mean a *theoretical* proposition, not demonstrable as such, but which is an inseparable result of an unconditional *a priori practical* law).[156]

In essence, Kant agrees with the argument Mendelssohn advanced in the third dialogue of *Phädon*, as well as with his view that the immortality of the soul is required as a consequence of the fact that the moral perfection rational beings strive to attain cannot be achieved in this life.[157]

---

155. Kant, *Critique of Practical Reason*, Pt. 1, Bk. II, ch. 2, §5, 220–22 ("The *summum bonum* is possible in the world only on the supposition of a Supreme Being having a causality corresponding to moral character."). See Jones, *History of Western Philosophy*, 4:91–92.

156. Kant, *Critique of Practical Reason*, Pt. 1, Bk. II, ch. 2, §4, 218–19 (emphasis original). See Jones, *History of Western Philosophy*, 4:92. Jones provides two main objections to these proofs. See Jones, *History of Western Philosophy*, 4:92–93.

157. See Copleston, *History of Philosophy*, VI, part 2, 130–31.

11.

In the Nineteenth and Twentieth Centuries, Reform Judaism Presents a Hodgepodge of Conflicting and Confused Ideas about the Soul, Resurrection, and the Afterlife

IN THE YEARS FOLLOWING the emergence of the *Haskalah*, there was a rapid expansion of secular education among the Jews of Western Europe and a growing interest in replacing "inherited dogma" with "the rational truths of natural religion."[1] David Friedländer, a disciple of Mendelssohn, came to deny Mendelssohn's claim that there is a revealed ceremonial law; for Friedländer there were only the eternal truths of reason.[2] And Saul Ascher sought to transform Judaism into a religion, not a nationality.[3] In keeping with Ascher's views, proponents of Jewish educational reform produced catechisms setting forth those beliefs they claimed to constitute the essence of Jewish religion.[4] Many, if not most, of these catechisms specify Maimonides's Thirteen Principles as the creedal affirmations of Judaism.[5] A catechism authored by Hirsch Baer Fassel, however, contained an elaboration of the Maimonidean principles that included the immortality of the soul as well as resurrection.[6] Ben Ze'eb's *Yesode ha-*

---

1. See Meyer, *Response to Modernity*, 17; Meyer, *Origins of the Modern Jew*, 157.

2. See Meyer, *Response to Modernity*, 44–45; Meyer, *Origins of the Modern Jew*, 58–59.

3. Meyer, *Response to Modernity*, 22. See Meyer, *Origins of the Modern Jew*, 122–23 ("Ascher insists that there must be some difference between Judaism and pure natural religion, and he claims to find this distinction in certain dogmas which constitute the essence of Judaism and the sole reason for its preservation.").

4. See generally Petuchowski, "Manuals and Catechisms of the Jewish Religion," 47–58; Meyer, *Origins of the Modern Jew*, 125; Meyer, *Response to Modernity*, 23.

5. See Petuchowski, "Manuals and Catechisms of the Jewish Religion," 47; Meyer, *Origins of the Modern Jew*, 125. See also Meyer, *Response to Modernity*, 38–40.

6. Petuchowski, "Manuals and Catechisms of the Jewish Religion," 56–57.

Dath went further, *replacing* a belief in bodily resurrection with the immortality of the soul.[7] This change was adopted by the Reform movement.

The rise of the reform movement in Germany, and then elsewhere in Western Europe and in America, led to further denominational divisions in Judaism—Conservatism and Orthodoxy. Meanwhile, a very different movement called Hasidism developed in Eastern Europe. As Neusner describes the modern situation, a single Judaism became many Judaisms. The several Judaisms had varying views about the soul, resurrection, and the afterlife, and major differences even emerged within a single movement. In this chapter the reform movement will be discussed; the other movements will be discussed in the next chapter.

A. The Reform Movement in Germany Rejects Belief in Bodily Resurrection, Accepting Only Immortality of the Soul

1. Early advocates of liturgical reform retain prayers for the resurrection of the dead

Hand in hand with the reformation of Jewish religious education, the *maskilim* sought a reformation of the worship service in order to make it more consistent with enlightenment thinking and the goal of political emancipation.[8] A reform-minded group of Jews in Hamburg formed a "New Israelite Temple Association," and in 1818 the association built a house of worship which they called a "temple."[9] The Hamburg temple developed a prayerbook which was the first comprehensive reform liturgy.[10] All succeeding prayerbooks of the reform movement were based on this one.[11] Of particular interest is the fact that the liturgy "retained intact, both in Hebrew and German, the references to the resurrection of the dead."[12] Such liturgical references include, primarily, the *Gevurot* benediction of the *Amidah,* specifically in its closing words which praise God Who "revives the dead (*"mehaye hametim"*)."[13] The retention of references to the resurrection of the dead was probably due to a desire to limit objection from traditionalists.[14]

    7. Petuchowski, "Manuals and Catechisms of the Jewish Religion," 56–57.

    8. See generally Scheindlin, *Short History of the Jewish People*, 168–69.

    9. See Meyer, *Response to Modernity*, 53–55; Meyer, *Origins of the Modern Jew*, 135–36.

    10. See Millgram, *Jewish Worship*, 583.

    11. See Idelsohn, *Jewish Liturgy and Its Development*, 269–70.

    12. Meyer, *Response to Modernity*, 56. See Meyer, *Origins of the Modern Jew*, 136.

    13. See generally Gillman, *Death of Death*, 193–96, 198. The meaning of the phrase *mehaye hametim* is enigmatic. Gillman writes: "What did the liturgist mean in penning these words? Bodily resurrection alone? Restoring the soul to the resurrected body? We don't really know. It is precisely this indeterminacy in meaning which gave modern liturgists the latitude to interpret the words in ways consistent with their own convictions" (Gillman, *Death of Death*, 195–96). See also Idelsohn, *Jewish Liturgy and Its Development*, 92–109; Millgram, *Jewish Worship*, 102.

    14. See Millgram, *Jewish Worship*, 583.

2. Jewish intellectuals and reformers, influenced by German cultural trends, adopt an historical approach to truth, and wed this approach to science

By as early as 1780, there arose among German philosophers a conception of truth which challenged the Enlightenment idea that truth is something eternal and unchanging. Johann Gottfried Herder argued, for example, that people's concepts, beliefs, sensations, etc. differ in deep ways from one period (or culture) to another.[15] Some years later, Georg Wilhelm Friedrich Hegel would contend in a more systematic fashion that truth is not static, but evolves in a dialectic process: "In Hegel's philosophy we find, for the first time, a thoroughgoing attempt to view all philosophical problems and concepts, including the concept of reason itself, in essentially historical terms. No idea, for Hegel, has a fixed meaning, no form of understanding an eternal, unchanging validity."[16] Gradually, German philosophy "became absorbed in a new and more comprehensive ideal . . . the ideal of *Wissenschaft*. The German term means much more than empirical science, although it includes it; it makes room for speculation but tempers it with historical fact."[17]

The ideal of *Wissenschaft* was embraced by German Jewish intellectuals and applied to Jewish sources.[18] The person most responsible for this application is Leopold Zunz, the founder of *Wissenschaft des Judentums*. Zunz "came to see his life's task to create a Jewish philology utilizing the principles and methods of modern scholarship."[19] Together with other like-minded Jewish intellectuals, Zunz, in 1819, founded the Society for Culture and Scientific Study of the Jews, and went on to become "the most universally respected modern Jewish scholar of the nineteenth century."[20] By demonstrating that Jewish religious practices were often the evolving customs of their times, *Wissenschaft des Judentums* "dealt a serious blow to the Orthodox *status quo* of the nineteenth century."[21] Zunz himself gradually despaired of achieving religious reform,[22] but the historical approach to Judaism that he initiated became vital to the reform effort led by Zunz's friend Abraham Geiger.[23]

---

15. See Meyer, *Origins of the Modern Jew*, 145.

16. Aiken, *Age of Ideology*, 72. See also Meyer, *Origins of the Modern Jew*, 145 ("In nineteenth-century Germany . . . [a]ttention was drawn away from the 'eternal verities' of metaphysics toward the individual facts of history.").

17. Meyer, *Origins of the Modern Jew*, 145. See Meyer, *Response to Modernity*, 75–76.

18. See generally Sachar, *Course of Modern Jewish History*, 149–50.

19. Meyer, *Origins of the Modern Jew*, 160.

20. Meyer, *Response to Modernity*, 75–76. See generally Meyer, *Origins of the Modern Jew*, 162–80; Sachar, *Course of Modern Jewish History*, 151–52.

21. Sachar, *Course of Modern Jewish History*, 153.

22. Meyer, *Response to Modernity*, 76. See Meyer, *Origins of the Modern Jew*, 180–81.

23. See Sachar, *Course of Modern Jewish History*, 153 (the historical approach was to be used by the new generation of reformers; "they sought . . . to substitute history for rationalism. History would decide what point of evolution Judaism had reached; it would decide what should be saved and what should be discarded. For did history not prove that there had always been adjustments and change in

3. Abraham Geiger emphasizes historical knowledge as the essential prerequisite to reform and makes scientific truth, not faith, the ultimate standard by which to judge beliefs and practices

Abraham Geiger assumed his first pulpit—serving the Jewish community of Wiesbaden—in 1832 when he was only twenty-two. In 1839, he was elected as second rabbi of the Breslau community which desired a more progressive leadership. Meyer writes: "To Geiger, if to anyone, belongs the title 'founding father of the Reform movement.' Although Reform ideas and liturgical innovations did not begin with him, it was he . . . who more than anyone drew together the strands and wove them into an ideology for the movement . . . Geiger could set no limits to Wissenschaft; scientific truth, not faith, remained his ultimate standard."[24] Geiger studied philosophy and history at the University of Bonn.[25] He was drawn to Herder's "philosophically informed historical studies of human spiritual development," and Herder's works, as well as Lessing's, "influenced him deeply."[26] Additionally, "Geiger had early and carefully studied Spinoza's biblical criticism and he kept up with what Christian scholars were writing [regarding the critical and historical study of the Hebrew Bible]."[27]

Geiger founded a critical journal called the *Scientific Journal for Jewish Theology,* which began publication in 1835.[28] In his writings, Geiger tried to show that Judaism was constantly "evolving" and that historical knowledge

> was the essential prerequisite for reform. It liberated the present from the shackles of a timeless tradition even as it created the basis for a new sense of continuity with the past. As Geiger saw it, contemporary Judaism was bereft of historical consciousness. It lived in a 'long present,' which had not so much grown out of the past as fully absorbed it . . . The inner history of Israel was commonly seen to be essentially uniform . . . But if the opposite could be shown, if Judaism had in fact displayed extraordinary variety, . . . then reform in the present would represent not an arbitrary break with the past but its logical continuation.[29]

Judaism?").

24. Meyer, *Response to Modernity*, 89. See Sachar, *Course of Modern Jewish History*, 153; Plaut, *Rise of Reform Judaism*, 18. See generally Kaplan, *Greater Judaism in the Making*, 231–46.

25. Meyer, *Response to Modernity*, 89.

26. Meyer, *Response to Modernity*, 89.

27. Meyer, *Response to Modernity*, 93.

28. See Sachar, *Course of Modern Jewish History*, 153–54; Plaut, *Rise of Reform Judaism*, 18.

29. Meyer, *Response to Modernity*, 92. See Meyer, *Response to Modernity*, 94.

4. By the mid-nineteenth century, Geiger advocates that the hope for an afterlife should not be expressed in terms which suggest bodily resurrection but only in terms of "the immortality of the human soul"[30]

Liturgical references to resurrection in German reform prayerbooks changed in 1854. That was when Geiger, then serving as rabbi in Breslau, prepared a prayerbook that was "more radical in its German paraphrases than its Hebrew text."[31] While keeping the Hebrew text of the *Gevurot* benediction, the German translation of the Hebrew phrase *mehaye hametim* states, not that God "revives the dead," but that God "renews life" or, more literally, "bestows life here and there," suggesting that God bestows life "in this age and in the age to come."[32] The preface to this prayerbook laid down certain guiding liturgical principles, among which was that "the belief in bodily resurrection must be eliminated"; it "must be expressed in such a way as to include the concept of spiritual immortality."[33] Geiger had held this view for quite some time. At a conference of Reform rabbis held in the city of Brunswick in 1844, Geiger had stated:

> many religious concepts have taken on a more spiritual character and, therefore, their expression in prayer must be more spiritual. From now on the hope for an after-life should not be expressed in terms which suggest a future revival, a resurrection of the body; rather, they must stress the immortality of the human soul.[34]

At that same Brunswick rabbinical conference Joseph Maier argued for the establishment of a commission for the creation of a new prayerbook.[35] He said that their "ordinary prayer book... suffers in formal as well as material respects from so many ailments that it is no longer in a position to satisfy the religious needs of a progressively educated generation."[36] Regarding the prayerbook's material defects, Maier said that it contained "prayers and pieces which are in contradiction to the beliefs of a large part of the congregation."[37] Although Maier does not specifically mention the *Gevurot*, the fact that the prayerbook edited by Geiger in 1854 was the one "which gained

---

30. Plaut, *Rise of Reform Judaism*, 158 (quoting Geiger).

31. Meyer, *Response to Modernity*, 186.

32. See Meyer, *Response to Modernity*, 186; Gillman, *Death of Death*, 198–99; Levenson, *Resurrection and the Restoration of Israel*, 7.

33. Idelsohn, *Jewish Liturgy and Its Development*, 276. See Gillman, *Death of Death*, 199 (There is in Geiger only "an intuitive sense that physical resurrection is not worthy of serious consideration... Nor is there a clear exposition of what the alternative doctrine really says.").

34. Plaut, *Rise of Reform Judaism*, 156–58. See Gillman, *Death of Death*, 198.

35. Plaut, *Rise of Reform Judaism*, 154. See generally Meyer, *Response to Modernity*, 132–36; Plaut, *Rise of Reform Judaism*, 74–79.

36. Plaut, *Rise of Reform Judaism*, 154.

37. Plaut, *Rise of Reform Judaism*, 155.

most popularity" suggests that bodily resurrection was, indeed, a belief rejected by most, if not all, reformers.[38]

5. Reformers did not accept belief in transmigration of souls, intercessory efforts to aid the souls of departed loved ones, or other superstitious beliefs and practices

Plaut asserts that "Reform . . . must boldly expose all superstitions and magical elements in Judaism" and he refers to an anonymous letter of a "Jewish Householder" that appeared in an 1837 journal.[39] The householder indicates in his letter that superstitious practices, such as seeking intercession at the graves of rabbis, were still prevalent, and he argues that reform efforts must be more directed toward the eradication of such superstitious beliefs and practices.[40] The concern to eliminate superstitious practices related to the dead is also evidenced in *Torat Hayyim* by Rabbi Leopold Stein. *Torat Hayyim* is a catalogue of religious duties included at the end of Stein's two-volume work on the theology of Judaism, *Die Schrift des Lebens*.[41] In *Torat Hayyim*, in the context of discussing mourning rituals, Stein asserts that the recitation of the Mourner's Kaddish should "be encouraged, *not* because its recital would ensure the happiness of the souls of our departed (this is a point of view which is un-Jewish and should be abandoned), but so that children be constantly reminded of their high duty to sanctify the name of God among men in their parents' stead, and to help bring about His heavenly kingdom on earth."[42] Other well-established mourning practices were likewise condemned as inconsistent with enlightened views about sin, the immortality of the soul, and the nature of the afterlife.[43]

---

38. Idelsohn, *Jewish Liturgy and Its Development*, 275. See also Meyer, *Response to Modernity*, 186.

39. Plaut, *Rise of Reform Judaism*, 100.

40. Plaut, *Rise of Reform Judaism*, 101–2 (citing *Die Allegemeine Zeitung des Judenthums*, I, no. 75 (1837) 297).

41. Plaut, *Rise of Reform Judaism*, 260.

42. Plaut, *Rise of Reform Judaism*, 265 (Stein source material, *Torat Hayim*; emphasis added).

43. See Plaut, *Rise of Reform Judaism*, 223–24.

B. The Reform Movement in America Initially Rejected Belief in Bodily Resurrection, *Gehenna*, and *Gan Eden* as "Not Rooted in Judaism,"[44] and Endorsed Belief in the Immortality of the Soul; but Recently the Reform Movement has Encouraged a Wide Array of Diverse Views

It was in America that the reform movement, and liturgical changes initiated by that movement, became most dominant.[45] Jews had lived in America since 1654 when twenty-four Jews from the Dutch colony of Recife, Brazil were forced to leave after the colony fell to the Portuguese. They boarded the tiny vessel *St. Charles*, landing on Manhattan Island in early September.[46] By the eve of the American Revolution the Jews of North America numbered about two or three thousand scattered along the Atlantic seaboard, with organized Jewish congregations in New York, Savannah, Charleston, and Philadelphia.[47] In the first decade of the nineteenth century the largest Jewish community in the United States, numbering 600 persons, was Charleston, South Carolina.[48]

1. The first reformed congregation in America adopts a creed substituting immortality of the soul for bodily resurrection

In 1750, the Charleston Jews formed Kaal Kodesh Beth Elohim, the fifth American Jewish congregation, and by 1794 they constructed a synagogue.[49] In November of 1824, a "considerable proportion" of Beth Elohim's membership signed a petition requesting certain liturgical reforms; they were rebuffed, and so, in January of 1825, they established an independent Reformed Society of Israelites.[50] The society adopted a ten-point creed based on Maimonides's Thirteen Articles of Faith but differing from it on four salient points, including the substitution of immortality of the soul for the resurrection of the dead.[51] With reference to the society's prayerbook printed in 1830, Idelsohn states: "The stress laid in the Charleston Prayerbook on the immortality of

---

44. Meyer, *Response to Modernity*, 388.

45. See Meyer, *Response to Modernity*, 225. See generally Kaplan, *Greater Judaism in the Making*, 272–315.

46. Sachar, *Course of Modern Jewish History*, 160–61.

47. Sachar, *Course of Modern Jewish History*, 163–64. See Scheindlin, *Short History of the Jewish People*, 187.

48. Meyer, *Response to Modernity*, 228.

49. Meyer, *Response to Modernity*, 228.

50. Meyer, *Response to Modernity*, 228–29. See Millgram, *Jewish Worship*, 584–85. See generally Sachar, *Course of Modern Jewish History*, 176.

51. Meyer, *Response to Modernity*, 229. See Gillman, *Death of Death*, 199–200.

the soul and the ethical and universal character of Judaism appears as a distinctive feature in all subsequent Reform rituals."[52]

In 1836, Beth Elohim, still under the control of avowed traditionalists, hired a new *hazan*, Gustavus Poznanski, whom they expected would strengthen the practice of Orthodox Judaism.[53] Poznanski was known for the meticulous observance of ceremonial law but turned into a proponent of reform ideas and practices.[54] Sometime after a new synagogue was built in 1841, Poznanski "formulated a new English version of the Maimonidean creed which was inscribed in golden letters on white tablets and permanently displayed in the synagogue . . . The thirteenth principle, however, clearly substituted immortality of the soul for resurrection of the body."[55] Although the creed was criticized by some, Beth Elohim eventually became a Reform congregation.

2. The prayerbooks of David Einhorn and Isaac Mayer Wise adopt differing approaches to the resurrection issue

By the 1840s, "the impulse for religious reform began to spread in America . . . By 1855 there were congregations with varying degrees of reformed ritual [not only] in Charleston, [but in] Baltimore, New York, Albany, and Cincinnati. In succeeding years, the number and size of Reform congregations would increase at a rapid pace and reforms would become more radical."[56] By 1885, all Reform congregations would substitute belief in the immortality of the soul for belief in the resurrection of the body. The two people most influential with respect to this substitution were Isaac Mayer Wise and David Einhorn, both of whom emigrated to America in the mid-1800s along with tens of thousands other German-Jewish and Central European Jewish immigrants.[57]

As early as 1847, Wise had prepared an outline for what he called a *Minhag America*, an "American Rite," which he wanted to be uniformly used by all American congregations in place of the various rituals that Jewish immigrants brought with them from their places of origin, but *Minhag America* was not published until 1857.[58]

---

52. Idelsohn, *Jewish Liturgy and Its Development*, 277 (quoting article in the *Journal of Jewish Philosophy and Lore*). See also Millgram, *Jewish Worship*, 585.

53. Meyer, *Response to Modernity*, 233.

54. Meyer, *Response to Modernity*, 233.

55. Meyer, *Response to Modernity*, 234.

56. Meyer, *Response to Modernity*, 235. See Sachar, *Course of Modern Jewish History*, 172 ("Reform Judaism . . . entered its greatest period of expansion after the [Civil War]. By the 1880's the German-Jewish immigrants of the early and mid-nineteenth century had virtually completed the process of acculturation.").

57. See generally Sachar, *Course of Modern Jewish History*, 165–74. See also Scheindlin, *Short History of the Jewish People*, 188–89.

58. See Scheindlin, *Short History of the Jewish People*, 253–54; Sachar, *Course of Modern Jewish History*, 177. Cf. Idelsohn, *Jewish Liturgy and Its Development*, 277.

As Meyer notes, "Although . . . Wise did not believe in bodily resurrection, *Minhag America* sidestepped that controversial issue by leaving the Hebrew text intact, altering only the vernacular renditions. Consistency and uniformity of ideology were clearly less important [to Wise] than devising a prayer-book that could gain entry into the largest number of congregations."[59]

Meanwhile, in 1856, Einhorn published the first part of his own liturgy entitled *Prayerbook for Israelite Reform Congregations*.[60] The completed prayerbook, called *Olat Tamid* (*The Daily Offering*), was published in 1858. *Olat Tamid* replaced the Hebrew phrase *mehaye hametim* ("revives the dead"), which closes the traditional *Gevurot* benediction, with the new Hebrew phrase *notea betoheinu haye olam* ("implanted within us eternal life"), so that the closing sentence of the *Gevurot* benediction now read "Praised be Thou, O Lord, who hast implanted within us eternal life."[61] The new Hebrew phrase used by Einhorn was a modification of the traditional second benediction recited by one who is called to the reading of the Torah.[62]

In 1869, Einhorn (who was then serving as a rabbi in New York) and other "radical Reformers" published a call for a rabbinical conference which ultimately met in Philadelphia in November of that year.[63] Attendees included Wise, Einhorn, Kaufmann Kohler, Samuel Hirsch,[64] and nine others; nearly all of the thirteen attendees belonged to the "radical faction."[65] Seven principles intended to distinguish reform Judaism from traditional Judaism were adopted by the conference; one of these adopted principles was that "the belief in bodily resurrection must give way entirely to the idea of spiritual immortality."[66] When traditionalists attacked these principles,

---

59. Meyer, *Response to Modernity*, 254–55. See also Gillman, *Death of Death*, 200 (*Minhag America* "reflected the more conservative wing of American Reform, [and] maintained the traditional form of [the *Gevurot*] benediction.").

60. See generally Meyer, *Response to Modernity*, 245–50, 253.

61. See Meyer, *Response to Modernity*, 254 (Einhorn "transformed the concept of resurrection ('who revives the dead') into immortality of the soul ('who plants within us eternal life')."); Gillman, *Death of Death*, 201 ("Einhorn's prayer book . . . replaces the doctrine of resurrection with 'the idea of a purely spiritual immortality.' His version of [the *Gevurot*] benediction replaces the traditional closing with a new Hebrew phrase which praises God 'Who has planted immortal life within us.'").

62. See Gillman, *Death of Death*, 201 n14; Levenson, *Resurrection and the Restoration*, 8.

63. Meyer, *Response to Modernity*, 255–56.

64. For a discussion of Hirsch, who was the rabbi of the Reform Congregation, Knesset Israel, in Philadelphia, and served as president of the 1869 rabbinical conference in that city, see Kaplan, *Greater Judaism in the Making*, 258–64. Kaplan writes that in his *Die Religionsphilosophie der Juden* Hirsch "definitely repudiates the otherworldly outlook of Rabbinic Judaism. That outlook, according to Hirsch, developed in Judaism when it came under Persian influence, and should be dissociated once again from it. Not otherworldliness, but Messianism, expresses the inherent goal of Judaism" (Kaplan, *Greater Judaism in the Making*, 263).

65. Meyer, *Response to Modernity*, 256.

66. Meyer, *Response to Modernity*, 256. See Gillman, *Death of Death*, 202 ("The sixth article of the Philadelphia statement reads: 'The belief in the bodily resurrection has no religious foundation, and the doctrine of immortality refers to the after-existence of the soul only.'").

"Wise complained that the meeting had had to be 'eminently Einhornian or nothing' and that the principles . . . should have been expressed more positively . . . It was, for example, possible to express belief in the immortality of the soul without explicitly rejecting resurrection."[67] Ultimately, however, at a conference held in Pittsburgh in 1885, the rejection of resurrection was reaffirmed.

3. The Pittsburgh Platform flatly rejects belief in bodily resurrection but leaves many questions about the soul and the afterlife unanswered

In the closing decades of the nineteenth century, Reform Judaism was challenged by a wholly nonsectarian universalism on the one side and by traditional expressions of Judaism on the other.[68] A major universalist challenge came from the New York Society for Ethical Culture founded in 1876/77 by Felix Adler, the son of Rabbi Samuel Adler of Temple Emanu-El in New York. Felix Adler, who taught philosophy at Columbia University from 1902 until his death in 1933, attacked Reform Judaism as a halfway house between an untenable orthodoxy and a complete liberation from religious authority.[69] Adler gave weekly Sunday morning lectures which drew enormous crowds; prominent among those attracted were Reform Jews whose Jewish identity had become marginal.[70] As Meyer comments, "Although Ethical Culture's tangible attraction for Reform Jews was mainly limited to New York, its arguments were a challenge to Reform Judaism everywhere,"[71] and Adler was condemned by leaders of the Reform movement. The most agitated response came from Kaufmann Kohler who "denounced [Adler] as 'a man who has deserted the Jewish flag, and openly professes his disbelief in God *and immortality*."[72]

The traditionalist challenge came especially from Alexander Kohut and the nascent Conservative Movement. Kohut was a Hungarian-born rabbi, ordained at the Jewish Theological Seminary of Breslau, who came to New York in 1885 to serve as rabbi for Ahavath Chesed in New York.[73] As Gillman notes: "Six months before the Pittsburgh Conference, Kohut began a series of lectures from his pulpit, sharply attacking the emerging shape of American Reform and presenting his own ideology as a more authentic alternative. Kohut's attack on Reform had an enormous impact. It impelled an equally passionate rebuttal in the form of sermons delivered by Kaufmann Kohler."[74]

---

67. Meyer, *Response to Modernity*, 258.
68. See Meyer, *Response to Modernity*, 265.
69. Meyer, *Response to Modernity*, 266.
70. Meyer, *Response to Modernity*, 265.
71. Meyer, *Response to Modernity*, 266.
72. Meyer, *Response to Modernity*, 266 (quoting Kaufmann Kohler; emphasis added).
73. See Gillman, *Conservative Judaism*, 29; Meyer, *Response to Modernity*, 267.
74. Gillman, *Conservative Judaism*, 29. See Meyer, *Response to Modernity*, 267 ("In declaring

The challenges to Reform Judaism posed by Kohut and Felix Adler convinced Kohler that a clear, succinct, and positive self-definition of Reform Judaism was required, and so he invited to a conference to be held in Pittsburgh in November of 1885 "all such American rabbis as advocate reform and progress and are in favor of united action in all matters pertaining to the welfare of American Judaism."[75] Nineteen rabbis attended the conference and elected Wise to chair it, but it was Kohler who dominated the proceedings.[76] The outcome of the conference was a document referred to as the Pittsburgh Platform. The Pittsburgh Platform sets forth eight principles agreed upon by the attendees. The following two principles are most relevant in the present context:

> Sixth. We recognize in Judaism a progressive religion, ever striving to be in accord with the postulates of reason . . .
>
> Seventh. We assert the doctrine of Judaism that the soul of man is immortal, grounding this belief on the divine nature of the human spirit, which forever finds bliss in righteousness and misery in wickedness. We reject, as ideas not rooted in Judaism, the beliefs both in bodily resurrection and in Gehenna and Eden (Hell and paradise) as abodes for everlasting punishment and reward.[77]

Noticeably absent from the Platform is any statement concerning the nature of the soul or any affirmative account of the nature of the afterlife. *Gehenna* and *Eden* are rejected as "abodes" for punishment and reward but, apparently, a postmortem punishment or reward is not rejected since it is stated that the soul finds bliss in righteousness and misery in wickedness "forever."[78] The text is silent, however, as to the nature of such bliss and misery, as well as to all other related questions such as: "which souls are subject to such bliss and misery?" (just Jews, or all humans?); "is there any possibility of postmortem purgation to avoid misery 'forever'?"; and "is the soul able to transmigrate to different bodies?" Nor is it at all clear what exactly counts as "righteousness" and "wickedness." The Platform accepts the "moral laws" of the Hebrew Bible as "binding"[79] but precisely which are these "moral laws"? Do they include the stoning of adulterers and rebellious children? Presumably not, but no criteria for distinguishing the moral laws from the nonmoral laws is given. Nor is

---

Reform Jews essentially non-Jews, Kohut was pressing from the other side a similar case to that which Felix Adler was making from the vantage point of Ethical Culture . . . [Kohler] jumped into the breach. In his own series of lectures during that same summer of 1885, [Kohler] launched a spirited defense of the Reform Judaism that Kohut had so tellingly attacked."). See also Gillman, *Conservative Judaism*, 29 ("The Kohut-Kohler Controversy dominated the pages of the American Jewish press throughout the summer of 1885.").

75. Meyer, *Response to Modernity*, 268.

76. See Meyer, *Response to Modernity*, 268; Gillman, *Conservative Judaism*, 27.

77. The text of the Pittsburgh Platform is contained in Meyer, *Response to Modernity*, 387–88. See Gillman, *Death of Death*, 202.

78. Meyer, *Response to Modernity*, 338.

79. Pittsburgh Platform [1885], Third Principle. See Meyer, *Response to Modernity*, 388.

there any explanation as to why belief in resurrection and the abodes of *Gehenna* and *Eden* are "not rooted in Judaism."

In 1895, the Central Conference of American Rabbis (CCAR), under the chairmanship of Kohler, published an official prayerbook for the American Reform synagogues, entitled *The Union Prayer Book*, which implemented the theology espoused in the Pittsburgh Platform.[80] Consequently, "[t]he doctrine of the resurrection of the dead was replaced by the immortality of the soul."[81] More specifically, following Einhorn, the second benediction of the *Amidah* concludes with "Who has implanted within us immortal life."[82] Similarly, the silent meditation for the Day of Atonement contains the statement: "'In all my doings make me to recognize every day and every hour that I am shaping for weal or for woe the destiny of my immortal soul.'"[83] The *Union Prayer Book* was revised and slightly reshaped from time to time "but was not fundamentally altered for eighty years."[84]

4. Kaufmann Kohler's *Jewish Theology* provides limited clarification or justification of the Reform position on the soul and the afterlife, and seems rather to deemphasize belief in any afterlife or postmortem reward and punishment

Kohler's main work, *Jewish Theology Systematically and Historically Considered*, was published in 1918. By an historic consideration of Jewish theology Kohler means the tracing of "the various doctrines of [Judaism] through the different epochs and stages of culture, showing their historical process of growth and development," while a systematic consideration "presents these same doctrines in comprehensive form as a fixed system."[85] Yet, since "Judaism is a religion of *historical* growth, which far from claiming to be a final truth, is ever regenerated anew at each turning point of history,"[86]

---

80. See Millgram, *Jewish Worship*, 586; Idelsohn, *Jewish Liturgy and Its Development*, 278. See generally Meyer, *Response to Modernity*, 279 ("By 1890 Reform congregations were worshiping not only from versions of Wise's *Minhag America* and Einhorn's *Olat Tamid*, but from a variety of prayer books compiled by individual rabbis for their own use . . . The solution reached was to create something new: a *Union Prayer Book* . . . which drew especially on Einhorn's work.").

81. Millgram, *Jewish Worship*, 588. See also Levenson, *Resurrection and the Restoration of Israel*, 8–9 ("*The Union Prayer book* (1895), pursues several strategies to affirm continued existence of the dead while sidestepping the rabbinic expectation that they will be miraculously revived.").

82. See Idelsohn, *Jewish Liturgy and Its Development*, 281.

83. Idelsohn, *Jewish Liturgy and Its Development*, 290. See also Idelsohn, *Jewish Liturgy and Its Development*, 293; Levenson, *Resurrection and the Restoration*, 8 ("afterlife is defined as the memory that the living have of the dead and the positive influence that the departed have on those who survive them. Not only is resurrection nowhere to be found, but even immortality has . . . been massively redefined and drastically curtailed.").

84. Meyer, *Response to Modernity*, 279.

85. Kohler, *Jewish Theology*, 1.

86. Kohler, *Jewish Theology*, 4 (emphasis original).

a systematic theology of Judaism must "content itself with presenting Jewish doctrine and belief in relation to the most advanced scientific and philosophic ideas of the age . . . but it by no means claims for them the character of finality."[87]

Elaborating on the notion of an historical consideration, Kohler writes that modern critical and historical research "has taught us to distinguish the products of different periods and stages of development . . . and therefore compels us to reject the idea of a uniform origin of the Law, and also of an uninterrupted chain of tradition reaching back to Moses on Sinai," and requires us to "attach still more importance to the process of transformation which Judaism had to undergo through the centuries."[88] The process of transformation included the assimilation of new ideas under the influence of "Babylonia and Persia, then of Greece and Rome, [and] finally of the Occidental powers."[89] As an example, Kohler states that Judaism "adopted the Babylonian and Persian views of the hereafter, of the upper and the nether world."[90]

Regarding Jewish articles of faith, the doctrine of the One and Only God, says Kohler, stands in the foreground.[91] A second fundamental article of the Jewish faith is divine revelation; however, the modern historical view "rejects altogether the assumption of a supernatural origin of either the written or the oral Torah."[92] Next, Kohler asserts:

> The third fundamental article of the Jewish faith is belief in a moral government of the world, which manifests itself in the reward of good and the punishment of evil, either here or hereafter . . . Closely connected with retribution is the belief in the resurrection of the dead [which] . . . Maimonides . . . transformed . . . into a belief in the continuity of the soul after death. In this form, however, it is actually a postulate or corollary, of the belief in retribution.[93]

In a chapter entitled "The Immortal Soul of Man," Kohler provides a very brief account of the development of the concept of the soul in Jewish thought. He finds some scriptural support for the idea of immortality in what he concedes to be "a rather obscure and probably corrupt passage"—Proverbs 12:28.[94] He then contends that there is "more solid foundation for the view that the verse, 'God created man in

---

87. Kohler, *Jewish Theology*, 6.

88. Kohler, *Jewish Theology*, 12.

89. Kohler, *Jewish Theology*, 12. See Kohler, *Jewish Theology*, 9 (Judaism "manifests a mighty impulse to come into close touch with the various civilized nations, partly in order to disseminate among them its sublime truths, . . . partly to clarify and deepen those truths by assimilating the wisdom and culture of those very nations.").

90. Kohler, *Jewish Theology*, 12.

91. Kohler, *Jewish Theology*, 21.

92. Kohler, *Jewish Theology*, 23–24.

93. Kohler, *Jewish Theology*, 24. Kohler rejects any belief in bodily resurrection. See Kohler, *Jewish Theology*, 395 ("the belief in the resurrection of the body . . . is in such utter contradiction to our entire attitude toward both science and religion, that it may be considered obsolete for the modern Jew.").

94. Kohler, *Jewish Theology*, 286.

His own image' implies that there is an imperishable divine essence in man."[95] Referring to Genesis 2:7, Kohler sees in the Bible two related ideas which, he says, have given rise in various ancient cultures to "diverse definitions of the soul."[96] One idea is that the soul leaves man at his death, flying toward heaven; the other is that "the soul descends into the nether world as a shadowy image of the body, there to continue a dull existence."[97] He continues:

> This was the point of departure for the development of the conception of immortality in one or another direction, according to whether the body was considered a part of the personality which somehow survives after death, or only the spiritual substance of the soul was thought to live on in celestial regions as something divine. The former led to the theory of the resurrection of the body and its reunion with the soul; the latter to the belief in a future life for the soul, after it had been separated or released from the body.[98]

Notwithstanding this discussion, Kohler makes it very clear that until "long after the exile the Jewish people shared the view of the entire ancient world . . . that the dead continue to exist in the shadowy realm of the nether world (*Sheol*), the land of no return (*Beliyaal*) of eternal silence (*Dumah*), and oblivion (*Neshiyah*), a dull, ghostly existence without clear consciousness and without any awakening to a better life."[99] No attempt was made during this biblical period, he adds,

> to transform the nether world into a place of divine judgment, of recompense for the good and evil deeds accomplished on earth, as did the Babylonians and Egyptians. Both the prophets and the Mosaic code persist in applying their promises and threats, in fact, their entire view of retribution, to this world, nor do they indicate by a single word the belief in a judgment or a weighing of actions in the world to come . . . Biblical Judaism evinced such a powerful impetus toward a complete and blissful life with God, that the center and purpose of existence could not be transferred to the hereafter, as in other systems of belief, but was found in the desire to work out the life here on earth to its fullest possible development.[100]

According to Kohler's account, "a tremendous process of transformation in Judaism" began with the *hasidim* or pious ones of the Second Temple period and their successors, the Pharisees.[101] Kohler asserts that, under the influence of the Persians, the Pharisees developed the concept of a divine judgment day after death when the

---

95. Kohler, *Jewish Theology*, 286.
96. Kohler, *Jewish Theology*, 287.
97. Kohler, *Jewish Theology*, 287.
98. Kohler, *Jewish Theology*, 287
99. Kohler, *Jewish Theology*, 279.
100. Kohler, *Jewish Theology*, 279-81.
101. Kohler, *Jewish Theology*, 283.

just were to awaken to eternal life, and the unjust to everlasting contempt.[102] Kohler further says that, "This *advanced moral view* ... transformed the ancient Semitic Sheol from the realm of shades to a place of punishment for sinners, and thus invested it with an ethical purpose."[103] Despite his attribution to external Persian influence,[104] Kohler recognizes that the transformation resulted when the abandonment of the primitive belief that the family or clan could be held responsible for the crime of an individual[105] gave rise to the need for a solution to the problem of moral evil. He states: "Under the severe political and social oppression that came upon the Jewish people, the pious ones failed to see a just equation of man's doings and his destiny in this life. The bitter disappointment which they experienced made them look to the God of justice for a future, when virtue would receive its due reward and vice its befitting punishment."[106]

Once the solution of a postmortem reward and punishment was hit upon, "[a]ll the [biblical] promises and threats of the law and the prophets, [not receiving fulfillment] in this world, appeared now to point forward to the world to come."[107] The Pharisees then looked for biblical support for this new view; they "made use of every reference, however slight, to the future life—even of such passages as those which speak of the Patriarchs as receiving the promise of possessing the Holy Land, as if they were still alive—as proofs of the continued life of the dead, or of their resurrection."[108] Kohler also mentions the words of Isaiah 26:19 (which he suggests "were inserted by a later hand") and the vision of Ezekiel 37:1–14.[109] Having formulated the belief in resurrection of the dead, the Pharisees then incorporated it into their daily prayers.[110]

Returning to his discussion of the soul, Kohler mentions a couple of rabbinic references to the soul, commenting that "no clear, consistent view of the soul prevailed yet in the rabbinic age ... [and that the] first clear idea of the nature of the soul came with the philosophically trained thinkers, who were dependent either on Plato, main founder of the doctrine of the immortality of the soul, or on Aristotle"; he identifies Philo and Saadia as among these "philosophically trained thinkers."[111] With the medieval Jewish philosophers, the conception "that the soul is a substance derived from the luminous primal matter, like the heavenly spheres and the angels, was ... persistently

---

102. Kohler, *Jewish Theology*, 283.

103. Kohler, *Jewish Theology*, 283 (emphasis added).

104. See Kohler, *Jewish Theology*, 283 ("the Jewish people were . . prepared to adopt the Persian belief in the resurrection of the dead."), 301 ("The whole system of eschatology in connection with resurrection arose undoubtedly from the Persian doctrine.").

105. See Kohler, *Jewish Theology*, 298–99.

106. Kohler, *Jewish Theology*, 282.

107. Kohler, *Jewish Theology*, 284.

108. Kohler, *Jewish Theology*, 284.

109. Kohler, *Jewish Theology*, 282–33.

110. Kohler, *Jewish Theology*, 284–35.

111. Kohler, *Jewish Theology*, 288–91.

maintained . . . [and used to explain] its immortality."¹¹² While some of these Jewish thinkers "expected the human soul to be absorbed in the divine soul, the active intellect, . . . [others] shrank from the logical conclusion of denying individuality to the soul . . . Not so Maimonides."¹¹³ Kohler further remarks that (1) Maimonides's view "that a certain measure of immortality is granted only to the wise—though they must be morally perfect as well—aroused great opposition," and (2) that all of these thinkers "find the future life either expressed or suggested in the Scripture as a truth based upon reason."¹¹⁴

Continuing his historical account of the soul, Kohler notes that the Platonic view forms the basis of the kabbalistic concept of the soul, so that the soul in the Kabbalah is seen as "an emanation from the divine intellect with a luminous character just like the philosophers," and "the soul yearns toward the Primal Source of light, finally to find freedom with God."¹¹⁵ The Kabbalah also divided the soul into three different substances "according to the three biblical names, [assigned] their origins to the three different spheres of the universe, and [reiterated] the Platonic theory of the preexistence of the soul and its future transmigration."¹¹⁶

He concludes his historical discussion of the soul with praise for Mendelssohn, whom Kohler credits with fostering "a new attitude toward the nature and destiny of the soul . . . in Judaism" in that Mendelssohn attempts "to show from the harmonious plan which pervades and controls all of God's creation, that the soul may enter a sphere of existence greater in extent and content than the little span of earthly life."¹¹⁷ Kohler is taken with Mendelssohn's argument that, since the striving for "moral and spiritual perfection" is "unsatisfied in this life," there must be a continued striving for perfection in an afterlife" to justify God's own perfection.¹¹⁸

Unfortunately, when Kohler discusses his own views about the soul, resurrection, and the afterlife, he is less than clear. He poses two questions: "What is the eternal divine element in man?" and "Where and how does divine retribution—reward and punishment—take place in human life?," and he states that the modern answer to these questions "can be neither that of rabbinic Judaism, which rests upon Persian dualism, nor that of medieval philosophy, which was under the Platonic-Aristotelian influence."¹¹⁹ By the answer of rabbinic Judaism Kohler means bodily resurrection. He rejects resurrection both because of its alleged Persian origin and because he views it

---

112. Kohler, *Jewish Theology*, 291.
113. Kohler, *Jewish Theology*, 291–92.
114. Kohler, *Jewish Theology*, 292–93.
115. Kohler, *Jewish Theology*, 294.
116. Kohler, *Jewish Theology*, 294.
117. Kohler, *Jewish Theology*, 295.
118. Kohler, *Jewish Theology*, 295.
119. Kohler, *Jewish Theology*, 285.

as contrary to the natural order of things as scientifically understood.[120] But what does Kohler mean by rejecting the answer of "medieval philosophy?" Is he rejecting any belief in the immortality of the soul, or only a belief based on "Platonic-Aristotelian influence?" After concluding his historical account, Kohler writes: "In the light of modern investigation, body and soul are seen to be indissolubly bound together by a reciprocal relation which either benefits or impedes them both."[121] This seems to preclude an independent existence for the soul.

Elsewhere, however, he appears to suggest that the human soul—the divine element in man—is to be equated with the ego ("self-conscious, morally active personality"), and he further states that this divine element "bears within itself the proof and promise of its future life."[122] That the divine element in man is the ego is not problematic; but how does the ego bear within itself proof of its immortality? As to this, Kohler seems to be at a loss, for he concludes the entire discussion of the soul's immortality with the sentence: "The question where, and how, this self-same ego is to continue, will be left for the power of the imagination to answer ever anew."[123]

Kohler follows the chapter on the soul's immortality with a chapter on divine retribution. After presenting an historical account of how postmortem reward and punishment in heaven and hell have been depicted in Jewish thought, he concludes his account with mention of Joseph Albo's consideration of the question of whether the eternal duration of the tortures of hell is reconcilable with divine mercy, and states that, for moderns, the question is "superfluous and superseded."[124] He then writes: "Our modern conceptions of time and space admit neither a place or a world-period for the reward and punishment of souls, nor the intolerable conception of eternal joy without useful action and eternal agony without any moral purpose. Modern man knows that he bears heaven and hell within his own bosom."[125] This seems to preclude any postmortem reward and punishment for the divine element in man, whether the divine element is called the ego or soul.

That Kohler, by 1918, was moving away from any emphasis on the afterlife is suggested in several places in the introductory chapters of *Jewish Theology*. In the very

120. See Kohler, *Jewish Theology*, 297 ("Whoever . . . still sees God's greatness . . . revealed through miracles, that is, through interruptions of the natural order of life, may cling to the traditional belief in resurrection . . . On the other hand, he who recognizes the unchangeable will of an all-wise, all-ruling God in the immutable laws of nature must find it impossible to praise God according to the traditional formula as the 'Reviver of the dead,' but will avail himself instead of the expression used in the Union Prayer Book after the pattern of Einhorn, 'He who has implanted within us immortal life.'"). See also Levenson, *Resurrection and the Restoration*, 15–16.

121. Kohler, *Jewish Theology*, 295–96.

122. Kohler, *Jewish Theology*, 295.

123. Kohler, *Jewish Theology*, 296. See also Gillman, *Death of Death*, 203 ("the closest Kohler comes to a serious theological inquiry into the weight of the two doctrines of resurrection and immortality of the soul is in his rejecting resurrection as contrary to the immutable laws of nature").

124. Kohler, *Jewish Theology*, 309.

125. Kohler, *Jewish Theology*, 309.

first chapter on the meaning of theology, Kohler writes: "The truth of the matter is that the aim and end of Judaism is not so much the salvation of the soul in the hereafter as the salvation of humanity in history."[126]

5. Samuel S. Cohon emphasizes a this-worldly approach to the problem of moral evil, and Cohon's views find expression in the 1937 Columbus Platform and the 1940 *Union Prayerbook*

In 1923, Samuel S. Cohon was appointed by Hebrew Union College to its chair in theology, succeeding Kaufmann Kohler, a position that Cohon held until 1956. In 1948, he published his seminal work, *Judaism, A Way of Life: An Introduction to the Basic Ideas of Judaism*. In a chapter entitled "Deliverance from Evil," Cohon states that the existence of evil poses a problem "in a theistic system of thought" and that "Judaism, ... while essentially a religion of law and moral discipline, directs much of its attention to the question how to face evil."[127] He acknowledges that "[t]he rabbis ... found ... comfort in the belief that the injustices of this life will be righted in the next."[128] But instead of endorsing the rabbinic response, Cohon turns to Maimonides whom, he says,

> introduced a new and enlightening note into the discussion of this subject by calling attention to the fact that the whole problem of evil grows out of the anthropomorphic view of the world ... Taking a larger cosmic view of things and abandoning the notion that man is the final measure of existence, the ground for our complaining against what seems to us evil is in large measure removed. What is injurious to man may be useful to other parts of nature or to the universe at large.[129]

Moreover, Maimonides insists, says Cohon, that the chief evils that befall man are due to his own actions.[130] Accordingly, Cohon ends the chapter with a discussion of what he refers to as "the modern view of evil" which redirects attention to overcoming evil in this life instead of righting evil in some other life.[131]

---

126. Kohler, *Jewish Theology*, 6. See also Kohler, *Jewish Theology*, 17–18 (Judaism "is a religion of *life*, which it wishes to sanctify by duty rather than by laying stress on the hereafter"; emphasis original); Kohler, *Jewish Theology*, 232 (The kingdom of God "is not ... a kingdom of heaven in the world to come, which men enter only after death ... Judaism points to God's Kingdom on *earth* as the goal and hope of mankind"; emphasis original).

127. Cohon, *Judaism, a Way of Life*, 49.

128. Cohon, *Judaism, a Way of Life*, 56. See Cohon, *Judaism, a Way of Life*, 124.

129. Cohon, *Judaism, a Way of Life*, 59–60. This idea has roots in Stoicism, which distinguished between the part and the whole. See e.g., Long, *Hellenistic Philosophy*, 179–84.

130. Cohon, *Judaism, a Way of Life*, 62.

131. See Cohon, *Judaism, a Way of Life*, 63–67.

Cohon's chapter on "Motives and Sanctions" is fully consistent with his discussion of the problem of moral evil. Relying again on Maimonides, Cohon contends that the true lover of God should not perform meritorious actions to obtain a reward or avoid doing evil in order to prevent punishment. According to Cohen, "The true lover of God must outgrow these pedagogical crutches. He must love truth and follow virtue not because of any worldly or otherworldly emoluments but because of their intrinsic value..."[132] Cohon had expressed similar sentiments some twenty-five years earlier in an article entitled "The Mission of Reform Judaism." In this article, Cohon suggests that immortality is primarily a matter of the influence one has had on others:

> In former ages our people made much of the resurrection of the body and of the bliss of the soul in the hereafter. Men like Maimonides long ago came to look upon the Gan Eden and Gehenna as mere desires on the part of man but not names of actualities... *The righteous live even after death. Their work remains behind them; their noble spirits, their hopes, their prayers and—what is greatest of all—their examples live on as blessings*... We, as men and as Jews, must promote the cause of justice on earth, defend the weak, and relieve the oppressed.[133]

Cohon's views deemphasizing retribution in a world to come and emphasizing the removal of evils in this world were given voice in a new general statement of the principles of Reform Judaism referred to as the Columbus Platform. Cohon was chairman of the committee tasked with formulating the platform and was primarily responsible for the draft statement presented at the 1937 Columbus convention of the CCAR.[134] The statement approved was officially called "Guiding Principles of Reform Judaism." In pertinent part, it states:

> Judaism affirms that man is created in the Divine image. His spirit is immortal. He is an active co-worker with God. As a child of God, he is endowed with moral freedom and is charged with the responsibility of overcoming evil and striving after ideal ends.[135]

In contrast to the Pittsburgh Platform which asserts that the *soul* of man is immortal, the Columbus Platform asserts that man's *spirit* is immortal. This change is significant. It signals acknowledgment that talk of a man's soul is problematic since "soul" suggests a substance that is separate and apart from the body. Kohler had noted back in 1918 that "modern investigation" teaches that "body and soul [or mind] are

---

132. Cohon, *Judaism, a Way of Life*, 130. See also Cohon, *Judaism, a Way of Life*, 133–82.

133. Cohon, "Mission of Reform Judaism," 42 (emphasis added). See also Cohon, *What We Jews Believe*, 183–86; Cohon, "Our Immortality," 182–83.

134. See Meyer, *Response to Modernity*, 318–19.

135. The Columbus Platform: "Guiding Principles of Reform Judaism" (1937), Principle A, 3. See Meyer, *Response to Modernity*, 389.

seen to be indissolubly bound together by a reciprocal relation."[136] That one's "spirit" is immortal may mean no more than that one continues to serve as an example to others. Also reflecting Cohon's views is the *Union Prayerbook* of 1940. As originally published, and in revised editions, it contains repeated mention of the need to be a co-worker with God to eradicate evil in *this* world, and it omits any mention of a reward or punishment in an afterlife.[137] Further, it speaks of immortality in terms of one's memory abiding as a lasting inspiration and moving the living to noble deeds.[138]

Cohon's *Jewish Theology: A Historical and Systematic Interpretation of Judaism and its Foundations* was published more than a decade after Cohon's death.[139] In *Jewish Theology*, Cohon reiterates an emphasis on eliminating evil in this life, but also *does* profess a belief in the "deathlessness of the human soul."[140] In the third section of this work, bearing the heading "The Nature and Destiny of Man," there are two chapters concerning the soul and its immortality. The first of these chapters provides an historical account of the development of Jewish ideas concerning resurrection, judgment and hell, and the origin and destiny of the soul, as well as the relationship of these ideas to Platonic and Aristotelian concepts of the soul.[141] Here Cohon asserts that the soul "is the life-principle and innermost self of man," that it is "the flowering of the divine in man, his moral and spiritual self, the imperishable core and center of his being."[142] In the second of the chapters, Cohon admits that the belief in the immortality of the soul "derives ... from the will to live, more than from conscious reflection."[143] He then briefly discusses what he terms four "forms" of the belief: (1) the continuance of the dead "within the family and the people," which is not a "personal continuance"; (2) transmigration, in which the soul of the departed "reincarnates itself in an offspring, kinsman or stranger," considered by Cohon "as a form of [personal] continuance"; (3) resurrection; and (4) a "spiritual" form which includes the "philosophical ideas of the soul's *immortality*."[144] Cohon claims that of the four forms "only resurrection of the

---

136. Kohler, *Jewish Theology*, 295–96.

137. See e.g., Central Conference of American Rabbis, *Union Prayerbook for Jewish Worship*, 45, 132–33.

138. See Central Conference of American Rabbis, *Union Prayerbook for Jewish Worship*, 76, 152, 204, 276, 308, 370. See also Central Conference of American Rabbis, *Union Prayerbook for Jewish Worship*, 46; Cohon, "Our Immortality," 183.

139. See generally Jacobs, *Jewish Theology*, vii ("Cohon's *Jewish Theology* [was] published posthumously from an incomplete manuscript.").

140. Cohon, *Jewish Theology*, xiv.

141. See Cohon, *Jewish Theology*, 345–415.

142. Cohon, *Jewish Theology*, 346.

143. Cohon, *Jewish Theology*, 426.

144. Cohon, *Jewish Theology*, 427–29 (emphasis original).

body attained the rank of a cardinal doctrine in Judaism"[145]; but he adds that while Orthodox Judaism still cherishes "this faith," Reform Judaism does not.[146] He explains:

> In line with the purer teachings of Maimonides and of Mendelssohn, Reform Judaism has eliminated from its liturgy, references to a future resurrection of the body, and emphasizes instead the immortality of the soul . . .
>
> We feel that what gives man preeminence over all living beings is his reflective reason, his ethical and spiritual idealism, his creative will. Coupled with freedom these gifts of heart and mind give man a godlike power. Constituting the chief elements of his distinctive humanism, they are of the essence of his self and give him whatever worth he possesses in life and death. The hope of immortality is, therefore, associated with the inward self rather than with the corporeal being. For us only the immortality of the spirit has sanctifying power and moral value. The consciousness that there is something at the core of one's being that is imperishable invests life with abiding worth.[147]

Cohon further states: "Our immortality . . . recommends itself to us as (1) natural, (2) reasonable and (3) helpful."[148] Cohon's assertion that immortality is "natural" is based on an alleged inability "to conceive of nonexistence," and he takes the "naturalness of the feeling of continuance beyond the grave . . . as a strong proof of the reality of that continuance."[149] Cohon's position that immortality is a "reasonable doctrine" is based on his definition of the soul as the divine element in man. He writes: "By virtue of his reason, his creative power and moral sense, [man] shares with God in the work of creation. Being one with him in life, man cannot be cast off in death. God delivers the soul from destruction."[150] In addition to this "theological" argument, Cohon says that there are "ethical arguments" which are "not based on proof in the scientific or philosophic sense" but are "deduced from empirical data."[151] The "simplest and most prevalent form" of this ethical argument relates to the problem of moral evil—"otherworldly retribution" enables (1) the "sinner who flouted justice on earth

---

145. Cohon, *Jewish Theology*, 429. Cohon adds that serious consideration was given to the condition of the resurrected body. "Will it arise with all its earthly defects or in a perfect state? Will it be old and worn or renewed in unfading youth? The hope was strong that while the raised body will be the same as during its days on earth, it will yet be new, rebuilt and refashioned. The mortal and corruptible frame will be exchanged for an immortal and incorruptible one. It may even be invested with celestial and angelic qualities" (Cohon, *Jewish Theology*, 429–30).

146. Cohon, *Jewish Theology*, 430.

147. Cohon, *Jewish Theology*, 430–31.

148. Cohon, *Jewish Theology*, 431.

149. See Cohon, *Jewish Theology*, 431–32. Cohon refers to Taylor, *Faith of a Moralist*, 1:268–71, as offering "a modern appraisal of this proof" (Cohon, *Jewish Theology*, 432n1). But Taylor's "modern appraisal" doesn't support Cohon's reliance on the naturalness argument. Taylor states that arguments for the "natural immortality" of the human mind are both of little value and inconclusive, though Taylor *does* make a "moral argument" for immortality. See Taylor, *Faith of a Moralist*, 1:255–332.

150. Cohon, *Jewish Theology*, 435.

151. See Cohon, *Jewish Theology*, 437–40.

[to] reap the harvest of evil in the beyond," and (2) "the righteous person who pursued the paths of justice [on earth to] enjoy the fruit of his doings in the hereafter."[152] Regarding the "helpfulness" of the belief in immortality, Cohon contends that, if you deny immortality, "you remove thereby the strongest prop of human endeavor."[153] He cautions that "moral paralysis . . . creeps over us with the abandonment of this belief," and he claims that the "decline of the belief in immortality . . . accounts, in great part, for the frightful disregard of the sanctity and worth of the individual in many lands."[154]

6. Under the leadership of Eugene Borowitz, the CCAR adopts the 1976 San Francisco Platform which removes mention of an "immortal spirit"; Borowitz later comes to favor belief in bodily resurrection

As Kohler had been a dominating influence on the committee that drafted the Pittsburgh Platform and Cohon had been a dominating influence on the committee that drafted the Columbus Platform, so Eugene Borowitz greatly influenced a new platform for American Reform Judaism that was adopted by the CCAR in 1976, the San Francisco Platform, formally called "Reform Judaism—A Centenary Perspective."[155] Only a single sentence relates to the soul, resurrection, or afterlife. It is:

> Amid the mystery we call life, we affirm that human beings, created in God's image, share in God's eternity despite the mystery we call death.[156]

Reference to a "spirit" that is immortal has been omitted. It thus seems to reflect the view that human beings themselves are not really immortal. While there is no mention as to precisely how human beings "share in God's eternity," the phrase echoes Cohon's view that human beings imitate God through their creative and moral powers to combat evil and form a better world.[157] Yet, the vagueness of the language permits one to read immortality into it. As Meyer states, the language was chosen as a way to "achieve consensus" by failing to take "a clear theological position."[158]

Borowitz saw fit to express his own view of the San Francisco Platform in a book entitled *Reform Judaism Today: What We Believe* (1977). In a chapter called "Of Life after Death," Borowitz discusses the language quoted above. He notes that pursuant to "the scientific view of life and thus death . . . there is no special thing present to survive

---

152. Cohon, *Jewish Theology*, 439.
153. Cohon, *Jewish Theology*, 442.
154. Cohon, *Jewish Theology*, 443. It is difficult to reconcile these claims about the helpfulness of immortality with the claim that we must love truth and follow virtue not because of any worldly or otherworldly emoluments but because of their intrinsic value.
155. See Meyer, *Response to Modernity*, 383–84.
156. See Meyer, *Response to Modernity*, 392.
157. See Cohon, *Judaism, a Way of Life*, 149–50.
158. Meyer, *Response to Modernity*, 384. See also Borowitz, *Reform Judaism Today*, 6 (Had the committee tried to say much more than it did, "it would have passed into the realm of controversy.").

the death of . . . a human being."¹⁵⁹ According to Borowitz, the "scientific way of looking at life is dramatically confirmed with every new discovery in molecular biology"; this, coupled with the inability to validate claims to have contacted someone who has died, or to have had a previous existence, and reinforced by "the modern religious thinker's concern to keep the focus of religion on this world and our responsibilities in it," has led "most Jews in our time [to] avoid speaking about personal survival after death."¹⁶⁰ Moreover, "[i]f one wants to talk about survival after death, . . . [one must] be able to say just what [it is that] survives"¹⁶¹; but the "notion of such a substance as a soul is no longer intellectually tenable for most modern thinkers."¹⁶² Although earlier in the twentieth century, Reform Judaism felt it was still possible to use the term *spirit*, now, says Borowitz, "*spirit* has gone the way of *soul*. We still use both words—but only poetically."¹⁶³ Despite his inability to identify any thing that survives death, Borowitz is unwilling to completely reject the concept of an afterlife. He writes: "We cannot say very clearly what we believe, yet we do not propose to abandon our faith that the God who gave us life will yet give us life after death."¹⁶⁴

Seven years after *Reform Judaism Today*, Borowitz wrote *Liberal Judaism* (1984). In the latter work, Borowitz revisit's the topic of life after death and again expresses his reluctance to abandon the notion of an afterlife. He reiterates his lack of clarity about the afterlife—he does not know "how [he] will survive, what sort of judgment awaits [him], or what [he] shall do in eternity."¹⁶⁵ But he then states: "I am, however, inclined to think that my hope is better spoken of as resurrection rather than immortality for I do not know myself as a soul without a body but only as a psychosomatic self. Perhaps even that is more than I can honestly say."¹⁶⁶

7. Richard Levy urges belief in bodily resurrection but the 1999 Pittsburgh Platform reintroduces the notion of an "eternal spirit"

Richard N. Levy urged Reform Judaism to adopt belief in bodily resurrection in an article which appeared in 1982. Levy begins the article bemoaning the fact that Wise and Einhorn had expunged *mehaye hametim* from Reform theology and had introduced

159. Borowitz, *Reform Judaism Today*, 42–43.
160. Borowitz, *Reform Judaism Today*, 43–44.
161. Borowitz, *Reform Judaism Today*, 46.
162. Borowitz, *Reform Judaism Today*, 45–46.
163. Borowitz, *Reform Judaism Today*, 45–46 (emphasis original). Yet, shortly after the 1976 San Francisco Platform was adopted, the CCAR adopted a new statement of principles that refers to man's "spirit" being eternal. See Levy, *Vision of Holiness*, xv–xix.
164. Borowitz, *Reform Judaism Today*, 48–49.
165. Borowitz, *Liberal Judaism*, 222.
166. Borowitz, *Liberal Judaism*, 222. Nevertheless, Borowitz readily admits that "in modern times" there has been a "loss of our belief in personal survival after death" (Borowitz, *Choices in Modern Jewish Thought*, 284).

alternative language in the *Gevurot* prayer in the *Amidah*.[167] He regrets that an attempt to reintroduce *mehaye hametim* into the liturgy "was defeated soundly by a vote of the CCAR Executive Board in the early 1970s,"[168] and that the concept has been written off "as 'a doctrine not accepted by Liberal Judaism.'"[169] Despite acknowledging that resurrection is "an embarrassing . . . belief," Levy urges its acceptance by the Reform movement.[170]

According to Levy, belief in resurrection "has at least three things to recommend it: (1) it is faithful to the nature of our being as creations of God; (2) it is compatible with the basic covenantal promise that has bound our people with God since the days of Abraham; and (3) by its connection with the messianic promise, it binds us to Eretz Yisrael in a manner that political or cultural Zionism fails to do."[171] The first of these three things is based on the biblical view that humans being are created from the dust of the earth and "the soul-breath [*neshamah*] God breathed into us."[172] Consequently, as Levy sees it, the nature of our being requires that, if the *neshamah* is eternal, so too must be the dust of the earth. There is something "unsettling," he asserts, about the view that at death our *neshamah* "loses all the individuality provided by our bodies."[173] The second thing that recommends resurrection, according to Levy, is its "compatibility" with the covenantal promise to make Abraham's seed as innumerable as "the dust of the earth." Equating the "dust of the earth" to the dust which human beings become after death, Levy claims that the covenantal promise entails that "the dust which we become after death . . . be transformed [at the time of the coming of the Messiah] into the uncountable people we were promised to be."[174] Third, Levy claims that belief in resurrection binds us to Israel because it is upon the earth of Israel that "the miracle of [resurrection], the miracle of the fulfillment of the covenant, will take place."[175]

Initially, Levy's drive for reacceptance of the concept of bodily resurrection did not gain much traction. When Levy, as President of the CCAR, shepherded the adoption of a new Reform Statement of Principles at its 1999 Pittsburgh convention, no mention is made of resurrection. The single statement of the 1999 Pittsburgh Platform referring to the afterlife affirms: "We trust in our tradition's promise that, although God created us as finite beings, the spirit within us is eternal."[176] Subsequently, how-

---

167. See Levy, "Upon Arising," 12.
168. Levy, "Upon Arising," 12.
169. Levy, "Upon Arising," 13 (quoting *Gates of Understanding*).
170. Levy, "Upon Arising," 14.
171. Levy, "Upon Arising," 14.
172. See Levy, "Upon Arising," 14–15.
173. Levy, "Upon Arising," 16.
174. Levy, "Upon Arising," 17–18.
175. Levy, "Upon Arising," 19–20.
176. *Reform Judaism: Modern Statement of Principles*, God. See Levy, *Vision of Holiness*, xvii.

ever, with a new Reform prayerbook called *Mishkan T'filah: A Reform Siddur* (2007), the idea of bodily resurrection was included in Reform liturgy as an option.[177]

8. Reform rabbis today espouse a wide variety of views about the soul, resurrection, and the afterlife

In 2014, the CCAR published a book, edited by Paul Citrin, entitled *Lights in the Forest: Rabbis Respond to Twelve Essential Jewish Questions*. The book contains the responses of a cross-section of Reform rabbis to questions including "What is your concept of soul and afterlife?"[178] Analysis of these views yields important points about the attitudes of Reform rabbis toward the soul and the afterlife. First, none of the respondents suggest that bodily resurrection is a doctrine they might accept. The single mention of bodily resurrection is made in a disparaging manner.[179]

Second, most, but not all, specifically express a belief that there exists something which they call the "soul," but few are very clear about what they mean by this word. Two associate the soul with "our *n'shamah* . . . which is the breath of God that lives within each person" and say that "our breath [is] the essence of our soul" and that our soul is the essence of our inner being."[180] One associates it with a person's "values, dreams and personality, breathed into [them] by God on the day [they are] born."[181] Several equate the soul with "energy."[182] One baldly proclaims: "In Judaism, the soul has been perceived as the quality that enables us to see the sacred in others and in ourselves."[183] Those who conceive of the soul as breath or energy presumably believe that the soul is a material substance but they don't specifically say so. One specifically says that the soul is not a material substance,[184] and a second says that he is "attracted to Maimonides's notion of . . . the afterlife, as a non-physical, purely intellectual existence."[185] A third person recognizes that all attempts to talk about a soul are problematic—it raises questions which, he says, "are impossible to answer and threaten to undo the entire Jewish concept of the human soul."[186] This statement is interesting for a number of reasons, not the least of which being that it presumes there *is* a "Jewish

---

177. See sec. B, 9.
178. Citrin, *Lights in the Forest*, 73.
179. See Citrin, *Lights in the Forest*, 114.
180. Citrin, *Lights in the Forest*, 96–97. See Citrin, *Lights in the Forest*, 91.
181. Citrin, *Lights in the Forest*, 131.
182. See Citrin, *Lights in the Forest*, 97, 115, 136.
183. Citrin, *Lights in the Forest*, 79.
184. Citrin, *Lights in the Forest*, 79.
185. Citrin, *Lights in the Forest*, 108.
186. Citrin, *Lights in the Forest*, 108–9.

concept of the soul." One respondent goes so far as to associate our souls simply with the "stories" about us which continue to exist after we die.[187]

Third, most of the rabbis make no mention of the concept of "spirit." Much less is any distinction made between the concepts of "soul" and "spirit," though this distinction seems to have been at issue in the wording of the most recent Reform Platforms. One respondent who *does* mention the concept of "spirit" uses it interchangeably with "soul," associating both English words with the Hebrew word *neshamah*.[188] Another person refers to "our spiritual soul" but fails to explain how it is distinguished from our nonspiritual soul.[189]

Fourth, four rabbis explicitly profess a belief in the immortality or eternality of the soul.[190] These make clear that what they mean by this is that after death the soul or spirit (however conceived) "returns to God."[191] Others implicitly suggest that the soul is, *or might be*, immortal claiming that it "does not die"[192] or that it "*perhaps . . .* returns to its Source and unites with the Holy One."[193] Nearly all those who profess to believe that the soul is immortal in a literal sense admit that their belief lacks a reasonable basis in fact; that it is based on "faith," not science, on "hopes," not philosophical reasoning.[194] The one or two who don't make such an explicit admission fail to provide, or even refer to, any scientific or rational basis justifying their belief in immortality. Indeed, the sole argument that is made in support of the soul's immortality is the wholly unsatisfactory theological argument that, if God is all powerful, God must triumph over death.[195]

Fifth, many of the rabbis who profess a belief in the immortality of the soul do not mean it in a literal sense. Rather, they only mean something like the memory or deeds of the departed survive. Thus, they really believe that there is no afterlife at all. So, for instance, one says that he knows that our "loved ones live on in our memories, and those memories can inspire us to live better lives."[196] A second, who equates the soul/spirit with our breath and claims that the "spirit returns to God who gave it," goes on to speculate:

> The idea, perhaps, is that the souls of our departed loved ones live on in our very breath. They survive in our reminiscing of the time shared. They survive

---

187. See Citrin, *Lights in the Forest*, 120–21.
188. See Citrin, *Lights in the Forest*, 90–91.
189. See Citrin, *Lights in the Forest*, 148–49.
190. See e.g., Citrin, *Lights in the Forest*, 85, 91, 96, 121.
191. See Citrin, *Lights in the Forest*, 86, 90, 97, 121.
192. Citrin, *Lights in the Forest*, 136.
193. Citrin, *Lights in the Forest*, 149 (emphasis added). See Citrin, *Lights in the Forest*, 136.
194. See e.g., Citrin, *Lights in the Forest*, 85, 102, 108, 126, 136, 143.
195. See Citrin, *Lights in the Forest*, 143.
196. Citrin, *Lights in the Forest*, 102.

> in the stories we continue to tell with heavy hearts . . . They survive in the tender invocation of their names at our celebrations and milestones.[197]

The notion of one achieving immortality by having stories told about you is mentioned by another rabbi who expands on the idea by saying that the souls of the deceased "live on" in the worldviews of those who learned from them.[198] Yet another focuses on the "values" of the deceased which "find new expression" in the lives of their children.[199] Interestingly, one of the rabbis takes strong objection to those who accept immortality in a nonliteral sense. Relying on a remark of Neil Gillman disparaging "the popular notion that one's immortality rests in the memories one leaves behind, in the impact of one's life on friends, family and community [etc.]," he writes: "I share this dissatisfaction with such notions of 'practical' immortality. While the language and images I use to communicate my belief in a life after this one may be metaphoric, they point to something real."[200]

Sixth, not all those who profess a literal belief in the soul's immortality believe that its immortality is a personal one. Rather, they speak of the energy that constitutes the soul being "absorbed and reunited" with "the Energy that we call God."[201] It is unclear if even those who speak in a less nonpersonal manner—saying only that the spirit reunites with God—believe in a personal immortality since they often are unclear as to what this spirit actually is or includes. If it does not include consciousness, memory, etc., it can hardly be considered a personal immortality.

Seventh, many of the respondents make a point of emphasizing that we can have no idea as to the nature of the afterlife. For example, one asserts: "I believe there is an afterlife. Yet I am also convinced that this afterlife is unimaginable and unknowable."[202] Another puts it this way: "I believe that there is an existence that follows earthly life. What this existence is, I cannot say. I take all teachings concerning . . . 'the world-to-come' to be metaphors for a reality beyond human conception."[203] In the words of a third: "I am not sure if there is a heaven or a world-to-come."[204] A fourth echoes the language of the San Francisco Platform: "In the face of the great mystery [of death], the religious Jew asserts not that he knows exactly what awaits him."[205] Those who do

---

197. Citrin, *Lights in the Forest*, 91.

198. See Citrin, *Lights in the Forest*, 120–21.

199. See Citrin, *Lights in the Forest*, 131. See also Citrin, *Lights in the Forest*, 114 ("'The departed . . . still live on earth in the acts of goodness they performed and in the hearts of those who cherish their memory,'" quoting *Union Prayerbook for Jewish Worship*).

200. Citrin, *Lights in the Forest*, 142–143 (quoting Gillman, *Death of Death*, 244–45).

201. Citrin, *Lights in the Forest*, 97. See also Citrin, *Lights in the Forest*, 115.

202. Citrin, *Lights in the Forest*, 80.

203. Citrin, *Lights in the Forest*, 142. Cf. Goldberg, *Mishkan HaNefesh—Rosh Hashanah*, xx–xxi.

204. Citrin, *Lights in the Forest*, 85.

205. Citrin, *Lights in the Forest*, 126 (also saying that "we are *not* granted access to what . . . [the] afterlife may consist of . . . Death is the great mystery . . . [and we are unable] to know what lies beyond," emphasis original).

not specifically admit to ignorance of the nature of the afterlife fail to describe it in any way. In particular, except for one, the rabbis say nothing about any postmortem reward or punishment. At least one specifically proclaims that we cannot know "in what way [the afterlife] is connected to our earthly, time-bound consciousness,"[206] suggesting that we cannot know if what we do in this life has any consequences for us in the afterlife. The sole rabbi saying anything about a postmortem reward or punishment says only: "I *hope* . . . that good people receive in some way rewards from God in a realm beyond the grave."[207] Since Reform rabbis lack confidence in a postmortem reward and punishment, one wonders what practical significance their belief in an afterlife may have for them.

Eighth, consistent with the afterlife having little, if any, practical significance, it is emphasized that "Judaism . . . is focused primarily on how we live our life in the present, and less so on *olam haba*,"[208] and that "Liberal Jewish thought focuses more on this life than on the afterlife."[209]

Last, one, but only one, expresses belief in the possibility of *gilgul*, reincarnation.[210]

9. Differing views on the afterlife are reflected in liturgical changes in Reform prayerbooks

At about the same time that the San Francisco Platform enunciated a new statement of principles for Reform Judaism, related liturgical changes were incorporated in *Gates of Prayer: The New Union Prayerbook*, published in 1975. The overall approach of *Gates of Prayer* was to provide a variety of differing viewpoints on all matters.[211] Consistent with this overall approach, *Gates of Prayer* contains ten different versions of the Sabbath Evening Service, with each version containing its own approach to the *Gevurot* prayer. The first version of the Sabbath Evening Service in *Gates of Prayer* contains the same Hebrew *Gevurot* as the *Union Prayerbook,* replacing *mehaye hametim* with *mehaye hakol,* but it replaces the ending blessing "Praised be Thou, O Lord, who hast implanted within us eternal life" with "Blessed is the Lord, the Source of life [*mehaye hakol*]."[212] The remaining versions of the Sabbath Evening Service contain, for the most part,[213] the same Hebrew version of *Gevurot*, but use very different English translations,

---

206. Citrin, *Lights in the Forest*, 126.
207. Citrin, *Lights in the Forest*, 102 (emphasis added).
208. Citrin, *Lights in the Forest*, 126.
209. Citrin, *Lights in the Forest*, 148.
210. See Citrin, *Lights in the Forest*, 136.
211. Stern, *Gates of Prayer*, xi–xii. See generally Meyer, *Response to Modernity*, 318–19.
212. See Stern, *Gates of Prayer*, 134–35. It also goes back to the English translation "keep faith with those who sleep in the dust" (Stern, *Gates of Prayer*, 135). See Levenson, *Resurrection and the Restoration*, 9.
213. The fourth version contains only a condensed *Gevurot*, and the ninth version entirely omits the *Gevurot*. See Stern, *Gates of Prayer*, 186, 260–68.

ones that refer to neither bodily resurrection nor the soul's immortality, and focus less on God's power than on man's responsibility to serve as God's co-worker.[214] In short, *Gates of Prayer* seems to reinforce the reluctance to take a clear theological position on the afterlife and emphasizes the need for man to improve his current life.[215]

In 2007, the CCAR published *Mishkan T'filah: A Reform Siddur*. *Mishkan T'filah* reflects an effort on the part of some reform rabbis to reintroduce the concept of resurrection into the liturgy of the Reform movement.[216] The two versions of the Sabbath Evening Service contained in *Mishkan T'filah* have the identical Hebrew for the *Gevurot*. It is sharply different than the *Gevurot* in *Gates of Prayer* in that it reintroduces the concept of bodily resurrection. Specifically, *mehaye hametim* is included as an alternative to *mehaye hakol*, reading "*mehaye hakol (metim)*" at all relevant places.[217] Footnotes included in the *Gevurot* for both Shabbat Evening Services suggest that the alternative reading is not to be taken literally. One footnote states:

> *G'vurot* ("God's might")—The second *T'fillah* benediction acknowledges divine power . . . Classical Reform prayerbooks replaced this benediction's image of physical resurrection of the dead (*m'chayei meitim*) with more generalized imagery expressing the hope for spiritual immortality. *Mishkan T'fillah* provides the original language as an option, acknowledging its metaphorical power.[218]

But the understanding that resurrection of the dead is to be taken metaphorically is rendered problematic by the following footnote contained in the *Gevurot* for the Shabbat Morning I service:

> *G'vurot* emphasizes God's ability to renew us in the future. The resurrection of the dead, *which may be taken literally*, is best understood as a powerful metaphor for understanding the miracle of hope.[219]

Despite having identical Hebrew versions of the *Gevurot*, the English translation for each evening service is very different. Shabbat Evening I emphasizes bodily resurrection of the dead, while Shabbat Evening II emphasizes the immortality of the soul.

---

214. See Stern, *Gates of Prayer*, 153, 170, 199, 213, 230, 255–56, 277. See also Gillman, *Death of Death*, 195 ("rarely does its English capture the precise literal sense of the Hebrew"); Levenson, *Resurrection and the Restoration*, 9.

215. See generally Levenson, *Resurrection and the Restoration*, 9–10 ("the rabbinic tradition . . . views the resurrection of the dead as a normative and defining doctrine, not simply as one option among many that a Jew may or may not elect").

216. Richard Levy is listed as being a member of the Siddur Discussion Group of 1985 to 1993, as well as a member of the Editorial Committee of 1999 to 2005. Frishman, *Mishkan T'filah*, xii.

217. See Frishman, *Mishkan T'filah*, 168, 275. Cf. Frishman, *Mishkan T'filah*, 78 (Weekday T'filah), 246 (Shabbat Morning I), 325 (Shabbat Morning II), 348 (Shabbat Afternoon), 472 (Festival T'filah).

218. Frishman, *Mishkan T'filah*, 276. Cf. Frishman, *Mishkan T'filah*, 326. See also Frishman, *Mishkan T'filah*, 169. Cf., Frishman, *Mishkan T'filah*, 79, 349.

219. Frishman, *Mishkan T'filah*, 246, 472 (emphasis added).

Eight years after publication of *Mishkan T'filah*, the CCAR published *Mishkan HaNefesh: Machzor for the Days of Awe*. *Mishkan HaNefesh* uses the same Hebrew and English versions of the *Gevurot* throughout.[220] The Hebrew version is also the same as the one that appears in *Mishkan T'filah* except that (1) it begins with an explicit direction to "choose either hakol or meitim," and (2) no preference is given to *hakol*. *Mishkan HaNefesh* also has, in one place, the following footnote to explain *mehaye ha metim*:

> The traditional wording of the *G'vurot* prayer speaks of God as *m'chayeih meitim* (Reviver of the dead), viewing bodily resurrection as the ultimate expression of God's compassion. The One who gives and sustains life does not abandon us, but remains faithful until the end of days. We might also understand these words to mean that God 'revives' the dead by keeping them vibrantly present in our memory, inspiring us to live in a way that honors them.[221]

The English translation of the *Gevurot* in *Mishkan HaNefesh* replaces the literal translation found in *Mishkan T'filah* (which includes "reviving the dead" as alternative language for "giving life to all") with a nonliteral translation that makes no mention of reviving the dead.[222] Elsewhere, standard language in Reform prayerbooks referring to the immortality of the soul, and God implanting within us eternal life, may be found.[223]

In summary, changes in the Reform liturgy present a hodgepodge of conflicting and confused ideas about the soul, resurrection, and the afterlife. These confused ideas include confusion between a soul and a spirit, confusion between the immortality of the soul and resurrection of the body, confusion as to whether resurrection of the body is to be understood literally or only metaphorically, and confusion as to whether there is any afterlife at all.

---

220. See Goldberg, *Mishkan HaNefesh—Rosh Hashanah*, 46, 170, 310; Goldberg, *Mishkan Hanefesh—Yom Kippur*, 50, 204, 364.

221. Goldberg, *Mishkan Hanefesh—Rosh Hashanah*, 47.

222. See Goldberg, *Mishkan Hanefesh—Rosh Hashanah*, 46, 170, 310; Goldberg, *Mishkan Hanefesh–Yom Kippur*, 50, 204, 364.

223. See e.g., Goldberg, *Mishkan Hanefesh—Rosh Hashanah*, 297; Goldberg, *Mishkan Hanefesh—Yom Kippur*, 158 ("Someday, when this soul returns to You, I will find a place in eternity.").

12.

Conservative Judaism, Orthodoxy, and Hasidism Take Varying Approaches to the Soul, Resurrection, and the Afterlife

THE CONSERVATIVE MOVEMENT, WHEN founded, adhered to liturgy referring to *mehaye hametim*. In the twentieth century, however, differing views regarding the soul, resurrection, and the afterlife emerged. Today, the official teaching of the movement accepts either immortality of the soul or bodily resurrection. However, since the acceptance of these doctrines in a figurative fashion is condoned, many Conservative Jews do not actually believe in an afterlife at all. The belief of many Orthodox Jews is similar. Cohn-Sherbok concludes an analysis of contemporary Jewish belief on the afterlife with these words: "Whereas the rabbis put the belief in an Afterlife at the center of their religious system, modern Jewish thinkers, *both Orthodox and Reform*, have abandoned such an otherworldly outlook, even to the point of denying the existence of such doctrines."[1] Among those Conservative and Orthodox Jews who affirm an afterlife, few accept transmigration of souls; Hasidic Jews, however, embrace it.

A. In Conservative Judaism a Variety of Views Regarding the Soul, Resurrection, and the Afterlife Have Emerged

1. Initially, Conservative Judaism accepted bodily resurrection

The Conservative Movement in America began with the founding of The Jewish Theological Seminary of New York (later changed to "of America") (JTS) on January 31, 1886.[2] While the reform movement rejected belief in bodily resurrection, the

---

1. Cohn-Sherbok, *Issues in Contemporary Judaism*, 29 (emphasis added).
2. Gillman, *Conservative Judaism*, 28, 31. See Millgram, *Jewish Worship*, 591–92; Gillman, *Death of Death*, 205.

conservatives did not.³ When a congregational arm of the Conservative movement developed, the affiliated congregations all kept the traditional *Gevurot* benediction.⁴ The first liturgical publication of the Conservative movement, the 1927 *Festival Prayer Book*, translates the closing phrase of the *Gevurot* benediction "who quickest the dead."⁵

2. In the twentieth century, many Conservative Jews opted to believe in the immortality of the soul rather than bodily resurrection

In 1946, the Conservative movement published its *Sabbath and Festival Prayer Book* "which quickly became omnipresent in Conservative congregations until the publication of *Siddur Sim Shalom* (1985)."⁶ The chairman of the commission that was responsible for the publication of the *Sabbath and Festival Prayer Book* was Robert Gordis, recognized as the leading philosopher of the Conservative movement.⁷ That Gordis and others began to have doubts about the doctrine of bodily resurrection is evidenced by the change in the translation of the *Gevurot* benediction. The relevant portion of the benediction is translated "who calls the dead to life everlasting." The foreword of the prayerbook, written by Gordis, explains the translation:

> The rendering of the phrase *mehayyai hameitim* 'who calls the dead to life everlasting' is linguistically sound and rich in meaning for those who cherish the faith in human immortality, as much as for those who maintain the belief in resurrection.⁸

In a work entitled *A Faith for Moderns* (1971), Gordis recognizes that the Hebrew Bible espouses a "this-worldly religion."⁹ Faith in an afterlife developed, he notes, only when "men's concern with their own personal destiny" came to be emphasized over

---

3. See Gillman, *Conservative Judaism*, 42. But see Kaplan, *Greater Judaism in the Making*, 346 (The conception of immortality held by Sabato Morais, who served as the Jewish Theological Seminary's first president, "was no longer identified with the naïve belief in a bodily resurrection and in a hereafter in some heaven, or in a physically transformed earth. He did believe, however, in the personal survival of the soul after death. Though he realized that we could at best have a vague idea of the soul, he, nevertheless, argued that the soul was capable of independent existence and was indestructible.").

4. See Millgram, *Jewish Worship*, 592.

5. Gillman, *Death of Death*, 205–6.

6. Gillman, *Death of Death*, 205.

7. See Gillman, *Conservative Judaism*, 85, 89, 92, 153.

8. Gillman, *Conservative Judaism*, 206. Gillman comments that this explanation captures conservative Judaism's predilection for "handling a liturgy that no longer reflects your theology" by keeping the Hebrew text but "shad[ing] the translation to accommodate your new interpretation of the doctrine" (Gillman, *Conservative Judaism*, 193, 206). See also Levenson, *Resurrection and the Restoration*, 10–11.

9. Gordis, *Faith for Moderns*, 239.

and above "the earlier biblical conception of group solidarity."[10] This sense of individuality, coupled with the consciousness of unjust suffering, gave rise to "the faith that this imperfect world could not be all; that there was another world . . . where . . . the just would be rewarded, and the wicked punished."[11] According to Gordis, although the earliest liturgy praises God as *mehaye hametim*, the Hebrew phrase "was general enough to permit a variety of interpretations," and the concept of resurrection "never succeeded in dislodging the this-worldly emphasis of the earlier biblical religion."[12] Gordis concludes his discussion by setting forth his own convictions on the issue.[13] Ignoring any mention of bodily resurrection, he writes:

> We believe that the spirit of man is too miraculous to perish utterly . . . [J]ust as man's spirit knows no bounds of space, but is able, through his intelligence, to embrace worlds seen and unseen, so his spirit *may well* transcend the limits of time . . . Man's soul, 'a portion of God on high,' would thus, like its Source, be endowed with the attribute of eternity as well as of infinity. Since man is fashioned in the image of God, he must partake in some degree of this aspect of the Divine. The facet in man's nature which is deathless, the vital spark, the breath of life, we call soul.[14]

Gillman concedes that "if Gordis' contemporaries in the Conservative rabbinate had been polled, they would have found [Gordis's statement of personal belief] to be entirely congruent with their own views at that time."[15]

3. A statement of principles adopted by Conservative Judaism accepts all manner of belief about the soul, resurrection, and the afterlife

In about 1984, rabbis in the Conservative movement felt that a statement of principles was needed.[16] A Joint Commission, chaired by Gordis, met on October 15, 1985, and, after ten further sessions, presented a document to the Rabbinical Assembly called *Emet Ve'Emunah: Statement of Principles of Conservative Judaism*.[17] Regarding the soul, resurrection, and the afterlife, the document states:

> For the individual human being, we affirm that death does not mean extinction and oblivion. This conviction is articulated in our tradition in the two

---

10. Gordis, *Faith for Moderns*, 242.
11. Gordis, *Faith for Moderns*, 242–43.
12. Gordis, *Faith for Moderns*, 244–45.
13. Gordis, *Faith for Moderns*, 251.
14. Gordis, *Faith for Moderns*, 251–52 (emphasis added).
15. Gillman, *Death of Death*, 208.
16. See Abelson, "Foreword," 4. See generally Gillman, *Conservative Judaism*, 108–23.
17. See Gillman, *Conservative Judaism*, 154. See generally Gillman, *Conservative Judaism*, 155–69; Abelson, "Foreword," 4–6; Gordis, "Introduction," 9–16.

doctrines of the bodily resurrection of the dead and the continuing existence, after death and through eternity, of the individual soul. In the course of our history, both of these doctrines have been understood in widely varying ways. For some of us, they are literal truths which enable us to confront death and the death of our loved ones with courage and equanimity. Others understand these teachings in a more figurative way. The doctrine of the resurrection of the dead, omnipresent in our liturgy, affirms in a striking way the value Judaism accords to our bodily existence in our concrete historical and social setting. Beyond this, we know that our genetic make-up will persist through our progeny, long after our deaths and as long as humankind survives. The doctrine of the immortality of the soul affirms that our identities and our ability to touch other people and society does not end with the physical death of our bodies. Great personalities from the beginning of history remain potent influences in the world. On a more personal level, our friends and the members of our families who are gone are still palpably alive for us to this day.[18]

This statement makes belief in the immortality of soul as acceptable in Conservative Judaism as belief in bodily resurrection. Further, it makes no attempt to define the soul in any manner, or to say anything about the nature of postmortem existence. Finally, it condones interpreting both bodily resurrection and the continuing existence of the soul in a figurative manner which essentially condones the denial of any afterlife. In short, the statement evidences no less a hodgepodge of notions about the soul, resurrection, and the afterlife than exists in Reform Judaism.

4. Neil Gillman asserts that Judaism "demands the death of death"[19]; he embraces bodily resurrection but only symbolically

In *The Death of Death* (1997) Neil Gillman (who taught at JTS) contends that, beginning with the medieval Jewish philosophers, the doctrine of the immortality of the soul begins to triumph over the doctrine of bodily resurrection, and that Mendelssohn foreshadows the ultimate triumph of spiritual immortality.[20] Gillman then states that in the late twentieth century there has been a renewed interest in the doctrine of bodily resurrection.[21] Relying extensively on Will Herberg's *Judaism and Modern Man: An Interpretation of Jewish Religion* (1951), as well as on articles by Arthur A. Cohen and Steven Schwarzschild, Gillman suggests that the renewed interest in

---

18. *Emet Ve'Emunah*, 26.
19. Gillman, *Death of Death*, 259.
20. See Gillman, *Death of Death*, 190–211. But see ch. 10, sec. D, 1 (Mendelssohn actually believed a disembodied soul to be an impossibility.).
21. Gillman, *Death of Death*, 215–16.

resurrection is a consequence of "Jewish thinkers' appropriation of the notion of myth as the way to characterize much of theological thinking and speaking."[22]

Herberg, for instance, argues that the concept of resurrection should not be associated with "the literalistic pseudo-biological fantasies that have gathered around it through the centuries" but should be taken as a symbol.[23] He asserts that the doctrine of resurrection symbolizes the belief that the redemption promised by what he calls transworldly messianism is totally dependent on God, involves the redemption of the *whole* man (not a disembodied soul), and involves "the salvation of [all] mankind."[24] Paradoxically, Herberg says that the end time associated with transworldly messianism is "not some far-off event in the indeterminate future" but "a dynamic force within life and history, here and now."[25] The kingdom of God may be said to be here "in *this* age wherever and to the degree that men are transformed in love of God and the acknowledgment of his total sovereignty."[26] The doctrine of resurrection, as the *symbol* of the kingdom of God, is indispensable, in Herberg's view, because it assures us that "our present life [is not] meaningless but will be completed and fulfilled" and "that in the very midst of the tragedy and frustrations of the historical process, the divine power is at work, redeeming temporal existence and leading it forward to fulfilment in a 'new age' in which life will at last realize all its potentialities and be transfigured in the fulness of the love of God."[27]

Herberg's understanding of human destiny is actually the same as Cohon's—that we find our *full* realization as persons in our creative efforts *in this life* to serve as co-workers with God in the eradication of evil and the establishment of good.[28] Yet, Cohon rejects the doctrine of resurrection; so bodily resurrection is not, as Herberg insists, an *indispensable* symbol.[29] Maintaining the doctrine of resurrection may also have an adverse consequence—misleading people into accepting the "pseudo-biological

---

22. Gillman, *Death of Death*, 216. See Gillman, *Death of Death*, 220–28.

23. Herberg, *Judaism and Modern Man*, 229–30. See Gillman, *Death of Death*, 224 (Gillman argues that to say, as Herberg does, that the doctrine of resurrection is a symbol "is to adopt the language of myth current in recent theological writing, for one definition of myth views it as a series of symbols, extended and systematized.").

24. Herberg, *Judaism and Modern Man*, 229.

25. Herberg, *Judaism and Modern Man*, 234–35.

26. Herberg, *Judaism and Modern Man*, 234 (emphasis original).

27. Herberg, *Judaism and Modern Man*, 234–36 (emphasis added). See Herberg, *Judaism and Modern Man*, 229–30 ("the doctrine of the resurrection of the dead . . . is a doctrine with which we cannot dispense"); Gillman, *Death of Death*, 221.

28. See ch. 11, sec. B, 5.

29. See also Jacobs, *Principles of the Jewish Faith*, 417–19 (Herberg's three points regarding the *whole* man and *all* men saved by the grace of God are well taken. But to safeguard these we have only to extend the idea of immortality to the whole person (i.e. the continuation of individual consciousness), to *all* men and to see the process as part of God's grace . . . The more straightforward attitude for moderns is to admit that the doctrine of the resurrection is not really significant and that what matters is that the soul of the man who had striven during his lifetime to lead the good life is immortal and near to God for all eternity.").

fantasies" that Herberg rejects.[30] Articles by Cohen and Schwarzschild offer little to support the indispensability of resurrection. Cohen concedes that the doctrine of resurrection is "alogical" and "antirational"; and Schwarzschild merely uses the doctrine of resurrection "to assert what is nowadays called the psychosomatic unity . . . of the human individual and the infinite ethical tasks incumbent upon him or her."[31]

Gillman begins a statement of what he himself believes by commenting that there are three types of "data" that he chooses to ignore: (1) "arguments for and against human immortality couched in the language of academic philosophy and psychology" because such arguments are "difficult to convey to readers" who lack "a grounding in classical philosophical literature"; (2) literature that finds "convincing arguments for immortality" in "parapsychology, near-death experiences, and alleged communications between the dead and the living" because Gillman "remain[s] unconvinced by [such] evidence"; and (3) "the popular notion that one's immortality rests in the memories one leaves behind, in the impact of one's life on friends, family and community, in children and grandchildren, in the institutions one helped to build, the students one taught or the books one published" because this notion "does not acknowledge [one's] concrete individuality."[32]

Then, Gillman asserts that human life would be "meaningless" without an afterlife because human life "cannot be fulfilled here on earth."[33] There is "an intuitive sense," he argues, "that since humans are born with an impulse to lead fulfilled lives, God must provide a setting for that fulfillment to be achieved, if not now, then in an afterlife."[34] Though this language seems to suggest that Gillman believes in an actual afterlife of some sort, in the very next sentence Gillman asserts: "The surest way to trivialize any eschatological doctrine is to understand it as literal truth."[35] He goes on to express his belief that Jewish teachings about the ultimate destiny of individual human beings may most fruitfully be understood as "part of Judaism's classic religious myth."[36] He states that there are "two core arguments for the indispensability of a doctrine of the afterlife. One is theological, the other is anthropological."[37] Gillman's theological argument is that, if God is all powerful, and, if the age to come is to mark "the ultimate manifestation of God's [power and] sovereignty over all creation," then the age to come must include "God's eschatological triumph over death."[38] Gillman's

30. See Jacobs, *Principles of the Jewish Faith*, 417–19 ("Herberg admits that 'pseudo-biological fantasies' have gathered around the doctrine of the resurrection through the centuries and apparently rejects these. He does not tell us how we can have the doctrine without these fantasies.").

31. See Gillman, *Death of Death*, 225–28.

32. Gillman, *Death of Death*, 244–45.

33. Gillman, *Death of Death*, 249.

34. Gillman, *Death of Death*, 249.

35. Gillman, *Death of Death*, 249.

36. Gillman, *Death of Death*, 250.

37. Gillman, *Death of Death*, 250.

38. See Gillman, *Death of Death*, 256–57.

anthropological argument is really an argument as to why the myth of an afterlife which he accepts on theological grounds must be bodily resurrection. He asserts that the "Jewish view of the human person" is "as a psycho-physical unity."[39] He rejects the Platonic idea that the soul alone constitutes the real person.[40] Rather, he views the soul "as a construct, an imaginative unification of the dimensions of [one's] inner life," including one's self-consciousness and thoughts.[41] Moreover, even if the soul *were* a distinct metaphysical entity, to say that it could be intrinsically immortal, Gillman believes,

> takes God out of the eschatological picture. If the soul is intrinsically immortal, then God has nothing to do with my soul at the end of days, other than reuniting it with my body. But the whole point of Jewish thinking on the afterlife is that it affirms God's ultimate power, the final manifestation of God's unfettered sovereignty. The doctrine of bodily resurrection preserves that affirmation. The doctrine of the intrinsic immortality of the soul does not.[42]

B. Orthodox Views about the Afterlife Include Both Immortality of the Soul and Resurrection of the Body

What came to be considered Orthodox Judaism had its roots in the opposition of German traditionalists, most notably Samson Raphael Hirsch, to the views of reformers regarding the divine authority of the Bible. Hirsch and his fellow traditionalists rejected the reformers' contention that Jewish law had developed in response to changing historical conditions, and could therefore be changed as well by future generations. For Hirsch, the whole of the Torah is divine and unalterable.

1. In nineteenth century Germany, Orthodox Jews expressed their belief in both the immortality of the soul and the resurrection of the dead

In his influential Torah commentary, *Uebersetzung und Erklärung des Penteteuchs* (1867/68), Hirsch expresses his belief in the immortality of the soul. Commenting on the death of Abraham described in Genesis 25:8–9, Hirsch states: "Our Torah does not *teach* the immortality of the soul. To a people which adheres to the Torah the immortality of the soul is an understood presupposition: the soul is immortal because it is the Divine spark which G-d breathes into the body [Gen 2:7]; it is the Divine

---

39. Gillman, *Death of Death*, 260.

40. See Gillman, *Death of Death*, 266–68 ("The problem with [a] sharp body/soul dualism is that it is counter-intuitive . . . We . . . feel intuitively that these two dimensions of our being form one concrete individuality.").

41. Gillman, *Death of Death*, 269.

42. Gillman, *Death of Death*, 270.

driving-power that enables man to strive for liberty and to serve the Divine Will in freedom. Judaism of the Torah is unthinkable without this precept."[43] Commenting on the burial of Jacob, Hirsch puts the matter succinctly: "The soul is immortal and only the body dies."[44]

Hirsch's belief in bodily resurrection is stated in his prayerbook commentary published posthumously. Regarding the traditional *Gevurot* benediction, Hirsch writes:

> [*You are all powerful.*] If God is our shield, then we need fear nothing, not even in death. For God is mightier than death; He can reawaken even the dead to renewed life . . . [*keeps His faith with the slumberers in the dust*] could be construed as indicating any one, or perhaps all, of these three thoughts: 1) Even if the person himself should die without receiving the salvation for which he had looked to God, God will still keep faith with him even in the world to come, and with his children who will live after him. 2) God is sure to fulfill the promise which He made to those who would be loyal to Him, namely, the pledge that He will reward the children and even grandchildren for the good deed of the parents, even though the parents themselves might long since have joined the slumberers in the dust. 3) God, in unchanging faithfulness, will fulfill the promise He had given the slumberers in the dust that He will one day awaken them and cause them to rise again to new life . . . [*Blessed be you, God, Who revives the dead.*] There can hardly be another thought that can so inspire man firmly to resolve to live a life so vigorous, unwavering, fearless and unswervingly dutiful than the belief in [bodily resurrection]. This is the firm conviction that to God not even the dead are lost forever, and that, even for the physical body, death is not the end but only a transition period from one life to the next.[45]

2. Orthodox Jews today hold varying views on the afterlife

Orthodox Jews today hold views about the afterlife that are just as diverse as the views held by Reform and Conservative Jews. While many maintain views that are similar to those held by Hirsch, others reject belief in resurrection, and some reject belief in any afterlife whatsoever.[46] With specific regard to rejection of the belief in bodily resurrection, Cohn-Sherbok asserts:

> the doctrine of the resurrection of the dead has in modern times been largely replaced in both Orthodox and non-Orthodox Judaism by the belief in the

---

43. Breuer, *Introduction to Hirsch's Commentary on the Torah*, 94–95 (emphasis original). See also Breuer, *Introduction to Hirsch's Commentary on the Torah*, 15, 19, 31.
44. Breuer, *Introduction to Hirsch's Commentary on the Torah*, 75.
45. Hirsch, *Hirsch Siddur*, 132–33.
46. See Cohn-Sherbok, *Issues in Contemporary Judaism*, 28–29.

immortality of the soul. The original belief in resurrection was an eschatological hope bound up with the rebirth of the nation in the Days of the Messiah, but as this Messianic concept faded into the background so also did this doctrine. For most Jews physical resurrection is simply inconceivable in the light of scientific understanding. The late Chief Rabbi [of the United Kingdom], Dr J.H. Hertz, for example, argued that what really matters is the doctrine of the immortality of the soul. Thus he wrote: 'Many and various are the folk beliefs and poetical fancies in the rabbinical writings concerning Heaven, *Gan Eden*, and Hell, *Gehinnom*. Our most authoritative religious guides, however, proclaim that no eye hath seen, nor can mortal fathom, what awaited us in the Hereafter; but that even the tarnished soul will not forever be denied spiritual bliss.'[47]

Similarly,

> the Orthodox thinker, Dr. Joseph Seliger, attacks the doctrine of the resurrection of the body as unduly materialistic and vigorously advocates the belief in the immortality of the soul . . . Seliger admits that it is possible for the physical resurrection to take place but he sees the whole conception as a popular folk-belief not really suitable for the philosophic mind to entertain. Basically, he concludes, this belief has far more in common with the ancient Egyptian belief than with the Law of Moses which rules that the corpse defiles. Seliger [argues] . . . that the 'resurrection of the dead' (i.e. the thirteenth principle of the faith [according to Maimonides]) does not refer to a physical resurrection but to the immortality of the soul.[48]

Although Orthodox prayerbooks retain the traditional language of the *Gevurot* benediction, this should not be taken to mean that all, or even most, members of the congregation believe in resurrection. As Levenson explains:

> In general, Orthodox Jews are more comfortable speaking of the laws of prayer than they are of the content of the prayers. My experience is that among Orthodox Jews, the recitation of liturgical texts affirming resurrection is often seen solely as a fulfillment of halakhic obligation, without concern for the theological character or credibility of the affirmations themselves and that it is not unusual to find Orthodox Jews who privately express attitudes toward the resurrection of the dead similar to those of the non-Orthodox."[49]

---

47. Cohn-Sherbok, *Issues in Contemporary Judaism*, 28. See Jacobs, *Principles of the Jewish Faith*, 415–16 (discussing Hertz's opinion that "the belief in the resurrection of the dead is of secondary importance and that what really matters is the doctrine of the immortality of the soul."). See also Jacobs, *Principles of the Jewish Faith*, 447 ("it might be argued convincingly that thanks to Mendelssohn it was the doctrine of the soul's immortality rather than that of bodily resurrection which came to be stressed even in Orthodox Jewish circles.").

48. Jacobs, *Principles of the Jewish Faith*, 414–15.

49. Levenson, *Resurrection and the Restoration*, 11n28.

Against those who reject any notion of an afterlife, Joseph B. Solveitchik holds that beliefs in an afterlife

> can be deduced logically from the proposition that God is just and merciful. God's attributes of absolute justice and mercy require that we provide rewards and punishments and that he redeem himself by being merciful to those most in need of mercy, that is, to the dead. Solveitchik holds with Nahmanides that the immortality of the soul after death is to be distinguished from a this-worldly resurrection of the dead in a post-messianic period, itself only intended to establish international peace and order.[50]

3. Recently, Jon Levenson has vigorously contended that the belief in bodily resurrection is indispensable to Jewish theology

Jon D. Levinson of Harvard University authored *Resurrection and the Restoration of Israel: The Ultimate Victory of the God of Life* (2006). In this book Levinson argues that belief in resurrection is *central* to the Judaism that the rabbis bequeathed later generations of Jews.[51] In particular, resurrection is associated with the ultimate victory of God over human evil. The source of human evil, the innate impulse that the rabbis called the "Evil Inclination," can, in the here and now, at best, be suppressed by adherence to the Torah but cannot be overcome.[52] "According to a number of rabbinic texts," asserts Levenson, "the human struggle against the Evil Inclination serves the larger purpose of contributing to the ultimate victory of God over human evil."[53] However, the final victory "requires the intervention of the Creator to uproot the Evil Inclination that he implanted within us in the beginning,"[54] and this is to be accomplished at the time of the resurrection which will subject the risen dead "to a process of recreation that renders them fit for life after death."[55] In this way, resurrection is

---

50. Rackman, "Orthodox Judaism," 680–81.
51. See Levenson, *Resurrection and the Restoration*, 218–29.
52. See Levenson, *Resurrection and the Restoration*, 220–21.
53. Levenson, *Resurrection and the Restoration*, 223.
54. Levenson, *Resurrection and the Restoration*, 224.
55. Levenson, *Resurrection and the Restoration*, 225. Levenson quotes Num. Rab. 15:16 which ends: "In the World-to-Come, I will uproot it [viz., the Evil Inclination] from you: 'I will remove the heart of stone ['eben] from your body and give [you a heart of flesh]' (Ezek 36:26)." Levenson then states: "The last verse cited comes from an oracle in which the prophet Ezekiel speaks of God's future repatriation and restoration of Israel. For Ezekiel, however, human nature is so incorrigibly evil that there are no grounds to imagine human beings in the state of righteousness that such a restoration requires. Without such righteousness, the sins that resulted in exile would immediately manifest themselves anew, and the restoration . . . would be exceedingly short-lived. The answer is nothing short of a re-creation of human beings, in which God replaces their stony hearts with fleshy ones, that is, hearts that are sensitive and obedient to the divine will . . . The notion of a re-creation of human beings to render them fit for life in the World-to-Come naturally calls to mind the resurrection of the dead. For . . . resurrection, too, is in the nature of a new creation" (Levenson, *Resurrection and the*

linked with the restoration and redemption of Israel.[56] Elsewhere in *Resurrection and the Restoration of Israel*, he puts it this way:

> The classical Jewish doctrine of resurrection . . . expresses the faith that the God who created will also recreate, and the miraculous potentials he activated at the beginning will again be seen at the end, when he restores the flesh-and-blood people Israel to their land and station, renders justice to Jew and gentile alike, reverses the very real tragedy of death, and ushers in a better world without it.[57]

Levenson admits that belief in the immortality of the soul is, as resurrection, also to be found in classical rabbinic Judaism and, to some degree, has precedents in biblical and Second Temple sources.[58] Thus, he says, neither resurrection nor immortality of the soul need be seen as exclusive of each other; rather, "they can and did coexist without tension."[59] However, such coexistence requires, Levenson believes, that immortality be defined

> as the state of those who have died and await their restoration into embodiment, that is, into full human existence . . . [I]f immortality is defined in connection with an indestructible core of the self that death cannot threaten (and may even liberate), then resurrection and immortality are at odds. Imported into Judaism, that version of immortality looks not forward to a new creation in a miraculous end-time but backward to the original creation . . . Whereas history in the classical Jewish vision of resurrection will culminate in God's supernatural triumph over death, this second idea of immortality assumes a very different scenario: individuals at various times and without relationship to each other quietly shed their perishable casings to continue in an unbroken communion with their benevolent creator.[60]

In short, Levenson rejects any hope for a disembodied mode of survival because he sees it as "a hope to shed Jewishness in this life. For to be a Jew means to be a member of a natural family, the people of Israel, the descendants of Abraham, Isaac and Jacob.

Restoration, 224).

56. See generally Levenson, *Resurrection and the Restoration*, 7 ("the resurrection of the dead belongs with other elements of Jewish eschatological expectation, such as the liberation of the Jews from subjugation to Gentile rule, the ingathering of the exile to the Land of Israel, the enthronement of the God of Israel, the reconstruction of Jerusalem as God's dwelling, and the coming of the messianic king").

57. Levenson, *Resurrection and the Restoration*, 22.

58. See Levenson, *Resurrection and the Restoration*, 20.

59. Levenson, *Resurrection and the Restoration*, 20.

60. Levenson, *Resurrection and the Restoration*, 21. See Levenson, "World Repaired, Remade," para. 7 ("The resurrection of the dead . . . is a divine intervention in the course of things at one moment in time . . . It also consummates history. The . . . immortality of the soul . . . doesn't imply a consummation of history or providential intervention into it.").

It is, in other words, a bodily state and not exclusively a spiritual or intellectual one ... To live as a disembodied spirit ... is to live in disconnection from peoplehood."[61]

All attempts by so-called Jewish modernists to foster liturgical pluralism in which belief in bodily resurrection becomes optional are seen by Levenson as misguided because "the rabbinic tradition ... views the resurrection of the dead as a normative and defining doctrine, not simply as one option among many that a Jew may or may not elect without destroying the central claims of Judaism. To the rabbis who formulated or canonized Gevurot, the resurrection of the dead was not dispensable."[62] In Levenson's view, the rejection of "the key rabbinic doctrine of resurrection" and the acceptance of the idea that "human beings can [themselves] build the messianic kingdom on earth" or can "exist forever in the presence of God in the form of disembodied spirits" is to

> purge the classical rabbinic vision of the end-time of its *redemptive* dimension. Redemption, God's reparative, restorative, and triumphant intervention into the tragedy of fleshly, historical life, [is] replaced by the ethical striving of individual persons overcoming evil in a world in which the potencies of God's goodness are, happily, already completely actualized ... When redemption is collapsed into ethics in this way, human beings, in one sense, take the place of God.[63]

Levenson rightly associates the denigration of resurrection by "Jewish modernists" with the rise of naturalism and scientism.[64] Though Levenson recognizes that belief in resurrection conflicts with naturalism and scientism, he offers little reason to

---

61. Levenson, *Resurrection and the Restoration*, 22.

62. Levenson, *Resurrection and the Restoration*, 10. Although it may be true that the rabbis who formulated the *Gevurot* did not view resurrection as dispensable, they likely had differing views as to what resurrection meant, and some may not even have accepted *bodily* resurrection. More important, many Jews, contemporaries as well as Jews who lived either before or after these rabbis lived, disagreed with them.

63. Levenson, *Resurrection and the Restoration*, 16–17 (emphasis original).

64. Levenson, *Resurrection and the Restoration*, 11, 21. See also Levenson, "World Repaired, Remade," para. 4, 6, and 9 ("[I]f you want Judaism to look progressive, scientific, and naturalistic, then the resurrection of the dead will have to be jettisoned ... If you're committed to a totally naturalistic universe without a personal creator God, an active God who actually does things, then the best you can do with the resurrection of the dead is to say that it's a symbol of hope, but a hope that ends at the grave ... Many modern people find eschatology problematic because they can't imagine a definitive end to evil and a transformation and recreation of realities as they stand now. Nothing in science suggests that this is what we're headed for. Science does not provide a happy view of ultimate destiny. These biblical affirmations are based, instead, on promises that don't have any unassailable empirical evidence.").

reject naturalism and scientism in favor of resurrection.[65] Nor is Levenson prepared to say very much about what life in the world to come would look like.[66]

C. Hasidic Sects Emphasize Reincarnation and Other Kabbalistic Points of View Concerning the Fate of the Disembodied Soul

Hasidism is a popular communal mysticism that arose and flourished among the Jews of Eastern Europe in the eighteenth and nineteenth centuries. The emergence of Hasidism was fueled by the disappointments following the collapse of the pseudo-messianism of Sabbatai Zevi and Jacob Frank, and by the spread of practical Kabbalah by the followers of Isaac Luria.[67] The spark that ignited these various embers was the person of the Baal Shem Tov. As Raphael notes, "By emphasizing devotional ecstasy and religious fervor over and above scholarship and legalism" the Baal Shem Tov founded a movement which challenged "the over intellectualized severity of Talmudic Judaism."[68] This anti-intellectual movement maintained most of the superstitions about the soul and the afterlife that had existed in Kabbalah for centuries. Paramount in this regard is belief in the transmigration of souls. But one need not be a member of a Hasidic sect to maintain belief in the transmigration of souls. For example, in what is purported to have been "one of the most popular works of mussar of the last three hundred years,"[69] *Kav HaYashar* (*The Just Measure*), first published in 1705, it is taught that, if at the time of death a human being has failed to fulfill all 613 commandments, or failed to "study the Torah, the statutes and the laws pertaining them," then "the soul must return to earth to be reincarnated in another body that it may fulfill its task and make good its deficiency."[70]

---

65. He says only that to conceive the essence of Judaism as this-worldly "severs practice from theology in ways for which classical Judaism (biblical and rabbinic) offers scant precedent." Levenson, *Resurrection and the Restoration*, 21. Elsewhere he recognizes, however, that the dominant theology in biblical sources, which is also found in postexilic sources, finds God's promise of "life" fulfilled in *this* world, not in a World-to-Come. See e.g., Levenson, *Resurrection and the Restoration*, 169–71, 194–95; Levenson, "World Repaired, Remade," para. 14 (The theologically older model "saw God's justice vindicated or realized with descendants, a postmortem vindication that does not involve the resurrection.").

66. See Levenson, "World Repaired, Remade," para. 18 ("any effort to envision the World-to-Come necessarily entails mythopoetic language, while attempts to account for this mode of being rationalistically and empirically come across as silly").

67. See Sachar, *Course of Modern Jewish History*, 75–76; Scholem, *Major Trends in Jewish Mysticism*, 327–29. See also Buber, *Origin and Meaning of Hasidism*, 24–57; Buber, *Tales of the Hasidim*, 1:2–3. But see Idel, *Hasidism*, 3–29.

68. Raphael, *Jewish Views of the Afterlife*, 329. See Scheindlin, *Short History of the Jewish People*, 177, 180.

69. Davis, "Foreword," xxv.

70. Kaidanover, *Kav HaYashar*, 235–36.

1. As taught by Hasidic tales, individuals are redeemed through transmigrations of their individual soul and its reaching higher levels of existence

As the newest phase in Jewish mysticism, Hasidism essentially preserves certain elements of Kabbalism. In particular, "Hasidism develops the late-Kabbalistic theory of the divine sparks that have fallen into the [realm of] things and can be 'uplifted' by man. It is for such uplifting that the *mitzvoth* are enjoined to man. He who performs a *mitsva* with perfect *kavana*, that is, he who accomplishes the action in such a manner that his whole existence is concentrated in it and is directed in it to God, works on the hallowing of the world, on its conquest for God."[71] Buber distinguishes four kinds of exile and redemption. They are: (1) "the exile of the 'holy sparks' and their redemption," (2) "the exile of the individual and the redemption of the individual through 'transmigrations' of the individual soul and its transformation in this way into higher stages," (3) "national exile and redemption," and (4) "the exile of the Shekina and its redemption."[72]

These four kinds of exile and redemption are said by Buber to "converge" in Hasidism.[73] Thus, the exile of the nation is connected with the both the exile of the holy sparks and with the exile of the individual soul, and the redemption of the holy sparks and the individual soul are connected with the nation's redemption. Buber notes that, according to Rabbi Nachman of Bratslav, "'The main purpose of the [national] exile . . . is to gather the "discarded ones," who are the sparks that were discarded into the "shells" of the *kelipot*, as it is said, "Israel was exiled for the sake of winning proselytes . . ."'"[74] Buber goes on to say,

> Just as the sparks are in exile, so also are the souls of the people. Their transmigrations from lower to higher stages are merely the result of the soul's aspiration to reach perfection. And here, too, the exile and redemption of the nation are connected in their depth with those of the soul. The exile of Israel is meant for the purification of the souls, which helps them to ascend to a higher stage of existence, and the redemption of Israel cannot be fulfilled without this uplifting of the souls and their perfection.[75]

2. Numerous Hasidic legends refer to the transmigration of souls

Adopting the concept of *gilgul* from Kabbalah, it was not uncommon for Hasidic legends to assert that a *tzaddik*, or saint, had experienced one or more previous incarnations. As Raphael comments:

71. Buber, *Origin and Meaning of Hasidism*, 50.
72. Buber, *Origin and Meaning of Hasidism*, 203.
73. See Buber, *Origin and Meaning of Hasidism*, 203–18.
74. Buber, *Origin and Meaning of Hasidism*, 206–7.
75. Buber, *Origin and Meaning of Hasidism*, 209.

The Baal Shem Tov himself claimed to be a reincarnation of Rabbi Saadia Gaon; Dov Baer of Mezhirich was said to be the reincarnation of Rabbi Akiba; and Reb Israel Stolin had the soul of the famous tenth-century scholar Rashi. Reb Mosche Teitelbaum, the Satmarer Rebbe, was aware of numerous previous lives. He spoke of having been alive in ancient times—as one of the sheep of Jacob when he worked for his father-in-law Laban, as one of the many Jews who left Egypt with Moses, and as a witness to the destruction of the Temple. In this latter incarnation, he claimed to be the prophet Jeremiah.[76]

Typical of such legends is the following one, referring to a disciple of Dov Baer:

> On the second day of Iyyar of the year 5538, Rabbi Shmelke summoned his disciples. He was sitting very erect in his big chair, his face was radiant, and his eyes as unclouded as always. He said to them: 'Today, you must know, is the day of my death.' They began to weep, but he bade them stop, and continued: 'You must know that the soul of the prophet is within me. For this there are three outward signs: my name is Samuel; I am a Levite, as he was; and my life has lasted fifty-two years, just as his. But he was called Samuel, and I Schmelke, and so I remained Schmelke.' Soon after this, he told his weeping disciples to leave him, leaned back, and died.[77]

Of a similar ilk is a legend about Abraham Joshua Heschel of Apt:

> On the Day of Atonement, when Rabbi Abraham Yehoshua would recite the Avodah, the prayer that repeats the service of the high priest in the Temple of Jerusalem, and would come to the passage: 'And thus he spoke,' he would never say these words, but would say: 'And thus I spoke.' For he had not forgotten the time his soul was in the body of a high priest of Jerusalem ... Once he himself related: 'Ten times I have been in this world. I was a high priest, I was a prince, I was a king, I was an exilic. I was ten different kind of dignitary. But I never learned to love mankind perfectly. And so I was sent forth again and again in order to perfect my love. If I succeed this time, I shall never return again.[78]

Other legends refer indirectly to *gilgul*. In several of these it is suggested that someone's soul will be reincarnated in the body of one of their descendants. Such is the case in a legend about the Seer, the rabbi of Lublin:

> It was at the wedding of his granddaughter Hinda. At the very moment the gifts were presented, Rabbi Jacob Yitzhak put his head in his hands, and seemed to fall asleep. The master of ceremonies called out again and again: 'Wedding gifts from the family of the bride,' and waited for the rabbi, but he

---

76. Raphael, *Jewish Views of the Afterlife*, (citing *inter alia*, *Shivhei Ha-Besht*).
77. Buber, *Tales of the Hasidim*, 1:194.
78. Buber, *Tales of the Hasidim*, 2:118. See Heschel, *Passion for Truth*, xiii ("The Apter Rav claimed that his soul had lived in several incarnations, and for his descendants it was as if he had never died.").

did not move. All fell silent and waited for him to wake up. When half an hour had passed, his son whispered in his ear: 'Father, they are calling for wedding gifts from the bride's family.' The old man started up from his meditations and replied: 'Then I give myself. After thirteen years, the gift will be brought.' After thirteen years, when Hinda bore a son, he was called Jacob Yitzhak after his grandfather. When he grew up he resembled him in every feature, his right eye, for instance, was a little bigger than his left, just like that of the rabbi of Lublin.[79]

One of the purposes of *gilgul* in Hasidism is to enable atonement for sin. This is made clear in the following story concerning the birth of Zev Wolf of Zbarazh, the son of Yehiel Mikhal of Zlotchov:

On a certain New Year's night, the maggid of Zlotchov saw a man who had been a reader in his city, and who had died a short time ago. 'What are you doing here?' he asked. 'The rabbi knows,' said the dead man, 'that in this night, souls are incarnated anew. I am such a soul. 'And why were you sent out again?' asked the maggid. 'I led an impeccable life here on earth,' the dead man told him. 'And yet you are forced to live once more?' the maggid went on to ask. 'Before my death,' said the man, 'I thought over everything I had done and found that I had always acted in just the right way. Because of this, my heart swelled with satisfaction and in the midst of this feeling I died. So now they have sent me back into the world to atone for my pride.' At that time a son was born to the maggid. His name was Rabbi Wolf. He was very humble.[80]

Transmigration of a soul into another body was apparently considered, by some *tzadikkim*, a harsher form of punishment than being sent to *Gehenna*, suggesting that both options were available, to wit:

This story is about Reb Noah . . . He died and came to the Court of Heaven. They looked into his case and they found out that all his life he had observed everything that he should in the highest way. Angels came who were born from his good deeds and they were witnesses for him . . . And the Court was going to decide that he should go immediately to [Gan Eden].

All of a sudden an angel appeared and he said, 'Wait a second! I have to tell something about him.' And he said, 'I was created from one bad deed that this *tzaddik* did in his lifetime.' And he brought out what he did.

The Court of Heaven deliberated and they said he should have either one half hour in Gehenna or he should be reborn on earth to fix what he had failed to do the first time. Reb Noah answered the court that all his life everything he had to decide he asked his Rebbe. He never did anything without asking

---

79. Buber, *Tales of the Hasidim*, 2:318.

80. Buber, *Tales of the Hasidim*, 2:158. See Raphael, *Jewish Views of the Afterlife*, 354–55 (in this story "an individual is reborn to atone for misdeeds of a previous lifetime").

the Rebbe; therefore, he wanted to ask the Rebbe to tell now what he should decide . . .

The Rebbe, Rabbi Shneur Zalman, was sitting with his *hasidim* and he said to them, 'Reb Noah is asking now what he should select: either Gehenna, a half hour of hell, or be reborn in the world a second time.' They had nothing to say. They were waiting. And the Rebbe put his holy hand on his forehead and he rested his head on the table a short time. Then he said: 'Gehenna . . . Gehenna.'[81]

3. Hasidic tales frequently refer to *Gehenna* and *Gan Eden*

As evidenced by the preceding tale, references to *Gehenna* as a place of purgation existed alongside belief in *gilgul*. As Raphael notes, "The *hasidim*, like the kabbalists and Talmudic Rabbis, saw Gehenna as a realm of purification for one's earthly sins. In order to avoid the purgations of Gehenna, the *hasidim* practiced God's commandments, the *mitzvoth*, and regularly evaluated their lives (*heshbon ha-nefesh*, literally, an 'accounting of the soul') in order to correct their unrighteous ways."[82] References to *Gehenna* in the Hasidic tales also refer to efforts by *tzaddikim* to rescue souls from *Gehenna*.[83]

Tales refer to *Gan Eden* as well as to *Gehenna*. As Raphael notes, "All the Hasidic tales on Gan Eden point out one essential teaching: what will be experienced in the postmortem realms of paradise is a direct reflection of one's experience and spiritual awareness."[84] That *Gan Eden* is conceived as a place of ecstasy, and that for a soul to experience the ecstasy of *Gan Eden* requires it to have experienced ecstasy while still embodied, is evidenced by the following teaching of Shelomo of Karlin:

> Rabbi Shelomo of Karlin said: 'When he, who has done all the commandments of the Torah, but has not felt the blaze of holy ecstasy in so doing, comes to that other world, they open the gates of paradise for him. But because he has not felt the blaze of ecstasy in this world, he does not feel the ecstasy of paradise. Now, if he is a fool, and complains, and grumbles: "And they make so much to-do about paradise!" he is instantly thrown out. But if he is wise, he leaves of his own accord, and goes to the zaddik, and he teaches the poor soul how to feel ecstasy.'[85]

---

81. Raphael, *Jewish Views of the Afterlife*, 347–48 (citing Mintz, *Legends of the Hasidim*, 251–52).
82. Raphael, *Jewish Views of the Afterlife*, 345–46.
83. See Raphael, *Jewish Views of the Afterlife*, 346–47.
84. Raphael, *Jewish Views of the Afterlife*, 348.
85. Buber, *Tales of the Hasidim*, 1:276–77.

4. Hasidic thought maintained many of the superstitious beliefs about the soul and spirits that existed in kabbalistic thought

Consistent with kabbalistic superstitions about disembodied souls, the *hasidim* continued to believe that "after physical death the soul remains close to the body for some time . . . Those souls who remain attached to the physical body and the material world find themselves in 'the world of confusion,' *olam ha-tohu*."[86] It was also accepted that the souls of the dead, even souls in paradise, could remain in contact with the living. As Raphael asserts: "There are numerous stories documenting encounters with those who have died either through dreams or spirit visitations."[87] An example of such a story is the one mentioned above about Yehiel Mikhal of Zlotchov seeing a reader from his congregation who had died but needed to atone for his sin of pride. Another concerns the soul of a *tzaddik* returning to this world from the highest regions of *Gan Eden* to rejoice with his family at his granddaughter's wedding.[88]

5. Simcha Paull Raphael advocates "a contemporary Jewish model of life after death"[89] incorporating Hasidic notions about the soul and *gilgul*

In the preface for the second edition of *Jewish Views of the Afterlife* (2009), Raphael writes that "the notion of a Jewish belief in an afterlife has slowly penetrated the normative, mainstream of Jewish community life . . . [and] the misconception that Judaism does not believe in an afterlife has begun to slowly dissolve and dissipate."[90] Raphael (who describes himself as a transpersonal psychotherapist, bereavement counselor, and rabbinic pastor ordained by Zalman Schacter-Shalomi) connects this perceived change in Jewish attitudes about the afterlife to a much broader change in American culture as a whole. As he sees it, America is "in the midst of psycho-spiritual transformation with regard to attitudes toward death, dying, afterlife, and spirituality in general."[91] He attributes this "psycho-spiritual transformation" to three factors: (1) "the idea that the soul survives the body has become infused in popular culture," and he points to, *inter alia*, television programs in which "living people and the souls of the dead are in communication"; (2) the dissemination of the work of Elisabeth Kübler-Ross on death and dying, and the work of Raymond Moody on near-death experiences, as well as "changes in caring for the dying"; and (3) "a powerful transformation . . . [in] the whole area of spirituality."[92] The body of Raphael's book is

---

86. Raphael, *Jewish Views of the Afterlife*, 344–45.
87. Raphael, *Jewish Views of the Afterlife*, 351.
88. Buber, *Tales of the Hasidim*, 2:94–95.
89. Raphael, *Jewish Views of the Afterlife*, 359.
90. Raphael, *Jewish Views of the Afterlife*, xxxix.
91. Raphael, *Jewish Views of the Afterlife*, xl.
92. Raphael, *Jewish Views of the Afterlife*, xl–xliii. See also Raphael, *Jewish Views of the Afterlife*, 31–32.

devoted to discussing those Jewish sources and texts that concern visionary tours of heaven and hell, and descriptions of *Gehenna* and *Gan Eden*.

Consistent with his desire to propagate kabbalistic/Hasidic beliefs about the soul and the afterlife, Raphael offers what he calls "a contemporary psychological model of the afterlife" which draws on "research on near-death experiences," "certain elements of Tibetan Buddhist philosophy of postmortem survival," and "contemporary transpersonal psychology."[93] Raphael's contemporary psychological model consists of seven "Transit Stages" of the soul's postmortem journey which he correlates to five "levels of the soul" in Kabbalah (*nephesh, ruach, nehamah, hayyah,* and *yehidah*, as well as to four kabbalistic metaphysical concepts (viz., the four "levels of reality"—the "worlds" of *Atzilut* or Emanation, *Beriyah* or Creation, *Yetzirah* or Formation, and *Assiyah* or Function), which are, in turn, related to what he calls four "states of consciousness" ("physical, emotional, mental, and spiritual"), and to the four letters of the Divine Name YHVH (*yod, hey, vav, hey*).[94] In the first stage of the soul's journey, per Raphael's model, the soul (1) experiences visions, (2) encounters "angelic spirits and deceased relatives" who "initiate the neophyte into the realm of postmortem consciousness," and (3) is subjected to a "life review." This is followed, in the second stage, by "separation from the physical body"; in the third stage, by "emotional purification" which "corresponds with Gehenna"; in the fourth stage, by the experience of "a world of bliss" in Lower *Gan Eden*; in the fifth stage, by the attainment of "heavenly repose" in Upper *Gan Eden*; in the sixth stage, by "being with God"; and, in the final stage, by *gilgul*.[95] Raphael concludes his depiction of the soul's postmortem journey by saying: "With the birth of a new being into the world, the postmortem journey is complete. A soul has finished its transition through the afterlife; another life of physical incarnation begins."[96] In short, Raphael accepts belief in the transmigration of souls. Raphael claims that actions taken by the bereaved have "the capacity to influence the postmortem fate of the dead" and, in particular, may serve "to either free or hinder the soul of the deceased in Gehenna."[97] Thus, for example, according to Raphael, "saying *Kaddish* functions as a way of assisting the disembodied soul through its purgation in Gehenna."[98]

Lacking from Raphael's contemporary psychological model of the afterlife are any arguments that would enable it to pass rational muster. For example, Raphael fails even to provide any sophisticated analysis of what precisely he takes a soul to be, other than associating the soul with consciousness. With regard to the belief that the soul, however understood, survives the death of the body, Raphael relies entirely on

---

93. See Raphael, *Jewish Views of the Afterlife*, 359–63.
94. See Raphael, *Jewish Views of the Afterlife*, 364–94.
95. See Raphael, *Jewish Views of the Afterlife*, 364–94.
96. Raphael, *Jewish Views of the Afterlife*, 394.
97. Raphael, *Jewish Views of the Afterlife*, 387.
98. Raphael, *Jewish Views of the Afterlife*, 387. Cf. ch. 6, sec. C, 3; ch. 11, sec. A, 5.

the observations of Raymond Moody, Jr. about "near-death experiences."⁹⁹ However, Raphael makes no mention of the voluminous research that has been done debunking any reliance on such experiences as evidence of a person's postmortem existence.¹⁰⁰

Leaving aside the merits of Raphael's beliefs, it must be admitted that his general attitudes about the soul and its postmortem existence, as well as about communication with dead people, are not without appeal to many Jews. And support for Raphael's description of the growth of so-called "spirituality" among Jews may be found in an article by Yaakov Ariel entitled "Jews and New Religious Movements." Ariel discusses the various twentieth-century religious movements, both within a Jewish context and outside a Jewish context, that have attracted an increasing number of young Jews in America and Israel who were "yearning for spirituality in their lives."¹⁰¹ He mentions, for example, Jews who joined American variants of Buddhist, Hindu, or Sufi groups, the Transcendental Meditation Movement of Maharishi Mahesh Yogi, the Unification Church, and Scientology. Ariel also discusses at some length what he refers to as a neo-Hasidic movement initiated as an outreach program of Rebbe Joseph Isaac Schneerson and his successor Menahem Mendel Schneerson, leaders of the Habad Hasidic community.¹⁰² As recounted by Ariel, two of Habad's "early emissaries, Shlomo Carlbach and [Zalman Schacter-Shalomi], helped develop liberal Hasidic-inspired and spiritually oriented new Jewish movements."¹⁰³

6. Elie Kaplan Spitz, a Conservative rabbi, enthusiastically supports reincarnation

Evidence for the intrusion of Hasidic views about the soul and reincarnation into Conservative congregations comes in the person of Elie Kaplan Spitz who is the rabbi of a such a congregation. In his book, *Does the Soul Survive? A Jewish Journey to Belief in Afterlife, Past Lives & Living with Purpose* (2000), Kaplan recounts his two-year long journey from denying reincarnation to being an enthusiastic advocate of reincarnation. The opening pages of Spitz's book contain endorsements and high praise from Rabbi David Ellenson, Rabbi David Wolpe, and Rabbi Bradley Shavit Artson. Spitz states that while attending the University of Judaism, and then JTS, he "never

---

99. See Raphael, *Jewish Views of the Afterlife*, 359–60. According to Raphael, the nature of the near-death experience "indicates that there is an awareness that transcends the limitations of the physical body and continues to exist even after the biological functions have ceased" (Raphael, *Jewish Views of the Afterlife*, 360).

100. See e.g., Blackmore, *Dying to Live*, 1–254; Lester, *Is There Life After Death?*, 27–101. See also sec. C, 6.

101. Ariel, "Jews and New Religious Movements," 10.

102. See Ariel, "Jews and New Religious Movements," 9–10. See also Scheindlin, *Short History of the Jewish People*, 253–54.

103. Ariel, "Jews and New Religious Movements," 10.

heard a discussion on survival of the soul."[104] Then, in his work as a rabbi, he heard stories of "mental telepathy" concerning recently deceased relatives.[105] Exposure to such telepathic stories lead Spitz to read material on so-called near-death experiences, especially *Life After Life* (1975) by Dr. Raymond Moody Jr., and Elisabeth Kübler-Ross's *Death and Dying* (1969) and *On Life After Death* (1991).[106] Although recognizing that near-death experiences "are not proof for the existence or survival of the soul," Spitz found that "the accumulated anecdotes . . . support the concept of a realm of life beyond this one."[107]

In early 1996, Spitz's secretary gave him a book by Dr. Brian Weiss titled *Many Lives, Many Masters* (1988).[108] The book concerns Weiss's work in what is termed "past-life regression." In past-life regression, patients under hypnosis refer to themselves as persons, different from who they really are, who lived in earlier times. So, for example, Weiss discusses a patient named Catherine who, under hypnosis, "referred to herself as Aronda and placed herself in the year 1863 B.C.E."[109] Later in 1996, Spitz attended a one-day seminar with Weiss.[110] This was followed by Spitz attending a weeklong training seminar offered by Weiss.[111] "Throughout the week Weiss . . . gently and adeptly led a variety of people to uncover their past-life traumas"; Spitz left the seminar quite in awe of Weiss.[112] According to Spitz, "Brian Weiss has much data to share and a solid *faith* in the survival of the soul and reincarnation."[113] Spitz comments that "much of the material generated in past-life regression is not true past-life memory, yet it remains potentially helpful."[114] Spitz's interest in reincarnation grew even more when he learned that Rabbi Joseph Telushkin "had a videotape of a past-life regression that he had conducted with a young Jewish woman," and Spitz went to Telushkin's home to view the videotape.[115]

Finally, Spitz recounts that several members of his community who had lost children provided him with exposure to the work of mediums.[116] In one case, a child had died suddenly at the age of seven from an asthma attack. The father had gone to a medium named George Anderson who had purportedly "conjured up" the child.[117] A

---

104. Spitz, *Does the Soul Survive?*, 2–3.
105. See Spitz, *Does the Soul Survive?*, 3–8.
106. See Spitz, *Does the Soul Survive?*, 13–21.
107. Spitz, *Does the Soul Survive?*, 13.
108. Spitz, *Does the Soul Survive?*, 57.
109. See Spitz, *Does the Soul Survive?*, 58–59.
110. Spitz, *Does the Soul Survive?*, 61.
111. See *Spitz, Does the Soul Survive?*, 65–80.
112. See Spitz, *Does the Soul Survive?*, 75.
113. Spitz, *Does the Soul Survive?*, 75 (emphasis added).
114. Spitz, *Does the Soul Survive?*, 77.
115. Spitz, *Does the Soul Survive?*, 62–63.
116. Spitz, *Does the Soul Survive?*, 103.
117. Spitz, *Does the Soul Survive?*, 103.

couple from Spitz's own congregation, mourning the death of their twenty-five-year-old daughter in a car accident, and feeling guilty about it, also had a "session" with George Anderson.[118] As Spitz writes, "On [the daughter's] behalf [Anderson] asked [the couple] that they not feel guilty, for they had been fine parents."[119] The couple came away "believers in Anderson's ability to communicate with their daughter. They found her words to be a great source of comfort and healing."[120] Spitz was prompted to attend a workshop, offered in 1997 by one James Van Praagh, a medium who is a friend of Brian Weiss.[121] The workshop was entitled "Developing Your Psychic Gifts." Spitz was impressed. He writes: "Watching Van Praagh up close revealing information about a loved one was a turning point for me in verifying survival of the soul. This last experience fit neatly with many of my other encounters over the previous two years, including graveside [telepathic] mysteries and past-life regressions."[122] Spitz states further that he "grew to believe that another realm does exist, to which our souls pass upon death and from which they may return into a new physical life."[123]

In chapter 13 of Spitz's book, entitled "Weighing the Evidence," Spitz gushes that he was "astounded" by Van Praagh's accuracy, and that the "ability of mediums to communicate with the dead supported Weiss's assertion that he had regressed [a patient under hypnosis] to a state 'between lives' in which [the patient was able to provide previously unknown facts, and] said that 'masters' in the realm beyond were the source of her knowledge."[124] Spitz concludes that mediums "can *apparently* reach into that realm from a wakeful state."[125] He then asserts: "The evidence of mediums *apparently* conferring with spirits reinforces my *faith* in survival of the soul."[126] Continuing, Spitz mentions Ian Stevenson, the "most experienced researcher in past-life memory that [Spitz knows]," and Spitz provides "two brief sketches of spontaneous memories of children culled from Stevenson's voluminous reporting that demonstrate the corroboration of past-life memories with verifiable facts."[127] Spitz also offers instances of xenoglossy, "the ability to speak a foreign language that the speaker cannot account for," noting that such instances "impressed [him] greatly" and "powerfully reinforce the notion of reincarnation."[128] Despite the strong impression that this material had on Spitz's belief in reincarnation, he ends chapter 13 by saying that there are "endless

---

118. See Spitz, *Does the Soul Survive?*, 111–13.
119. Spitz, *Does the Soul Survive?*, 112.
120. Spitz, *Does the Soul Survive?*, 112–13.
121. Spitz, *Does the Soul Survive?*, 111.
122. Spitz, *Does the Soul Survive?*, 123.
123. Spitz, *Does the Soul Survive?*, 125.
124. Spitz, *Does the Soul Survive?*, 125–26.
125. Spitz, *Does the Soul Survive?*, 125–26 (emphasis added).
126. Spitz, *Does the Soul Survive?*, 125–26 (emphasis added).
127. Spitz, *Does the Soul Survive?*, 128.
128. See Spitz, *Does the Soul Survive?*, 129–31.

CHAPTER 12.

questions that may be asked of each account that render their significance uncertain" and that "a host of [more general] questions emerged."[129] In the end, however, Spitz accepts reincarnation:

> Despite differences in accounts, I am persuaded of the reality of soul survival by the compelling similarities in descriptions of the afterlife in Jewish mystical texts, texts of ancient cultures such as Tibetan Buddhism, and contemporary findings. These divergent systems of wisdom affirm the survival of the soul and describe stages following death that include being drawn into light, life review, purification, levels of soul achievement, and reincarnation . . .
>
> In sum, my personal experiences and reading have led me to believe in the reality of the soul, its survival, and reincarnation. *My faith* is reinforced by traditional Jewish and contemporary accounts.[130]

Spitz explicitly rejects belief in bodily resurrection, seeing it as mutually exclusive with reincarnation.[131] Admitting that resurrection is a fundamental tenet of rabbinic Judaism, he argues that, over time, it "lost its importance for many Jewish thinkers," and that, in modern times, "the whole topic of resurrection has been largely ignored."[132] Moreover, he says, an emphasis on reincarnation "has traditional roots, too," gaining "popular acceptance after the thirteenth century."[133] According to Spitz, some prayerbook commentators have reinterpreted the *Gevurot* benediction to refer to "the promise of reincarnation," but he provides no reference.[134]

Spitz's reliance on near-death experiences, so-called past-life memories, the purported ability of mediums to conjure up spirits and the like to support a belief in reincarnation is misguided. As he himself admits, none of these phenomena constitute scientific proof of anything; they are not procedures conducted in accordance with the scientific method. Indeed, Spitz even fails to provide an adequate definition

129. Spitz, *Does the Soul Survive?*, 132–33.
130. Spitz, *Does the Soul Survive?*, 142–45 (emphasis added).
131. Spitz, *Does the Soul Survive?*, 54–55.
132. See Spitz, *Does the Soul Survive?*, 49–53.
133. Spitz, *Does the Soul Survive?*, 55. Several chapters of the book are devoted to a presentation of Jewish views on the survival of the soul, reincarnation, and the use of mediums to call on the "spirits" of the departed. See Spitz, *Does the Soul Survive?*, 33–39, 81–109. Regarding the use of mediums, Spitz notes the generally understood Jewish position that Jews are *not* permitted to consult with mediums. See Spitz, *Does the Soul Survive?*, 103–5. However, as Jewish mysticism grew in importance, Spitz claims, necromancy came to be accepted if the medium "conjured up the dead through the use of holy names" (Spitz, *Does the Soul Survive?*, 106). After a brief discussion of the use of mediums to contact the dead after about 1600, he concludes: "several streams of Judaism permit calling on the spirit of the departed and the use of mediums. The biblical prohibition against necromancy is limited to calling on the dead as an idolatrous religious act . . . Conjuring up the dead through the use of Jewishly acceptable mystical techniques, such as recombinations of the letters of God's name, is seen as a sacred act. Jewish tradition also discourages the use of mediums to foretell the future, for to do so contradicts the basic Jewish tenets of free will and individual responsibility for the future" (Spitz, *Does the Soul Survive?*, 108–9).
134. Spitz, *Does the Soul Survive?*, 55.

of what he means by the term "soul." He claims that the soul "is not an object" and that we "engage soul with the aid of imagination."[135] But such claims, without more, are gibberish. As Eugene Borowitz has well noted: "If one wants to talk about survival after death, it would be helpful to be able to say just what [it is that] survives."[136] If the soul is not an object, as Spitz asserts, Spitz must tell us precisely what it is. Whatever it is, he must further explain precisely what its relationship is to the numerous persons with whom it is purportedly associated. Instead of providing any such definition or explanation, Spitz confesses: "My reading of contemporary authors and Jewish sacred texts left me humbled in trying to define the soul. Any attempt to define soul in clear, unequivocal terms resulted either in distortion or glibness."[137]

Equally significant, the various phenomena upon which Spitz relies to support his faith in reincarnation can be adequately explained without resort to reincarnation. For example, the phenomenon of near-death experience has been extensively and carefully studied by Susan Blackmore, an Oxford-trained psychologist with a PhD in parapsychology. In her book *Dying to Live: Near-Death Experiences* (1993), Blackmore examines the several aspects of near-death experiences, including visions of a tunnel, bright lights, out-of-body sensations, sensations of peace and joy, and life-review, all in the context of a scientific understanding of what is happening to a dying brain. She considers two hypotheses to account for the several aspects of near-death experience, the "Afterlife Hypothesis" and the "Dying Brain Hypothesis." The first hypothesis is that there is a "soul or spirit" which is "freed from its earthly ties" and travels "in a nonmaterial world beyond the limitations of space and time."[138] The second hypothesis is that all the phenomena of a near-death experience are the "products of the dying brain; hallucinations, imaginings and mental constructions that will ultimately stop when the brain's activity stops."[139] If the second hypothesis is true, she says, then near-death experiences "tell us nothing about life after death."[140] After several hundred pages discussing the data, as well as the arguments advanced by proponents of each hypothesis, Blackmore concludes that "the evidence and the arguments are overwhelming" in favor of the Dying Brain Hypothesis.[141]

More expansive than Blackmore's book is *Reincarnation: A Critical Examination* (1996) by Paul Edwards. Edwards considers not only near-death experiences but also hypnotic regressions and memories of past lives. He devotes a significant portion of his book specifically to Kübler-Ross, Moody Jr., and Stephenson. Although he does not discuss xenoglossy, that is only because he felt that the topic had been excellently

---

135. Spitz, *Does the Soul Survive?*, 23, 24.
136. Borowitz, *Reform Judaism Today*, 46. See ch. 11, sec. B, 6.
137. Spitz, *Does the Soul Survive?*, 32.
138. Blackmore, *Dying to Live*, 3–4.
139. Blackmore, *Dying to Live*, 4.
140. Blackmore, *Dying to Live*, 4.
141. See Blackmore, *Dying to Live*, 260–64.

CHAPTER 12.

treated by Ian Wilson in *Mind Out of Time* (1982), and in two articles by Professor Sarah G. Thomason, a professional linguist.[142] The gist of Edwards's argument is succinctly summarized in the book's introduction:

> It is well-known that the main philosophical tenets of Christianity and Judaism—belief in God, life after death, and miracles—have been subjected to a devastating critical examination by a number of the greatest Western philosophers . . . No Western philosopher has offered a similarly detailed critique of reincarnation and the related doctrine of Karma probably because very few people in the West had taken these theories seriously. Unfortunately this is no longer true. The belief in reincarnation and Karma has been steadily gaining support in recent decades. This is . . . one aspect of the tide of irrationalism that has been flooding the Western World, especially the United States. There is an urgent need for a comprehensive and systematic evaluation of reincarnation and Karma and the present volume is designed to fill this gap.
>
> I have attempted to state, fairly and fully, all the main arguments offered in support of reincarnation and Karma. I have tried to show that this evidence is worthless. It has been claimed that such facts as child prodigies, déjà vu experiences, hypnotic regressions, and the reincarnation memories of a number of children, mainly in India and in other countries where belief in reincarnation is widespread, can only be explained by reincarnation. None of these claims stands up under critical examination.
>
> I also try to show that there are grave conceptual problems connected with these doctrines . . . There is . . . the altogether fatal problem of specifying a credible way in which a person can come to inhabit another body after its original body has died . . . Finally, we have enormous evidence that the mind or consciousness cannot exist without the brain . . .
>
> I refer to the problems of finding a way in which the mind of a human being could make its transition from one body to another as the '*modus operandi* problem.' . . . I don't think that believers have an answer.[143]

---

142. See Edwards, *Reincarnation*, 8.

143. Edwards, *Reincarnation*, 7–8. See also Elbert, *Are Souls Real?*, 113–368; Lester, *Is There Life After Death?*, 101–207.

13.

The Principle of Immanence Comes to Dominate the Intellectual Landscape of the Nineteenth and Twentieth Centuries

BARUCH SPINOZA GENERATED A philosophical revolution that had as its underlying principle what Yirmiyahu Yovel calls immanence. As Yovel describes it:

> This principle views this-worldly existence as the only actual being, and the unique source of ethical value and political authority. All being is this-worldly and there is nothing beyond it, neither a personal creator-God who imposes His divine will on man, nor supernatural powers or values of any kind. The laws of morality and politics, too, and even religion, stem from this world by the natural power of reason; and recognizing this is the prelude and precondition for human emancipation . . .
>
> Spinoza's immanent revolution was as slow in leaving its mark on future thought as its principle was radical. For over a century after his death, Spinoza was excluded from respectable circles, either abhorred or ignored . . . His influence, though already penetrating, remained marginal and half-underground . . .
>
> It was only in late eighteenth century Germany that Spinoza emerged into prominence, both among poet-philosophers like Goethe, Lessing, and later Heine, and within major trends of post-Kantian philosophy from Fichte to Hegel and beyond . . . [I]t is no accident that some of the most unorthodox and innovative minds in the last two centuries . . . have either been what may we may call root-Spinozoists, or operated, as Freud defined it, within Spinoza's 'climate of ideas.'[1]

---

1. Yovel, *Adventures of Immanence*, ix–xi. See also Yovel, *Marrano of Reason*, x ("Since the late eighteenth century, Spinoza's philosophy of immanence has tacitly or expressly penetrated the major currents of modern thought and has helped to shape the modern mind far beyond what is usually recognized . . . [M]uch of the history of modern thought can be retold—and illuminated—from the standpoint of Spinoza's immanent revolution."); ch. 9, sec. F. See generally Schwartz, *First Modern Jew*,

CHAPTER 13.

A. Nineteenth-Century Positivists, Empiricists, Materialists, Evolutionists, and Liberals Reject Belief in an Afterlife as Scientifically Unfounded

Most nineteenth-century philosophers, however different, shared the belief that an objective knowledge of man is attainable by applying the methods of empirical science to the study of social and psychological processes. They were frequently optimists and meliorists who looked forward to the steady improvement in the well-being of mankind. Such thinkers "were convinced that scientific knowledge, which they conceived of in the broadest sense as an empirical method, could be brought to bear on the solution of grave social problems."[2] Interest in social problems resulted in the application of science to the study of society and human mentality. Thus, the sciences of sociology and psychology were born. People lacking despair in this life have less reason to focus on another, so these nineteenth-century philosophers frequently rejected belief in any afterlife—"it was in this world, not in the next, they held, that man lived and moved and had his being."[3]

Wladyslaw Tatarkiewicz supports this historical understanding. He characterizes nineteenth-century philosophy, after 1830, as minimalistic. He asserts that this type of philosophy "recognizes only the minima, only such theses as phenomenalism, empiricism, subjectivism, utilitarianism."[4] He writes:

> Auguste Comte's *Course of Positive Philosophy* [in France] and J.S. Mill's *The System of Logic* [in England] initiated the new period [of minimalism] in both countries. These two books were the philosophical foundations of the epoch. The next generation laid a third foundation—Herbert Spencer's *Synthetic Philosophy*.
>
> French positivism from the fourth decade of the nineteenth century, English empiricism from the fifth, and evolutionism from the sixth together created a minimalistic philosophy that became the authoritative mode of thinking in almost all of Europe. It drew from all three sources, but it most frequently took its name from Comte and called itself 'positivism.' The middle of the century (1830-1860) was the period of its formulation and the end of the century (1860-1900) the time of its predominance.
>
> ... [O]ne view was proclaimed from all sides: we acquire knowledge through the senses and only through the senses. The only source of knowledge

---

55–56 (Ludwig Philippson "was the sole Jew to pay written tribute to Spinoza in 1832 [the bicentennial of Spinoza's birth]. The rest of the 1830s and 1840s, however, witnessed continued signs of a reentry of Spinoza into Jewish consciousness ... Two individuals within this early group of Spinoza admirers [were] ... the poet Heinrich Heine (1799-1856) and the pioneering German socialist later turned pioneering Jewish nationalist Moses Hess (1812-1875).").

2. Jones, *History of Western Philosophy*, 4:162.
3. Jones, *History of Western Philosophy*, 4:160.
4. Tatarkiewicz, *Nineteenth Century Philosophy*, 6.

is experience; the only method of science is induction; the only objects of inquiry are facts. No absolutes, no metaphysics, are allowed, for these produce errors and insanity...

This was the leading doctrine of the nineteenth century. It was characterized by intellectualism, indifference to metaphysics, and naturalism.[5]

1. The father of positivism is Auguste Comte

The major work of Auguste Comte, *Course of the Positive Philosophy*, presents his theory and methods of sociology and lays out a plan for the ideal human society. The first volume of this work presents Comte's "law of three stages" which asserts that each branch of human knowledge "passes successively through three different theoretical conditions: the Theological, or fictitious; the Metaphysical, or abstract; and the Scientific, or positive. In other words, the human mind, by its nature, employs in its progress three methods of philosophizing, the character of which is essentially different, and even radically opposed: viz., the theological method, the metaphysical, and the positive."[6] In man's first stage of development, the theological method is used; this method "supposes all phenomena to be produced by the immediate action of supernatural beings."[7] In the second, metaphysical, stage of development, "the mind supposes, instead of supernatural beings, abstract forces, veritable entities (that is, personified abstractions) inherent in all beings, and capable of producing all phenomena."[8] And "in the final, the positive state, the mind has given over the vain search after Absolute notions, the origin and destination of the universe, and the causes of phenomena, and applies itself to the study of their laws—that is, their invariable relations of succession and resemblance. Reasoning and observation, duly combined, are the means of this knowledge."[9]

---

5. Tatarkiewicz, *Nineteenth Century Philosophy*, 7–8.
6. Comte, *Course of the Positive Philosophy*, 124.
7. Comte, *Course of the Positive Philosophy*, 125.
8. Comte, *Course of the Positive Philosophy*, 125.
9. Comte, *Course of the Positive Philosophy*, 125 (emphasis original). See also Jones, *History of Western Philosophy*, 4:175 ("In the first stage, or *theological* phase, causal explanation is based on the idea of volition. This level was reached in physics when, for instance, thunder and lightning were attributed to Zeus's desire to frighten lesser gods and men. The second, or *metaphysical* phase, marks a distinct advance. Crude anthropomorphism is replaced by causal explanation based on abstract concepts. This was the level reached in physics when causes were 'taken to be abstract forces...'—when, that is, men believed that entelechies and vital forces caused stones to seek the center of the earth and acorns to grow up into oaks. The third and final stage, or *scientific* phase, is reached when the attempt to explain is abandoned for the attempt to describe. This stage was reached in physics when Galileo said it was his 'purpose merely to investigate... some of the properties of accelerated motion, whatever the cause of this acceleration may be.'"); Tatarkiewicz, *Nineteenth Century Philosophy*, 21–22; Aiken, *Age of Ideology*, 118–20.

Thus, in the scientific or positive stage of human development, the mind resists all attempts to go beyond the facts.[10] The objective of investigation becomes only "to discover the laws of phenomena," not to seek "causes, whether first or final."[11] According to Comte, the scientific or positive stage began "when the human mind was astir under the precepts of Bacon, the conceptions of Descartes, and the discoveries of Galileo."[12] However, not all branches of knowledge develop at the same rate; so, while Comte believed that astronomical, physical, chemical, and physiological categories of knowledge had entered the third stage of development, "social physics" had not.[13] Accordingly, it was his principal aim to establish a positive approach to social phenomena.[14]

Giving full allegiance to the scientific method, Comte was radically opposed to "mythical thinking," which he associated with traditional religion. As Comte saw it, traditional religion required the acceptance of unscientific beliefs and directed one's energies "away from the problems of individual and collective being '*in this world*' . . . In its place he sought to substitute the new religious ideal of a progressively enlightened humanity unselfishly dedicated to principles of service and love."[15] He, as many others in France and England, aspired to a completely humanistic culture, securely based on the foundation of modern science. For such people, belief in an immortal, immaterial soul, and belief in an afterlife of any kind, was an anathema.[16] Comte himself regarded the concept of "soul," as well as the concept of "matter," as a metaphysical fiction.[17]

---

10. See Tatarkiewicz, *Nineteenth Century Philosophy*, 22 ("The razor of positivistic philosophy was turned against all efforts to go beyond facts, in particular against searching for the causes of facts that lie beyond the facts themselves . . . The true task of science is to elaborate and establish fixed relationships between facts, in other words, to establish laws."); Aiken, *Age of Ideology*, 120 (At the positive stage, explanation "is conceived solely in terms of empirical hypotheses or laws which describe the constant relations which hold among classes of observable phenomena."); Miller, *Psychology*, 10–11(Comte limited himself "strictly to facts whose truth was unquestionable, whose validity was insured by the recognized methods of science . . . Any speculation about transcendental powers, hidden essences, or ultimate causes is dismissed as sophistry and illusion . . . A positive philosophy accepts as real only those things that can be known.").

11. Comte, *Course of the Positive Philosophy*, 127–28.

12. Comte, *Course of the Positive Philosophy*, 129.

13. Comte, *Course of the Positive Philosophy*, 130.

14. Comte, *Course of the Positive Philosophy*, 130. See also Tatarkiewicz, *Nineteenth Century Philosophy*, 24 (Comte identified six abstract sciences, sciences that "deal with general laws governing the elementary facts of nature"—mathematics, astronomy, physics, chemistry, biology and sociology. "In Comte's time the first five of these sciences were already formed and developed. Only the sixth, sociology, did not yet exist. Nevertheless, Comte postulated it . . .").

15. Aiken, *Age of Ideology*, 122–23 (emphasis added).

16. See generally Aiken, *Age of Ideology*, 122 (For Comte "there are, at bottom, only two basic sciences of human behavior, physiology and sociology. Any third discipline which purports to deal with some special 'psychical' phenomena [he] regards as pure mythology.").

17. Tatarkiewicz, *Nineteenth Century Philosophy*, 25 ("matter," conceived as the cause of phenomena, is incapable of being the object of experience, and, thus, is "the same kind of metaphysical fiction

2. John Stuart Mill, an empiricist and utilitarian, contends that happiness is attainable in this life, and that belief in human immortality is not grounded on scientific arguments

One of the first Englishmen to appreciate the importance of Comte's philosophy was John Stuart Mill.[18] Mill studied Comte and wrote a book discussing Comte's views entitled *Auguste Comte and Positivism* (1865). Comte's positivism complemented Mill's own empiricism, and Mill helped to link positivism with English empiricism. Mill was no less troubled by the concepts of matter and soul than was Comte. According to Mill's view, which is sometimes called phenomenalism,

> every statement of fact is, in principle, reducible to a conjunction of statements about actual or possible sense-impressions. And, on this view, there is no term of reference which does not designate some potentially experienceable item of sensation or feeling. What we call 'matter' is merely one system of uniformities among sensations, and what we call 'mind' is another. In referring, therefore, to the human mind, we are not talking about some immaterial substance that lies behind the world of sense, but only, as Hume put it, about a 'bundle of impressions.'[19]

Continuing the critique of "substance" begun by Locke and Hume, Mill asserted that the terms "mind" and "soul" served only to stress the permanence of internal sensations, just as the terms "matter" and "substance" stressed the permanence of our external sensations.[20]

Mill also shared Comte's emphasis on improving conditions in this life rather than concerning oneself with any afterlife. Mill advocated the ethical doctrine of utilitarianism. This doctrine "accepts as the foundation of morals 'utility' or the 'greatest happiness principle' [and] holds that actions are right in proportion as they tend to promote happiness; wrong as they tend to produce the reverse of happiness. By happiness is intended pleasure and the absence of pain; by unhappiness, pain and the privation of pleasure."[21] In his book *Utilitarianism* (1863), Mill contended that, unless denied the liberty to use resources at their disposal, people could all find happiness in this life so long as they escaped what he called "the positive evils of life" such as disease and poverty, and that these positive evils could themselves be largely overcome by

---

as 'soul.'").

18. See generally Merz, *History of European Thought*, 1:18–19 ("the philosophy of Auguste Comte, published between the years 1830 and 1840, remained without much influence in his own country, whereas, mainly through the writings of J.S. Mill and his school, it became, as it were, a centre of thought, an embodiment of a circle of modern ideas in [England], whence it was riposted into France nearly a generation after its first appearance.").

19. Aiken, *Age of Ideology*, 145.
20. Tatarkiewicz, *Nineteenth Century Philosophy*, 40.
21. Mill, *Utilitarianism*, 10.

advances in science and improvements in social arrangements and institutions.[22] In *On Liberty* (1859) he argued that what is most needed for enlightenment and happiness is liberty, and he voiced opposition to legal requirements obligating people to profess belief in God and in an afterlife.[23]

Mill's *Three Essays on Religion* was published posthumously. In the essay "Utility of Religion," Mill acknowledges that an advantage of what he calls "supernatural religions" over what he calls the "Religion of Humanity," which he prefers,[24] is the former's hope of "a life after death."[25] Nevertheless, he contended that "as the condition of mankind becomes improved, as [people] grow happier in their lives, and more capable of deriving happiness from unselfish sources, they will care less and less for [the expectation of an afterlife]."[26] In the essay "Theism," Mill addresses the issue of the soul's immortality. He divides arguments supporting immortality in two classes: "Those which are independent of any theory respecting the Creator and his intentions, and those which depend upon an antecedent belief on the subject."[27] The first class of arguments for immortality are dismissed by Mill as being premised on a false belief that the thinking principle in man constitutes a simple substance, distinct from the body, which is not susceptible of dissolution. In fact, the thinking principle in man, as Mill and other "moderns" see it, is not a separate substance at all, and thinking cannot be separated from bodily operations.[28] With regard to the second class of arguments in support of the immortality of the soul, Mill contends that the existence of a Creator is supported by no more than a "preponderance of probability" and that of his benevolence there is "a considerably less preponderance."[29] Nevertheless, assuming the truth of these premises, Mill concludes that, apart from revelation, no inference may be drawn from them supporting a future life.[30]

---

22. Mill, *Utilitarianism*, 19–20.

23. See Mill, *On Liberty*, 42–43.

24. The "Religion of Humanity" is based upon the strong and earnest direction of human emotions and desires toward the improvement of the human species. See Mill, *Three Essays on Religion*, 106–9.

25. See Mill, *Three Essays on Religion*, 118 ("One advantage . . . the supernatural religions must always possess over the Religion of Humanity; the prospect they hold out to the individual of a life after death."), 104 ("In that other life each hopes to find the good which he has failed to find on earth, or the better which is suggested to him by the good which on earth he has partially seen and known . . . So long as earthly life is full of sufferings, so long there will be need of consolations, which the hope of heaven affords to the selfish, the love of God to the tender and grateful. The value, therefore, of religion to the individual . . . as a source of personal satisfaction and of elevated feelings, is not to be disputed.").

26. Mill, *Three Essays on Religion*, 118. See also Mill, *Three Essays on Religion*, 118–22.

27. Mill, *Three Essays on Religion*, 196. See Edwards, *Immortality*, 172–76 (containing relevant excerpts from "Theism").

28. Mill, *Three Essays on Religion*, 196–203.

29. Mill, *Three Essays on Religion*, 208.

30. Mill, *Three Essays on Religion*, 208–11.

3. Herbert Spencer combined positivism, empiricism, and materialism with evolutionism

The leading concept of the philosophy of Herbert Spencer is evolution, or development. As Tatarkiewicz explains, "This concept [first introduced in *The Developmental Hypothesis*, published in 1852] contains three ideas: (1) that matter is subject to development; it is changeable; (2) that its changes take place continually and by stages; and (3) that changes take place in one direction, according to one law . . . that development is the universal law of the world. The name evolutionism was applied to this position."[31]

Spencer was a materialist:

> He understood the world mechanistically, according to the functions of matter, movement, and forces. In particular, he understood evolution in this way. He reinterpreted biology according to the action of mechanical forces. He believed that the phenomena of life, the mind, and the social order develop in the same way mechanical structures do . . . He saw mechanical process in every kind of development: this was the most characteristic feature of the evolutionism he created and passed on to the nineteenth century.[32]

Thus, Spencer described biological and psychological phenomena in mechanistic terms. There was no need to resort to the metaphysical concept of the soul to explain life, or mental activity. Not surprisingly, there is no mention in Spencer's work of an immortal soul or of an afterlife as these are outside the bounds of what is scientifically knowable. Put differently, Spencer "regards all positive knowledge as limited to phenomena appearing in space and time."[33]

Evolutionism, already encompassing materialism, allied itself with positivism and empiricism, forming an amalgam that Tatarkiewicz says "created a certain common view for people of this epoch [that] is most frequently called 'positivism,' in the broad and popular meaning of this term," but is more correctly termed "scientism."[34] Scientism "had thousands of representatives in various countries."[35] Typical of these

---

31. Tatarkiewicz, *Nineteenth Century Philosophy*, 99.

32. Tatarkiewicz, *Nineteenth Century Philosophy*, 100–1.

33. Aiken, *Age of Ideology*, 164.

34. Tatarkiewicz, *Nineteenth Century Philosophy*, 106–7. See Jones, *History of Western Philosophy*, 4:162 ("the theory of evolution . . . seemed to show that man is a part of nature and is thus subject to its laws. Indeed, the new triumphs of biology led to a rather facile belief in science and its 'iron laws,' and to an assumption on the part of some thinkers that science provides simple, straightforward answers to all philosophical problems. This point of view, which may be described as 'scientism,' became increasingly dominant in the second half of the nineteenth century."), 199 (identification of current scientific theories with truth may be called scientism). See also Tatarkiewicz, *Nineteenth Century Philosophy*, 106 ("The evolutionists conducted many debates with the empiricists of Mill's school and the positivists of Comte's school. For the most part, however, these were family quarrels; in most cases, the groups formed a common front. Positivism . . . arose from the union of their doctrines.").

35. Tatarkiewicz, *Nineteenth Century Philosophy*, 107.

men was Karl Pearson, whose most influential work is *The Grammar of Science* (1892), "a fully developed statement of the version of science commonly accepted at the end of the nineteenth century."[36] As expressed by Pearson, one of the goals of science "is to eliminate all unfounded judgments appealing to faith rather than knowledge"[37] which unfounded judgments presumably included those concerning an immortal soul and an afterlife.

B. Advances in Nineteenth-Century Empirical Psychology and in Biology Lead to the Adoption of a Psycho-Physical View of Nature and the Abandonment of the Concept of Soul by Psychologists and Biologists

In the eighteenth century, psychology, as the science of the mind, separated from biology, as the science of life, due to the fading of an Aristotelian conception of the soul.[38] Furthermore, eighteenth-century philosophy distinguished two kinds of psychology, or rather two ways of acquiring knowledge on matters connected with the new Cartesian conception of the soul or mind: rational psychology and empirical psychology.[39] As Merz explains:

> Empirical psychology dealt with detailed facts and phenomena in the life of the soul [that is, it dealt with science], rational psychology dealt with questions of principle and with fundamentals [that is, it dealt with metaphysics]. Whilst in Germany, up to the beginning of the nineteenth century, little methodical work was done in empirical psychology, English, and notably Scotch, thinkers had devoted themselves almost exclusively to the cultivation of this field.[40]

---

36. Tatarkiewicz, *Nineteenth Century Philosophy*, 107.

37. Tatarkiewicz, *Nineteenth Century Philosophy*, 108.

38. See Hatfield, "Psychology," 243; Vidal, *Sciences of the Soul*, 74 (The rejection of teleological explanations and animism helped to foster the empirical study of human beings as machines. While the notion of a soul persisted, the study of the soul *in its relationship to the body* came to be seen as part of physics, not metaphysics, and "psychology" became increasingly associated with "an empirical investigation of the rational soul united with the body.").

39. See Merz, *History of European Thought*, 3:200.

40. Merz, *History of European Thought*, 3:202. But see Hatfield, "Psychology," 246 ("Abel, Schmid, and other philosophical psychologists in late eighteenth-century Germany insisted that the cognitive faculties of the mind can be studied empirically.").

1. Bell and Müller help change the old, metaphysical, or rational psychology to a new, empirical psychology—psychology as a laboratory science, or psychology without a soul

The study of the interaction of the mind and body by scientific methods came to be variously designated by the terms "physiological psychology," "mental physiology," "psycho-physiology," or "physiology of the soul."[41] The eighteenth century saw the initiation of isolated researches of an experimental or mathematical nature regarding this mind/body interaction but on the whole little progress was made; however, "the end of the eighteenth and the beginning of the following century brought several important discoveries."[42]

One such discovery was by the Scottish surgeon, anatomist, and physiologist Charles Bell.[43] Bell published the results of his detailed studies of the nervous system in 1811 in his privately circulated book *An Idea of a New Anatomy of the Brain*.[44] As discussed in this work, Bell's research of the brain evidenced an "anatomical difference between the anterior and posterior roots of the nerves of the spine."[45] This helped lead to the distinction between sensory and motor nerves: "the anterior nerves of the spine are employed to carry the nervous stimulus outward to the different organs (efferent or motor nerves), the posterior and better protected nerves serving to carry the peripheral stimuli of the senses inward to the nervous centres (sensory or afferent nerves)."[46] Bell's work also described distinct regions of the brain and relations between the nervous system and the brain.[47]

Shortly after *An Idea of a New Anatomy of the Brain* was written, Johannes Müller, a German physiologist, introduced the doctrine of the "specific energies," which also concerns the action of the sensory nervous apparatus, namely,

---

41. Merz, *History of European Thought*, 2:469n1.

42. Merz, *History of European Thought*, 2:473–74.

43. See generally Miller, *Psychology*, 175–76 (Beginning in the eighteenth century "a brilliant array of men—philosophers, physicians, natural scientists—contributed to the growing knowledge about the structure and function of the nervous system. The most significant step forward was probably the discovery, early in the nineteenth century, that the nerves attached to the spinal cord had a clear division of function. Sir Charles Bell in England and Francois Magendie in France were able to show that the nerves entering the back side of the spinal cord were important for sensory processes, and nerves entering the front side were important for muscular movements.").

44. A reprint of Bell's work, together with excerpts from related letters he wrote to his brother between the years 1807 and 1821, appeared in the *Journal of Anatomy and Physiology* of November 1868. Bell explained his task by stating: "I have found some of my friends so mistaken in their conception of the object of the demonstrations which I have delivered in my lectures, that I wish to vindicate myself at all hazards. They would have it that I am in search of the seat of the soul; but I wish only to investigate the structure of the brain, as we examine the structure of the eye and ear" (Bell, "Idea of a New Anatomy of the Brain," 153.

45. Merz, *History of European Thought*, 2:481.

46. Merz, *History of European Thought*, 2:481–82.

47. Bell, "Idea of a New Anatomy of the Brain," 154.

'that by the stimulus of any single nerve-fibre, only such sensations can be produced as belong to the qualitative—or order—region of one definite sense, and that every stimulus which can at all affect this nerve fibre produces only sensations belonging to this definite order.' This means that, for instance, any effective stimulus of the optic nerve apparatus produces only and always the sensation of light, whereas the same stimulus would in the auditory nerve apparatus, if effective, produce the sensation of sound.[48]

Müller's *magnum opus, Handbuch der Physiologie des Menschen,* appeared between 1833 and 1840, and, translated into English as *Elements of Physiology,* was published in London between 1837 and 1843. The book became the leading textbook in physiology for much of the nineteenth century.

Following in the wake of physiologists such as Bell and Müller the discipline of psychology as "the study of the mind" was born.[49] By the end of the nineteenth century a "new psychology"—"psychology as a laboratory science"—developed out of "the old, metaphysical psychology."[50] Ultimately, a psycho-physical view of human beings was accepted by both German and English psychologists. It is this common understanding of human beings as psycho-physical unities (instead of composites of body and soul) that leads to the abandonment of the concept of soul by those engaged in the new science of psychology. As explained by Hatfield, by the end of the nineteenth century, most authorities "considered psychology to be a natural science, which meant ceasing to talk of 'the mind' as its subject matter, or perhaps regarding 'mind' as a natural activity of the organism . . . The new psychology was, in Lange's oft-repeated phrase, a 'psychology without a soul.'"[51]

2. William James explicitly abandons the idea of soul

William James was primarily a psychologist but in later life was also "the recognized leader of American philosophy."[52] His *Principles of Psychology* (1890) "was a

48. Merz, *History of European Thought,* 2:482–83 (quoting Helmholtz, *Handbuch der Physiologischen Optik,* 233). See Hatfield, "Psychology," 253–54 (discussing Müller and describing his law of specific nerve energies). See generally Merz, *History of European Thought,* 2:485–92 (discussing Helmholtz and "his two great treatises on the psycho-physics of the Eye and the Ear, of Vision and of Music").

49. See Hatfield, "Psychology: Old and New," 93 ("Psychology as the study of mind was an established subject throughout the nineteenth century in Britain, Germany, France, and the United States.").

50. Hatfield, "Psychology: Old and New," 94. According to Hatfield: "During the period from 1870 to 1914 the existing discipline of psychology was transformed . . . In Germany and the United States a tradition of psychology as a laboratory science soon developed, which is called a 'new psychology' by contrast with the old, metaphysical psychology . . ." (Hatfield, "Psychology: Old and New," 94).

51. Hatfield, "Psychology: Old and New," 103–4.

52. Russell, *History of Western Philosophy,* 811. See Jones, *History of Western Philosophy,* 4:296 ("James was primarily a psychologist—a truly original one—and an advocate and preacher—an

pioneering work that greatly influenced the development of the science; his popular lectures made him the best-known philosopher of time."[53] The first volume of James's *Principles of Psychology* contains a discussion of the soul in which he concludes that the word "soul" should be discarded from psychology since it is superfluous for scientific purposes. He writes:

> [The] substantialist view of the soul was essentially the view of Plato and of Aristotle. It received its completely formal elaboration in the middle ages. It was believed by Hobbes, Descartes, Lock, Leibnitz, Wolf, Berkeley, and is now defended by the entire modern dualistic or spiritualistic or common-sense school...
>
> *My final conclusion, then, about the substantial Soul is that it explains nothing and guarantees nothing.* Its successive thoughts are the only intelligible and verifiable things about it, and definitely to ascertain the correlations of these brain-processes is much as psychology can empirically do... *I therefore feel entirely free to discard the word Soul from the rest of this book.* If I ever use it, it will be in the vaguest and most popular way. The reader who finds any comfort in the idea of the Soul, is, however, perfectly free to continue to believe in it; for our reasonings have not established the nonexistence of the Soul; they have only proved its superfluity for scientific purposes.[54]

Nearly fifteen years after publication of the *Principles of Psychology*, James addressed the concept of consciousness in an article entitled "Does 'Consciousness' Exist?," published in 1904 in the *Journal of Philosophy, Psychology and Scientific Methods*. Here, James suggests that while the concept of a soul had been "undermined," the concept of consciousness was still being used to refer to a "spiritual principle."[55] James argues that the time had come to assert that consciousness "does not denote a special stuff or way of being."[56] As explained by Bertrand Russell: "What [James] is denying might be put crudely as the view that consciousness is a 'thing.' He holds that there is

---

immensely persuasive one. He was also a philosopher."). For a summary of James's life, thought, and place in the development of psychology, see Miller, *Psychology*, 60–78.

53. Jones, *History of Western Philosophy*, 4:296n1. See generally Perry, *Thought and Character of William James*, 181–99 ("The *Principles of Psychology*... was widely read.").

54. James, *Principles of Psychology*, 178, 182–83 (emphasis original). But in the Ingersoll Lecture that James gave in 1898 entitled "Human Immortality: Two Supposed Objections to the Doctrine," he argued that "even though our soul's life... may be in literal strictness the function of a brain that perishes, yet it is not at all impossible... that the life may still continue when the brain itself is dead" (James, "Ingersoll Lecture," 284).

55. James, "Does 'Consciousness' Exist?," 207–8.

56. James, "Does 'Consciousness' Exist?," 216. See James, "Does 'Consciousness' Exist?," 207–8. Despite arguing that thought is a function of the brain, James also contends that immortality is not incompatible "with the brain-function theory of our present mundane consciousness" (James, "Ingersoll Lecture," 282–91). See also Perry, *Thought and Character of William James*, 267–68 ("He was concerned to defend the theoretical possibility of immortality," but he himself "was never 'keen'" on the belief until 1904 when he "acquired a feeling of its 'probability.'").

'only one primal stuff or material,' out of which everything in the world is composed. This stuff he calls 'pure experience'... He defines 'pure experience' as 'the immediate flux of life which furnishes the material to our later reflection.' *It will be seen that this doctrine abolishes the distinction between mind and matter, if regarded as a distinction between two different kinds of what James calls 'stuff.'*"[57] The affinity between James's position (which came to be termed "neutral monism") and the position of Spinoza should be readily apparent.[58] Thus, while James may not have referred to Spinoza or directly relied on Spinoza, James (and the adherents of neutral monism) are certainly heirs of Spinoza.

James prepared the way for an American approach to psychology that is called functionalism. Indeed, James's *Principles of Psychology* has been called a classic statement of the functionalist point of view. However, it was John Dewey and others at the University of Chicago and at Columbia University who fully developed the functionalist approach.[59] Functionalists emphasized that behavior and mental processes are adaptive—they enable an individual to adjust to a changing environment. Thus, they sought to study the adaptive functions of behavior and mental processes, not merely their structure. To study functions, the functionalists extended experimental methods to include not only the method of introspection (which was limited to the description and analysis of sensory experience) but also the observation of behavior—what a person does.[60]

3. The science of biology supported psychology's abandonment of the concept of soul

In the same way that the new science of psychology abandoned reliance on the concept of soul to explain mental activity, biologists in the nineteenth century abandoned the concept of soul to explain the phenomenon of life itself. The

> complex phenomenon in the higher organisms was analysed into various mechanical and physical processes, each connected with some well-defined organ which was more and more recognized as possessing the properties of a physical apparatus. A great deal of the work of the numerous members of

---

57. Russell, *History of Western Philosophy*, 812–13 (emphasis added).

58. See e.g., Kim, *Philosophy of Mind*, 96 ("A modern form of [Spinoza's] approach is known as neutral monism, according to which the fundamental reality is neutral in the sense that it is intrinsically neither physical nor mental.").

59. See generally Miller, *Psychology*, 65–67.

60. See generally Miller, *Psychology*, 65–67 ("By broadening the definition of psychology, the American functionalists ... were able to supplement introspection by other methods of collecting data ... By the time of Wundt's death in 1920 the purely introspective, experimental science he founded in Leipzig was merely a small part of, and had been overshadowed by, the larger and more pragmatic American science of psychology. Ten years later the victory of the functional psychologists was complete. In the U.S. today functional psychology *is* psychology"; emphasis original).

this school consisted in unraveling with the microscope the structure of such organic apparatus, and studying its action by physical measurements and experiments... One of the immediate consequences of these varied researches—all tending to show how the conception formerly established in chemistry, physics and dynamics could be utilized in the description of the phenomena of living matter, how the complex phenomenon of life could be split up into a number of separate chemical and physical processes, which could be imitated in the laboratory, and how the living organism could be analysed into a complex of separate apparatus or machines, acting on intelligible mechanical and physical principles—was a radical change in the conception of vital force and the vital principle. It ceased in the opinion of many to be opposed to other nonliving forces...; according to others it was nonexistent, or at all events useless... A popular philosophy... promulgated the notion that science had succeeded in banishing all spiritual entities, and was able to explain everything on purely mechanical principles. Vitalism and animism were at an end; there only remained mechanism and materialism.[61]

Representative of the materialism of those biologists who abandoned the notion that a vital force, or soul, is responsible for life is Ernst Haeckel, a biologist who taught at the University of Jena. Haeckel's views are reminiscent of those of Spinoza in that Haeckel was a monist who denied the existence of "the various nonmaterial substances—minds, souls, and so on—of traditional philosophy."[62] As Jones comments, "Haeckel believed that science had indubitably proved that 'the universe, or the cosmos, is eternal, infinite, and illimitable, [and that] its substance, with its two attributes (matter and energy), fills infinite space, and is in eternal motion...'"[63] Haeckel was one of the many scientists who came to believe that life could be explained in strictly physico-chemical terms. This view was given added support by the work of Charles Darwin.

---

61. Merz, *History of European Thought*, 2:397–99. Cf. Merz, *History of European Thought*, 2:400–2 ("It seemed time to abandon the familiar conception of a special vital force, and to hand over physiological problems likewise to the physicist, the chemist, and the microscopist...; and an impression was created in the minds of thinking outsiders that a purely mechanical explanation of life and mind was finally decided on, and within possible reach... Among those who assisted in bringing about this impression, I need only single out two names—those of Hermann Lotze... and of Emil Du Bois-Reymond... Both agreed in denouncing the conception of a vital force... as illogical, and moreover as scientifically useless."). But see Jones, *History of Western Philosophy*, 4:201 ("Such mechanistic solutions to life's 'riddles' were attacked by another school of metaphysician-scientists called vitalists. These thinkers held life to be *sui generis* and inexplicable in terms of physical and chemical laws... Representative of this version of scientism was Hans Driesch [1867-1941]"; according to Driesch, an organism "differs from a machine because it operates as a whole, as an individual; hence it cannot be explained mechanistically."). See generally Merz, *History of European Thought*, 2:368–464 (discussing vitalistic view of nature).

62. Jones, *History of Western Philosophy*, 4:199.

63. Jones, *History of Western Philosophy*, 4:199 (quoting Haeckel).

Hans Reichenbach, writing in 1951 and alluding to the work of nineteenth-century molecular biologists and their successors, explained that the move from teleology to causality resulted in the rejection of the concept of soul:

> Compared with the blind functioning of the inorganic world . . . the activities of living organisms appear to be controlled by a plan, to be directed toward a certain purpose. The inorganic world is controlled by the laws of cause and effect . . .
>
> It was the great discovery of Charles Darwin that the apparent teleology of living organisms can be explained in a similar way by a combination of chance and selection . . .
>
> The problem of life does not involve contradictions to the principles of an empiricist philosophy—such is the result of the biology of the nineteenth century. Life can be explained along with all other natural phenomena, and biology requires no principles that violate the laws of physics. The apparent teleology of living organisms is reducible to causality. Life does not call for the existence of an immaterial substance, a *vital force*, an *entelechy*, or whatever names have been proposed for such a supernatural entity.[64]

C. Philosophers, Psychologists, and Neuroscientists in the Twentieth and Twenty-First Centuries Continue to Mostly Reject or Ignore the Ideas of a Soul, Resurrection, and an Afterlife

The concept of soul fared no better among philosophers and psychologists in the twentieth century than it had in the nineteenth. Among psychologists, early in the twentieth century John B. Watson advocated an approach to the study of human behavior that eliminated any need for introspection of mental states or consideration of any nonphysical things such as the soul or even consciousness. His approach, called behaviorism, became near universally accepted. Philosophers in the twentieth century similarly rejected notions of a soul or an afterlife. The second half of the twentieth century witnessed the virtual abandonment by philosophers of all talk of a soul or of resurrection. Recent works of relevance published in the twenty-first century are those by Owen Flanagan and Antonio Damasio.

---

64. Reichenbach, *Rise of Scientific Philosophy*, 192–202. See generally Merz, *History of European Thought*, 2:416–42 (discussing nineteenth-century biological theories of the cell, of metabolism, and natural selection, and stating that Theodor Schwann "not only conceived the cell to be the morphological unit of all living matter, but he also saw that 'cell formation must be the general principle of organic development, and that there can be only one such principle.' In the third section of his 'Microscopical Researches' [1839] he . . . 'rejects . . . all teleological explanations based upon a vital force acting according to final purposes.' He thus showed 'that the only essential property of all living matter—viz., growth—is not inaccessible to a physical explanation.'").

1. In the first half of the twentieth century, Dewey, the logical positivists, and Ryle all reject the idea of a soul and of an afterlife

In America, early in the century, John Dewey was an exponent of pragmatism, a point of view allied with positivism and empiricism. Dewey opposed the notion that truth is fixed, final, eternal, and divorced from experience, and supported the notion that truth is concrete, specific, changing, and tied to the scientific method. Accordingly, Dewey rejected any notion of a supernatural, eternal, immaterial world, any heavenly realm beyond human experience, or any immortal soul. He believed that one should not wait for some supernatural being to alleviate evil conditions that exist in the world; nor wait for an afterlife in which the evil conditions wouldn't exist. Rather, one should use intelligence to ameliorate whatever adversity is confronted.[65]

In Europe, philosophers in the first half of the twentieth century wed positivism with logical analysis, developing a point of view that came to be called logical positivism. The logical positivists, such as A. J. Ayer and Hans Reichenbach, maintained that metaphysical statements, including those concerning an immortal soul or an afterlife, are "meaningless."[66] Gilbert Ryle used philosophical analysis to argue that the traditional conception of human beings as composed of a body and a soul is based on a logical error that he called a "category mistake."[67]

2. Philosophers in the late twentieth and early twenty-first centuries continue to reject substance dualism and immortality

Since Ryle's *Concept of Mind* (1949) philosophers have focused on the concept of "mind" to a great extent, and it has become a main area of philosophical attention, an area called "the philosophy of mind." All talk of a soul has been virtually abandoned. The only relevant concept is that of a mind. The issues which are subsumed within the philosophy of mind include:

1. What is it to be a creature with a mind, or what exactly are mental phenomena as opposed to physical phenomena?
2. What kinds of mental phenomena, or mental states, are there?
3. What is the relation between mental and physical phenomena, between minds and bodies, and how can mental states or events have physical effects, and vice versa?
4. What is consciousness?

---

65. See generally Dewey, *Reconstruction in Philosophy*, 287–346; Dewey, *Liberalism and Social Action*, 50–55, Dewey, *Common Faith*, 77–78.

66. See e.g., Ayer, *Language, Truth and Logic*, 31, 115, 117; Reichenbach, *Rise of Scientific Philosophy*, 252–72.

67. See Ryle, *Concept of Mind*, 11–22.

While a full discussion of what philosophers specializing in the philosophy of mind have contended since 1949 is well beyond our present scope, some key points are very relevant.[68] First and foremost,

> materialism, or physicalism, broadly understood is the basic framework in which contemporary philosophy of mind has been debated . . . Materialism is the doctrine that all things that exist in the world are bits of matter or aggregates of bits of matter. There is no thing that isn't material—no transcendental beings . . . or immaterial minds. Physicalism is the contemporary successor to materialism. The thought is that the traditional notion of material stuff [is] ill-suited to what we now know about the material world from contemporary physics. For example, the concept of a 'field' is widely used in physics, but it is unclear whether fields would count as material things in the traditional sense. Physicalism is the doctrine that all things that exist are entities recognized by the science of physics, or systems aggregated out of such entities.[69]

This is to say that most contemporary philosophers of mind reject Cartesian substance dualism—they reject the idea that human beings are composite beings formed from the union of a material body and an immaterial mind or soul.[70] In particular, they reject the idea of immaterial minds or disembodied minds.[71] Rather than assuming that mental phenomena occur in an immaterial substance, whether called a mind or soul, it is now assumed that the body is the thing that does the thinking. This is essentially a Spinozistic idea.[72] In particular, philosophers such as J. J. C. Smart have argued that the mind is identical with the brain and that for a creature to have mental states, events, or processes is to have a brain with appropriate structure and capacities.[73] Indeed, "we now

---

68. For a good introduction to the philosophy of mind, see Kim, *Philosophy of Mind*.

69. Kim, *Philosophy of Mind*, 11.

70. See Kim, *Philosophy of Mind*, 13, 57 ("substance dualism has played a small role in contemporary philosophy of mind. Philosophical attention has focused instead on mental activities and functions—or mental events, states, and processes—and the mind-body problem has turned into the problem of understanding how these mental events, states, and processes are related to physical and biological events, states, and processes, or how mental or psychological capacities and functions are related to the nature of our physical structure and capacities."). See also Kim, *Philosophy of Mind*, 31–60 (discussing Cartesian substance dualism and comparing it to what contemporary philosophers call "property dualism").

71. See generally Edwards, *Immortality*, 46–53 (discussing challenges to the idea of a disembodied mind).

72. See Edwards, *Immortality*, 325 ("The eighteenth-century debate on whether matter can think took as its point of departure Locke's declaration that there was no contradiction in supposing that God could 'superadd to matter a faculty of thinking.' However, several decades before Locke, Spinoza had offered a similar suggestion. 'No one has hitherto laid down the limits of the body,' Spinoza had written, 'no one has yet been taught by experience what the body can accomplish solely by the laws of nature.'"). See also Edwards, *Immortality*, 38–42.

73. See Smart, "Sensations and Brain Processes," 142 ("It seems to me that science is increasingly giving us a viewpoint whereby organisms are able to be seen as physico-chemical mechanisms: it seems that even the behavior of man himself will one day be explicable in mechanistic terms. There

have overwhelming scientific evidence attesting to the centrality of the brain and its activities as determinants of our mental life."⁷⁴

Once it is accepted that the mind is identical with the brain belief in immortality is adversely impacted.⁷⁵ Edwards writes:

> The basic idea has been stated very clearly by Bertrand Russell. 'All the evidence goes to show,' Russell writes, 'that what we regard as our mental life is bound up with the brain structure and organized bodily energy.' At the same time we know that the brain is not immortal and that the organized energy of the living body becomes demobilized at death. Therefore, 'it is rational to suppose that mental life ceases when bodily life ceases.' . . . After learning something about the way in which thoughts and feelings depend on the brain, a great many people, including psychologists and brain physiologists, find the notion of disembodied mental states utterly fantastic.⁷⁶

Furthermore, if the mind-body dependence argument is valid, "it shows more than that a person's consciousness cannot exist without a *brain*; it shows that it cannot exist without the *current* brain, and this refutes reincarnation no less than the belief in the survival of the disembodied mind."⁷⁷

---

does seem to be, so far as science is concerned, nothing in the world but increasingly complex arrangements of physical constituents. All except for one place: in consciousness. That is, for a full description of what is going on in a man you would have to mention not only the physical processes in his tissue, glands, nervous system, and so forth, but also his states of consciousness: his visual, auditory, and tactual sensations, his aches and pains. That these should be correlated with brain processes does not help, for to say that they are correlated is to say that they are something 'over and above.' You cannot correlate something with itself. You correlate footprints with burglars, but not Bill Sikes the burglar with Bill Sikes the burglar. So sensations, states of consciousness, do seem to be the one sort of thing left outside the physicalist picture, and for various reasons I just cannot believe that this can be so. That everything should be explicable in terms of physics . . . except the occurrence of sensations seems to me to be frankly unbelievable."). See also Kim, *Philosophy of Mind*, 91–127 (discussing the psychoneural identity theory).

74. Kim, *Philosophy of Mind*, 92.

75. Edwards, "Dependence of Consciousness on the Brain," 294 ("'If parts of the mind depend for their existence upon parts of the brain, then the whole of the mind must so depend too. Hence the soul dies with the brain, which is to say it is mortal," quoting Colin McGinn).

76. Edwards, *Immortality*, 52. See also Edwards, *Reincarnation*, 292–307.

77. Edwards, *Immortality*, 19 (emphasis original). See generally Edwards, *Immortality*, 5–19, 317–19 (discussing reincarnation); Edwards, "Dependence of Consciousness on the Brain," 294 (the mind-body dependence argument "equally rules out reincarnation and the . . . replica-version of resurrectionism. If my mind is finished when my brain dies, then it cannot transmigrate to any other body. Similarly, if God created a duplicate [or replica] of my body containing a duplicate of my brain, *my* mind would not be able to make use of it since it stopped existing with the death of my original body"; emphasis original). For a discussion of resurrection, including what Edwards calls the "replica-version," see sec. C, 3. Edwards provides a full critique of the evidence in favor of reincarnation in his book *Reincarnation*.

CHAPTER 13.

3. Belief in bodily resurrection is ridiculed by most philosophers, and finds support only for theological reasons

Bodily resurrection has nothing to do with the philosophy of mind and is not generally addressed by contemporary philosophers standing outside of a theological tradition. It is, however, addressed by Paul Edwards.[78] Edwards distinguishes between "resurrection in a literal sense" and what he refers to as the "replica version" of resurrection. He notes that "the leading Christian existentialists, Rudolf Bultmann and Paul Tillich . . . reject . . . resurrection in any literal sense" and that "it is doubtful if they and their numerous followers believe in survival at all."[79] Edwards then adds: "Several of the best-known Christian philosophers in Anglo-Saxon countries—Richard Swinburne, [Peter] Thomas Geach, and John Hick—are supporters of [resurrection], maintaining that it and not belief in the disembodied mind is the doctrine taught in the Bible."[80] According to Edwards:

> Whatever its own difficulties, belief in resurrection of the body avoids many of the objections which have been leveled against belief in survival of the disembodied mind . . . Since resurrection bodies presumably possess brains, this doctrine is also quite consistent with the dependence of consciousness on the brain. Finally, survivors with resurrection bodies would not be condemned to the lonely existence of disembodied minds.[81]

The literal version of resurrection maintains, says Edwards, "that the vehicles of survival are the very bodies human beings had in this life," and, among contemporary philosophers, Peter van Inwagen and Peter Geach "are ardent defenders of this view."[82] John Hick is "one of the most articulate spokesmen of [the replica version of resurrection]."[83] According to Hick, the resurrection of the dead "has nothing to do with the resuscitation of corpses in the cemetery. It concerns God's recreation or reconstitution of the psychophysical individual, not as the organism that has died but as . . . an exact replica of him."[84]

Edwards asserts that "resurrectionism has been ridiculed by many writers," including C. J. Ducasse, who "was scathing in his dismissal of the resurrection doctrine."[85] Several of the philosophic objections to resurrection are briefly discussed by Edwards, including what he calls "the age regression problem" which "equally confronts the

---

78. See Edwards, *Immortality*, 53–62, 328–31.
79. Edwards, *Immortality*, 53.
80. Edwards, *Immortality*, 53.
81. Edwards, *Immortality*, 54.
82. Edwards, *Immortality*, 54.
83. Edwards, *Immortality*, 56.
84. Hick, *Philosophy of Religion*, 278. See Edwards, *Immortality*, 56–59.
85. Edwards, *Immortality*, 55.

believer in the disembodied mind."[86] With regard to this problem, Edwards quotes from a work by W. T. Stace called *Man Against Darkness* (1967):

> 'When an old man dies, what kind of consciousness is supposed to survive? Is it his consciousness as it was just before death, which may perhaps have become imbecile? Or is it the consciousness of his mature middle age? Or is it the infant mind that he had when he was a baby? The point of these questions is not that we do not know the answers to them. The point is that all possible answers are equally senseless. Suppose we suggest that it is the mature consciousness which will survive because it is best. Then will the old man who dies suddenly revert to his middle years after death? And will the infant who dies suddenly become mature?'[87]

Commenting on responses to this problem, including that of John Hick who supposes "that in the resurrection world [the replica] will be 'subjected to processes of healing and repair which bring it into a state of health and activity . . . [and that for people who died in old age we may] conceive of a process of growing physically younger to an optimum age,'" Edwards states: "We have obviously now reached a cuckoo land in which all the most delightful dreams will become reality . . . It is salutary to remind resurrectionists of all stripes that resurrections have never been observed and, by their own stipulation, cannot be observed in 'this space' [which is to say that there is no empirical evidence which supports it]."[88]

Those few philosophers who argue in favor of belief in bodily resurrection do so primarily, if not solely, on theological grounds. For instance, Hicks argues that since World War II "the Cartesian mind-matter dualism, having been taken for granted for many centuries, has been strongly criticized by philosophers of the contemporary analytic school [citing Ryle]" and that, as a result, "mid-twentieth-century philosophy has come to see man in the way he is seen in the biblical writings, not as an eternal soul temporarily attached to a mortal body, but as a form of finite, mortal, psychophysical life."[89] Accordingly, says Hick, if God is to fulfill his purpose for man, and if the problem of evil is to be resolved, there must be a bodily resurrection. He asks: "What is the basis for this Judaic-Christian belief in the divine recreation or reconstitution of the human personality after death?"[90] His answer:

> [B]elief in the resurrection arises as a corollary of faith in the sovereign purpose of God . . . [I]f it be God's plan to create finite persons to exist in fellowship with himself, then it contradicts both his own intention and his love for

---

86. See Edwards, *Immortality*, 55–62.
87. Edwards, *Immortality*, 60. See Edwards, *Immortality*, 331.
88. Edwards, *Immortality*, 61. See Edwards, *Immortality*, 330–31. See also, *supra*, n. 77.
89. Hick, *Philosophy of Religion*, 237.
90. Hick, *Philosophy of Religion*, 239.

the creatures made in his image if he allows men to pass out of existence when his purpose for them remains largely unfulfilled.

It is this promised fulfillment of God's purpose for man, in which the full possibilities of human nature will be realized, that constitutes the 'heaven' symbolized in the New Testament as a joyous banquet in which all and sundry rejoice together. As we saw when discussing the problem of evil, no theodicy can succeed without drawing into itself this eschatological faith in an eternal, and therefore infinite, good which thus outweighs all the pains and sorrows that have been endured on the way to it.[91]

Similarly, Peter Geach argues against the idea of disembodied minds. He does so on the grounds that, even were it possible for the disembodied mind of person "x" to survive, it would not constitute the survival of person "x"—"there would not even be a surviving individuality."[92] Thus, the possibility of life after death hinges on belief in resurrection. Geach writes:

> There is of course no philosophical reason to expect that from a human corpse there will arise at some future date a new human body, continuous in some way with the corpse, and in some particular cases there appear strong empirical objections. But apart from the *possibility* of resurrection, it seems to me a mere illusion to have any hope for life after death.[93]

Resurrection is not only rejected or ignored by most philosophers and scientists but by most educated people in general. Edwards asserts:

> There are indeed vast numbers of fundamentalists and also a few pious philosophers who believe or say they believe in resurrection in [a] literal sense, but to the great majority of scientists and philosophers and of educated persons generally it seems totally incredible.[94]

The journalist Lisa Miller agrees, commenting that "ever since the idea of resurrection took hold in monotheistic religion, it has strained credulity."[95] Citing polling data, Miller claims that only about 26 percent of Americans believe in resurrection.[96]

---

91. Hick, *Philosophy of Religion*, 239–40. It is worth noting that Hick argues against the idea of an eternal torment for sinners in hell. "If hell is construed as eternal torment, the theological motive behind the idea is directly at variance with the urge to seek a theodicy . . . If, on the other hand, 'hell' means a continuation of the purgatorial suffering often experienced in this life, and leading eventually to the high good of heaven, it no longer stands in conflict with the needs of theodicy" (Hick, *Philosophy of Religion*, 240).

92. Geach, *God and Soul*, 227–30. See also Edwards, "Dependence of Consciousness on the Brain," 307 ("if there were such a thing as the spiritual substance or the metaphysical soul, it would not be what anybody means by 'I.'").

93. Geach, *God and Soul* 233–34 (emphasis original).

94. Edwards, "Dependence of Consciousness on the Brain," 294–95.

95. Miller, *Heaven*, 110.

96. Miller, *Heaven*, 107.

Further, belief in resurrection has been declining; this is evidenced by the fact that cremations in America are rising. Writing in 2010, Miller notes: "Thirty years ago, almost no one chose to be cremated; now almost half of Americans say they'd prefer cremation to burial."[97]

4. Owen Flanagan argues that belief in souls has been subverted by the development of contemporary brain science

In 2002, Owen Flanagan, a philosopher at Duke University, published *The Problem of the Soul: Two Visions of Mind and How to Reconcile Them*. The two "visions of mind" referenced in the title are essentially (1) the viewpoint that Ryle called the official doctrine which postulates the existence of an immaterial soul which is synonymous with the mind, and (2) a form of physicalism similar to that espoused by Smart which identifies the mind with the brain and rejects the existence of an immaterial soul. Flanagan relates these two "visions of mind" to two competing conceptual schemes about human nature: the "humanistic image" and the "scientific image."[98] According to Flanagan:

> The humanistic image says that we are spiritual beings endowed with free will ... 'In doing what we do, we cause certain things to happen, and nothing—or no one—causes us to cause those events to happen.' The scientific image says that we are animals that evolved according to the principles of natural selection. Although we are extraordinary animals we possess no capacity that permits us to circumvent the laws of cause and effect ...
>
> One image says humans are possessed of a spiritual part—an incorporeal mind or soul—and that one's life and eternal fate turn on the state of this soul. The other image says that there is no such thing as the soul and thus that nothing—nothing at all—depends on its state.[99]

The humanistic image, as Flanagan describes it, is also associated with belief in a supernatural God, miracles, and a heavenly abode for the immortal soul.[100]

What is most relevant for present purposes is Flanagan's discussion of the reasons that lead to the positing of a soul in the first place. Those reasons are, he says, a need to posit an ego "to be the site where experiences come together," a need for personal

---

97. Miller, *Heaven*, 107.

98. Flanagan also refers to the "manifest image." He explains: "[Wilfred] Sellars uses the term *manifest image* to refer to the ordinary, commonsense image that takes as its subject both human nature and the nature of the external world. We can think of it as the composite set of all the folk theories of ordinary people. What I have been calling the humanistic image is the part of the manifest image that concerns the nature of persons" (Flanagan, *Problem of the Soul*, 38).

99. Flanagan, *Problem of the Soul*, ix.

100. See e.g., Flanagan, *Problem of the Soul*, xiii.

identity, and a desire for personal immortality.[101] After discussing these reasons, he comes to the conclusion that they are insufficient to provide a basis to accept that the belief in a permanent, immutable soul is a true belief.[102] He states:

> The upshot [of analyzing the arguments advanced in support of positing a soul] is this: Most people believe they possess immutable souls, and that this soul constitutes their essence. But the arguments we have just examined—the best arguments ever produced—give no reason to think this. Perhaps there are other ways to gain the desired conclusion, but I think not. The very idea of a soul is in conflict with the way the scientific image conceives things.[103]

5. The neuroscientist Antonio Damasio explains that mental phenomena are dependent on the operation of many specific systems of brain circuits, not on a soul

A year after Flanagan's book appeared, Antonio Damasio published *Looking for Spinoza: Joy, Sorrow, and the Feeling Brain* (2003). In *Looking for Spinoza*, Damasio explains the neurobiology of emotions and feelings based on the most recent scientific evidence. In a chapter called "Body, Brain, and Mind," Damasio addresses the mind-body problem. He acknowledges that the mind seems to be a different kind of thing than the objects around us and from the parts of our own bodies that we see and touch.[104] It is this seeming difference that gave rise to the view known as substance dualism, the view that the body and its parts are physical while the mind is not. Although Damasio thinks that this view is today probably accepted by most people, it is "no longer mainstream in science or philosophy."[105] Damasio states that substance dualism "is the account that Descartes helped to dignify" but Descartes never adequately addressed the shortcomings inherent in this account.[106] Descartes never explained in any satisfactory way, for example, how there could be any interaction between something physical and something nonphysical. Damasio explains the rejection of substance dualism by neuroscientists in the following manner:

> In spite of its scientific shortcomings, the view identified with Descartes resonates well with the awe and wonder we deservedly have for our minds ... But awe and wonder at the human mind are compatible with other views of the relation between body and mind and do not make Descartes' views any more correct.

---

101. Flanagan, *Problem of the Soul*, 165–66.
102. See Flanagan, *Problem of the Soul*, 172.
103. Flanagan, *Problem of the Soul*, 180.
104. See Damasio, *Looking for Spinoza*, 187.
105. Damasio, *Looking for Spinoza*, 187.
106. See Damasio, *Looking for Spinoza*, 187–88.

As the observations made possible by introspection became increasingly informed by the modern scientific facts of neurobiology, the substance dualistic view of the mind-body problem lost its appeal. Mental phenomena were revealed as closely dependent on the operation of many specific systems of brain circuits. For example: Seeing depends on several specific neural regions located along pathways from the retina to the cerebral hemispheres. When one of those regions is removed, vision is disturbed. When *all* of the vision-related neural regions are removed, vision is compromised in its entirety. Likewise for hearing, smelling, moving, speaking, or whatever mental function you fancy. Even minor perturbations of the specific neural systems entail a major modification of mental phenomena. Perturbations caused by circumscribed damage to the nerve cells of certain neural regions—as occurs in a stroke, which causes a lesion—markedly change the content and form of feelings and thoughts . . . And so, perhaps for most scientists working on the mind and brain, the fact that the mind depends closely on the workings of the brain is no longer in question.[107]

Finally, Damasio pays homage to Spinoza. According to Damasio, although Descartes was, in his time and in later centuries, honored, while Spinoza was derided, Spinoza was correct in rejecting Descartes's substance dualism. "Spinoza was changing the perspective he inherited from Descartes when he said, in *The Ethics*, Part I, that thought and extension, while distinguishable, are nonetheless attributes of the same substance, God or Nature."[108] Damasio writes:

> In my interpretation, Spinoza was making a bold attempt at penetrating the mystery . . . Spinoza may have intuited the general anatomical and functional arrangement that the body must assume for the mind to occur together with it, or, more precisely with and within it . . .
>
> The real breakthrough, as I see it, regards Spinoza's notion of the human mind, which he defines transparently as consisting of *the idea of the human body*.[109]

After devoting some eight pages to unpacking Spinoza's notion, Damasio asserts: "If my interpretation of Spinoza's statements is even faintly correct, his insight was revolutionary for its time but it had no impact in science."[110] At least, until now. Equally revolutionary is Spinoza's rejection of

> the notion that the prospect of after-death rewards or punishments was a proper incentive for ethical behavior. In a telling letter he lamented the man

---

107. Damasio, *Looking for Spinoza*, 189–90.

108. Damasio, *Looking for Spinoza*, 209. See also Damasio, *Looking for Spinoza*, 15–16 (Spinoza's thoughts on the mind and the body was not only "profoundly opposed to the thinking of most of his contemporaries, but remarkably current three hundred and some years later").

109. Damasio, *Looking for Spinoza*, 210–11 (emphasis original).

110. Damasio, *Looking for Spinoza*, 217.

whose behavior is so guided: 'He is one of those who would follow after his own lusts, if he were not restrained by the fear of hell. He abstains from evil actions and fulfills God's commands like a slave against his will, and for his bondage he expects to be rewarded by God with gifts far more to his taste than Divine love, and great in proportion to his original dislike of virtue.'[111]

---

111. Damasio, *Looking for Spinoza*, 273–74 (quoting Spinoza correspondence).

14.

Increasing Numbers of Jews in the Nineteenth and Twentieth Centuries Reject Belief in a Soul, Resurrection, and an Afterlife as Unfounded, Unscientific, and Superstitious, and Emphasize that Virtue Is its Own Reward

IN THE MID-NINETEENTH CENTURY Jews began to be influenced by Spinoza's metaphysical views and by his teaching that the hope of reward or the fear of punishment in an afterlife are improper incentives for ethical behavior, and this influence continued into the twentieth century. Some, such as Moses Hess and Morris Raphael Cohen, were avid readers and devotees of Spinoza and were *directly* influenced by his words. Others, such as Sigmund Freud and Jacques Loeb, were psychologists or biologists influenced *indirectly* as a consequence of the psycho-physical view of human nature that Spinoza's ideas helped to foster. Still others, such as Hermann Cohen, accepted the principle of immanence as a result of the impact of post-Enlightenment philosophical schools of thought. These intellectuals were not necessarily religiously observant. Nonobservance in the nineteenth and twentieth centuries was restricted neither to intellectuals nor to Jews. Sachar states:

> [I]f modern science, Darwinism, biblical criticism, psychiatry, et. al., were making serious inroads on the religious loyalties of Jewish and Christian intellectuals, they had their effect, as well, on the religious convictions of nonintellectuals. In the face of these new developments, many Western Europeans repudiated or profoundly modified their traditional religious beliefs and practices. There were others, perhaps a majority, who remained nominally within their churches and synagogues, who continued to profess Christianity and Judaism, but who sought somehow to reconcile their inherited doctrines of faith and morals with the modern spirit of science and materialism.[1]

---

1. Sachar, *Course of Modern Jewish History*, 410–11. See also Sachar, *Course of Modern Jewish History*, 524 ("The impact of American secularism was largely responsible ... for the decline in religious

CHAPTER 14.

A. Moses Hess Equates the Principle of Immanence with Authentic Judaism in Which Immortality Is Not Individual Immortality but the Immortality of the People Israel

Moses Hess was born in Bonn, Germany in 1812. His father was "thoroughly orthodox" and on his mother's side he descended from a line of rabbis and Jewish scholars.[2] Hess attended the Bonn University and became attracted to theories proposing changes in the distribution of wealth that were to become associated with socialism.[3] In 1837, he published his first work, entitled *The Sacred History of Humanity*, whose author is identified, not by name, but as a Young Disciple of Spinoza. As Waxman notes, "In this work, Hess develops his Philosophy of History, which is, in its essence, a combined product of Spinozism and Hegelianism."[4] In all his early works, Hess espouses a "messianic socialism" in which both Judaism and Christianity are replaced "with a global and pantheistic religion of reason, in which the alienation between spirit and matter, and the social hierarchy and inequality that was the necessary counterpart to this divide, would be permanently overcome."[5]

His Jewish nationalism was fostered to a great extent by the Damascus Affair of 1840.[6] In 1862, he published *Rome and Jerusalem, a Study in Jewish Nationalism*, his *magnum opus*, in which he calls for the regeneration of the Jewish nation, the Jewish colonization of Palestine, and the restoration of a Jewish State. In *Rome and Jerusalem* Hess pays repeated homage to Spinoza whom he understands as expressing points of view which are not only fully consistent with "Jewish Monotheism"[7] but which represent the essence of the Jewish message and serve as the latest and most powerful manifestation of that message. For example, Hess writes:

> The basic idea of the system of Spinoza, namely, that God is the only substance, the ground and origin of all being, is the fundamental expression of the Jewish genius, which has ever manifested itself in divine revelations from the time of Moses and the Prophets, down to modern days. These manifestations of the Jewish genius are not a supernatural phenomenon, but form a part of

---

observance among the second generation of Russian-Jewish immigrants. After the first World War organized religion in general suffered a perceptible diminution of strength in the United States . . . Agnosticism was common enough to go largely unnoticed. People who attended devotional services regularly did so more in response to social convention than out of religious conviction.").

2. Waxman, "Introduction," 18–19.

3. Waxman, "Introduction," 11, 19. See generally Waxman, "Introduction," 11–18 (discussing German social and political movements in the 1830s); Sachar, *Course of Modern Jewish History*, 284–304 (discussing the growth of Jewish socialism).

4. Waxman, "Introduction," 20.

5. Schwartz, *First Modern Jew*, 120.

6. See Schwartz, *First Modern Jew*, 67–70. See also Kaplan, *Greater Judaism in the Making*, 409 ("The immediate cause of his Jewish reawakening was undoubtedly his realization that the German people would not permit the Jews to be integrated into the German nation.").

7. Hess, *Rome and Jerusalem*, 215.

the great eternal law which governs all three life spheres, the cosmic, organic and social.[8]

The great eternal law which Hess sees as governing all three life spheres, that is, all aspects of the world, seems to be that God is the "ground of Nature and Thought," that "in the world of Nature and life" there is "one creative force" which is in "continual operation."[9] This law is related to what Hess calls "the genetic view of the world," or "our Jewish genetic view," which he contrasts with what he calls the "anti-genetic, pagan view of the world."[10] The later worldview teaches "the eternity of being"; the former worldview teaches that everything in the world is constantly changing, developing.[11] Hess contends that the anti-genetic, pagan view was at that time giving way to the genetic, Jewish view:

> The hypothesis of the eternity of the atoms of matter and their rigidity and exchangeability does not explain all phenomena of the behavior of matter under certain conditions, and is gradually giving way to the genetic view, which sees everywhere only movements and no fixed atoms nor any stable cosmic ether. Chemical atoms have not existed from eternity, but, like organic germs, were once generated and are subject to the great law of growth and decay. They arose through the act of creation, by the same act which successively calls into existence every being and continues to form centers of gravity, which in the cosmic world we name atoms; in the organic, germs; and in the social, revelations.[12]

Hess also equates the anti-genetic, pagan view with dualism, including the dualism of material and spiritual substance, body and soul, Creator and creation, individual and nation, nation and humanity as a whole, and this world and the world to come. By way of contrast, he equates the genetic, Jewish view with monism, unity, responsibility to family, nation, and humanity, and this-worldliness.[13] As Hess under-

---

8. See Hess, *Rome and Jerusalem*, 212. See also Hess, *Rome and Jerusalem*, 75 ("Today, as ever, I still believe that the present great epoch in universal history had its first manifestation . . . in the teachings of Spinoza.").

9. See Hess, *Rome and Jerusalem*, 212–13.

10. See generally Hess, *Rome and Jerusalem*, 211–16, 251–52.

11. See Hess, *Rome and Jerusalem*, 211–16, 251–52.

12. Hess, *Rome and Jerusalem*, 213.

13. See Waxman, "Introduction," 25–26, 32 ("The fundamental principle of Hess's thought is what he terms 'the genetic view.' It is based on the teaching of Spinoza, of which he was a devoted follower . . . According to his view, the world, in spite of its multiplicity and variety of phases, is a unity. There is no place in it for a dualism of matter and spirit, or other divisions; it is all one—an undivided whole . . . Behind this unity there is the all-embracing force which unifies the phenomena of the universe—the Creator or God. God is not outside of the world but within it, its essence and substance . . . The Jews have taught humanity true religion, a religion which is neither materialistic nor spiritualistic, which has for its aim, unlike Christianity, not the salvation of the individual in the other world, but the perfection of social life in this world.").

stands it, the truly Jewish belief in immortality relates not to the immortality of the individual person but to the immortality of the people of Israel. Similarly, the truly Jewish belief in resurrection relates not to the resurrection of the individual person but to the rebirth of the Jewish nation in the messianic age.[14] He sees the belief in an *individual* immortality of any sort as a pagan perversion of Judaism brought about by Christianity.[15] Accordingly, he sees Spinoza's rejection of the immortality of the soul and rejection of an afterlife of any kind as a return to authentic Judaism. In Hess's words, contained in the third letter of *Rome and Jerusalem*:[16]

> You wonder why it is that there is no mention of the doctrine of immortality in the Old Testament . . . You argue, that if Moses and the Prophets had believed in a life beyond the grave, in the Christian sense, they would have stated the fact as explicitly as did the writers of the New Testament, and would not have limited reward and punishment to the life of this world alone. I do not deny the fact that there is no mention of immortality in the Old Testament. But if you reproach our Holy Scriptures for passing over such an important doctrine in silence, you . . . overlook the point of our sacred history, namely, the genetic conception which never separated the individual from the race, the nation from humanity, and the created world from the Creator. You forget that the part of the Sacred Scriptures wherein there is no mention of immortality was written at a time when the Jewish nation was still in existence, and therefore there was no need of a belief in a resurrection. The Jewish belief in immortality is inseparable from the national humanitarian Messianic idea . . . [T]he Rabbis never separated the idea of a future world from the conception of the Messianic reign. Nachmanides insists, in contradiction to Maimonides, upon the identity of *Olom Habbo*, 'the world to come,' with the Messianic reign.
>
> . . . It was only when Judaism was threatened with the possibility of national destruction . . . that . . there arose the idea of the immortality of the individual. The Prophet Isaiah already draws a sharp line of distinction between those nations which are doomed to eternal death and Israel which is destined to be resurrected. The momentary death of Israel, the people of the spirit, is only the preliminary stage for a future eternal life. [Isa. 36:14–19]
>
> Even in primitive Christianity, as long as it did not separate itself completely from Judaism and the historical cult, the Jewish conception still survived, the 'Kingdom of Heaven,' and 'the world to come' are identical with the Messianic age, the rebirth of the Jewish nation . . .

---

14. See generally Hess, *Rome and Jerusalem*, 137–38 (in the messianic era the Jewish nation "will rise again to new life"; to refer to this time as "the time of the 'resurrection of the dead'" is to use a "symbolic expression").

15. See Hess, *Rome and Jerusalem*, 211 ("as a result of the combination of a Judaism devoid of its element of worldliness and a Godless Paganism, there was born the Christian view, according to which a Jewish saint in the garb of a pagan man, had come to raise and prepare the nations for a better, divine world which, however, possesses all the characteristics of otherworldliness.").

16. *Rome and Jerusalem* consists of a series of twelve letters and an epilogue.

Even the latest expression of the Jewish genius concerning life and death, namely, the teaching of Spinoza, has nothing in common with the sickly atomistic conception of immortality, a conception which dissolves the unity of life either in a spiritualistic way [the immortality of the soul] or in a materialistic manner [bodily resurrection], and whose highest religious and moral principle is the egoistic maxim, 'everyone for himself.' No nation was ever so far from this egoistic principle as was the Jewish people. With the Jews, solidarity and social responsibility were always the fundamental principal of life and conduct.

In the *Sayings of the Fathers*, the rule of bourgeois morality—'everyone for himself'—is severely condemned, and is declared to be a wicked rule of conduct.[17] In the teaching of Spinoza, as in the teaching of the Jewish saints, the individual is not treated as a separate entity, but as a part of a whole. According to Spinoza, eternity does not begin with our death, but always exists, is always present even as God himself.[18]

At the end of the fourth letter of *Rome and Jerusalem*, Hess elaborates on the idea that in authentic Judaism immortality is not *individual* immortality but the immortality of the people of Israel:

> You can discern clearly the source of the Jewish belief in immortality; it is the product of our remarkable family love. Our immortality extends back into the past as far as the Patriarchs, and in the future to the Messiah's reign . . . This belief . . . has, in the course of ages, shrunk to the belief in the atomistic immortality of the individual soul; and thus, torn from its roots and trunk, has withered and decayed. It is only in the Jewish conception of the family that the former living belief is still retained. When modern dualism of spirit and matter, the result of the separation of Christianity from Judaism, had found its highest expression in the works of the last Christian philosopher, Descartes, and had threatened to kill all unity of life, there arose again out of Judaism the belief in the existence of one eternal force in Nature and History . . . Just as Christian dualism received its mortal blow from the teachings of Spinoza, so does the existence of the ancient Jewish people, with its model of family life, act as an antidote against this disease of dualism in practical life.[19]

It is precisely because Hess believed in a collective, this-worldly salvation of a utopian socialist society, not an individual, otherworldly salvation experienced after death, that Hess came to see Jewish nationalism and the reestablishment of a Jewish

---

17. Here Hess cites, *inter alia*, the saying in *Pirqe Avot* that "we should not be like the servants who serve for the sake of reward but like children who perform their duty because of reverence inspired in them by the majesty of the father of all being," which saying, Hess says, "seems to be indifferent to the doctrine of [personal] immortality" (Hess, *Rome and Jerusalem*, 53n3).

18. Hess, *Rome and Jerusalem*, 50–53.

19. Hess, *Rome and Jerusalem*, 65–66.

state as vital.[20] This is to say that Hess came to identify the coming of the utopian socialist society with the coming of the messianic age, and came to believe that the Jewish people were "the triumphal arch of the future epoch" which would "destroy the weed of materialism together with its roots."[21] This mission of the Jewish people required a Jewish state, an exemplary socialist society in the ancient Jewish homeland.

Hess was, therefore, quite critical of Reform Jews.[22] He believed that so long as the reform movement denied that the Jewish people constituted a nation, and saw Jews as Germans of the Mosaic faith, the erroneous belief in an individual salvation would persist, and the messianic age would be postponed.[23] He argued that it was the dominance of German culture that kept Jews from authentic, this-worldly Judaism. "With the entrance of the German race, both natural and historical religion lost their hold over the human mind and their influence was replaced by an apotheosis of the individual . . . As long as the German race dominates in Europe," he believed, "there can be no development of [Jewish] national life. The 'religion of love,' separated from natural and historical life, had only the salvation of the individual soul in view."[24] The true prophet of the modern messianic movement was, for Hess, Spinoza since Spinoza opposed the dualism that was responsible for belief in individual salvation, belief in the immortality of an individual soul.[25]

Hess admired Spinoza, however, not only for his metaphysical position, but for his view of Jewish statehood. In particular, "Hess relied on a famous passage in chapter 3 of the *Theological-Political Treatise* where Spinoza invokes the possibility that the Jews will reestablish their state and 'God will again elect them.' Hess read this text in a modern Zionist vein, as did other Zionist writers and activists who admired Spinoza, like Nahum Sokolov, Joseph Klausner, and David Ben-Gurion . . ."[26]

20. See generally Yovel, *Adventures of Immanence*, 68, 72 (Hess "became the father of socialist Zionism." In *Rome and Jerusalem* Hess maintained that the Jews "will fulfill their universal mission in history not as assimilated individuals but as a national entity which assumes its place in the family of nations and, regaining political independence, will establish an exemplary socialist society in its ancient homeland.").

21. See Hess, *Rome and Jerusalem*, 159.

22. See Kaplan, *Greater Judaism in the Making*, 414 ("Hess spares no words in denouncing the Reform movement.").

23. See generally Hess, *Rome and Jerusalem*, 71 ("Those of our brethren who, for purposes of obtaining emancipation, endeavor to persuade themselves, as well as others, that modern Jews possess no trace of a national feeling, have really lost their heads."), 95–96.

24. Hess, *Rome and Jerusalem*, 85–86.

25. See Hess, *Rome and Jerusalem*, 83–84 ("Already at the beginning of the modern period, a Messianic movement . . . took hold of Eastern as well as Occidental Jews . . . whose true prophet was Spinoza."). See also Hess, *Rome and Jerusalem*, 137–38 ("The Messianic era is the present age, which began to germinate with the teachings of Spinoza"); Yovel, *Adventures of Immanence*, 73 (in his maturity, Hess "returned to Spinoza both as the prophet of modernity and the precursor of Jewish national emancipation."). It should be noted that, while claiming Spinoza as a prophet, Hess does not always accurately reflect Spinoza's viewpoints. See Yovel, *Adventures of Immanence*, 70–72.

26. Yovel, *Adventures of Immanence*, 73. See Schwartz, *First Modern Jew*, 120–21; Hess, *Rome and*

Since many Zionists were, as Hess, secularists, they, as Hess, also admired Spinoza for rejecting otherworldliness, and were participants in what Yovel calls "Spinoza's immanent revolution."[27] In 1938, Ben-Zion Dinur, then a lecturer in modern Jewish history at Hebrew University, published the first volume of his compendium of Zionist sources, *Sefer ha-Tsiyonut*, which was devoted to the "forerunners of Zionism."[28] As Schwartz comments, "At the very beginning of this development [Dinur] located Spinoza. By interpreting 'chosenness' as a civic instead of spiritual capacity, Spinoza became the first to secularize the messianic idea and to secure Jewish uniqueness on purely immanent as opposed to transcendent foundations."[29] Secular Zionists, "who rejected literal belief in a personal and transcendent God, special providence, and the giving of the Torah at Sinai,"[30] were also free to reject belief in a soul or an afterlife.

B. Hermann Cohen Adopts the Principle of Immanence as a Consequence of His Neo-Kantian Viewpoint in Which Virtue Is Its Own Reward

Born in 1842 in Coswig, Germany, Hermann Cohen was raised in an observant family. His father was a synagogue cantor and Cohen left *Gymnasium* in order to attend a rabbinical seminary in Breslau, Poland.[31] However, he decided against becoming a rabbi and enrolled instead in a German university, first in Breslau and then in Berlin. He, ultimately, received his doctorate from the University of Halle. In 1873, less than two years after publishing an essay and a book defending philosophical positions of Immanuel Kant against Kantian critics, Cohen was appointed lecturer at the University of Marburg.[32] Three years later, he was promoted to full professor, a rank that was at that time in Germany almost never granted to unconverted Jews in philosophy departments.[33] Cohen remained at Marburg for close to forty years, becoming a noted Kantian philosopher.[34]

Jerusalem, 64.

27. See generally Schwartz, *First Modern Jew*, 114–53 (discussing the Zionist rehabilitation of Spinoza).

28. Schwartz, *First Modern Jew*, 123.

29. Schwartz, *First Modern Jew*, 123.

30. Schwartz, *First Modern Jew*, 130.

31. Agus, *Modern Philosophies of Judaism*, 57; Scott, "Hermann Cohen," §1.

32. See Agus, *Modern Philosophies of Judaism*, 57; Scott, "Hermann Cohen," §1.

33. Scott, "Hermann Cohen," §1.

34. Agus, *Modern Philosophies of Judaism*, 58–59 ("The 'Marburg School' in philosophy is nearly synonymous with the works of Cohen and his disciples."). See also Tatarkiewicz, *Nineteenth Century Philosophy*, 128–30. ("Kantianism remained the leading philosophy in Germany until the end of the [nineteenth] century . . . At the beginning of the twentieth century Kantians were still in the vanguard of the philosophical movement, but they had split into many camps and deviated significantly from the original variety of neo-Kantianism . . . Some Kantians crossed the metaphysical boundary and became idealists or realists; others moved further from metaphysics and approached positivism. The

CHAPTER 14.

At Marburg, Cohen devoted little attention to Jewish thought or affairs until after 1879, when the German historian and politician Heinrich von Treitschke published an article justifying the anti-Semitic movement that had emerged in Germany.[35] As Kaplan writes, "The older Cohen grew, the more fervently he devoted himself to Jewish religious problems, on which he wrote extensively. Part of these writings were collected posthumously (1924) in the three volumes of the *Jüdische Schriften* [Jewish Writings]."[36] After retiring from Marburg in 1912, Cohen moved to Berlin to teach at a rabbinical seminary, the *Hochschule für die Wissenschaft des Judentums*, or Higher Institute for Jewish Studies. It was at that time that he wrote his most famous work devoted to Judaism, *Die Religion der Vernuft aus den Quellen des Judentums* [*Religion of Reason Out of the Sources of Judaism*] which appeared posthumously in 1919. The English translation by Simon Kaplan was not published until 1972. As Seeskin asserts, "Cohen was the central figure in Jewish philosophy for more than 60 years."[37]

In sharp contrast to Moses Hess, Cohen was neither a Zionist nor an admirer of Spinoza's metaphysics.[38] Yet, with regard to the afterlife, Cohen, out of his neo-Kantian philosophical position, reached a conclusion similar to that of Hess, that the truly Jewish belief in immortality relates, not to the immortality of the *individual* person, but to the "immortality" (or eternal, historical continuance) of the people of Israel and

---

most important Kantian schools were the Marburg school (Cohen and Natorp) and the Baden school (Windelband and Rickert) . . . The essential difference between the positivists and the neo-Kantians was in their relationship to a priori elements of knowledge: the former denied them, the latter defended them. But both groups held some common minimalistic beliefs."). See generally Tatarkiewicz, *Nineteenth Century Philosophy*, 122–23 (discussing Neo-Kantianism).

35. Agus, *Modern Philosophies of Judaism*, 59. Treitschke's article argued that the danger of Jewish domination in Germany posed a great threat. As a result of Treitschke's endorsement, anti-Semitic agitation, which until then had been considered vulgar, especially in intellectual circles, now received the imprimatur of one of the most illustrious thinkers in Germany, thereby gaining a degree of respectability.

36. Kaplan, "Introduction," xii.

37. Seeskin, "How to Read *Religion of Reason*," 23. For analyses of *Religion of Reason*, see Guttmann, *Philosophies of Judaism*, 400–16; Agus, *Modern Philosophies of Judaism*, 57–128.

38. Cohen opposed Zionism and the establishment of a Jewish state because he believed they were inconsistent with the mission of Israel: "to be an eternal witness to pure monotheism, to be *the* martyr, to be the suffering servant of the Lord" (Strauss, "Introductory Essay," xxxiii; emphasis original). See also Cohen, *Religion of Reason*, 253 ("That the state declined, while the people were preserved, is a providential symbol of Messianism; it is the sign of the truth of monotheism No state, but yet a people. But this people is less for the sake of its own nation than as a symbol of mankind. A unique symbol for the unique idea: the individual peoples have to strive to the unique unity of mankind."). Cohen opposed Spinoza's metaphysics because he believed that pantheism is inconsistent with monotheism. The essence of monotheism, for Cohen, is God's uniqueness, rather than his oneness. Cohen, *Religion of Reason*, 35. God's uniqueness consists in incomparability, and as such the unique being of God does not admit of any connection with sensible experience (Cohen, *Religion of Reason*, 44–45). Thus, Spinoza's thesis *Deus sive natura* entails a contradiction since "nature must not be set up in being together with God. Nature is subject to the limitations of space and time . . Space [and time], however, cannot be a limitation of God's being" (Cohen, *Religion of Reason*, 45). See also Guttmann, *Philosophies of Judaism*, 405.

of humanity in general, and that the truly Jewish belief in resurrection relates not to the resurrection of the *individual* person, but to the "eternal sequence of generations of men in the historical unity of the peoples in general, and of the messianic people in particular."[39]

Cohen's rejection of an immortal soul is due to his agreement with Kant's "transcendental criticism" of those concepts which exceed what can be known on the bases of sense experience—concepts which result when *pure reason* strives to transcend the bounds of sense experience in its pursuit of speculative knowledge.[40] Kant, however, had relied on *practical reason* to establish the existence of an immortal soul.[41] Kant argued that happiness must be proportional to virtue and, since there is no such proportionality in this life, there must be an afterlife.[42] Cohen flatly and vigorously rejects this Kantian argument for the immortality of the individual soul.

For one thing, Cohen recognized that the attempt to make happiness proportional to virtue violated Kant's own ethical position. Kant's ethical position is that any action done in order to satisfy some desire or inclination (which would include the desire for happiness) has no moral worth. To have moral worth, for Kant, an action must be done *solely* because it accords with the demands of reason, which is to say that it must be done out of duty, out of respect for the law, and *not* because it is a means of achieving happiness.[43]

Secondly, Cohen's position is that monotheism precludes any relationship between ethical conduct and happiness, and precludes happiness being proportional to virtue. Or, to put it in terms used by Cohen: "Opposition to *eudaemonism* is ... deeply rooted in monotheism."[44] Indeed, Cohen sees Jewish ethics as fully consistent with

39. Strauss, "Introductory Essay," xxxiv.
40. See ch. 10, sec. D, 2.
41. See ch. 10, sec. D, 2.
42. See ch. 10, sec. D, 2.
43. See Kant, *Groundwork of the Metaphysics of Morals*, 67–69 (emphasis original) ("An action done from duty has its moral worth, *not in the purpose* to be attained by it, but in the maxim in accordance with which it is decided upon; it depends therefore, not on the realization of the object of the action, but solely on the *principle* of *volition* in accordance with which, irrespective of all objects of the faculty of desire, the action has been performed ... *Duty is the necessity to act out of reverence for the law* ... Now an action done from duty has to set aside altogether the influence of inclination ... so there is nothing left able to determine the will except objectively the *law* and subjectively *pure reverence* for this practical law, and therefore the maxim of obeying this law even to the detriment of all my inclinations"; emphasis original). See generally Kant, *Lectures on Ethics*, 52–57 (discussing reward and punishment, distinguishing two kinds of *praemia* (rewards)—*auctorantia* and *remunerantia*, and stating that: "It is not right for religion to represent its *praemia* as *auctorantia*, to tell us to be moral for the sake of future reward. No man can demand that God should reward and make him happy. He may hope for reward from the Supreme Being, he may expect that God will see to it that he does not suffer for his good deeds, but reward must not be the impulsive ground of his action. Man may hope for happiness, but this hope ought not to be his incentive, merely his consolation."). See also Jones, *History of Western Philosophy*, 4:92–93 (discussing objections to Kant's proof of the immortality of the soul, including the objection that it contradicts Kant's position that virtue is its own reward).

44. Cohen, *Religion of Reason*, 46 (emphasis original).

Kantian ethics, and thus as opposed to eudaemonism, opposed, that is, to any attempt to make the attainment of happiness the reason for performing God's commands.[45] Cohen asserts that to seek a reward for following God's commands "belongs to the prohibited land of eudaemonism."[46] He continues:

> There is only one reward that does not fall under this verdict, and this is the one which is identical with the good act itself. This identity the Mishnah expressed in a great passage: "The reward of duty is the duty." Spinoza translated this passage of the Mishnah literally without mentioning the source: *praemium virtutis virtus* [virtue is its own reward].[47] There is no other reward, and there can and should be no other reward, than the infinite, unceasing task of morality itself. Any other reward is heterogeneous to morality and therefore injures its purity.[48]

Although Cohen sees the "presence" of the pagan myth of the soul's immortality in the biblical concept of *Sheol*, he believes that immortality "must gain an entirely different meaning in monotheism."[49] Pointing to biblical references describing burial as being "gathered to [one's] people," Cohen writes:

> If man enters into the abode of his fathers, he is thereby elevated above the character of an individual being . . . [I]t is the *people*, it is the people's soul into which the individual soul enters. The people does not die, but has a history which continues. And *history*, the history of one's people, gives duration and continuity to the individual soul. *Immortality acquires the meaning of the historical living-on of the individual in the historical continuity of his people . . .*
>
> Since we have recognized the historical meaning of immortality, it can further be understood that *resurrection* could become a lever for the formulation

---

45. Cohen argues that the people of Israel are to be understood as the suffering servant of Isaiah, and that their suffering symbolizes monotheism's rejection of eudaemonism. See Cohen, *Religion of Reason*, 268 ("Considered from the point of view of eudaemonism, the suffering of the Jews is, to be sure, a misfortune. But the messianic calling of Israel sheds another light on its own earthly history. As Israel suffers, according to the prophet, for the pagan worshippers, so Israel to this very day suffers vicariously for the faults and wrongs which still hinder the realization of monotheism."), 283–84 ("to suffer for the dissemination of monotheism, as the Jews do, is not a sorrowful fate; the suffering is, rather, its tragic calling, for it proves the heartfelt desire for the conversion of the other peoples, which the faithful people feels . . . The tragic suffering has the final good as its end, and therefore despises all transitory, eudaemonistic prosperity.")

46. Cohen, *Religion of Reason*, 321.

47. Cf. ch. 9, sec. D.

48. Cohen, *Religion of Reason*, 321–24. See Guttmann, *Philosophies of Judaism*, 401–2.

49. Cohen, *Religion of Reason*, 300–1. A different meaning of immortality is required because immortality in a netherworld for the purpose of punishment by the gods of the netherworld contradicts the monotheistic idea of "the God of forgiveness." Cohen, *Religion of Reason*, 300–1. See also Cohen, *Religion of Reason*, 290 ("the idea of immortality in no way remained alien to the biblical spirit but was invigorated and spiritualized anew by it.").

of immortality ... Ezekiel interpreted immortality as the immortality of the people: 'These bones are the whole house of Israel' [Ezek 37:10]. Thus, the image of resurrection even more than that of immortality could make clear the idea of ... the continuous duration of individual souls in the historical unity of the people.[50]

This meaning of immortality is connected by Cohen with what is for him the most significant concept in Judaism after monotheism—messianism.[51] According to Cohen, "under the Persian influence immortality and resurrection became alive in the Jewish mind and were connected with one another, [and] both concepts were soon connected with the concept of the Messianic age."[52] As Cohen sees it, the original understanding of messianism—the hope for an individual person, a king, who would reestablish the political nation of the Jews—gives way to the idea that the "remnant of Israel," through its vicarious suffering "for the faults and wrongs which still hinder the realization of monotheism," will bring about the universal acceptance of monotheism, the removal of "external doctrinal and national limits," the "unity of mankind," and "the warding off of the idea of eudaemonism."[53] Through messianism, and its link to monotheism, all humanity may achieve immortality through each person's participation in the development of the human race.[54]

Several additional points made by Cohen relating to the afterlife are worth mentioning. First, Cohen adamantly opposes the mystical ideal of the souls of the righteous uniting, after death, with God. Such a union would undermine both God's uniqueness and the individual's humanity.[55] Second, Cohen is equally opposed to

---

50. Cohen, *Religion of Reason*, 301–2 (emphasis original). See also Cohen, *Religion of Reason*, 281 (Ezekiel "is able to recognize in the notion of resurrection, which became known to him in Persia, the resurrection of the people.").

51. The messianic era becomes for Cohen the "unending work of ethical perfecting" (Guttmann, *Philosophies of Judaism*, 404).

52. Cohen, *Religion of Reason*, 309.

53. See Cohen, *Religion of Reason*, 236–95. See also Agus, *Modern Philosophies of Judaism*, 118–20 ("Immortality ... finds its concrete expression in Judaism, in the ideal of the Messiah. The hope for 'the days of the Messiah' is really an expression of the belief that human society will advance perpetually along the endless road to perfection ... To the extent that it accepts ... evil visitations as its contribution to the evolution of the perfect society, Israel is the Messiah.").

54. See Strauss, "Introductory Essay," xxxiv ("On the basis of messianism, immortality comes to mean the survival of the soul in the historical process of the human race."). See also Cohen, *Religion of Reason*, 301, 308–9 ("What a perspective Messianism now opens up for the historical meaning of immortality, according to which the individual soul acquires its immortality in the historical continuation of the human race!").

55. See Cohen, *Religion of Reason*, 306 (Properly understood, "the immortality of the human spirit separates religion from those dangers of mythology contained in mysticism. The return to God is not a union with God ... [Holiness does not] make man and God identical ... God remains the Unique One ... Monotheism ... does not save the immortality of the human soul at the expense of infringing on God's uniqueness ... The individual as human would be nullified, if it could come to a union with God.").

reading into any Jewish source the idea of eternal punishment.[56] Such postmortem punishment undermines a central element of Cohen's understanding of the religion of reason and Judaism, namely that there is divine forgiveness and human repentance.[57] Last, Cohen interprets the mishnaic teaching that "All Israel has a share in the world to come" as meaning that all mankind is immortal. This is because the "whole of Israel stands here for the concept of man in general."[58]

C. For Sigmund Freud Belief in an Afterlife Is an Illusion

Sigmund Freud "was a nonreligious Jew, a heretical Jew, but a Jew nevertheless, as he regarded himself and was seen by other Jews and by non-Jews as well."[59] The emergence of anti-Semitism in Vienna, and Freud's encounter with it, had the effect of causing Freud to abandon hopes for social integration and of invigorating his connection to

---

56. Cohen's objection to the eternality of punishment was not anything new. In seventeenth-century Amsterdam, the *hakhamim* Saul Levi Morteira and Isaac Aboab de Fonseca had a heated, public dispute concerning whether punishment in the afterlife is eternal or not. See Altmann, "Eternality of Punishment," 2–4; Rosenbloom, "Menasseh Ben Israel," 241; Nadler, *Spinoza*, 52–54. The importance of the Morteira-Aboab dispute is evidenced by the fact that the lay leaders of the community requested the intervention of the Venice rabbinate to resolve it. Morteira's position is contained in an appeal to the *Beth Din* of Venice (preserved in manuscript), and Aboab's view is set forth in an unpublished treatise entitled *Nishmat Hayyim* (*The Breath* [or *Soul*] *of Life*) dealing with reward and punishment in the hereafter. The position advanced by Aboab is that all Israelites have a share in the world to come, although, following Lurianic Kabbalah, the souls of certain Jews go through a process of purification before they receive their share in that world, with such process of purification being *gilgul*.

57. See Cohen, *Religion of Reason*, 312 ("In the rabbinical writings some passages are found that eliminate any positive or negative eudaemonism from reward as well as from punishment . . . Particularly characteristic . . . is the expression of Resh Lakish in the Talmud [b. Ned. 8b] according to which there will no longer be any hell in the Messianic Age. The principle of self-perfection in the development of man is not compatible with the principle of retributive punishment: the latter is replaced by the former and therefore there can no longer be a hell in the Messianic Age. Moreover, hell is not to be thought of as a permanent place of retribution, for after purification the sinners are supposed to go to heaven. Therefore, a necessary consequence became valid: there are no eternal punishments of hell. This consequence follows from the connection of divine forgiveness with the human work of repentance and its effect on the development of the human race. The messianic future thus has overcome and eliminated the share of punishment in immortality."), 326–27 ("The Mishnah does not say that all Israel is equally good, but it grants to all Israel, without individual distinction, a share in the eternal life. This share is mediated and secured by repentance. It is in every man's power to repent; therefore everyone has a share in eternal life. The threat of eternal hell does not exist for anyone. This specific form of punishment does not exist at all in the Jewish notion of retribution.").

58. Cohen, *Religion of Reason*, 336. See also Cohen, *Religion of Reason*, 337 ("To the eternity of God corresponds, as an anthropomorphic consequence, the eternity of man. Liberated of the anthropomorphic setting, this eternity of man means only the infinite continuation of the correlation of man and God. Without immortality God's creation, revelation, and providence could not have existence. Thus Messianism is only an analogy of immortality, while monotheism itself in its correlation of God and man has immortality as its necessary consequence.").

59. Yovel, *Adventures of Immanence*, 165. Freud said in a letter expressing support for Zionism: "Although I have been alienated from the religion of my forebears for a long time, I have never lost the feeling of solidarity with my people . . ." (Robert, *From Oedipus to Moses*, 40–41).

the Jewish people.[60] As Klein comments, "Freud's early reaction to anti-Semitism was . . . a mixture of disappointment and the determination to defend himself as a Jew . . . He expressed renewed appreciation of his Jewish heritage . . ."[61] In a short period of time "Freud's Jewish consciousness developed from an anxious and erratic self-defense to an all-embracing sensibility inspiring deep passions."[62] Nevertheless, "he remained firmly opposed to religious dogmas" and to what he disparaged as "foolish superstitions."[63]

On September 29, 1897, Freud joined the Viennese lodge of the International Order of the *B'nai B'rith* (the *Israelitische Humanitäts-Verein "Wein" B'nai B'rith*) which had been founded on October 13, 1895, as the order's 449th membership lodge.[64] Among the most active members of the Viennese lodge were Solomon Ehrman, a friend of Freud's since 1874 when they both were students at the medical school, and William Knöpfmacher, another old friend from the days of Freud's secondary and university education.[65] Ehrman supported the society's stress on fellowship, and, along with Freud and other members of the *Wien*, "considered religion obsolete or, at most, ancillary."[66] In a 1902 article by Ehrman included in the society's *Quarterly Report*, Ehrman said that, rather than being an observance of laws and customs,

> Judaism rests upon 'the active support of the ideals of humanity which our prophets laid down but which have been ignored by European mankind' . . . Judaism, as 'a principle of unlimited development and eternal progress,' always had a liberating influence on the rest of mankind, especially in philosophy and the sciences. Spinoza, for example, a 'Jew even in his way of thinking,' had contributed to excellence and freedom by pursuing knowledge and truth. Ehrman noted that more recently, Jews had smoothed the way in all lands for the development of modern technology and remained in the forefront of biological research.[67]

While a student, Freud "received a thorough grounding in the positivistic science of the nineteenth century. First he concentrated on biology . . . Next he moved to physiology."[68] He was trained in the Helmholtz school of medicine which viewed

---

60. See Klein, *Jewish Origins of the Psychoanalytic Movement*, 48–55.
61. Klein, *Jewish Origins of the Psychoanalytic Movement*, 55–57.
62. Klein, *Jewish Origins of the Psychoanalytic Movement*, 59.
63. Klein, *Jewish Origins of the Psychoanalytic Movement*, 59–60.
64. Klein, *Jewish Origins of the Psychoanalytic Movement*, 72, 75. B'nai B'rith had been founded in New York City fifty-two years earlier as an organization that "stressed the value of unity and fellowship, rather than the religion of Judaism . . . In Europe, the impetus for the founding of the B'nai B'rith was the spread of anti-Semitism" (Klein, *Jewish Origins of the Psychoanalytic Movement*, 75).
65. See Klein, *Jewish Origins of the Psychoanalytic Movement*, 48, 73.
66. See Klein, *Jewish Origins of the Psychoanalytic Movement*, 81–82.
67. Klein, *Jewish Origins of the Psychoanalytic Movement*, 81–84.
68. Klein, *Jewish Origins of the Psychoanalytic Movement*, 233.

the living organism as operating solely according to physical-chemical principles, omitting any reliance on vitalism, that is the existence of any immaterial substance or vital force to explain any of the organism's activities.[69] Specifically, at medical school Freud studied physiology with Ernst Brücke.[70] Brücke had worked together with Hermann Helmholtz and Emil Du Bois-Reymond as students in the laboratory of Johannes Müller, and in 1845 they formed the Berlin Physical Society, dedicated to destroying vitalism.[71] The three also agreed to the "Reymond-Brücke oath," a vow of allegiance to the view that only physicochemical forces, in opposition to any and all "life force" (or vitalism) theories, operate in organisms.[72] Accordingly, Freud was fully knowledgeable of the advances in nineteenth-century empirical psychology, and in biology, that lead to the adoption of a psycho-physical view of nature and the abandonment of the concept of soul by psychologists and biologists: "He was convinced that all mental events are completely determined—even mistakes have a cause. And to the end of his life he used the mechanical, electrical, hydraulic terminology of his positivistic teachers. Thus we must classify him as loyal to the positivistic tradition."[73]

Freud explains all human activity, both normal and abnormal, both physical and mental, on the bases of natural, scientifically knowable processes, without the need to postulate the existence of an immaterial soul. In this regard Yovel sees Freud as a follower of Spinoza:

> Freud and Spinoza became uncompromising critics of historical religion, adhering to a radical philosophy of immanence while denying any transcendental horizon to existence. There are only natural phenomena, though the

69. See Klein, *Jewish Origins of the Psychoanalytic Movement*, 173–74, 246 ("During the last half of the nineteenth century the Helmholtz school of medicine, brandishing its materialistic credo, completely dominated physiological and medical thinking."); Bernfeld, "Freud's Earliest Theories," 348–50. But see Cranefield, "Freud and the 'School of Helmholtz,'" 35–39 (Although, "Freud's belief in psychic determinism may well owe much to the determinism of his teachers and especially to Brücke," reference to the "School of Helmholtz" is misleading).

70. Miller, *Psychology*, 174 ("Freud was Brücke's student"); Bernfeld, "Freud's Earliest Theories," 348 (When Freud entered medical school, he studied at the Physiological Institute of Brücke.).

71. See generally Miller, *Psychology*, 173–74 ("In Germany . . . the science of physiology was controlled by four men: Hermann Ludwig von Helmholtz, Emil Du Bois-Redmond, Ernst Brücke, and Carl Ludwig. These four men formed a private club in Berlin whose members were pledged to destroy vitalism . . .").

72. See Bernfeld, "Freud's Earliest Theories," 348–49. The oath was, specifically: "[We pledge] to put in power this truth: no other forces than the common physical chemical ones are active within the organism. In those cases which cannot at the time be explained by these forces one has either to find a specific way or form of their action by means of physical mathematical method, or to assume new forces equal in dignity to the chemical-physical forces inherent in matter, reducible to the force of attraction and repulsion" (Bernfeld, "Freud's Earliest Theories," 348). "This pledge expresses materialism in a pure form, flatly denying that life might involve vital forces transcending 'the force of attraction and repulsion'" (Miller, *Psychology*, 174).

73. Miller, *Psychology*, 246–47. See Bernfeld, "Freud's Earliest Theories," 356 ("In spite of the new revolutionary features of psychoanalysis, its core is a continuation of the work that Freud did for Brücke.").

meaning of nature is expanded by both thinkers to include the psychic domain
... Freud shares Spinoza's refutation of the image of man as endowed with
a God-given soul, selfless motives, or a transcendental mind separate from
nature and capable of modifying and manipulating nature from without. Human beings are fully integrated in nature and are moved by a dominant natural striving or source of energy (*conatus* in Spinoza, *libido* in Freud), which
streams forth in a variety of outlets, and which knowledge and the products
of high culture are but sublimated configurations. This has an irritating ring
in the ears of traditional believers, whether religious or metaphysical, who are
used to thinking of man as halfway between animal and angel ...

The climate of ideas that Freud shares with Spinoza is naturalistic and
deterministic, yet the meaning of 'nature' is expanded in both to include the
psychic (even the logical) domain. Nature acquires an additional depth dimension; in Freud it includes psychological depths of the unconscious, and
in Spinoza it takes the form of the attribute of 'thought,' in which nature is
internally reflected and which is considered an integral part of nature.[74]

The principle of immanence is most forcefully argued for by Freud in *The Future of an Illusion* (1928). In the fifth and sixth chapters of *The Future of an Illusion* Freud examines the "psychological significance" of "religious ideas." He contends that no valid, logical bases for believing these ideas exists, and the fact that these ideas were believed by our ancestors is not an adequate reason for *us* to believe them since our ancestors believed in many things that we could not possibly accept any longer, and the "proofs they have bequeathed to us ... are full of contradictions, revisions, and interpolations."[75] In particular, says Freud, "spiritualists ... are convinced of the immortality of the individual soul, and they would demonstrate to us that this one article of religious teaching is free from doubt."[76] Yet, he claims, "they have not succeeded in

74. Yovel, *Adventures of Immanence*, 142–47. See also Yovel, *Adventures of Immanence*, 160 ("As Spinoza had maintained overtly, so Freud implies tacitly: psychic changes have their bodily correspondents. The early Freud was anxious to secure an autonomous scientific role for psychoanalysis, independent of anatomy and bodily medicine; hence he resorted to language that ignored the somatic parallels of psychic events. But the older Freud no longer hesitated to refer to the body as the locus of psychoanalytic structures and processes. The 'ego,' he says, 'is first and foremost a bodily ego'; it has spatial dimension even in the 'anatomical' sense ... As in Spinoza, in order to maintain a strict philosophy of immanence while refusing to simply reduce mental phenomena to bodily states, some sort of mind-body parallelism must be admitted, whereby the psychic and somatic aspects of the organism are two complementary expressions of the same [phenomenon]. Or putting it differently: if the mind is to be the object of autonomous study and interpretation, without admitting a transcendent ground for it, then the mind must be both attached to a body and irreducible to the terms by which the body is studied. This is, fundamentally, also Spinoza's position."). According to Damasio, Spinoza "had an important influence on Freud" (Damasio, *Looking for Spinoza*, 260). In 1932, Freud said of Spinoza: "'I have had, for my entire life, an extraordinary esteem for the person and for the thinking of that great philosopher'" (Damasio, *Looking for Spinoza*, 260, quoting Freud in correspondence to Siegfried Hessing).

75. See Freud, *Future of an Illusion*, 45–47.

76. Freud, *Future of an Illusion*, 48.

disproving the fact that the appearances and utterances of their spirits are merely the productions of their own mental activity."[77]

He, therefore, considers the "psychological origin of religious ideas" and determines that these ideas, "which profess to be dogmas, are not the residue of experience or the final result of reflection; [but, rather] they are illusions, fulfilments of the oldest, strongest and most insistent wishes of mankind."[78] He elaborates as follows:

> Thus, the benevolent rule of divine providence allays our anxiety in the face of life's dangers, the establishment of a moral world order ensures the fulfilment of the demands of justice, which within human culture have so often remained unfulfilled, and the prolongation of earthly existence by a future life provides in addition the local and temporal setting for these wish-fulfilments.[79]

Freud concludes that, because religious doctrines (including doctrines about an immortal soul, resurrection, and an afterlife) "are all illusions [and] do not admit of proof . . . no one can be compelled to consider them as true or to believe them. Some of them are so improbable, so very incompatible with everything we have laboriously discovered about the reality of the world, that we may compare them . . . to delusions."[80] At any rate, truths about the nature of the world can only be known through science.[81] In fact, Freud opines that it is precisely due to the "increase in the scientific spirit in the higher strata of human society" that "religion no longer has the same influence on men that it used to have."[82]

D. On the Basis of Experimental Biology Jacques Loeb Abandons Belief in an Immortal Soul or Any Afterlife

Jacques Loeb was a leading biologist who taught that life can be explained in physico-chemical terms. Accordingly, he agreed with those nineteenth-century biologists who abandoned the notion of a soul to explain life. As Freud, Loeb was deeply devoted to the well-being of the Jewish people. According to Deichman, Loeb was "appalled by the suppression and persecution of Jews in Russia, he supported the activities of Zionists, and served as an advisor for the development of science-related institutions

---

77. Freud, *Future of an Illusion*, 48.

78. Freud, *Future of an Illusion*, 52. Freud distinguishes illusions from delusions. "It is characteristic of the illusion that it is derived from men's wishes; in this respect it approaches the psychiatric delusion, but it is to be distinguished from this . . . In the delusion we emphasize as essential the conflict with reality; the illusion need not be necessarily false, that is to say, unrealizable or incompatible with reality . . . Thus we call a belief an illusion when wish-fulfilment is a prominent factor in its motivation, while disregarding its relations to reality, just as the illusion itself does" (Freud, *Future of an Illusion*, 54–55).

79. Freud, *Future of an Illusion*, 52–53.

80. Freud, *Future of an Illusion*, 55.

81. See Freud, *Future of an Illusion*, 55.

82. Freud, *Future of an Illusion*, 67.

in Palestine."[83] The Jacques Loeb Centre for the History and Philosophy of the Life Sciences at Ben-Gurion University of the Negev is named after him.

After attaining his medical degree, Loeb began working as an assistant for Adolf Fick, a physiology professor at Wurzburg. At that time, 1886, Loeb also met Julius von Sachs, a famous botanist. Von Sachs was researching plant tropism, the ability of plants to respond like simple machines to external stimuli, such as light or gravity. Loeb decided to apply similar ideas to animals. His first experiment in animal tropisms involved caterpillars' reaction to light. When caterpillars hatch from cocoons they climb to the tips of branches for food. It was believed that caterpillars had an instinct for where to find food. Loeb, however, had a more mechanistic hypothesis. He believed that the caterpillars had no such instinct and were simply responding to the external stimulus of light. His experiments proved his theory correct. Caterpillars were given the choice of light or food and they chose light even though they starved to death. Loeb worked feverishly on this idea for two years until he published his first paper on animal tropisms.

He immigrated to the United States in 1891, and "There he was successful; he occupied positions at Bryn Mawr, Chicago, Berkeley, and, from 1910, at the Rockefeller Institute for Medical Research in New York, with summers spent in the marine laboratories at Pacific Grove or Woods Hole."[84] Loeb's interests gradually shifted from physiology to experimental embryology, where, shortly after his emigration to America, he conducted his most famous experiment involving the artificial parthenogenesis (reproduction without fertilization) in sea urchins.[85] He subjected eggs to both chemical and physical stimuli and discovered several methods by which an egg could develop without sperm fertilization. Loeb's work on artificial parthenogenesis established him as a major figure in biology, and he was nominated for the Nobel Prize in 1901.

In 1912, Loeb published a collection of his essays in a volume titled *The Mechanistic Conception of Life*, his most famous work. The book's title is also the title of its first essay. The object of the essay, states Loeb, is to "discuss whether our present knowledge gives us any hope that ultimately life . . . can be explained in physico-chemical terms."[86] He then discusses what constitutes truth in scientific biology (and science in general). This is followed by a brief mention of the beginning of scientific biology with the work of Laplace and Lavoisier in 1780. Regarding this work, Loeb states that it touched on the core of the "riddle of life," by which he means the "desire to know how life originates and what death is."[87] Scientific biologists know, says Loeb, that every living thing is able to transform food-stuffs into living matter, that the compounds that are formed in the animal body can be produced artificially, and

83. Deichmann, "Introductory Remarks," 7.
84. Deichmann, "Introductory Remarks," 3.
85. See Deichmann, "Introductory Remarks," 5.
86. Loeb, *Mechanist Conception of Life*, 3.
87. Loeb, *Mechanist Conception of Life*, 5.

that chemical reactions that occur in living organisms can be repeated at the same rate and temperature in the laboratory, but they don't know the chemical character of the catalyzers. Loeb then asserts: "Nothing indicates, however, at present that the artificial production of living matter is beyond the possibilities of science."[88]

Loeb then goes on to talk about the activation of the egg, stating that twelve years earlier biologists did not know how spermatozoon caused an egg to develop into a new individual, but that they now do; the activation of the egg has been reduced to physico-chemical terms. He next describes (1) the process of cell activation by spermatozoon, (2) his own experiments with sea urchins in which unfertilized eggs were activated with sea water, and (3) subsequent developments. He concludes that, given what had been learned in the past twelve years, biologists have a right to hope that remaining riddles will soon be solved.

In a section of the essay entitled "Nature of Life and Death" Loeb writes:

> The nature of life and death are questions which occupy the interest of the layman to a greater extent than possibly any other purely theoretical problem; and we can well understand that humanity did not wait for experimental biology to furnish an answer. The answer assumed the anthropomorphic form characteristic of all explanations of nature in the prescientific period. Life was assumed to begin with the entrance of a 'life principle' into the body; that individual life begins with the egg was of course unknown to primitive or prescientific man. Death was presumed to be due to the departure of this 'life principle' from the body.
>
> Scientifically, however, individual life begins . . . with the acceleration of the rate of oxidation in the egg, and this acceleration begins after the destruction of its cortical layer. Life of warm blooded animals—man included—ends with the cessation of oxidation in the body . . . The problem of the beginning and end of individual life is physico-chemically clear. It is therefore unwarranted to continue the statement that in addition to the acceleration of oxidations the beginning of individual life is determined by the entrance of a metaphysical 'life principle' [a soul] into the egg; and that death is determined, aside from the cessation of oxidations, by the departure of this 'principle' from the body. In the case of the evaporation of water we are satisfied with the explanation given by the kinetic theory of gases and do not demand—to repeat a well-known jest of Huxley—the disappearance of the 'aquosity' be also taken into consideration.[89]

---

88. Loeb, *Mechanist Conception of Life*, 5.
89. Loeb, *Mechanist Conception of Life*, 14–15.

E. Morris Raphael Cohen's Faith in Liberalism and Science Leads Him to Challenge Inherited Beliefs about Resurrection and Immortality, and to View Hope in an Afterlife as Illusory

Morris Raphael Cohen was a leading American philosopher.[90] He "adhered to agnosticism all of his life" and was not known to have attended religious services.[91] Yet, he has been called one of "the two most intensely Jewish thinkers ... in the entire sweep of American history."[92] Cohen taught philosophy at the City College of New York from 1912 to 1938. He was a fierce defender of rationalism, naturalism, and the scientific method, and an equally fierce opponent of supernaturalism and superstition. In his most well-known work, *Reason and Nature: An Essay on the Meaning of Scientific Method* (1931), Cohen states:

> It is frequently asserted that the principle of scientific method cannot rule out in advance the possibility of any fact, no matter how strange or miraculous. This is true ... Actually, however, certain types of explanation cannot be admitted within the body of scientific knowledge. Any attempt, for instance, to explain physical phenomenon as directly due to Providence or disembodied spirits, is incompatible with the principle of rational determinism. For the nature of these entities is not sufficiently determinate to enable us to deduce definite experimental consequences from them. The Will of Providence, for instance, will explain everything whether it happens one way or another. Hence, no experiment can possibly overthrow it. An hypothesis, however, which we cannot possibly refute cannot possibly be experimentally verified.[93]

The two most important pillars of Cohen's philosophy are his commitments to the scientific method and to liberalism. He saw both pillars as intimately connected.[94] The critical examination of one's beliefs that is common to both liberalism and science means, for Cohen, that they both require, and foster, the virtues of tolerance and humility.[95] The belief in toleration was, in fact, described by Cohen, in "The Future of

---

90. Konvitz, *Nine American Jewish Thinkers*, 23. Konvitz, "Morris Raphael Cohen," 487 (Cohen was "'an almost legendary figure in American philosophy, education, and the liberal tradition,'" quoting *The New York Times*).

91. Rosenfield, *Portrait of a Philosopher*, 209. See Konvitz, *Nine American Jewish Thinkers*, 33 ("Cohen was an agnostic, or what used to be called, especially in England, a rationalist.").

92. Konvitz, *Nine American Jewish Thinkers*, 24.

93. Cohen, *Reason and Nature*, 158–59.

94. Cohen, *Dreamer's Journey*, 171. See also Cohen, *Faith of a Liberal*, 14 ("the policies of liberalism aim to liberate the energies of human nature by the free and fearless use of reason. Liberalism disregards dogmas and rules that hinder the freedom of scientific inquiry and the questioning of accepted truths. Prophets, priestly hierarchies, sacred books, and sanctified traditions must submit their claims to the court of human reason and experience. In this way mankind is liberated from superstitious fears.").

95. See Konvitz, "Morris Raphael Cohen," 497 ("A fundamental tenet of his liberalism is that an individual may never assume that he has the whole truth in his possession. Moral humility, tolerance,

American Liberalism," as one of the "two fundamental ideas of liberalism," the other being "the belief in progress."[96] In that same essay, Cohen also said that the belief in tolerance "is very closely connected with scientific method" for tolerance implies the willingness to consider opposing points of view, and the scientific method "is largely a method that consists in the development of the consequences of differing hypotheses."[97] Similarly, the virtue of humility implied, for Cohen, the recognition that one's ability to know whether one's inherited beliefs are, in fact, true is limited. Arrayed against humility is the vice of pride—the assumption, without adequate evidence, that one's inherited beliefs must be true.[98]

Cohen viewed religion to be antithetical to science and liberalism. In an essay called "The Dark Side of Religion," Cohen contended:

> To religion, agreement is a practical and emotional necessity, and doubt is a challenge and an offense. We cannot tolerate those who wish to interfere or break up the hallowed customs of our group. Science, on the other hand, is a game in which opposing claims only add zest and opportunity . . . Thus it comes to pass that religion passionately clings to traditional beliefs which science may overthrow.
>
> . . .[R]eligion never preaches the duty of critical thought, of searching or investigating supposed facts.[99]

Cohen goes on to discuss "some actual forms of superstition [that is, irrational, unscientific beliefs] that have been strengthened by religion," such as demonic possession.[100] More specifically, he discusses the "persistence of the belief in disembodied spirits, benevolent and malevolent," stating that "all existing religions involve the belief in such supernatural beings, called gods, ghosts, spirits of ancestors, demons, angels, etc." and that "religion is largely based on and develops credulity in this domain."[101]

In this same essay, Cohen disputes the claim that religion is "the protector of morals and that the breakdown of [religion] inevitably leads to an enduring decline in morality."[102] He argues instead that "religious morality' must be criticized for emphasizing "the sanctions of fear—the terrifying consequences of disobedience."[103] He

---

a belief in the scientific method, freedom of speech and inquiry—a faith in these qualities of mind and action was at the heart of his liberalism.").

96. Cohen, *Faith of a Liberal*, 449.

97. Cohen, *Faith of a Liberal*, 453–54.

98. See generally Rosenfield, *Portrait of a Philosopher*, 207 (the cardinal sin is spiritual pride—the assumption of knowledge where knowledge is impossible).

99. Cohen, *Faith of a Liberal*, 342, 345. Cf. Spinoza, *Theological-Political Treatise*, 4 ("faith has become identical with credulity and biased dogma . . . completely inhibiting man's free judgment and capacity to distinguish true from false").

100. See Cohen, *Faith of a Liberal*, 342–43.

101. Cohen, *Faith of a Liberal*, 343.

102. See Cohen, *Faith of a Liberal*, 347–53.

103. Cohen, *Faith of a Liberal*, 348.

asserts that the "predominant emphasis on the motive of fear for the enforcement of absolute commands has made religious morality develop the intensest cruelty that the human heart has known."[104] In this regard, he criticizes, in particular, the development of, and stress placed upon, "the doctrine of Hell, of eternal and most terrifying punishment."[105] Finally, Cohen criticizes religion for holding out the hope of an afterlife. He states that "hopes may be illusory or ill-founded—they may even attach to what is demonstrably impossible. Such, in light of modern science, is the hope of the actual resurrection of the body."[106] Worse yet, depending upon how the afterlife is envisioned, hope for an afterlife may be "thoroughly unworthy and even sordid."[107]

The criticism of religious morality (which emphasizes the fear of eternal punishment and the illusory hope of resurrection for the purpose of a material reward) expressed in "The Dark Side of Religion" was presaged in Cohen's review of Paul Elmer More's book, *Platonism*, which first appeared in *The New Republic* of August 31, 1918.[108] Here, Cohen criticizes More's general illiberal, unscientific point of view, and then extends that criticism to More's attempt "to make of Plato an orthodox Calvinistic moralist."[109] Cohen asserts that More's own Calvinistic philosophy underlies his analysis of Plato, and Cohen says that, while More's Calvinistic moral conception is "still most powerfully entrenched" and "still taught in all our Sunday and week-day schools, and in almost all of our colleges," it is nevertheless against "the current of the day."[110] The Calvinistic moral conception, as Cohen understood it, assumes that "none of us would be 'good' or moral unless we were promised some reward or threatened with punishment."[111] And, says Cohen, "there are few doctrines so intellectually dishonest as doctrines concerning the rewards and punishments of the moral life ... That those who suffer must have been wicked, and that those who triumph must have been virtuous, is one of the most inhuman beliefs in history."[112]

---

104. Cohen, *Faith of a Liberal*, 349.

105. Cohen, *Faith of a Liberal*, 348. See also Cohen, *Faith of a Liberal*, 350 ("intense hatred for the enemies of God (i.e., those not of our own religion) has invented and developed the terrors of Hell, and condemned almost all mankind to suffer them eternally—all, that is, except a few members of our own particular religion.").

106. Cohen, *Faith of a Liberal*, 354.

107. Cohen, *Faith of a Liberal*, 354.

108. See Cohen, *Faith of a Liberal*, 72–77. See generally Cohen, *Dreamer's Journey*, 182–83 (discussing Cohen's involvement with *The New Republic*, and stating that in the years between 1914 and 1921 he was "a fairly regular contributor").

109. Cohen, *Faith of a Liberal*, 72.

110. Cohen, *Faith of a Liberal*, 73. According to Cohen, Calvinism cannot "stand the light of that mode of thought which we call modern science, but which has its roots in ancient Greece. The spirit of free inquiry has no room for that reliance on and craving for 'authority higher than reason' which is at the heart of Mr. More's whole effort" (Cohen, *Faith of a Liberal*, 73).

111. Cohen, *Faith of a Liberal*, 75.

112. Cohen, *Faith of a Liberal*, 75.

Within a year of Cohen's review of More, he revisited the theme of reward and punishment in a review of Felix Adler's *An Ethical Philosophy of Life*, also appearing in *The New Republic*.[113] Cohen praises Adler for being "too enlightened to share the orthodox belief that all the atrocious evil of life will be compensated in some 'hereafter.'"[114] Cohen states further that "the importance which Professor Adler rightly attaches to the instrumentalities of life clearly suggests the need of a radical transformation of the traditional view according to which the business of life is the saving of one's soul in a universe which is a transcendental wage system designed to reward men according to their effort and sacrifices."[115]

In yet another essay for *The New Republic,* entitled "Dante as a Moral Teacher,"[116] Cohen argues that Dante's "otherworldly morality" makes Dante's *Divine Comedy* "more alien to the modern spirit than the more distant but more human world of Homer."[117] Modern morality, Cohen believes, is "positive" in recognizing that the human heart desires "the peace and order that nourishes an ever-growing harmonious human life *on this earth*."[118] Dante's otherworldly morality is "essentially negative" and "has little sympathy with the earthly joys and sorrows that fill our life here."[119] Dante has "no conception of the multitudinous forces within the community that intelligent direction can harmonize into a brighter and fuller life."[120] The different moralities are due, in part, to the fact that the modern view of the world has been widened by science. Today,

> the idea that some men are all perfect and deserve eternal blessedness, while others are all wickedness and deserve eternal damnation, cannot be justified in the forum of enlightened human experience . . . The whole idea that God created men and women knowing that they will sin and thus subject them to eternal torture is odious today . . . The idea of an eternal suffering is horrible enough, but to glorify it and call it, as Dante does, 'supreme wisdom and primal love' makes us ashamed of the human nature that is capable of entertaining such horrible perversity and disloyalty to human nature.[121]

In sum, Cohen not only views resurrection as scientifically impossible, but he disapproves of postulating an afterlife in which the wicked are punished and the righteous

---

113. *The New Republic* 19 (June 25, 1919), in Cohen, *Faith of a Liberal*, 78–84. Cohen was a student of Felix Adler when Cohen was a graduate student in philosophy at Columbia University, and Adler invited Cohen to participate in the meetings of Adler's Ethical Cultural Society. See Cohen, *Dreamer's Journey*, 128, 129.

114. Cohen, *Faith of a Liberal*, 79.

115. Cohen, *Faith of a Liberal*, 83.

116. *The New Republic* 28 (October 12, 1921), in Cohen, *Faith of a Liberal*, 234–41.

117. Cohen, *Faith of a Liberal*, 241.

118. Cohen, *Faith of a Liberal*, 241 (emphasis added).

119. Cohen, *Faith of a Liberal*, 236.

120. Cohen, *Faith of a Liberal*, 237.

121. Cohen, *Faith of a Liberal*, 237–39.

are rewarded. He rejects the very notion that the wicked must be punished and the righteous must be rewarded—he rejects religious morality. Life, for Cohen, is not about saving one's soul for a reward in a *future* life, or about avoiding a future punishment; it is about working for progress in *this* life, about doing what we can to make this life better. Nor is immortality as the mere continuance of life in and of itself valuable; rather, there is value to be found in such life as we experience in the here and now.[122]

In *Reason and Nature*, Cohen discusses rationality and the scientific method at great length. In a chapter titled "Mechanism and Causality in Physics," Cohen criticizes the view that all physical phenomena can be explained solely on the basis of a mechanical view of nature. This is because the "term *mechanics* as used by physicists denotes [only] that branch of physics which studies the motion of masses" and "there are physical phenomena such as light, magnetism, etc., which are not prima facie phenomena of motion, and no physicist claims that all these have . . . been satisfactorily explained on mechanical principles."[123] Nevertheless, "all nature does behave in conformity with logical and mathematical principles."[124]

In the very next chapter, titled "Law and Purpose in Biology," Cohen considers the case for vitalism, the position "that there is a radical discontinuity between vital and nonvital phenomena, [and] that biological laws are different in character from the laws of the inorganic world."[125] He concludes: "vitalism cares so much for the sense of mystery that it dogmatically blocks the path of rational physical research and it keeps its door open to arbitrary and wilful dreams. Like other attempts to cling to our primitive feelings, it is delightful but childish and barren . . . In the end, . . . [mechanism] keeps the essential faith in the rational concatenation of things according to universal law."[126] He concludes his discussion with an attack on the belief that the righteous must be rewarded and the wicked must be punished in an afterlife:

---

122. In a letter to his wife written in August of 1907, Cohen said: ". . . As an attitude to life agnosticism [is] summed up in [the] saying of Micah—to do justice, to love mercy & [to] *walk humbly with the Lord*. Agnosticism makes much of intellectual honesty and courage. According to it, the cardinal sin is spiritual pride—the assumption of knowledge where knowledge is impossible . . . With regard to the nature of the world as a whole we must remain ignorant in large measure. But though we cannot know God we can *be* godly, at any rate strive to act the godly. Everybody admits certain things are good & others bad. Let us join forces & work for the good & against the evil—As to immortality as a religious doctrine its value consists in making life valuable, but life cannot get its value simply from its continuance. (Hence the recognition that certain parts of life *are* valuable is for the agnostic as good as immortality.)" (Rosenfield, *Portrait of a Philosopher*, 207, emphasis original). See also Rosenfield, *Portrait of a Philosopher*, 237 (referring to Cohen's "philosophical otherworldliness [being unassociated] with belief in monotheism, resurrection, or a day of judgment, but [being] impregnated with a concept of eternity.").

123. Cohen, *Reason and Nature*, 207 (emphasis original).

124. Cohen, *Reason and Nature*, 226.

125. Cohen, *Reason and Nature*, 249.

126. Cohen, *Reason and Nature*, 282.

For the purposes of currently prevailing religion, it is not enough that the world should be merely purposive. It must be purposive in the interests of humanity and in accordance with a definite scheme as to what our best interests are. A purposive world in which the fate of humanity is a mere incident . . . offers little more support to current religion than a dogmatic materialism. Yet so ingrained is the fear of empty spaces and so strong the human desire for a conscious spectator of our intense but often incommunicable inner strivings, that millions have preferred to believe in a demoniac world, designed to torture all but a few of the elect rather than in a world that indifferently pours its beneficent and destructive rains on the just and the unjust [alike].[127]

Cohen begins a chapter of *Reason and Nature* titled "Psychology as a Natural Science" by dismissing "common-sense psychology" as "confused and inadequate."[128] He writes:

The confusion and inconsistency of common-sense psychology is perhaps best seen when we ask what it means by the terms *mind*, *soul*, or *spirit*. The answer will generally be found to contain an unstable mixture of supernaturalism and naïve materialism.

The soul is an ethereal or divine essence so utterly distinct from the earthly body as to be capable of continuing its separate career when the latter disintegrates. But on the other hand common sense cannot conceive of the soul except as some sort of body in space . . .

When we become aware of these inconsistencies and begin to question the assumptions of popular psychology and seek methods of testing them we take the first step in the type of reflection called the philosophy of mind. But such a philosophy cannot develop prosperously without additional and more accurate factual knowledge.[129]

Historically, according to Cohen, the passage from "a common-sense and practical psychology to science begins in Greek philosophy"[130]; but progress in psychology as a science "was hampered by the fact that the immortality of the individual human soul became a religious dogma. The "modern revival of psychology as a science," claims Cohen, was due to two movements.[131] First, the reintroduction of "the experimental methods or attitudes of the natural sciences into psychology through processes of self-observation or introspection" by the British and French followers of Hobbes, Locke, and Hume.[132] Second, the development of psychology "from the physiological side . . . in the nineteenth century" which was "one of the results of the

---

127. Cohen, *Reason and Nature*, 291–92.
128. Cohen, *Reason and Nature*, 295.
129. Cohen, *Reason and Nature*, 295.
130. Cohen, *Reason and Nature*, 296.
131. Cohen, *Reason and Nature*, 296.
132. Cohen, *Reason and Nature*, 296.

rapid expansion of physiology, especially the physiology of the nervous system."[133] Regarding the second movement, Cohen notes that men like Müller, Weber, Helmholtz, Fechner, and Wundt "laid the foundations for a definite science of psychophysics or physiological psychology."[134] Cohen also states that this physiological movement that had begun in Germany spread to the United States, and that William James's *Principles of Psychology*, which united introspection with physiology and treated psychology as a natural science, marks the end of the period of the modern revival of psychology as a science.[135]

In the second section of "Psychology as a Natural Science," Cohen considers the subject-matter of psychology. He begins by considering the concept of the *psyche* or soul. He states: "though the vast majority of men not only have no doubt as to the existence of the soul but believe it survives the body (and may even have had a previous career) most scientific psychologists have rejected this conception as too metaphysical or even mythologic."[136] He briefly considers the arguments for this rejection, concluding:

> we set ourselves against the fallacy of reification, of supposing that because we can speak of the soul as a noun or subject of discourse it must necessarily be an existing thing in which properties inhere. This fallacy of reification is not avoided if for the word *soul* we substitute any other term such as the *conscious* or *unconscious mind, the nonempirical self, the psychic organism independent of the body*, or the like. Conscious life is a series of events in the history of an organism. It is not a separate nonempirical thing. Some realization of this led William James to reject consciousness as an entity though not as a function.[137]

Rejecting "the notion of a substantial mind implies, of course, a rejection of that dualism which conceives of the mind and the 'external' world as two independent substances."[138]

Although the mind or soul is not a "substantial thing," there still exists mental or conscious phenomena (such as perceptions and thoughts). Some who espouse a view that Cohen calls "mentalism" deny that mental phenomena are "events in a physical space," wishing "to destroy the mechanistic view of the world."[139] Opposed to mentalism

---

133. Cohen, *Reason and Nature*, 296.
134. Cohen, *Reason and Nature*, 298.
135. Cohen, *Reason and Nature*, 298.
136. Cohen, *Reason and Nature*, 300.
137. Cohen, *Reason and Nature*, 302 (emphasis original).
138. Cohen, *Reason and Nature*, 322n21. See also Cohen, *Reason and Nature*, xiii ("I reject . . . all monisms which identify the whole totality of things with matter, mind, or any element in it. But I also reject the common dualism which conceives *the* mind and *the* external world as confronting each other like two mutually exclusive spatial bodies. I believe in the Aristotelian distinction between matter and form. But I am willing to be called a materialist if that means one who disbelieves in disembodied spirits; and I should refer to spiritists who localize spirits in space as crypto-materialists"; emphasis original).
139. Cohen, *Reason and Nature*, 311. Cohen adds that "by insisting that 'there is no such thing

CHAPTER 14.

is behaviorism or materialism; behaviorists, says Cohen, "vainly try to wipe out a real difference [between conscious phenomena and physical phenomena] by stretching a word to cover two entities or aspects that need to be distinguished."[140] Cohen discusses these opposing positions at some length. In the end, he rejects both points of view, adopting a position that has some affinity with Spinozism:

> We may, in summary, note that those who seek to eliminate the concept of consciousness entirely have more in common with those who reduce the whole world to forms of consciousness than is generally recognized. In general, any argument as to whether the world falls within one or the other of opposite categories must be largely verbal. But the common element of mentalism and behaviourism may be seen more precisely if we consider their relation to the primitive error of reifying the soul or mind . . . If, upon the assumption that the mind is a substantial thing, we look for its constituent elements, we find only such bilateral facts as seeing, desiring and wondering, in all of which 'external reality' is implicated. Now either these relations are internal and constitutive of our original mind-substance, in which case the universe becomes an attribute of mind, or they are external, in which case there can be no empirical evidence for the existence of mind itself . . . In both cases the position assumed is explicable only if we conceive the mind as a substantial thing. With that assumption rejected, there is no difficulty in supposing that the bilateral facts of experience give us knowledge of two aspects of the universe. The existence of these distinct aspects is the first postulate of a scientific psychology.[141]

Given Cohen's nondualistic metaphysics, eagerness to question inherited beliefs, and this-worldly focus, it is not surprising that Cohen greatly admired Spinoza and titled a 1927 essay "Spinoza: Prophet of Liberalism."[142] In that essay, Cohen said:

> It is true that Spinoza rejects the idea of an anthropomorphic God, who will respond to our flattering prayers, reward us for our unsuccessful efforts, and in general compensate us for the harshness of the natural order and the weakness of our reason . . . If, however, religion, consists in humility (as a sense of infinite powers beyond our scope), charity or love (as a sense of the mystic potency in our fellow human beings), and spirituality (as a sense of the limitations of all that is merely material, actual or even attainable), then no one was more deeply religious than Spinoza . . .
>
> Spinoza has little regard for the immortality which means the postponement of certain human gratifications to a period beyond our natural life. He does, however, believe in the immortality which we achieve when we live in

---

as a physical world existing apart from consciousness' [mentalists] prevent due consideration of the physical conditions of the latter" (Cohen, *Reason and Nature*, 311).

140. Cohen, *Reason and Nature*, 314.
141. Cohen, *Reason and Nature*, 321–22.
142. *The New Republic* 50 (March 30, 1927), in Cohen, *Faith of a Liberal*, 13–19.

the eternal present or identify ourselves with those human values that the process of time can never adequately realize or destroy.[143]

---

143. Cohen, *Faith of a Liberal*, 19. Accord, Cohen, *Dreamer's Journey*, 217. See also Cohen, *Faith of a Liberal*, 307–19.

15.

Mordecai Kaplan, the Founder of Reconstructionism, Advocates Naturalism and This-Worldliness, as Does Sherwin Wine, the Leading Voice in Humanistic Judaism

THE REVOLUTION THAT WAS initiated by Spinoza, and that came to fruition in the nineteenth and twentieth centuries, found its most influential Jewish voice in Mordecai Kaplan. Kaplan agreed with Spinoza that the Hebrew Bible is not the literal word of God, and that one should avoid reading one's own prejudiced ideas into the Hebrew Bible.[1] Kaplan also agreed with Spinoza's naturalism—associating God with the forces of nature that enable human beings to achieve a this-worldly salvation, not with a supernatural being.[2] For both Spinoza and Kaplan, "God does not intervene in history or formulate laws. God does not reward or punish."[3] Then too, Kaplan, as Spinoza, taught that salvation is attained in *this* world, not in an afterlife. Kaplan believed that Jewish survival in the twentieth century required a this-worldly focus because one could not be a modern person without it, and because Judaism would not survive, he thought, if it remained at odds with modernity.[4] Kaplan wrote:

---

1. Scult, *Radical American Judaism of Mordecai M. Kaplan*, 23. Just as Spinoza taught that people had to be "liberated from the authority of the Bible and its interpreters so that they might pursue the truth through a life of reason," so Kaplan "sought to free the Jewish people from the authority of tradition" (Scult, *Radical American Judaism of Mordecai M. Kaplan*, 23).

2. See e.g., Kaplan, *Meaning of God*, 40–103; Agus, *Modern Philosophies of Judaism*, 300 (In *Judaism as a Civilization* Kaplan "[identifies] God with nature, taken as a whole . . . In this sense, God is the natura naturans of Spinoza, the underlying unceasing energy of the universe.").

3. Scult, *Radical American Judaism of Mordecai M. Kaplan*, 25. See generally Scult, *Radical American Judaism of Mordecai M. Kaplan*, 25–26 (comparing Spinoza's concept of God with Kaplan's concept of God).

4. See Kaplan, *Greater Judaism in the Making*, 425 ("Salvation, or human self-fulfillment, came to be conceived as realizable in the here-and-now, rather than in the hereafter or in a world-to-come. The otherworldly outlook . . . was viewed as irrelevant for modern times.' ").

Throughout the post-biblical period until modern times, salvation was conceived as achievable only in the hereafter. In recent times such postponement has come to be regarded as evasion of the duty to improve living conditions and abolish exploitation and war in the here and now.[5]

Although Kaplan took issue with what he perceived as Spinoza's scorn for the Jewish people, he "embraced much of [Spinoza's] philosophy."[6] As a student, Kaplan studied "the history of philosophy and devoted himself particularly to the study of Spinoza, Kant, and the major philosophers of the nineteenth century."[7] Later, when Kaplan was associated with the Jewish Theological Seminary, he taught a course for rabbinical students called "Philosophies of Judaism" which included a discussion of Spinoza.[8] Kaplan's notes for this course contains the following appraisal of Spinoza:

> Spinoza's importance consists in his crystallizing the spirit of modernism . . . He altered radically the [traditional] universe of thought and has virtually established the contemporary universe.[9]

In short, as Kaplan's biographer and leading commentator notes, "we can sum up much of Kaplan's philosophy by calling it a Spinozist approach to God and religion in the service of saving the Jewish people."[10]

It is noteworthy that just as Spinoza's unorthodox views led to his excommunication, so was Kaplan excommunicated by a Jewish religious body because of his unorthodox views.[11] This chapter summarizes the relevant parts of some of Kaplan's most important works. These are *Judaism as a Civilization: Toward a Reconstruction of American-Jewish Life* (1934), *The Meaning of God in Modern Jewish Religion* (1937), *The Greater Judaism in the Making: A Study of the Modern Evolution of Judaism* (1960), and *The Religion of Ethical Nationhood: Judaism's Contribution to World Peace* (1970). After these summaries, attention will be paid to the liturgical works of the Reconstructionist movement founded by Kaplan. Finally, mention will be made of the thought of Sherwin Wine, the founder of Humanistic Judaism, a new movement which, as Reconstructionism, may be seen as arising as a result of the influence of Spinoza.

---

5. Kaplan, *Greater Judaism in the Making*, 480.
6. Scult, *Radical American Judaism of Mordecai M. Kaplan*, 20.
7. Scult, *Judaism Faces the Twentieth Century*, 53.
8. Scult, *Radical American Judaism of Mordecai M. Kaplan*, 21n33.
9. Scult, *Radical American Judaism of Mordecai M. Kaplan*, 21 (quoting Kaplan's notes).
10. Scult, *Radical American Judaism of Mordecai M. Kaplan*, 22.
11. See Silver, "Excommunication of Mordecai Kaplan," 21–25; Gurock and Schacter, *Modern Heretic and a Traditional Community*, 140–41. See also Scult, *Radical American Judaism of Mordecai M. Kaplan*, 11–27 (comparing the excommunication and thought of Kaplan to that of Spinoza, "one of Kaplan's intellectual inspirations").

CHAPTER 15.

A. *Judaism as a Civilization* Envisions Judaism as Dynamic and as Entering a New Stage of Development in Which the Center of Gravity Will Again Be on the Here and Now, Not the Afterlife

JTS Chancellor Arnold Eisen considered *Judaism as a Civilization* "'the single most influential book of its generation.'"[12] Its publication resulted in a small group of Kaplan's friends launching the Reconstructionist magazine in January 1935, which, in turn, "started the Reconstructionist movement which 'is dedicated to the advancement of Judaism as a religious civilization, to the upbuilding of Eretz Yisrael, and to the furtherance of universal freedom, justice and peace.'"[13]

The introductory chapter of *Judaism as a Civilization* sets forth the circumstances underlying what Kaplan saw as a "crisis in Judaism."[14] Whereas before the nineteenth century all Jews regarded Judaism as a privilege, "since then," Kaplan contends, "most Jews have come to regard it as a burden."[15] A sense of inferiority and self-contempt, Kaplan believed, was the result of a changed environment, a new world outlook, faced, not only by Jews, but by all peoples. "Before the enlightenment the one dominant concern of human beings was their fate in the hereafter . . . The prospect of attaining bliss in the world to come, which constituted the Jews' conception of salvation, was . . . in keeping with the conception of salvation which until recently prevailed throughout the world with which Jews came in contact . . . The only way in which the Jew believed it was possible for him to achieve salvation was by remaining loyal to his people, for it was only by sharing their life in this world that he was certain to share their life in the next world. This belief was the great cohesive force of Jewish life in the past."[16]

Part one of *Judaism as a Civilization*, subtitled "The Factors in the Crises," consists in a discussion of (1) those factors promoting Jewish disintegration, (2) those factors promoting conservation of Judaism, and (3) a "decisive factor" related to a "program of reconstruction."[17] The factors promoting disintegration are political, economic, and ideological. Most relevant in the present discussion are the ideological factors. Here Kaplan identifies three ideological tendencies which "distinguish modernism from medievalism."[18] These include the tendency to adopt the scientific approach to ascertain the truth, the tendency to set up human social well-being as the criterion of the good for man (instead of the revealed will of God), and the tendency to regard esthetic enjoyment and self-expression as of ultimate value, not of mere incidental worth.[19]

---

12. Silver, "Excommunication of Mordecai Kaplan," 21n3.
13. Kaplan, *Judaism as a Civilization*, ix.
14. See Kaplan, *Judaism as a Civilization*, 3–15.
15. Kaplan, *Judaism as a Civilization*, 3.
16. Kaplan, *Judaism as a Civilization*, 6, 8.
17. See, Kaplan, *Judaism as a Civilization*, 19–87.
18. Kaplan, *Judaism as a Civilization*, 36.
19. Kaplan, *Judaism as a Civilization*, 36–37.

These modern standards of what are true, good, and beautiful clash with traditional Jewish values far more violently than did medieval standards.[20] Significantly, Kaplan views modern aesthetic values as being the antithesis to the belief in otherworldliness, for "that belief declares the fulfillments of this world to be vanity."[21]

With respect to factors promoting conservation of Judaism, Kaplan writes:

> Although the primary cohesive force which held the Jewish people together—the traditional conception of otherworldly salvation—*has practically become inoperative*, there has developed in the course of the centuries of living, thinking and suffering together, a secondary cohesive force which manifests in the will to maintain and perpetuate Jewish life as something desirable in and for itself.[22]

The forces of disintegration and conservation are said by Kaplan to be equally balanced.[23] He asserts: "In order that Judaism shall survive, Jews must focus their mind and heart upon the task of giving purpose and direction to what is at present little more than a blind urge to live as Jews."[24] What is required, he believes, is a program (related to a new version of Judaism) that will enable the individual Jew to achieve "Jewish self-fulfillment."[25] Before setting forth this program in part three of the book, Kaplan, in part two, explains why the "current versions of Judaism" are inadequate to achieve the desired goal. These current versions are said to be: (1) Reformist, (2) Conservative, right-wing Reformist, (3) Neo-Orthodox, and (4) Conservative, left-wing Neo-Orthodox.

Kaplan acknowledges that the Reformist version of Judaism recognized the merit of the change in world outlook, and saw the need for Judaism to adjust to it. He writes:

> Reformism sees in the shifting of the center of gravity from interest in the hereafter to interest in transforming the world we live in, and in the substitution of the authority of reason for the authority of tradition, permanent and ineluctable gains of the human spirit. It therefore assumes that Judaism should welcome the necessity which compels it to readjust itself and to reconstruct its teaching in light of the new developments in human life.[26]

Consequently, Reformism was able to prevent "thousands of Jews . . . from severing all connections with their people."[27] Nevertheless, Reformism is inadequate to provide

---

20. Kaplan, *Judaism as a Civilization*, 37.
21. Kaplan, *Judaism as a Civilization*, 41.
22. Kaplan, *Judaism as a Civilization*, 47 (emphasis added).
23. Kaplan, *Judaism as a Civilization*, 80.
24. Kaplan, *Judaism as a Civilization*, 84.
25. Kaplan, *Judaism as a Civilization*, 84.
26. Kaplan, *Judaism as a Civilization*, 91–92. See Kaplan, *Judaism as a Civilization*, 109 (the Reformist movement "represents a deliberate and purposeful effort in social and spiritual adjustment.").
27. Kaplan, *Judaism as a Civilization*, 108.

the necessary program for Jewish self-fulfillment that Kaplan desires.[28] According to Kaplan, Reformism has "failed to check the process of gradual self-elimination of Jews from Jewish life."[29] One of his main criticisms of this version of Judaism is that it has repudiated Jewish nationhood and reduced Judaism to an ideology.[30]

In contrast to Reformism, Neo-Orthodoxy has failed to directly face the crux of the problem confronting modern-day Jews. Even though "the center of interest has been shifted from life in the world to come to life in this world," Neo-Orthodoxy has "permitted the conception of otherworldly salvation to remain inert by neglecting to dwell upon the consequences and implications of that conception."[31] It has thus "mummified" what was in traditional Judaism a vital and functioning belief, relegating it "to the background."[32] Moreover, "Neo-Orthodoxy, like the Reformist movement which it is combatting, regards all institutions of national life as quite secondary in importance, if not altogether superfluous."[33]

The two Conservative versions of Judaism are seen by Kaplan as merely weaker, inconsistent versions of Reform and Neo-Orthodoxy, and are, accordingly, easily dismissed by him.[34] The version of Judaism advocated by Kaplan is one which sees Judaism as more than merely a religion, more than a matter of religious beliefs and practices. Rather, it conceives of Judaism as a complete civilization through which Jews can achieve self-fulfillment in this world. Kaplan explains:

> With this approach, the question of 'why be a Jew?' loses its relevance. If Jewish life is a unique way of experience, it needs no further justification. We may call this approach to Judaism the intuitional approach, in contrast with the traditional approach of Neo-Orthodoxy and the rational approach of Reformist Judaism.[35]

Implied in Kaplan's version of Judaism is the idea that the beliefs and practices of Jews have changed to adjust to differing environments. "As a civilization, Judaism is not a static system of beliefs and practices but a living and dynamic social process, the manifestations of which are conditioned by the nature of the environment."[36] Kaplan identifies three distinct stages in Jewish civilization: (1) the henotheistic stage, (2) the theocratic stage, and (3) the otherworldly stage.[37] The third stage, that of other-

---

28. See Kaplan, *Judaism as a Civilization*, 108–25 (critiquing the Reformist version of Judaism).
29. Kaplan, *Judaism as a Civilization*, 110.
30. See Kaplan, *Judaism as a Civilization*, 120–21, 124–25.
31. See Kaplan, *Judaism as a Civilization*, 155.
32. See Kaplan, *Judaism as a Civilization*, 155–56.
33. Kaplan, *Judaism as a Civilization*, 159.
34. See Kaplan, *Judaism as a Civilization*, 126–32, 160–69.
35. Kaplan, *Judaism as a Civilization*, 182.
36. Kaplan, *Judaism as a Civilization*, 209.
37. See Kaplan, *Judaism as a Civilization*, 210–14.

worldliness, "dominated Jewish thought during the eighteen centuries of traditional Judaism."[38] In that stage the *summum bonum* (the highest good) was transferred "from the present earthly environment to an environment which God will create at some future time."[39] According to Kaplan, the third stage is in the process of ending; consequently, he writes that "Judaism is now on the threshold of a fourth stage in its development, and the civilization into which it will grow will be humanistic and spiritual . . . [T]he next phase of Jewish civilization will constitute, in some respects, a return on a higher level to the first stage; *the center of gravity of the spiritual interests will again be the here and now.*"[40]

B. *The Meaning of God in Modern Jewish Religion* Claims That Salvation for Modern Man Is This-Worldly, Not Otherworldly, and Debunks the Notion That Human Beings Are a Composite of Body and Soul

In keeping with Kaplan's fundamental viewpoint that Judaism is a constantly evolving civilization, he recognizes that the concept of God in Jewish thought has been changing to adjust to new environments. In *The Meaning of God in Modern Jewish Religion*, Kaplan argues that a new change in the God concept is required to adjust Jewish beliefs about God to the modern environment. The God concept that he believes modernity requires is, in part, a consequence of modernity's disinterest in otherworldliness in favor of a concern for this-worldliness. Put differently, Kaplan understands the God concept as having *always* been functionally related to achieving salvation so that, because the modern idea of salvation has changed, the modern concept of God must change in a corresponding manner.[41]

Kaplan asserts that from the time of the destruction of the Second Temple in 70 CE until the Enlightenment period "the conception of salvation held by the Jews was otherworldly."[42] The future life was envisioned as "a posthumous existence of an

---

38. Kaplan, *Judaism as a Civilization*, 212.

39. Kaplan, *Judaism as a Civilization*, 213.

40. Kaplan, *Judaism as a Civilization*, 214 (emphasis added).

41. Kaplan believes that modernity also requires that we cease to think of God as a "being" and as, in any way, supernatural. He writes that: "In thinking about God we must avoid all those mental habits which issue in logical fallacies. The most common of these is the habit of hypostasis, or assuming the separate identifiable existence of anything for which language has a name . . . The divine is no less real, no less dependable for our personal salvation or self-realization, if we think of it as a quality than if we think of it as an entity or being" (Kaplan, *Meaning of God*, 21–25). Regarding supernaturalism he writes: "To the modern man, religion can no longer be a matter of entering into relationship with the supernatural. The only kind of religion that can help him live and get the most out of life will be the one which will teach him to identify as divine or holy whatever in human nature or in the world about him enhances human life" (Kaplan, *Meaning of God*, 25).

42. Kaplan, *Meaning of God*, 43.

CHAPTER 15.

entirely different order from life as it is encountered here on earth."[43] Life on earth is a struggle for survival, and a struggle against the sinful nature of mankind; and life on earth ends in death.[44] "In the world to come," however, 'there would not only be no death, but there would be no toil. Life would sustain itself, according to one version, without food or drink."[45] According to another version, "men would eat the fruits of the earth as in this life, but these would be brought forth in abundance, without men's having to toil to produce them.'"[46] In addition to changes in the physical environment, Kaplan notes, in the world to come, human nature itself would be transformed: "God [will] destroy the Evil *Yezer*, all those passions and appetites that tempted man to evil-doing, so that he [will] no longer be in danger of falling from grace, and there [will] be no bar to his perfect and direct communion with God."[47] In short, the ideal envisioned by reference to the world to come is "the ultimate fulfillment of . . . human yearnings for a harmonious and cooperative social order."[48]

The conduct of people today, however, claims Kaplan, is not motivated by a yearning for an ideal existence in a *future* world. It has "dawned upon man that he can transform his physical and social environment and deliberately change the conditions under which he lives."[49] Consequently, modern people are motivated "by the desire to win for themselves a share of life in *this* world, to win success, honor, love and everything that contributes to human well-being and self-fulfillment *on earth*."[50] Modern man conceives of a situation in which his wants are satisfied in the here and now, and he endeavors to affect his present environment, and human behavior, so that they conform to such conception. This is what is meant by having "ideals."[51]

Kaplan argues that people today *should* seek salvation in this world, and not in an afterlife. In the past, belief in a future, posthumous world was required because man had become so acutely aware of "evil which seemed to him irremediable that he might have been driven to despair, had he not been able to hope for salvation in the hereafter. By preserving the ideal of salvation, so to speak, in heaven, man could bring that ideal

---

43. Kaplan, *Meaning of God*, 50.

44. Kaplan, *Meaning of God*, 46.

45. Kaplan, *Meaning of God*, 47 (citing b. Ber. 17a). "There would, of course, be no begetting of children, . . . so that the curse of Eve as well as the curse of Adam would be removed" (Kaplan, *Meaning of God*, 47, citing b. Yabam. 62a).

46. Kaplan, *Meaning of God*, 47 (citing Exod. Rab. 25:21).

47. Kaplan, *Meaning of God*, 48.

48. Kaplan, *Meaning of God*, 51. See also Kaplan, *Meaning of God*, 44–45 ("The terms in which our fathers conceived of [the future] bliss were very concrete, and were projections of whatever men found desirable on earth.").

49. Kaplan, *Meaning of God*, 50. Cf. ch.13, sec. C, 1 (discussing John Dewey).

50. Kaplan, *Meaning of God*, 44 (emphasis added).

51. See Kaplan, *Meaning of God*, 51–52. Cf. Dewey, *Common Faith*, 23 ("all endeavor for the better is moved by faith in what is possible, not by adherence to the actual."). See also Kaplan, *Meaning of God*, 53–55.

down to earth as soon as he learned enough about himself and the world he lived in to be able to improve both."⁵² At the present time, however, the effect of the

> opiate of otherworldliness . . . is to keep us from the attainment of salvation on earth. This is equally true whether we think in terms of personal salvation or of social salvation . . . Religion must no longer betray the hopes of men for the abolition of poverty, oppression and war on this earth by regarding these evils as mere 'trials and tribulations' or 'chastisements of love,' for which we shall be compensated in another world. It must cease waiting for an act of miraculous intervention to remove these evils 'in the end of days.' It must [rather] encourage men with faith and hope to apply human intelligence and good-will to the removal of these evils in the achievement of the social salvation of mankind.⁵³

Just as it is fallacious to hypostasize the concept of God,⁵⁴ so it is fallacious to hypostasize the concept of the soul. More specifically, Kaplan states that the divine "is no less real, no less dependable for our personal salvation or self-realization, if we think of it as a quality [rather] than . . . as an entity or being."⁵⁵ Then he continues: "Human personality may serve as an illustration. It is no less real, if we think of it in psychological terms, as a system of behavior patterns in which the human organism reacts to the world, than if we think of it as a sort of invisible spiritual man that inhabits the physical man and determines his behavior."⁵⁶ Kaplan thus recognizes that modern science has debunked the notion that a human being is a combination of body and soul; rather, a human being is a psychosomatic unity.⁵⁷ In this point of view, Kaplan was no doubt influenced by John Dewey who railed against the dualism of mind and body, thought and action, intelligence and habit.⁵⁸

---

52. Kaplan, *Meaning of God*, 55.

53. Kaplan, *Meaning of God*, 55–57. The new idea of salvation corresponds, for Kaplan, to a new understanding of the Sabbath. The Sabbath has always functioned in the Jewish consciousness as a symbol of salvation. See Kaplan, *Meaning of God*, 41–42. Today, says Kaplan, "*the Sabbath should serve as the symbol of this-worldly salvation*" (Kaplan, *Meaning of God*, 57, emphasis original). It should remind us that "we can transform the evils of the world, if they are within our control, and transcend them, if they are beyond our control" (Kaplan, *Meaning of God*, 63).

54. See Kaplan, *Meaning of God*, 21; *supra*, n. 41.

55. Kaplan, *Meaning of God*, 25.

56. Kaplan, *Meaning of God*, 25.

57. See Kaplan, *Meaning of God*, 88 (Modern science has again reconstructed our picture of the universe and destroyed the dichotomy of body and soul, matter and spirit, physical and metaphysical, which characterized the Middle Ages.).

58. See Dewey, *Human Nature and Conduct*, 63–69 (decrying separation of body and mind, practice and theory, actualities and ideals, habit and thought). A strong affinity in the thought of Dewey and Kaplan has been noted by many Jewish thinkers. See Lazaroff, "Kaplan and Dewey," 173n1. But see Lazaroff, "Kaplan and Dewey," 181–82 (Lazaroff contends that Kaplan's transnaturalism "is quite distinct from Dewey's naturalism").

CHAPTER 15.

C. *The Greater Judaism in the Making* Reiterates Kaplan's Views

The Greater Judaism in the Making: A Study of the Modern Evolution of Judaism is, essentially, a fuller account of views originally set forth in *Judaism as a Civilization*, including an account of (1) the change in worldview from medieval times to the modern era, (2) the failure of existing "versions of Judaism" (viz., Reform Judaism, Orthodox Judaism, Conservative Judaism and Zionism) to adequately meet the challenge to traditional Judaism arising from the modern worldview, and (3) Kaplan's proscription for a more viable Judaism that incorporates and synthesizes those elements in the existing versions of Judaism that are "in keeping with what is most likely to enable the Jews as individuals and as a people to contribute their share to the betterment of human life."[59]

In the book's preface, Kaplan asserts that the challenge to Jews and to Judaism comes from "modern naturalism" which is in conflict with "the supernaturalism inherent in the traditional religions *and with their doctrine that salvation is achievable only in the hereafter and not in this world*."[60] To meet the challenge of the modern world, says Kaplan, Jewish leaders have proposed four different solutions: Reform, Orthodoxy, Conservatism, and Zionism. These differing responses to the challenge posed to Judaism by modernity suggest that, if Judaism is to survive, "it will have to emerge as a Greater Judaism, and that the present chaos in Jewish life is the process of creation which should be properly described as 'the Greater Judaism in the making.'"[61]

The first three chapters of the book describe the "world of traditional Judaism" and includes a chapter on the "salvational aspect of traditional Judaism."[62] This chapter discusses at some length the otherworldliness of traditional Judaism. Kaplan stresses that otherworldliness was not part of biblical Judaism, and just as rabbinic Judaism altered biblical Judaism to incorporate the otherworldliness that had become dominant during the Second Temple period, so the greater Judaism in the making must alter rabbinic Judaism to incorporate the naturalism that has become dominant in the modern period:

> [T]he otherworldly outlook on life, God, and man which became an integral part of the Jewish tradition was not originally a part of that tradition, but came to it from without. This shows that a religious tradition, no matter how sacrosanct, cannot remain uninfluenced by a dominant world outlook, however alien to the tradition's original character. Naturalism has become as dominant a world outlook as otherworldly supernaturalism was in the days when the Pharisees had to reinterpret the Torah in keeping with the then prevailing otherworldly outlook. If, therefore, the Jewish religious tradition is to function

---

59. Kaplan, *Greater Judaism in the Making*, 450.
60. Kaplan, *Greater Judaism in the Making*, vii–viii (emphasis added).
61. Kaplan, *Greater Judaism in the Making*, x.
62. Kaplan, *Greater Judaism in the Making*, 3–111.

in our day, it has to come to terms with naturalism. That is the next metamorphosis it has to undergo.[63]

After the chapters discussing the worldview of rabbinic Judaism there follows a chapter on medieval Judaism. Here Kaplan discusses two distinct trends developed during the Middle Ages which altered the general worldview of rabbinic Judaism, namely rationalism and mysticism. Regarding rationalism, beginning with Saadia and continuing through the fifteenth century, Kaplan identifies eleven ways in which rabbinic Judaism underwent metamorphosis by synthesizing Greek philosophy.[64] Two of the changes are particularly relevant to the soul, resurrection, and the afterlife: (1) a sharp distinction is drawn between the body and the soul, and the soul "is conceived in philosophical terms suggested by Aristotle" with that part of the soul associated with the intellect surviving the destruction of the body, and (2) while belief in bodily resurrection continues, the "theologians . . . find resurrection a troublesome belief," with Maimonides refusing to accept unqualifiedly the traditional idea concerning resurrection but, rather, assuming that the reunification of soul and body is not eternal because the body, being a compound substance, "must ultimately disintegrate and fall away from the soul."[65]

According to Kaplan,

> even the pronouncedly intellectual elements of Jewish mysticism, such as those which have to do with the conception of God, of the world, or of the soul, are definitely extraneous in origin . . . Alien notions, such as those concerning the resurrection of the dead, or of the world to come, unconsciously transformed the thought-pattern of biblical religion during the era of the Second Commonwealth. So did alien notions about emanation, 'sparks,' and metempsychosis, which unconsciously found their way later into Jewish tradition as interpreted by the mystics. The *Tannaim* of the *Mishnah* were so certain that the doctrine of resurrection was contained in the Torah that they consigned to perdition anyone who denied such origin. The Jewish mystics would similarly have condemned anyone who would have questioned the Torah origin of such beliefs as those concerning the *Sefirot* or concerning metempsychosis.[66]

Kaplan traces the origins of Jewish mysticism, going back to the first century BCE.[67] Three of the many observations that Kaplan makes about Jewish mysticism deserve mention. First, whereas Jewish philosophers were on the whole treated with aversion in premodern Judaism, Kabbalah enjoyed great prestige.[68] Second, Jewish

---

63. Kaplan, *Greater Judaism in the Making*, 86.
64. See Kaplan, *Greater Judaism in the Making*, 116–20.
65. Kaplan, *Greater Judaism in the Making*, 119–20.
66. Kaplan, *Greater Judaism in the Making*, 124.
67. See Kaplan, *Greater Judaism in the Making*, 130–43.
68. Kaplan, *Greater Judaism in the Making*, 125–26.

mysticism "not only recognized the reality of evil, but was preoccupied with the problem of combating it in *this* world."⁶⁹ Third, Jewish mysticism "strongly accentuated . . . the redemption of Israel and the salvation of the individual."⁷⁰

Next, Kaplan describes the cultural and scientific revolutions that began with the Renaissance.⁷¹ He states that the result of these revolutions "is the naturalist approach to reality, in contrast with the thought-world of supernaturalism and otherworldly salvation."⁷² He writes:

> The modern challenge to Judaism differs radically from the one which the Jewish People encountered in the past. That challenge emanates from the spirit of this-worldliness, or secularism, which permeates contemporary human life. The transfer of the center of gravity of human existence from the other world to this world is both the cause and the effect of modern man's desire to acquire mastery over the forces of nature and his growing ability to render the world he lives in more habitable . .
>
> Formerly, the evils in the world, both natural and social, presented an impregnable wall against which man seemed to dash himself in vain. Hence, the more aware of his helplessness man grew, the more he found it necessary to look to another world than the present one for the meaning of his existence. This led him to conclude that affliction and misery were part of the divine plan as means of rendering man worthy of bliss in the hereafter . . . But once man realized what power he possessed to make this world more habitable by manipulating the forces of nature, he tended to abandon the idea that all of life's evils were inevitable. He began to think of eliminating those evils instead of trying to find some plausible explanation for them.⁷³

D. Kaplan Addresses the Soul and Its Immortality in *The Religion of Ethical Nationhood*

In *The Religion of Ethical Nationhood: Judaism's Contribution to World Peace*, Kaplan discusses his notion that the soul is a "trans-natural process." He makes it clear that his intent is *not* to imply a capacity to "overstep the limits of nature", rather, he means

---

69. Kaplan, *Greater Judaism in the Making*, 128 (emphasis original).

70. Kaplan, *Greater Judaism in the Making*, 130.

71. See *Kaplan, Greater Judaism in the Making*, 144–220.

72. Kaplan, *Greater Judaism in the Making*, x.

73. Kaplan, *Greater Judaism in the Making*, 150–51. See Kaplan, *Greater Judaism in the Making*, 167 ("As soon as Renaissance humanism and Enlightenment rationalism began to undermine the belief in otherworldly salvation, the human mind began to explore the possibilities of this-worldly, or secular, salvation."), 183 ("As in general life, so in Jewish life, Enlightenment meant reliance upon personal initiative and effort as a means of bettering one's lot, individually and collectively, instead of passively waiting for divine help.").

only to assert that human beings are different than other species of animals.[74] In particular, human beings have "personality," the ability to consciously and creatively strive to achieve self-fulfillment through self-control of their baser instincts and cooperation with their fellow man. Put differently, human beings can transcend their purely material and individual desires and act rationally, creatively, and ethically for the betterment of society as a whole and to achieve goals that are not purely material.[75]

Kaplan further asserts that a human being "transcends mechanistic and scientific law" in the sense that, unlike subhuman species, human beings have values.[76] Values are

> a manifestation of self-consciousness . . . By *conscious* striving to develop his latent talents a person achieves that *differentia* which determines his essential nature in contrast to the essential nature of other living creatures. The human experience of selfhood manifests itself in a sense of responsibility for what one thinks, feels or does; a sense of responsibility is experienced emotionally as an imperative call for expression and action . . . Personality is thus experienced emotionally as self-identity or responsibility. Insofar as it has direct bearing on man's striving for salvation or self-fulfillment, personality is generally referred to as a *soul*.[77]

Man's self-consciousness, his awareness of his potential to set goals related to his values, and to work cooperatively and creatively with others to overcome obstacles and achieve his goals (that is, to achieve salvation or self-fulfillment), is thus associated by Kaplan with man's personality or soul. It is this aspect of human nature that Kaplan calls "spiritual."[78] It is perfectly clear that Kaplan does not conceive the soul to be a separate entity distinct from the body that continues to exist after the body's

---

74. See Kaplan, *Religion of Ethical Nationhood*, 89 ("Transcendence does not imply overstepping the limits of natural law. It merely implies taking into account a dimension within human nature which some scientists ignore. That is the dimension of value which differentiates human nature from subhuman nature.").

75. See Kaplan, *Religion of Ethical Nationhood*, 88–92. See also Kaplan, *Future of the American Jew*, 246–54 (discussing what Kaplan refers to as "spiritual selection," which is a term he coined to indicate that humans cannot achieve their destiny, cannot achieve self-fulfillment, unless they keep their inclinations or desires in check, subject them to the control of reason or a transcendent law, and bring them "into a pattern of integrated personality and cooperative society," and stating: "the doctrine of spiritual selection sees in man's reason and ethical aspirations the evidence of a different destiny from that of other species and stresses the human differentia . . . Man has, as it were, been selected from among all orders of existence to find survival and self-realization through rational self-control and disinterested love. Man thus *transcends* the rest of nature in introducing a new method of survival"; emphasis added); Kaplan, *Meaning of God*, 85–86 (the response of nonhumans to their environment "is instinctive and involves a minimum of conscious evaluation" whereas humans, owing to memory, imagination, and speech, are aware of the possibility of transcending limitations the environment imposes on the realization of their aims).

76. Kaplan, *Religion of Ethical Nationhood*, 88–92.

77. Kaplan, *Religion of Ethical Nationhood*, 89–90 (emphasis original).

78. See *supra*, n. 75.

decompensation.[79] Kaplan specifically refers to such concept as being "premodern."[80] He then states: "In modern psychological terms, immortality might be transmuted into the assumption that man's spiritual dimension or moral responsibility lives on through an endless chain of creative consequences. Those consequences constitute immortality for the person and society."[81]

E. Current Reconstructionist Liturgy Departs from Kaplanian Views about the Soul and the Afterlife

Kaplan's *Sabbath Prayer Book* was published in 1945. As one would expect, traditional prayers are altered by Kaplan to reflect his this-worldly point of view. Surprisingly, after Kaplan's death, the movement he founded saw fit to adopt a new series of prayerbooks that is notably less emphatic in stressing the principle of immanence championed by Kaplan. The willingness to permit allusion to otherworldliness no doubt reflects the influence of what Raphael calls "the Jewish renewal movement" of the 1970s and 1980s.[82]

1. The *Sabbath Prayer Book* eliminates the doctrine of resurrection and affirms a Kaplanian version of the immortality of the soul

In the program for reconstruction of Judaism set forth in *The Future of the American Jew* (1967), Kaplan asserts that the revitalization of the Jewish religion requires that its "*sancta*" be reinterpreted so as to be relevant to the needs of moderns.[83] This reinterpretation requires the elimination of any association with magic and supernaturalism.[84] Kaplan believed that whenever possible, traditional forms of worship should be retained. It was only when a traditional text "ran counter to scientifically established fact" that it had to be expunged.[85] This general sentiment is expressed in the introduc-

---

79. See generally Lazaroff, "Kaplan and Dewey," 181 (although Kaplan "speaks of the soul as the infinitely creative plus in human beings beyond nature . . . [he also] insists that the spiritual and rational is neither supernatural nor transcendent . . . Kaplan's transnaturalism is thus more appropriately not a dualism but rather a distinction between a higher and lower form of being.").

80. Kaplan, *Religion of Ethical Nationhood*, 94.

81. Kaplan, *Religion of Ethical Nationhood*, 94.

82. Raphael, *Jewish Views of the Afterlife*, xlii. See ch. 12, sec. C, 5

83. Kaplan, *Future of the American Jew*, 48–49.

84. Kaplan, *Future of the American Jew*, 48–49.

85. See Eisenstein, "Kaplan as Liturgist," 325. See also Eisenstein, "Kaplan as Liturgist," 329–30 ("Kaplan drew a line at affirming as true, or even seeming to affirm as true, what he believed with certainty to be untrue, such as statements about the historicity of miracles as operations that involved suspension of natural law."); Caplan, *From Ideology to Liturgy*, 54 ("The refusal to alter tradition in light of modern belief and values is a dangerous form of nostalgia that will 'hasten the inner disintegration of Jewish life' as many Jews abandon their heritage because of its archaic views"; quoting the *New Haggadah*, 18).

tion to the *Sabbath Prayer Book*.[86] The introduction also expresses opposition to the practice of retaining traditional prayers that are objectionable but "reading into them meanings completely at variance with what they meant to those who framed them."[87] To use English translations to read meanings into traditional Hebrew prayers that are at variance with the Hebrew text would "violate the principle of forthrightness" and confuse the "average worshipper."[88]

Having set forth these and other general principles, the introduction discusses changes made to the Sabbath liturgy with regard to specific doctrines. Of relevance in the present context is the discussion of the doctrine of resurrection. It is stated:

> *The Doctrine of Resurrection*: Men and women brought up in the atmosphere of modern science no longer accept the doctrine that the dead will one day come to life. To equate that doctrine with the belief in the immortality of the soul is to read into the text a meaning which the words do not express. That the soul is immortal in the sense that death cannot defeat it, that the human spirit, in cleaving to God, transcends the brief span of the individual life and shares in the eternity of the Divine Life can and should be expressed in our prayers. But we do not need for this purpose to use a traditional text which requires a forced interpretation. This prayer book, therefore, omits the references to the resurrection of the body, but affirms the immortality of the soul, *in terms that are in keeping with what modern-minded men can accept as true*.[89]

The immortality of the soul affirmed in the *Sabbath Prayer Book* as being "in keeping with what modern-minded men can accept" did not entail that there is an entity—the soul—which is separate from, and survives the decomposition of, the body. Indeed, this is *not* what is being affirmed. As is suggested elsewhere in the introduction, what is being affirmed is that we must live for ends "that link us with the life of all mankind, and, beyond that, with the life of the universe, with God."[90] We must do so because "[h]uman life has worth only when its interests extend beyond the service of the self. Only then do we feel that we are fulfilling our destiny as human beings and find joy in that fulfillment. Only by serving God can we achieve salvation."[91] All

---

86. Kaplan and Kohn, *Sabbath Prayer Book*, xvii, xxiii.

87. Kaplan and Kohn, *Sabbath Prayer Book*, xxiii. See Caplan, *From Ideology to Liturgy*, 54 ("Kaplan also rejected the approach to liturgy that . . . seeks to reconcile modern views and troubling aspects of the siddur text by making the English translation reflect current understandings while leaving the Hebrew words unchanged. For Kaplan, a siddur should state clearly, in both Hebrew and English, what a Jew ought to believe about God, Israel and the Torah.").

88. Kaplan and Kohn, *Sabbath Prayer Book*, xxiii.

89. Kaplan and Kohn, *Sabbath Prayer Book*, xxvii–xxviii (emphasis added).

90. Kaplan and Kohn, *Sabbath Prayer Book*, xix.

91. Kaplan and Kohn, *Sabbath Prayer Book*, xix–xx. See Caplan, *From Ideology to Liturgy*, 58 ("while Kaplan did believe that the soul (understood metaphorically as human personality) lived on after death through the memories and values of those touched by the deceased, he was unwilling to associate this view with the belief in resurrection prevalent in the traditional siddur text."). See also

references to the "soul" are presumably meant to refer to the human "personality," to the "self," not to some immaterial entity.

In accordance with the rejection of the doctrine of resurrection, the references to resurrection in the *Gevurot* benediction of the *Amidah* are removed. The first reference is simply omitted, and the second is replaced by a Hebrew verse taken from the traditional High Holiday liturgy for this benediction which, in English translation, is rendered "Blessed be Thou, O Lord, who in love rememberest Thy creatures unto life."[92] Reference to resurrection is also removed from the closing stanza of the *Yigdal* hymn.[93] "God, in his great mercy, will revive the dead" is rewritten as "God, in his great mercy, sustains the living [*hayim mehalkel*]."[94]

A meditation inserted before the Mourner's *Kaddish*

> attempts to provide mourners with a rationale for not despairing of the goodness of the world as a result of their recent suffering. It argues that there is still cause for optimism since 'those qualities which have made the souls [personalities] of the departed so dear to their survivors have not lost their power or virtue; life can still reveal the divine love which mourners once experienced in the cherished companionship of the departed.'[95]

2. Beginning in 1981, a new Reconstructionist Prayerbook Series is considered, and eventually adopted, called *Kol Haneshamah*, which opens the door to Hasidic ideas about the soul and is accepting of otherworldliness

In the fall of 1981, the Reconstructionist movement established a commission to create a new Reconstructionist liturgy.[96] It had previously been expressed that Kaplanian liturgical viewpoints were no longer dominant in the movement he founded; that among students at the Reconstructionist Rabbinical College (RRC) one is more likely to hear certain traditional prayers than the corresponding Reconstructionist versions, including "the second blessing of the *'Amidah* [the *Gevurot*]."[97] The publication of

---

Gillman, *Death of Death*, 210 ("Kaplan concedes that the wish for immortality stems from a 'divine urge in man not to live only for himself and the moment, but also for mankind and its future.' He continues, 'Insofar as the good we do while alive bears fruit after we are gone, we have a share in the world to come.' That is about as much immortality as Kaplan is prepared to concede"; quoting Kaplan, *Questions Jews Ask: Reconstructionist Answers*, 180).

92. Kaplan and Kohn, *Sabbath Prayer Book*, 44–45, 126–27, 220–21. See Caplan, *From Ideology to Liturgy*, 58–59; Gillman, *Death of Death*, 210.

93. See Caplan, *From Ideology to Liturgy*, 59.

94. Caplan, *From Ideology to Liturgy*, 59. The translation is actually rendered by Caplan "because the SPB provides Israel Zangwill's nonliteral, poetic rendering of the hymn" (Caplan, *From Ideology to Liturgy*, 59n65).

95. Caplan, *From Ideology to Liturgy*, 89, quoting Kaplan and Kohn, *Sabbath Prayer Book*, 61, 197).

96. See Caplan, *From Ideology to Liturgy*, 165–66.

97. See Caplan, *From Ideology to Liturgy*, 167–68.

tentative principles for a new Reconstructionist liturgy "triggered considerable debate within the movement, much of which focused on the desirability of reinstating aspects of the liturgy that Kaplan had removed."[98] The Prayerbook Commission disbanded shortly after the formulation of its working principles, but a new Commission was created in 1987. The new Commission oversaw a series of prayerbooks published under the title of *Kol Haneshamah*.[99] The first book in the series was *Kol Haneshamah: Shabbat Eve*, a siddur for Friday night. This was "an experimental edition [published in 1989] to solicit feedback that was used to mold the subsequent siddurim."[100] An article about this new siddur, appearing in *The New York Times* on February 14, 1989, is titled "Reconstructionist Jews Turn to the Supernatural." According to the article, Reconstructionism had moved "increasingly toward the mystical . . . [by] borrow[ing] liberally from the spiritual tradition of Hasidic Jews."[101] While startling, such a change should have been expected since Arthur Green, who together with Zalman Schacter [later Schacter-Shalomi] had helped to initiate a neo-Hasidic movement in 1968, had become dean and then president of RRC in 1984, and Schacter had taught at RRC in the 1970s. The article in the *Times* states that the new liturgy restores mention of miracles, like the parting of the Red Sea, which Kaplan had eliminated from his liturgical material. It quotes Green as saying that "the 'language of myth' speaks powerfully to many people, even if they do not believe in the literal details."[102]

The experimental *Shabbat Eve* edition was followed in 1994 by *Kol Haneshamah: Shabbat Vehagim*, a Sabbath and festival prayerbook, which includes a revised version of most of the Friday night book; then by *Kol Haneshamah: Limot Hol*, the daily prayerbook, released in 1996; followed by *Kol Haneshamah: Mahzor Leyamim Nora'im*, a High Holiday prayerbook published in 1999; and, last, by *Kol Haneshamah: Prayers for a House of Mourning and a Guide to Mourning Practices*, put out in 2001. Green, who "served as Hebrew editor of most of the Sabbath and festival material" until his departure from RRC in 1993, "was, for the most part in favor of reinstating the traditional *nusaḥ*. The other rabbis on the Commission were divided, depending on the issue."[103]

There are numerous references in *Kol Haneshamah* to a *soul*, some of which can be interpreted by an "average worshipper"[104] to be referring to the soul and its immortal-

---

98. Caplan, *From Ideology to Liturgy*, 169.

99. See Caplan, *From Ideology to Liturgy*, 170–71. The name of the series "comes from Psalm 150— *Kol haneshamah tehalel Yah* that is often translated, 'Let every soul praise God.' But *kol haneshamah* could also mean, 'all the soul'" (Teutsch, *Shabbat Vehagim*, xxvi).

100. Caplan, *From Ideology to Liturgy*, 171.

101. Goldman, "Reconstructionist Jews."

102. See also Caplan, *From Ideology to Liturgy*, 201–2 (discussing the Prayerbook Commission's decision to reinstate references to the Red Sea miracle, and stating that, for "Arthur Green, 'religion is about a sense of the miraculous . . . The religious mind sees the natural as supernatural.'").

103. Caplan, *From Ideology to Liturgy*, 172–74.

104. Kaplan and Kohn, *Sabbath Prayer Book*, xxiii.

ity in a Platonic sense, and to an otherworldly salvation. Nowhere in *Kol Haneshamah* is there an adequate discussion of what is meant by a "soul," so a worshipper, lacking knowledge that (for Kaplan, at least) "soul" means simply "personality" (or the self), could easily interpret the word "soul" to refer to an entity existing separate from the body. Indeed, several liturgical texts, and commentaries explaining the texts, invite such misunderstanding. For example, *Kol Haneshamah: Shabbat Vehagim* reinstates *'Elohai Neshamah*, a text which the *Sabbath Prayer Book* omitted. The language of the prayer refers to the soul as a *thing* that is separate from the person. It states: "the soul you gave me is pure. You have created it, you shaped it, and you breathed it into me, and you preserve it deep inside of me. And someday you will take it from me, restoring it to everlasting life."[105] Similarly, a Derash offered by the editors refers to the soul as a thing which is separate from us, separate from our personhood.[106] In sum, everything about the language of this blessing, and the comments offered to explain the language, suggests a concept of the soul as an independent entity that survives the destruction of the body and continues on for eternity.[107]

One might have thought that, given the various ways in which *Shabbat Vehagim* presents the risk that worshippers may understand the liturgical text to be referring to an immortal soul which is separate and apart from the body, and to a future world in which the "pure souls" return to a God (which is separate and apart from the natural world), the editors have been somewhat careless. But it turns out that the editors may have actually acted with an *intent* to make multiple understandings of the text possible. This possibility arises in light of a discussion of the afterlife contained in *Kol Haneshamah: Prayers for a House of Mourning And a Guide to Mourning Practices*. This prayerbook contains a guide "to suggest basic *Reconstructionists* practices ... for mourners and for those who comfort mourners."[108] The guide contains the following teaching about life after death:

> As an evolving religious tradition, Judaism has passed through several stages in its thinking about the afterlife. In the biblical period, life was understood as primarily this-worldly, and whatever afterlife may have been envisioned was vaguely understood as a shadowy and ethereal semi-existence in a place called Sheol ... [T]he death of the individual was seen as final, and ... eternity was understood to be in the ongoing life of the Jewish people.
>
> With the rise of the rabbinic period ... a more focused concern on the fate of the individual emerged. Evidence from this period ... points to an

105. Teutsch, *Shabbat Vehagim*, 164.

106. Teutsch, *Shabbat Vehagim*, 164 ("God, the healer, returns our souls to us"). See also Teutsch, *Shabbat Vehagim*, 166 (expressing the kabbalistic thought: "When we each accept the purity of our own souls and the purity of the souls of others, *tikun olam* will have been achieved."), 168 ("We ... celebrate the purity of the soul that is implanted within us.").

107. See also Teutsch, *Shabbat Vehagim*, 136 (stating that "God shall deliver all, upon the end of time" and "God wakes all beings to life").

108. Teutsch, *Prayers for a House of Mourning*, 138 (emphasis added).

emerging belief in *teḥiyat hametim*/resurrection of the dead and *olam habah*/the [heavenly] world to come. Other teachers and authorities affirmed the eternality of the soul while denying the resurrection of the body. Some medieval forms of Jewish mysticism, as well as some forms of contemporary Hasidism, support belief in *gilgul nefashot*/reincarnation . . .

With the rise of modernity, the belief in bodily resurrection and a heavenly realm receded before science, reason and rationality. The early Reform and the later Reconstructionist prayerbooks eliminated references to resurrection and the world to come . . .

Reconstructionist Judaism . . . sees the current period in Jewish life as a this-worldly period . . . While no longer affirming many of the traditional ideas about life beyond death, Reconstructionist Judaism recognizes that eternality and immortality remain important spiritual concepts that can be understood from naturalist and humanistic perspectives.

Like our biblical ancestors, we affirm faith in the eternality of the Jewish people . . . And like our rabbinic ancestors, we affirm that beyond the limits of human life and the human body are our individual neshamot/souls with which we are graced and for which we are responsible. At death, the body comes to rest, but the soul returns to God.

. . . Some understand each soul to be as a wave, drawn back into the ocean from which it was essentially never separate. A smaller number of Reconstructionists . . . find comfort and meaning in the more traditional ideas of a world to come . . .[109]

Pursuant to this statement, Reconstructionists may now be understood to accept any view about the soul, resurrection, and the afterlife, no matter how unscientific, baseless, or irrational. It is doubtful that Kaplan would approve.

F. Late in the Twentieth Century, Sherwin Wine Founded the Society for Humanistic Judaism Which Discards the Concept of God and Rejects Belief in an Afterlife

Sherwin Wine believed that Jews could and should abandon the concept of God. Of course, well before Wine there had been Jewish atheists and agnostics, but Wine was different. First of all, Wine was a rabbi; second, Wine believed that Jewish observance and ritual could and should be maintained without the concept of God.[110] Wine founded what he called "Humanistic Judaism," and in 1969 helped to establish the

109. Teutsch, *Prayers for a House of Mourning*, 158–59 (emphasis added).

110. In other words, unlike Kaplan, Wine believed that one could be a rabbi on the basis of nontheistic religion. Corresponding to this difference is a different view about Jewish identity. Whereas Kaplan thought that Jewish identity requires belief in God, a central thesis of Wine is that Jewish identity does not require such a belief. See Wine, *Judaism Beyond God*, 86–104 (discussing Jewish identity). According to Wine: "The old Judaism finds theological value in Jewish identity. The new Judaism finds *humanistic* value in Jewish identity" (Wine, *Judaism Beyond God*, 100–1, emphasis original).

CHAPTER 15.

Society for Humanistic Judaism as a national outreach for the new movement.[111] Others have preferred the term "Secular Judaism" to Humanistic Judaism and, combining both terms, the International Federation for Secular Humanistic Judaism and the related International Institute for Secular Humanistic Judaism (providing training for rabbis and leaders of the new movement) came into being in the mid-1980s. Included in the tenets of Secular Humanistic Judaism is the rejection of belief in an afterlife. Indeed, according to Adam Chalom, Dean of the Institute, one meaning of the word "secular" is "this-worldly, naturalistic."[112] Chalom considers Secular Humanistic Judaism to be comparable to other organized Jewish religious groups in that it celebrates "Jewish culture through communities of shared values, traditions, holidays, life-cycle ceremonies and positive beliefs."[113]

When it became known that Wine was leading a congregation that didn't recognize God, controversy ensued:

> *The Detroit Free Press* ran an article in December 1964 with the headline 'Suburban Rabbi: I am an Atheist.' This was followed by stories in *Time* magazine and *The New York Times*. Wine explained that his views were not precisely atheistic. Rather, reflecting his acceptance of the basic outlook of the logical positivists, he declared that it was not possible empirically to prove or disprove the existence of God and, therefore, the concept was meaningless.[114] He referred to this stance as 'ignosticism' rather than atheism.[115]

In 1985, Wine's book *Judaism Beyond God* was published. The central thesis of *Judaism Beyond God* is that rabbinic Judaism "has lost most of its believing public" as

---

111. See also Scult, *Radical American Judaism of Mordecai M. Kaplan*, 112 ("Colleagues and students who misunderstand Kaplan's theology often call him a humanist. The ordinary use of the term *humanism* means that religion is restricted completely to the human realm. In this sense, Kaplan was definitely not a humanist. Because peoplehood was so central to his concept of religion and because he seemed to equate God with the ideals of the group, many think that he completely dismissed the transcendent and the nonhuman realm. Nothing could be further from the truth."). Scult distinguishes between what he calls "secular humanism" and what he calls "religious humanism," and he sees Kaplan as conforming with the latter and explicitly dismissing the former. According to Scult: "We might describe Kaplan as believing in religion with a decidedly humanistic emphasis, but he was nonetheless a theist" (Scult, *Radical American Judaism of Mordecai M. Kaplan*, 112).

112. Chalom, "Foreword," 2.

113. Wine, *Judaism Beyond God*, 2.

114. Of course, the logical positivists considered the concept of a soul to be equally meaningless. See Ayer, *Language, Truth and Logic*, 31 ("To test whether a sentence expresses a genuine empirical hypothesis, I adopt what might be called a modified verification principle. For I require of an empirical hypothesis, not indeed that it should be conclusively verifiable, but that some sense-experience should be relevant to a determination of its truth or falsehood. If a putative proposition fails to satisfy this principle, and is not a tautology, then I hold that it is metaphysical, and that, being metaphysical, it is neither true nor false but literally senseless. It will be found that much of what ordinarily passes for philosophy is metaphysical according to this criterion, and in particular, that *it can not be significantly asserted that . . . men have immortal souls*, or that there is a transcendent God"; emphasis added).

115. See www.sherwinwine.com/careerhighlights.

a result of the "Secular Revolution."[116] Rabbinic Judaism is described by Wine in the book's second chapter as having been created "out of priestly Judaism by an ambitious scholar class that promised more than the priests offered. Rabbinic rewards included political independence and personal immortality."[117] Rabbinic Judaism postulates an omnipotent, omniscient God who promised the Jews postmortem rewards if they adhered to Jewish religious law. According to Wine, until modern times the "story" of rabbinic Judaism "had no real competition" and "convinced most Jews to remain Jews."[118] However, continues Wine, "the creators of the Secular Revolution" undermined the story told by rabbinic Judaism and "in this day age . . . [the story] is not very believable."[119]

Wine identifies the creators of the Secular Revolution as the "devotees of the Enlightenment, the Age of Reason, the Era of Science," and suggests that the revolution has been going on for "the past four centuries."[120] Central to the revolution is the awareness that human beings have the power "to control their environment" and feel "less of a need to turn to supernatural help [or] to rely on worship."[121] Wine summarizes the history of the Secular Revolution's "subversion of [the] . . . myth" of rabbinic Judaism from the beginning of the revolution until the twentieth century, mentioning Spinoza as one of those who "discarded religious faith as an essential path to truth and publicly embraced secular reason."[122]

Wine essentially contends that the Secular Revolution brought about a transvaluation of values. Faith and obedience, which had been held in the highest esteem before the Secular Revolution, were replaced by reason and dignity.[123] Faith, according to Wine, "prescribes a method for discovering truth"; "it recommends that people trust the advice of their ancestors . . . [and] insists that the wisdom of the past is still true and that the authority of the past is still reliable."[124] In contrast, reason refers to a method of discovering truth that is based on logic and the scientific method.[125] With the advent of reason in the form of modern science "a divine father figure with a personal interest in planet Earth became less believable."[126]

116. Wine, *Judaism Beyond God*, 15.
117. Wine, *Judaism Beyond God*, 9.
118. Wine, *Judaism Beyond God*, 12.
119. Wine, *Judaism Beyond God*, 15.
120. Wine, *Judaism Beyond God*, 15.
121. Wine, *Judaism Beyond God*, 15–16.
122. Wine, *Judaism Beyond God*, 16–17.
123. See Wine, *Judaism Beyond God*, 19–20.
124. Wine, *Judaism Beyond God*, 19.
125. See Wine, *Judaism Beyond God*, 22–23 ("The word *reason* . . . refers to two different thinking processes. The first is best called *formal* reason. The second is called *practical* reason. Formal reason is logic . . . Practical reason . . . is called the *scientific method*. In the world of philosophy, it is known as *empiricism*"; emphasis original).
126. Wine, *Judaism Beyond God*, 29.

Wine notes that replacing reliance on faith as the means to truth with reliance on reason not only influenced attitudes about God but also influenced attitudes about salvation and an afterlife. Specifically, he states: "The men of reason believed that the life [of] reason would dispel superstition and would provide 'salvation' through the truths of the new science. Made aware of its power, humanity would seize the opportunity to transform the human condition and to pursue human happiness in the only life that was ours to live."[127] Wine addresses the afterlife more fully in the last half of the book which deals, *inter alia*, with Jewish humanist approaches to the celebration of holidays and life-cycle events. Wine states:

> Traditional rabbinic mourning customs all derive from [a] denial of death . . . The preservation of the body, even in its skeletal form, was an act of faith in the forthcoming resurrection . . .
>
> As you can well imagine, Humanistic Jews find most of these procedures offensive. Since the secular vision begins with the recognition that death is real, rituals that seek to deny death would compromise human dignity. And the willingness to confront unpleasant truth is part of that dignity. *The Humanistic Jew starts with mortality as an unavoidable and final event.* Life is valuable because it does not go on forever. Happiness is an urgent matter because it will not be available after we die. If there is "immortality," it is purely figurative. Only memory survives in the minds of others.[128]

Judaism Beyond God closes with a list of ten guidelines for believers in Humanistic Judaism. The third guideline states: "From the fundamentalist perspective, preparing yourself for the afterlife is desperately important; from the humanistic perspective, training yourself to make the most out of your life here on earth is equally important."[129]

Secular Humanistic Judaism has grown significantly in the fifty years since Wine formed the first Humanistic congregation, the Birmingham Temple. According to the website of the Society for Humanistic Judaism, there currently are about twenty-six affiliated congregations, communities, and *havurot* in sixteen states, the District of Columbia and Canada, with several more in the process of formation. An Association of Humanistic Rabbis in North America was formed by Wine in 1967 and presently has twenty rabbis as members. It is fitting that an anthology of secular humanistic thought published by the Institute contains as its first entry an excerpt from Spinoza's *Theological-Political Treatise*, and claims Spinoza as a "precursor" of Secular Humanistic Judaism.[130]

---

127. Wine, *Judaism Beyond God*, 32.
128. Wine, *Judaism Beyond God*, 196 (emphasis added).
129. Wine, *Judaism Beyond God*, 226.
130. See Kogel and Katz, *Judaism in a Secular Age*, xxx–xxxi.

16.

Concluding Considerations Regarding the History of Jewish Thought with Respect to the Soul, Resurrection, and the Afterlife

THIS CHAPTER SETS FORTH in sections A to E five claims that may be derived from the history of Jewish thought concerning the soul, resurrection, and the afterlife. Each of these claims is an important take-away from the history recounted herein. The chapter continues in sections F and G with a brief discussion of dogma in Judaism and a statement of the author's position as to what dogmas regarding the soul, resurrection, and the afterlife Jews should accept. In brief, it is argued that (1) Jews, as all people, should believe that which is true, (2) truths about the nature of the world must be established on the basis of science (that is, through the scientific method), and (3) science has not established that human beings possess a Platonic soul, will be resurrected, or will experience a postmortem existence of any kind.

A. There Is No View of the Soul, Resurrection, or the Afterlife that Properly May Be Called Normative in the Jewish Community

The history of Jewish thought makes it abundantly clear that there does not presently exist, and there has never existed, a specific, detailed view of the soul, of resurrection, or of an afterlife that can be said to be, or to have been, normative for all Jewish people. Rather, from biblical times to the present, the Jewish people have held a wide variety of differing, conflicting, and even contradictory ideas about these matters.

The idea of a soul, for example, never existed among the ancient Israelites. More specifically, the Hebrew Bible evidences no notion of a belief that human beings possess, or are to be identified with, an immaterial entity that is responsible for all mental activity, that constitutes one's personality, that exists separate and apart from the body, and that survives the destruction of the body to receive a reward or punishment. To the contrary, the Hebrew Bible presents a view of human beings as psycho-physical wholes, shunning the dualism of soul and body. Further, after the idea of a soul entered into Jewish thought, due to the influence of Greek culture and a need to resolve the problem of moral evil, there developed no clear and agreed upon view as to precisely how to understand this idea. This is not surprising as the Greek concept of *psyche* was itself unclear and confusing.

During the rabbinic period, it came to be generally accepted that souls exist but rabbinic texts offer no well-defined view as to what exactly the rabbis understood a soul to be. Nor were the rabbis particularly interested in such metaphysical issues. In the medieval period, Jewish philosophers, influenced by the Neoplatonism or Aristotelianism of their Islamic counterparts, held relatively clearly defined views about the soul and its postmortem existence but their views neither agreed with each other nor agreed with the views of the less philosophical members of the Jewish community. Then too, the views held by Nahmanides and later kabbalists were very different than those held by most other Jews due to the former's acceptance of *metempsychosis*, which had not been accepted by the rabbis, had been explicitly rejected by Saadia (among others), and was at odds with Neoplatonism and Aristotelianism.

In the Enlightenment period, Spinoza and Mendelssohn held opinions about the soul and its postmortem existence that were very different from any earlier Jew, and very different from each other; and their ideas influenced subsequent generations of Jews. Finally, with the scientific revolution of the nineteenth and twentieth centuries, as well as with the rise of positivism, empiricism, scientism, and liberalism, vast numbers of Jews came to reject the idea of a soul altogether, returning to the biblical view that human beings are psycho-physical wholes. Even among those Jews who continued to accept the idea of a soul there was little clarity or agreement as to what the soul is or what happens to it after death. A major disagreement exists, for example, as to the acceptance of *metempsychosis*. In sum, there is no view of the soul that is, or has been, normative within the entire Jewish community.

Nor has any specific and detailed view of resurrection ever been normative within the entire Jewish community. The Hebrew Bible, for the most part, offers no belief that, in the ordinary course of events, human beings who die will be brought back to life. After the idea of resurrection entered into Jewish thought, largely in response to the problem of moral evil, and perhaps also due to the influence of Persian culture, no uniform view of resurrection ever emerged. From the start, a segment of the Jewish people—the Sadducees, among others—rejected the concept of resurrection. And from that time to the present day there has continued to be Jews who effectively rejected any belief in resurrection. Moreover, among those Jews who accepted a belief in resurrection, there has never been unanimity concerning important aspects of this belief. For instance, there have always been differences concerning precisely who would be resurrected and when any resurrection would occur. Perhaps most importantly, there has never been any clear idea as to what type of body the resurrected person would have, or even whether the resurrected person would have a body or be a person. Some believed that the resurrected body would be exactly like the body before death (needing food and water); others thought the resurrected body would be of an entirely different nature; and still others believed in astral resurrection according to which we would become celestial objects or angels.

During the Middle Ages, Neoplatonic Jewish philosophers abandoned any belief in resurrection, preferring to accept the idea that one's soul returns to the heavenly region from whence it originated. And these Neoplatonic ideas spread among large swaths of Jews who were not philosophically sophisticated. Jewish Aristotelians held views about the soul and its postmortem existence which were quite different than those of the Neoplatonists but by and large they agreed with the Neoplatonists in effectively rejecting any belief in bodily resurrection. With the Enlightenment, increasing numbers of Jews abandoned the concept of resurrection, and this became the official position of those Jews who initiated the reform movement in the nineteenth century. Moreover, while the many Jews embracing Kabbalah or Hasidism may have paid lip service to a belief in bodily resurrection, bodily resurrection is hard to square with their primary allegiance to *metempsychosis*.

Similarly, there is not now, and never has there been, a normative Jewish belief concerning the nature of any afterlife. To a large extent, the absence of uniform beliefs with regard to the nature of an afterlife is a function of the absence of uniform beliefs with respect to the soul and resurrection. The nature of the afterlife for those Jews who accept the immortality of the soul but reject bodily resurrection differs from the nature of the afterlife for those Jews who accept bodily resurrection. But there are also differences within each of these two groups. So, for instance, among those who accept bodily resurrection, the nature of the afterlife envisioned depends upon the nature of the resurrected body that is accepted. This difference accounts for two of the most well-known rabbinic depictions of the afterlife—that of b. Berakhot 17a (which envisions neither eating, drinking, nor sexual activity) and that of b. Ketubbot 111b (which envisions the continued existence of such activities but without effort). A myriad of other issues exists among those who accept resurrection. For example, there are differences of opinion as to the fate of the soul after death but before reunification with the resurrected body. Does the soul stay dormant, as Saadia maintained, or does it receive some sort of reward or punishment, and where does it go? Differences also exist concerning such matters as whether resurrection occurs both at the end of days and at the beginning of the messianic age, as Saadia maintained, or only at the former, and whether punishment is eternal or not.

As for those who accept the immortality of the soul but not resurrection, there were major differences between Neoplatonists and Aristotelians, as well as major differences within each of these two subgroups. For instance, among the Jewish Aristotelians there was a dispute as to whether the postmortem existence of the acquired intellect would, when it united with the active intellect, constitute the continued existence of the person who had lived (the view of Gersonides and Hillel ben Samuel of Verona) or whether the acquired intellect would completely merge with the active intellect destroying all individuality and personhood (the view of Maimonides and Shem Tov ben Yosef Ibn Falaquera).[1] The view of the Neoplatonists differed from the Aristotelians since the former did not have any notion of an acquired intellect merging with an active intellect. But the Neoplatonists also differed among themselves. For instance, the afterlife for Ibn Gabirol, but not for Israeli, included purgation for the sins committed when the soul was embodied. Then too, Mendelssohn's view of the soul was totally unlike that of the medieval Jewish philosophers. And today's Reform rabbis hold a great variety of divergent views as to the nature of the soul and its postmortem existence.

B. Jewish Views of the Soul, Resurrection, and the Afterlife Have Been Evolving, in Large Part Due to External Influences

The history of Jewish thought also makes it abundantly clear that Jewish views of the soul, resurrection, and the afterlife have been evolving, and have been doing so in part because of new ideas from non-Jewish sources. So, the Hebrew Bible evidences no notion of a soul as that term is commonly understood, and presents a nondualistic view of human beings. Nor, for the most part, does the Hebrew Bible evidence any belief in a general resurrection of the dead at some time in the future, or of an afterlife other than a dreary, unanimated existence in *Sheol*. Post-biblical Jewish texts, however, due to the penetration into Jewish thought of Greek ideas, generally adopt dualistic views, seeing human beings as composed of a soul and a body, and offering a variety of afterlife depictions. Some of these texts express a belief in the immortality of the soul and some express, perhaps due to Persian influence, a belief in bodily resurrection. Rabbinic texts develop these postbiblical ideas in a variety of ways, but no attempt is made to present a uniform, systematic view of the soul, resurrection, and the afterlife until Saadia in the tenth century, who relied on reason as well as revelation to arrive at truth.

During the Middle Ages, Jewish views of the soul, resurrection, and the afterlife develop in a variety of ways that are different than, and sometimes in contradiction to, the views of Saadia. Under the influence of Islamic philosophers, some Jewish philosophers accept Neoplatonic views, while others accept views that are considered to be Aristotelian. Many others, attracted to Kabbalah, accept views that have Neoplatonic roots but, unlike those classified as Neoplatonists, include a belief in *metempsychosis*. Furthermore, within each of these groups—Neoplatonists, Aristotelians, and Kabbalists—there are significant divergences, and further development takes place. Among Neoplatonists, for example, Israeli envisions a return to the supernal regions for the souls of the righteous and a place of perpetual torment for the souls of the wicked,

---

1. See ch. 7, nn. 9 and 10.

but Ibn Gabirol develops a system that includes, in addition to places of postmortem punishment for the souls of the wicked, places of postmortem purgation. Among Aristotelians, some envision a personal immortality while others envision a merging of the acquired intellect with the active intellect. Among kabbalists, there was, among many other developments, an expansion in the use of *metempsychosis*.

During the Enlightenment, Cartesian views of human nature and the soul (now equated with the mind and consciousness) replace Aristotelian views for both Jews and gentiles alike. Leibniz significantly alters Cartesian views, and Mendelssohn, under the influence of Leibniz, develops a view of the soul that is quite different than the view of Jewish medieval philosophers. In the nineteenth century, with the development of the sciences of psychology and biology, as well as with the spread of empiricism, positivism, and scientism in western democracies, many Jews came to reject any notion of a soul, resurrection, or an afterlife; and under the influence of liberalism and actual improvements in the quality of life, many Jews came to emphasize improving conditions in this world instead of waiting for a better life in another world.

C. The Evolution of Jewish Views of the Soul, Resurrection, and the Afterlife Has Been Closely Tied to the Problem of Moral Evil

The notions of the immortality of the soul, resurrection, and a postmortem reward or punishment entered into Jewish thought in response to the problem of moral evil that arose after the abandonment of a belief in intergenerational and collective reward and punishment in about the sixth century BCE. With the teaching of Ezekiel, Jeremiah, and the Deuteronomic code of law that each individual is rewarded or punished by God for their own conduct, the prosperity of the wicked and the adversity of the righteous became a problem. This problem became acute during the reign of Antiochus IV in the second century BCE. At that time the righteous—those Jews who refused to violate any of God's commandments—were persecuted and killed, and the wicked—those Jews who became hellenized and assented to the demands of Antiochus requiring violation of God's commandments—were rewarded with material well-being. This breach of divine justice required an explanation, and the primary explanation hit upon was that there would be a postmortem reward and punishment. In an afterlife, the righteous and the wicked would receive their proper desserts.

Not only did the problem of moral evil give birth to a belief in another world in which an immortal soul or a resurrected person would be rewarded or punished, but the problem of moral evil largely accounts for the persistence of this belief. After the destruction of the Second Temple, the rabbis sought to ensure absolute fidelity and obedience to rabbinic interpretations of the Torah. Since adherence to their interpretations might not result in one's material well-being while alive, the rabbis realized that adherence could be enhanced if reward in an afterlife depended on it. Therefore, rabbinic texts are replete with references to obedience to Torah as the means of achieving a reward after death, and disrespect for rabbinic authority is said to cause one's loss of such postmortem reward. References to reward in the world to come for obedience completely overshadow rabbinic teaching that God's laws should be followed without the expectation of a reward.

In the tenth century, Saadia presented rational arguments to support rabbinic teachings about reward and punishment in an afterlife. Saadia's reasoned arguments are based on the problem of moral evil. He takes it as given that God is omnipotent and just, and these qualities mandate that God reward the righteous and punish the wicked. However, in this life, says Saadia, the righteous are not always rewarded and the wicked are not always punished. Therefore, God "must perforce have reserved for them a second abode in which justice would be restored in their relationship to each other, reward being remitted to the one corresponding to the pain he has suffered at the hand of him that wronged, and punishment being brought down upon the other corresponding to the pleasure derived by his nature from his wrongdoing and violence."[2]

In the twelfth century, Maimonides similarly assumes that there is an ultimate good that is derived from fulfilling the commandments but argues that such ultimate good does not consist in physical pleasures, so the fact that the righteous lacked material well-being in this life did not present a major problem for him so long as intellectual and moral perfection were not prevented. In the thirteenth century, however, Nahmanides directly considers the problem of moral evil, and accepts *metempsychosis* as a means of resolving what he considers the most vexing examples of the problem—Job and Rabbi Akiba.

Mendelssohn's eighteenth-century attempt to prove the immortality of the soul similarly hinges to a great degree on resolving the problem of moral evil. He argues that because human beings cannot achieve perfection in their lifetime, it must be part of God's plan that they be permitted to achieve perfection in a postmortem existence. To say otherwise, argues Mendelssohn, would undermine God's wisdom, goodness, or omnipotence. It would likewise undermine God's wisdom, goodness, or omnipotence, he asserts, to deny that one who has fulfilled his duty here on earth with steadfastness in defiance of misfortune would not receive a postmortem recompense, or to deny that the evil deeds of the wicked in this life would not lead to a postmortem felicity.

Most recently, in the twenty-first century, Levenson argues that resurrection is necessary in order for God to achieve an ultimate victory over human evil. This final victory "requires the intervention of the Creator to uproot the Evil Inclination that he implanted within us in the beginning," and requires a time when God "renders justice to Jew and gentile alike."[3]

Conversely, the abandonment by many Jews of a belief in an afterlife is associated with the rejection of the belief that righteousness must result in some external

---

2. Saadia, *Book of Beliefs and Opinions*, 325–26.
3. Levenson, *Resurrection and the Restoration*, 22, 224.

reward or that there must be a time when God renders justice. True, it had long been acknowledged that one must serve God without the expectation of a reward. This teaching may be found, for example, in the Mishnah. Yet, the Torah clearly promises material well-being for obedience and the opposite for disobedience; and rabbinic texts stress external rewards and punishments for allegiance to rabbinic interpretation of God's law in an afterlife, if not in this life, far more frequently than they mention allegiance without the expectation of a reward. Post-rabbinic texts are no different. Maimonides, for example, teaches service to God without the expectation of a reward but acknowledges that the masses need to be told about external rewards.

Such mixed messages finally ended with Spinoza in the late seventeenth century. Spinoza was, arguably, the first Jew to unequivocally and strenuously object to any reliance on external rewards for virtuous behavior. He repeatedly emphasized that virtue is its own reward, and he writes with disgust and contempt of the appeal of conventional religious morality to supernatural rewards and punishments. For Spinoza all such appeals are unworthy of adult intelligence. After Spinoza's work became more widely known to Jews in the nineteenth century, his teaching that virtue is its own reward was increasingly accepted. One of the strongest proponents of this point of view was Hermann Cohen. Cohen, a famous Neo-Kantian philosopher, maintained that monotheism precludes any relationship between ethical conduct and happiness, precludes happiness being proportional to virtue. He strongly opposed any attempt to make the attainment of happiness a reason for performing God's commands. More recently, Mordecai Kaplan has followed Spinoza in asserting that God does not reward or punish. Consistent with the teaching that virtue is its own reward, neither Spinoza, Cohen, nor Kaplan was much concerned with the problem of moral evil, and they all rejected belief in any reward or punishment in an afterlife.

D. Reliance on Biblical or Rabbinic Texts to Justify One's Relevant Beliefs Is Counterproductive Since These Texts May be Interpreted in Ways That Support Virtually Any Belief about the Soul, Resurrection, or the Afterlife

Philo and other Jewish Hellenists relied upon allegorical interpretations of the Bible to read their views about the immortality of the soul into biblical literature. Similarly, the rabbis justified their views about resurrection through fanciful interpretations of biblical texts. For Saadia, the source of correct belief about the soul, resurrection, and the afterlife is revelation as well as reason. Therefore, Saadia cites biblical and rabbinic authority to support the views he espouses. He believes that every statement found in the Bible must be understood in its literal sense, except in four instances, including when the biblical statement conflicts with reason.[4] Unfortunately, despite Saadia's view

---

4. Saadia, *Book of Beliefs and Opinions*, 265–66. Accord, Saadia, *Book of Beliefs and Opinions*, 415–16. See Efros, "Saadia's Theory of Knowledge," 163 ("whenever a Biblical passage seems in its

of biblical interpretation, the biblical passages he cites often support his position only because he creatively interprets those passages in a nonliteral fashion; and rabbinic tradition can be said to support his positions only by ignoring rabbinic texts that do not support his positions. He contends that interpretations of biblical and rabbinic texts which are at odds with his views are erroneous interpretations but, arguably, his interpretations are no less erroneous than those of his opponents.

Maimonides similarly confronts the issue of textual interpretation. He describes five different positions as to the ultimate good to be derived from adherence to the commandments, and he states that the proponents of each position support their opinion by adducing proofs based on statements found in traditional Jewish sources. Accordingly, he observes, a correct interpretation of traditional Jewish sources is required to arrive at a correct opinion regarding the ultimate good to be obtained by adherence to God's commandments. He argues that the traditional texts should *not* be interpreted literally, permitting him to read into these texts the ideas he believes to be in accord with Aristotelianism. In advocating a nonliteral interpretation of traditional texts Maimonides is in essential agreement with Philo but not with Saadia. The Maimonidean view of textual interpretation was a source of controversy for centuries, with Maimonideans favoring allegorical interpretations and non-Maimonideans contending that allegorical interpretations are forbidden.

Since one can use creative interpretations of biblical and rabbinic texts to support virtually any view of the soul, resurrection, or the afterlife that one wishes, reliance on these texts to support one's view of such matters is not helpful. Spinoza vigorously condemned the practice of reading the "delusions of the Greeks"[5] into Scripture. He asserted that, properly understood, there are no revealed truths in the Hebrew Bible having anything to do with such things as the immortality of the soul, resurrection, or the nature of any afterlife because the aim of revelation is not to impart knowledge concerning philosophy or what may be called "scientific knowledge."

E. Baruch Spinoza Occupies a Central Place in the History of Jewish Thought Concerning the Soul, Resurrection, and the Afterlife

By insisting that there are no revealed truths concerning the soul, resurrection, or the afterlife, and by contending that philosophy should neither be made to conform to Scripture nor be made ancillary to Scripture, Spinoza played a seminal role in the history of Jewish thought, and, more broadly, in the history of human thought. Freed from the constraints of biblical exegesis, Spinoza relied solely on the "natural light

---

literal sense to run counter to reason or tradition, it must be interpreted and harmonized therewith."); Guttmann, *Philosophies of Judaism*, 72 ("Saadia declares agreement with reason to be a necessary precondition for the acceptance of any doctrine claiming the status of revelation."); Efros, *Studies in Medieval Jewish Philosophy*, 113–14; Malter, *Saadia Gaon*, 234.

5. Spinoza, *Theological-Political Treatise*, 5.

of reason"⁶ to understand the natural world. His logical reasoning led him to the conclusion that the soul, or mind, is not an entity that exists separate and apart from the body and survives the destruction of the body in any personal sense. Rather, the mind and the body are modes of a single, infinite substance, and there is no personal immortality.

These seminal ideas were accompanied by the related, seminal idea that has been called the principle of immanence. The principle of immanence refers to Spinoza's contention that there is only a this-worldly existence—there is no personal afterlife. This principle, of course, entails as a corollary that there is no reward or punishment in an afterlife. Thus, Spinoza challenged the well-established Jewish theodicy (first expressed by the early rabbis, reformulated and systematized by Saadia, and followed by subsequent Jewish philosophers, both medieval and modern) that the righteous are rewarded and the wicked are punished in an afterlife. Indeed, Spinoza argued that it is wrongheaded to act righteously for the sake of any external reward at all, whether in an afterlife or in our this-worldly existence. Spinoza opposed the idea that we require the hope of reward and fear of punishment as a motive to be virtuous or to act rightly. Virtue is its own reward in the strict sense that the best life is necessarily the happiest. The reward for being virtuous is not material well-being in this world or blessedness in the world to come, but virtuous living itself.

In the last two centuries the principle of immanence has become accepted by an increasingly larger number of Jews. It cannot be denied that many Jews still maintain a belief in a postmortem reward and punishment, but, arguably, such a belief is no longer dominant. Nor is such a belief consistent with modern, science-based, worldviews. It is precisely because of this fact that Mordecai Kaplan embraced much of Spinoza's philosophy. Kaplan argued that salvation is attained in *this* world, not in an afterlife; and Jews should act to improve conditions in this world, not to achieve well-being in some other world. Samuel Cohon was expressing essentially the same Spinozist point of view by talking about the modern approach to evil and emphasizing that we are God's co-workers in the eradication of evil. The true lover of God, he stated, must be virtuous, not because of any worldly or otherworldly emoluments, but because of their intrinsic value.

F. Are There Any Jewish Dogmas?

"Dogma," says Kellner, "typically means a belief ordained by a recognized religious authority, acceptance of which is a necessary condition both for membership in the faith community under discussion and for the achievement of personal redemption, however that may be defined."⁷ Pursuant to this definition, Judaism clearly has no dogmas because there exists no religious authority recognized by all Jews. Thus, Cohon has

---

6. Spinoza, *Theological-Political Treatise*, 6.
7. Kellner, *Must a Jew Believe Anything?*, 24.

flatly stated: "Judaism . . . possesses no beliefs whose binding character derives solely from the circumstance that they were decreed by an authoritative body, and which a Jew must profess in order to be saved."[8] Yet, for Cohon, Judaism does have dogmas in the sense of "underlying principles"—"premises upon which the religious life [of Jews] rests."[9] He writes that "in Judaism attention was paid to underlying ideas rather than to the stereotyped formulas."[10]

Cohon goes on to provide an account of what he refers to as the "evolution" of dogma in Judaism, which is to say the evolution of Judaism's underlying principles.[11] In other words, while claiming that Judaism has underlying principles or dogmas, Cohon believes that these dogmas have changed from time to time. Cohon states that while the Torah offers "no concisely formulated set of doctrines," it nevertheless "rests on a doctrinal basis."[12] The Prophets and the Writings, according to Cohon, "rest on virtually the same dogmatic foundations" as the Torah.[13] In postexilic times, these dogmatic foundations were altered, on Cohon's account, due to contact with Hellenism and internal conflicts among Jews.[14] Ultimately, continuing with Cohon's account, in the rabbinic period, Judaism's dogmas were set forth in Mishnah Sanhedrin 10:1 and in the official liturgy of the synagogue.[15]

Cohon claims that acceptance of any particular dogma was not seen as a condition of being Jewish but only as a condition of having nonheretical views. As Cohon expresses this point, because "Judaism is the religion of a people rather than of a Church," the denial of "this or that belief" of Judaism "makes for heresy, but not for exclusion from the fold."[16] Schechter makes substantially the same point when he states:

> The Rabbis did not maintain that he who gave up the belief in Revelation and Resurrection, and treated irreverently the teachers of Israel, severed his

---

8. Cohon, *Jewish Theology*, 91. Accord, Jacobs, *Principles of the Jewish Faith*, 10 ("dogmas in the Catholic sense . . . are impossible in Judaism because Judaism has no Church, no central authority with the power to formulate beliefs.").

9. Cohon, *Jewish Theology*, 93.

10. Cohon, *Jewish Theology*, 91–92.

11. See Cohon, *Jewish Theology*, 94–101.

12. Cohon, *Jewish Theology*, 95. Cf. Kellner, *Must a Jew Believe Anything?*, 16–18 ("the Torah teaches . . . certain beliefs about God, the universe, and human beings; notwithstanding this, the Torah has no systematic theology."). See also Schechter, "Dogmas of Judaism," 52–54; Jacobs, *Principles of the Jewish Faith*, 8.

13. Cohon, *Jewish Theology*, 95.

14. See Cohon, *Jewish Theology*, 95–98. See also Jacobs, *Principles of the Jewish Faith*, 8–9 ("Philo . . . was the first Jew, so far as we know, to formulate articles of faith.").

15. See Cohon, *Jewish Theology*, 98–101. See also Schechter, "Dogmas of Judaism," 54–57; Jacobs, *Principles of the Jewish Faith*, 10–13.

16. Cohon, *Jewish Theology*, 91–92.

connection with the Jewish nation, but that, for his crime, he was going to suffer the heaviest punishment. He was to be excluded from the world to come.[17]

Kellner's view differs somewhat from Cohon's. While acknowledging the claim of some that Mishnah Sanhedrin 10:1 represents an attempt by the rabbis to set down certain dogmas, Kellner asserts that "classical Judaism has no dogmas."[18] As Kellner sees it, it was not until the twelfth century that we find "the first comprehensive account of the dogmas of Judaism"; more specifically, Kellner states that Maimonides "was the first non-Karaite Jewish author systematically, self-consciously, and explicitly to posit specific beliefs which all Jews *qua* Jews had to accept."[19] These specific beliefs are the so-called Thirteen Principles.

Kellner, Cohon, and Schechter all discuss the Maimonidean creed as well as the numerous differing creeds of subsequent medieval Jewish thinkers, such as Shimon ben Zemah Duran, Hasdai Crescas, and Joseph Albo.[20] While all these creeds set forth first principles of Judaism, they differed as to the number and nature of these first principles. As Schechter puts it, these thinkers agree with Maimonides that Judaism has dogmas but "differ from him as to what these dogmas are, or . . . give a different enumeration of them."[21] Schechter contrasts these thinkers with others, like Isaac Abravanel, who denied that Judaism has any dogmas. Abravanel, in *Rosh Amanah* (1495), argued that "the whole procedure . . . of formulating dogmas or first principles from which to deduce Jewish beliefs and practices is foreign to Judaism's nature."[22] For Abravanel, there are no specific first principles underlying Judaism "beyond the general acceptance of the Torah."[23]

In the nineteenth century, early reformers produced catechisms setting forth those beliefs they claimed to constitute the essence of the Jewish religion.[24] Some of these catechisms adopted the Maimonidean creed but replaced belief in bodily resurrection with the immortality of the soul. Many other Jews in the nineteenth century, however, were not interested in setting forth dogmas of Judaism. Following what they

---

17. Schechter, "Dogmas of Judaism," 57.

18. Kellner, *Must a Jew Believe Anything?*, 24, 33. Accord, Kohler, *Jewish Theology*, 19–20 (Neither Scripture nor the rabbis demanded the formal acceptance of a prescribed belief; "Judaism lays all stress upon conduct, not confession; upon a hallowed life, not a hollow creed."). See generally Kellner, *Must a Jew Believe Anything?*, 26–38 ("Systematic thinking and formulation . . . were foreign to the rabbis . . ., and it would be surprising if we were to find 'settled doctrines' about anything [in rabbinic literature].").

19. Kellner, *Dogma in Medieval Jewish Thought*, 1 (emphasis original).

20. See Kellner, *Dogma in Medieval Jewish Thought*, 10–156; Cohon, *Jewish Theology*, 104–11; Schechter, "Dogmas of Judaism," 59–61, 115–21. See also Jacobs, *Principles of the Jewish Faith*, 14–23.

21. Schechter, "Dogmas of Judaism," 115.

22. Cohon, *Jewish Theology*, 111. See Schechter, "Dogmas of Judaism," 121–23; Kellner, *Dogma in Medieval Jewish Thought*, 179–95; Jacobs, *Principles of the Jewish Faith*, 23–24.

23. Kellner, *Dogma in Medieval Jewish Thought*, 194.

24. See ch. 11.

took to be Mendelssohn's position, they denied that Judaism even has dogmas.[25] Writing in 1888, Schechter, who served as the president of JTS, discusses the causes for the neglect of dogma in Judaism, and bemoans that the "great dogma of dogmalessness" has been accepted by the majority of Jewish theologians.[26] Standing in opposition to these theologians, Schechter argues in favor of Jewish dogma, writing:

> We usually urge that in Judaism religion means life; but we forget that a life without guiding principles and thoughts is an existence not worth living. At least it was so considered by our greatest thinkers, and hence their efforts to formulate the creed of Judaism, so that men would not only be able to do the right thing, but also to think the right thing.[27]

In the mid-twentieth century, Jacobs, also a leader in the Conservative movement, took the same position as Schechter. In the introduction to *Principles of the Jewish Faith: An Analytical Study* (1964), Jacob disagrees with the statement attributed to Mendelssohn that Judaism has no dogmas, and agrees with Schechter "that there *are* dogmas in Judaism."[28] Jacobs proposes "to take up the matter where Schechter left off and ask ourselves what these dogmas are and if and how they can be reinterpreted for the Jew today."[29] Since Jacobs sought to "reinterpret" Jewish dogmas, he presumably believed that Jewish dogmas are subject to change or, to use Cohon's word, evolution. In fact, Jacobs explicitly states that "the question of what a modern Jew can, and should believe, is to be found in an examination of Maimonides' Creed, with the all-important proviso that Maimonides' formulation requires much reinterpretation *and revision* in light of the new knowledge God has given man since the twelfth century."[30] The substance of *Principles of the Jewish Faith* analyzes each of the thirteen principles formulated by Maimonides, discussing the difficulties they present for moderns, and examining "the possibility of reinterpretation."[31] Thus, for example, in a chapter discussing the thirteenth principle of Maimonides—resurrection of the dead—Jacobs concludes that this principle is "best interpreted today as belief in the immortality of the soul, provided that this is understood to mean that the whole personality of man, his complete individuality, shares in God's eternal goodness."[32]

25. See Cohon, *Jewish Theology*, 88–90; Schechter, "Dogmas of Judaism," 48.
26. Schechter, "Dogmas of Judaism," 48–51. See Cohon, *Jewish Theology*, 90.
27. Schechter, "Dogmas of Judaism," 127.
28. Jacobs, *Principles of the Jewish Faith*, 7 (emphasis original). See Jacobs, *Principles of the Jewish Faith*, 4, 8.
29. Jacobs, *Principles of the Jewish Faith*, 7.
30. Jacobs, *Principles of the Jewish Faith*, 6 (emphasis added).
31. Jacobs, *Principles of the Jewish Faith*, 29–30.
32. Jacobs, *Principles of the Jewish Faith*, 459. The main reason offered by Jacobs for acceptance of this principle is based on the problem of moral evil. How can the justice of God be realized, he asks, "unless all who have striven for the good eventually find it" (Jacobs, *Principles of the Jewish Faith*, 449). While acknowledging that it is difficult to conceive how the mind can exist without the bodily organs through which it functions, Jacobs states that "man only requires the brain as his instrument here on

As Schechter and Jacobs, Cohon, a leader in Reform Judaism, takes issue with Mendelssohn's view "that Judaism seeks to regulate the deeds of man rather than his beliefs," and bemoans that Mendelssohn's authority "has been invoked for the purpose of dismissing all precepts as well as dogmas, as inconsequential."[33] He then adds: "The cry 'Deed not Creed,' raised in [many] quarters, ignores the elementary truth that without religious convictions, beliefs, or creed, there can be no religious deeds."[34] Although emphasizing the importance of Jewish dogmas, Cohon, as already mentioned, believes that these dogmas have evolved and should continue to evolve. "A Jewish doctrine," he writes, must be determined "in the life of the Jewish people. It must further stand the test of reason and of conscience. Thus, the changing political and social status of the Jews in emancipated lands and the widening philosophical and scientific horizon called for a reform or reconstruction of the patterns of Jewish living and for a [corresponding] restatement of the principles of Jewish belief."[35]

The issue of whether Judaism has any dogmas has most recently been addressed by Kellner, an Orthodox Jew addressing himself to other Orthodox Jews. In contrast to Jacobs and Cohon, Kellner is not prepared to say that the underlying principles of Judaism have evolved or have changed in any way. To the contrary, in *Must a Jew Believe Anything?*, first published in 1999, Kellner proclaims that "Judaism teaches truth and there is one absolute [unchanging] truth."[36] This is precisely why Kellner rejects what he calls "Maimonides' dogmatic version of Judaism." This version defines a Jew "as a person who adheres to a strictly defined set of dogmas"—it requires an Orthodox Jew to dismiss all non-Orthodox Jews as heretics.[37] Yet, while rejecting this "theological definition of Judaism," Kellner is unwilling to accept an "essentialist definition of Judaism" which turns Judaism "into a kind of religious nationalism," making beliefs completely unimportant.[38] Instead, Kellner proposes a "halakhic definition" of Judaism which defines Jews "as persons born Jewish (i.e. born to a Jewish mother) or

---

earth, in the world of matter, space and time. In the realm of eternity," he is confident, "the soul can function without these aids" (Jacobs, *Principles of the Jewish Faith*, 449–50). Perhaps, if Jacobs knew of contemporary neuroscience, he would not be so confident. See also Jacobs, *Principles of the Jewish Faith*, 398–454 (discussing the history of Jewish thought concerning the soul, resurrection, and the afterlife, and noting that Jewish viewpoints about these topics have varied and evolved).

33. Cohon, *Jewish Theology*, 89–90.

34. Cohon, *Jewish Theology*, 90.

35. Cohon, *Jewish Theology*, 113–14. Cf. Kohler, *Jewish Theology*, 27 ("We must do as Maimonides did—as Jews have always done—point out anew the really fundamental doctrines, and discard those which have lost their [hold] on the modern Jew, or which conflict directly with his religious consciousness... Judaism... must again reshape its religious truths in harmony with the dominant ideas of the age.").

36. Kellner, *Must a Jew Believe Anything?*, 113. See Kellner, *Must a Jew Believe Anything?*, 5.

37. Kellner, *Must a Jew Believe Anything?*, 7, 113 ("For Maimonides, persons born to a Jewish mother are not thereby truly Jewish until they consciously accept the essential doctrines taught by Judaism."). See Kellner, *Must a Jew Believe Anything?*, 2 ("If Judaism is defined in terms of dogmatic orthodoxy, non-Orthodox Jews automatically become heretics.").

38. Kellner, *Must a Jew Believe Anything?*, 4–5, 112–13.

converted to Judaism."³⁹ The halakhic definition "disallows Maimonides' theological reading of what constitutes a Jew, since it counts as Jews those persons born to Jewish mothers who are unaware of the theological teachings of the Torah, mistaken about them, or even unwilling to accept them."⁴⁰ Yet, it also acknowledges that Judaism has a theological, absolutely true content that may be accepted by a convert. With regard to the question posed by the title of Kellner's book, Kellner answers: "If 'belief' is the intellectual acquiescence in carefully defined statements of dogma, the answer is that there is nothing that a Jew *must* believe."⁴¹

G. What *Should* Jews Believe about the Soul, Resurrection, and the Afterlife?

Focusing solely on dogmas, principles, or beliefs about the soul, resurrection, and the afterlife, I agree with Kellner that there is nothing that a Jew *must* believe. This is primarily because I view being Jewish as belonging to a people, not a church. As with most, if not all, peoples or national/cultural groups, membership does not require adherence to a specific creed or set of dogmas, even if certain values and/or certain principles are widely shared and promulgated within the group. But, in addition, there is nothing that a Jew, *qua* Jew, *must* believe about the soul, resurrection, or the afterlife because, as has been shown, there is nothing that all Jews agree on with respect to these matters. To the contrary, Jews presently accept a wide variety of differing and even conflicting and contradictory ideas about the soul, resurrection, and the afterlife. Moreover, Jewish institutions, organizations, and leaders do not at present teach, and have never taught, one specific, detailed, absolute, unchanging truth with respect to these matters. But, while there is nothing that a Jew, *qua* Jew, *must* believe about the soul, resurrection, or the afterlife, one may still query: Is there anything that a Jew, *qua* Jew, *should* believe about these matters? This question is relevant whether or not one believes that Judaism has dogmas.

If one were to agree with Jacobs and Cohon that Judaism has always had, and should now have, a set of underlying principles or dogmas to be adhered to by all Jews, *qua* Jews, and if one thought that such dogmas should include dogmas about the soul, resurrection, and the afterlife, the question becomes "What should these dogmas be?" Jacobs and Cohon admit that Jewish dogmas have evolved, and that inherited dogmas need to be reinterpreted or revised. So how should the multitude of Jewish ideas about the soul, resurrection, and the afterlife be reinterpreted and/or revised? According to Cohon, inherited dogmas must "stand the test of reason" and must be in accord with today's wider "philosophical and scientific horizon."⁴² Nevertheless, in *Jewish Theol-*

---

39. Kellner, *Must a Jew Believe Anything?*, 113.
40. Kellner, *Must a Jew Believe Anything?*, 113.
41. Kellner, *Must a Jew Believe Anything?*, 9 (emphasis original).
42. Cohon, *Jewish Theology*, 113–14.

ogy, Cohon accepts the immortality of the soul as "reasonable" because of "ethical arguments" which are "not based on proof in the scientific or philosophic sense"—which is to say arguments permitting resolution of the problem of moral evil.[43] In Jacobs's opinion, inherited dogmas must be revised in light of "new knowledge."[44] This position led Jacobs to reject bodily resurrection and accept the immortality of the soul on the basis of his understanding that mental activity does *not* require the brain.[45] But new knowledge—current philosophy and neuroscience—teaches that mental activity *does* require the brain. In short, while the criteria Cohon and Jacobs offer for revising inherited beliefs may be unobjectionable, their application of the criteria is clearly flawed.

I begin *my* response to the question of what Jews *should* believe about the soul, resurrection, and the afterlife by expressing agreement with Schechter that life without thoughts—without thinking—is an existence not worth living.[46] In other words, Jews, as well as all other people, should certainly think about these matters. I would add that, while Jews hold, and have held, differing beliefs concerning the soul, resurrection, and the afterlife, it has *always and consistently* been a Jewish *value* to be truthful, and this entails being truthful to oneself, or believing that which is true. This value has been expressed most succinctly and forcibly by Maimonides in the introduction to his commentary on Pirqe Avot, the Eight Chapters, where he writes: "Hear the truth from whoever says it."[47] I would, similarly, urge all Jews to hear the truth from whoever says it, and to believe that which is true about the soul, resurrection, and the afterlife from whoever says it.

But what is the truth? While a full and complete answer to this question is well beyond the scope of this book, for present purposes we need only refer to Spinoza. Spinoza asserted that truths about the natural world (which includes truths about the soul, resurrection, and the afterlife) cannot be derived from faith—from Scripture or traditional texts—but only from philosophy—from what was then called the natural light of reason. Today we call it science and the scientific method. Thus, my answer to the question of what Jews *should* believe about the soul, resurrection, and the afterlife is that they should believe only what is established to be true through science, through use of the scientific method. This criterion requires rejection of any belief in a soul, in resurrection, or in any afterlife since the truth of these things has not been established by science.[48]

---

43. See ch. 11, sec. B, 5. Yet, this position is inconsistent with Cohon's position in *Judaism, a Way of Life*. See ch. 11, sec. B, 5.

44. Jacobs, *Principles of the Jewish Faith*, 6.

45. See *supra*, n. 32.

46. Schechter offers a restatement of the Socratic maxim that the unexamined life is not worth living. See Plato, *Apology* 38a5–6.

47. Maimonides, *Eight Chapters*, 60. See also e.g., Kohler, *Jewish Theology*, 23 ("The Jewish conception of God . . . makes *truth* . . . a moral duty for man"; emphasis original).

48. Cf. ch. 14, sec. E (discussing Morris Raphael Cohen's *Reason and Nature*).

CHAPTER 16.

To those who object that human beings need illusions to endure the cruelty of reality, and that, in particular they need the comfort of believing in an afterlife, I refer them to Freud. Freud countered such objections by arguing that in place of the illusions of religion, human beings need an "education to reality."[49] This is to say that, if one chooses to ignore that which is true, chooses to ignore reality, one does so at one's own peril. To those who object that an afterlife is needed to deal with the problem of moral evil, and that the fear of eternal punishment is required to motivate people to be virtuous, I refer them to Spinoza. Spinoza said that people must be taught that an individual's "reward" for being virtuous is not to be equated with the maximum amount of their individual material well-being in this world, nor with their blessedness in a future world, but with "virtuous living itself."

---

49. Freud, *Future of an Illusion*, 85.

Bibliography

Abelson, Kassel. "Foreword." In *Emet Ve'Emunah: Statement of Principles of Conservative Judaism*, 4–6. New York: The Jewish Theological Seminary of America, The Rabbinical Assembly, and The United Synagogue of America, 1988.

Adamson, Peter. *Philosophy in the Islamic World*. Oxford: Oxford University Press, 2016.

Adkins, Arthur W. H. *From the Many to the One: A Study of Personality and Views of Human Nature in the Context of Ancient Greek Society, Values and Beliefs*. London: Constable and Company, 1970.

———. *Moral Values and Political Behaviour in Ancient Greece*. New York: Norton, 1972.

Agus, Jacob B. *Modern Philosophies of Judaism*. New York: Behrman's, 1941.

Aiken, Henry David, ed. *The Age of Ideology: The 19th Century Philosophers*. New York: The New American Library, 1956.

Altmann, Alexander. "Eternality of Punishment: A Theological Controversy Within the Amsterdam Rabbinate in the Thirties of the Seventeenth Century." *Proceedings of the American Academy for Jewish Research* 40 (1972) 1–88.

———. *Moses Mendelssohn: A Biographical Study*. Portland, OR: The Littman Library of Jewish Civilization, 1998.

———. *Studies in Religious Philosophy and Mysticism*. Ithaca, NY: Cornell University Press, 1969.

Altmann, Alexander, and Samuel Miklos Stern. *Isaac Israeli: A Neoplatonic Philosopher of the Early Tenth Century*. Chicago: The University of Chicago Press, 2009.

Ariel, Yaakov. "Jews and New Religious Movements: An Introductory Essay." *Nova Religio* 15.1 (2011) 5–21.

Aristotle. *Nicomachian Ethics*. Translated by Terrence Irwin. 2nd ed. Indianapolis: Hackett, 1999.

Avery-Peck, Alan J. "Death and the Afterlife in the Early Rabbinic Sources: The Mishnah, Tosefta, and Early Midrash Compilations." In *Judaism in Late Antiquity: Death, Life-After Death, Resurrection & The World to Come in the Judaisms of Antiquity*, edited by Alan J. Avery-Peck and Jacob Neusner, 243–66. Leiden: Brill, 2000.

Ayer, Alfred Jules. *Language, Truth and Logic*. 2nd ed. New York: Dover, 1946.

Beiser, Frederick C. "Mendelssohn Versus Herder on the Vocation of Man." In *Moses Mendelssohn's Metaphysics and Aesthetics*, edited by Reinier Munk, 235–44. Dordrecht, Netherlands: Springer, 2011.

Bell, Charles. "Idea of a New Anatomy of the Brain." *Journal of Anatomy and Physiology* 3.1 (November 1868) 147–82.

Bernfeld, Siegfried. "Freud's Earliest Theories and the School of Helmholtz." *Psychoanalytic Quarterly* 13 (1944) 314–62.

Bernstein, Alan E. *The Formation of Hell: Death and Retribution in the Ancient and Early Christian Worlds.* Ithaca, NY: Cornell University Press, 1993.

Blackmore, Susan. *Dying to Live: Near Death Experiences.* Buffalo, NY: Prometheus, 1993.

Borowitz, Eugene B. *Choices in Modern Jewish Thought.* New York: Behrman House, 1983.

———. *Liberal Judaism.* New York: Union of American Hebrew Congregations, 1984.

———. *Reform Judaism Today, What We Believe.* New York: Behrman House, 1977.

Bostock, David. *Plato's Phaedo.* Oxford: Oxford University Press, 1986.

Bremmer, Jan N. *The Early Greek Concept of the Soul.* Princeton, NJ: Princeton University Press, 1983.

Brenton, Lancelot. *The Septuagint with Apocrypha: Greek and English.* Peabody, MA: Hendrickson, 1986.

Breuer, Joseph. *Introduction to Rabbi Samson Raphael Hirsch's Commentary on the Torah.* New York: Feldheim, 1948.

Brichto, Herbert Chanan. "Kin, Cult, Land and Afterlife—A Biblical Complex." *Hebrew Union College Annual* 44 (1973) 1–54.

Buber, Martin. *The Origin and Meaning of Hasidism.* Edited and translated by Maurice Friedman. New York: Horizon, 1960.

———. *Tales of the Hasidim.* Translated by Olga Marx. 2 vols. New York: Schocken, 1947.

Burkert, Walter. *Greek Religion.* Cambridge, MA: Harvard University Press, 1985.

Bynum, Caroline Walker. *The Resurrection of the Body in Western Christianity, 200–1336.* New York: Columbia University Press, 1995.

Caplan, Eric. *From Ideology to Liturgy: Reconstructionist Worship and American Liberal Judaism.* Cincinnati: Hebrew Union College Press, 2002.

Central Conference of American Rabbis (CCAR), eds. *The Union Prayerbook for Jewish Worship.* Newly rev. ed. New York: CCAR, 1957.

Chajes, J. H. *Between Two Worlds: Dybbuks, Exorcists, and Early Modern Judaism.* Philadelphia: University of Pennsylvania Press, 2003.

Chalom, Adam. "Foreword." In *Judaism Beyond God*, by Sherwin Wine, 1–3. Lincolnshire, IL: International Institute for Secular Humanistic Judaism, 1995.

Charles, Robert H. *The Book of Enoch.* Oxford: Clarendon, 1893.

Chilton, Bruce. "Resurrection in the Gospels." In *Judaism in Late Antiquity: Death, Life-After Death, Resurrection & The World to Come in the Judaisms of Antiquity*, edited by Alan J. Avery-Peck and Jacob Neusner, 215–39. Leiden: Brill, 2000.

Citrin, Paul J., ed. *Lights in the Forest: Rabbis Respond to Twelve Essential Jewish Questions.* New York: Central Conference of American Rabbis, 2014.

Clarke, Ernest G. *The Wisdom of Solomon.* Cambridge: Cambridge University Press 1973.

Claus, David B. *Toward the Soul: An Inquiry into the Meaning of [Psyche] before Plato.* New Haven, CT: Yale University Press, 1981.

Cohen, Hermann. *Religion of Reason Out of the Sources of Judaism.* Translated by Simon Kaplan. Atlanta: Scholars, 1995.

Cohen, Morris Raphael. *A Dreamer's Journey: Autobiography of Morris Raphael Cohen.* Glencoe, IL: Free Press, 1949.

———. *The Faith of a Liberal.* New Brunswick, NJ: Transaction, 1993.

———. *Reason and Nature: An Essay on the Meaning of Scientific Method.* 2nd ed. New York: Dover, 1978.

Cohen, Shaye J. D. *From the Maccabees to the Mishnah*. 2nd ed. Louisville: Westminster John Knox, 2006.

Cohn-Sherbok, Dan. *Issues in Contemporary Judaism*. New York: St. Martin's, 1991.

Cohon, Samuel S. *Jewish Theology: A Historical and Systematic Interpretation of Judaism and its Foundations*. Edited by H. J. Prakke and H. M. G. Prakke. Assen, The Netherlands: Royal Vangorcum, 1971.

———. *Judaism, a Way of Life: An Introduction to the Basic Ideas of Judaism*. New York: Schocken, 1962.

———. "The Mission of Reform Judaism." *The Journal of Religion* 2.1 (1922) 27–43.

———. "Our Immortality." In *Religious Affirmations*, edited by The Union of American Hebrew Congregations, 176–83. Los Angeles: n.p., 1983.

———. *What We Jews Believe*. Cincinnati: The Union of American Hebrew Congregations, 1931.

Collins, John J. "The Afterlife in Apocalyptic Literature." In *Judaism in Late Antiquity: Death, Life-After Death, Resurrection & The World to Come in the Judaisms of Antiquity*, edited by Alan J. Avery-Peck and Jacob Neusner, 119–39. Leiden: Brill, 2000.

———. *Jewish Wisdom in the Hellenistic Age*. Louisville: Westminster John Knox, 1997.

Comte, Auguste. *Course of the Positive Philosophy*. In *The Age of Ideology: The 19th Century Philosophers*, edited by Henry Aiken, 124–37. New York: The New American Library, 1956.

Copleston, Frederick. *A History of Philosophy*. New rev. ed. 7 vols. Garden City, NY: Image, 1962.

Cranefield, Paul F. "Freud and the 'School of Helmholtz.'" *Swiss Journal of the History of Medicine and Sciences* 23 (1966) 35–39.

Cronbach, Abraham. "Social Thinking in Sefer Hasidim." *Hebrew Union College Annual* 22 (1949) 1–147.

Curley, Edwin. *Behind the Geometrical Method: A Reading of Spinoza's Ethics*. Princeton, NJ: Princeton University Press, 1988.

———. "The Immortality of the Soul in Descartes and Spinoza." *Proceedings of the American Catholic Philosophical Association* 75 (2001) 27–41.

———, ed. *The Collected Works of Spinoza*. Vol. 1. Princeton, NJ: Princeton University Press, 1985.

Da Costa, Uriel. *Examination of Pharisaic Traditions Compared with the Written Law*. In *Uriel Da Costa, Examination of Pharisaic Traditions*, translated and edited by H. P. Salomon and I. S. D. Sassoon, 267–425. Leiden: Brill, 1993.

Damasio, Antonio. *Looking for Spinoza: Joy, Sorrow, and the Feeling Brain*. Orlando, FL: Harcourt, 2003.

Davidson, Herbert A. *Alfarabi, Avicenna and Averroes, On Intellect: Their Cosmologies, Theories of the Active Intellect, and Theories of Human Intellect*. New York: Oxford University Press, 1992.

———. "Saadia's List of Theories of the Soul." In *Jewish Medieval and Renaissance Studies*, edited by Alexander Altmann, 75–94. Cambridge, MA: Harvard University Press, 1967.

Davies, Philip R. "Death, Resurrection, and Life After Death in the Qumran Scrolls." In *Judaism in Late Antiquity: Death, Life-After Death, Resurrection & The World to Come in the Judaisms of Antiquity*, edited by Alan J. Avery-Peck and Jacob Neusner, 189–214. Leiden: Brill, 2000.

Davis, Avrohom. "Foreword." In *Kav HaYashar (The Just Measure)* by Tzvi H. Kaidanover. Translated by Avrohom Davis, xxv–xxxi. Monsey, NY: Eastern 2007.

Deichmann, Ute. "Introductory Remarks at the Inauguration of the Jacques Loeb Centre for the History and Philosophy of the Life Sciences." https://in.bgu.ac.il/en/loeb/Site Assets/Pages/Inauguration-Ceremony/inauguralspeech.pdf.

DeSouza, Nigel, "The Soul-Body Relationship and the Foundations of Morality: Herder Contra Mendelssohn." *Herder Yearbook/Jahrbuch* (2014) 145–61.

Dewey, John. *A Common Faith*. New Haven, CT: Yale University Press, 1934.

———. *Human Nature and Conduct: An Introduction to Social Psychology*. New York: Random House, 1922.

———. *Liberalism and Social Action*. New York: Capricorn, 1963.

———. *Reconstruction in Philosophy*. In *Philosophy in the Twentieth Century: Pragmatism and America's Philosophical Coming of Age*, edited by Henry Aiken and William Barrett, 287–346. New York: Harper & Row, 1962.

Dweck, Yaacob. *The Scandal of Kabbalah: Leon Modena, Jewish Mysticism, Early Modern Venice*. Princeton, NJ: Princeton University Press, 2011.

Edwards, Paul. "The Dependence of Consciousness on the Brain." In *Immortality*, edited by Paul Edwards, 292–307. Amherst, NY: Prometheus, 1997.

———. *Reincarnation: A Critical Examination*. Amherst, NY: Prometheus, 1996.

———, ed. *Immortality*. Amherst, NY: Prometheus, 1997.

Efros, Israel. "Saadia's Theory of Knowledge." *The Jewish Quarterly Review* 33.2 (Oct. 1942) 133–70.

———. *Studies in Medieval Jewish Philosophy*. New York: Columbia University Press, 1974.

Eichrodt, Walther. *Theology of the Old Testament*. 2 vols. Translated by John A. Baker. Philadelphia: Westminster, 1967.

Eisenstein, Ira. "Kaplan as Liturgist." In *The American Judaism of Mordecai M. Kaplan*, edited by Emanuel S. Goldsmith et al., 319–31. New York: New York University Press, 1990.

Elbert, Jerome W. *Are Souls Real?* Amherst, NY: Prometheus, 2000.

Emet Ve'Emunah: Statement of Principles of Conservative Judaism. New York: The Jewish Theological Seminary of America, The Rabbinical Assembly, and The United Synagogue of America, 1988.

Eylon, Dina Ripsman. *Reincarnation in Jewish Mysticism and Gnosticism*. Lewiston, NY: Edwin Mellon, 2003.

Feldman, Seymour. "Introduction" In *Theological-Political Treatise*, by Baruch Spinoza, translated by S. Shirley, vii–xlvii. Indianapolis: Hackett, 1998.

Flanagan, Owen. *The Problem of the Soul: Two Visions of Mind and How to Reconcile Them*. New York: Basic, 2002.

Flesher, Paul V. M. "The Resurrection of the Dead and the Sources of the Palestinian Targums to the Pentateuch." In *Judaism in Late Antiquity: Death, Life-After Death, Resurrection & The World to Come in the Judaisms of Antiquity*, edited by Alan J. Avery-Peck and Jacob Neusner, 311–31. Leiden: Brill, 2000.

Fontaine, T. A. M. *In Defense of Judaism: Abraham Ibn Daud*. Assen, Netherlands: Van Gorcum, 1990.

Forstrom, K. Joanna S. *John Locke and Personal Identity: Immortality and Bodily Resurrection in 17th-Century Philosophy*. New York: Continuum International, 2010.

Frazer, James George. *The Golden Bough*. New York: Touchstone, 1950.

Freud, Sigmund. *The Future of an Illusion*. Translated by W. D. Robson-Scott. New York: Liveright, 1955.

Freudenthal, Gad. "Stoic Physics in the Writings of R. Saadia Gaon Al-Fayyumi and Its Aftermath in Medieval Jewish Mysticism." *Arabic Sciences and Philosophy* 6 (1996) 113–36.

Freudenthal, J. "Are There Traces of Greek Philosophy in the Septuagint?" *Jewish Quarterly Review* 2.3 (April 1890) 205–22.

Friedman, Richard Elliot. *The Bible with Sources Revealed*. New York: Harper Collins, 2003.

Friedman, Richard Elliot, and Shawna Dolansky Overton. "Death and Afterlife: The Biblical Silence." In *Judaism in Late Antiquity: Death, Life-After Death, Resurrection & The World to Come in the Judaisms of Antiquity*, edited by Alan J. Avery-Peck and Jacob Neusner, 35–59. Leiden: Brill, 2000.

Frishman, Elyse D., ed. *Mishkan T'Filah, A Reform Siddur—Weekdays, Shabbat, Festivals and Other Occasions of Public Worship*. New York: Central Conference of American Rabbis, 2007.

Gastor, Theodore. *Festivals of the Jewish Year*. 3rd ed. New York: Sloane, 1966.

Geach, Peter. *God and Soul*. In *Immortality*, edited by Paul Edwards, 225–34. Amherst, NY: Prometheus, 1997.

Gillman, Neil. *Conservative Judaism: The New Century*. West Orange, NJ: Behrman House, 1993.

———. *The Death of Death: Resurrection and Immortality in Jewish Thought*. Woodstock, VT: Jewish Lights, 1997.

Glatzer, Nahum. *Hillel the Elder: The Emergence of Classical Judaism*. New York: Schocken, 1956.

Goetz, Stewart, and Charles Taliaferro. *A Brief History of the Soul*. Chichester, UK: Wiley-Blackwell, 2011.

Goldberg, Edwin, et. al., eds. *Mishkan Hanefesh: Machzor for the Days of Awe—Rosh Hashanah*. New York: Central Conference of American Rabbis, 2015.

———, eds. *Mishkan Hanefesh: Machzor for the Days of Awe—Yom Kippur*. New York: Central Conference of American Rabbis, 2015.

Goldman, Ari L. "Reconstructionist Jews Turn to the Supernatural." *New York Times*, February 14, 1989.

Gordis, Robert. *A Faith for Moderns*. 2nd augmented ed. New York: Bloch, 1971.

———. "Introduction." In *Emet Ve'Emunah: Statement of Principles of Conservative Judaism*, 9–16. New York: The Jewish Theological Seminary of America, The Rabbinical Assembly, and The United Synagogue of America, 1988.

Gottlieb, Micah, ed. *Moses Mendelssohn: Writings on Judaism, Christianity, & The Bible*. Waltham, MA: Brandeis University Press, 2011.

Grabbe, Lester L. "Eschatology in Philo and Josephus." In *Judaism in Late Antiquity: Death, Life-After Death, Resurrection & The World to Come in the Judaisms of Antiquity*, edited by Alan J. Avery-Peck and Jacob Neusner, 163–85. Leiden: Brill, 2000.

———. *Judaic Religion in the Second Temple Period*. London: Routledge, 2000.

Gurock, Jeffrey S., and Jacob J. Schacter. *A Modern Heretic and a Traditional Community: Mordecai M. Kaplan, Orthodoxy, and American Judaism*. New York: Columbia University Press, 1997.

Guthrie, W. K. C. *Orpheus and Greek Religion: A Study of the Orphic Movement*. Princeton, NJ: Princeton University Press, 1993.

Guttmann, Julius. *Philosophies of Judaism.* Translated by David Silverman. Garden City, NY: Doubleday, 1964.

Hallote, Rachel S. *Death, Burial, and Afterlife in the Biblical World: How the Israelites and Their Neighbors Treated the Dead.* Chicago: Dee, 2001.

Hampshire, Stuart. *Spinoza.* Baltimore: Penguin, 1951.

Harvey, Stephen. "Islamic Philosophy and Jewish Philosophy." In *The Cambridge Companion to Arabic Philosophy,* edited by Peter Adamson and Richard Taylor, 349–70. Cambridge: Cambridge University Press, 2005.

Harvey, Warren Zev. "Hasdai Crescas's Critique of the Theory of the Acquired Intellect." PhD diss., Columbia University, 1973.

———. "A Portrait of Spinoza as a Maimonidean." *Journal of the History of Philosophy* 19.2 (April 1981) 151–72.

Hatfield, Gary. "Psychology." In *The Cambridge History of Philosophy in the Nineteenth Century (1790–1870),* edited by Allen Wood and Songsuk Hahn, 241–62. Cambridge: Cambridge University Press, 2012.

———. "Psychology: Old and New." In *The Cambridge History of Philosophy 1870–1945,* edited by Thomas Baldwin, 93–107. Cambridge: Cambridge University Press, 2003.

Herberg, Will. *Judaism and Modern Man: An Interpretation of Jewish Religion.* 1951. Reprint, Philadelphia: The Jewish Publication Society of America, 1959.

Heschel, Abraham Joshua. *A Passion for Truth.* New York: Farrar, Straus and Giroux, 1973.

———. "The Quest for Certainty in Saadia's Philosophy." *The Jewish Quarterly Review* 33.3 (January 1943) 265–313.

———. "Reason and Revelation in Saadia's Philosophy." *The Jewish Quarterly Review* 34.4 (April 1944) 391–408.

Hess, Moses. *Rome and Jerusalem, A Study in Jewish Nationalism.* Translated by Meyer Waxman. New York: Bloch, 1918.

Hett, Walter S., trans. *Aristotle: On the Soul, Parva Naturalia, On Breath.* Revised and reprinted. Cambridge, MA: Harvard University Press, 1957.

Hick, John. *Philosophy of Religion,* 2nd ed. In *Immortality,* edited by Paul Edwards, 235–41. Amherst, NY: Prometheus, 1997.

Hirsch, Samson Raphael. *The Hirsch Siddur.* Translated by The Samson Raphael Hirsch Publication Society. New York: Feldheim, 1969.

Hirsch, W. *Rabbinic Psychology: Beliefs about the Soul in Rabbinic Literature of the Talmudic Period.* London: Edward Goldston, 1947.

Husik, Isaac. *A History of Mediaeval Jewish Philosophy.* New York: Atheneum, 1969.

Hyman, Arthur. *Eschatological Themes in Medieval Jewish Philosophy.* Milwaukee, WI: Marquette University Press, 2002.

———. "Maimonides' 'Thirteen Principles.'" In *Jewish Medieval and Renaissance Studies,* edited by Alexander Altmann, 119–44. Cambridge, MA: Harvard University Press, 1967.

Ibn Gabirol, Solomon ben Judah. *The Fountain of Life (Fons Vitae).* Translated by Alfred Jacob. Stanwood, WA: Sabian, 1987.

———. *The Kingly Crown (Keter Malkhut).* Translated by Bernard Lewis. Notre Dame: University of Notre Dame Press, 2003.

Ibn Pakuda, Bahya ben Joseph. *The Book of Direction to the Duties of the Heart.* Translated by Menahem Mansoor. Portland, OR: The Littman Library of Jewish Civilization, 2004.

Idel, Moshe. *Hasidism: Between Ecstasy and Magic.* Albany: State University of New York Press, 1995.

Idelsohn. Abraham Z. *Jewish Liturgy and Its Development.* New York: Schocken, 1960.
Israeli, Isaac. *The Book of Definitions.* In *Isaac Israeli: A Neoplatonic Philosopher of the Early Tenth Century*, edited by Alexander Altmann and Samuel Miklos Stern, 10–78. Translated by Samuel Miklos Stern. Chicago: The University of Chicago Press, 2009.
———. *The Book of Substances.* In *Isaac Israeli: A Neoplatonic Philosopher of the Early Tenth Century*, edited by Alexander Altmann and Samuel Miklos Stern, 81–105. Translated by Samuel Miklos Stern. Chicago: The University of Chicago Press, 2009.
———. *Book on the Elements.* In *Isaac Israeli: A Neoplatonic Philosopher of the Early Tenth Century*, edited by Alexander Altmann and Samuel Miklos Stern, 133–45. Translated by Alexander Altmann. Chicago: The University of Chicago Press, 2009.
———. *The Book on Spirit and Soul,* Pages 108–114 in *Isaac Israeli: A Neoplatonic Philosopher of the Early Tenth Century.* Edited by Alexander Altmann and Samuel Miklos Stern. Translated by Samuel Miklos Stern. Chicago: The University of Chicago Press, 2009.
———. *The Mantua Text.* Pages 119–32 in *Isaac Israeli: A Neoplatonic Philosopher of the Early Tenth Century.* Edited by Alexander Altmann and Samuel Miklos Stern. Translated by Alexander Altmann. Chicago: The University of Chicago Press, 2009.
Jacobs, Louis. *A Jewish Theology.* New York: Behrman House, 1973.
———. *Principles of the Jewish Faith: An Analytical Study.* New York: Basic, 1964.
James, William. "Does 'Consciousness' Exist?" In *Philosophy in the Twentieth Century: Pragmatism and America's Philosophical Coming of Age,* edited by Henry Aiken and William Barrett 207–21. New York: Harper & Row, 1962.
———. "Ingersoll Lecture." In *Immortality,* edited by Paul Edwards, 282–91. Amherst, NY: Prometheus, 1997.
———. *The Principles of Psychology.* In *Immortality,* edited by Paul Edwards, 177–83. 2 vols. Amherst, NY: Prometheus, 1997.
Johnson, Aubrey R. *The Vitality of the Individual in the Thought of Ancient Israel.* 2nd ed. Cardiff: University of Wales Press, 1964.
Johnston, Philip S. *Shades of Sheol: Death and Afterlife in the Old Testament.* Downers Grove, IL: InterVarsity, 2002.
Jones, William T. *A History of Western Philosophy.* 2nd rev. ed. 5 vols. Belmont, CA: Wadsworth Group/Thomson Learning, 1975.
Kaidanover, Tzvi Hirsch. *Kav HaYashar (The Just Measure).* Translated by Avrohom Davis. Monsey, NY: Eastern 2007.
Kamesar, Adam. "Biblical Interpretation in Philo." In *The Cambridge Companion to Philo*, edited by Adam Kamesar, 65–94. Cambridge: Cambridge University Press, 2009.
Kant, Immanuel. *Critique of Practical Reason.* Translated by Thomas K. Abbott. London: Longmans Green, 1927.
———. *Critique of Pure Reason.* Translated by Norman K. Smith. New York: St. Martin's, 1965.
———. *Groundwork of the Metaphysics of Morals.* Translated by Herbert J. Paton. New York: Harper & Row, 1964.
———. *Lectures on Ethics.* Translated by Louis Infield. Indianapolis: Hackett, 1963.
Kaplan, Mordecai, M. *The Future of the American Jew.* New York: The Reconstructionist, 1967.
———. *The Greater Judaism in the Making: A Study of the Modern Evolution of Judaism.* New York: The Reconstructionist, 1960.

———. *Judaism as a Civilization: Toward a Reconstruction of American-Jewish Life.* New York: Schocken, 1967.

———. *The Meaning of God in Modern Jewish Religion.* New York: The Reconstructionist, 1962.

———. *The Religion of Ethical Nationhood: Judaism's Contribution to World Peace.* New York: Macmillan, 1970.

———. *Questions Jews Ask: Reconstructionist Answers.* New York: Reconstructionist, 1956.

Kaplan, Mordecai M., and Eugene Kohn, eds. *Sabbath Prayer Book.* New York: The Jewish Reconstructionist Foundation, 1945.

Kaplan, Simon. "Introduction." In *Religion of Reason Out of the Sources of Judaism*, by Hermann Cohen, translated by Simon Kaplan, xi–xxii. Atlanta: Scholars, 1995.

Kasher, Asa, and Shlomo Biderman. "Why Was Spinoza Excommunicated?" In *Sceptics, Millenarians and Jews*, edited by David Katz and Jonathan Israel, 98–141. Leiden: Brill, 1990.

Kellner, Menachem. *Dogma in Medieval Jewish Thought: From Maimonides to Abravanel.* Portland, OR: The Littman Library of Jewish Civilization, 2004.

———. *Maimonides on Human Perfection.* Atlanta: Scholars, 1990.

———. *Must a Jew Believe Anything?* 2nd ed. Portland, OR: The Littman Library of Jewish Civilization, 2006.

Kenny, Anthony. *A New History of Western Philosophy.* 3 vols. Oxford: Clarendon, 2004.

Kim, Jaegwon. *Philosophy of Mind*, 3rd ed. Boulder, CO: Westview, 2011.

Klein, Dennis B. *Jewish Origins of the Psychoanalytic Movement.* New York: Praeger, 1981.

Kogel, Renee, and Zev Katz, eds. *Judaism in a Secular Age: An Anthology of Secular Humanistic Thought.* Farmington Hills, MI: International Institute for Secular Humanistic Judaism, 1995.

Kohler, Kaufmann. *Heaven and Hell in Comparative Religion.* New York: Macmillan, 1923.

———. *Jewish Theology Systematically and Historically Considered.* New York: Macmillan, 1918.

Kohler, Kaufman, and Isaac Broyde. "Transmigration of Souls." jewishencyclopedia.com/articles/14479-transmigration-of-souls.

Konvitz, Milton R. "Morris Raphael Cohen." *The Antioch Review* 7.4 (Winter 1947) 487–501.

———. *Nine American Jewish Thinkers.* New Brunswick, NJ: Transaction, 2000.

Kraye, Jill. "British Philosophy Before Locke." In *A Companion to Early Modern Philosophy*, edited by Steven Nadler, 283–97. Malden, MA: Blackwell. 2008.

Lazaroff, Allan. "Kaplan and Dewey." In *The American Judaism of Mordecai M. Kaplan*, edited by Emanuel S. Goldsmith et al., 173–96. New York: New York University Press, 1990.

Le Goff, Jacques. *The Birth of Purgatory.* Translated by Arthur Goldhammer. Chicago: University of Chicago Press, 1981.

Leibniz, Gottfried Wilhelm. *The Monadology.* In *Leibniz: Philosophical Writings*, translated by Mary Morris, 3–20. London: Dent & Sons, 1965.

———. *New System of the Nature and Communication of the Substances, as Well as the Union Consisting Between the Soul and the Body.* In *Leibniz: Philosophical Writings*, translated by Mary Morris, 97–109. London: Dent & Sons, 1965.

———. *Principles of Nature and Grace, Founded on Reason.* In *Leibniz: Philosophical Writings*, translated by Mary Morris, 21–31. London: Dent & Sons, 1965.

Lester, David. *Is There Life After Death? An Examination of the Empirical Evidence.* Jefferson, NC: McFarland, 2005.

Levenson, Jon D. *Resurrection and the Restoration of Israel: The Ultimate Victory of the God of Life*. New Haven, CT: Yale University Press, 2006.

———. "The World Repaired, Remade: An Interview with Jon D. Levenson." https://bulletin.hds.harvard.edu/articles/winter2007/world-repaired-remade.

Levin, Leonard, and R. David Walker. "Isaac Israeli." The Stanford Encyclopedia of Philosophy (Spring 2013 Edition). Edited by Edward Zalta. http://plato.stanford.edu/archives/spr2013/entries/israeli/.

Levy, Richard N. "Upon Arising: An Affirmation of *Techiyat Hameitim*." *Journal of Reform Judaism* (Fall 1982) 12–20.

———. *A Vision of Holiness: The Future of Reform Judaism*. New York: URJ, 2005.

Lewis, Theodore J. *Cults of the Dead in Ancient Israel and Ugarit*. Atlanta: Scholars 1989.

Loeb, Jacques. *The Mechanist Conception of Life*. Chicago: University of Chicago Press, 1912.

Loewe, Raphael. *Ibn Gabirol*. London: Peter Halban, 1989.

Long, Anthony A. *Hellenistic Philosophy: Stoics, Epicureans, Sceptics*. 2nd ed. Berkeley: The University of California Press, 1986.

Macdonald, Paul S. *The History of the Concept of Mind: Speculations about Soul, Mind and Spirit from Homer to Hume*. Burlington, VT: Ashgate, 2003.

Madigan, Kevin J., and Jon D. Levenson. *Resurrection: The Power of God for Christians and Jews*. New Haven, CT: Yale University Press, 2008.

Maimonides, Moses. *The Book of Knowledge*. Translated by Moses Hyamson. New York: Feldheim, 1974.

———. *Eight Chapters*. In *Ethical Writings of Maimonides*, edited by Raymond L. Weiss and Charles Butterworth, 59–104. New York: Dover, 1975.

———. *The Guide of the Perplexed*. 2 vols. Translated by Shlomo Pines. Chicago: The University of Chicago Press, 1963.

———. *Maimonides' Commentary on the Mishnah Tractate Sanhedrin*. Translated by Fred Rosner. New York: Sepher-Hermon, 1981.

———. *Moses Maimonides' Treatise on Resurrection*. Translated by Fred Rosner. New York: KTAV, 1982.

Malter, Henry. *Saadia Gaon: His Life and Works*. Philadelphia: The Jewish Publication Society of America, 1921.

Mansoor, Menahem. "Introduction." In *The Book of Direction to the Duties of the Heart* by Bahya ibn Pakuda, translated by Menahem Mansoor, 1–82. Portland, OR: The Littman Library of Jewish Civilization, 2004.

Mendelsohn, Moses, *Jerusalem*. In *Moses Mendelssohn: Writings on Judaism, Christianity, & The Bible*, edited by Michah Gottlieb, 72–123. Waltham, MA: Brandeis University Press, 2011.

———. "Letter to Rabbi Jacob Emden." In *Moses Mendelssohn: Writings on Judaism, Christianity, & The Bible*, edited by Michah Gottlieb, 32–35. Waltham, MA: Brandeis University Press, 2011.

———. "Open Letter to Lavatar." In *Moses Mendelssohn: Writings on Judaism, Christianity, & The Bible*, edited by Michah Gottlieb, 6–15. Waltham, MA: Brandeis University Press, 2011.

———. *Phädon, or On the Immortality of the Soul*. Translated by Patricia Noble. New York: Lang, 2007.

Merz, John Theodore, *A History of European Thought in the Nineteenth Century*. 4 vols. New York: Dover, 1965.

Meyer, Michael A. *The Origins of the Modern Jew: Jewish Identity and European Culture in Germany, 1749–1824*. Detroit: Wayne State University Press, 1967.

———. *Response to Modernity: A History of the Reform Movement in Judaism*. Detroit: Wayne State University Press, 1988.

Milgrom, Jacob. *The JPS Torah Commentary: Numbers*. Philadelphia: The Jewish Publication Society, 1990.

Mill, John Stuart. *On Liberty*. Chicago: Regnery, 1955.

———. *Three Essays on Religion*. London: Longmans, Green, Reader and Dyer, 1874.

———. *Utilitarianism*. Indianapolis: Bobbs-Merrill, 1957.

Miller, George A. *Psychology: The Science of Mental Life*. New York: Harper & Row, 1962.

Miller, Lisa. *Heaven: Our Enduring Fascination with the Afterlife*. New York: HarperCollins, 2010.

Millgram, Jacob. *Jewish Worship*. Philadelphia: The Jewish Publication Society of America, 1971.

Mintz, Jerome. *Legends of the Hasidim: An Introduction to Hasidic Culture and Oral Tradition in the New World*. Chicago: University of Chicago Press, 1968.

Moore, George Foot. *Judaism in the First Centuries of the Christian Era*. 2 vols. New York: Schoken, 1958.

Nadler, Steven. *A Book Forged in Hell: Spinoza's Scandalous Treatise and the Birth of the Secular Age*. Princeton, NJ: Princeton University Press, 2011.

———. *Spinoza: A Life*. Cambridge: Cambridge University Press, 1999.

———. *Spinoza's Heresy: Immortality and the Jewish Mind*. Oxford: Oxford University Press, 2001.

Nahmanides (Moses ben Nahman). *Commentary on the Torah*. 5 vols. Translated by Charles B. Chavel. Brooklyn, NY: Shilo, 1999.

———. "Discourse on *Rosh Ha-Shanah*." In *Writings of the Ramban*, translated by Charles B. Chavel, 13–137. Brooklyn, NY: Shilo, 1999.

———. *The Gate of Reward*. Translated by Charles B. Chavel. New York: Shilo, 1983.

———. "Letter to the French Rabbis." In *Writings of the Ramban*, translated by Charles B. Chavel. Brooklyn, NY: Shilo, 1999.

Neusner, Jacob. "Death and Afterlife in the Later Rabbinic Sources: The Two Talmuds and the Associated Midrash-Compilations." In *Judaism in Late Antiquity: Death, Life-After Death, Resurrection & The World to Come in the Judaisms of Antiquity*, edited by Alan J. Avery-Peck and Jacob Neusner, 267–91. Leiden: Brill, 2000.

———. *From Politics to Piety: The Emergence of Pharisaic Judaism*. Englewood Cliffs, NJ: Prentice-Hall, 1973.

———. *Jerusalem and Athens: The Congruity of Talmudic and Classical Philosophy*. Leiden: Brill, 1997.

Nickelsburg, George W. E. *1 Enoch 1: A Commentary on the Book of 1 Enoch Chapters –1–36, 81–108*. Minneapolis: Fortress, 2001.

———. *Jewish Literature between the Bible and the Mishnah*. 2nd ed. Minneapolis: Fortress, 2005.

———. "Judgment, Life-After-Death, and Resurrection in the Apocrypha and the Non-Apocalyptic Pseudepigrapha." In *Judaism in Late Antiquity: Death, Life-After Death, Resurrection & The World to Come in the Judaisms of Antiquity*, edited by Alan J. Avery-Peck and Jacob Neusner, 141–62. Leiden: Brill, 2000.

———. *Resurrection, Immortality, and Eternal Life in Intertestamental Judaism and Early Christianity.* Expanded ed. Cambridge, MA: Harvard University Press 2006.

Perry, Ralph Barton. *The Thought and Character of William James.* Cambridge, MA: Harvard University Press, 1948.

Pessin, Sarah. "Solomon Ibn Gabirol [Avicebron]." The Stanford Encyclopedia of Philosophy (Summer 2014 Edition). Edited by Edward Zalta. http://plato.stanford.edu/archives/sum2014/entries/ibn-gabirol/.

Petuchowski, Jakob J. "Manuals and Catechisms of the Jewish Religion in the Early Period of Emancipation." In *Studies in Nineteenth-Century Jewish Intellectual History*, edited by Alexander Altmann, 47–64. Cambridge, MA: Harvard University Press, 1964.

Pietersma, Albert, and Benjamin G. Wright, eds. *A New English Translation of the Septuagint.* Oxford: Oxford University Press, 2007.

Pines, Shlomo. "Introduction." In *The Guide of the Perplexed*, by Moses Maimonides, lvii–cxxxiv. Translated by Shlomo Pines. Chicago: The University of Chicago Press, 1963.

Plato. *Phaedo.* Translated by Reginald Hackforth. Cambridge: Bobbs-Merrill, 1955.

Plaut, W. Gunther, ed. *The Rise of Reform Judaism: A Sourcebook of Its European Origins.* 50th anniv. ed. Lincoln: University of Nebraska Press, 2015.

Pomponazzi, Pietro. *On the Immortality of the Soul.* In *The Renaissance Philosophy of Man*, edited by Ernst Cassirer et al., 280–381. Translated by William Hay II. Revised by John H. Randall Jr. Chicago: The University of Chicago Press, 1948.

Pope, Marvin. *The Anchor Bible: Job.* Garden City, NY: Doubleday, 1965.

Popkin, Richard H., ed. *The Philosophy of the 16th and 17th Centuries.* New York: The Free Press, 1966.

Porter, Frank Chamberlin. "The Pre-Existence of the Soul in the Book of Wisdom and in the Rabbinical Writings." *The American Journal of Theology* 12 (1908) 53–115.

Proops, Ian. "Kant's First Paralogism." *The Philosophical Review* 119.4 (October 2010) 449–95.

Rackman, Emmanuel. "Orthodox Judaism." In *Contemporary Jewish Religious Thought*, edited by Arthur Cohen and Paul Mendes-Flohr, 679–84. New York: Scribner's Sons, 1987.

Randall, John Herman, Jr. "Introduction." In *The Renaissance Philosophy of Man*, edited by Ernst Cassirer et al., 257–79. Chicago: The University of Chicago Press, 1948.

Raphael, Simcha Paull. *Jewish Views of the Afterlife.* 2nd ed. Lanham, MD: Rowman & Littlefield, 2009.

Reichenbach, Hans. *The Rise of Scientific Philosophy.* Berkeley: University of California Press, 1951.

Robert, Marthe. *From Oedipus to Moses: Freud's Jewish Identity.* Translated by Ralph Manheim. New York: Anchor 1976.

Robinson, James T. "Soul and Intellect." In *The Cambridge History of Jewish Philosophy: From Antiquity through the Seventeenth Century*, edited by Steven Nadler and Tamar Rudavsky, 524–60. Cambridge: Cambridge University Press, 2009.

Robinson, Thomas M. *Plato's Psychology.* Toronto: University of Toronto Press, 1970.

Rohde, Erwin. *Psyche: The Cult of Souls and Belief in Immortality among the Greeks.* 2 vols. Translated from the eighth edition by W. B. Hillis. Reprint, Eugene, OR: Wipf & Stock, 2006.

Rosenbloom, Noah H. "Menasseh Ben Israel and the Eternality of Punishment Issue." *Proceedings of the American Academy for Jewish Research* 60 (1994) 241–62.

Rosenfield, Leonora Cohen. *Portrait of a Philosopher: Morris R. Cohen in Life and Letters.* New York: Harcourt, Brace & World, 1962.

Rosner, Fred. "Brief Description of the Treatise." In *Moses Maimonides' Treatise on Resurrection*, translated by Fred Rosner, 15–20. New York: KTAV, 1982.

———. *Moses Maimonides' Treatise on Resurrection.* New York: KTAV, 1982.

Royse, James R. "The Works of Philo." In *The Cambridge Companion to Philo*, edited by Adam Kamesar, 32–64. Cambridge: Cambridge University Press, 2009.

Rudavsky, Tamar M. *Maimonides.* Malden, MA: Wiley-Blackwell, 2010.

Ruderman, David B. "On Divine Justice, Metempsychosis, and Purgatory: Ruminations of a Sixteenth-Century Italian Jew." *Jewish History* 1.1 (Spring 1986) 9–30.

Russell, Bertrand. *A History of Western Philosophy.* New York: Simon & Schuster, 1972.

Ryle, Gilbert. *The Concept of Mind.* New York: Barnes & Noble, 1949.

Saadia. *The Book of Beliefs and Opinions.* Translated by Samuel Rosenblatt. New Haven, CT: Yale University Press, 1948.

———. *The Book of Doctrines and Beliefs.* Translated by Alexander Altmann. Indianapolis: Hackett, 2002.

Sachar, Howard Morley. *The Course of Modern Jewish History.* New York: Dell, 1958.

Salomon, Herman P., and Isaac S. D. Sassoon. "Introduction." In *Uriel da Costa's Examination of Pharisaic Traditions Supplemented by Semuel da Silva's Treatise on the Immortality of the Soul*, translated by H. P. Salomon and I. S. D. Sassoon, 1–50. Leiden: Brill, 1993.

Sarna, Nahum M. *The JPS Torah Commentary: Genesis.* Philadelphia: The Jewish Publication Society, 1989.

Schechter, Solomon, "The Dogmas of Judaism," *The Jewish Quarterly Review*, 1.1 (Oct. 1888) 48–61; 1.2 (Nov. 1888) 115–27.

Scheindlin, Raymond P. *A Short History of the Jewish People: From Legendary Times to Modern Statehood.* Oxford: Oxford University Press, 1998.

Scholem, Gershom G. *Kabbalah.* New York: New American Library, 1978.

———. *Major Trends in Jewish Mysticism.* New York: Schocken, 1961.

———. *On the Mystical Shape of the Godhead: Basic Concepts in the Kabbalah.* Translated by Joachim Neugroschel. New York: Schocken, 1991.

———. *Origins of the Kabbalah.* Translated by Allan Arkish. Princeton, NJ: Princeton University Press, 1987.

———, ed. *Zohar: The Book of Splendor: Basic Readings from the Kabbalah.* New York: Schocken, 1949.

Scholer, David M. "An Introduction to Philo Judaeus of Alexandria." In *The Works of Philo: New Updated Edition*, translated by Charles D. Yonge, ix–xvii. Peabody, MA: Hendrickson, 1993.

Schwartz, Daniel B. *The First Modern Jew: Spinoza and the History of an Image.* Princeton, NJ: Princeton University Press, 2012.

Schwartz, Daniel R. "Philo, His Family, and His Times." In *The Cambridge Companion to Philo*, edited by Adam Kamesar, 9–31. Cambridge: Cambridge University Press, 2009.

Scott, Edgar. "Hermann Cohen." *The Stanford Encyclopedia of Philosophy* (Fall 2015 Edition). Edited by Edward Zalta. https://plato.stanford.edu/archives/fall2015/entries/cohen/.

Scult, Mel. *Judaism Faces the Twentieth Century: A Biography of Mordecai M. Kaplan.* Detroit: Wayne State University Press, 1993.

———. *The Radical American Judaism of Mordecai M. Kaplan.* Bloomington: Indiana University Press, 2013.

Seeskin, Kenneth. "How to Read *Religion of Reason*." In *Religion of Reason Out of the Sources of Judaism*, by Hermann Cohen, 21–42. Translated by Simon Kaplan. Atlanta: Scholars, 1995.

Segal, Alan F. *Life After Death: A History of the Afterlife in Western Religion*. New York: Doubleday, 2004.

Setzer, Claudia. *Resurrection of the Body in Early Judaism and Early Christianity: Doctrine, Community, and Self-Definition*. Boston, MA: Brill Academic 2004.

Shakespeare, William. *All's Well that Ends Well*. Oxford: Oxford University Press, 1993.

Shyovitz, David I. "'You Have Saved Me from the Judgment of Gehenna': The Origins of the Mourner's Kaddish in Medieval Ashkenaz." *AJS Review* 39.1 (2015) 49–73.

Silver, Daniel Jeremy. *Maimonidean Criticism and the Maimonidean Controversy 1180–1240*. Leiden: Brill, 1965.

Silver, Zachary. "The Excommunication of Mordecai Kaplan." *American Jewish Archives Journal* 22.1 (2010) 21–48.

Sirat, Colette. *A History of Jewish Philosophy in the Middle Ages*. Cambridge: Cambridge University Press, 1985.

Smart, John J. C. "Sensations and Brain Processes." *The Philosophical Review* 68.2 (April 1959) 141–56.

Smith, Norman Kemp. *A Commentary to Kant's "Critique of Pure Reason."* New York: Humanities, 1962.

Speiser, Ephraim A. *The Anchor Bible: Genesis*. Garden City, NY: Doubleday, 1964.

Spinoza, Baruch. *Ethics*. In *The Collected Works of Spinoza*, edited and translated by Edwin Curley, 408–617. 2 vols. Princeton, NJ: Princeton University Press, 1985.

———. *Short Treatise on God, Man, and His Well-Being*. In *The Collected Works of Spinoza*, edited and translated by Edwin Curley, 53–156. 2 vols. Princeton, NJ: Princeton University Press, 1985.

———. *Theological-Political Treatise*. Translated by Samuel Shirley. Indianapolis: Hackett, 1998.

Spitz, Elie Kaplan. *Does the Soul Survive? A Jewish Journey to Belief in Afterlife, Past Lives & Living with Purpose*. Woodstock, VT: Jewish Lights, 2000.

Steiner, Richard. *Disembodied Souls: The Nefesh in Israel and Kindred Spirits in the Ancient Near East, with an Appendix on the Katumuwa Inscription*. Ancient Near East Monographs, 11. Atlanta: SBL, 2015.

Stern, Chaim, ed. *Gates of Prayer: The New Union Prayerbook—Weekdays, Sabbaths, and Festivals*. New York: Central Conference of American Rabbis, 1975.

Stern, S. M. "Ibn Ḥasdāy's Neoplatonist. A Neoplatonic Treatise and Its Influence on Isaac Israeli and the Longer Version of the Theology of Aristotle." *Oriens* 13/14 (1960–61) 58–120.

Strauss, Leo. "Introductory Essay." In *Religion of Reason Out of the Sources of Judaism*, by Hermann Cohen, xxiii–xxxvii. Translated by Simon Kaplan. Atlanta: Scholars, 1995.

Tatarkiewicz, Wladyslaw. *Nineteenth Century Philosophy*. Translated by Chester Kisiel. Belmont, CA: Wadsworth, 1973.

Taylor, Alfred E. *The Faith of a Moralist*. 2 vols. London: Macmillan, 1930.

Termini, Cristina. "Philo's Thought within the Context of Middle Judaism." In *The Cambridge Companion to Philo*, edited by Adam Kamesar, 95–123. Cambridge: Cambridge University Press, 2009.

Teutsch, David, ed. *Kol Haneshamah: Prayers for a House of Mourning and a Guide to Mourning Practices.* Elkins Park, PA: The Reconstructionist, 2001.

———. *Kol Haneshamah: Shabbat Vehagim.* Wyncote, PA: The Reconstructionist, 1994.

Tigay, Jeffrey H. *The JPS Torah Commentary: Deuteronomy.* Philadelphia: The Jewish Publication Society, 1996.

Tomasoni, Francesco. "Mendelssohn's Concept of the Human Soul in Comparison with Those of Georg Friedrich Meier and Kant." In *Moses Mendelssohn's Metaphysics and Aesthetics,* edited by Reinier Munk, 131–57. Dordrecht, the Netherlands: Springer, 2011.

Twersky, Isadore. "Introduction." In *From Philo to Spinoza: Two Studies in Religious Philosophy,* by Harry Austryn Wolfson, 1–14. New York: Behrman House, 1977.

Urbach, Ephraim E. *The Sages: Their Concepts and Beliefs.* 2 vols. Translated by Israel Abrahams. Jerusalem: Magnes, 1987.

Verman, Mark. *The Books of Contemplation: Medieval Jewish Mystical Sources.* Albany: State University of New York Press, 1992.

Vidal, Fernando. *The Sciences of the Soul: The Early Modern Origins of Psychology.* Translated by Saskia Brown. Chicago: The University of Chicago Press, 2011.

Wallis, Richard T. *Neoplatonism.* 2nd ed. Indianapolis: Hackett, 1995.

Waxman, Meyer. "Introduction." In *Rome and Jerusalem: A Study in Jewish Nationalism,* by Moses Hess, 9–34. Translated by Meyer Waxman. New York: Bloch, 1918.

Weiss, Raymond L. and Charles Butterworth, eds. *Ethical Writings of Maimonides.* New York: Dover, 1975.

Wine, Sherwin T. *Judaism Beyond God.* Lincolnshire, IL: International Institute for Secular Humanistic Judaism, 1995.

Winston, David. *Logos and Mystical Theology in Philo of Alexandria.* Cincinnati: Hebrew Union College Press, 1985.

———. *The Wisdom of Solomon.* New York: Doubleday, 1979.

Wolfson, Harry Austryn. *From Philo to Spinoza: Two Studies in Religious Philosophy.* New York: Behrman House, 1977.

———. "Immortality and Resurrection in the Philosophy of the Church Fathers." In *Immortality and Resurrection,* edited by Krister Stendahl, 54–96. New York: Macmillan, 1965.

———. *Philo: Foundations of Religious Philosophy in Judaism, Christianity, and Islam.* Cambridge, MA: Harvard University Press, 1968.

———. *The Philosophy of Spinoza: Unfolding the Latent Processes of His Reasoning.* New York: Schocken, 1969.

Yonge, Charles D., trans. *The Works of Philo: New Updated Edition.* Peabody, MA: Hendrickson, 1993.

Yovel, Yirmiyahu. *Spinoza and Other Heretics: The Adventures of Immanence.* Princeton, NJ: Princeton University Press, 1992.

———. *Spinoza and Other Heretics: The Marrano of Reason.* Princeton, NJ: Princeton University Press, 1992.

Zeller, Dieter. "The Life and Death of the Soul in Philo of Alexandria." *Studio Philonica Annual* 7 (1995) 19–55.

www.ingramcontent.com/pod-product-compliance
Lightning Source LLC
Chambersburg PA
CBHW081755300426
44116CB00014B/2123